Axel-Volkmar Jaeger • Götz-Sebastian Hök

FIDIC-A Guide for Practitioners

 Springer

Axel-Volkmar Jaeger
Moitzfeldstraße 11
51069 Köln
Germany
consultingservices@online.de

Dr. Götz-Sebastian Hök
Eschenallee 22
14050 Berlin
Germany
kanzlei@dr-hoek.de

ISBN 978-3-642-02099-5   e-ISBN 978-3-642-02100-8
DOI 10.1007/978-3-642-02100-8
Springer Heidelberg Dordrecht London New York

Library of Congress Control Number: 2009929206

Cover design: WMXDesign GmbH, Heidelberg, Germany

Printed on acid-free paper

Springer is part of Springer Science+Business Media (www.springer.com)

Foreword

In 1999, a suite of three new conditions of contract was published by FIDIC, following the basic structure and wording harmonised and updated around the previous FIDIC Design-Build and Turnkey Contract (the 1992 "Orange Book").

These conditions, known as the "FIDIC rainbow, were the Conditions of Contract for:

- Construction, the so-called Red Book, for works designed by the Employer
- Plant and Design-Build, the so-called Yellow Book, for works designed by the Contractor
- EPC/Turnkey Projects, the so-called Silver Book, for works designed by the Contractor

The first is intended for construction works where the Employer is responsible for the design, as for per the previous so-called Red Book 4th Edition (1987), with an important role for the Engineer.

The other two conditions of contract are intended for situations when the Contractor is responsible for the design. The Plant and Design-Build Contract has the traditional Engineer while the EPC/Turnkey Contract has a two-party arrangement, generally with an Employer's Representative as one of the parties.

The 1999 Conditions of Contract for Plant and Design/Build retained the essential elements of the earlier Orange Book. It had been noted, however, that new trends in project financing and management, especially related to PFI and BOT, required a different set of conditions, and the Conditions of Contract for EPC/Turnkey Projects were drafted to cater for to this. The EPC/Turnkey Contract complements, but does not replace, the Plant and Design/Build Contract in that it was intended to be used in a rather specific context.

While it was recognised that there were alternative scenarios encompassing the Design, Build and Operate Service (DBO), the so-called Gold Book concept, FIDIC recognised that the various scenarios required different contract conditions that could be used where long-term operation was involved. The Conditions of Contract for Design, Build and Operate Projects, the so-called Gold Book, for works designed by the Contractor were published in 2008.

Understanding the FIDIC Conditions of Contract is the key to preparing and managing FIDIC contracts. Only a keen and comprehensive understanding of the contracts will help in avoiding disputes and the accompanying cost and time overruns.

However, even though the FIDIC suite of contracts enjoys a worldwide reputation because they are widely accepted by employers, contractors, international financing organizations, engineers and lawyers, regrettably, misunderstanding and poor practices lead to avoidable disputes.

It is with great pleasure that I draw the attention of users of FIDIC contracts to this FIDIC Guide for Practitioners. The authors have shared their huge wide knowledge of the contracts and their implementation in various countries with the FIDIC community. Both are well known and experienced experts and accredited FIDIC trainers, as well as being adjudicators and arbitrators. They have made a major contribution in seeking to give guidance on the use of FIDIC forms of contract. This Guide is easy to read, and engineers, as well as legal advisors, employers and contractors will find it very helpful in daily practice.

In particular, those practitioners in civil law countries will benefit greatly from this Guide, which shows how FIDIC contracts should be interpreted against a civil code background. Common law practitioners will also welcome the Guide as a valuable source of information on how to address issues raised by the FIDIC contracts in a common law jurisdiction. Sample letters, checklists and other features will help to ensure that the Guide will meet with success all over the world.

In summary, I believe the Guide represents an invaluable resource that will raise the awareness of practitioners in the international construction industry to the rights and responsibilities of the parties under an FIDIC contract. Informative and accessible, the Guide provides employers, contractors and engineers with the means to manage FIDIC-based contracts properly and in accordance to with best-practice principles.

Gregs G. Thomopulos
President, FIDIC

Preface

The idea for this book was born out of the belief that the increasing dissemination of FIDIC forms of contract throughout the Civil Law world requires a different approach to the subject matter than that which is found under the Common Law. An English native speaker will naturally not encounter many difficulties when reading the FIDIC forms, although of course the wording used will sometimes be subject to interpretation. Again an English native speaker will usually be familiar with the underlying legal principles, which mostly derive from Common Law, despite the fact that some Civil Law-inspired features have been incorporated in the FIDIC books. Thus there is a clear need to explain Common Law concepts and legal terms in the context of Civil Law. This may often prove to be difficult as the very nature of Civil Law language is in many respects different from Common Law language. Both systems have terms which are often difficult to translate literally because of the fact that the terms reflect legal concepts which are unknown in the other legal world.

Although many difficulties in understanding the wording may be overcome if the terms and concepts are carefully explained, the English wording may sometimes be in direct contradiction to Civil Law concepts and practice. Whether the FIDIC wording will then prevail depends on the strength of the pacta sunt servanda principle. Civil Law systems usually determine and categorise the very nature of a contract. If the contract falls within the limits of a nominated contract, the relevant default rules (lois supplétives, dispositives Recht) and additionally the relevant mandatory rules will apply. Whether the FIDIC based contract will be recognized as an agreement sui generis or at least as a valid agreement although being in contradiction to the law must be ascertained on a case by case basis.

On the other hand, English native speakers will hopefully appreciate this book as a means of understanding better the members of the constructing team originating from Civil Law nations. Common Law practitioners should realise that the export of services does not always follow the export of Common Law practice. Common Law practitioners will encounter unknown legal concepts, such as pre-contractual duties, specific performance, duties to negotiate in good faith and judicial powers to adapt contracts to changed circumstances. They will also become aware of different approaches as to the designer's scope of service, its content and the resulting duties and obligations.

The authors have combined both practical experiences and an academic approach. They have also combined the views of an engineer with the views of a lawyer, which sometimes proves to be difficult. However, lawyers should understand that the practical needs are sometimes stronger than any sophisticated legal thinking can envisage. Engineers should accept that the law is a useful and a necessary feature because it makes decisions predictable and therefore calculable. It is the law which gives the engineer the powers to do what the parties expect him to do, although it is also the law which places constraints and limits on him when acting as a certifier or decision maker. Thus an exchange of ideas, impressions and experiences between lawyers and engineers appears to be not only helpful, but even essential.

Both authors wish to emphasize that a contract is not only a means to solve misunderstandings and disputes. Thus it should be read and prepared with the common understanding to follow its provisions from the outset. Only then can the contract provide easy answers. Legal help will then quite often be unnecessary. However, if, as is too often the case, the Parties ignore the contract on a day to day basis until it proves difficult to find a common understanding, sophisticated and expensive legal solutions have to be worked out and disputes will then become unavoidable.

The authors are further of the unanimous opinion that even though standard forms of contract may be as good and balanced as possible and even better, they are as good as worthless if the project is badly prepared and if in particular the bespoke documents such as the specifications, schedules, bills of quantities and/or employer's requirements do not reflect the intentions of the employer in a comprehensive and unambiguous way and if the aforementioned documents ignore the basic requirements of a FIDIC contract. Preparing a contract means taking into account that a FIDIC contract includes specific documents, defines terms, contains references to sub-clauses and comprises fall-back clauses. Multiple details must be specified in the documents and they should be implemented as provided and required by the FIDIC documents. It should be the primary interest of both parties to the contract to do so in order to avoid misunderstandings, lacunas and the debate and disputes which will inevitably result.

Finally the authors wish to apologise to their wives and families for the time spent on this book, and neglecting their needs and hopes, and also wish to thank all those who have contributed to this book, in particular Mr. Robert Leadbeater and Mr. Henry Stieglmeier.

Berlin and Cologne
September 2009

Axel-Volkmar Jaeger
Dr. Götz-Sebastian Hök

Contents

Cases

English Cases

Adams v. Richardson and Starling Ltd	(1969) 2 All ER 1221	Chap. 16 Fn 11
AIC Ltd v. Its Testing Services (UK) Ltd	[2005] EWHC 2122 (Comm) (07 October 2005)	Chap. 14 Fn 1
Air Foyle Ltd & Anor v. Center Capital Ltd	[2002] EWHC 2535 (Comm) (03 December 2002)	Chap. 2 Fn 11
Alfred McAlpine Capital Projects Ltd v. Tilebox Ltd	[2005] EWHC 281 (TCC); [2005] BLR 271	Chap. 7 Fn 14; Chap. 12 Fn 6
Antaios Compania Naviera SA v. Salen Rederierna AB	[1985] AC 191	Chap. 1; Chap. 7 Fn 4
Apple Corps Ltd v. Apple Computer, Inc	[2004] EWHC 768 (Ch)	Chap. 1 Fn 11
Balfour Beatty Building Ltd v. Chestermount Properties Ltd	(1993) 62 BLR 12	Chap. 7 Fn 17; Chap. 12 Fn 16
Barrett Bros (Taxis) Ltd v. Davies Lickiss and Milestone Motor Policies at Lloyd's, Third Parties	[1966] 1 WLR 1334	Chap. 21 Fn 12
Beaufort Developments (NI) Ltd v. Gilbert-Ash NI Ltd and Others	[1998] 2 All ER 778; [1999] 1 AC 266	Chap. 11; Chap. 13 Fn 4
Bernhard's Rugby Landscapes Ltd v. Stockley Park Consortium Ltd	[1998] EWHC (TCC) (22 April 1998)	Chap. 1 Fn 22
Beximco Pharmaceuticals Ltd & Others v. Shamil Bank of Bahrain EC	[2004] EWCA Civ 19 (28 January 2004)	Chap. 1 Fn 54, 55, 59
Billyack v. Leyland Construction Company Ltd	[1968] 1 All ER 783	Chap. 16 Fn 9
Blackpool and Fylde Aero Club v. Blackpool Borough Council	[1990] 1 WLR 1195	Chap. 5 Fn 3
Bouygues (UK) Ltd v. Dahl-Jensen (UK) Ltd	[2000] BLR 522, CA	Chap. 22 Fn 8
Boys v. Chaplin	[1971] AC 356	Chap. 2
Breas of Doune Wind Farm (Scotland) Ltd v. Alfred McAlpine Business Services Ltd	[2008] EWHC 426 (TCC)	Chap. 12 Fn 26

Irish Cases

French Cases

Cour de Cassation,	11.06.1985	JCP (G) 1985 IV, 295	Chap. 19 Fn 7
Cour de Cassation	03.10.2001	RD. Imm. 2001, 498	Chap. 19 Fn 7
Cour de Cassation	16.02.2005	Mon TP 2005, 104	Chap. 19 Fn 7
Cour de Cassation	19.03.1986	file number 84-17.424	Chap. 19 Fn 8
Cour de Cassation	17.11.1999	RD imm. 2000, 52	Chap. 19 Fn 9
Cour de Cassation	15.01.2003	RD imm. 2003, 259	Chap. 19 Fn 10
CA Paris	20.06.1996	(1996) Rev.arb. 657	Chap. 1 Fn 28
Cour de Cassation	15.11.1972	file number 71-11.651, Bull.civ. III no. 611	Chap. 21 Fn 4
Cour de Cassation	11.05.2006	file number 04-18.092	Chap. 21 Fn 5
Cour de Cassation	8.10.1974	file no. 73-12.347, Bull.civ. III no. 337	Chap. 18 Fn 3
Cour de Cassation	20.1.1982	file no. 80-16.415, Bull.civ. III no. 20	Chap. 18 Fn 4
Cour de Cassation	27.09.2006	file no. 05-13.808, D. 2006, 2416	Chap. 1 Fn 26
Cour de Cassation	20.11.2002	file no. 00-14.423, RD imm. 2003, 60	Chap. 1 Fn 27
Cour de Cassation, mixed chamber	30.11.2007	file no. 06-14006	Chap. 1 Fn 31
Cour de Cassation	04.08.1915	(1916) D.P. 1, 22	Chap. 18 Fn 8

German Cases

BAG	December 12th, 2001; file no. 5 AZR 255/00; [2003] IPRax 258	Chap. 2 Fn 2
BGH	June 7th, 1984; file no. IX ZR 66/83; [91] BGHZ 325	Chap. 1 Fn 33
BGH	February 27th, 2003; file no. VII ZR 169/02; [2003] ZfBR 367	Chap. 11 Fn 8
BGH	November 24th, 1969; file no. VII ZR 177/67; [1970] NJW 421	Chap. 18 Fn 2
BGH	November 24th, 1969; file no. VII ZR 177/69; [1970] NJW 421	Chap. 1 Fn 44, 47; Chap. 15 Fn 1
BGH	September 8th, 1998; file no. X ZR 4/97; [1998] NJW 3636 at 3636 et seq.	Chap. 5 Fn 17
BGH	May 17th, 1967; file no. VIII ZR 58/66; [48] BGHZ 25	Chap. 6 Fn 1
BGH	January 27th, 1971; file no. VIII ZR 151/69; [55] BGHZ 248	Chap. 6 Fn 1
BGH	Schäfer-Finnern, Z 2.311 Bl. 22 and 29	Chap. 6 Fn 2
BGH	October 22th, 1981; file no. VII ZR 310/79; [82] BGHZ 100	Chap. 7 Fn 1; Chap. 19 Fn 13
BGH	February 14th, 2001; file no. VII ZR 176/99; [2001] NJW 1196	Chap. 7 Fn 1
BGH	October 8th, 1969; file no. VIII ZR 20/68; [1970] NJW 29	Chap. 7 Fn 15
BGH	November 8th, 2007; file no. VII ZR 183/05; [2008] IBR 77	Chap. 9 Fn 3
BGH	January 14th, 1993; file no. VII ZR 185/91; [1993] IBR 368	Chap. 12 Fn 9

USA Cases

Canadian Cases

Best Cleaners & Contractors Ltd v. R. in Right of Canada	[1985] 2 FCR 29	Chap. 5 Fn 6
Ellis-Don Ltd v. The Parking Authority of Toronto	(1978) 28 BLR 98, HC (Ont)	Chap. 2
Northern Construction v. Gloge Heating & Plumbing	(1986) 27 DLR (4th) 265	Chap. 5 Fn 5
The Queen in the Right of Ontario v. Ron Engineering & Construction (Eastern) Ltd	[1981] 1 SCR 111	Chap. 5 Fn 4

Australian Cases

Alucraft Pty Ltd v. Grocon Ltd (no. 2)	[1996] 2 VR 386	Chap. 16 Fn 13
Baltic Shipping Co v. Dillon	(1993) 176 CLR 344	Chap. 7
Chinook Aggregates Limited v. Abbotsford (Municipal Districts)	(1989) 35 CLR 241	Chap. 5 Fn 7
Emery Construction Limited v. St John's (City) Roman Catholic School Board	(1996) 28 CLR (2d) 1	Chap. 5 Fn 10
Gaymark Investments Pty Ltd v. Walter Construction Group Ltd	[1999] NTSC 143; (2005) 21 Const. LJ 71	Chap. 12 Fn 1; Chap. 21 Fn 2
GEC Marconi Systems Pty Ltd v. BHP Information Technology Pty Ltd	[2003] FCA 50	Chap. 7
Onerati v. Phillips Constructions Pty Ltd (in liq)	(1989) 16 NSWLR 730	Chap. 9 Fn 21
Ownit Homes Pty Ltd v. Batchelor	[1983] 2 Qd R 124	Chap. 7
Pavey & Matthews Pty Ltd v. Paul	(1987) 162 CLR 221	Chap. 2
Peninsula Balmain Pty Ltd v. Abigroup Contractors Pty Ltd	[2002] NSWCA 211	Chap. 12 Fn 3
Perini Corporation v. Commonwealth of Australia	[1969] 12 BLR 82	Chap. 11
Phillips v. Ellinson Brothers Pty Ltd	(1941) 65 CLR 221	Chap. 7
S.M.K. Cabinets v. Hili Modern Electrics Pty Ltd	[1984] VR 391	Chap. 12
Speno Rail Maintenance Australia v. Hamersley Iron Pty Ltd	[2000] WASCA 408	Chap. 19 Fn 15
Steele v. Tardiani	(1946) 72 CLR 386	Chap. 7
Tan Hung Nguyen v. Luxury Design Homes	[2004] NSWCA 178	Chap. 7 Fn 11, 12
Turner Corporation Ltd (Receiver and Manager Appointed) v. Austotel Pty Ltd (2nd June 1994)	(1997) 13 BCL 378	Chap. 21 Fn 1
Walsh v. Kinnear	(1876) 14 SCR (NSW) 434	Chap. 7

Scottish Cases

Malaysian Cases

South African Cases

Trinidad and Tobago Case

India Cases

English Abbreviations

AC	See "LRAC"
All ER	All England Law Reports
App Cas	See L.R.App.Cas.
Arb Intl	Arbitration International
BCA	Building and Construction Authority
BCL	Building and Construction Law (Australia)
BLR	Building Law Reports
Ch	Law Reports, Chancery Division (Third Series)
Chi-Kent L. Rev.	Chicago Kent Law Review
Cl.Ct.	United States Claims Court Reporter (USA)
CLJ	Cambridge Law Journal
CLR	Commonwealth Law Reports (Australia)
Colo	Colorado Reports (USA)
Com Cas	Commercial Cases
Con LR	Construction Law Reports
Const LJ	Construction Law Journal
Const. & Eng. L.	Construction & Engineering Law
Ct Cl	Court of claims Report (USA)
DLR (3d)	Dominion Law Reports, Third Series (Canada)
DLR (4th)	Dominion Law Reports, Fourth Series
ENG BCA	Engineers Board of Contract Appeals
EWCA Civ	Media neutral citation from the Court of Appeal (Civil Division)
EWHC	Media neutral citation from the High Court
Ex D	See LREx
F.2d	Federal Reporter, Second Series (USA)
F.3d	Federal Reporter, Third Series (USA)
FCA	Federal Court of Australia (Neutral Citation) (Australia)
FCR	Canada Federal Court Reports (Canada)
Fed.Cl.	Federal Claims Reporter (USA)
H & N	Hurlston & Norman
ICLR	International Construction Law Review (International)
IEHC	High Court of Ireland [Neutral Citation] (Ireland)
IR	Irish Reports (Ireland)
J.Int.Arb.	Journal of international Arbitration
KB	See LRKB
L.R.App.Cas.	Law Reports (Second Series) Appeal Cases
Lloyd's Rep	Lloyd's Law Reports
LRAC	Law Reports (Third Series) Appeal Cases

LRCP	Law Reports (First Series) Common Pleas Cases
LREx	Law Reports (First Series) Exchequer Cases
LRKB	Law Reports, King's Bench
LT	Law Times Report
NSWCA	New South Wales Court of Appeal [Neutral Citation] (Australia)
NSWLR	New South Wales Law Reports (Australia)
NTSC	Northern Territory Supreme Court [Neutral Citation] (Australia)
P.2d	Pacific Reports, Second Series (USA)
PD	Law Reports, Probate, Divorce & Admiralty Division
QB	Quenns Bench (LR)
Qd R	Queensland Report (Australia)
SA	South African Law Report (South Africa)
SCR (NSW)	Supreme Court Reports, New South Wales (Australia)
SLT	Scots Law Time (Scotland)
So.2d	Southern Reporter, Second Series (USA)
TCC	Tax Court of Canada (Canada)
UKHL	United Kingdom House of Lords [Neutral Citation]
VR	Victorian Reports (Australia)
WASCA	Western Australia Supreme Court: Court of Appeal (Australia)
WLR	Weekly Law Reports
ZAWCHC	South Africa: Western Cape High Court, Cape Town

German Abbreviations

BAG	Bundesarbeitsgericht, Federal Labour Court
BauR	Baurecht, Construction Law Journal
BGB	Bürgerliches Gesetzbuch, German Civil Code
BGH	Bundesgerichtshof, Federal Court of Justice
BGHZ	Bundesgerichtshofentscheidungen Zivilsachen, Official case collection of the Federal Court of Justice in civil matters
BVerfG	Bundesverfassungsgericht, Federal Constitutional Court
BVerwG	Bundesverwaltungsgericht, Federal Administration Court
BVerwGE	Bundesverwaltungsgerichtsentscheidungen, Official case collection of the Federal Administration Court
DB	Der Betrieb, Law Journal
DNotZ	Deutsche Notar Zeitschrift, Law Journal
IBR	Immobilien & Baurecht, Law Journal
IPRax	Praxis des Internationalen Privat- und Verfahrensrechts, Law Journal
KG	Kammergericht (Court of Appeal Berlin), See "OLG"
LAG	Landesarbeitsgericht, Higher Labour Court
LG	Landgericht, High Court
NJW	Neue Juristische Wochenschrift, Law Journal (New Weekly Law Report)
NJW – RR	Neue Juristische Wochenschrift Rechtssprechungsreport, Law Journal (New weekly Law Report, case collection)
NWVBI	Nordrhein-Westfälische Verwaltungsblätter, Official Journal of Nordhren-Westfalen
NZBau	Neue Zeitschrift für Baurecht und Vergaberecht, Law Journal (New Construction and Procurement Law Journal)
OLG	Oberlandesgericht, Appellate Court (Court of Appeal)
RG	Reichsgericht, Imperial Court (1879–1945)
RGZ	Offizielle Sammlung der Entscheidungen des Reichsgerichts in Zivilsachen, Official collection of cases of the Imperial Court
VergabeR	Vergaberecht, Law Journal (Procurement Law)
VG	Verwaltungsgericht, Administration Court
ZfBR	Zeitschrift für deutsches und internationales Bau- und Vergaberecht, Law Journal (German and International Construction and Procurement Law)

French Abbreviations

Bull. or bull. civ.	Bulletin civil, Official collection of cases of the Court of Cassation
CA	Cour d'appel, Court of Appeal
D.	Recueil Dalloz, Law Journal
JCP (G)	Jurisclasseur périodique, édition générale (*ou «la semaine juridique»*), Law Journal
Mon TP	Moniteur des travaux publics et du bâtiment, Law Journal
RD imm.	Revue de droit immobilier, Law Journal
Rev Crit Dr Intern Priv	Revue Critique de Droit International Privé (International), Law Journal
Rev. arb.	Revue de l'arbitrage, Law Journal
RJT	La Revue Juridique Themis (Canada), Law Journal

Chapter 1
Legal Systems

The proper law of the contract has a great deal of influence on each and every contract. The law which governs the contract provides for:

- Concepts, which must be known in order to understand the effects of the contract and its underlying mechanisms
- Legal language and terminology, which is highly influenced by the law, and may sometimes prove difficult to translate and understand
- Legal rules which may clarify any remaining gaps
- Mandatory legal rules
- Rules of contract interpretation

As ignorance of the law is usually no excuse, Contractors, in particular those coming from abroad must familiarise themselves with the applicable law, its concepts and language. Engineers often believe that they have a "common language", which consists of drawings. However even drawings must be interpreted and understood in their legal context. Civil law and common law concepts often also differ from each other to a considerable extent and a simple translation of words constitutes no sufficient basis for a common understanding. As English has become the leading language for international construction projects both civil law and common law practitioners must carefully analyse whether any given wording means exactly what it appears to mean.

However, understanding legal terms also means taking into account the fact that legal systems differ from each other as to the underlying principles and in further detailed analysis. The Common law, which is the legal system developed in those nations which trace their legal heritage to Britain, is primarily contrasted with civil law, which is based on former Roman law. Both legal systems have over time developed their own traditions and characteristics. Moreover there is Islamic law also referred to as Shari'a law, which comprises all of the legal framework within which the public and private aspects of life are regulated for those living in a legal system based on Islamic principles of jurisprudence, as well as for Muslims living outside the domain. The concept of Shari'a consists of the Qur'an and Sunnah. For some, it also includes classical fiqh. Shari'a is often explained as law based upon the Qur'an, the Sunna, and classical fiqh derived from consensus (ijma) and analogy

A.-V. Jaeger and G.-S. Hök, *FIDIC-A Guide for Practitioners*,
DOI 10.1007/978-3-642-02100-8_1, © Springer-Verlag Berlin Heidelberg 2010

(qiyas). Most Arab countries refer to the Qur'an or Islamic principles in their existing Civil Codes as a primary source of enlightenment.[1]

It is a common understanding worldwide that contracts are binding instruments being enforceable at court. The primary duty of a court in construing a written contract is to endeavour to discover the intention of the parties from the words of the instrument in which the contract is embodied. However, the manner of doing so varies from country to country. In Civil Law countries a construction contract will usually be understood as a nominate contract having its legal background in Roman Law, even though the specific legal shape of the contract may vary from country to country. Thus, it is worthwhile to emphasize some basic ideas of Roman law in order to help us understand the Civil law approach.

In later classical Roman law there were two common types of contract (*emptio-venditio* and locatio-conductio). According to Roman Law a construction contract is a contract of letting and hiring (*locatio conductio operis*). Under a locatio conductio operis the conductor operis is normally obliged to carry out the work which he is engaged to do before the contract money can be claimed from the locator (the employer). In such a case the obligation to pay the money is conditional on the preperformance of the obligation to carry out the work, but, of course, the converse does not apply.[2] The principle of reciprocity would normally apply to such a contract unless there are indications to the contrary.[3]

The wording of locatio conductio operis is a bit confusing and shall therefore be explained.[4] The term derives from locatio conductio (letting and hiring). Locatio conductio may be defined as a contract whereby one person agrees to give another the use or the use and enjoyment of a thing or his services or his labour in return for a remuneration. Three types of letting and hiring were distinguished:

- The hire of a thing (locatio conductio rei)
- The hire of services (locatio conductio operarum or locatio operarum)
- The hire of a piece of work (locatio conductio operis or locatio operis faciendi)

In the third case the person who gives the order for the work, and pays for it, is the locator (one could say he places the order or the works), whilst it is the conductor who executes the works. This perplexed terminology is due to the different meanings of locare. It is therefore useful to give an example: The work (*opus*) let out would be the installation of the unit. The lessor (*locator*) would be the employer (locator) who let out the work and was obliged to pay for it, whereas the lessee (*conductor*) would be the contractor, who did the installation.[5] Under Scottish law,

---

[1] Compare Art. 1 of the Algerian Civil Code and Art. 1 of the Egyptian Civil Code.

[2] See, e.g. Kamaludin v. Gihwala, [1956] (2) SA 323 (C) at p. 326; de Wet and Yeats (1978, p. 139).

[3] BK Tooling (Edms) Bpk v. Scope Precision Engineering (Edms) Bpk [1979] (1) SA 391 (A) at 418 B–C.

[4] Oxonica Energy Ltd v. Neuftec Ltd [2008] EWHC 2127 (Pat) (05 September 2008).

[5] B C Plant Hire cc t/a B C Carriers v. Grenco (SA) (PTY) Ltd (1090/2002) [2003] ZAWCHC 70 (12 December 2003); see Gaius Institutes 3.147 Institutes 3.24.4 Digest 18.1.20, 19.2.2.1.

so far as building works are concerned, one of the characteristics of a contract *locatio operis faciendi* is that the worker (conductor) is hired to do work on the property of the hirer (locator).[6]

In some Civil Law jurisdictions Roman Law is still an important source of law, like in South Africa, Scotland or Malta, in others, like Germany or France Roman Law has been incorporated in the respective Civil Codes. Thus for example under Scottish law old Roman law is still used in order to determine the obligations of the parties of a contract and even in tort. Thus Scottish courts have said:[7]

> If a person is employed under a contract *locatio operis faciendi,* "for services" rather than "of service", the law does not hold the employer vicariously liable for wrongs committed by the contractor in the course of the employment. Such a person is an independent contractor, and is personally liable only, not being subject to detailed direction or control from the employer in the manner of performing the work. His contract is not to serve, but to bring about a required result in his own way, and if, in so doing, he injures a third party, he alone is responsible.

However, even in Turkish law, the term locatio conduction operis still operates, when it is necessary to assess the legal nature of a given agreement.[8] As defined in article 355 of the Turkish Law on Obligations: "the 'Manufacturing Contract' is a contract where one of the parties (the Contractor) undertakes the production of goods in exchange for the price that the other side (the Employer) undertakes to pay".

Unfortunately and although most Civil law countries derive their current legislation from the old Roman law and although the locatio conductio operis did not merely cover work on goods but also the construction of buildings, current legislation largely ignores the specific requirements and needs of a contract for works to be carried out on land. Also for a long time the export of construction services was rather the exception than the rule. Largely distinct local markets have emerged from this fact and the involved contractors, employers, architects and engineers have widely developed local self made law of industry which crystallizes in local standard terms and practises supported by case law.

1.1   English Contract Law

1.1.1   Relevant Provisions

The main legal provisions concerning the English law of contract are contained in English case law. Otherwise, there are special provisions stipulated in a number of distinct Acts of Parliament, such as:

The Housing Grants, Construction and Regeneration Act 1996

---

[6] Marjandi Ltd v. Bon Accord Glass Ltd [1998] ScotSC 55 (15 October 2007).

[7] Stewart & Anor v. Malik [2008] ScotSC 12 (29 April 2008).

[8] T Comedy (UK) Ltd v. Easy Managed Transport Ltd [2007] EWHC 611 (Comm) (28 March 2007).

1.1.2   English Legal System

The English legal system is a Common Law legal system. By this it is meant that many of its primary legal principles have been made and developed by judges on a case by case basis in what is called a system of precedent. Historically two distinct court systems have co-existed: courts in common law and courts in equity. Both branches were unified in 1873 but remedies in equity still exist parallel to those in common law. Additionally statutory rules, such as Acts of Parliament and other statutory instruments and by-laws exist.

Construction law as a whole is ruled by statutory instruments and by case law. Most of planning law and procedure is ruled by statutory instruments and by-laws. Construction contract law is mainly case law based, with the exception of the Contract Scheme contained in the Housing Grants, Construction and Regeneration Act 1996. The Act provides mandatory implied terms of construction contracts within the scope of the Act.

1.1.3   Entering a Contract

A contract is an agreement which legally binds the parties. Sometimes contracts are referred to as "enforceable agreements". This is rather misleading since one party cannot usually force the other to fulfil his part of the bargain. The usual remedy is and always has been damages (see below breach of contract).

1.1.3.1   Elements of Contracts

The essential elements of a contract are:

(a) That an agreement is made as a result of an offer and acceptance.
(b) The agreement contains an element of value known as consideration, although a gratuitous promise is binding if it is made by deed.
(c) The parties intend to create legal relations.

Incidentally, it has become increasingly common in recent years in the construction industry for a form of *letter of intent* to be employed which, while it does indeed contain a request to a contractor to commence the execution of works, also seeks to circumscribe the remuneration to which he will be entitled in respect of work done pursuant to the request in the event that no contract is concluded.

The English position has been explained by Steyn LJ in *Percy Trentham Ltd v. Archital Luxfer Ltd.* [1993] 1 Lloyd's Rep 25 at page 27:

> Before I turn to the facts it is important to consider briefly the approach to be adopted to the issue of contract formation in this case. It seems to me that four matters are of importance. The first is the fact that English law generally adopts an objective theory of contract

formation. That means that in practice our law generally ignores the subjective expectations and the unexpressed mental reservations of the parties. Instead the governing criterion is the reasonable expectations of honest men. And in the present case that means that the yardstick is the reasonable expectations of sensible businessmen. Secondly, it is true that the coincidence of offer and acceptance will in the vast majority of cases represent the mechanism of contract formation. It is so in the case of a contract alleged to have been made by an exchange of correspondence. But it is not necessarily so in the case of a contract alleged to have come into existence during and as a result of performance. See Brogden v. Metropolitan Railway (1877) 2 AC 666; New Zealand Shipping Co Ltd v. A. M. Satterthwaite & Co Ltd [1974] 1 Lloyd's Rep 534 at p. 539 col.1 [1975] AC 154 at p. 167 D-E; Gibson v. Manchester City Council [1979] 1 WLR 294. The third matter is the impact of the fact that the transaction is executed rather than executory. It is a consideration of the first importance on a number of levels. See British Bank for Foreign Trade Ltd v. Novinex [1949] 1 KB 628 at p. 630. The fact that the transaction was performed on both sides will often make it unrealistic to argue that there was no intention to enter into legal relations. It will often make it difficult to submit that the contract is void for vagueness or uncertainty. Specifically, the fact that the transaction is executed makes it easier to imply a term resolving any uncertainty, or, alternatively, it may make it possible to treat a matter not finalised in negotiations as inessential. In this case fully executed transactions are under consideration. Clearly, similar considerations may sometimes be relevant in partly executed transactions. Fourthly, if a contract only comes into existence during and as a result of performance of the transaction it will frequently be possible to hold that the contract impliedly and retrospectively covers pre-contractual performance. See Trollope & Colls Ltd v. Atomic Power Constructions Ltd [1963] 1 WLR 333.

1.1.3.2 Offer and Acceptance

The underlying theory is that a contract is the outcome of "consenting minds", each party being free to accept or reject the terms of the other. However, whether in a case a contract has come into existence must depend upon the true construction of the relevant communications which have passed between the parties and the effect (if any) of their actions pursuant to those communications[9] The principles to be applied to the construction of communications between parties in order to determine whether they have made a contract by correspondence are those principles suggested by Lord Hoffman in Investors Compensation Scheme Ltd v. West Bromwich Building Society [1998] 1 WLR 896 at pages 912H–913F in relation to the construction of a contract in writing. As enunciated by Lord Hoffman:

The principles may be summarised as follows:

(1) Interpretation is the ascertainment of the meaning which the document would convey to a reasonable person having all the background knowledge which would reasonably have been available to the parties in the situation in which they were at the time of the contract.
(2) The background was famously referred to by Lord Wilberforce as the "matrix of fact", but this phrase is, if anything, an understated description of what the background may

---

[9]British Steel Corporation v. Cleveland Bridge and Engineering Co. Ltd [1984] 1 All ER 504, at 509, in which it was held that the effect of the *letter of intent* in that case was that it was a mere request without any contractual force.

include. Subject to the requirement that it should have been reasonably available to the parties and to the exception to be mentioned next, it includes absolutely anything which would have affected the way in which the language of the document would have been understood by a reasonable man.

(3) The law excludes from the admissible background the previous negotiations of the parties and their declarations of subjective intent. They are admissible only in an action for rectification. The law makes this distinction for reasons of practical policy and, in this respect only, legal interpretation differs from the way we would interpret utterances in ordinary life. The boundaries of this exception are in some respects unclear. But this is not the occasion on which to explore them.

(4) The meaning which a document (or any other utterance) would convey to a reasonable man is not the same thing as the meaning of its words. The meaning of words is a matter of dictionaries and grammars: the meaning of the document is what the parties using those words against the relevant background would reasonably have been understood to mean. The background may not merely enable the reasonable man to choose between the possible meanings of words which are ambiguous but even (as occasionally happens in ordinary life) to conclude that the parties must, for whatever reason, have used the wrong words or syntax: see Mannai Investments Co Ltd v. Eagle Star Life Assurance Co Ltd [1997] AC 749.

(5) The "rule" that words should be given their "natural and ordinary meaning" reflects the common sense proposition that we do not easily accept that people have made linguistic mistakes, particularly in formal documents. On the other hand, if one would nevertheless conclude from the background that something must have gone wrong with the language, the law does not require judges to attribute to the parties an intention which they plainly could not have had. Lord Diplock made this point more vigorously when he said in Antaios Compania Naviera SA v. Salen Rederierna AB [1985] AC 191,201:

if detailed semantic and syntactical analysis of words in a commercial contract is going to lead to a conclusion that flouts business commonsense, it must be made to yield to business commonsense.

There must be offer and acceptance. The offer must be addressed to the offeree, either as an individual or as a member of a class or of the public. The acceptance must come from one who is so addressed and must itself be addressed to the offeror.

Illustration: The classic case of Cundy v. Lindsay (1873) 3 App Cas 459, was one in which the acceptance was not addressed to the offeror. The offer was addressed to a person who held himself out as willing to do business. But the offer was made by Blenkarn and the acceptance addressed to Blenkiron. The fact that there was a real Blenkiron whom Blenkark was pretending to be showed that it was not a case of *falsa demonstratio nonnocet.*

Where instantaneous forms of communication are concerned a contract is made where the acceptance is received.[10] In a case where the two parties to a contract are not in the same location at the time of contracting, the notion of where the contract is made is essentially a lawyer's construction. It seldom matters of course, but where it does matter (principally for the purposes of jurisdiction under English law) the law has to provide some answers where an application of the experience of

---

[10]Entores v. Miles Far East Corporation [1955] 2 QB 327; Brinkibon Ltd v. Stahag Stahl [1983] 2 AC 34.

everyday life does not enable one to provide them. HHJ Mann pronounced it in this way: A contract can be made in two places at once.[11]

In this case the process of drafting ended up with drafts of the agreement being in place, signed by each party, and countersigned by one but not the other, in the offices of Frere Cholmeley, solicitors for Apple, and with Mr Lagod, counsel for Computer in California. On 9 October 1991 there was a conversation to arrange completion. Computer says that the telephone call ended with (in effect) Mr Lagod in California proposing completion and Mr Zeffman (of Frere Cholmeley) agreeing to that. If correct, that would amount to an offer from Mr Lagod, accepted by Mr Zeffman. Corps puts the final events the other way round – Mr Zeffman offered, and Mr Lagod accepted, so the acceptance was received in London and the contract was made there.

Offer: An offer is a definite promise to be bound on certain specific terms. It cannot be vague as in Gunthing v. Lynn (1831), where the offeror promised to pay a further sum for a horse if it was "lucky". However if an apparently vague offer is capable of being made certain, either by implying terms or by reference to previous dealings between the parties, or within the trade, then it will be regarded as certain. Thus in Hillas v. Arcos (1932) 38 Com Cas 23, a contract for the sale of timber "of fair specification" between persons well acquainted with the timber trade was upheld.

Two particular issues as to offers should be mentioned:

Invitations to Treat or Bid. An offer must be carefully distinguished from an invitation to treat, which is an invitation to another person to make an offer. The main distinction between the two is that an offer can be converted into a contract by acceptance, provided the other requirements of a valid contract are present, whereas an invitation to treat cannot be "accepted". There are several types of invitations to treat.

Revocation, for example withdrawal of the offer. Beware that a promise to keep an offer open for a fixed period does not prevent its revocation within that period. However a person may buy a promise to keep an offer open for a fixed period, ie he may buy an option to purchase a parcel of land within a specified time if and when he so chooses. The offer cannot then be revoked without breach of this "option contract". This tool is useful for developers in their attempt to piece together a development site.

Acceptance: The acceptance may be in writing, or oral, or it may be inferred from conduct, for example by dispatching goods in response to an offer to buy. The acceptance must be unqualified and must correspond to the terms of the offer. Accordingly:

• A counter offer is insufficient and, as stated above, causes the original offer to lapse.
• A conditional assent is not enough, for example when an offer is accepted "subject to contract".

---

[11] Apple Corps Ltd v. Apple Computer, Inc [2004] EWHC 768 (Ch).

However, subject to the actual facts it is permissible to conclude that the terms of the contract are agreed between the parties either expressly or by the conduct of the contractor in carrying out the work and that there are no essential terms which had been left unagreed.[12]

Acceptance must be unqualified. A conditional acceptance is deemed to be a new offer. Note that the traditional form of acceptance "subject to mutual agreement" or "subject to contract" is not binding.

Letter of Intent: In the construction industry typically the *letter of intent* will seek to provide that the remuneration of the contractor will not include any element of profit in addition to out of pocket expenses incurred in doing the relevant work or that the remuneration payable will be ascertained by someone like a quantity surveyor employed by the person making the request for work to be done. It is also likely to request that the addressee indicates his agreement to the terms set out in the *letter of intent*. The natural interpretation of such kind of a *letter of intent* is that it is an offer to engage the addressee to commence the execution of work which it is anticipated will, in due course, be the subject of a more formal or detailed contract, but upon terms that, unless and until the more formal or detailed contract is made, the requesting party reserves the right to withdraw the request and its only obligation in respect of the making of payment for work done before the more formal or detailed contract is made is that spelled out in the *letter of intent*. If an offer in those terms is accepted either expressly, as, for example, it could be by countersigning and returning a copy of the *letter of intent* to indicate agreement to its terms, or by conduct in acting upon the request contained in the letter, it would seem that a binding contract is thereby made, albeit one of simple content.[13]

Postal rules. Where the parties contemplate acceptance by post, acceptance is complete when the letter is posted, even if the letter is lost in the post. In Household Fire Insurance Co v. Grant (1879) 3 Ex D 216 D applied for share in the company. A letter of allotment (the acceptance) was posted to him, but it never arrived. The company later went into liquidation and D was called upon to pay the amount outstanding on his shares. It was held that he had to do so. There was a contract between the company and himself which was completed when the letter of allotment was posted, regardless of the fact that it was lost in the post.

1.1.3.3   Consideration

A promise is only legally binding if it is made in return for another promise or an act (either a positive act or something given up), for example if it is part of a bargain. The requirement of "something for something" is called *consideration*.

---

[12] Pagnan S p A v. Feed Products Ltd [1987] 2 Lloyd's Rep 601 for the principles set out by Lloyd LJ at page 619; Smith v. Hughes (1871) LR 6 QB 597, and Percy Trentham Ltd v. Archital Luxfer Ltd [1993] 1 Lloyd's Rep 25.

[13] Tesco Stores Ltd v. Costain Construction Ltd & Ors [2003] EWHC 1487 (TCC) (02 July 2003), at no. 162.

It may be defined as some benefit accruing to one party, or some detriment suffered by the other. There have been several case law definitions, for example from Currie v. Misa (1875). The most common forms of consideration as to a construction contract are payment of money and performance of work or services. Beware that anything which has already been done is no consideration. Thus amendment to contracts should be made in advance in order to avoid the defence of lack of consideration.

1.1.4 Validity of Contract

The validity of a contract may be affected by the following factors:

(a) *Capacity.* Some persons, for example children have limited capacity to make contracts.
(b) *Form.* Most contracts can be made orally, but others must be in writing or by deed. Some verbal contracts must be supported by written evidence.
(c) *Content.* The parties may generally agree any terms, although they must be reasonably precise and complete. In addition some terms will be implied by the courts, custom or statute and some express terms may be overridden by statute (ie, statutory provisions ruling on a contractor's duty of fitness for purpose and reasonable skill and care).
(d) *Genuine consent.* Misrepresentation, mistake, duress and undue influence may invalidate a contract.
(e) *Illegality.* A contract will be void if it is illegal or contrary to public policy.

Note that generally construction contracts and contracts for services do not require a contract by deed, if there is reasonable consideration. Parties can simply enter into a contract by deed by making that intention clear on the face of the document, together with a signature and attestation. The main characteristics of deeds are that they do not require consideration and that they have a twelve year limitation period instead of a six year limitation period for simple written contracts.

1.1.5 Express Term or Representation

A statement may be an express term of the contract or a representation inducing its formation. The importance of the distinction is that different remedies are available if a term is broken or a representation is untrue. Which it is depends on the intention of the parties (objectively assessed).

A misrepresentation is an untrue statement of fact which is one of the causes which induces the contract.

1.1.6   Implied Terms

Terms may be implied by custom, the courts, or by statue.

The courts will imply two types into contracts. Firstly terms which are so obvious that the parties of it must have intended them to be included. These are called terms implied in fact. Secondly terms which are implied to maintain a standard of behaviour, even though the parties may not have intended them to be included. These are called terms implied in law.

There is for example in principle an implied contractual obligation of the architect or engineer with regard to the timing and programming of its design work to exercise reasonable skill and care in carrying out the design work. The obligation involving strict liability and amounting to a warranty to perform its design services by the stipulated time and within the stipulated timescale whether or not this was possible or feasible, can only arise from an express and directly imposed contractual obligation. Strict liability is rarely imposed on a professional and, where it is, these result from both clearly expressed contractual obligations that arise in the unusual situation where there is a perceived necessity for such a provision, for example, if a contractor, subject to a design and build obligation in relation to a warehouse, engages a structural engineer to design the structural floor.[14]

By contrast contractors usually are liable for fitness for purpose: If the contractor is to supply materials he warrants that the materials will be reasonably fit for the intended purposes. Where the employer makes known to the contractor the particular purpose for which the works is to be done and the work is of a kind which the contractor holds himself out as possessing a contractor's skill and judgment in the matter, there is an implied warranty that the completed work will be reasonably fit for the purposes (Keating on Construction Contracts, note 3-060). Thus depending on the merits of the case it may be appropriate to imply into a construction contract a term that the structure to be erected will, when complete, be reasonably fit for its intended purpose, but that will only be so if and insofar as the structure is to be designed by the contractor. The existence of the term in that type of case was explained by Lord Denning MR in Greaves & Co. (Contractors) Ltd v. Baynham Meikle and Partners [1975] 1 WLR 1095 at page 1098. However, it is clear from the decision of the Court of Appeal in Lynch v. Thorne [1956] 1 WLR 303 that there is no such implied term in a case in which the contractor undertakes to build to a particular specification already, at the date of the relevant contract, devised by or on behalf of the employer, and it must follow that there is no such implied term if the contractor agrees to build in accordance with plans or specifications to be produced in the future by others.[15]

---

[14] See Greaves (Contractors) v. Baynam Meikle (1975) 4 BLR 4, CA.

[15] See also Tesco Stores Ltd v. Costain Construction Ltd & Ors [2003] EWHC 1487 (TCC) (02 July 2003).

1.1.7 Discharge

There are in principle four ways by which the rights and obligations of the parties may come to an end, in particular performance, agreement, frustration and breach.

Performance: Generally, full and complete performance is required to discharge contractual obligations. Under the doctrine of substantial performance also referred to as substantial completion, illustrated by the well-known case of Hoenig v. Isaacs [1952] 2 All ER 176, if a party to a contract has substantially performed his obligations under the contract, he is entitled to payment, although he still remains exposed to a claim for damages in relation to those aspects in which the performance of his obligations is less than complete.

Illustration: Perhaps the most helpful case is the one of Hoenig v. Isaacs. That was a case where the plaintiff was an interior decorator and designer of furniture who had entered into a contract to decorate and furnish the defendant's flat for a sum of £750; and, as appears from the statement of facts on page 177, the Official Referee who tried the case at first instance found that the door of a wardrobe required replacing, that a book-shelf which was too short would have to be re-made, which would require alterations being made to a book-case, and that the cost of remedying the defects was £55. 18s. 2d. That is on a £750 contract. The ground on which the Court of Appeal in that case held that the plaintiff was entitled to succeed, notwithstanding that there was not complete performance of the contract, was that there was substantial performance of the contract and that the defects in the work which there existed were not sufficient to amount to a substantial degree of non-performance.

When interpreting a contract there are nevertheless possible issues of construction such as the meaning of "substantial completion" and "contract completion". Most contract forms provide clauses defining the conditions under which completion occurs.

Agreement: Release from contractual liability can be achieved by express agreement or waiver. Quite often construction contracts provide stipulations in order to prevent waivers, for example as to instructions or certificates issued by the engineer. Note that the fact that one party does not insist on the fulfilment of an obligation does not lead to an agreement, because there is no consideration. However if the other party has acted on the agreement the court may treat it as a binding waiver (see Uff, Construction Law, p. 256).

Frustration: The general rule is that if a person contracts to do something he is not discharged if performance proves to be impossible. The basic principles are as follows:

1. Actual physical impossibility of performing is an excuse for non performance.[16]
2. A contract is not frustrated if it becomes unexpectedly more expensive or burdensome to one of the parties. Thus unexpected difficulty or expense is no excuse for non performance.

---

[16]Clifford v. Watts (1870) LR 5 CP 577.

3. If the contract is to be discharged performance must become "radically different". This may be the case if the soil upon which the works shall be carried out is destroyed by flooding.
4. However, destruction of the work itself by fire, flood or landslip before substantial completion and taking over does not release the contractor from his obligation under the contract.

Breach of contract occurs:

1. If a party fails to perform one of his obligations under a contract, for example he does not perform on the agreed date, or he delivers goods of inferior quality.
2. If a party, before the date fixed for performance, indicates that he will not perform on the agreed date. This is an anticipatory (or repudiatory)breach.

Breach does not automatically discharge the contract. Breach of warranty only entitles the innocent party to damages. By contrast breach of condition entitles the innocent party to damages, and gives him an option to treat the contract as subsisting or discharged. In other words the contract becomes repudiated.

A party commits a repudiatory breach of contract where he threatens to, or does, breach the contract in such a way "as to show that he does not mean to accept the obligations of the contract any further".[17] Such a breach occurs:[18]

1. Where the contracting parties have agreed, whether by express words or implication of law that any breach of the contractual term in question shall entitle the other party to elect to put an end to all remaining primary obligations of both parties, i.e. were there is a breach of condition
2. Where the event resulting from the breach of contract has the effect of depriving the other party of substantially the whole benefit which it was the intention of the parties that he should obtain from the contract, i.e. where there has been a fundamental breach of contract

Note that repudiation is a drastic conclusion which should only be held to arise in clear cases of a refusal, in a matter going to the root of the contract, to perform contractual obligations. An absolute refusal to carry out the work or an abandonment of the work before it is substantially completed, without any lawful excuse, is treated as repudiation.[19]

Repudiation by one party standing alone does not terminate the contract. Repudiation must be accepted by the suffering or innocent party. Where a party affirms a contract after becoming aware of repudiatory breach by the other party, he cannot

---

[17] Heyman v. Darwins [1942] AC 356 at 378 & 398, HL.

[18] Photo Production v. Securicor [1989] AC 827 at 849, HL.

[19] Mersey Steel & Iron Co Ltd v. Naylor (1884) 9 APP Cas 434, HL; CFW Architects (A Firm) v. Cowlin Construction Ltd [2006] EWHC 6 (TCC) (23 January 2006).

thereafter rely on that breach in order to discharge his obligation to perform the contract.[20]

Apart from repudiation, there are both common law and equitable remedies for breach of contract. The common law remedies are damages, an action for an agreed sum, and a quantum meruit claim. The equitable remedies are specific performance and injunction. By far the most commonly sought remedy is damages.

As to damages the basic principles are as follows:

1. A claimant is entitled to be compensated by being given such sum of money as will put it in the position which it would have been in if it had not sustained the wrong for which it is being compensated – see Livingstone v. Rawyards Coal Co (1880) 5 App Cas 25 at 39.
2. This principle was reaffirmed by Lord Haldane in British Westinghouse v. The Underground Railway of London [1912] AC 673 at 689 together with the principle that it is the duty of a claimant to take all reasonable steps to mitigate the loss consequent on the breach.
3. The damages in respect of which compensation is given must have been caused by the defendant's breach and must be of a type which was foreseen or should reasonably have been foreseen by the claimant.[21]
4. It follows that if the whole or part of the claim does not arise out of a defendant's wrongdoing but from some independent cause the claimant cannot recover damages arising from that cause. The independent cause may be an event which breaks the chain of causation or takes the form of negligent advice on which the claimant has acted. See, e.g. The Board of Governors of the Hospital for Sick Children v. McLaughlin & Harvey plc [1987] 19 Con L R 25 at 96.
5. The courts have made it clear that where a claimant has undertaken work to remedy a wrongful act the court should be very slow to accept an objection by the wrongdoer as to the method used by the claimant to repair the injury.

1.1.8 Common Features of English Construction Contracts

Three common features of English construction contracts are:

1. Provisions for an independent third party (The Engineer, also referred to as the Construction Manager, the Supervisor, the Architect or similar) to issue *certificates* signifying particular events
2. Liquidated damages clauses, ensuring payments for non compliance with quality and time requirements
3. Dispute Adjudication clauses

---

[20] Peyman v. Lanjani [1985] Ch 457; CFW Architects (A Firm) v. Cowlin Construction Ltd [2006] EWHC 6 (TCC) (23 January 2006).

[21] See The Wagon Mound [1961] AC 388 and The Wagon Mound No. 2 [1967] 1 AC 617.

Certificates are merely a manifestation of the parties' agreement and its effects are no more than the parties have agreed them to be. The function of a certificate is usually nothing more than to record factual events. Whether a certificate is conclusive as to what it purports to certify depends on the wording of the certificate. Usually construction contracts distinguish between interim and final certificates.

It is not uncommon to find the following or similar clauses within a construction contract:[22]

(1) The Construction Manager has no authority to issue and he shall not issue without the prior written approval of the Client, or of the Design Team Leader on the Client's behalf, an instruction to any Trade Contractor varying the design or specification of work, materials and/or goods or the quality or quantity thereof as shown or described in any Trade Contract. The Construction Manager has no authority to consent to or agree to any amendment to the terms of any Trade Contract with any Trade Contractor nor to consent to or agree to any waiver or release of any obligation of any Trade Contractor under and in connection with a Trade Contract without the prior written approval of the Client.

(2) The Construction Manager has no authority to approve any design carried out by any Trade Contractor or to approve the quality of materials or the standards of workmanship where and to the extent that the Trade Contract requires that such approval is a matter for the opinion of the Design Team Leader without, in either case, the prior written approval of the Design Team Leader.

(3) The Construction Manager shall not grant any extension of time to any Trade Contractor nor shall he agree to accept any financial claim of any kind whatsoever pursuant to the terms of any Trade Contract without having first consulted the Design Team Leader and having taken due account of its comments and without having first reported on the same to the Client.

(4) The Construction Manager has no authority to issue any certificate whatsoever (including, but without limitation, interim and final certificates and certificates of practical completion and making good defects) to any Trade Contractor unless the same has been duly signed by the Design Team Leader.

(5) The Construction Manager has no authority to issue any instruction or give any approval or do any other thing pursuant to a Trade Contract which would or might alter the cost of the Development to the Client by more than £1,000 in respect of any one such event without first referring the matter in writing to the Design Team Leader and to the Client, with his comments....

(6) The Construction Manager shall have no authority to give any notice of default pursuant to any condition of the Trade Contract that provides for the

---

[22] See Bernhard's Rugby Landscapes Ltd v. Stockley Park Consortium Ltd [1998] EWHC Technology 326 (22 April 1998).

determination of the employment of a Trade Contractor by the Client, without having first consulted the Design Team Leader and the Client.

It will depend on the construction of the contract whether any certificate is binding and final or only interim in nature.

Liquidated damages clauses intend to fix damages for identified and specified events, such as delayed completion or failure to achieve performance criteria which have been warranted. Liquidated damages are pre-estimated amounts or a sum definitely ascertainable for breach of contract. The substitution of a larger sum as liquidated damages is regarded, not as a pre-estimate of damages, but as a penalty in the nature of a penal payment. Penalties are unenforceable. In dealing with the circumstances in which an agreed sum might be held to be a penalty instead of liquidated damages, the following principles will be fundamental:[23]

1. It will be held to be a penalty if the sum stipulated for is extravagant and unconscionable in amount in comparison with the greatest loss that could conceivably be proved to have followed from the breach.
2. It will be held to be a penalty if the breach consists only in not paying a sum of money, and the sum stipulated is a sum greater than the sum which ought to have been paid.

The question whether a sum stipulated is a penalty or liquidated damages is a question of construction to be decided upon the terms and inherent circumstances of each particular contract, judged of as at the time of the making of the contract, not at the time of the breach.[24] Although the parties to a contract who used the words "penalty" or liquidated damages may *prima facie* be supposed to mean what they say, yet the expression used is not conclusive. The Court must find out whether the payment stipulated is in truth a penalty or liquidated damages. The essence of a penalty is a payment of money stipulated as *in terrorem* of the offending party whereas the essence of liquidated damages is a genuine covenanted pre-estimate of damage.

Dispute Adjudication: Since the enactment of the HGCRA 1996 dispute adjudication is compulsory for all parties to a construction contract where the site is situated within England and Wales. Dispute Adjudication is a modern method of dispute resolution. In short, as has been confirmed by Lord Justice May in Quietfield Ltd v. Vascroft Construction Ltd [2006] EWCA Civ 1737 (20 December 2006) dispute adjudication is intended to provide a speedy and proportionate temporary decision of disputes arising under construction contracts. The idea behind this is in essence that such a decision may settle the dispute for the time being in a fair way, and help the parties, if possible, to finally resolve their disputes by agreement without the need for protracted and often very expensive arbitration or litigation.

---

[23] Compare Campus and Stadium Ireland Development Ltd v. Dublin Waterworld Ltd [2006] IEHC 200 (21 March 2006).

[24] Dunlop Pneumatic Tyre Company v. New Garage and Motor Company Ltd [1915] AC 79, at p. 86.

The general understanding is that the statutory provisions have been reasonably successful. But it is well known that there have been problems with some large contracts; as if huge disputes scarcely amenable to speedy, even temporary, determination are nevertheless referred wholesale for adjudication; or if a procedure which is supposed to be speedy turns into something more akin to protracted and more expensive litigation or arbitration. The key features of English dispute adjudication are:

- Short delay of 28 days within which the adjudicator must render his decision
- Limited control of interim binding adjudication decisions
- Enforceability of dispute adjudication decisions by summary judgments

The relevant provision of the HGCRA reads as follows:

> A party to a construction contract has the right to refer a dispute under the contract for adjudication under a procedure complying with this section. For this purpose "dispute" includes any difference.

An adjudicator derives his jurisdiction from his appointment. That appointment is governed by the statutory provisions of the HGCRA which require there to be a dispute that has already arisen between parties to a construction contract.

1.2   Finnish Contract Law

The Finnish Contracts Act and other Finnish law do not contain any particular provisions for construction contracts. However contractual freedom allows the parties to decide the content of any contract. In Finland most commonly works become awarded by main contracts with nominated sub-contracts, separate trade contracts with a project manager, design-and-construct contracts as well as CM contracting contracts and CM consulting contracts. However, if the contract parties do not make detailed provisions in the contract itself, any remaining gaps are filled by general principles of contract law. As a matter of fact these general principles of contract law are generally not very suitable for the management of construction projects.

Due to the above mentioned fact that Finnish law lacks any detailed legislation as to construction contracts, a collection of provisions for such contracts in Finland has been developed. These are the YSE terms (at present in the version of 1998 YSE 98). These terms do not have the character of a law, but are standardised general contract terms that have been drafted by a public committee. YSE terms are also in use in some other countries such as Estonia. When drafting construction agreements in Estonia it is common to refer to either FIDIC standard contract forms, less frequently also to the YSE, the Finnish standard terms of contracts.

YSE terms are applicable only if the parties to a construction contract expressly agree to incorporate them into the contract. Actually, they are generally regarded as being balanced and fair, and are agreed upon in most Finnish construction contracts. Therefore, in practice there is usually no way around YSE terms, even for foreign contractors and investors, and they must accordingly be taken into account when drafting the contract.

Section 1.1 of the YSE (1998) sets out a contractor's principal obligation to carry out all works as specified in contract documents. Section 1.2 states further that the contract includes all works required to achieve the agreed finished result. Additionally, articles 7 and 8 of YSE (1998) provide the mode of cooperation and collaboration between contract stakeholders, respectively.

According to section 29 of the YSE 98 terms, the guarantee period for buildings is only two years. Following expiration of the guarantee period, the contractor may remain liable for a period of up to ten years following delivery in the circumstances set out below:

- A defect has been caused by the contractor's gross negligence or there has been serious neglect of agreed quality assurance, or work has been left entirely uncompleted.
- The client could not reasonably be expected to have noticed the defects in the handover inspection or during the guarantee period.

1.3   French Contract Law

1.3.1   Relevant Provisions

The main provisions concerning the French law of contract are contained in the French Civil Code (hereinafter Code Civil). Otherwise, there are special provisions in a number of distinct acts such as:

Law no. 75-1334 as to sub-contracting
Law no. 78-12 as to liability and insurance in the construction field

The French Civil Code is still an archetype for legislators in various jurisdictions and has been adopted by many countries, such as Belgium, Cameroon, Luxembourg, Malta and Romania. French law still strongly influences its former colonies, protectorates and condominiums such as Algeria, Morocco, Tunisia and other parts of Africa including the OHADA.

OHADA is the French acronym for "Organisation pour l'Harmonisation du Droit des Affaires en Afrique" translated in English as the "Organization for the Harmonisation of Business Law in Africa". This organisation was founded on 17 October 1993 in Port Louis (Mauritius). The OHADA Treaty is today made up of 16 Africans states. Initially fourteen African countries signed the treaty, with two countries subsequently adhering to the treaty (Comoros and Guinea) and a third the Democratic Republic of Congo) due to adhere shortly.

1.3.2 Entering a Contract

1.3.2.1 Definition of Contract Under French Law

According to Art. 1101 Code Civil, a contract is an *agreement* by which one or several persons bind themselves, towards one or several others, to transfer (e.g. property in the sales of goods), to do (e.g. contract of manufacture/of employment) or not to do something. A contract may be synallagmatic (where the contracting parties bind themselves mutually towards each other), or unilateral (where one or more persons are bound towards one or several others, without any obligation of the latter, e.g. loan, gift) (Art.1102, 1103 Code Civil).

A construction contract will usually be considered as a "contrat de louage d'ouvrage", whereby one instructs a person to do a work, whether it is agreed that he will furnish his work or his industry only, or that he will also furnish the material (Art. 1787 Code Civil). The French legal wording as to construction contracts is still very close to the old Roman law which can be seen from the use of the term louage d'ouvrage which in fact is a "locatio conductio", whereby a locator (employer = maître de l'ouvrage) lets the work to the conductor (contractor = entrepreneur).

For the purposes of the French Law no. 75-1334, subcontracting shall be understood to mean the process by which a contractor entrusts, by means of a subcontract, and under their responsibility, all or part of the execution of a works contract or public contract concluded with the client to another person known as the subcontractor. Also for the purposes of the aforementioned law subcontractors shall be considered as the main contractor with regard to their own subcontractors.

Such an agreement lawfully entered into take the place of the law for those who have made it. It may be revoked only by mutual consent, or for causes authorized by law and must be performed in good faith (Art. 1134 Code Civil). It should be retained that agreements are binding not only as to what is therein expressed, but also as to all the consequences which equity, usage or statute give to the obligation according to its nature (Art. 1135 Code Civil). Therefore, thorough attention should be paid to the mandatory provisions of the proper law of the contract (*ordre public*).

For example, a contractor in France should bear in mind while taking an insurance policy that the statutory liability of a contractor lasts 10 years under French law, insofar as stability and security of the building are affected by latent defects (*garantie décennale*). Although the Cour de Cassation had not yet the occasion to qualify the *garantie décennale* as belonging to *ordre public international*, the majority of the doctrine shares this opinion; on the contrary, the remedy of the subcontractor against the employer (*action directe du sous-traitant*, see below) belongs in to the *ordre public interne*.[25] As a matter of the fact, the parties may derogate from the rule of *action directe* while setting another law as French law as applicable to a contract, but not from that of the decennial guarantee.

---

[25] Cour de Cassation 23.01.2007, no.04-10897: Juris–Data no. 2007-037027.

Moreover, one should pay attention to the *customary rules* (regional/international), as according to Art. 1160 Code Civil, terms which are customary shall be supplemented in the contract, even though they are not expressed there. Other sources are the *international provisions that are part of the French national law*, e.g. among others the United Nations Convention on contracts for the International Sale of Goods (CISG) is part of French substantive law and should apply whenever an international sales agreement is made; the domestic sales are subject to the national provisions.

1.3.2.2   Are There Any Formal Requirements for Contracts?

Although most non-lawyers think of contracts as written documents, generally, unless it is provided by a statute, a formal expression of a contract (written contract) is not necessary for lawfully creating a contractual obligation and it is merely necessary in order to prove the existence of a contract. However, some contracts may be executed only in written form and may need an authentic instrument (e.g. conveyance of real estate, mortgage on real property).

Where a written document is required for the validity of a legal transaction, it may be established and stored in electronic form; exception to that is made in regard to instruments relating to family law, to the law of succession and to instruments relating to securities or real charge. Some contracts may require under French law the handing over of the contract's material object (e.g. pawn, deposit, loan, called *contrats réels*); if there is promise without handing over, the creditor is entitled to damages.

1.3.2.3   Validity of Contracts

The following elements are essential for the validity of an agreement (Art. 1108 Code civil):

1. *The* consent *of the party who binds himself:* there is no valid consent, where the consent was given only by error (erreur), or where it was extorted by duress (violence) or abused by deception (dol) (Art. 1109 Code civil). An agreement entered into by error, duress or deception is not void by the law (Art. 1117 Code Civil); it only gives rise to an action for annulment or rescision.
2. The capacity *to enter a contract:* Provisions relating to the capacity of persons are contained in Art. 1123–1125 and 489 Code Civil. Various cases of incapacity are enumerated in the Art.903, 907, 908, etc. of Code civil.
3. *A definite* object *which forms the subject-matter of the undertaking:* the object of the contract represents the performance due by each party; it has to be lawful which means it should not derogate from the mandatory statutory provisions (*lois d'ordre public*).
4. *A lawful* cause *in the obligation:* the cause represents the reason a person is engaged for, the mere reason of her consent. The French doctrine distinguishes

between the "objective cause" (also "cause of the obligation", which is the same for each category of contracting party) and the "subjective cause" (also "cause of the contract", which is specific to a party of a given contract). In synallagmatic contracts, the French "*cause de l'obligation*" corresponds in part to the English concept of "consideration", as both reveal the expectation of the counter-performance by the other party. One cannot compare both concepts, as for example a gift is made without consideration, but it has a cause though (the intention of gratifying a person, *l'intention libérale*). Under French law, an obligation without cause (in synallagmatic contracts, with a ridiculous counter-performance) or having a false cause (e.g. taking an insurance for goods already lost) are null and void (*nullité absolue*). Another good example of lack of cause is the lack of risk in the so-called *aleatory* contracts (in Civil Law, an aleatory contract is a mutual agreement, of which the effects, with respect both to the advantages and losses, whether to all the parties, or to some of them, depend on an uncertain event, e.g. an insurance). The sole instruments allowed creating an obligation without having a cause are the so-called *actes abstraits*, like cheques, bills of exchange, etc.(all *effets de commerce*). As to the "cause du contrat", it has be "lawful", which means not violating the *ordre public et les bonnes moeurs,* as a contract with an unlawful subjective cause is also null and void *(nullité absolue)* (e.g. selling one's elector vote).

1.3.3 Contract Interpretation

Contracts shall be construed according to the common intention of the parties, which is given priority rather than the literal meaning of the terms (Art. 1156 Code civil). When a common intention cannot be established, reference is made to the understanding which a reasonable man would have of the disputed term. Ambiguous clauses shall be given the meaning which allows them have some effect and not the contrary (Art.1157 Code civil); they should be taken in the meaning which best suits the subject matter of the contract (Art.1158 Code civil). It should be noticed that in case of doubt, an agreement shall be interpreted against the one who has stipulated, and in favour of the one who has contracted the obligation (Art. 1162 Code civil). It is also provided that interpretation has to be in accordance with good faith and fair dealing.

French courts usually first of all qualify or characterize the nature of the agreement. If the agreement meets the elements of one of the nominated contracts its content will be largely determined by the relevant default rules (lois supplétives). And even if it has the nature of an innominate contract (a contract sui generis) its incidents will be derived from the nominate contracts to which it is most analogous. Once the legal character of an agreement has been determined the courts will make a distinction between an "obligation de moyens" and an "obligation de résultat". The rationale for this is that in principle liability for non performance is traditionally based on fault. The distinction between "obligation de moyens" and an "obligation de résultat" makes it possible to put a contractor either under an obligation to exercise skill and care (obligation de moyens) or to achieve a specific result (obligation de résultat). It is common place that a contract for works (contrat de louage d'ouvrage or contrat d'entreprise) comprises the promise to achieve a specific result. Whether a contract comprises an "obligation de moyens" or an "obligation de résultat" is a matter of law. The criterion which is most commonly acknowledged by the authorities for the determination of the nature of an obligation is that of the aleatory or otherwise character of the debtor's undertaking. If the promised performance can in the ordinary course of events be expected to be achieved, the obligation is de résultat. If not, it is an obligation de moyens. The obligation of an architect or engineer is sometimes said to be obligation de Moyens, but in any case its obligations are de résultat in so far as the French decennial liability is concerned.

1.3.4   Effects of a Contract

According to Art. 1134 Code Civil, agreements lawfully entered into take the place of the law for those who have made them. They may be revoked only by mutual consent, or for reasons provided by law. As a rule, one may bind oneself and stipulate in his own name, only for oneself (Art. 1119 Code civil), so that agreements produce effect only between the contracting parties; they cannot harm a third party (Art. 1165 Code Civil). An exception to this rule is the representation, e.g. the mandatary (*mandataire*) is acting in the name of a third party, the *mandant*.

Under French law, in contrast with the anglo-saxon concept of the privity of contract, contracts may create enforceable obligations even for third parties. For example, under French law, even if there is no direct relationship between the employer and the subcontractor (one who has contracted with the original contractor for the performance of a part of the work), the subcontractor is entitled to ask payment from the employer in the case the original contractor refuses to pay (so-called "action directe du sous-traitant", art. 12 of the Statute concerning the sub-contracting, of 31 December 1975 – Law no. 75-1334).

Another example of *action directe* is laid down in Art. 1166 Code Civil: creditors may exercise their debtor's rights and actions, except those which are exclusively dependent on the person (*action oblique*); furthermore, they are entitled by Art. 1167 Code Civil to attack on their own behalf transactions made by their debtor in fraud of their rights (*action paulienne*). The French law provides another few examples of *action directe*: that of the victim against the insurance provider, that of the landlord against the sub-tenant.

As a contract is a legally binding agreement the parties to it are bound to perform it. Thus contractual liability is in principle absolute. As such according to Art. 1147 Code Civil the debtor is condemned, where appropriate, to the payment of damages, either on account of the non performance of the obligation or on account of delay in its performance, whenever he does not show that the non performance is due to an external cause which cannot be imputed to him, even if there is no bad faith on his part. No doctrine of change of circumstances or economic impossibility or disappearance of the foundation of the contract has been accepted by French courts. However, the term of sujétions imprévus has been adopted for public works contracts, which comprises insurmountable obstacles, which had very gravely disturbed the economy of the contract. The civil courts only accept a « bouleversement de l'économie du contrat », which requires proving that the performed works are radically different from those which have been originally agreed and that the scope of the works has changed. Also the Cour de Cassation requires that the employer has either expressly instructed the works before they have been carried out or that he has unequivocally accepted them after their execution.[26] As a rule any unforeseeable circumstances do not have the nature to result in a modification of a lump sum price.[27]

1.3.5 Limitation Periods

The French law concerning limitation has recently been reformed. According to Art. 2262 Code Civil (old version), the *general limitation period* under French law lasted *30 years. Claims for tort liability* were barred after *10 years* from the manifestation of the injury or of its aggravation (Art. 2270-1 Code Civil – old version). Since 2008 the general limitation period under French law lasts 5 years (Art. 2224 Code Civil). The time limit for tort claims is still ten years (Art. 2226 Code Civil).

Any natural or juridical person who may be liable under Articles 1792 to 1792-4 of the Civil Code is discharged from the liabilities and warranties by which they are weighed down in application of Articles 1792 to 1792-2 Civil Code, after ten years from the approval of the works or, in application of Article 1792-3, on the expiry of the period referred to in this Article (Art. 1792-4-1 Code Civil). Other Claims against constructors in the sense of Art. 1792 and 1792 Code Civil falling outside the scope of Art. 1792-3, 1792-4-1 and 1792-4-2 Code Civil are barred after ten years from the approval of the works (Art. 1792-4-3 Code Civil).

Claims for liability directed against subcontractors for reason of damages affecting a work or elements of equipment of a work specified in Art. 1792 and 1792-2 Code Civil are barred after *ten years* as from the approval of the works and, as to the damages affecting those of the elements of equipment specified in Art.1792-3, after two years as from that same approval (Art. 2270-2 Code Civil old version = Art. 1792-4-2 Code Civil).

---

[26]Cour de Cassation, decision from 27 September 2006, file no. 05-13.808, D. 2006, 2416.

[27]Cour de Cassation, decision from 20 November 2002, file no. 00-14.423, RD imm. 2003, 60.

There is a special limitation period of 10 years for claims which arises in the relationship between merchants or between merchants and non-merchants (Art. L.110-4 Code de Commerce). Shorter limitation periods are provided for claims resulting of the sale of goods and services to non-merchants (2 years, Art. L-137-2 Code de la Consommation replacing the former Art. 2272(4) Code Civil) and for those resulting of everything which is payable periodically (5 years, Art. 2277 Code Civil old version replaced by Art. 2224 Code Civil).

1.3.6   Pre-contractual Liability

French courts imposed under certain circumstances tortious liability (Art.1382 and 1383 Code civil) when unfair behaviour of one of the parties at the pre-contractual stage led to the failure to enter into the agreement (*rupture abusive des pourparlers*).

1.3.7   Good Faith

According to Art.1134(3) Code Civil, the obligations resulting from contracts "must be performed in good faith". The concept of "good faith" is explained neither by the French case-law nor by statutes, but obviously means "with the loyalty inherent to the contractual dealings", without fraud, deception or malevolence.[28] Violating the duty of good faith and fair dealing gives rise to a tort action which is different from the contractual remedies.

1.3.8   Performance

1.3.8.1   What Does "Non-performance" Mean?

Under French law, the non-performance may occur in different ways: it may be total (e.g. the contractor who did not build anything), partial (e.g. the contractor who executed only the masonry works); moreover, a defective performance (e.g. delayed or malfunctioning works) is equal to a non-performance. As a matter of fact, the creditor is entitled, alternatively, to seek proper enforcement (if possible), to perform the debtor's obligation by himself but at the debtor's costs, or terminate the contract (*résolution du contrat*). If economic loss occurs as a result of the non-performance, the creditor may be awarded damages (*dommages-intérêts*).

---

[28] CA Paris 20 juin 1996, Rev.arb. 1996.657, Cour de Casssation 2 juillet 1975, Bull.III, p.1978.

1.3.8.2   What Are the Available Remedies in Case of Non-performance?

The *exceptio non adimpleti contractus* or *exception d'inexécution*, under which a party who has not received the contractual performance to which it is entitled may withhold its own performance. However, it has to be proportionate to the non-performance occurred (*bonne foi du créancier*). The contract is not terminated, but just suspended: if the faulty party resumes the performance, the party withholding its performance should equally resume the performance.

A contract may be terminated may through amiable settlement or, if not possible, by judiciary means (Art.1184 Code Civil), which is the most frequent way of termination in France. Termination may occur even if there is no fault of the debtor, without regard to the degree of the non-performance. The judge has a large discrepancy as to the remedies he pronounces: he may grant the debtor an extension of time, or refuse to terminate the contract but to award damages to the creditor, or terminate the contract partially or totally while awarding or not awarding damages to the creditor. Otherwise, termination may occur also through a terminating clause inserted in the contract (*clause résolutoire*), or by the virtue of a law (e.g. in *intuitu personae* contracts as mandate or insurance).

1.3.8.3   Specific Remedies Available Against the Builder:
The Decennial Liability

Art. 1792 Code Civil provides that any builder of a work is liable as of right, towards the building owner or purchaser, for damages, even resulting from a defect of the ground, which imperil the strength of the building or which, affecting it in one of its constituent parts or one of its elements of equipment, render it unsuitable for its purposes. Are deemed builders of the work any architect, contractor, technician or other person bound to the building owner by a contract of hire of work (art. 1792-1 Code Civil).

It is however necessary to note that the French liability system is much more complete than that. Under French law the contractor also warrants a "garantie de bon fonctionnement" of 2 years (Art. 1792-3 Code Civil) and according to Art. 1792-6 Code Civil a warranty of perfected completion ("garantie de parfait achievement"), to which a contractor is held liable during a period of 1 year.

The decennial liability concerns all defects, whether apparent or hidden. Such liability does not take place where the builder proves that the damages were caused by an extraneous event.

Foreign contractors have to be aware of the decennial liability even if the proper law of the contract is not the law of the country where the site is situated. As a rule the decennial liability overrules choice of law clauses and is applicable by law in the country where the site is located if and when the laws of this country provide the decennial liability (see explanatory note "The definition of the contract under French Law").

1.3.9 Damages and Limitation of Liability

1.3.9.1 Extent of Damages

Damages due to a creditor are, as a rule, for the loss which he has suffered and the profit which he has been deprived of (Art. 1149 Code Civil). Damages may include only what is an immediate and direct consequence of the non-performance of the agreement (Art. 1152 Code Civil).The party entitled to damages may not be awarded a greater or lesser sum; nevertheless, the judge may even of his own motion moderate or increase the agreed penalty, where it is obviously dispropor-tionate.

In all matters, the award of compensation involves interest at the statutory rate even failing a claim or a specific provision in the judgment (Art.1153-1 Code Civil). Damages are due only where a debtor is given notice to fulfil his obligation (Art.1146 Code Civil). As in the case of the penalty clauses (see below), notice of default may follow from a letter missive where a sufficient requisition results from it.

1.3.9.2 Cases of Exemption

According to Art.1147 Code civil, "If the debtor does not prove that the non-performance/the delay in performing is due to an external cause, he shall be ordered to pay damages even in absence of bad faith". The corollary of this rule is that damages should not be due if the debtor was prevented from performing by reason of *force majeure* or of a fortuitous event (Art. 1148 Code Civil).

Nevertheless, the *concept of force-majeure does not include the unforeseeable physical conditions*, e.g. those related to the ground (*risque du sol*). The most important consequence of this rule is that in the case of *lump sum contracts* (*marché à forfait*), the contract price is quasi-untouchable, as additional works caused by unforeseeable conditions have to be carried by the contractor as long they are necessary and do not affect the object and general economy of the contract.[29]

According to the Code de la Construction et de l'Habitation (CCH), the respon-sibility for unforeseeable physical conditions related to the ground shall be taken by the contractor, who has a general duty of inspecting the site while working in the so-called *secteur protégé*. Therefore, under French consumer law the employer doesn't have to bear additional costs related to unforeseeable physical conditions of the soil[30].

---

[29] Cour de Cassation. 27.09.2006, D.2006, I.R. 2416.

[30] Cour de Cassation, 20 janv. 1993, no. 91-10-900/C, no. 115 P + F, Voisin c/ Correia : Bull. civ. III, no. 5.

1.3.10   Penalty Clauses

According to art. 1226 Code Civil, "a penalty is a clause by which a person, in order to ensure performance of an agreement, binds himself to something in case of non-performance." A penalty clause is a compensation for the damages which the creditor suffers from the non-performance of the principal obligation. The penalty clauses with purely punitive aims are usual on the continent, but are prohibited under Common Law and as a result are not enforceable by the courts.

The difference between the penalty clause and the liquidated damages is that the sum to be paid when breaking a promise under Common Law has to be reasonably estimated at the time of contracting, taking into account the actual damage that will probably ensue from breach. On the contrary, under French Contract Law there isn't any relationship between the actual damage and the sum to be paid as a penalty. A creditor may not claim at the same time the principal and the penalty, unless it was stipulated for a mere delay; instead of claiming the penalty stipulated against the debtor who is under notice of default, a creditor may proceed with the performance of the principal obligation.

It is important to notice that the penalty is incurred only where the debtor is under notice of default (Art. 1230 Code Civil), whether the original obligation contains or not a term within which it must be performed, in proportion to the interest which the part performance has procured for the creditor, without prejudice to the application of Article 1152 Code Civil. Any stipulation to the contrary shall be deemed not written (null and void). A debtor is given notice of default either through a demand or other equivalent act such as a letter missive, where a sufficient requisition results from its terms or by the effect of the agreement where it provides that the debtor will be put in default without any notice and through the mere expiry of time (Art. 1139 Code Civil).

1.3.11   Subcontracting

French law protects subcontractors by Law no. 75-1334. According to Art. 6 of this law subcontractors who have been accepted and whose conditions of payment have been approved by the client shall be paid directly by the latter for the part of the contract executed by the former. Pursuant to Art. 12 of the law the subcontractor shall be able to take direct action against the client, should the main contractor fail to pay the monies due by virtue of the subcontract, one month after notice to pay is given. A copy of this notice to pay shall be sent to the client. Any waiver of direct payment shall be considered invalid. This direct action shall apply even if the main contractor is in liquidation, receivership or temporary suspension of proceedings. Also the provisions of the second subparagraph of Article 1799-1 of the Civil Code shall apply to subcontractors who fulfil the conditions laid down in this article.

After a long period of uncertainty the French Supreme Court has decided that the aforementioned direct claim has a nature which justifies applying it in all cases where the place of performance of the works is situated in France, even though the proper law of the subcontract and the proper law of the main contract is another law.[31] Thus the direct action is part of the French ordre public.

1.4 German Contract Law

1.4.1 Relevant Provisions

The main provisions concerning the German law of contract are contained in the German Civil Code (hereinafter Civil Code), adopted in 1900. Since then the Code has been reformed several times, in particular in 2001 and 2009.

1.4.2 German Legal System

The German legal system is a civil law legal system. By this it is meant that most of its primary legal principles have been adopted, made or developed by acts of parliament. German law has been subject to many influences over the centuries. In fact, German law has its roots in former Salic law, Roman law and French law. The first landmark event was the enactment of the Prussian General National Law for the Prussian States (Preußisches Allgemeines Landrecht, 1874) followed by the German Civil Code (Bürgerliches Gesetzbuch) in 1900.

For the purposes of this book it is not appropriate immerse too far into a detailed analysis. However, some preliminary remarks as to German contract law must be emphasized. German contract law is a sophisticated system which is clearly structured and based on a set of concepts and definitions. Obligations may be created by law or by contract. An obligation presupposes a legal relationship concerning an obligation (Schuldverhältnis). A contract is the result of declarations of intentions (Willenserklärungen). The subject matter of contracts is part of the doctrine of legal transactions (Rechtsgeschäftslehre). A contract is a legal transaction which may constitute an obligation or even more precisely a relationship of obligation (Schuldverhältnis). However a contract may also transfer a legal title or a right which leads to one of the main and characteristic German legal principles, which is the abstraction principle which includes the distinction principle. Both principles dominate the entire Civil Code and are vital for the understanding of how the German Civil Code treats legal transactions, such as contracts. According to this system, ownership is not transferred by a contract of sale, as for example is the case in France. Instead, a contract of sale merely obliges the seller to transfer ownership of the good sold to the purchaser, while the purchaser is obliged to pay the agreed price.

---

[31] Cour de Cassation, mixed chamber, decision from 30 November 2007, file no. 06-14006.

For transfer of ownership, a further contract is necessary which is governed by Sections 929 et seq. The sales contract and the contract by which ownership becomes transferred to the purchaser are distinct contracts (distinction principle). According to the abstraction principle both contracts do not suffer the same destiny. Thus either the sales contract or the contract concerning transfer of ownership may be invalid without having an effect on the other contract. However German courts have much influence on the interpretation of the law. Thus in practice case law is quite important. For the avoidance of ambiguity the following paragraph concerns only contractual relationships of obligations.

German contract law is of course based on the principle of freedom of contract. The Motive (Vol. I, p. 126) pronounced that a legal transaction is a private declaration of intention aiming at the legal consequence which the law sanctions because it is intended. In line with this the current Section 311 para. 1 German Civil Code provides that "unless otherwise provided by statute, a contract between the parties is necessary in order to create an obligation by legal transaction or to alter the content of an obligation". Thus it must be doubted that German law recognises contractual freedom as being the principle according to which a contract is the outcome of consenting mind, which forms the law of the parties, being enforceable at court. Instead contractual freedom means first of all that the parties are free to decide whether they wish to enter into a contract or not. Once they have done so the courts will ascertain the nature of the legal transaction depending on the subject matter of the transaction and the common intentions of the parties. According to the nature of the transaction the existing default rules as provided by law for this type of contract will apply unless the parties expressly or tacitly deviate from them to the extent that is possible and permitted. In other words, entering into a contract means that the parties accept what the law provides for the particular type of contract involved which the parties intended to conclude. One could also say that the parties are free to enter into a contract which is governed by the law, or alternatively that the formation of a contract is necessary in order for the law to apply. Thus the content of each contract is more or less pre-defined unless a court is willing to consider that a particular contract is a contract sui generis, which is rarely the case. The socio economic developments in Germany since 1900 led to the current consensus that the principle of good faith justifies policing the content of each contract. Thus as a rule contractual freedom only exists within the limits of good faith and according to Section 307 German Civil Code any contract term incorporated in standard terms which is not compatible with the essential principles of statutory regulation from which it deviates, or limits essential rights or duties inherent in the nature of the contract to such an extent that attainment of the contractual objective is jeopardised, is void. Bespoke contracts are still an admissible and valid alternative but to negotiate a contract means much more than to honour it. Thus a consultancy agreement based on standard terms would not be considered to be a bespoke contract simply because the contracting party has not made any objections to it or the standard terms have been discussed with them. By contrast negotiations which exclude judicial control under Section 307 Civil Code mean that "the user first seriously puts on the table the core content which is contrary to statute law in his general conditions of contract … and gives the negotiating party freedom of formulation for protection of his own interests, with at least a real possibility of influencing the shaping of the content of the contractual conditions".[32] The negotiating party must clearly and seriously declare himself prepared to make envisaged amendments to the individual clauses.

It can be summarized that freedom of contract is not understood as the power of the parties to create a legal relationship, the terms of which follow from the intentions of the parties but a being a freedom which can be exercised within the limits of the framework of a special type of contract and an under a comprehensive judicial control. It follows from this that more or less the so called legal Leitmotiv has become a dogma. One could say that the parties are invited to define their common intentions in order to determine the applicable law. Even though it is not mandatory as such it will be enforced if the parties are not willing to shoulder the burden of lengthy and thorough negotiations.

German law distinguishes between single sided transactions and double sided transactions. A single sided transaction requires only one declaration of intention, for example a termination notice or a rescission notice. Such kind of transaction does not create obligations. In order to create an obligation out of a contract two declarations of intention are required.

Finally German law distinguishes between one sided contracts (gift contract whereby the donor becomes obliged to transfer the gift to the donee), which create only one obligation and doubled sided contracts which usually create reciprocal obligations (sales contracts, leasehold contracts, etc.).

1.4.3   Entering a Contract

As aforementioned under German law there is no legal definition as to the term "contract". However Section 311 para. 1 Civil Code provides as follows: Unless otherwise provided by statute, a contract between the parties is necessary in order to create an obligation by legal transaction or to alter the content of an obligation. But an obligation with duties under section 241(2) Civil Code also comes about by:

1. The commencement of contract negotiations
2. The initiation of a contract where the one party, with regard to any possible contractual relationship, grants or entrusts to the other party the possibility of affecting his rights, legally protected interests and other interests
3. Similar business contacts

Moreover, pursuant to Section 311 para. 3 Civil Code an obligation with duties in accordance with section 241(2) may also arise towards persons who are not intended to be parties to the contract. Such an obligation arises in particular, if

---

[32] BGH [1987] NJW-RR 144.

the third party by enlisting a particularly high degree of reliance materially influences the contractual negotiations or the conclusion of the contract.

The necessary elements of a contract consist in an offer made by one party and in an acceptance given by the other one. There must be the intention of both parties to create a legal relationship. Under German law a declaration which was actually given without consciousness which the recipient might understand as legally effective, is initially effective but can be challenged as a mistaken declaration in accordance with Sec. 119, 120, 121 Civil Code.[33] The intention to create a contract must be expressed so that the other party is informed of it. It may be declared either express or implied. Thus a contract may be concluded either by the acceptance of an offer or by conduct of the parties that is sufficient to show agreement. In some jurisdictions additional requirements must be fulfilled. If French law governs the contract there must be *cause*. If English law governs the contract there must be *consideration*.

An offer is a legal act that declares the intention of the offeror to be bound in case of acceptance. It must be sufficiently definite. Acceptance is a legal act that declares the assent to an offer. It can be made expressly or impliedly. The above mentioned legal acts or so called declarations of intention must correspond. Until the parties have agreed on all points of a contract on which an agreement was required to be reached according to the declaration of even only one party, the contract is, in case of doubt, not entered into. As a rule an offer made to a person who is present may be accepted only immediately. In the construction industry however quite often an offer is made to a person who is not present. In this event the question is whether the offer may be revoked or not. Two different approaches exist. Under German law an offer becomes effective at the moment when this declaration reaches the other party. It cannot be revoked after the offer has reached the other party, unless the offeror has excluded being bound to it. By contrast under common law any offer can be revoked until acceptance.

It may happen that the way to conclude a contract is ruled by special provisions. Some contracts must be concluded in writing (for example a gift contract), some must be made in front of a notary public (for example a real estate sales contract governed by German law).

1.4.4 Contract Interpretation

According to German law contracts have to be interpreted subject to the requirements of good faith, taking common usage into consideration. When interpreting a declaration of intent, the true intention is to be sought irrespective of the literal meaning of the declaration. Even tough Section 133 German Civil Code forbids a literal interpretation any interpretation has to be drawn down from the literal

---

[33] [91] BGHZ 325.

meaning. In general the common literal meaning is authoritative. Once having determined the literal meaning the interpreter shall then take into consideration the collateral circumstances. Hence he shall bear in mind the genesis of the contractual relationship and the existing interests of the parties. In the event of doubt each interpretation shall come to a reasonable result. Thus German Courts are willing to look at past correspondence and conduct in order to ascertain the true intention of the parties and to come to a most reasonable result of interpretation with regard to the circumstances. In summary the objective meaning shall be determined from the perspective of the addressee of the declaration by taking into account the particular circumstances of the position of the person making the declaration as far as they were or should have been known to the addressee. However, where the shared or common subjective understanding deviates from the objective understanding the subjective one prevails.[34]

1.4.5 Construction Contract

A construction contract is a contract for work and services subject to Sections 631 et seq. Civil Code (Palandt and Sprau 2009, Section 631, note 16), whereby the contractor promises to do the work in consideration of an agreed remuneration. However the scope of Sections 631 et seq. Civil Code is much broader than that. Through the use of a contract for work and services the contractor is bound to produce the work or render the service promised and the customer is bound to pay the remuneration agreed. It is commonplace that site supervision services as well as design services usually have the nature of a contract for works and services (Messerschmidt and Voit 2008, note B 3).

By means of a German construction contract the Contractor assumes to complete the Works free from defects (see Section 633 Civil Code). It lays within its discretion how to achieve the result (Bamberger et al. 2008, Section 631, note 4). However in German practise the latter seems to be partially ignored because various authors undertook to say that the agreed amount of work and the agreed price for it may be incongruent with the result to be achieved by the Contractor which may cause an entitlement of the Contractor to additional payment (Motzke 2002, p. 641, 642; see also Leupertz 2005 p. 775 et seqq.; Oberhauser 2005, p. 919 et seqq).

Unlike in the UK there are no standard forms of contract commonly used in Germany, which have been developed and published by private organisations. Even though a large number of German engineering and architects' associations exist, neither of these have published commonly recognised standard forms. Thus the terms of a construction contract are usually determined by statutory regulations and are frequently complemented by the Award Rules for Building Works ("Vergabe- und Vertragsordnung für Bauleistung", "VOB"). The German Award and Contract

---

[34] RG [99] RGZ 147.

Committee for Building Work ("Deutscher Vergabe- und Vertragsausschuss für Bauleistungen") is responsible for the current and subsequent revision of these award rules, which are composed of three parts, part A through C.

Part A of the VOB, also referred to as the "General Provisions on the awarding of contracts for construction work", contains a set of rules dealing with the procurement procedures for public works contracts. However public procurement law embodies a number of further laws, such as Sect. 97 et seq. of the German Act on Restraints on Competition and the Regulations on the Award of Public Contracts.

Part B of the VOB ("VOB/B"), also referred to as the General Contractual Conditions for the Performance of construction work, contains general provisions regulating the legal relationship between the employer and the contractor from the time of conclusion of the construction contract until discharge. The provisions of VOB/B having the nature of standard terms of contract are only applicable if the parties expressly agree their contract to be governed by them. They modify and complement the regulations under the BGB in order to make them more suitable for the needs and particularities of a construction contract, e.g. the unilateral order of change in performance under Sect. 1 no. 3 and 4 VOB/B or detailed provisions concerning defects liability and payment or the method of invoicing the work. The BGB regulations remain applicable unless the VOB/B derogates from them. However, in principle the VOB/B follow the risk allocation policy ruled by law, e.g. they do not shift the risk for unforeseen soil conditions to the contractor. Moreover the VOB/B do not provide for a third party to the contract, who has to execute powers under the construction contract as it is the case under FIDIC conditions. Alternative dispute resolution is not yet incorporated.

Part C of the VOB, also referred to as the General contractual technical conditions for construction work, contains a considerable number of technical rules and standards.

1.4.6 German Legal Concepts as to Construction Contracts

A construction contract by its very nature creates reciprocal obligations. The reciprocity is one sided in that the complete performance of his contractual obligation by the contractor and acceptance of it by the employer is a condition precedent to the performance of the reciprocal obligation by the employer. In other words the obligations, though inter dependent, fall to be performed consecutively. Thus the contractor is normally obliged to carry out the work which he is engaged to do before the contract money can be claimed. The obligation to pay the money is conditional on the pre-performance of the obligation to carry out the work. The remuneration falls due at the time of acceptance of the works (Section 641 para. 1 Civil Code). Where the nature of the works is such that acceptance is impossible, the completion of the works replaces acceptance of it (Section 646 Civil Code). Even though it may be stipulated that the payments shall be made in instalments, it arises from the very nature of the contract that nevertheless any instalment shall only become due dependent on the further development of the transaction.[35] Where either the common intention of parties to a contract or its nature is that there should be a reciprocal performance of all or certain of their respective obligations the exceptio non adimpleti contractus operates as a defence for a defendant sued on a contract by a plaintiff who has not performed, or tendered to perform, such of his obligations as are reciprocal to the performance sought from the defendant.

1.4.6.1 Duty to Achieve a Specific Result

According to Section 631 German Civil Code the contractor promises to the employer to build the works as defined by the contract against payment of the agreed fee which becomes due after completion of the works and its acceptance by the employer. Thus the Civil Code imposes on the contractor a duty to pre-perform.

The duty to pre-perform exists subject to the doctrine of clausula rebus sic stantibus, according to which a contract ceases to be binding if matters did not remain the same as they were at the time of contracting. Thus under a reciprocal or synallagmatic contract a party to it may refuse to perform it if, after the conclusion of the contract a serious deterioration in the financial position of the other party occurs which comprises the claim for payment.

The central characteristic of a contract for works is the obligation to achieve a specific result (Section 631 para. 2 Civil Code). The contractor remains free to decide how to achieve the result (Bamberger et al. 2008, Section 631, note 4). Thus in principle the individual responsibility of the contractor and the fact that the contractor is not generally bound to directives of the employer are constitutive elements of a contract for works. The responsibility of the contractor includes scrutinising the employer's requirements and any materials provided by the employer. In addition the works must be fit for use together with the existing facilities. When completed the works must be fit for running. In a summary and in accordance with Section 633 Civil Code the contractor must meet the agreed conditions or, if not agreed, the mutually assumed purpose. Any of the works is defective if it is not in accordance with the contract or if there is a functional discrepancy or a technical deficiency or if it proves that the contractor did not comply with recognised technical rules. The work is defective irrespective of its cause (Bamberger et al. 2008, Section 633 note 18). If the work is defective there is breach of contract (Bamberger et al. 2008, Section 633 note 18). However, although Sections 633 et seq. apply to defects whether they occur prior to acceptance of the works or after acceptance of the works, the right to request the remedy of any defect prior to acceptance of the works is slightly restricted and subject to the discretion of the contractor (Boldt 2004, note 241). Prior to acceptance of the works it lies within

---

[35] RG [83] RGZ 279.

the discretion of the contractor when to remedy a defect. It may prove appropriate to do so later than expected by the employer.

One could believe that Section 631 para. 1 Civil Code would include the clear message that the result is due against payment of the agreed price. However, some misleading vocabulary has been introduced to the discussion. It has been argued that even though the contractor is bound to achieve a specific result, the agreed price in consideration of which the contractor has accepted to achieve it does not cover all of the works needed. Instead the price covers only a specific quota, the so called construction quota (Bausoll) which corresponds with the work which can be derived from the specifications and BoQ.[36] The opposite of the construction quota is the construction result quota (Bauerfolgssoll) comprising all of the work needed to achieve the result. The courts however not using the term unanimously held that the specific work to be done by the contractor shall be ascertained from the contract including the specifications and BoQ.[37] The intentions of the parties will be ascertained from the perspective of the addressee of the bid by taking in account the particular circumstances of the position of the bidder. Whilst in principle it is legally possible to specify the works by reference to a functional description[38] quite often employers prefer to refer to a detailed description. Thus in the event of a lump sum price the contract has either the nature of a global lump sum price or a detailed lump sum price. If in the latter case the BoQ and specifications clearly and obviously disclose any pricing risk and the bidder submits its offer while being aware of it, he bears all of the calculation risk.[39] If not, the agreed price may not cover all of the works needed. The agreed price will then only cover the construction quota (Bausoll).

The aforementioned approach seems to be in contradiction with the nature of a construction contract, whereby a contractor promises to execute the works in order to achieve an agreed result. If he has accepted a lump sum price for doing so any specifications or BoQ which were incorporated in the contract should not excuse the contractor who already accepted the risk of achieving a result. Presumably the aforementioned construction quota theory derives from the German VOB/B which include the following provision:

> Services not comprised in the contract, although necessary for the execution of the works, shall be performed by the contractor on request of the employer unless its undertaking is not prepared to execute such services.

This wording clearly includes the assumption that the contract may cover work which is not yet covered by the agreed price although it also derives from the contract that the contractor already accepted to achieve the agreed result. On the other hand it is beyond doubt that the contractor will be liable for any defects which

---

[36] Compare OLG Düsseldorf [2008] IBR 633 Karczewski; BGH [2002] IBR 231 Putzier.

[37] BGH [2002] IBR 231 Putzier.

[38] BGH [1996] IBR 487 Schulze-Hagen.

[39] BGH [1996] IBR 487 Schulze-Hagen; OLG Celle [2005] IBR 520 Schwenker.

are due to omissions by the contractor. In line with this the Court of Appeal of Dresden[40] recently held that a contractor was liable to carry out the work fit for the purposes by rejecting the purported defence of the contractor that the contract documents did not provide for an insulation of the cellar, which, according to the evidence which was shown, was apparently an error caused by the designer. However, due to the fact that according to Section 278 Civil Code the employer was responsible for the default of persons whom he employed in fulfilling its obligations (including for example designers) to the same extent as for his own faults, the contractor could rely on the fact that the design was defective. Thus the court held that the damages should be mitigated and apportioned between the parties and that the employer should bear 50% of the damages which he incurred for the remedy of the defect.

1.4.6.2 Risk Allocation

By means of a construction contract the contractor assumes several risks. German doctrine distinguishes between the risk of performance (Leistungsgefahr) and the risk of counter performance (Vergütungsgefahr). Under a contract for works the contractor bears the risk of performance. If the works are accidentally destroyed before the employer has accepted it being in accordance with the contract (see below) the contractor will be obliged to replace the works which have been destroyed at his cost and risk. However, if the contractor is released from his obligation to complete the works for whichever reason the question arises whether the employer is equally released from his obligation to pay the price. The answer to question depends on whether the risk of counter performance is borne by the employer.

Sections 644 and 645 of the Civil Code deal with the risk of counter performance only. Pursuant to Section 644 para. 1 sentence 1 Civil Code the contractor bears the risk until the work is accepted. However, if the employer falls into delay with acceptance the risk passes to him. Also the contractor is not liable for any accidental loss or accidental deterioration of material supplied by the employer. Pursuant to Section 645 para. 1 Civil Code, in the event of destruction or deterioration of the work prior to acceptance or if the work cannot be completed because of a defect in materials supplied by the customer or because of an instruction given by him and if no circumstance has contributed to this for which the contractor is liable, the contractor is entitled to demand a part of the remuneration which corresponds to the work performed as well as to reimbursement of those expenses which are not included in the remuneration. However, according to Section 645 para. 2 Civil Code any further liability of the employer beyond this due to fault remain unaffected.

---

[40] OLG Dresden [2009] IBR 71 Heiland, further appeal rejected by the Federal Court of Justice.

According to German case law the term "material supplied by the employer" as used in Section 645 para. 1 Civil Code also covers the site.[41] This is the reason why it is commonplace to say that the employer bears the risk of unforeseen physical conditions,[42] although the Federal Supreme Court was always reluctant to use the term "soil risk" (Baugrundrisiko). However, a claim for extra payment will only be confirmed, when the encountered challenge was unforeseeable for the contractor, which will be denied if the specifications or BoQ were obviously fragmentary.[43]

1.4.6.3 Taking Over

Also under German law the contractor will be discharged from all further liability for the principal obligations which arise from the contract, if he has completed the works. However completion is not sufficient. The law requires that the works shall be delivered to and must be accepted by the employer (Section 640 Civil Code).

Thus the contractor shall deliver the works to the employer. Under a construction contract delivery will be replaced by handing over. The employer will then be obliged to accept the works. Both, handing over and acceptance of the works are enforceable rights. Subject to Section 640 paragraph 1 BGB *the employer is obliged to accept the work produced in accordance with the contract save where the nature of the work precludes such acceptance. Acceptance may not be refused on account of insubstantial defects. Failure by the customer to accept the work within a period of time specified by the contractor even though he is under a duty to do so is equivalent to acceptance of the work.*

Reception or acceptance of the works means a declaration by the employer to the contractor that the latter has essentially completed the works in accordance with the contract.[44] In the words of the former Empire Court acceptance means the act of physical reception of the contractor's performance by the employer, accompanied by the express or tacit declaration of the employer that, in substance, he acknowledges the work as a performance in compliance with the contract.[45] His declaration covers not only compliance of the works with the contractual technical requirements but also compliance with the contractual timely requirements. If the employer refuses to accept the works even though they have been completed in accordance with the contract, upon request of the contractor the court will declare acceptance on behalf of the employer. In practice this will happen implicitly when the contractor refers its claim for payment to the court.

If the customer accepts the works according to Section 640 paragraph 1 sentence 1 BGB, even though he is aware of a defect, he waives his rights referred to in

---

[41] OLG Naumburg [2004] IBR 481 Fuchs.

[42] OLG Hamm [1994] IBR 95 Englert.

[43] OLG Brandenburg [2008] IBR 636 Orthmann; OLG Jena [2003] IBR 122 Schwenker.

[44] See BGH [1970] NJW 421.

[45] RG [110] RGZ 404, 406.

Section 634 nos. 1–3 BGB unless, upon accepting the work, he reserves his rights in respect of the defect. Thus acceptance of the works commutes the contractual relations between the contractor and the employer. Whereas prior to acceptance of the works the contractor is in charge to execute the works and to show evidence that the completed works are in accordance with the contract, on the date of acceptance the burden proof becomes shifted to the employer who must then prove that there is a defect. Acceptance of the works confines the duty of the contractor to the accepted works and eventual complementary remedies, such as the entitlement to demand the repair of defects which were not yet accepted.

Thus, at the time of reception the employer must reserve its right to assert claims for defects and for liquidated damages or penalties in order to save its entitlement to damages and other forms of relief, in particular its entitlement to liquidated damages and penalties for non compliance with time for completion.[46]

Reception means therefore *acceptance of the works*. As a rule the consequences of acceptance are:

- The acceptance date represents the start of the legal warranty period according to Sect. 63a BGB for all parts of the works covered by the declaration of reception.
- At the reception date the burden of proof for latent defects becomes shifted to the employer
- According to Sect. 641 BGB the remuneration of the contractor becomes due.
- Subject to Sect. 644 BGB at the reception date the risk for accidental damage to the works becomes shifted to the employer.

1.4.6.4   Taking Over Under FIDIC Contracts

Under a FIDIC contract the date on which the Employer issues the Taking-Over Certificate is taken to be Completion (Sub-clauses 10.1, 8.2). This will have several significant effects. The *defects notification period* starts (Sub-clause 1.1.3.7), half the retention fund becomes payable (Sub-clause 14.9), the liability to pay liquidated damages ceases, the Contractor's obligation to reinstate the works if these are damaged by any but the excepted risks ceases (Sub-Clause 17.2, 18) and the period within which the Statement at Completion must be submitted by the Contractor starts to run (Sub-Clause 14.10).

However Taking Over according to FIDIC Conditions must not be confused with "reception" or "acceptance" of the Works according to French or German legislation. According to German and French law only *acceptance of the Works* by the employer discharges the contractor from his obligation to carry out the Works. Thus in principle the contractor remains liable to perform the Works and he is not released from care for the Works until the employer declares *acceptance of the Works*. According to German law acceptance is a declaration by the employer to the contractor that the latter has substantially completed the agreed Works in compliance with the

---

[46] See OLG Naumburg [2004] BauR 1831; [2004] ZfBR 791.

contract.[47] This declaration covers both, the Works themselves and compliance with time for completion. If the Employer does not make any reservations as to apparent defects or non compliance with time for completion any claims for liquidated or delay damages according to Sub-Clause 8.7 FIDIC Conditions and any claims based on apparent defective works will be foreclosed. One main effect of acceptance of the Works is that the post contractual legal liability period starts.

As under German law specific performance is a legal remedy usually no additional defects notification period is necessary. The Employer is allowed to claim for the remedying of any defects which occur after acceptance of the works. This is by the way the reason why it is not uncommon that civil law lawyers misunderstand the nature of the defects notification period which is ruled in Clause 11 FIDIC Conditions. They quite often assume that the *defects notification period* replaces the legal defects liability according to their law, which is obviously wrong. The defects notification period is an *additional period of time* during which the duty to perform the Contract continues to exist. This can clearly be seen in Sub-Clauses 11.1 and 11.2. According to these Sub-Clauses the Contractor is still under the obligation to carry out any work which becomes instructed by the Employer, to the extent that a defect occurs which is not attributable to the Contractor.

Thus, in principle under a FIDIC contract governed by German law the issue of the Performance Certificate according to Sub-Clause 11.9 GC will constitute acceptance of the works. At the taking over date only the risk of coincidental (accidental) damage to the Works will be shifted to the Contractor. However the Contractor will remain responsible for care of the works for outstanding work and work which he will perform subject to Sub-Clause 11.2 (see Sub-Clause 17.2 2nd paragraph).

1.4.6.5 Breach of Contract

To the contrary of English law German law prefers specific performance as a cure for breach of contract. Thus the employer may demand performance in specie. The contractor then may show evidence for the defence that performance is impossible without prejudice to innocent party's other remedies. Breach of contract comprises any breach of a duty including delay, impossibility and non conformity. The range of remedies is broad, including the entitlement to terminate or to rescind the contract, the right to demand conforming performance, the recovery of cost of reinstatement, the right to reduce the price and the entitlement to damages. Until reception of the works the employer is entitled to specific performance. As he did not yet accept the works the contractor must then show evidence that the work is in accordance with the contract. After reception of the works the burden of proof shifts to the employer who will then be in charge to show evidence that any purported defect exists.

By virtue of a construction contract the contractor promises to build the works free from physical and legal defects (Section 633 para. 1 Civil Code). Work is

---

[47] BGH [1970] NJW 421, see above.

defective if it has not the agreed composition. In so far as the composition is not agreed, the work is free from physical defects, when it is appropriate for the intended use under the contract or otherwise for the usual use having a composition which is usual for works of the same kind and which an employer can expect according to the type of work. Performance under a construction contract is not yet defective if it does not comply with the state of the technical art (Stand der Technik) but only if it does not comply with the recognised technical rules (Regeln der Technik).[48] According to the authorities,[49] in the event of failure of the parties to agree a composition the test is whether the works are done in a manner that they are free from defects which neutralize or reduce its fitness for usual use. Thereby the recognised technical rules are of significant importance. The employer may honestly expect that the works meet those quality standards which other comparable works meet which have been completed and accepted at the same time. The contractor usually promises tacitly to comply with these standards. Thus in general the state of the recognised technical rules (Stand der anerkannten Regeln der Technik) on the time of completion and acceptance of the works is decisive. This includes for example compliance with other legal standards such as the German Energy Savings Regulation (Energieeinsparverordnung)[50] or technical recommendations such as the VDE standards.[51]

According to Section 634 Civil Code the available remedies of the employer in the event of defective work are:

- The demand of subsequent performance under Section 635 Civil Code (Section 634 no. 1 Civil Code)
- The entitlement to eliminate any defect by himself including the reimbursement of any necessary expenditure as a result of this (Section 634 no. 2 Civil Code)
- The rescission of the contract under Sections 636, 323 and 326 Civil Code or reduction of the remuneration (Section 634 no. 3 Civil Code)
- The demand of compensation under Sections 636, 280, 281, 283 and 311a Civil Code (Section 634 no. 4 Civil Code)

The contractor may refuse subsequent performance if it is only possible with disproportionate cost (Section 635 para. 3 Civil Code).

1.4.6.6 Defects Liability Period

Under German law the legal defects liability period is clearly regulated by law. Section 634a BGB, establishing a unitary approach to prescription of claims for defective work, reads as follows:

---

[48] OLG Düsseldorf [1998] IBR 437 Kieserling; BGH [1998] BauR 872.

[49] BGH [1998] BauR 872; OLG Stuttgart [2008] IBR 433 Weyer, further appeal denied (BGH, decision from 10 April 2008; file no. VII ZR 159/07).

[50] OLG Brandenburg [2008] IBR 724 Reichert.

[51] OLG Hamm [1990] BauR 104; compare LG Duisburg [2007] IBR 246 Heisiep.

(1) The claims cited in Section 634 nos. 1, 2 and 4 are time-barred:

  1. With reservation made for no. 2 in two years with a work, the result of which consists of manufacture, servicing or alteration of a thing or in the performance of planning or monitoring services for this purpose
  2. In five years with construction work and a work, the result of which consists of performance of planning or monitoring services for this purpose
  3. In other respects in the regular limitation period

(2) In cases falling under subsection (1) nos. 1 and 2, limitation begins when the work or service is accepted.
(3) In derogation from subsection (1) nos. 1 and 2, and subsection (2), claims are time-barred after the standard limitation period if the contractor fraudulently concealed the defect. However, in the case of subsection (1) no. 2, claims are not time-barred before the expiry of the period there specified.
(4) Section 218 applies to the right of withdrawal referred to in section 634. Notwithstanding the ineffectiveness of withdrawal under section 218(1), the customer may refuse to pay the remuneration in so far as he would be entitled to do so by virtue of withdrawal. If he makes use of that right, the contractor may withdraw from contract.
(5) Section 218 and subsection (4) sentence 2 above apply with the necessary modifications to the right to reduce the price specified in section 634.

The normal limitation period is three years. The warranty period is not a clear cut-off period. From the legal point of view the warranty period within the meaning of Section 634a BGB is a *limitation period* subject to Sections 194 et seq. BGB. According to Sections 203 et seq. BGB the limitation period can be suspended as follows:

Section 203 BGB

If negotiations between the obligor and the obligee are being conducted with regard to the claim or the circumstances on which the claim is based, the limitation period is suspended until the one or the other party refuses to continue the negotiations. The claim is not barred until at least three months have elapsed after the end of the suspension.

Section 204 BGB

(1) Limitation is suspended by:

  1. The bringing of an action for performance or for a declaration of the existence of a claim, for the attachment of an execution certificate or for the issue of an order for execution.
  2. ...
  3. The service of a demand for payment in summary proceedings for recovery of debt.
  4. Arranging for notice to be given of an application for conciliation filed with a conciliation body established or recognised by the administration of justice of a *Land* (state) or, if the parties agree to seek conciliation, with

any other conciliation body which settles disputes; if notice is arranged to be given shortly after the filing of the application, the limitation period is suspended immediately on the giving of notice.

5. The assertion of a right to set off the claim in the course of a lawsuit.
6. The service of third-party notice.
7. The service of an application for an independent procedure for the taking of evidence.
8. The beginning of an agreed expert appraisal procedure.
9. The service of an application for an attachment order, an interim injunction or an interim order, or, if the application is not served, the filing thereof if the order for attachment, the interim injunction or the interim order is served on the obligor within one month of its being made or of its service on the obligee.
10. The filing of a claim in insolvency proceedings or in proceedings for the distribution of assets under maritime law.
11. The beginning of the arbitration proceedings.
12. The filing of an application with a public authority, if the admissibility of the action depends on a preliminary decision by this authority and the action is brought within three months after the application has been dealt with; this applies with the necessary modifications to applications required to be made to a court or a conciliation body referred to in no. 4 above, the admissibility of which depends on a preliminary decision by an authority.
13. The filing of an application with a higher court, if it is for that higher court to decide upon the court with jurisdiction over the claim and, within three months after the application has been dealt with, the action is brought or the application for which a decision on jurisdiction was necessary is filed.
14. Arranging for notice to be given of the first application for the grant of legal aid; if notice is arranged shortly after the filing of the application, the suspension of the limitation period takes effect immediately when the application is filed.

(2) Suspension under subsection (1) above ends six months after a final decision has been made in respect of the proceedings commenced or after their cessation in some other manner. If the proceedings come to a halt because of inaction by the parties, the date of the last step in the proceedings taken by the parties, the court or other body responsible for the proceedings applies instead of the date of cessation of the proceedings.
Suspension begins anew if one of the parties pursues the proceedings further.
(3) Sections 206, 210 and 211 apply with the necessary modifications to subsection (1), nos. 9, 12 and 13 above.

According to Sect. 13 VOB/B (General contractual conditions for the performance of (public) construction work) the following limitation periods apply:

If no limitation period as to defects has been agreed in the contract, it is four years for civil works, for other works two years and for insulation works one year.

1.4.6.7 Time for Completion

The original FIDIC concept of time for completion is based on Clause 8 GC FIDIC
Conditions. According to this concept the parties agree on a period of time for
completion, which is usually indicated in the Appendix to Tender or the Particular
Conditions. Time for completion starts when the Employer has notified the commencement date, which he shall do within 42 days after the contract has been
executed (Sub-Clause 8.1 GC). Subject to Sub-Clause 1.1.3.3 Time for Completion
means the time for completing the Works or a Section (as the case may be) under
Sub-Clause 8.2, as stated in the Appendix to Tender or the Particular Conditions
(with any extension under Sub-Clause 8.4, calculated from the Commencement
Date. According to Sub-Clause 8.2 the Contractor shall complete the whole of
the Works within the Time for Completion for the Works including completing
all work which is stated in the Contract as being required for the Works or Section
to be considered to be completed for the purposes of taking-over under Sub-
Clause 10.1. In other words, the Contractor complies with the requirements for
Time for Completion if he completes the Works within Time for Completion if the
Taking Over Certificate becomes issued until the end of Time for Completion and
not later.

Failure to comply with Time for Completion will lead to the entitlement of delay
damages according to Sub-clause 8.7 GC. However if and when the Contractor is
prevented from carrying out the works or if the Employer causes delay to the
progress with effect to time for completion the Contractor is subject to the GC
entitled to claim for extension of time (EOT). This concept has been adopted from
English law, where time remains only of the essence if and when the contract
provides for time extension claims for those events attributable to the employer,
which cause delay and disruption. Failure to provide such claims leads to time at
large, which will mean that the Employer looses his entitlement to delay damages.
Thus EOT claims release the Contractor from his liability for delay damages and
protect the Employer against the loss of his entitlement to delay damages in the
event that the Contractor fails to comply with time for completion.

This English concept includes the presumption that there is an effective contractual system for time extension, including that the Employer grants EOT in accordance with the contract whenever an EOT claims becomes notified by the
Contractor. Failure to comply with the contractual system of EOT management
rules may also lead to *time at large*.

The whole concept leads to a number of conclusions, summarised as follows:

- Firstly delay damages must in principle be understood as a limitation of liability
  for delay.
- Secondly there is no space for so called milestone damages, which are quite
  often encountered by Contractors. Milestone provisions in FIDIC contracts
  should be avoided. They do not fit within the structure of FIDIC Conditions,
  because it is not possible to apply the concept of EOT to them. Instead FIDIC
  Conditions recommend so called Sections, which must be agreed by the parties

and which are compatible with the concept of EOT. Remember in so far that EOT creates a win-win situation, through which the Employer is protected against the loss of delay damages and the Contractor becomes released from liability for delay damages. As complementary milestone provisions are not compatible with this system it is suggested that they lead to time at large.

- Thirdly delay damages do not fall under national legislation concerning *penalties*. They have nothing to do with the compensation for a time overrun. By contrast they include a promise to pay a certain amount of money for non compliance with this particular agreement only.
- Fourthly, if and when delay damages are related to milestones they become due even though the Contractor complies with time for completion. In so far it should be taken into consideration, that according to FIDIC Conditions the Contractor has to submit and maintain a programme (see Sub-clause 8.3) according to which he shall proceed to carry out the Works. This means that the Contractor has absolute discretion as to how the work is planned and performed. Milestone agreements are therefore in contradiction to the whole concept of the contract and include constraints on the ability of the Contractor to carry out the works in accordance with the contract.

According to German law an obligor may promise a penalty in the event that he fails to fulfil his obligation. If he fails to fulfil his obligations, the obligee may demand the forfeited penalty in lieu of fulfilment. If the obligee declares to the obligor that he is demanding the penalty, the claim to fulfilment is excluded. However the obligor may demand the forfeited penalty as the minimum amount of the damage. The entitlement to further damages is not excluded. Thus in principle the obligor can choose between penalties and damages. Penalties are due even though no damage occurred. If actual damages are higher than the agreed penalty the obligor is entitled to further damages up to the amount of damages which are due for the compensation of the whole damage (see Palandt and Grüneberg 2009, Section 340, note 7).

Subject to Sect. 343 BGB a penalty which is unreasonably high may be reduced by the courts. But subject to Sect. 348 Commercial Code (HGB) a contract penalty which a merchant has agreed to in the operation of his business ay not be reduced by reason of Sect. 343 BGB. However if and when the penalty clause has the nature of a standard term as defined in Sect. 305 BGB penalties are subject to court control anyway. Thus in principle a penalty clause shall not penalise the contractor unreasonably. The courts have held that penalty clauses are valid up to 0.2–0.3% of the contract price per day. In addition a cap shall be agreed. The courts usually hold that a cap of 5% of the contract price is reasonable. If no such cap is agreed the penalty clause usually will be declared void.

However if FIDIC terms become construed against its original legal background Sub-Clause 8.7 must be understood as genuine pre-estimated damages and not as penalties. As it is also possible under German law to agree to a fixed amount of damages for an event which is clearly expressed within the terms of the contract, again under German law Sub-Clause 8.7 should be understood as it is, a genuine pre-estimated amount of money which becomes due in the event of failure to comply with Time for Completion.

1.4.6.8 Caps

Since a recent adaptation of Sect. 639 BGB it seems to be possible to create a proper system of liability. Until the reform Section 639 read as follows:

The contractor may not rely on an agreement by which the customer's rights in respect of a defect are excluded or restricted *if* he fraudulently concealed the defect or *if* he has guaranteed the nature of the work.

It now reads: "The contractor may not rely on an agreement by which the customer's rights in respect of a defect are excluded or restricted *as far as* he fraudulently concealed the defect or *as far as* he has guaranteed the nature of the work".

Thus the contractor is allowed to guarantee a specific result and to limit his liability in this respect. Thus in principle the cap according to Sub-Clause 17.6 GC covers further damages for delay.

Under German law legal "delay damages" (not to be confused with pre-estimated delay damages under FIDIC contracts) are subject to Sect. 280, 286 BGB. According to Sections 280 paragraph 2 and 286 BGB, only compensation for the damage caused *by the delay* is due. This does not include consequential losses. However it is the unanimous position of the German courts that Sect. 280 paragraph 1 BGB applies if the damage was caused by another reason, such as poor performance. It was always beyond doubt that a contractor owes compensation for loss of production and other consequential losses if the employer shows evidence that the contractor was in breach of contract.

1.4.6.9 Termination

Furthermore another interesting feature of German law is worthwhile to be emphasized, which is the right of the employer to terminate the contract by convenience (Section 649 Civil Code). Whilst under English law the concept of repudiation prevails if either of the parties refuses to perform the contract, under German law the employer is not in breach of contract if he terminates the contract prematurely. However, according to Section 649 Civil Code the contractor then will be entitled to claim for the agreed fee subject to a deduction of the amount saved as a result of the premature termination of the contract, which in fact leads to the result that he is entitled to what he failed to earn as a result of the deliberate termination or omission. In practice the fee will often be pre-estimated and fixed in the contract. Since the last reform Section 649 Civil Code provides that the contractor will be deemed to be entitled to 5% of the part of the remuneration which remains unperformed on the date when the notice becomes effective. However, he is allowed to show evidence of a higher loss of profit.

1.4.6.10   Security Mortgage and Other Securities

Section 648 Civil Code provides for an enforceable entitlement of the builder to claim for an entry in the land registry of a security mortgage in respect of its demands under the construction contract against the land of the owner on which the works shall be executed. Upon demand of the contractor the courts may grant an interlocutory and provisional measure in order to secure the entry of the security mortgage.

In addition Section 648a Civil Code provides for an entitlement of the contractor to demand for the provision of a security in respect of any unpaid remuneration. The security may either be provided in cash or by a guarantee or other promise of payment by a credit institute or credit insurer authorised to carry on business in the area of application of this statutory provision. Any financial charges as to the security will be borne by the contractor up to a maximum rate of 2% per annum. In the event that the employer does not provide the security within a period to be specified in the notice of demand the contractor may suspend the progress of the works and terminate the contract. If the contractor gives such a notice he will be entitled to be paid for all the work performed and to what he failed to earn as a result of the termination. Since the last reform Section 648a paragraph 5 Civil Code provides that the contractor will be deemed to be entitled to 5% of the part of the remuneration which remains unperformed on the date when the notice becomes effective. However, he is allowed to show evidence of a higher loss of profit.

1.4.6.11   Subcontracting

Subcontracting is a widespread feature in the German construction industry. German traditions as to the organisation of the craftsmen's industry led to the understanding that works should be carried out intuitu personae but not by the craftsman himself but by his employees and under his control (Compare Staudinger and Peters 2003, before Section 631 note 42). However, according to current authorities a contract for works is no longer concluded intuitu personae, thus generally spoken subcontracting is admitted. On the other hand according to the VOB/B prior written authorisation by the employer is a condition precedent of admissible subcontracting (Section 4 no. 8 VOB/B). According to the principle of privity of contract no contractual relations between the employer and the subcontractor exist. However the subcontractor is usually considered being a contractual assistant for the purpose of fulfilling the obligations of the main contractor towards the employer (compare Section 278 German Civil Code). Hence the main contractor's liability will cover the faults of its subcontractors because he employs the subcontractor for that he performs the part of the subcontracted works. To which extent he will be liable to supervise and control the performance of the subcontractor depends on the merits of the case. According to Section 242 Civil Code the main contractor owes a duty to effect performance in the manner required by good faith, having regard to custom. Thus for the purposes of performance the parties to a contract are obliged to cooperate in order to establish the premises of performance (Palandt and Heinrichs

2009, Section 242, Rn. 32). A duty of assistance, protection and clarification follows from this finding. The Federal Supreme Court perpetually holds that a contractor, who carries out the work partially by himself and partially through subcontractors, shall establish the organizational premises enabling him to check whether at completion the works are in compliance and conformity of the contract.[52] However a main contractor may rely on the fact that a subcontractor takes all necessary steps for carrying out the work in a workmanlike manner and for final testing the work under the premises that he has carefully singled the subcontractor.[53] Thus the employer is protected against the risk that the main contractor selects an incompetent or inefficient subcontractor.

1.5 Romanian Law

1.5.1 Relevant Provisions

The main provisions concerning the Romanian law of contract are contained in the Romanian Civil Code (hereinafter Cod civil), adopted in 1854, which is widely inspired by the French Civil Code (hereinafter Code civil). Otherwise, there are special provisions in some distinct acts such as:

– Law nr.193/2000 relating to unfair clauses contained in contracts between consumers and merchants
– Law no.469 of 9 July 2002 relating to the contractual discipline
– O.U.G. nr. 54/2006 on concession of goods belonging to public property contracts
– O.U.G. nr. 34/2006 concerning the awarding of public acquisition contracts, of public works' concession contracts and of services concession contracts
– O.G. nr.9/22-01-2004 relating to some financial warranty contracts, and others

1.5.2 Definition of Contract Under Romanian Law

According to Art.942 Cod civil, a contract is an *agreement* between two or several persons in order to create or dissolve a legal relationship. This definition apparently excludes unilateral agreements from the category of contracts, but Art.944 Cod civil gives a definition thereof. As under French law, there are four essential conditions for the validity of an agreement (Art. 948 Cod civil): the *consent* of the party who binds himself, its *capacity* to enter a contract (provisions relating to

---

[52] BGH [117] BGHZ 318; BGH [2005] IBR 80 Vogel; BGH [2008] NJW 145 = BGH [2008] IBR 17 = BGH [2008] IBR 18; BGH [2009] IBR 90 Knychalla.
[53] BGH [2008] NJW 145 = BGH [2008] IBR 17 = BGH [2008] IBR 18 Steiner; compare OLG München [2009] IBR 39 Averhaus.

the capacity of persons are contained in Art. 9–11 of the Decree nr. 31/1954 concerning the persons and the corporations [B. Of. nr. 8 din 30 ianuarie 1954]), a definite *object* and a lawful *cause* in the obligation (for further explanations as to the concept of cause see comments on French contract law). A written contract is not necessary for lawfully creating a contractual obligation and it is merely necessary in order to prove the existence of a contract. However, some contracts may be carried out only in the written form and may need an authentic instrument (e.g. conveyance of real estate, mortgage on real property).

For principles of interpretation of contracts, see comments on French contract law.

1.5.3 Effects of the Contract

Art. 969 Cod Civil is a faithful copy of Art. 1134 of French Code civil, according to which agreements lawfully entered into take the place of the law for those who have made them. As a result, agreements only produce effect between the contracting parties (Art.973 Cod civil). Nevertheless, there are, as under French law, some exceptions to this principle, as the direct action of the subcontractor (where an unpaid subcontractor is entitled to demand payment directly from the employer in the case that the original contractor refuses to pay, rom. "actiunea directa a subantreprenorului", art.1488 Cod civil).

1.5.4 Limitation Periods

The general limitation period for all kinds of actions resulting of contracts lasts three years (§ 3 of the Decree nr. 67 of 10/04/1958).

1.5.5 Does Romanian Law Recognize Pre-contractual Liability?

Although theoretically possible on grounds of tortious liability, the pre-contractual liability of negotiating parties is regarded with some degree of scepticism by Romanian judges.

1.5.6 Non-performance Remedies

1.5.6.1 Normal Remedies

Remedies such as the suspension of the contract or terminating the contract are similar to those commented in the French law overview. The *exceptio non adimpleti contractus* or *exceptia de inexecutare* is a remedy allowing a party who has not received the contractual performance to which it is entitled to withhold its own performance, thus suspending the contract.

A contract may be also terminated through amiable settlement or, if not possible, by judicial means, through a terminating clause inserted in the contract (*clauza rezolutorie*), or by virtue of a law (e.g. in *intuito personae* contracts as mandate or insurance).

1.5.6.2   Specific Remedies Available Against the Builder: The Decennial Liability

A provision similar to that of Art.1792 of the French Code civil before the reforms of 1967, 1978 and 2005 may be found in Article 1843 of Romanian Cod civil. Nonetheless, the legal ground of the decennial liability is to be found in art.29 of the *Law nr.10/1995 about the quality in constructions, M.O. nr. 12 of 24 January 1995*). It is very important to mention, that the decennial liability of Art.29 refers exclusively to the construction's latent defects; as to the defects affecting the resistance structures caused by the disregard of the legislation in force, the Law provides a responsibility for the entire "lifetime" of the construction (such extreme cases of liability only arise in rather exceptional cases under French law, as is the case of deception from the contractor). Art.29 of the Law nr.10/1995 will be part of the new Construction code, to be adopted in 2007.

1.5.7   Damages and Limitation of Liability

The Romanian Cod Civil contains a provision without equivalent in the French Code civil: Art 1073 provides that the creditor is entitled to seek the exact performance of the obligation and if the contrary occurs, he is entitled to compensation. But as to the extent of damages and the cases of liability limitation, the provisions of both Codes are similar.

Damages due to a creditor are, as a rule, for the loss which he has suffered and the profit which he has been deprived of (Art. 1084 Cod civil). The debtor is only liable for the damages which could be provided at the moment of entering the contract, unless the non-performance is due to deception (Art.1085 Cod civil). Damages may include only what is an immediate and direct consequence of the non-performance of the agreement, even if the non-performance is due to deception (Art. 1086 Cod civil). The party entitled to damages may not be awarded a greater or lesser sum (Art.1087 Cod civil). The damages resulting of the obligation to pay a sum are due without the proof of any creditor's losses being necessary (Art.1088(2) Cod civil) and begin to be due from the day on which the creditor's application has been lodged within a court, unless otherwise stipulated by the law. According to Art.1082 Cod civil, "If the debtor does not prove that the non-performance/the delay in performing is due to an external cause, he shall be ordered to pay damages even in absence of bad faith". The corollary of this rule is that damages should not be due if the debtor was prevented from performing by reason of *force-majeure* or of a fortuitous event (Art. 1083 Cod civil).

1.5.8 Penalty Clauses

Penalty clauses are permitted under Romanian law (Art.1066 Cod civil, "a penalty is a clause by which a person, in order to ensure performance of an agreement, binds himself to give something in case of non-performance"), excepting in loan contracts (*Law nr. 313/1879 for annulment of penal clauses in some contracts – M.O. nr. 40 of 20 February 1879*), where only the statutory interest may apply (between individuals, 6% per annum – Decree nr. 311/1954 concerning the statutory interest, B.O. nr. 38 of 9 August 1954). The penalty clause and the principal obligation are separated as to their validity (Art. 1067 Cod civil) and cannot be claimed together by the creditor (Art.1068, 1069(1) Cod civil), unless the penalty was stipulated for belated performance. As in French law, the penalty is incurred only where the debtor is under notice of default (Art. 1230 Cod civil).

Between merchants, the Law no. 469 of 9 July 2002 relating to the contractual discipline provides that penalties which are due for non-performance begin only after 30 days of non-performance after the completion date, which means for example that the creditor is not entitled to penalties if the debtor performs his obligation 27 days after the completion day stipulated by the contract.

1.6 Islamic Law

Whether Shari'a law is sufficiently certain in order to be applied as the proper law of a contract has been discussed in detail in Musawi v. Re International (UK) and others.[54] In *Shamil Bank of Bahrain EC v Beximico Pharmaceuticals Ltd* the English Court of Appeal held that a choice of the principles of Shari'a law was not a choice of law of a country for the purposes of the Rome Convention.[55] However and despite this judgment Islamic Law is not an unsophisticated, obscure and defective system. Instead it is a basic element of the Islamic society. As Asaf Fyzee (1949) noted:

> Islamic law is not a systematic code, but a living and growing organism; nevertheless there is amongst its different schools a large measure of agreement, because the starting point and

---

[54] [2007] EWHC 2981 (Ch); see also Beximco Pharmaceuticals Ltd & Ors v. Shamil Bank of Bahrain EC [2004] EWCA Civ 19 (28 January 2004).

[55] Beximco Pharmaceuticals Ltd & Ors v. Shamil Bank of Bahrain EC [2004] EWCA Civ 19 (28 January 2004); However see also Halpern & Ors v. Halpern & Anor [2007] EWCA Civ 291 (03 April 2007) concerning the incorporation of Jewish law.

the basic principles are identical. The differences that exist are due to historical, political, economic and cultural reasons, and it is, therefore, obvious that this system cannot be studied without a proper regard to its historical development.

As a matter of fact Shari'a law is a part of the law in most Islamic countries. Whilst most Islamic countries such as Algeria, Egypt, Iraq, Lebanon, Morocco, Tunisia, Turkey, United Arab Emirates have used modern legislation and codification in order to complement its provisions, some like Saudi Arabia apply directly the Shari'a principles. Again other Islamic countries are heavily influenced by common law, such as Pakistan and Malaysia. However, usually Islamic legislation refers to the Shari'a as a legal source. Thus art. 1(2) of the Egyptian Civil Code refers, in the absence of usage, to Islamic Law principles. According to art. 1(2) of the Algerian Civil Code, in the absence of a legal provision a judge shall rely on the principles of the Islamic Law Principles. As Professor M. Ballantyne (1989, p. 269 et seq.) notes:

> Even where the *Shari'a* is not applied in current practice, there could be a reversion to it in any particular case...Without doubt, a knowledge of the *Shari'a* will become increasingly important for practitioner, not only in Saudi Arabia, but in the other Muslim jurisdictions.

Given that the legal systems of the Middle Eastern and of the Maghreb nations incorporate *Shari'a* principles to varying degrees, it is worthwhile to have a look on it:

The two fundamental sources of Islamic law are Qur'an and Sunna also referred to as the Hadith. The Sunna is the most important source of the Islamic faith after the Qur'an and refers essentially to the Prophet's example as indicated by the practice of the faith. The only way to know the Sunna is through the collection of Hadith, which consists of reports about the sayings, deeds and reactions of the Prophet. The two subsidiary sources of Islamic law are Ijima (derived from consensus among Muslim scholars) and Qiyas (derived from analogy). Detailed practical rules drawn from these sources are called *Fiqh* (or "Islamic jurisprudence").

Some of the aforementioned key words describe only the sources of law. Others cover Islamic Law methodology. Thus *Qiyas* is reasoning by analogy to solve a new legal problem. *Qiyas* comprises the a fortiori argument in both its occurrences, the a *minori ad maius* and a *maiori ad minus, reductio ad absurdum* and *induction*. The only argument not included is the *argmentum e contrario*, which is considered a linguistic argument in usul al fiqh. This is quite important to know, because Islamic law permits legal rules to be changed and modified in accordance with changing circumstances.

However this is the place to speak about contracts and the principles of Islamic Law as to contracts. Under Islamic law a contract is a binding instrument. Generally speaking, Muslims must comply with any agreements that they make. Allah said about the believers:

> "...And those who fulfill their pacts when they make one..."[56] and "O you who believe fulfill your contracts...".[57]

---

[56] Al-Baqara:177.

[57] Al-Ma'idah:1.

The Prophet said:

Muslims are bound by their stipulations.[58]

Thus the contract is the law of the parties as expressed in art. 147 para. 1 Civil Code Egypt. It shall not be revoked or amended except with the agreement of the two parties, or for the reasons prescribed by law.

One further principle expressly stated in the Qur'an and Sunnah is that the charging of interest upon a loan, in whatever form, is "Riba" and is contrary to the Shari'a.[59] At Sura II, 275–79 of the Qur'an it is stated that:

> ... Allah has made buying and selling lawful and has made the taking of interest unlawful. Remember, therefore, that he who desists because of the admonition that has come to him from his Lord, may retain what he has received in the past; and his affair is committed to Allah. But those who revert to the practice, they are the inmates of the fire; therein shall they abide. ... O Ye who believe, be mindful of your duty to Allah and relinquish your claim to what remains of interest, if you are truly believers. But if you do not, then beware of war from the side of Allah and his Messenger. If, however, you desist, you will still have your capital sums; thus you will commit no wrong, nor suffer any wrong yourself.

Sura III 130 states that:

> O Ye who believe, devour not interest, for it goes on multiplying itself; and be mindful of your obligation to Allah that you may prosper. (*The Quran, translated by Muhammad Zafrulla Khan, Curzon Press, 1971*)

Another principle derived from the Qur'an and Sunna is the avoidance of Gharar or unacceptable risk. Sometimes translated as "trading in risk", the *Hadith* discusses *Gharar* at length. Intrinsically, the limitation on *Gharar* is related to the Islamic prohibition on gambling. Etymologically, *Gharar* means uncertainty and ambiguity and, separately, can also include elements of deceit. *Shari'a* prohibits transactions that are subject to excessive uncertainty. However, some level of risk remains a fundamental aspect of commercial life. Thus risk allocation is a necessary component of Islamic law. Only disproportionate risk, speculative trading and transactions meeting exceeding limitations are considered *Gharar*. The concept of Gharar arose in early Islamic times where *Gharar* was often associated in the *Hadith* with the sale of unborn livestock or unripened fruit on trees, or the payment of a fixed price upfront for a fisherman's prospective catch. However, hiring the fisherman to go fishing for you and paying him for his labor would be acceptable, as labor is not an uncertain concept. In line with *Gharar*, Islamic scholars typically forbid the use of conventional forward contracts. However certain types of *Shari'a*-compliant forward sales, called *Bai Al-Salam*, and Istisna, which means a purchase/sale transaction in which a buyer places an order for the manufacture of an object for delivery at a future date and at an agreed price, are allowed.

---

[58] Abu Daud & Al-Hakim (sahih).

[59] Beximco Pharmaceuticals Ltd & Ors v. Shamil Bank of Bahrain EC [2004] EWCA Civ 19 (28 January 2004).

Shari'a contract law differentiates between nominate contracts (those which are specifically named in the Qu'ran) and innominate contracts (those which are not specifically named in the Qu'ran). Contracts for works draw their origin in Islamic law from Istisna. They are also known as aqd muqawala, which are innominate contracts. Accordingly art. 872 Civil Code UAE provides, that a Muqawala is a contract whereby one of the parties thereto undertakes to make a thing or to perform work in consideration which the other party undertakes . . .. As Shari'a law prohibits dealing with matters which are not in existence at the time of making the agreement according to the principle of "Gharar" the subject matter of a contract for works and the price to be paid in consideration must be clearly defined.

Some further principles of Islamic law are known as the principles of good faith and due process (see art. 148 Civil Code Egypt). Also the concept of unforeseen and exceptional events should be mentioned. If general unforeseen and exceptional events occur and their occurrence results in rendering the implementation of the contract, though not impossible, an exhausting factor for the debtor threatening him with an enormous loss, the judge shall, according to conditions of the case and after balancing between the interests of the two parties, restore the exhausting obligation to the plausible limit (see art. 147 Civil Code Egypt). However, in principle a contract shall not be revoked except by mutual consent. Also termination of the contract under "faskh" must be distinguished from its termination under "iqala" in that "faskh" affects invalid or imperfect contracts, whereas "iqala" terminates the perfectly valid contract by mutual agreement of the parties. In legal terminology, *iqala* means the dissolution of a transaction of sale in consideration of an equivalent of the original price. However, rescission of the contract (Iqala) is permissible according to prophet's saying – Peace and prayers be upon him –:"that who rescinds the sale contract (Iqala) because he feels repentant, Allah will forgive him in doomsday" (Yagi 2004, p. 169).

The majority of Islamic countries have adopted the French decennial liability as covered by art. 1792 et seq. Civil Code France. This is the case in Algeria, Egypt, Iraq, Jordan, Kuwait, Lebanon, Morocco, Qatar, Saudia Arabia, Tunisia and the United Arab Emirates. Decennial liability (responsabilité décennale in French) is a form of strict construction liability under which no proof of negligence is required. The builder and usually also the architect jointly guarantee that during a period of ten years the building will not be demolished, wholly or in part, even if the demolition results from a defect in the land itself (see art. 651 Civil Code Egypt; art. 880 Civil Code UAE, art. 692 Civil Code Kuwait).

Finally it should be emphasised that the Qur'an is extremely in favour of amicable settlements. Sura IV 128 states that:

Settlement (sulh) is best.

This statement comes from a verse from the Qur'an which suggests amicable divorce when a wife fears ill-treatment.[60] It reads as follows:

It shall not be wrong for the two to set things peacefully to rights between them: for sulh is best.

---

[60] Sura IV 128.

Thus "sulh" is an independent system which is permissible in the Shari'a. It has been ordained by the Shari'a to settle and terminate mutual disputes. Judges will often have in mind that "sulh" is near to justice. Thus, in practice judges will often actively, even forcefully, exhort the parties to reach a settlement if they consider that it is where justice lies (Vogel 2000, p. 156). In addition it is common sense that "sulh" confers religious blamelessness on the parties and the judge and avoids animosity between the parties, which might be caused by any judgment.

References

Ballantyne WM (1989) Book review of commercial arbitration in the Arab Middle East (A study in Sharia and Statute Law). Arb Inl 269

Boldt A (2004) Der neue Bauvertrag, 2nd edn. Carl Heyemanns, Köln

de Wet JC, Yeats JP (1978) Die Suid-Afrikaanse kontraktereg en handelsreg, 4th edn. Butterworth, Durban

Fyzee AA (1949) Outlines of Muhammadan Law, 3rd edn. Oxford University Press, London

Grüneberg C (2009) in: Palandt (ed) Commentary to BGB, 68th edn. C.H. Beck, München

Heinrichs H (2009) in: Palandt (ed) Commentary to BGB, 68th edn. C.H. Beck, München

Leupertz S (2005) Der Anspruch des Unternehmers auf Bezahlung unbestellter Bauleistungen beim BGB – Bauvertrag. BauR 775 et seqq.

Messerschmidt B, Voit W (2008) Privates Baurecht. C.H. Beck, München

Motzke G (2002) Parameter für Zusatzvergütung bei zusätzlichen Leistungen. NZBau 641

Oberhauser I (2005) Ansprüche des Auftragnehmers auf Bezahlung nicht "bestellter" Leistungen beim Bauvertrag auf der Basis der VOB/B. BauR 919 et seqq.

Peters F (2003) in: Staudinger (ed) Commentary to BGB, 15th edn. De Gruyter, Berlin

Sprau H (2009) in: Palandt (ed) Commentary to BGB, 68th edn. C.H. Beck, München

Vogel FE (2000) Islamic law and legal system. Brill, London

Voit W (2008) in: Bamberger, Roth (eds) Commentary to BGB, 2nd edn. C.H. Beck, München

Yagi A (2004) Droit musulman. Publisud, Paris

Chapter 2
Conflict of Laws

2.1 Introduction

In any case which involves a foreign element it may prove necessary to decide which system of law is to be applied, either to the case as a whole or to a particular issue or issues. Such foreign elements may be constituted by the central administration or headquarters of each of the parties being located in different countries or by the fact that the site is located in a country different from the home country of either of the parties.

The identification of the appropriate law may be viewed as involving a three-stage process: (1) characterisation or classification of the relevant issue; (2) selection of the rule of conflict of laws which lays down a connecting factor for that issue; and (3) identification of the system of law which is tied by that connecting factor to that issue.[1] In practise, in particular at pre-contract stage, the approach should be a bit more sophisticated, as such:

- Identification of the forum (which is either stipulated or not)
- Identification of the applicable set of conflict of laws rules (determined by the seat of the forum)
- Characterisation or classification of the relevant issue (contract issue, pre-contract issue, tort issue, power of attorney issue, formal requirement issue, etc.)
- Selection of the rule of conflict of laws which lays down a connecting factor for that issue
- Identification of the system of law which is tied by that connecting factor to that issue

At a first stage the jurisdiction of a court must be determined. The conflict of laws rules of this court shall be applied to decide which system of law is to be applied.

---

[1] See Macmillan Inc v. Bishopsgate Investment Trust Plc [1996] 1 WLR 387, 391–2 per Staughton LJ; *Raiffeisen Zentralbank Österreich AG v. Five Star Trading LLC ("The Mount I")* [2001] QB 825 at 840B to 841B.

A.-V. Jaeger and G.-S. Hök, *FIDIC-A Guide for Practitioners*,
DOI 10.1007/978-3-642-02100-8_2, © Springer-Verlag Berlin Heidelberg 2010

At a second stage the judge or the presumed judge is likely to commence by asking himself what is the nature of the problem which confronts him. In other words he must classify the "cause of action" in order to determine the applicable conflict of laws rule. This way has been explained by Cheshire and North (North and Fawcett 2005, p. 36) as follows:

> This "classification of the cause of action" means the allocation of the question raised by the factual situation before the court to its correct legal category. Its object is to reveal the relevant rule for the choice of law. The rules of any given system of law are arranged under different categories, some being concerned with status, others with succession, procedure, contract, tort and so on, and until a judge, faced with a case involving a foreign element, has determined the particular category into which the question before him falls, he can make no progress, for he will not know what choice of law rule to apply. He must discover the true basis of the claim being made. He must decide, for instance, whether the question relates to the administration of assets or to succession, for in the case of movables left by a deceased person, the former is governed by the law of the forum, the latter by the law of the domicile. Whether undertaken consciously or unconsciously, this process of classification must always be performed. It is usually done automatically and without difficulty.

Once the proper conflict of laws rule has been identified that connects the question identified by classification of the cause of action to a particular system of law, this being referred to as the "connecting factor", the applicable system of law which is tied by the connecting factor must be applied. Finally the judge shall identify which set of rules from or part of that system should be applied to determine the dispute. If a contractual cause of the action has been identified the following principles of the so called Rome Convention (or as of the 17 December 2009 on the so-called Regulation EC/593/2008 of the European Parliament and the Council of 17 June 2008 on the law applicable to contractual obligations, also referred to as Rome I Regulation) shall apply:

2.2 Nature of the Cause of Action

As a first step the relevant cause of action must be identified and qualified in order to determine the applicable choice-of-law rule of the forum. Contractual claims must be considered according to the proper law of the contract. If the relevant cause of action has the nature of a claim in tort then the lex loci commissi applies. Questions concerning the property as to movables and immovables follow the lex situs rule.

Under the new Rome II Regulation which has come into force 11 January 2009, *culpa in contrahendo* is an autonomous concept and should not necessarily be interpreted within the meaning of national law. It should include the violation of the duty of disclosure and the breakdown of contractual negotiations. Article 12 of the Regulation covers only non-contractual obligations presenting a direct link with the dealings prior to the conclusion of a contract. This means that if, while a contract is being negotiated, a person suffers personal injury, Article 4 of the Rome II Regulation or other relevant provisions of this Regulation should apply.

2.3 Pre-contractual Stage

According to Article 8 Rome Convention (compare art. 9 Rome I Regulation) the existence and validity of a contract, or of any term of a contract, shall be determined by the law which would govern it under the Convention if the contract or term were valid. Thus in principle the answer to the question of whether a call for tenders is an offer or an invitation ad offerendum will depend on the presumptive proper law of the contract. Another issue is whether the procurement rules of a state which invites tenderers to submit offers fall within this regime. It is suggested that procurement rules as to how to procure a contract for works have the nature of procedural rules relating to the conduct of public bodies and authorities. If so, the law of the state applies according to the *auctor regit actum* principle. Whether substantial procurement law prevails over the proper law of the contract, if this is different to the proper law of the contract, depends on the nature of the substantial rules. In most cases substantial procurement law, such as German budget law and related ordinances according to which German public bodies shall incorporate the VOB/B in any construction contract will not have the nature of mandatory law within the meaning of art. 7 Rome Convention (compare Art. 8 Rome I Regulation), although of course German public bodies are in principle bound to it. German courts are reluctant to apply Article 7(2) Rome Convention. It is a common position that Article 7(2) Rome Convention is not in itself a conflict of laws rule. It presupposes the existence of a rule which is mandatory irrespective of the law otherwise applicable. Examples where the German legislator has expressly ruled that a provision has this nature are extremely rare (for example Section 130(2) German Cartle law). If there is no such express rule the test is whether according to its purpose and telos it has the nature of a rule which is mandatory irrespective of the law otherwise applicable. This is a matter of interpretation of law. According to the German authorities the concerned rule must be legitimised by public interest concerns. It is not sufficient that the concerned rule aims to protect individual interests.[2] Whereas public procurement procedure rules are aimed to ensure a fair procurement procedure in the interest of both, the public body and the bidders, substantial law aims to balance risks and duties. Hence German public budget law is not aimed at ensuring fair and non-discriminatory conditions of competition for suppliers. It is aimed at an efficient use of public funds in order to ensure value for money on public procurement financed out of general taxation.[3] Competition of suppliers becomes used in order to achieve this result but it is not the purpose of budget law.[4]

---

[2] BAG [2003] IPRax 258, p. 261.
[3] BVerfG, decision from 13 June 2006; file no. 1 BvR 1160/03.
[4] BVerfG, decision from 13 June 2006; file no. 1 BvR 1160/03.

2.4   Proper Law of the Contract

On the 17 December 2009 the Rome I Regulation will replace the Rome Convention. The United Kingdom and Ireland have opted to adhere to the Rome I Regulation. The Rome Convention therefore remains applicable only in cases which involve Denmark.

2.4.1   Rome Convention

At the present time in most European countries the proper law of the contract has to be determined in accordance with the so called Rome Convention. The Rome Convention has the force of law in the United Kingdom pursuant to Section 1 and Schedule 1 of the *Contracts (Applicable Law) Act 1990* and in Austria, Belgium, Denmark, Finland, France, Germany, Greece, Ireland, Italy, Luxemburg, Portugal, Sweden and Spain. Subsequently Estonia, Latvia, Poland, Malta, Slovenia, Hungry, Cyprus, Lithuania, Czech, Slovakia adhered. Its relevant provisions are as follows.

Article 3 (Freedom of Choice) provides:

1. A contract shall be governed by the law chosen by the parties. The choice must be expressed or demonstrated with reasonable certainty by the terms of the contract or the circumstances of the case. By their choice the parties can select the law applicable for the whole or a part only of the contract.

Under a FIDIC contract the parties usually choose the applicable law to the contract. This is what is suggested by Sub-Clause 1.4 and what usually happens by indication of the relevant law in the Appendix to Tender. However sometimes the parties to the contract ignore the fact that a country is split in different jurisdictions, such as is the case in the United Kingdom or the United States of America. In those cases the relevant jurisdiction instead of the relevant country must be indicated in order to determine the applicable law in a precise way, leaving no room for ambiguities.

In the absence of an express or implied choice of law by the parties, article 4(1) of the Rome Convention provides that the contract shall be governed by the law of the country with which it is most closely connected. Article 4(2) provides that, subject to the provisions of article 4(5), it shall be presumed that the contract is most closely connected with the country where the party who is to effect the performance which is characteristic of the contract has, at the time of the conclusion of the contract, his habitual residence, or, in the case of a body corporate or unincorporated, its central administration. Article 4(5) provides that article 4(2) shall not apply if the characteristic performance cannot be determined. Article 4(5) further provides that the presumptions in paragraphs (2), (3) and (4) shall be disregarded if it appears from the circumstances as a whole that the contract is more closely connected with another country. Articles 4(3) and (4) have no application to the present case. They make provision for particular presumptions in relation to certain specified contracts.

Article 4 (Applicable Law in the absence of choice) provides:

1. To the extent that law applicable to the contract has not been chosen in accordance with Article 3, the contract shall be governed by the law of the country with which it is most closely connected ...
2. Subject to the provisions of paragraph 5 of this Article, it shall be presumed that the contract is most closely connected with the country where the party who is to effect the performance which is characteristic of the contract has, at the time of conclusion of the contract, his habitual residence, or, in the case of a body corporate or un-incorporate, its central administration. However, if the contract is entered into the course of that party's trade or profession, that country shall be the country in which the principal place of business is situated or, where under the terms of the contract the performance is to be effected through a place of business other than the principal place of business, the country in which that other place of business is situated.
3. ...
4. ...
5. Paragraph 2 shall not apply if the characteristic performance cannot be determined and the presumptions of paragraphs 2, 3 and 4 shall be disregarded if it appears from the circumstances as a whole that the contract is more closely connected with another country.

However there is no unanimous position which prevails worldwide. Under the traditional conflict of laws rules in Florida (USA), it is well settled that "matters bearing on the validity and substantive obligation of contracts are determined by the law of the place where the contract is made (lex loci contractus),"[5] whilst Colorado has adopted the "most significant relationship" approach of the Restatement (Second) of Conflict of Laws for resolving questions in contract cases.[6] In some jurisdictions such as in France the place where the works were carried out is the preferred most significant relationship in contract cases (Rémy-Corlay 2001, p.670; Glavinis 1993, note 646 et seq.).

It has been decided to replace the Rome Convention by a new EC Regulation, also referred to as the Rome I Regulation. The Regulation aims at converting the Rome Convention on the law applicable to contractual obligations into a Community Regulation and to modernise some of its rules. A final draft of the Rome I Regulation is already available. According to the new Regulation a contract shall be governed by the law chosen by the parties. The choice shall be made expressly or clearly demonstrated by the terms of the contract or the circumstances of the case. To the extent that the law applicable to the contract has not been chosen, a contract for services shall be governed by the law of the country where the service provider

---

[5] Jemco, Inc v. United Parcel Service, Inc, 400 So.2d 499 (Fla.3d DCA 1981), review denied, 412 So.2d 466 (Fla.1982); Lincoln P. Tang-How, d/b/a Tang How Brothers, General Contractors v. Edward J. Gerrits, Inc and others 961 F.2d 174.

[6] Wood Bros. Homes, Inc v. Walker Adjustment Bureau 198 Colo 444, 601 P.2d 1369 (1979).

has his habitual residence. However, where it is clear from all the circumstances of the case that the contract is manifestly more closely connected with a country other than where the service provider has his habitual residence, the law of that other country shall apply. Thus in principle the legal situation does not change in substance. It is however worth to note that the new Regulation does not exclude the option to choose a non state body of law such as the European Principles of Contract law or the Unidroit Principles on commercial contracts.

Sometimes mandatory rules do exist the respect for which is regarded as crucial by a country for safeguarding its political, social or economic organisation to such an extent that they are applicable to any situation falling within their scope, irrespective of the law otherwise applicable to the contract. This type of rules prevails over the proper law of the contract. A good example for this type of rule is the French decennial liability according to art. 1792 et seq. French Civil Code, having been adopted by act of parliament in a number of other jurisdictions, such as Algeria, Angola, Belgium, Egypt, Luxemburg, Malta, Morocco, Spain, Romania, Tunisia, and the United Arab Emirates. The decennial liability has been enacted in order to guarantee the structural stability of building works, which is legitimised by public interest concerns. Whichever law the parties have agreed to apply to their contract, the decennial liability of the country where the site is located will apply.

2.4.2   Rome I Regulation

The Rome I Regulation slightly changes the existing conflict of laws rules as to contractual relationships. However, in principle the legal situation will be upheld.

According to Article 3 Rome I Regulation the parties to a contract may choose the applicable law. Consideration 13 of the new Regulation provides for a new option by stating that the Regulation does not preclude parties from incorporating by reference into their contract a non-State body of law or an international convention. Hence it will be possible to submit the contract to the Unidroit Principles for commercial contracts or the European Principles of Contract Law (EPCL). Although it has already been said by Prof. Molineaux (1997, p. 55 et seq.), that the FIDIC forms of contract are widely used and that their dissemination has already developed a degree of commonality or construction *lex mercatoria*, it is submitted that it will not be sufficient to refer to the FIDIC form of contract as such as they do cover all of the legal questions arising from a construction contract (Fig. 2.1).

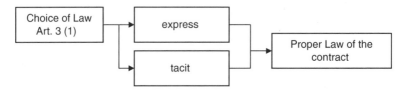

Fig. 2.1 Choice of Law

If the Parties did not choose the proper law of the contract, Article 4 Rome I Regulation applies. Therein a new system for the purposes of the determination of the proper law of the contract has been established, which distinguishes between nominate and innominate contracts. The proper law of the contract as to all types of contracts having been listed in Article 4 paragraph 1 Rome I Regulation shall be the one which has been ruled accordingly. In the case of an innominate contract the contract shall be governed by the law of the country where the party required to effect the characteristic performance of the contract has his habitual residence (Art. 4 paragraph 2 Rome I Regulation). Where it is clear from all the circumstances of the case, that the contract is manifestly more closely connected with a country other than that indicated in Article 4 paragraphs 1 or 2, the law of that other country shall apply. Finally, if the proper law of the contract cannot be determined pursuant to Article 4 paragraphs 1 or 2 Rome I Regulation, the contract shall be governed by the law of the country with which it is most closely connected.

As to construction contracts and consultancy agreements this will have the following effect:

According to Consideration no. 17 of the Rome I Regulation as far as the applicable law in the absence of choice is concerned, the concept of "provision of services" and "sale of goods" should be interpreted in the same way as when applying Article 5 of Regulation (EC) No 44/2001 in so far as sale of goods and provision of services are covered by that Regulation. By consequence all construction contracts and consultancy agreements will have the nature of a service agreement (Kropholler 2005, Art. 5 note 44) and they will be governed by the law of the country where the service provider has his habitual residence. Whether it will be possible to deviate from this rule depends on the merits of the case. If the contract is manifestly more closely connected to a country other than that indicated in Article 4 paragraphs 1 or 2 Rome I Regulation, it is still possible to apply the law of that country. In line with the famous German author Savigny it would be still possible to argue that a construction contract has its natural centre of gravity in the country

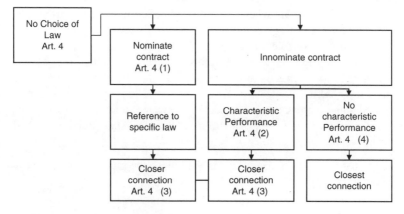

Fig. 2.2 Choice of Law without consent

where the works have to be executed. By the way it cannot be completely ignored that more or less all Civil law countries derive their concepts of a contract of letting and hiring from Roman law according to which the locator let the work to the conductor (locatio conductio operis) which meant that the employer placed the site in the hands of the contractor on which he was to expend his labour. This was and is still a main characteristic of a contract for works. To some extent the French decennial liability (see Art. 1792 et seq. Code Civil) shows that the place of working creates a particular responsibility for the stability of the structure also in order to protect the public. This finding constitutes the justification for this type of liability and underlines what Mr. Savigny said (Fig. 2.2).

2.5 Tort Law

In particular in construction cases the proper law of the contract governs only a part of the relevant causes of actions. Site accidents and other events need to be handled as well. However, although the principle of the *lex loci delicti commissi* is the basic solution for non-contractual obligations in virtually all the member States of the EU, the practical application of the principle where the component factors of the case are spread over several countries varies. In England one of the purposes of the Private International Law (Miscellaneous Provisions) Act 1995 was to make provision for choice of law rules in tort and delict, and the relevant provisions are contained in Part III (sections 9–15). The main purpose of Part III is to abolish the common law rules of double actionability, established in *Phillips v. Eyre* (1870) LR 6 QB 1 and developed by the House of Lords in *Boys v. Chaplin* [1971] AC 356, and the exceptions to it discussed in *Boys v. Chaplin* and *Red Sea Insurance Ltd v. Bouygues SA*,[7] and to establish a new general choice of law rule. The effect of the double actionability rule was, in short, that in order to bring proceedings in England in respect of a tort committed abroad, the acts or omissions of the defendant had to be actionable as a tort in England and actionable in the foreign country in which the tort was committed. Today where the cause of action has resulted from allegedly tortious conduct in a foreign country, it is no longer necessary for the case to be based on a tort actionable in England. The English courts must apply wider international tests and respect any remedies available under the "Applicable Law" or *lex causae* including any rules on who may claim and who the relevant defendant may be.

The first stage is for the court to decide where the tort occurred which may be difficult if relevant events took place in more than one state. Section 11(2) distinguishes between:

• Actions for personal injuries: This is the law of the place where the individual sustained the injury.

---

[7] (1995) 1 AC 190.

- Damage to property: this is the law of the place where the property was damaged.
- In any other case, this is the law of the place in which the most significant element or elements occurred.

In Germany the test for a cause of action resulting from allegedly tortious conduct with foreign elements is where the person who is liable to the injured party has committed the unlawful act. However art. 40 Introductory Law of the Civil Code lays down the so-called restricted *Ubiquitätsprinzip* (principle of ubiquity), according to which the injured party has the right, up to the final oral hearing in the court proceedings of first instance, to choose the law of the country where the loss was sustained instead of the law of the country where the person who is liable has acted, which best serves its interests.

Where a French Court qualifies the cause of action as a tort issue, the applicable law should be the law of the country where the tort was committed. French cases usually define the *lex loci delicti* as the place where the injury occurs. The French Cour de Cassation has held that the *lex loci delicti* should be the place where the injury initially occurs, whether or not tortious acts may have taken place elsewhere.[8]

However, Regulation EC/846/2007 of the European Parliament and of the Council on the law applicable to non-contractual obligations (Rome II) will change the conflict of law regime within all Member States of the EU except Denmark. According to Article 4(1) Rome II Regulation, coming in force on 11 January 2009, unless otherwise provided for in the Regulation, the law applicable to a non-contractual obligation arising out of a tort/delict shall be the law of the country in which the *damage occurs* irrespective of the country in which the event giving rise to the damage occurred and irrespective of the country or countries in which the indirect consequences of that event occur. Recital 11 declares that, since the concept of a non-contractual obligation varies from one Member State to another, for the purposes of the Regulation "non-contractual obligation" should be understood as an autonomous concept.

For the avoidance of doubt the Regulation makes it clear that the law applicable should be determined on the basis of where the *damage occurs*, regardless of the country or countries in which the indirect consequences could occur. Article 4(1) Rome II Regulation makes applicable "the law of the country in which the damage occurs irrespective of the country in which the event giving rise to the damage occurred and irrespective of the country or countries in which the indirect consequences of that event occur." Accordingly, in cases of personal injury or damage to property, the country in which the damage occurs should be the country where the injury was sustained or the property was damaged respectively.

However two exceptions have to be kept in mind according to Article 4(2) and (3):

---

[8] Cour de Cassation, Première chambre civile, 11 mai 1999.

Where the person claimed to be liable and the person sustaining damage both have their habitual residence in the same country at the time when the damage occurs, the law of that country shall apply. Thus if an employee of the Contractor suffers an injury, and both originate from the same country, the law of the common country of origin will apply.

Where it is clear from all the circumstances of the case that the tort/delict is manifestly more closely connected with a country other than that indicated in paragraphs 1 or 2, the law of that other country shall apply. A manifestly closer connection with another country might be based in particular on a pre-existing relationship between the parties, such as a contract, that is closely connected with the tort/delict in question.

2.6   Quasi Contracts

Besides tort law remedies another cause of action may be interesting for contractors. It may happen that the Engineer or the Employer will instruct the Contractor to carry out works even though there is not yet a contractual basis. Again it may happen that an amendment to the contract is null and void for different reasons. Thus if works have been carried out without a clear contractual background, the question arises whether the Contractor is nevertheless entitled to a payment. If the cause of action is a claim for restitution there is no claim in contract. In English law it is clear that a claim for restitution is a separate and distinct cause of action from a claim in contract. In *Fibrosa Spolka Akcyjna v. Fairbairn Lawson Combe Barbour Ltd* [1943] AC 32 at 61 Lord Wright stated:

> It is clear that any civilised system of law is bound to provide remedies for cases of what has been called unjust enrichment or unjust benefit, that is to prevent a man from retaining the money of or some benefit derived from another which it is against conscience that he should keep. Such remedies in English law are generically different from remedies in contract or in tort, and are now recognised to fall within a third category of the common law which has been called quasi-contract or restitution.

In *Westdeutsche Bank v. Islington* Lord Browne-Wilkinson stated:[9]

> The common law restitutionary claim is based not on implied contract but on unjust enrichment: in the circumstances the law imposes an obligation to repay rather than implying an entirely fictitious agreement to repay: *Fibrosa Spolka Akcyjna v. Fairbairn Lawson Combe Barbour Ltd.* [1943] AC 32, 63–64, *per* Lord Wright; *Pavey & Matthews Pty Ltd v. Paul* (1987) 162 CLR 221, 227, 255; *Lipkin Gorman v. Karpnale Ltd* [1991] 2 AC 548, 578C; *Woolwich Equitable Building Society v. Inland Revenue Commissioners* [1993] AC 70. In my judgment, your Lordships should now unequivocally and finally reject the concept that the claim for moneys had and received is based on an implied contract. I would overrule *Sinclair v. Brougham* on this point.

---

[9]Westdeutsche Bank v. Islington L.B.C. [1996] AC 669, 710E.

The proper law of an obligation to restore the benefit of an enrichment obtained to another person's expense is the presumptive proper law of contract if it arises in connection with a contract.[10]

From 11 January 2009 onwards, when the Rome II Regulation comes into force, unjust enrichment cases will be treated according to art. 10 of the Rome II Regulation. If a non-contractual obligation arising out of unjust enrichment, including payment of amounts wrongly received, concerns a relationship existing between the parties, such as one arising out of a contract or a tort/delict, that is closely connected with that unjust enrichment, it shall be governed by the law that governs that relationship.

2.7 Choice of Law as to Extra-contractual Claims

The new Rome II Regulation lays down choice of law rules for torts and restitutionary obligations. It is designed to complement the Rome I Regulation and the Rome Convention of 19 June 1980 on the Law Applicable to Contractual Obligations. It can be seen that, under art. 4(3) of the Rome II Regulation, a tort claim may in some cases be governed by the law which applies to a contract between the same parties, concluded before the events constituting the tort occurred, on the basis that the tort claim is manifestly most closely connected with the country whose law governs the contract.

Further art. 14 of the Rome II Regulation enables parties to reach an agreement, choosing the law applicable to a tort claim between them, except in respect of claims for unfair competition, restriction of competition, or infringement of an intellectual property right. Pursuant to art. 14(1) of the Rome II Regulation, the agreement may be entered into after the event giving rise to the damage has occurred. However, and this is completely new, where all the parties are pursuing a commercial activity, and the agreement is freely negotiated, the agreement may also be entered into before the event giving rise to the damage has occurred. The requirement of commercial activity appears to exclude agreements entered into with a consumer or an employee. As under art. 3 of the Rome I Regulation, the choice must be expressed or demonstrated with reasonable certainty by the circumstances of the case, and is not to prejudice the rights of third parties (such as liability insurers). Art. 14(2) specifies that where all the elements relevant to the situation at the time when the event giving rise to the damage occurs are located in a country other than the country whose law has been chosen, the choice of the parties is not to prejudice the application of provisions of the law of that country which cannot be derogated from by agreement. Finally art. 14(3) of the Rome II Regulation adds that where all the elements relevant to the situation at the time when the event giving

---

[10]Fibrosa Spolka Akcyjna v. Fairbairn Lawson Combe Barbour Ltd [1943] AC 32.

rise to the damage occurs are located in one or more of the EC Member States, the parties' choice of a law other than that of a Member State is not to prejudice the application of provisions of Community law, where appropriate as implemented in the Member State of the forum, which cannot be derogated from by agreement. Parties commonly include choice of law clauses to govern the contractual aspects of a dispute (e.g., breach of a warranty or obligation). An adjusted Sub-Clause 1.4 for a choice of law clause could be as such:

This Contract *and any non-contractual obligations arising out of or in connection with it* shall be governed by and construed in accordance with the law of the country or other jurisdiction) stated in the Appendix to Tender.

The aforementioned clause broadens the scope of the provision and includes non-contractual claims (e.g., a cause of action that arises out of a breach of a representation or a cause of action that arises out of the quantum principle).

2.8 In Rem Claims

Finally both of the parties are interested in knowing who is or becomes the owner of materials and equipment being delivered to the Site. The actual transfer or disposition of property is, in principle, a matter for the legislature and courts of the jurisdiction where the property *is situate*. In English and German private international law, the law of a country where a thing is situate *(the lex situs)* determines whether the thing is to be considered a movable or an immovable. As to the validity of a transfer of a tangible movable and its effect on property rights, the position in English conflict of laws is as follows:

The validity of a transfer of a tangible movable and its effect on the proprietary rights of the parties thereto and of those claiming under them in respect thereof are governed by the law of the country where the movable is at the time of the transfer *(lex situs)*. A transfer of a tangible movable which is valid and effective by the law of the country where the movable is at the time of the transfer is valid and effective in England. This Rule, long established beyond challenge, rests on a line of authority dating back to the leading case of Cammell v. Sewell (1860) 5 H&N 728.[11]

2.9 The Importance for Choice of Law Issues

Usually the parties determine the proper law of the contract in the Appendix to Tender. By doing this the parties accept that all of the complementary and supplemental statutory rules and implied terms which are included in the governing law will be incorporated in the contract. Complementary rules and implied terms may

---

[11] Air Foyle Ltd & Anor v. Center Capital Ltd [2002] EWHC 2535 (Comm) (03 December 2002).

either have the nature of mandatory or non mandatory rules or implied terms. Thus the parties who are not fully informed about the proper law of the contract will sometimes incorporate terms which they would not have incorporated if they had prior knowledge of them. Skill and care must therefore be taken to identify the complementary rules of the contract before the contract is executed. A second issue arises if and when the proper law of the contract comprises general risk allocation rules which are not known by one of the parties and probably not reflected in the intended standard form of contract. An example of this is the German rule concerning subsoil conditions. According to German law the Employer bears the risk of unforeseen subsoil conditions, which may have an impact on the understanding of Sub-clauses 4.10, 4.11 and 4.12. Finally the Parties may encounter the issue that the proper law of the contract remains silent as to critical points of the contract. If for example the proper law of the contract is one which belongs to the Islamic law family, it is fundamental to know that Islamic law in principle does not time bar any remedies at law. Thus the post contractual liability does not end unless statue law stipulates otherwise. As an example, in Iran time bar (statute of limitation) was objectionable to religious figures who argued that in Islamic law rights did not expire. In response, when it was incorporated in the Iranian Civil Code, the provision was written so as to avoid the concept of expiration: it merely says that beyond the specified time the court would not hear the claim.

It is critical to understand that choice of laws' issues are not only technical legal problems which may remain open to be discussed by lawyers in the event of disputes. It must be clear at tender stage which law will be applicable to the contract and to other causes of actions. Otherwise a complete risk assessment and the Contractor will not:

(a) Have satisfied himself as to the correctness and sufficiency of the Accepted Contract Amount, and
(b) Have based the Accepted Contract Amount on the data, interpretations, necessary information, inspections, examinations and satisfaction as to all relevant matters referred to in Sub-Clause 4.10 [*Site Data*]

as supposed by Sub-Clause 4.11. The reason for this lays in the applicable law and its characteristics. Any choice of law includes the whole of the law which has been chosen. This means that all of the applicable rules whether imposed by statute or by cases law or by usage will apply to the contract or the legal relationship in question. The proper law of the contract usually includes either implied terms as is the case in anglo-saxon jurisdictions or so called non mandatory but complementary rules. Whether the parties would have included such complementary rules in the event that they would have disclosed them before making their contract or not is not at all important. Only those rules which have been excluded either expressly or impliedly can not be relied on. Thus if the parties to the contract have ignored the characteristics of the proper law of the contract disputes are more probable to arise than otherwise. The applicable law may bring matching effects on the contract altering its character and causing and imbalance in the relationship of the parties (Bunni 2005, p. 22). In other words, the applicable law is obviously one of the most important facts which must be taken in consideration for the purposes of the calculation of the tender price.

The applicable law may include:

- Special risk allocation features, for example as to the ground conditions: In some jurisdictions the risk for unforeseen ground conditions may become allocated to the Contractor in others it may become allocated to the Employer
- Rules governing the termination by convenience as is the case in Germany
- Particular post contractual liabilities such as the decennial liability in Algeria, Angola, Belgium, Egypt, Luxemburg, Malta, Morocco, Romania, Tunisia, United Arab Emirates
- Particular remedies for incorrect tender data, which can be excluded by waiver clauses
- Particular provisions as to the protection of the contractor and in particular subcontractors, such as duty of the employer to provide a payment security on request of the contractor or the possibility of subcontractors to recover payment from the employer in the event that the main contractor should refrain to pay the subcontractor
- Particular requirements to provide insurance cover as it is the case in countries which have adopted the French decennial liability
- Special causes of action in the event of changed circumstances
- Limitation rules which provide for a much longer post contractual liability for latent defects than expected
- A variety of remedies in the event of defective work, such as a claim to remedy defects (specific performance) or the right to make deductions from the contract price
- Particular features which may constitute a waiver of claims for defective works
- Differing contract interpretation rules, allowing for example to consider pre contract negotiations or simply forbidding them

FIDIC does not exclude to rely on the proper law of the contract. Instead it presupposes that the parties to the contract are bound by the proper law of the contract and other applicable law. FIDIC even refers to remedies and claims under the applicable law by ruling that claims in connection with the contract and under the contract shall be dealt with equally.Each jurisdiction is a single and particular legal framework. Different jurisdictions often offer different solutions to the same issues. Although the results may sometimes be analogous, they may also at times be contradictory. Misunderstandings are commonplace. It is therefore strongly recommended to undertake legal research on a case by case basis and to ascertain the whole legal background of the contract. It is critical to learn about the local court practice, about local usages and experiences. Law is not a logical science. Instead it consists of the common conviction of a given community as to how daily life and trades shall be ruled and handled. Legislation and case law is an expression of this common conviction on an appointed day. Thus, with time, it may change.

Law is composed of different sections. A whole legal system consists of public law, procedural law and substantive private law. Within public law lies administrative law which denotes a whole section of law whose rules deal with two aspects in the relationship between authorities and the public (Bunni 2005, p. 26). The first aspect is the protection of individuals against infringements of their legal rights which most commonly have a constitutional basis. The second aspect is the requirement of an effective operation of the public service (Bunni 2005, p. 26). This part of administrative law has much impact on construction developments. Zoning law and building regulations are part of it. To some extent the law of procurement procedures for public works and even the award of contracts for public works were put under the regime of administrative law. Within its territory of origin public or administrative law usually applies to everybody but sometimes particular law exists which governs the way of life and the business of foreigners. It may then require special permissions and licences for doing the business or even requiring permissions for being in the country. Sub-Clause 1.13 requires the Contractor to comply with the Laws. To some extent this is self explanatory but to some extent it goes further than this, because the fact that the Contractor accepts to comply with laws is binding on him as a contractual obligation.

2.10 Compliance Rules

In the field of international construction the proper law of contract may be different from the local law to be applied at the site. Sub-Clause 1.13 of all of the FIDIC Books 1999 edition provides that the Contractor shall comply with the Laws, which means that all local laws ruling safety and health issues as well as quality issues must be met. It may prove difficult to identify the Laws. It is therefore critical to rely on Sub-Clause 2.2 according to which the Employer shall provide reasonable assistance to the Contractor by obtaining copies of the Laws which are relevant to the Contract but are not readily available. As the obligation is qualified as "reasonable" and the Employer being in the position to give assistance it is doubtful whether the Employer must give comprehensive and correct information. Again it must be doubted that Sub-Clause 2.2 will reduce the Contractor's obligation to comply with the Laws.

It is quite common for the law to require the parties to obtain a permit needed to allow the Contractor to commence the works. According to Sub-clause 1.13 the Employer owes a duty to obtain such permits, including the duty to make a proper application, requiring the deposit of appropriate drawings.

Illustration: In the Canadian case of *Ellis-Don Ltd v. The Parking Authority of Toronto* (1978) 28 BLR 98. Ellis-Don was a contractor engaged to build a parking facility for the Authority. Ellis-Don contended that the Authority had failed to obtain the excavation permit needed to allow Ellis-Don to commence the excavation works shortly after award of contract, causing delay. The Authority's argument that Ellis-Don should have been aware at tender stage that no permit had been issued and that it would not be issued until Ellis-Don prepared detailed shoring drawings was rejected. The court held that the Authority was under the obligation to make a proper application, including the deposit of appropriate drawings. It was held implicit in the wording of the contract that the Authority was to have obtained the required building permits at least as soon after the signing of the contract as to allow Ellis-Don to commence work when it was ready.

References

Bunni NG (2005) FIDIC forms of contract, 3rd edn. Blackwell, Oxford
Glavinis P (1993) Le contrat international de construction. GLN Joly Editions, Paris
Kropholler J (2005) Europäisches Zivilprozessrecht, 8th edn. Recht und Wirtschaft, Heidelberg
Molineaux C (1997) Moving toward a Lex Mercatoria - A Lex Constructionis. J Int Arb 14:55
North P, Fawcett JJ (2005) Cheshire and North's private international law, 13th edn. Oxford University Press, Oxford
Rémy-Corlay P (2001) Tribunal de Grande Instance Poitiers, 22.12.1999. Rev Crit Dr Intern Priv 670

Chapter 3
English and International Standard Forms of Contract

3.1 Introduction

Within the construction industry the use of standard forms has become common-place. They exist at the national level (for example JCT,[1] SIA,[2] AFNOR,[3] VOB/B[4]) but also for international purposes. Civil law standard forms, such as VOB/B, AFNOR, SIA, usually predominate national markets, whilst on the international level English speaking conditions of contract are preferred. For different reasons in the international field the most frequently used standard forms are those of the International Federation of Consulting Engineers (FIDIC). The FIDIC range of contract comprises three major forms which are usually known as Red Book, Yellow Book and Silver Book. All of them contain a set of General Conditions, a Guidance for Preparation of Particular Conditions and several model forms. But there is a larger choice than that. An also frequently used standard form has been published by the Institution of Civil Engineers (ICE) under the name of New Engineering Contract (NEC). The NEC contract family is even broader than that of FIDIC and is accompanied by guidance notes, flow charts and advisory docu-ments. In the field of technical and electrical plant the MF/1 form having been published by the Institution of Electrical Engineers for the Joint IMechE/IEE Committee on Model Forms of General Conditions of Contract has become quite common. This form has been made for home or overseas contracts for the supply and erection of electrical, electronic or mechanical plant and includes Forms of Tender, Agreement, Sub-Contract, Performance Bond and Defects Liability Demand Guarantee. Finally in the field of chemical plant the IChem model forms are recognised being a useful feature. The Institution of Chemical Engineers (IChem) offers a set of model forms, in particular the so called Red Book

---

[1] England.

[2] Switzerland.

[3] France.

[4] Germany.

A.-V. Jaeger and G.-S. Hök, *FIDIC-A Guide for Practitioners*,
DOI 10.1007/978-3-642-02100-8_3, © Springer-Verlag Berlin Heidelberg 2010

(Model Form of Conditions of Contract for Process Plants suitable for Lump Sum Contracts).

All the aforementioned standard forms originate from common law jurisdictions and/or are strongly influenced by common law doctrines and experiences. They have been drafted in English and no authentic translations exist. Only FIDIC has begun in recent years to change its policy and to licence translations. Great care should be taken when using translated standard forms due to the fact that it is quite a challenge to translate legal texts. As legal terms are part of a legal culture it is often the case that no exact translation is available for technical terms. The German concept of *Mängelgewährleistung* is not duly translated with *defects liability*. The English concept of titles in real estate is not comparable with the French term of *property of real estate*. The French or German concept of *reception of the works* has no correspondent in English law and other common law jurisdictions. By contrast English draftsmen must be aware of the fact that in civil law jurisdictions so called legal definitions exist, each of it having a precise meaning which is often specified by case law. Thus to translate the word *prompt* by the German term *unverzüglich* will lead to misunderstandings.

On the other hand standard forms are a useful feature. The relevant community is familiar with them and the frequent use of the forms result in common experiences and commentaries. Less misunderstandings and disputes are the result of it. But although it is common practice to rely on standard forms it is not essential. It can even be appropriate to draft a particular contract, for example in order to adapt local legislation or to mirror special interests or intentions not covered by any standard form. In such a case it is strongly recommended to take special advice as the drafting of construction contract demands great skill, knowledge and experience.

3.2   Types of Contracts

One of the most critical issues in apportioning risks is the way that prices are calculated and fixed in the contract. There are usually three ways to define the contract price which is to be paid to the contractor for carrying out the works:

By means of a lump sum contract the contractor agrees a fixed price (a lump sum price) for the execution of certain specified construction works. Payment is received either when the contractor has substantially completed the works or by instalments according to a payment schedule. The Lump sum price is usually agreed at the time of contract formulation when the work starts. The contractor bears the risk of any additional quantities compared with its estimation.

Cost Contracts are not based on a pre agreed price. The contractor is paid for the works that are expended together with an additional payment called a fee to cover profit and overheads of the contractor.

Remeasurement contracts are a combination of unit prices and measured quantities. The parties agree the rates of remuneration per unit but not the price of the work as a whole. The whole works become measured by a quantity surveyor or similar. The rate in the bill will be multiplied by the actual quantity of each item fixed. For example the Turkish Law on Public Procurement Contracts reads as follows:

> Art. 6 lit. c: Unit price contracts shall be made over the total price calculated by multiplying the quantity for each work of item specified in the schedule prepared by the contracting entity, with unit prices proposed by the tenderer for each corresponding work of item, on the basis of, preliminary or final projects and site lists thereof along with unit price definitions in procurement of works whereas on the basis of detailed specifications of the work involved in procurement of goods or services.

In order to facilitate the procurement of works most of the well known contract form providers have established model forms for each pricing method.

3.3   Common Characteristics of Standard Forms

The above mentioned internationally used standard forms have some common characteristics with which draftsmen and user should be familiar before using the forms.

3.3.1   The Position of the Engineer

All the abovementioned standard forms use the concept of certification and a certifier. The latter is a person or company, usually nominated by the employer, who is authorised to certify payments, completion of the works and to determine claims. The certifier, known under different names such as Engineer, Project Manager, Employer's Representative, Architect, etc., is a third person to the contract who is not a party to it. However the certifier derives its powers from the construction contract. The idea is that the parties to the contract agree that certain rights and obligations only exist under the condition that the certifier exercises his powers. Hence payment is only due if the certifier evaluates and certifies the relevant amount. A claim is given, if the certifier has determined it. The common understanding of such position is the following:

> The building owner and the contractor make their contract on the understanding that in all such matters the Engineer will act in a fair and unbiased manner and it must therefore be implicit in the owner's contract with the Engineer that he shall not only exercise due care and skill but also reach such decisions fairly, holding balance between his client and the contractor.[5]

---

[5] Sutcliffe v. Thackrah [1974] AC 727.

3.3.2   Certification

As seen above it is a common feature of construction contracts to provide for an independent third party to issue certificates signifying particular events and usually embodying administrative decisions. By means of the construction contract the parties to it agree that such kind of certificates will be issued. The effect of such a certificate is thus no more than the parties agree to it. Usually the function of the certificate is to record factual events involving the certifier to form a judgment or giving an opinion. Whilst such a certificate may be conclusive as to what it purports to certify, generally the parties confer only a power and duty to file interim binding certificates which can be challenged in further proceedings. On the other hand standard forms quite often require the existence or issuing of a certificate as a pre-condition for payments. It is usual to provide a contract provision for evaluation and payment certification by the contract administrator. If no such certificate exists the employer will be entitled to refuse payment. This leads to the question of what happens when the certifier improperly refuses to issue the certificate. It is not at all astonishing that a considerable number of court cases exist, where the alleged improper conduct of a certifier has been dealt with. In such circumstances the English courts usually held that the certifier was considered to be disqualified and that the contractor was entitled to recover payment even in the absence of a certificate (see Uff 2005, p. 283).

3.3.3   Time

The parties to a contract may make time of the essence. They do this when they fix time for completion or a fixed day of completion. If they have done so, they usually also agree to liquidated damages (LAD) for failure to comply with time for completion. But what happens if the employer prevents the contractor from complying with the time limits, either by instructions or by failure to grant possession of the site? In this event there is a risk to slip into time at large, which means that the employer looses his right to sue for liquidated damages in the event of delay by the contractor. At common law the usual approach to preserve the employer's entitlement to liquidated damages is that the contractor becomes entitled to require time extension, if and when delay and disruption occurs which is attributable to the employer.

Usually the certifier has the power to determine whether the contractor is allowed to ask for time extensions. In order to make his decisions transparent and comprehensible a sophisticated system has been established. Quite often networks techniques are used showing the critical path of the works. If and when delay and disruption has any impact to the critical path time extension has to be granted. It depends on the contract wording whether time extension will be given for each impediment or not. Most often only events which directly causes a delay on time for completion will be considered to be decisive. So called floating time will be owner owned and thus consumed in favour of the employer before any time extension can be granted.

3.3.4 Programming

Programming is the central feature to manage progress of the works. In general the contractor has to provide the programme and to update it. It depends on the contract wording whether network techniques have to be used. In such a case the critical path method as referred to in the Delay and Disruption Protocol of the English Society of Construction Law (SCL) will be applied.

3.3.5 Substantial Completion and Taking Over

All the abovementioned standard forms mirror the common law concept of substantial completion. Taking over will be certified by the certifier, but normally the certificate will not release the contractor from any contractual obligations. Only by issuing the so called Performance Certificate the contractual obligations will be deemed to be performed. However, any legal liability will remain binding. Thus, if such a contract form becomes combined with civil law the exact date of reception must be carefully ascertained in order to determine the beginning of any legal defects liability, especially for those countries where the so called decennial liability (French: responsabilité décennale[6]) has been introduced by the legislator. If a FIDIC form of contract has been used by the parties the commencement date of the decennial liability will therefore be the date of the issuing of the Performance Certificate only.

3.3.6 Liquidated Damages

The common law approach as to compensation for delay is that of delay or liquidated damages. By contrast in civil law jurisdictions the doctrine of penalty prevails. Care has to be taken that in an international contract a penalty clause may be considered invalid, when common law is the proper law of the contract. Common law courts permanently hold that penalty clauses are not equitable and therefore void. Thus it is strongly recommended not to use penalty clauses in international contracts. Liquidated damages are where a specific, usually pre-agreed, sum is requested, which must correspond to a genuine pre-estimated

---

[6]See Art. 1792 et seq. French Civil Code.

amount for compensation of a probable delay. Thus, under common law, any general wording in standard forms providing for a specific amount or percentage of the contract amount being due for delay will be void, because it cannot be pre-estimated. LAD cover comprehensively all damages resulting from delay.

3.3.7 Claims

In common law based contract forms it is usual to provide a set of claim-management rules. Compliance with such kind of management rules is critical because in general non compliance with claim management rules will lead to the foreclosure of the concerned claim or may influence the assessment of the claim. It is therefore crucial to establish a well organised contract management which requires experienced staff. A good example for such kind of clauses is contained within the FIDIC Red Book. Two major claim management requirements are ruled there, one of which is the respect of the notification delay and the other is the requirement to keep contemporary records (see sub-clause 20.1). Failure to comply with the claim management requirements leads to the foreclosure of the concerned claim. Skill and care should be taken in order to establish a claim management which covers all contractual management requirements. Civil law practitioners must understand that the timely notification of claims is a necessary part of daily work.

3.3.8 Dispute Resolution

In most of the common law standard forms alternative dispute resolution mechanisms have been introduced. For a long time, only arbitration has been used as an alternative to national courts. But today it is quite common to refer to mediation, dispute reviewing or dispute adjudication at a first step. Parties to an international contract should familiarise themselves with such modern forms of dispute resolution. This trend in "preventive law" has been taking hold all over the world, saving time, project costs, and legal fees.

Mediation is a procedure normally presided by a mediator who tries to moderate negotiations and to support any endeavour to find an amicable settlement. The mediator never decides a dispute but he may be asked for his opinion.

Dispute review boards, panels of three experienced, reputable, and impartial reviewers, take in all the facts and circumstances of a dispute and make recommendations on the basis of those facts and circumstances and the board's own expertise and experience.

Dispute adjudication leads to a decision of the adjudicator or Dispute Adjudication Board, if any. The idea of dispute adjudication is to come to a quick result, which should be binding on the parties until revision by arbitration or court proceedings. However dispute adjudication should not be confused with arbitration.

Thus the decision of an adjudicator is enforceable but subject to a following court or arbitration proceedings.

For large, complex projects, most often dispute adjudication is the preferred dispute resolution method. It can save enormous amounts of money and time compared with traditional court proceedings or even arbitration. Disputes are settled contemporaneously with the construction project, which allows the parties to free up time and resources and allows personnel to work on more productive things.

All bespoken contract forms provide Dispute Adjudication except the MF/1 form. There disputes shall be referred directly to arbitration whilst FIDIC and NEC have adopted dispute adjudication clauses. Any dispute arising form or in connection with the contract must first be referred to the Adjudicator or the Dispute Adjudication Board. Under the MF/1 form however, the parties are not allowed to go directly to arbitration when they dispute or question any decision, instruction or order of the Engineer before having given the opportunity to the Engineer to produce relief (compare Cl. 2.6 MF/1).

3.4 Contract Forms Overview

FIDIC forms of contract, the MF/1 form of contract and the NEC family of contracts comprise each a full set of model forms, based on recommended General Conditions which can be adapted and altered for special purposes. The FIDIC and NEC contracts respond to the need of a diversified range of contract forms. Thus the FIDIC contract forms and the NEC family of forms provide different forms for different procurement routes. For example FIDIC has published a measurement contract form for the procurement of works designed by the employer (so called Red Book) and two design & build contract forms (the Yellow and the Silver Book). A new Design–Build–Operate Contract form is available since 2007. Additionally FIDIC has published a special Dredging and Reclamation works form in 2006 and a Consultant Agreement Model Form, 4th edition 2006. The NEC family is even more sophisticated and comprises modules for management contracting, cost plus fee contracts, etc. The MF contracts are focused on electrical and mechanical works only. The MF/1 form is envisaged for the supply and erection of electrical, electronic or mechanical plant designed by the contractor.

FIDIC, NEC3 and MF/1 forms are administered by a nominated contract administrator. Under a FIDIC form the contract administrator is called Engineer. NEC3 has split the function of the contract administrator in a Supervisor and a Project Manager, who are required to be impartial, when acting as a certifier (Costain Ltd and others v. Bechtel[7]). According to the MF/1 form an Engineer will be appointed for contract administration purposes and especially as a certifier.

---

[7] (1) Costain Ltd, (2) O'Rourke Civil Engineering Ltd, (3) Bachy Soletanche Limited, (4) Emcor Drake & Scull Group plc v. (1) Bechtel Ltd, (2) Mr Fady Bassily [2005] EWHC 1018 (TCC).

All three of the standard forms provide detailed provisions as to the certification of events and claims. The duty of issuing the certificates is given to the concerned contract administrator. Sub-Clause 3.5 of the FIDIC forms expressly rules that the Engineer (the certifier) has to act fairly taking due regard to all relevant circumstances. No such express contract term exists in the NEC3 form.

Contracts rarely attempt to specify all the obligations of the parties. Some contracts, such as the MF/1 form even exclude implied terms by stating that the obligations, rights and liabilities of the parties are only those as expressly stated. Others exclude implied terms only on particular issues. Civil law contractors and consultants are used to be held liable for fit for purpose as to the works and the design whilst common law contractors and consultants usually expect as to their design duties to be protected by the standard of due diligence and care. The difference is the following: If a duty of care exists, it is necessary to establish a breach of that duty in order to recover damages. If the contractor or consultant is under a duty of fit for purpose, the design must result in works that fulfil the purpose for which they are intended (Huse 2002, note 9-02). Thus the designer will not escape liability by showing that his design satisfies accepted standards of engineering (Huse 2002, note 9-02). Although it is generally accepted at common law that in the absence of express provisions to the contrary there is an implied term in the design and build contract that the finished works will be reasonably fit for their intended purposes (see IBA v. EMI), the traditional approach under common law is that normally the law does not imply terms of fitness for purpose into contracts for professional services. The duty of a designer is thus to use reasonable skill and care only. It is therefore not astonishing that most of the contractors who come from common law countries try to escape from the standard fitness for purpose as to their design duties.

As a consequence it must be verified how the different standard forms deal with this issue. FIDIC rules the express obligation of fitness for purpose as to the design of the works (see Cl. 5.1 Yellow Book), whilst the MF/1 form and the ORGALIME Turn Key model refrain from doing so. Thus one of the main differences between FIDIC forms on the one side and the MF/1 and ORGALIME forms on the other side consists in the standard of liability. The ICE (NEC3) approach is bit more flexible. NEC3 does not have any limitation of liability in its core clauses. Thus the contractor's liability for his design is almost certainly on a fitness for purpose basis (Eggleston 2006, p.131). But it will depend for the special case whether there is an implied term of fit for purpose or not.

As stressed earlier common law generally does not entitle the parties to a contract to enforce any obligations in the way of specific performance. This is not very practical for construction contracts, where often some minor defects arise after substantial completion of the works. Therefore all common law influenced standard forms provide express provisions as to the remedy of defects during a special period of time after taking over, the name of which varies form standard form to standard form. As a rule the contractor is deemed to not having performed its obligations until expiry of this special period of time after taking over and sometimes even commissioning. Under the FIDIC form of contract this period is called defects notification period. The NEC3 form rules a defects correction period. In the MF/1 form a Defects Liability Period has been added.

References

Eggleston B (2006) The NEC3 engineering and construction contract, 2nd edn. Blackwell, Oxford
Huse JA (2002) Understanding and negotiating turnkey and EPC contracts, 2nd edn. Sweet & Maxwell, London
Uff J (2005) Construction law, 9th edn. Sweet & Maxwell, London

Chapter 4
Civil Law Business Terms

Using a typical national standard form of contract increases the risk for the adherent party who is not familiar with it. Moreover, using it in a translated version will result in additional risk due to linguistic misunderstandings and conceptual differences.

Finland is a good example for this risk which is inherent with the use of unknown standard terms. In Finland, the use of standardised contract terms is prevalent in many industries, and invitations to tender usually refer to such terms. Such terms are often substantially different from each other in their material content. For example, the KSE terms (General Conditions for Consulting) for planning and consulting, which have been jointly drawn up and ratified by the Finnish Association of Building Owners and Construction Clients, the Finnish Association of Consulting Firms SKOL and the Finnish Association of Architects SAFA stipulate that total liability of the provider may not exceed the total contract price while, on the other hand, the YSE terms (abbreviation for: Finnish general conditions for construction projects) provide for unlimited liability even for consequential damages. According to KSE terms the consultant's total price includes the following items: remuneration, special compensation and expenses. The total remuneration for the assignment or different parts thereof may be based on the following remuneration systems: percent-based remuneration, lump-sum remuneration, unit-based remuneration, time-work remuneration by group of persons, time-work remuneration based on consultant's own costs and other agreed remunerations.

Unlike in common law countries, there is also no variety of standard form contracts in common use in Germany. In most cases individually prepared contract terms for multiple applications are used, the stipulations of which are strongly influenced by case law. Thus the content of a construction contract is predominantly determined by statutory regulations, particularly by the regulations of sect. 631 et seq. German Civil Code, and frequently complementary application of the Award Rules for Building Works ("Vergabe- und Vertragsordnung für Bauleistung", "VOB"), at the outset envisaged for the award of public works but in fact used for both, private and public works contracts. Compared with other standard conditions having been issued by various associations the VOB/B are considered to be

A.-V. Jaeger and G.-S. Hök, *FIDIC-A Guide for Practitioners*,
DOI 10.1007/978-3-642-02100-8_4, © Springer-Verlag Berlin Heidelberg 2010

a fair set of rules, holding balance between the diverging interests of contractors and employers. The VOB includes three parts, in particular part A ruling the procurement procedure for public works, part B ruling standard terms for building contracts, and part C ruling technical standards. Only part B is in common use for private construction contracts. The German Award and Contract Committee for Building Work ("Deutscher Vergabe- und Vertragssausschuss") is responsible for the regular revision of these award rules. Part B of the VOB ("VOB/B") comprises a set of provisions regulating the legal relationship between the employer and the contractor from the time of conclusion of the construction contract until discharge. Whilst the provisions of VOB/B modify the regulations under the German Civil Code in order to make them more suitable for the particular needs and particularities of a construction contract, they do not alter them completely. Instead they are built upon the main legal policies and provide for additional features, for example the power of the employer to instruct unilateral change orders (see sect. 1 no. 3 and 4 VOB/B). All general risk allocation rules remain unchanged, such as the concept of acceptance of the works according to Section 640 Civil Code. The VOB/B only applies if the parties expressly agree so. However, Sections 631 et seq. German Civil Code remain applicable unless the VOB/B derogates from them. Some of the statutory provisions are already compulsory, such as Section 648a German Civil Code.

The VOB/B set of rules is in principle only suitable for use with a traditional procurement route. It covers in particular remeasurement and lump sum contracts. Design and build projects require considerable amendments to the VOB/B set of rules.

As to consultant contracts the situation in Germany is similar. However in this area the German Fee Structure for Architects and Engineers (Honorarordnung für Architekten und Ingenieure-HOAI) is predominant. No instrument comparable to VOB/B exists which is in common use for consultant contracts. The HOAI is quite a sophisticated instrument envisaged to rule the remuneration of engineers and architects for most of their services. It provides minimum fees and maximum fees in order to restrict defeating competition among architects and engineers and to restrict increasing rental prices.

Also in other civil law countries the situation seems to be similar. In France, Switzerland and Denmark particular standard terms do exist and are habitually used for national construction projects.[1] As in France public works are governed by the Code des Marchés publics and the award of a construction contract has the nature of an administrative act, there is a clearcut difference between public and private works. For private works usually the AFNOR-conditions (also referred to as P 03-001) will be used whilst for public works the CCAG (Cahiers des Clauses administratives Générales) and CCAP (Cahiers des Clauses administratives particulières) shall be incorporated. This type of conditions is not intended for use in international business.

Romania has adopted the FIDIC Red and Yellow Book for public works. However a Government Order from 2008 has been abrogated in May 2009.

---

[1] Switzerland: SIA; Denmark: AB/ABT; France: AFNOR.

Chapter 5
Development Stages

5.1 Overview

Depending on the contract form used the project can be divided into different stages:

1. Step: Pre-tender duties such as scrutiny of Employer's documents and requirements site surveys and visits
2. Step: Pre-contract design
3. Step: Final design
4. Step: Completion of the works
5. Step: Remedy of defects
6. Step: Post contractual liabilities
7. Step: Operation and Maintenance Services

At the very beginning of each project clear objectives must be determined. At this stage the developer or investor has to check up the location for the intended investment and the surrounding circumstances. A lot of factors have to be checked in order to find a suitable location, including tax issues, infrastructure issues, price and cost issues, financing issues, geological issues and legal issues.

The site must be investigated and surveyed in order to identify property conditions, boundaries, easements, covenants and any operational hazards. Usually then a kind of feasibility study will be made, covering zoning restrictions and preconditions, environmental conditions, including climatic and physical conditions.

If the location, the site surroundings and further investment conditions are met, the developer or investor will try to either become the legal owner or title holder of the interest or to ensure in a different way the consecutive and sustainable use of the land for the intended purposes by means of lease agreements, licences, etc.

Once feasibility has been confirmed and access to and use of the site has been ensured, a first outline proposal will be initiated, including cost evaluations. At this stage the decision has to be taken whether to award the works in a design and build

A.-V. Jaeger and G.-S. Hök, *FIDIC-A Guide for Practitioners*,
DOI 10.1007/978-3-642-02100-8_5, © Springer-Verlag Berlin Heidelberg 2010

contract or in a more traditional way. Depending on this decision the design will be developed from the outline proposal or so called Employer's Requirements will be defined.

Then a final design will be developed and approved, either by the design and build contractor or by the employer or on behalf of the employer. At the latest at this stage the works must be awarded to a contractor. This can be done either by way of an open tender procedure, a restrictive tender procedure or by way of direct negotiation. At the end of the awarding process a construction contract will be executed.

Once the contract has become binding on the parties the contractor will commence the performance of the works. At practical completion stage the works are carried out in accordance with the contract and in compliance with local laws and building regulations.

During the whole practical completion period any unforeseen events, which may happen or occur, have to be settled by means of the contract. Unforeseen conditions or circumstances are a critical point of each development. Construction and development contracts usually dedicate detailed provisions to the settlement of such events.

Unforeseen conditions may have an impact on time and cost. Sometimes they may prevent the parties form performing their contractual obligations, and other times they only make it harder or more costly to perform the contract. Some conditions are not really unforeseen but their occurrence is simply unexpected. In such a case the common approach is the following: an experienced contractor is only excused from his contractual obligations if he could not take precaution against the occurrence of the event or provide sufficient financial, technical or staff resources in order to overcome such a situation. Quite often the term "unforeseeable" is defined in the contract.

Some events are commonly known as hardship or force majeure events. The management and handling of such kind of events is in general subject to special contractual or legal provisions.

As time is usually of the essence for developers, construction contracts attempt to ensure compliance with time for completion. Time management, time control and time extension issues are therefore most often ruled in detail within the contract, usually accompanied by so called liquidated damages clauses, which sometimes are referred to as penalty clauses, which is wrong. Liquidated damages clauses shall ensure compensation for delay instead of punishing or disciplining the contractor. They are thus not punitive in nature. Instead they deal with pre-calculated damages in case of delay.

By consequence time progress has to be discussed within a framework of time control and time management as such and in the context of delay or liquidated damages. Whilst programming is a task of the contractor, the employer will normally refrain from instructions concerning the progress of the works. He can do so by acceleration instructions, which means that the employer requests the input of more staff, equipment, etc. If the contractor risks failure in complying with the time for completion, he will be obliged to bear any additional cost arising from such an instruction. By contrast if the employer simply wishes to achieve completion in advance, let's say before the agreed time for completion, he must bear the additional cost and probably also any further risk arising from his instruction, because usually it is up to the contractor to decide the methods and sequence of works.

If the contractor becomes handicapped or impeded by the employer and progress of the works therefore becomes delayed in comparison with the contractor's scheduled or proposed programme, the latter is normally entitled to ask for time extension, which has a double function. Firstly time extension leads to exoneration from liability for delay damages in the event of a time overrun and secondly the programme becomes adjusted.

Time for completion is increasingly managed by MS project and network techniques ensuring that a day-today critical path analysis can be made. Care has to be taken to provide clear rules as to the management of floating time, which is often supposed to be owner owned. As to this subject reference is made to the Delay and Disruption protocol of the English Society of Construction Law, which has been issued in 2003.

At the end of the performance period tests are usually carried out in order to control compliance of the works with the contract and if they are fit for the purposes. Successful tests will lead to acceptance of the works or the issue of a taking over certificate.

After substantial completion or taking over of the works, the contractor shall usually remedy any defects, which may occur during a special defects period, ensuring specific performance until final acceptance. Once this additional period has expired, the legal liability for either hidden defects (vices cachés) or simply for occurring defects starts. The duration of this period is subject to the applicable law and to mutual agreement of the parties, if the governing law is not compulsory.

Once the project has been completed it can be used according to the intended purposes. The facility management period commences and maintenance precautions have to be taken. Facility management itself comprises of several stages of services, including the award of rental contracts, building maintenance, technical maintenance, financial and tax reporting and last but not least marketing services, which may comprise the sale of the project, sale and lease back or other forms of product placement.

All the aforementioned project development stages have to be structured by contracts, which must be initiated, negotiated and awarded, performed and managed. None of the services to be needed will be available without a legally binding and enforceable contract, of course subject to exceptions which will have to be discussed later.

Depending on the subject matter service contracts, licence agreements, sales contracts, lease contracts, loan agreements and collateral agreements have to be drafted, negotiated and executed. All these different types of contracts are usually embedded in a national law or jurisdiction, which is called the governing law or proper law of the contract.

5.2   Pre-contract Stage

At pre-tender stage no contract exists. Thus the existence and the nature of any legal relationship between the parties generally depends on the applicable law. According to art. 8(1) of the Rome Convention the existence and validity of a contract, or any term of a contract, shall be determined by the law which would govern it under the Convention if the contract or term were valid. In other words whether an agreement has been reached depends on the future or presumptive proper law of the contract. Equally according to art. 10 para. 1 of the Rome I Regulation the existence and validity of a contract, or of any term of a contract, shall be determined by the law which would govern it under the Regulation if the contract or term were valid.

In practice at pre-tender stage the first contacts and communications or even negotiations between the parties of the later contract will happen. Usually it is critical to exchange as much information as possible concerning the future project. Sometimes this may lead to confidentiality problems because the transfer of information may include sensitive information and thus result in a considerable transfer of knowledge. Sometimes feasibility studies and other preparation works are necessary and won't become payable without the conclusion of any pre-contract. It is therefore quite common to enter in a letter of memorandum or similar (Heads of Agreement, Letter of Intent) in order to protect the information exchanged. Such kind of agreement is generally subject to contract and thus not binding unless stipulated otherwise. The words "subject to a contract" are normally used in order to ensure that a binding contract does not accidentally come into existence during negotiations.

Which kind of pre-tender stages can be isolated from each other depend on the procurement method which is used to manage the project. Under a traditional contract, where the design is made by or o behalf of the employer any feasibility studies, soil investigations and the design of the works will be prepared in more detail than under a design and build contract. If a design and build contract is used, the initial phase is that during which the Employer's Requirements are prepared. All steps which will be necessary for the preparation of the Employer's Requirements will be completed at the tender stage, because the Employer's Requirements are a necessary element of the tender documentation.

The contractor who likes to participate at a bidding procedure or to enter in direct negotiations with the employer will then start to prepare his so called Proposal which usually comprises a preliminary design for inclusion in the tender. Thus the contractor will be obliged to prepare an outline design or proposal taking in account the employer's requirements without any counter obligation from the part of the employer. Thus if no contract will eventually be concluded, the contractor will not be paid for this work. It is therefore understandable that the contractor will be reluctant to incur excessive tendering costs if the likelihood of success seems low. Final design for the works will therefore only be produced after the contract has been set in force. However the question may arise whether the contractor may recover the costs of tendering and a substantial part of the profit it would have made on the contract, if the contract is not awarded to him. Also the question of liability for misrepresentation may arise.

In any case the existence and validity of a contract and subsequent contractual relations presupposes an intention to create legal relations. An agreement is made as a result of an offer and an acceptance. Subject to the presumptive proper law of the contract an invitation for tenders usually does not amount to an offer to the person who responds to such a request. As HHJ Lloyd has held, an invitation to tender is by its nature not normally an offer; it solicits offers. It does not carry with it an obligation to accept any offer that is made in response to it, even if the customary disclaimer is not made.[1] This is in line with German law.[2]

Also even though there is an intention to create a legal relationship at tender or negotiation stage, there is not yet any contract. However the question may arise as to whether the existence of a reciprocal intention to create a contract which becomes apparent by serious negotiations or the response to a call for tenders does already constitute a legal relationship. This has been discussed in length in Blackpool and Flyde Club v. Blackpool Council[3] and later in Harmon Façade. However previous Canadian cases have set a benchmark. The leading case is Rom Engineering.[4] The case concerned the issue of whether the acceptance of a call for tenders for a construction job could constitute a binding contract. The Supreme Court of Canada held that indeed in many cases the submission of an offer in response to a call for tenders constitutes a contract separate from the eventual contract for the construction. It was held that a unilateral contract, contract A, arises automatically upon the submission of a tender between the contractor and the owner whereby the tenderer cannot withdraw the tender for a specified period of time, after which, if the tender is not accepted, the tender bond can be recovered by the tenderer. The principal term of contract A is the irrevocability of the bid and the corollary term is the obligation in both parties to enter into a construction contract, contract B, upon the acceptance of the tender. In examining the Canadian cases as it has been done by HHJ Lloyd in Harmon Façade, it is at first necessary to bear in mind that the key factor is the commitment of the tenderer to the person to whom the tender was submitted. In *Ron Engineering* the tender had been supported by a tender bond. Estey J said at page 122–123: "The principal term of Contract A is the irrevocability of the bid...". In a later case,[5] a sub-contractor was not able to withdraw a tender on the strength of which the main contractor had, to the sub-contractor's knowledge, submitted its own tender to an owner). However, a more

---

[1] Harmon CFEM Facades (UK) Ltd v. The Corporate Officer of the House of Commons [1999] EWHC Technology 199 (28 October 1999).

[2] VG Karlsruhe, decision from 14 June 2006; file no. 8 K 1437/06.

[3] Blackpool and Fylde Aero Club v. Blackpool Borough Council [1990] 1 WLR 1195.

[4] The Queen in the Right of Ontario v. Ron Engineering & Construction (Eastern) Limited [1981] 1 SCR 111.

[5] Northern Construction v. Gloge Heating & Plumbing (1986) 27 DLR (4th) 265.

generous approach was applied in Best Cleaners v. R. in Right of Canada[6] and in Chinook Aggregates Limited v. Abbotsford.[7] In the former case, after the tenders had been submitted, discussions took place with one tenderer about the possibility of awarding the contract for a longer period than that originally sought. The plaintiff was not consulted. In the event, the contract was awarded to the other tenderer but on the original basis. The decision turned on whether there should or should not be a new trial. The dissenting judgment of Pratt C.J. shows that he thought that there was an obligation to treat the tenderers fairly and equally, so the division of opinion was largely as to whether that had in fact occurred. In *Chinook* the plaintiff had not been informed that the defendant had a policy whereby if any local bidder was within 10% of the lowest price, then the local bidder would get the contract. However, with the release of the decision Ron Engineering, the tendering process practiced in Canada was fundamentally changed.

Meanwhile it was unclear, whether the Canadian approach would be acknowledged as a general principle of law. In Blackpool and Flyde Club v. Blackpool Council the English Court of Appeal held that it is possible to have exceptions to the rule that invitations to tender are not a contractual offer. In Harmon Façade[8] the claimant, a subsidiary of an American company, was the unsuccessful tenderer for the fenestration contract for a new building in London. The trial judge found that the claimant was in fact the lowest bidder but that the bids had been manipulated so as to prefer another bidder, which was a consortium that included a British partner. This was held to be a breach of contract. His Honour Judge Humphrey Lloyd QC[9] said:

> In the public sector where competitive tenders are sought and responded to, a contract comes into existence whereby the prospective employer impliedly agrees to consider all tenders fairly.

Also HHJ Lloyd held that the claimant could recover the costs of tendering and a substantial part of the profit it would have made on the contract. HHJ Lloyd drew the pre-contractual obligations from a contract to be implied from the procurement regime required by the European directives, as interpreted by the European Court, whereby the principles of fairness and equality form part of a preliminary contract. He added that the Emery[10] decision shows that such a contract may exist at common law against a statutory background which might otherwise provide the exclusive remedy. Furthermore he considered that it is clear in English law that in the public sector where competitive tenders are sought and responded to, a contract

---

[6] Best Cleaners & Contractors Limited v. R. in Right of Canada [1985] 2 FCR 293.

[7] Chinook Aggregates Limited v. Abbotsford (Municipal Districts) (1989) 35 CLR 241.

[8] Harmon CFEM Facades (UK) Ltd v. The Corporate Officer of the House of Commons [1999] EWHC Technology 199 (28 October 1999).

[9] Harmon CFEM Facades (UK) Ltd v. The Corporate Officer of the House of Commons [1999] EWHC Technology 199 (28 October 1999).

[10] Emery Construction Limited v. St John's (City) Roman Catholic School Board (1996) 28 CLR (2d) 1.

comes into existence whereby the prospective employer impliedly agrees to consider all tenderers fairly. However, he also said that there must be something more
than a request for a tender which is to be submitted competitively along with others.
However, the English position is clearly limited to the procurement regime required
by European directives and it will therefore be difficult to rely on Ron Engineering
as a general principle of law in the private sector because there is no general
principle of good faith under English law outside particular contracts.

In Interfoto v. Stiletto[11] Bingham J. said:

> In many civil law systems, and perhaps in most legal systems outside the common law
> world, the law of obligations recognises and enforces an overriding principle that in making
> and carrying out contracts parties should act in good faith. This does not simply mean that
> they should not deceive each other, a principle which any legal system must recognise; its
> effect is perhaps most aptly conveyed by such metaphorical colloquialisms as "playing
> fair", "coming clean" or "putting one's cards face upwards on the table". It is in essence a
> principle of fair and open dealing.. . .

> English law has, characteristically, committed itself to no such overriding principle but has
> developed piecemeal solutions in response to demonstrated problems of unfairness. Many
> examples could be given. Thus equity has intervened to strike down unconscionable
> bargains. Parliament has stepped in to regulate the imposition of exemption clauses and
> the form of certain hire purchase agreements. The common law also has made its contribu-
> tion, by holding that certain classes of contract require the utmost good faith, by treating as
> irrecoverable what purport to be agreed estimates of damage but are in truth a disguised
> penalty for breach, and in many other ways.

Nevertheless Prof. Christie has a different position as to tender contracts by
referring to the fact that HHJ Lloyd's position was allegedly simply an unnecessary
obiter (Christie 2008, p. 325).

Under German law, however, a relatively different approach exists. Since the
famous professor Rudolph v. Jhering has worked out in the nineteenth century the
existence of a mutual duty of care upon persons who were not yet in privity of
contract to negotiate with care, and not to lead a negotiating partner to act to his
detriment before a firm contract is executed German law acknowledges the doctrine
of "culpa in contrahendo" which literally means "culpable conduct during contract
negotiations". In line with this doctrine a party who, through culpable conduct,
prevents a contract from being formed or causes the contract to be invalid, is liable
for damages suffered by the innocent party who relied on the validity of the
forthcoming contract. These days the doctrine of culpa in contrahendo is ruled by
law (see Sect. 311a para. 2 German Civil Code).

To the contrary French law adopts a reluctant stance towards pre-contractual
duties. However, under French law, "liability typically lies where one party enters
into negotiations without having any intent to contract, yet creates a reasonable
expectation in the other party that a contract will be forthcoming so that the other
incurs substantial precontractual expenses". This type of liability also referred to as

---

[11] Interfoto Picture Library Ltd v. Stiletto Visual Programmes Ltd [1987] EWCA Civ 6
(12 November 1987).

"responsabilité pour pourparler" has the nature of tort (see Malaurie et al. 2007, note 1002).

The fact that pre-contractual behaviour is not treated equally in various countries leads to the question of which law applies in the event of failure to act either honestly or in compliance with procurement guidelines or in compliance with the given instructions for bidders. In order to determine the applicable law firstly the nature of the action must be ascertained. If the relief sought is based on tort the rule lex loci delicti commissi (subject to Regulation Rome II the law of the place where the direct damage occured) will apply. If the relief sought is based on contract the proper law of the contract will apply. Within Europe, according to art. 12 of the Regulation Rome II, the law applicable to a non-contractual obligation arising out of dealings prior to the conclusion of a contract, regardless of whether the contract was actually concluded or not, shall be the law that applies to the contract or that would have been applicable to it had it been entered into. Thus despite the nature of any pre-contractual fault or default.

Another issue arises as to the procurement law. Notwithstanding the fact that parts of the procurement law have been harmonised within Europe by means of directives, procurement law is still national law. As a matter of fact procurement law is quite a sophisticated body of law including procedural rules and substantive law.

According to German law taken as a whole and the therein embedded principle of equality, the legal rules governing contracts for public works would be characterised as pertaining to private law, which, consequently, implies the application of the German Civil Code. In principle also the procurement procedures, which prepare the contract award for public works and which shall lead to the choice of the appropriate contractor for the purposes of the contract award belong to private law. If so, German procurement law does not apply according to the principle auctor regit actum but by virtue of the relevant conflict of laws rules. Hence, if the tender documents would not include a choice-of-law clause in favour of German law German procurement law would not apply. However, this would be in clear contradiction to public policy and various laws which obviously impose a duty on German public authorities to proceed in accordance with public procurement law comprising Sect. 97 German Act on restraints on Competition (Gesetz gegen Wettbewerbsbeschränkungen) and the Regulation on the Award Public Contracts (Vergabeverordnung), both referring to VOB/A: General Terms and Conditions for the Award of Public Work Contracts, VOB/B: General Terms and Conditions for the Exececution of Public Work Contracts and VOB/C: General Technical Terms and Conditions for the Execution of Construction Work Contracts. Thus there is an issue. However, apparently there are no authorities at all dealing with the issue. The Regulation on the Award Public Contracts sets out a legal framework for all contracts above the pan European thresholds. Below the thresholds German public bodies are subject to German budget law.

Pursuant to Sect. 97 German Act on restraints on Competition public contracting entities shall procure goods, works and services in accordance with the subsequent provisions through competition and by way of transparent award procedures. All participants in an award procedure shall be treated equally unless discrimination is expressly required or allowed by the Act. Contracts shall be awarded to skilled, efficient and reliable undertakings; contractors may be expected to meet other or further requirements only if federal law or the laws of a Bundesland provides for this. The economically most advantageous tender shall be accepted. The German Federal Government is empowered to more precisely define, by regulation ... the procedure to be followed in awarding contracts, in particular concerning the notice, the course and the categories of awards, the selection and examination of under-takings and tenders, the conclusion of the contract as well as other issues relating to the award procedure. The undertakings have a right that the public contracting entities comply with the award procedure. Thus German procurement law is basically part of German competition law. Procurement under competitive condi-tions is the founding element of German public purchase. According to art. 6 para. 1 Rome II Regulation the law applicable to a non-contractual obligation arising out of an act of unfair competition shall be the law of the country where competitive relations or the collective interests of consumers are, or are likely to be, affected. Hence, in principle German public procurement law is not part of the presumptive proper law of the contract. With regard to public authorities, public procurement law is a code of conduct to be followed which has, more or less, the nature of procedural rules imposed on the contracting authorities. However, German pro-curement law has also much influence on the contract itself. It imposes a duty to award the contract against a reasonable price (Sect. 2 no. 1 VOB/A). Also the services shall be specified in a clear and exhausting way (Sect. 9 no. 1 VOB/A). Non compliance with this Sect. 9 no. 1 VOB/A may be contested during the procurement proceedings. If an unsuccessful bidder incurs damages as a result of such non compliance he may also recover such damages on the ground of culpa in contrahendo. Furthermore a successful bidder may recover additional cost which he will incur as a result of incomplete tender documents if he could not discover the lack of information at tender stage.[12] Finally German public authorities are obliged to incorporate the so called VOB/B in their contracts, which means that contractual freedom is partially limited. Thus a great part of German procurement law covers also substantial elements of the contract formation and the contract itself. This part of the law is obviously covered by the proper law of the contract.

In the event of a misrepresentation by or on behalf of the employer which is a cause which induces the contract, Common law refers to the authorities as to the liability for misrepresentation. They distinguish between fraudulent misrepresenta-tion, negligent misrepresentation and innocent misrepresentation. Civil law on the contrary refers to the doctrine of culpa in contrahendo, the law of mistake (Sections 119 et seq, 142 et seq. German Civil Code and the doctrine of disturbance of the foundation of the transaction (Wegfall der Geschäftsgrundlage, Section 313 German Civil Code), the latter empowering the courts to step in and change the terms of the contract where they believe that it is necessary to correct a disturbance of the foundation of the contract, which however will only happen in extreme cases

---

[12] BGH [1997] NJW 1577.

where it seems to be unreasonable that a party bears the risk of subsequent change of events.

In both, the Civil law and the Common law systems, the misrepresentation must induce the contract. Under German law, in the event of deceit or deception (Täuschung) the innocent party may set the contract aside (Section 123 Civil Code). In the event of a mere mistake a right to declare void one's declaration of intention arises (Section 119 Civil Code). Mere calculation errors are in principle irrelevant. Such an error usually will be considered as an error in motivation. However, this may be dealt differently if there is a common error in its broader sense, meaning that both of the parties share a mistaken motivation for entering into a contract. A difficulty arises in the event of a negligent misrepresentation which constitutes a mere motivation to enter into a contract, which is in principle irrelevant. However, German courts have filled up the gap by establishing a right to set aside the contract on the basis of culpa in contrahendo. Thus under German law a contractor who entered into a contract on the basis of negligent misrepresentation which were imputable to the employer and then being bound to it may either rescind the contract or claim for damages.

5.2.1 Base Date

The FIDIC feature of the "base date" as referred to in Sub-Clause 1.1.3.1 ensures that changes as to technical standards and laws occurring between the base date and the contract award will constitute a risk which, subject to the contract, is allocated to the Employer. If the tender documents contain a clause as referred to below, the risk of such changes will be shifted to the Contractor which seems to be unreasonable:

> The base date should be understood as the date of contract signature.

Care must be had as sometimes considerable time will pass between the submission of the offer and the contract award. It may prove difficult to adjust the offer during that time. Thus it is critical to shift the risk of legal and technical changes to the Employer.

The following Sub-Clauses of the General Conditions of the Silver Book refer to the Base Date:

Sub-Clause 4.10
Sub-Clause 5.1
Sub-Clause 5.4
Sub-Clause 13.7
Sub-Clause 14.15
Sub-Clause 17.5
Sub-Clause 18.2

In the Yellow and Red Book additionally Sub-Clause 13.8 refers to the Base Date.

5.2.2   *Information Transfer and Research*

The pre-contractual transfer of know-how and information is critical for the successful completion of the whole operation. The extent to which such kind of information is necessary depends however not only on the project and its specification but also on the applicable law. By submitting their tenders, tenderers are usually deemed to know all relevant laws, acts and regulations that may in any way affect or govern the operations and activities covered by the tender and the resulting contract. The presumptive or future proper law of the contract will govern the contractual risk allocation.

Usually the bidder is expected to examine all instructions, forms, terms, and specifications in the bidding documents. Under a FIDIC contract this follows from Sub-Clause 4.10. Failure to furnish all information or documentation required by the bidding documents may result in the rejection of the bid. However, a prospective bidder may require any clarification of the bidding documents. The employer shall then respond in writing to any request for clarification. The bidder will normally be advised to visit and examine the site of works and its surroundings and obtain for himself on his own responsibility all information that may be necessary for preparing the bid and entering into a contract for construction of the works. The costs of visiting the site will usually be at the bidder's own expense.

The quality of the answers may vary, depending on the contract type which will be used. Thus it's conceivable that the employer will not give a satisfactory answer. If for example the bidder requires additional information as to the "values for the jacket friction and the point bearing pressure contained in the geological report" in order to enable him to calculate the pile lengths, the answer may be that the geological report as included in the bidding documents with additional information is indicative only and is intended solely to assist the potential tenderers in preparing their tenders and that the bidder should comply with the contract provisions, thus performing geological surveys and submitting geological reports as stated therein. The simple reason for this answer was that the announced contract was a design and build contract under which the contractor carries out the design and the necessary soil investigations.

For a building or civil engineering contract, soil and sub-soil information is usually needed. Thus a site investigation is usually necessary, which typically includes boreholes and other sub-surface investigations. As to such kind of information great care has to be taken, because unlike in Germany and some other civil law countries at common law the risk of unforeseen site conditions is usually borne by the contractor. Failure to comply with the pre-tender or pre-contract obligation to investigate and survey the site may lead to a considerable pricing risk, if and when common law is the proper law of the contract. Standard forms which originate from common law countries thus normally comprise detailed provisions on the allocation of the soil risk. Ad hoc contracts often do not have any specific provisions, leaving the contractor at full risk. Thus the contractor should make the contract with the attempt to minimise the risk as much as possible. Usually a clause will be adopted which defines the term unforeseeable as anything that could not reasonably been foreseen at tender stage by an experienced contractor. The contract should also provide any necessary additional work due to soil obstructions and unforeseen physical conditions.

The report on site investigation, that the employer has usually commissioned to progress basic feasibility studies and initial outline design will be issued to (or otherwise made available for use by) the tenderers, preferably in its original form, in order to inform the tenderers about the soil conditions. Most employers will consider it to be unwise for them to take responsibility for the report by including it within the Tender Dossier. Thus such reports are often part of the "information documents" made available to the tenderers. Usually any tender enquiry documentation includes exclusion clauses stating that the employer accepts no responsibility for the accuracy of such investigation reports. It is also common and good practise from the point of view of an employer for the documentation to include the advice to the tenderers to carry out their own site survey and investigations.

It is common use (see Cl. 4.10 FIDIC Red Book, Cl. 5.1 MF/1) to adopt a contract clause according to which the contractor, to the extent which was practicable (taking account of cost and time), shall be deemed to have obtained all necessary information as to risks, contingencies and other circumstances (including for example health and safety regulations) which may influence or affect the tender or works. A complementary clause may be added according to which the contractor shall also be deemed to have inspected and examined the site, its surroundings, the above data and other available information, and to have been satisfied before submitting the tender as to all relevant matters, including (without limitation):

- The form and nature of the site, including sub-surface conditions
- The hydrological and climatic conditions
- The extent and nature of the work and goods necessary for the execution and completion of the works and the remedying of any defects
- The laws, procedures and labour practices of the country where the site is situated
- The contractor's requirements for access, accommodation, facilities, personnel, power, transport, water and other services

It is thus extremely important that the bidder surveys the site, its location and surroundings thoroughly before submitting the tender. Particular attention should be given to the ascertainment of local labour law, material specifications, plant and equipment requirements, conditions on employment including collective wage agreements, tax and royalty legislation, port unloading facilities and capacities, customs clearance procedures and finally transportation and logistics. It is also essential to gather information about local business customs and religious rites, which sometimes may overrule legal framework and international customs. Last but not least it is critical to obtain information about local requirements to buy national, which may considerably affect pricing.

5.2.3 Survey Report

As already mentioned above it is strongly recommended to prepare a comprehensive survey report including, but not limited to:

- Area information (location, routes, transport, access)
- Administration (Government, Local Government, etc.)
- Legal system and culture

  - Religion
  - Bilateral Investment Treaties
  - Tax Treaties
  - Civil law, common law, Sharia'h law, etc. (Codifications, etc.)
  - National expropriation law, etc.
  - Zoning, Building regulations, etc.

- Taxes, Currencies, Levies, Duties, Social contributions, etc.
- Exchange rates, currency importation and exportation
- Banking
- Licences (Construction Licence, Design Licence, etc.)
- Special area information (physical conditions, Climatic conditions, etc.)
- Special transportation data (loading restrictions, bridges, tunnels, etc.)
- Waste dispoal, excavation disposal
- Availability of Services (gas, water, sewage, electricity, communications)
- Availability of materials, services and goods
- Special legal requirements and constraints (decennial liability, subcontractor protection laws, corruption issues, health and safety rules, labour rules, etc.)
- Shipping and importation restrictions and constraints (embargos, importation constraints, etc.)
- Technical standards, workmanship, etc.
- Foreign workers and specialists
- Accommodation facilities, etc.
- Medical services

This is part of the risk assessment.

5.3 Tender Stage

At the latest at tender stage the employer must choose the procurement route, which means that he must determine the type of contract (for example FIDIC Red Book, FIDIC Yellow Book, FIDIC Gold Book) to be used. Whether he is bound to specific procurement procedures depends on the applicable law. Usually public authorities must follow specific procedures ruled by law. Financing institutions such as the World Bank and other multilateral development banks have issued specific procurement requirements to be followed by their borrowers. However, it is common sense in England,[13] France and Germany,[14] that the tendering process is such that:

(a) The issue of an invitation to tender by employers is an invitation to treat rather than an offer; except if the employer engages himself to award the tender to the bidder with the "best bid" (see Bénabent 2004, note 517).
(b) The submission of a tender in response to the invitation to tender by a tenderer amounts to an offer by that tenderer.
(c) No binding contract becomes effective between the parties until a tender is accepted by the party inviting tenders.

Other than in French law, according to German law a call for tenders for public works is not an administrative procedure but an invitation "ad offerendum".[15] Once the employer accepts one of the offers addressed to him, a contract becomes awarded accordingly without any changes.[16] However, at the moment of the submission of the tender a pre-contractual relationship arises. In the event of breach of this pre-contractual relationship the parties may be entitled to damages based on the principles of "culpa in contrahendo".[17]

5.4 Performance

Once the contract has been awarded the Contractor shall execute the Works including any design as stated in the Contract. All of the FIDIC Books provide for detailed rules concerning the execution of the Works and payment for it. The Works shall be completed within Time for Completion. If the Works are completed the Engineer will issue the Taking Over Certificate, which under the Gold Book has been renamed in Commissioning Certificate. After the expiry date of the latest of the relevant Defects Notification Period the Engineer shall issue the Performance Certificate (Fig. 5.1). The Gold Book, due to the fact that the Contractor assumes the responsibility for the Operation Service, provides for a Contract Completion Certificate.

For more details reference is made to Chap. 9 in this book.

---

[13] Harmon CFEM Facades (UK) Ltd v. The Corporate Officer of the House of Commons [1999] EWHC TCC 199, at no. 214.

[14] See Ellenberger (2009, Section 145, note 2) for Germany, Bénabent (2004, note 517) for France and Uff (2005, p. 170).

[15] VG Karlsruhe, decision from 14 June 2006; file no. 8 K 1437/06.

[16] See BVerwG, [35] BVerwGE 103 at 104; Tomerius and Kiser (2005, p. 557); Irmer (2006, p. 165); see again VG Gelsenkirchen NWVBl 40 et seq.

[17] See BGH [1998] NJW 3636 at 3636 et seq.

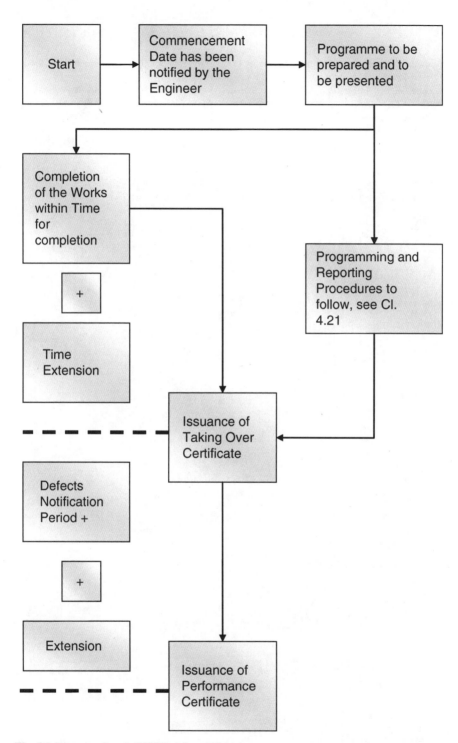

Fig. 5.1 Progress of work (1999 Rainbow Edition)

References

Bénabent A (2004) Les contrats spéciaux civils et commerciaux, 6th edn. Montchrestien, Paris

Christie RH (2008) Tendering procedure at common law. ICLR 321, 325

Ellenberger J (2009) in: Palandt (ed) Commentary to BGB, 68th edn. C.H. Beck, München

Irmer W (2006) Eröffnung des Verwaltungsrechtswegs bei Vergaben außerhalb des Anwendungsbereichs von § 100 GWB oder Aufgabe der Zweiteilung und Neuordnung des Vergaberechts. VergabeR 159

Malaurie P, Aynès L, Stoffel-Munck P (2007) Les obligations, Répertoire Defrénois, 3rd edn. Paris

Tomerius S, Kiser V (2005) Verwaltungsgerichtlicher Rechtsschutz bei nationalen Auftragsvergaben – auf dem Weg zur "unterschwelligen" Rechtswegspaltung? VergabeR 551

Uff J (2005) Construction law, 9th edn. Sweet & Maxwell, London

Chapter 6
Understanding FIDIC: A Civil Law Approach

6.1 Introduction

The 1999 FIDIC Rainbow edition constitutes a detailed and carefully crafted set of inter-related clauses that define a series of interlocking events and periods of time which involve the close collaboration and co-operation of the Parties and the Engineer which are intended to culminate in the issuing of the Performance Certificate as referred to in Sub-Clause 11.9. These events include the identification and making good of defects and any associated valuation of an abatement to take account of defects; the operation of the provisions concerned with the determination of the Contractor's extension of time entitlement; the carrying out of Tests on Completion; following the issue of the Taking-Over Certificate the Defects Notification Period; the finalisation of the completion date and the operation of the machinery concerned with the payment of liquidated damages by the Contractor; the accounting procedures, including the provision of documents (as built drawings, manuals, etc.), that lead to the finalisation of the Contract Price and, finally, the preparation and issuing of the Final Payment Certificate. All this must be read in a legal context.

As has recently been confirmed by HHJ Lloyd, FIDIC forms of contract are embedded in the common law notwithstanding the fact that some of its features may be influenced by civil law (Lloyd 2007, p. 505). In fact no specific endeavours and efforts have been made to emancipate FIDIC forms of contracts of its basic roots, which are undeniably identified as being the common law (Bunni 2005, p. 10). Its approach and language still reflect the common law, but presumably not English law alone (Lloyd 2007, p. 505).

However in most cases FIDIC forms of contract will be used in their original, English version, even though translations do exist and FIDIC terms of contract are often used in a Civil law context. Despite any contradictions with the applicable law, which may exist and must be recognised as the case may be, the use of English does not mean that the parties will understand the terms and clauses as an English native speaker will do. Instead at the outset some of the wording used by FIDIC will

A.-V. Jaeger and G.-S. Hök, *FIDIC-A Guide for Practitioners*,
DOI 10.1007/978-3-642-02100-8_6, © Springer-Verlag Berlin Heidelberg 2010

be either misleading or even not make sense. It is therefore critical to have prior knowledge of FIDIC's common law background in order to render it understandable to non native speakers. The examples for this are multiple:

- In most civil law countries the concepts of discharge and substantial completion are unknown. Instead civil law jurisdictions most commonly use the concept of acceptance of the works. This means that the employer is required to accept the works once they have been substantially completed. Thus the employer is required to declare that the works have been carried out in compliance with the contract. The effects of this kind of declaration by the employer are ruled at law. Usually care for the works shifts to the employer, the entitlement to payment becomes due and the defects liability period starts to run. In this context civil law contractors often misunderstand the significance of the taking-Over Certificate as being acceptance of the works, which is wrong because the Defects Notification Period is not identical to the post contractual defects liability.
- In most civil law countries the use of penalties is common practice. Penalty clauses are valid instruments and subject to judicial control by the courts. They usually do not limit the liability for delay. Civil law employers are not used to the concept that liquidated damages have the nature of a genuine pre-estimate of damage for delay, which often constitutes a cap for such kind of liability.
- The concept of "time is of the essence" and "time at large" which has been adopted by FIDIC is not a civil law concept and in most cases remains completely unknown in civil law countries. In civil law countries the parties usually agree to a programme and a delay which is attributable to the employer will be a defence against penalties. The extent to which the contractor will be excused will be discussed at the end of the construction period. No clear system of claims for extension of Time for Completion exists.
- Multiple terms and expressions which are not defined in Clause 1 but well known in common law countries are unknown to civil law contractors and engineers. The well-developed common law case law as to the term "reasonable" or the expression "workmanlike manner" is also completely unknown. The complicated use of the words "may" and "shall" is furthermore often ignored.
- Some terms or connotations, such as Force Majeure, seem to have a clear meaning, but in truth this is wrong. They are false friends (faux amis) and their meaning depends on legal definitions which may vary from country to country.
- The common law method of capitalising terms which are defined in the contract is not practicable in those countries which use capital letters for grammatical reasons. Translations often ignore the fact that the English version uses capital letters for defined terms, which makes it impossible to rely on definitions.
- The role of the Engineer having been developed in common law countries and being clearly described and ruled by common law courts is completely unknown in civil law countries. Most civil law contractors, engineers and employers will understand that the engineer is an agent of the employer being strictly dependent

on the employer's instructions. This is a clear misunderstanding but the experiences in Eastern European countries are not encouraging.

- Dispute adjudication having been invented by common law practitioners is not a commonly understood feature of dispute resolution and in most Eastern European countries employers are reluctant to accept this feature in particular for cost reasons.

6.2 Legal English

It is critical to realise that the English language used by FIDIC involves the understanding of legal English. Legal English is a professional language aimed at achieving certainty of meaning. Legal documents impose obligations and confer rights. Neither the parties to a contract nor the contract draftsmen have the last word in deciding exactly what those rights and obligations are. In the event of a dispute the courts will be involved, having the authority to interpret and settle the meaning of a word. If anyone is to be held irrevocably to meaning what he says, he must be very careful to say what he means. A document for legal purposes should be clear and precise. The use of terms of the art is quite usual including the use of words and phrases which derived from French and Latin. Some ordinary words are used in a particular sense, such as the word "consideration" which means, *an act, forbearance or promise by one party to a contract that constitutes the price for which the promise of the other party is bought* (Oxford Dictionary of Law). One of the most unusual aspects of old-fashioned legal drafting – particularly in conveyances and deeds – is the almost complete lack of punctuation. It is also quite usual to combine terms in order to express a single legal concept. Examples of this include the combination of to *promise, agree and covenant* or the expression *null and void.* Lack of statute based definitions has led to the drafting of extensive definitions in each contract. A number of further particularities can be identified. So called legalese is a kind of long-winded jargon used by lawyers which may prove difficult to understand. In particular contracts, insurance policies, and guarantees are among the documents in which legalese may be found. Thus it is critical to use legal dictionaries in order to understand the exact meaning of a contract term. Translations undertaken by non-legally educated translators are often misleading because of the fact that they do not fully understand the legal meaning behind a term. In addition some of the English legal terms derive from legal concepts which are unknown in civil law countries. It will then be difficult to find an exact homologue of the word in the translation language. On the other hand common law may lack legal concepts which are widely used in civil law jurisdictions. One of those concepts is "acceptance of the works", a concept which is expressly used and defined in Section 640 German Civil Code, Art. 643 Polish Civil Code and Art. 1792-6 French Civil Code.

According to Art. 1792-6 French Civil Code "approval" is the act by which the building owner declares that he accepts the work with or without reservation.

It occurs at the suit of the first requesting party, either amicably or, failing which, judicially. The effects of such an "approval" are multiple. Among others an unconditioned approval constitutes a waiver of further complaints concerning apparent defective works. Moreover the post contractual defects liability period starts running on the date of acceptance of the works.

Common law contractors should be aware of the fact that civil law jurisdictions provide for various remedies in the event of defective works. At the difference to common law specific performance is a common instrument in civil law. Thus according to Sect. 634a German Civil Code the Employer may:

1. Demand remedy of the defect under Sect. 635 German Civil Code.
2. Remedy the defect himself under Sect. 637 German Civil Code and demand compensation for required expenses.
3. Withdraw from the contract under Sections 636, 323 and 326(5) German Civil Code or reduce the Contract Price under Sect. 638 German Civil Code.
4. Under Sections 636, 280, 281, 283 and 311a German Civil Code demand damages or under Sect. 284 demand compensation for futile expenses.

According to art. 1792-6 French Civil Code the Contractor warrants perfect completion, to which a contractor is held during a period of one year, after the approval. His liability extends to the repairs of all shortcomings indicated by the building owner, either through reservations mentioned in the memorandum of approval, or by way of written notice as to those revealed after the approval. Also according to art. 1792-3 French Civil Code some elements of equipment of a "work" (Ord. no 2005-658 of 8 June 2005), are the subject of a warranty of good running for a minimum period of two years "as from its approval".

6.3   Conceptual Legal Background

It is well accepted that FIDIC forms of contract have a Common law background. Thus before using a FIDIC contract considerable clarification and explanation of Common law legal concepts is required. That does not entail a strict adoption of all common law ideas and to practise a FIDIC contract with regard to common law only. But it means first of all to identify the intentions which are behind the wording of each clause. Once having understood what is meant, the proper law of the contract shall be applied in order to implement the contract. An example of this procedure may be helpful:

Delay damages according to Sub-Clause 8.7 are intended to be a genuine pre estimate of damages for failure to comply with the Time for Completion. It is not intended as being an agreement to a penalty. Once this intention has been understood it must be verified whether the proper law of contract allows such a clause. If so, it must not be confused with a penalty clause and this for different reasons. Firstly under civil law only a penalty clause is subject to court control. Secondly under a delay damages clause the recovery of additional damages or actual damages is excluded. Thirdly it must be cleared up whether the fact that delay damages become due even though the time overrun is not attributable to the contractor will be accepted by the proper law of the contract. This is not obvious. It might be helpful in this context to know that the common law is more equitable than probably expected. This makes it necessary to have a further look at the common law concept of "time is of the essence".

Under English law the parties conclude their contract under the understanding that the Contractor's liability for delay damages is based on a concept which releases the Contractor from this liability to the extent which is ruled by the contract. However if the Contractor himself fails to comply with the contract management rules extension of time will not be granted (see Sub-clause 20.1 FIDIC Conditions) and his liability for delay damages continues to exist even though the Employer causes delay to Time for Completion. Time remains only of the essence if and when the contract provides for time extension claims for those events attributable to the Employer, which cause delay and disruption. Failure to provide such claims leads to time at large, which will mean that the Employer looses his entitlement to delay damages. Thus EOT claims release the Contractor from his liability for delay damages and protect the Employer against the loss of his entitlement to delay damages in the event that the Contractor fails to comply with Time for Completion. Thus it becomes clear that the whole concept of "extension of time for Time for Completion" is a balanced concept according to which the Contractor may escape from delay damages for delays which are not attributable to him.

Hence it is not arguable that the FIDIC concept of delay damages lays in contradiction to the civil law principle that an entitlement to damages should require a fault by the contractor. It is inherent to this system that the contractor may not become liable to pay damages for delay which is not attributable to him. The fact that FIDIC requires him to save his claims within the short period of time of 28 days by giving notice of claim is not a valid argument against this balanced principle. Compared to the requirements which the contractor must meet in order to save insurance cover in the event that a covered event occurs the FIDIC claims' procedure appears to be innocuous.

A second good example is the role of the Engineer within a FIDIC contract. Civil law contractors and employers used to understand the Engineer as an Employer's agent, who shall be under the strict control of the Employer. By this they ignore the fact that there is the reciprocal promise of the contractor and the employer to comply with the contract. All of the claims which arise out of the contract are in principle already given if and when the related event occurs. The role of the Engineer is only to determine the consequences of the event. In other words he determines whether there is under the terms of the Contrat and subject to the applicable law an event giving rise to a claim for additional time or money. Thus all of the claims are subject to his determination. It is not his role to create claims or to accept claims beyond the express conditions of the contract. However the Engineer also has the powers to give instructions and to initiate variations. This element of his task may create additional entitlements to payment. However his power to initiate variations is not unlimited. It exists within its power to give instructions. In addition most of the variations are either due to unilateral decisions of the Employer or either errors in the Employer's Requirements or the design which was prepared by him or on his behalf. As a matter of fact most current cost overruns are due to the fact that the design or the Employer's Requirements are incomplete, erroneous or simply badly prepared.

Thus placing the Engineer under strict control is often a consequence of the employer's previous bad experiences with cost overruns. But employers should not ignore that it is up to them to prepare the design or the Employer's Requirements in a skilful and appropriate manner. It is not the purpose of the contract to remedy such kind of omissions and faults committed by the employer and his consultants. It is not the role of the Engineer to shape a new contract by a one-sided and partial operation of his powers. However it is the role of the Engineer to encourage using best practice within the contractual framework.

Under a FIDIC contract the Engineer is supposed to be an independent and fair "decision-maker", using his skills for the purposes of the project. It is intended for the Engineer to use his skills not only as an agent of the employer but in the endeavour to reach good results. The Engineer shall ensure best practice for money. To some extent he is a form of instance of control and the centre of contract administration. In the former FIDIC forms of contract the works had to be to the satisfaction of the Engineer which made of him a quasi-arbitrator. Today the Engineer's powers are strictly described and limited by the contract. He has to act in accordance with the contract. The contract is not only the law of the parties but also the law of the Engineer. This is was the parties have promised to each other.

In fact he is not only the Employer's adviser who will make the decisions by himself, but is also the person responsible for a proper contract administration. His actions are binding on both of the parties. The parties to the contract shall verify in advance what are the rules of the game. The Employer should not be allowed to change these rules for whichever reason.

Common law courts have analysed in length the role of the Engineer of the type which has been adopted by FIDIC. They have made clear what it means to appoint an Engineer describing the consequences of the role of the Engineer. Thus civil law contractors and employers should have a look at the Engineer's legal position before making use of this feature. Again only after having understood this role it should be argued on the basis of the proper law of the contract. Most often the proper law of the contract does not explain this role firsthandedly. For example under German law it could be argued that Sections 317 et seq. Civil Code apply to the Engineer. Section 317 paragraph 1 Civil Code reads as follows: "Where specification of performance is left to a third party, in case of doubt, it must be assumed that the specification must be agreed with equitable discretion". German courts have held that in fact the specification by the third party leads to an amendment of the contract.[1] In other words Section 317 Civil Code replaces the

---

[1] [48] BGHZ 25; [55] BGHZ 248.

intention of the parties who have left the specification open for determination by a third party. The determination will be binding on the parties like the contract itself. It is suggested that this is not what is intended by FIDIC. FIDIC simply puts the claims and rights of the parties under the condition of fair determination by the Engineer. That makes the rights binding on the parties and enforceable. But in fact the relevant rights are pre-existing. Thus the role of the Engineer is to make the pre-existing rights temporarily enforceable because all of his determinations are subject to review by the Dispute Adjudication Board. This is in line with the Sub-Clause 3.1 where it is clearly stated that the Engineer has no authority to amend the contract. Whatever the Engineer will have to decide has already been agreed by the parties to the contract because the Engineer is strictly bound to it. If the contract remains silent there is no need for an action of the Engineer. But if the contract provides for a claim or additional payment then the Engineer will enforce the contract. Hence the Employer should refrain from putting most of the authorities of the Engineer under the condition of an approval. Even if there would be no Engineer the contract will be binding on the Employer. By consequence any restrictions to the authority of the Engineer will not constitute an effective prevention from additional charges because of the binding nature of the contract itself. Hence in principle any restriction to the authority of the Engineer will only be a feature of control, which may prevent the Engineer from faulty or wrongful acts and determinations.

Moreover it is worth to focus on a third source of misunderstanding. According to Sub-Clause 4.1 Yellow Book the Contractor shall design, execute and complete the Works in accordance with the Contract. Although Sub-Clause 1.13 allocates the responsibility for obtaining the zoning or construction permission to the Employer it may sometimes be argued that the Contractor has assumed to carry out all of the design work and will therefore be responsible for the preparation of the drawings and other documents composing the whole of the application for the zoning or construction permission. In Germany the designer's responsibility usually includes but is not limited to the so called preliminary design, the final design and the design necessary for the application of the building permission. The reason for this is that prior to any development building permission must be obtained which allows for the preventive control detailing whether the builder will be able to meet all of the requirements of the applicable Building Regulations, including fire protection and structural design. Some Eastern European countries, as is the case in Poland, have adopted the German building control system and sometimes employers argue that Sub-Clause 1.13 shall be read in conjunction with Sub-Clause 4.1 meaning that the Contractor will have to enable the Employer to apply for building permission. The Contractor being not prepared to comply with local administrative law requirements will not be amused about such a position. Disputes may easily arise in this context.

Finally the use of the term promptly may easily be misinterpreted. According to Sub-Clause 8.3 the Contractor shall give prompt notice about future probable events which may have an adverse effect on time and cost. In some eastern European countries it seems that this Sub-Clause was understood as a time bar.

Contractors who failed to give prompt notice have been faced with the argument that their claim should be rejected for this reason.

Thus civil law contractors and employers should not ignore the original legal background of FIDIC conditions. By contrast common law contractors and employers should not believe that the use of a FIDIC form of contract will enable them to escape from the particularities of the proper law of the contract.

6.4   Lex Mercatoria

Even though Prof. Molineaux (1997, p. 55 et seq.) has suggested that we should "recognize that there are construction law principles which, by reason of the activities of the multinational engineering firms (which draft contracts) and of the development banks (which standardize contract terms), already receive *de facto* recognition for international construction" and continued saying that "the forms of contract of the *Fédération Internationale des Ingénieurs-Conseils* (FIDIC) are widely used and their dissemination has already developed a degree of commonality or construction *lex mercatoria*", the aforementioned examples prove that in fact we are far from this. However, it is true that FIDIC has set an international standard which has developed a certain degree of homogeneity. But due to the enormous success of FIDIC in Eastern Europe and the increasing sudden use of FIDIC forms in those countries a split development appears to be established.

Where an international project involves civil law, differences are often of culture and style rather than of legal rules. There are a number of dissimilarities which must be taken in consideration.

The civil law practice of contract drafting is aimed at shaping an existing legal situation for the purposes of the parties. A contract is a means to fit an individual legal situation into a grid of legal rules which consist of entire codification, complementary statutes and ordinances (Hewitt 2005, note 20-13). Civil law lawyers will therefore attempt merely to adjust the legal framework as required by the individual case. It is often superfluous to cover every nook and cranny of each eventual possibility as is usual in common law practice. Hence civil law contracts tend to be shorter than common law contracts without being less precise and comprehensive. In other words civil law lawyers will rely on Civil Codes and Commercial Codes instead of so called boilerplates. Each contract clause must be read in conjunction with complementary statute law. As a consequence a full and comprehensive understanding of the individual contract requires the study of the whole Civil Code including general principles such as *culpa in contrahendo, good faith, force majeure, economic impossibility*, etc.

Not got accustomed to understand a contract as the law of the parties, being shaped by them according to the principle of freedom of contract, in some civil law countries the parties often do not familiarise themselves with the particular terms and concepts of a contract. They believe that most of the contract terms (should) strictly or principally comply with its legal background ignoring the fact that most of the legal framework of other countries is non mandatory and that quite often the law remains silent. Thus if the contract contains specific and peculiar approaches and features as is the case in FIDIC forms of contract having its roots in common law, civil law contractors must learn the whole adopted concept (for example the prevention principle as adopted by FIDIC in Sub-Clauses 8.4 and 8.7) instead of particular adjustments of a given legal situation. Where in addition the proper law of the contract relies on the "Leitmotiv" of statutory rules it may prove difficult to imagine and shape an independent little contract world, because if a clause in standard business terms is not compatible with the essential principles of statutory regulation from which it deviates, it may be null and void. This is the current situation in Germany according to Sections 305 et seq. Civil Code. Under German law it will therefore be necessary to explain the whole contract in order to render it clear that a particular clause does not place, contrary to the requirement of good faith, the contractual partner at an unreasonable disadvantage.

Hence it is not at all surprising that in particular German authors have argued that some of the FIDIC terms of contract are invalid for lack of conformity with the Leitmotiv of rules incorporated in the German Civil Code. For example it has been argued that Sub-Clauses 4.10 and 4.12 are in conflict with the Leitmotiv of Sections 644, 645 German Civil Code and shall therefore be invalid (Rosener and Dorner 2005, p. 101; Kus et al. 1999, p. 538), in particular because of the risk-shifting for all errors of the Employer to the Contractor and because of the fact that under German law the Contractor may rely on building specifications to the extent that they concern the site conditions. Those authors do not take into consideration the fact that FIDIC supposes – based on common law – that the so called soil risk is in principle borne by the Employer. In addition they ignore the fact that FIDIC forms of contract stem from a well recognised international association which invites all relevant interested groups, including the European International Contractors, to comment on the FIDIC contracts in advance, thus taking concerns into consideration at an early stage. Moreover it should be noted that even under German law it is not strictly forbidden to shift the soil risk to the Contractor and that the extent to which this risk becomes shifted to the Contractor is fairly limited to foreseeable risk. All of the unforeseeable risks as to the physical conditions of the site are borne by the Employer. Finally it must be doubted that Section 645 German Civil Code shifts the risk for the whole of the physical conditions to the Employer. In fact the Employer's risk comprises any deviation of the building ground from the composition of the ground to be expected and described in detail in the specifications (Rosener and Dorner 2005, p. 102). However not even the Employer is under a duty to carry out unreasonable survey efforts. If an obstruction occurs during the course of the works which could not have been discovered with reasonable efforts and which must be assumed to constitute a risk beyond the control of both of the parties, this type of risk must be shared according to the principles of hardship.[2]

---

[2]BGH, Schäfer-Finnern, Z 2.311 Bl. 22 and 29; Putzier (2002, p. 549); Hök (2007, p. 10); Werner and Pastor (2008, note 2497).

However the aforementioned points prove that despite of the incontestable worldwide dissemination of FIDIC forms of contract and the practical advantages in using such kind of internationally discussed standard forms national particularities exist which have much influence on the understanding and use of FIDIC contracts, which must be taken into consideration in international cases.

6.5   English and Other Legal Terms

Beware that all of the FIDIC forms of contract include definitions. Most of the important terms are already defined in Clause 1. However, the use of FIDIC forms of contract quite often requires a more sophisticated understanding of the used contract terms and complementary vocabulary and abbreviations.

6.6   FIDIC Contracts Guide, Time Lines and Other Support

When in 1999, the Fédération Internationale des Ingénieurs-Conseils ("FIDIC") published its three new forms of contract which are know as the 1999 Rainbow Edition, the Contracts Committee decided to publish a complementary guide. The three books of which are covered by this Guide and referred to as "CONS", "P&DB" and "EPCT".

This Guide was written by Peter L Booen and reviewed by the Contracts Committee which at that time comprised Michael Mortimer-Hawkins (Chairman), Christopher Wade, Axel-Volkmar Jaeger and Peter L Booen; together with John B Bowcock as Special Adviser and Christopher R Seppala as Legal Adviser. The commentary on Clause 18 was also reviewed by Mark Griffiths, Griffiths & Armour, UK.

Remember that each of the three Books is in three parts:

- General Conditions, the part which is intended to be incorporated (by reference) into each contract, and whose Sub-Clauses are often referred to in this Guide without the use of the word "Sub-Clause" (for example: "CONS 1.1").
- Guidance for the Preparation of the Particular Conditions, the part which is referred to in this Guide as "GPPC", which commences by proposing suitable wording to incorporate the appropriate General Conditions into a contract, and which concludes with annexed example forms of securities.
- Forms of Letter of Tender, Contract Agreement and Dispute Adjudication Agreement, the part which is referred to in this Guide as "the Example Form(s)".

In the FIDIC Contracts Guide, the texts in the Books are reproduced in a three-column layout. The Guide includes comments and recommendations as the case may be. It is not a comprehensive or conclusive clause by clause commentary but it gives extremely important advice and information about the books.

AB 1992	General Conditions of 1992 for Works and Supplies in the Building and Construction Industry (Almindelige Betingelser for Arbejder og Leverancer i Bygge- og Anlægsvirksomhed 1992) for use in Denmark in Sweden
ABT 1993	"Almindelige Betingelser for Totalentreprise" (ABT 93) (General Conditions for turnkey contracts) for use in Denmark in Sweden
AIA	American Institute of Architects, publishing a whole set of contract form for use in the Unites States of America
Arbitrary	By mere opinion; not according to reasoned judgment or rules; a decision made at the discretion of the judge, not the law
Arbitration	Method of dispute resolution presupposing an express agreement by which the parties of a dispute derogate the given jurisdiction of an otherwise competent state court. It is quite common to refer to an existing set of procedure rules, such as the rules of the International Chamber of Commerce (ICC) in Paris
Architect	Regulated profession. In France the mission of an architect lies in the interest of public order (see article 1 Act 1977). In England the use of the architect title is reserved by statute for professionals who are professionally entitled to it. In Germany the use of the professional title architect is reserved for those who are entered in the architects' list of the related chamber of architects. Some design services, such as submission of building permission planning are in principle reserved for architects or similar suitable professionals
Bill of quantity	A document which itemises the quantities of materials and labour in a construction project and is usually drawn up and specified by a cost professional called a quantity surveyor. They are prepared in advance to take into account the works required for a project and issued with the project specification, for use by contractors in submitting tenders. Usually quantities are measured from design drawings, to be used by the contractors for tendering and for progress payments, for variations and changes and ultimately for statistics, taxation and valuation
Bond	An undefined term. It is a debt instrument usually issued by a bank or insurer which constitutes a written guaranty submitted to the Employer by the Contractor on winning the tender ensuring payment of a sum of money in case the Contractor fails to perform the contract. Unlike on demand guarantees it is not payable on first demand but only on presentation of evidence proving the Contractor's non-performance. A bond usually covers 100% of the Contract Price. Unlike bonds unconditional on demand guarantees substitute a cash deposit and are payable on first demand. Whether a specific instrument is either an on demand guarantee or a bond must be derived from the particular wording of the instrument. Under Civil law bonds usually have the nature of an accessory guarantee or surety (Bürgschaft, Cautionnement) involving a triangular relationship between the creditor, the principal debtor and the surety. As a surety is accessory in nature the existence and extent of the principal debt creates and determines the extent of the surety. The surety is usually entitled to rely on all defences of the principal debtor against the creditor
Breach (of contract)	Violation of a right, duty or obligation arising from a contract by an act or omission, e.g. failure to perform according to a contract (delayed performance, defective work, etc.)
Care of works	Not really a legal term in English law but often used in construction contracts in order to express the responsibility for damage to the works, materials, plant and equipment, by making the contractor generally liable to take care for the works and to

compensate or to make good any damage irrespective of fault on his part. By contrast under German law care of works is more or less a legal term, expressing that the contractor bears the risk for the loss or damage of the work prior to acceptance including those due to events which are beyond the contractor's control and for which he is not responsible; risk which becomes partially transferred to the employer according to Sec. 7 no. 1 VOB/B

Common law	Common law jurisdictions are in widespread use, particularly in those nations which trace their legal heritage to Great Britain. It means the law refined by judges in common law jurisdictions. Common law in its broader sense divides into common law in its strict sense and equity. Before 1873, England had two parallel court systems, courts of "law" that could only award money damages and recognized only the legal owner of property, and courts of "equity" that could issue injunctive relief and recognized trusts of property
Condition precedent	A condition, that must be fulfilled before a contract or a right or obligation under a contract becomes effective, for example subject to according contract terms payment becomes due when a payment certificate has been issued
Consideration	An essential legal component of any contract governed by common law; a bargain. It means counter performance, something of legal value done, given or promised by the party seeking to enforce the contract. It is not necessary in a deed
Construction permit	Formal permission from the local building authority required in several jurisdictions to begin construction, demolition, addition or renovation on property and in some cases for modifications of uses. The owner shall usually apply for the grant of a construction permit and obtain it before starting any works. Subject to local law the authorities must review submitted plans to ensure that they comply with the local building codes, local zoning by-laws, and other applicable regulations. The right to submit planning documents is sometimes reserved for suitable professionals, such as architects and engineers (for example in German law)
Contract	A legally binding agreement, arising as a result of offer and acceptance, but subject to applicable law a number of other requirements must be satisfied for an agreement to be legally binding
Copyright	Copyright is an intangible property right; a form of protection provided by the law to the authors of "original works of authorship", including literary, dramatic, musical, artistic, and certain other intellectual works. Subject to applicable laws it consists of the exclusive right of reproducing any form of those works defined in applicable laws, including for example the design of a building. Licences may be granted in respect of Copyright by the owner. Whether it is transmissible by assignment depends on the applicable law. Under German law it is only transferable by heritage
Damages	Compensation awarded to a party suffering loss or damage caused by a third party. Under common law it is usually a monetary obligation, whilst under civil law specific performance is possible
DB (Design and Build)	Design and Build contracts are used in order to commit a contractor with both the design and the execution of works
DBO (Design Build Operate)	DBO is an innovative contracting method that reduces the time and owner risks associated with delivering major projects
Deed	Commonly referred to as a "contract under seal". In USA: a written instrument transferring interests in real property
Design	This is not a defined term. The extent of the design responsibility shall be specified by the Contract

Decennial liability	Strict liability for structural defects ruled by law, French origin and adopted by French law inspired jurisdictions all over the world
Discharge	Release, dismiss, free, or relieve from obligations under a contract
Dispute adjudication	An innovative form of dispute resolution not aimed to replace court proceedings or arbitration but to provide a complementary feature of dispute resolution. Usually the decisions given by an adjudicator or dispute adjudication board become temporarily binding until revised by an arbitral award
Doctrine of substantial performance	Doctrine of equity whereby substantial performance should be compensated, not only complete performance, meaning that minor defects are unremarkable
EJCDC	Engineers Joint Contract Documents Committee, publishing a whole set of contract forms for use in the United States of America
Engineer	In some standard contract forms (for example FIDIC forms of contract) this term is used in legal sense explained in Sutcliffe v. Thackrah. The Engineer is third part to a construction contract who owes duties under the construction contract, including tasks of determination of claims, certification of payments, etc. The wording may vary and some contracts refer to an architect, supervisor, contract manager but the role and function of this third party to a construction contract is always nearly the same
Equitable remedies	A legal remedy based on equity instead of common law, which is a specific common law distinction
Equity	Principles of justice or fairness applied to overcome any unjust result or consequence resulting from the application of common law in its strict sense
FIDIC	Fédération Internationale des Ingénieurs-Conseils, sitting in Geneva, represents the interests of Engineers worldwide. FIDIC has published a range of internationally recognised construction contract forms which are also recommended for use by the World Bank. Among those contract forms the FIDIC Red Book, Yellow Book and Silver Book are the most important ones
Float (floating time)	Contingency time allowance between the date on which the works have to be completed and the date when the contractor actually plans to complete. In major projects usually networks techniques are used in order to find the critical path of each activity which is required for completion. If floating time can be shown on the CPN the question arises of who is the owner of this float. According to the SCL Delay and Disruption Protocol float is owned by the employer
Force majeure	Legal term used to describe a situation under which non performance of a contract is excused, often referred to as act of god or act which is beyond the control of both parties of the contract but subject to local legislation including elements of frustration or impossibility to perform. Beware that in some jurisdictions force majeure is ruled by law, thus having a precise meaning. Boilerplate which is often used in international contracts
Forum	Court
Forum shopping	Practice adopted by a litigant to get his legal case heard in the court thought most likely to provide a favourable judgment
Gold Book	A FIDIC contract form for works, where the design, the execution of the works and the operation service is done by the contractor (see DBO)

Guarantee	An undertaking to perform some act, etc. A guarantee can be conditional or on demand. Depending on its nature it is only enforceable, if a condition is fulfilled, e.g. undertaking to "pay money back" if the main debtor fails to do so. In civil law jurisdictions conditional guarantees are ruled by law and referred to as Bürgschaft (German) or Cautionnement (French), both being "accessory"
ICE	Institution of Civil Engineers publishing a whole set of contract forms of use in the UK
Injunction	An equitable remedy under common law in which the court orders a party to perform or to desist from a particular act. An "interim" or "interlocutory" is an injunction issued prior to trial to prevent irreparable injury to the plaintiff while the court considers whether to grant permanent relief
JCT	Joint Contracts Tribunal publishing a whole set of contract forms for use in the UK
Joint and several obligation	An obligation entered into by two or more persons, so that each is liable severally, and all liable jointly, and a creditor or obligee may sue one or more severally, or all jointly, at his option. In some jurisdictions joint and several liability is provided by law, for example in France, where usually contractors and consultants assume joint and several liability under the decennial liability rule
Jurisdiction	Power or authority of a court over a person (in pesonam) or property (in rem); area of legal authority, often used as a synonym for legal system, especially where an individual state is divided in different jurisdictions, such as the United Kingdom, Canada or Australia
Koran (Qur'an)	First source of Law in Islamic countries. Islamic law is known as Shar'iah Law. Shari'ah means the path to follow God's Law, which means a much wider concept than for example Civil law because it includes the whole prescriptive side of religion. The second element of Shar'iah is referred to as the Sunna, including the teachings of the Prophet Mohammad not explicitly found in the Qur'an. Sunna's rules are a composite of the teachings of the Prophet and his works. Fiqh, Islamic jurisprudence, is an expansion of Islamic law, complemented by the rulings of Islamic jurists. Fiqh consists of detailed rules and is therefore closer to the concept of law than Shari'ah
Letter of intent (LOI)	A written, preliminary understanding between parties of how they intend to proceed in a particular matter. An LOI was not traditionally a contract, but rather a tentative expression of intentions. However, today some parts of an LOI may include contractual duties (e.g. confidentiality) and if worded in binding terms the court may hold an LOI to be contractually binding in part or whole
Lex causae	The law or laws chosen by the forum court from among the relevant legal systems to arrive at its judgment of an international case
Lex fori	The law of the forum or court before which a case is pending. More particularly the law relating to procedure or the formalities in force (adjective law) in a given place
Lex rei situs or sitae	The law of the situation of the thing
Liquidated damages (delay damages)	A pre-estimated amount of money specified in a contract to compensate a party for damages suffered because of a breach of contract by the other party to the agreement. It is also a limitation on liability for damages. Beware that liquidated damages should not be confused with so called penalties

May	Verb in English used to express a possibility, also used in legal texts as a synonym for shall leaving open to the addressee some discretion. Depending on the context "may" can mean "shall"
Mechanic's lien	A mechanic's lien (USA) is a "hold" against property that, if unpaid, allows a foreclosure action, forcing the sale of the property. Such kind of instruments are quite common within jurisdictions all over the world but their nature and way in which it becomes enforced differ quite a lot. In Germany for example the contractor is entitled to sue for registration of a so called workman's mortgage (or better hypothec), if he remains unpaid. In England however such kind of instrument is unknown
Memorandum of understanding	A document outlining areas of "agreement" or understanding. Not usually intended to be a binding contract, although, as with an LOI, if it is worded precisely in terms of rights and duties, etc., it may be binding
Misrepresentation (common law)	A false and misleading statement as to a material fact, which may be grounds for rescinding a contract or for the recovery of damages in contract or tort. The civil law approach is a bit different. German law has adopted the culpa in contrahendo doctrine according to which the innocent party may calim for damages as a result of a pre-contractual negligent false statement (of which the party should or could have known that the information was misleading)
Mortgage	Charge against land, often ruled in detail by law. According to German law the Contractor is entitled to a mortgage against the land of the owner in order to secure its entitlement to payment
NEC3	The New Engineering Contract Engineering and Construction Contract
Negligence	As a tort, negligence is the breach by the defendant of a legal duty to take care and diligence, which results in damage to the claimant
Nominate contracts	A contract that is given a special designation as to its purpose. Some jurisdictions, especially civil law jurisdictions and islamic jurisdictions make a difference between nominate and innominate contracts. Each nominate contract is governed by particular rules (whose content and form is regulated by statute, thus being a contract with a given special designation), whereas all innominate contracts are created as people exercise their freedom to contract in new situations. Thus innominate contracts evolve as a non-regulated variant of a regulated or nominate contract, such as a contract of sale or a loan contract. An innominate contract does create rights and obligations of the parties, which rights and obligations may be enforceable and demandable
Penalty	A punishment, usually referred to as a penalty clause by which one party of a contract promises to pay a predetermined amount of money for breach of contract in order to ensure strict compliance with the contract; a void contract term according to "equity" rules under common law, but usually binding under civil law
Performance	Fulfilment of one's obligations according to a contract
Privilege	Term describing a number of rules excluding evidence that would be adverse to a fundamental principle or relationship if it were disclosed; under French law a payment security, for example the contractor's or architect's privilege related to any payment claim against the employer

Pro forma invoice	A term coming from Latin which means "as a matter of form". In foreign trade transactions, a *pro forma* (or *proforma or proforma*) invoice is an invoice provided by a supplier in advance of providing the goods or service. It states a commitment from the supplier to provide goods or services to the purchaser (or client) at specified prices and terms and it is commonly used to declare the value of the transaction. Some of the advantages of a pro forma invoice to the purchaser include to show to his government for foreign currency allocation and most importantly, to have a detailed information on the transaction that can help him plan. The pro forma invoice is also often used by the purchaser to apply for a letter of credit (L/C). An accurate and professionally submitted pro forma invoice can help purchasers to make a decision and agree to the quotation. In fact it is not a true invoice, because it is not used to record accounts receivable for the supplier and accounts payable for the purchaser
Punitive damages (common law)	Award of damages intended to punish the defendant and deter future wrongdoing. Usually awarded when an action is aggravated by evil motives, gross negligence, or deliberate violence or oppression. Also called "exemplary damages" Available under torts but generally not under contract law
Quantity surveyor	Construction professionals, who are employed predominantly on major building and construction projects as consultants to the owner, in both the public and private sectors. They work closely with architects, financiers, engineers, contractors, suppliers, project owners, accountants, insurance underwriters, solicitors and Courts and with all levels of government authorities. They get their name from the Bill of Quantities. The profession of quantity surveyors is well known in common law countries but rarely known in civil law countries
Quantum meruit	Supposing a person employs another to do some work for him, without any binding contract as to his compensation, the law may imply a promise from the employer to the workman that he will pay him for his work, as much as he may deserve, based on merit
Real property	Land and buildings (or other permanent attachments to the land) as well as the rights arising out of land. Real property is different from "personal property", which is any movable property
Reasonable	Used in legal texts in order to express a standard of duty or the way in which a power or authorisation can or may be used. A reasonable man is presumed to be a careful man, a man of ordinary prudence. The reasonable man is a hypothetical individual who is intended to represent a sort of average citizen or professional. Within reasonable time means within appropriate and pertinent time, within the time which is needed. Reasonable time means at any time which is acceptable. Reasonably practicable means a level of precaution taking in account of the balance between the risk involved in a particular hazard and the cost involved in remedying it. Reasonable skill and care has been judged as the standard of an ordinary man exercising and professing to have that skill which is appropriate for the task committed to him
Reception	Noun form of receiving; under civil law a legal term meaning the acceptance of works under a construction contract followed by a couple of legal consequences, such as the transfer of care for the works to the owner and the commencement date of (legal) defects liability limitation
Red Book	A FIDIC contract form for works, where the design is done by the employer or on behalf of the employer

Rescission	The ending of a contract and the restoring of the parties to their respective positions before the contract started
Revocation	The cancellation of power or authority granted to another; the withdrawing of an offer to contract
Seal	A method of expressing consent to a written instrument by attaching to it wax impressed with a device, or now, more commonly, a paper seal
Set-off	Where a claim by a defendant to a sum of money (whether of an ascertained amount or not) is relied on as a defence to the whole or part of a claim made by the claimant, it may be included in the defence or counterclaim and set-off against the claimant's claim. Under some laws set-off presupposes an expressed or implied declaration, under some set-off requires only a situation where two counter claims exist
Shall	Modal verb in English used to express the future; also used in legal texts to express a duty or obligation (but see also "may")
Silver Book	A FIDIC contract form for turn key projects
Specific performance	Under common law an equitable remedy granted by a court whereby the court requires the breaching party to fulfil its obligations under a contract. In civil law jurisdictions specific performance is the rule whereas under common law it is an exceptional remedy which can be granted by court
Standard contract terms	Terms of contract which have been drafted for multiple use. In some countries standard contract terms are subject to legal control. In Germany even commercial contracts fall under the particular rules of court control (Sect. 305 et seq. German Civil Code), which sometimes is referred to as the "main rouge" principle
Statute of limitations	Statutes or laws which set out the maximum time periods within which various types of legal proceedings can be started or rights enforced, time bar of a claim.
Subject to	Connotation used to express that any obligation provided in a legal text will be become effective only when a contract has been executed. Example: "Subject to contract the contractor shall design and execute the works specified in the Bill of Quantity"
Substantial completion	A matter of fact which is required to discharge contractual obligations. The word "substantial" is not intended to convey the meaning of absolute exactness but to convey the concept of almost being complete, and that the state of completion is materially so to the extent that the building can serve the intended use. Usually construction contracts define what is meant and provide at this stage that either the engineer o the architect shall issue a completion certificate. But in principle completion does not mean automatically acceptance of the works or release from liability. Completion means in fact to permit the employer to take possession of the works and to allow the contractor to leave the site
Taking-Over (see also reception)	The term "taking-over" should be used with care. Civil law practitioners will sometimes hastily assume that taking-over means discharge or acceptance of the Works in accordance with domestic legislation. FIDIC uses the term in a slightly different sense
Termination	The ending or finishing of a contract for convenience and for breach as a result of an unilateral declaration, which must be distinguished from rescission, repudiation, avoidance, withdrawal
Time is of the essence	Stipulation in a contract which denotes the duty of one party to perform within a specified period of time, or else the other party may terminate the contract

Time extension	Construction contract forms which originate from common law jurisdictions usually provide claims for extension of time in order to ensure that the employer may sue for liquidated damages if the contractor fails to comply with the agreed time for completion. If and when the employer prevents the contractor to progress with the works the contractor is entitled to claim for time extension
Tort	Wrongful behaviour recognized by law suffered by somebody resulting in an injury or harm constituting the basis for a claim by the victim against the responsible person
To rescind	To annul, avoid, or cancel a contract, and restore the parties to the position they were in before the contract was entered into
VOB (*Verdingungsordnung für Bauleistungen* = *Vergabe und Vertragsordnung für Bauleistungen*)	Set of Rules developed and published by the German Award and Contract Committee for Construction Work. Primarily aimed to rule public works only today they are partially used by the whole industry and even for contracts with consumers. The so called Provisions on the awarding of construction works are divided in three parts, such as the General Provisions on the awarding of contracts for construction work (part A), General contractual conditions for the performance of construction work (part B) and the General technical contractual conditions for construction work (part C). Whereas part A contains regulation on procurement law for the award of public work contracts, part B and part C are in use in both sectors, private and public. The provisions of part B, not having a legal status, can be used as general Terms and Conditions, which do not underlie the "main rouge" principle which is ruled by law (Sect. 305 et seq. German Civil Code) to the extent that no contractual amendments to the provisions of the VOB/B have been made. VOB/B differs in various points from the rules of the German Civil Code
Void	Of no legal force or binding effect
Warranty	A promise or assurance. An agreement, for example, with reference to goods which are the subject of a contract of sale, but collateral to the main purpose of such contract, the breach of which gives rise to a claim for damages, but not to a right to reject the goods and treat the contract as void. A common usage of the term is to refer to a manufacturer's written promise or guarantee as to the extent to which he will repair, replace or otherwise compensate for defective goods
White Book	FIDIC contract form for consultants' services, 4th Edition 2006
Workmanship	Skill in an occupation or trade
Yellow Book	A FIDIC contract form for design and build projects
YSE	Finnish standard terms of contracts for works, also used from to time to time in Baltic states
Zoning	Key tool for carrying out planning policy, used in urban planning for a system of land-use regulation in various parts of the world. The expression is derived from the practice of determining the size and use of buildings, where they are located and, in large measure, the densities of the city's diverse neighbourhoods. Zoning is usually based on mapped zones which separate one set of developments from another. Zoning regulations fall under public policy rights governments and municipalities may exercise over real property

Also each of the books includes a Guidance for the Preparation of Particular Conditions which gives additional help. The reader will find therein commentaries as well as pre-formulated additional Sub-Clauses for particular use as it may be appropriate depending on the specific requirements of a project or any by virtue of the governing law.

Finally each of the books includes timelines. It is strongly recommended to have a view on it before entering into any contract. The timelines give a clear and comprehensive overview about all major events, such as the Commencement Date, the date on which the Taking-Over Certificate will be issued, the date on which the Performance Certificate will be issued or the date on which the Performance Security will be restored. The parties to the Contract will also be informed about the typical sequence of Payment Events and the typical sequence of Dispute Events. In the Gold Book this concept has been maintained and amplified. A further Guide to the Gold Book is in preparation.

In summary, FIDIC books should be read in their common law context having regard to the governing law. The meaning of any contract term which is not yet defined in Clause 1 should not be determined by mere translation. Using dictionaries without having in mind that the wording has a common law background may, and quite often will, lead to misunderstandings. FIDIC has obviously adopted a considerable number of common law concepts, such as the concepts of substantial completion and time at large. The rationale of some FIDIC features lies in the fact that common law lacks to provide appropriate remedies. This is for example the case concerning the obligation to remedy any defects. Whilst Common law provides only for damages as the normal and exclusive legal remedy for breach of contract, Civil law is much more sophisticated. However, the Defects Notification Period as referred to in Clause 11 of the 1999 FIDIC Rainbow Edition is a complementary relief and not exclusive at all.

Thus the following way of working is appropriate:

- Identify the relevant term
- Check definitions in Clause 1
- Check the common law legal background of the term or of the Sub-Clause which includes the term
- Take in account any relevant provisions of the governing law dealing with interpretation of contracts
- Identify the true meaning of the term in its contractual and legal context
- Try not to denature the original meaning of the term even though used in a Civil law context

How does this work in reality? The following examples will enlighten the recommended approach:

(1) Supposed a Contractor is to construct a waste water treatment plant in Poland. According to the Contract he shall pay delay damages to the Employer if he fails to comply with Time for Completion. The Contract is governed by Polish law.

The question may arise whether according to the contractual wording delay damages should be understood as a "genuine estimate of damages" in the event of failure to comply with the requirement of Time for Completion or whether additional damages may be claimed. The true meaning of delay damages in Common law is clear. It should be a genuine estimate of damages. No further damages will be due, because otherwise the clause will have the nature of a penalty clause which is null and void under Common law. However, in Poland penalty clauses are allowed. Following the aforementioned test the result will be that the Parties have made their contract with the understanding that delay damages are different from penalties. However, if the Parties have made their contract in Polish and the translator was not aware of the particular meaning of delay damages he might have used the term penalty instead of delay damages.[3] It will then be quite difficult to argue that the contractor did not intend to assume liability for penalties.

(2) Supposed the Contractor was to design, supply, construct and install 36 Wind Turbine Generators (WTGs) including all civil and building works, electrical works connecting the WTGs to the switch room and other connection works. Subject to Sub-Clause 1.4 Romanian law is the governing law. Due to defects in the ground which were unforeseeable the foundation works are defective. This was obvious when the Performance Certificate was issued, but no reservation was made. However, although the Performance Certificate has been issued the Employer instructs the Contractor to remedy the defect. The Contractor who is not really unwilling to do so however argues that he should be paid for this. He relies on the fact that the Performance Certificate was issued without any reservation.

The question is whether this is a good defence. According to English law a certificate may be conclusive as to what it purports to certify. However this is a question of contract interpretation. According to Sub-Clause 11.9 the Performance Certificate is deemed to constitute acceptance of the Works, but Sub-Clause 11.10 already states that although the Performance Certificate has been issued, each party remains liable for the fulfilment of any obligation which remains unperformed at that time. According to Romanian law approval or acceptance of the Works constitutes a waiver. On the other hand Romanian law provides for a so called decennial liability. Subject to Romanian law the issuing of the Taking-Over and the Performance Certificate by the Engineer is without prejudice to the Contractor's liability for latent defects of the Works during the periods of liability imposed by the applicable laws. According to art. 29 Law no. 10/1995 the designer, certified specialised project checker, manufactures and suppliers of construction materials und products, the contractor, the certified technical responsible, the specialised site engineer shall be responsible for any latent defect of the works which become apparent within a period of ten years as well during the whole life cycle of the construction, resulting from a failure in observing the design and performance regulations in force at the date of the execution of the works. Furthermore according to art. 1483 Romanian Civil Code, in the course of ten years any builder of a work is liable as of right, towards the building owner or purchaser, for damages, even

---

[3] Beware that in many bilingual dictionaries the connotation "liquidated damages" will be translated by using terms meaning in fact "penalty".

resulting from a defect of the ground, which imperil the strength of the building or which, affecting it in one of its constituent parts or one of its elements of equipment, render it unsuitable for its purposes.

Furthermore the delivery of the Taking-Over Certificate and the Performance Certificate may involve an adjustment of the General Conditions as such:

> The Engineer shall request the Employer to nominate a Taking-Over Commission that acting in accordance with the Applicable Laws shall issue and sign the Taking-Over Minutes upon Completion of Works.

Thus if in course of ten years a latent defect becomes apparent, even though no reservation has been made, the Contractor is liable to make good the defect. His claim for additional payment should therefore be dismissed.

Finally it is worthwhile to emphasise that using English or other languages is always dangerous if the text must be translated at a later date. Needless to say, translators often do an excellent job. However, at times translations are found to be incomplete, misleading or even wrong. In a recent case a German Court of Appeal[4] encountered such misleading translation. The parties to the dispute were bound to a sales contract according to which the seller was to deliver a machine for the production of refreshing tissues. A dispute arose and the purchaser started legal proceedings before the High Court of Stuttgart. The contract provided for an arbitration clause, which – in its English version which obviously was not written in perfect English – read as follows:

> 8. Arbitration
>
> The seller and the Buyer, hereinafter referred to a Parties, will take measures to settle amicably all disputes and differences which may arise under the present Contract or in connection with it. If Parties cannot agree upon an amicable settlement then all disputes and differences are to be submitted without recourse to the ordinary court to Stockholm, Sweden.
>
> The Award of the arbitration Commission will be final and bindin(g) upon both Parties.

The seller objected the jurisdiction of the court by relying on the arbitration clause. The contract was executed in English and Russian. The purchaser submitted a translation of the aforementioned clause which had been drawn from the Russian version. The translation (literally retranslated into English) read as follows:

> In case that the Parties cannot achieve an amicable settlement all disputed questions and differences, except the judicial competences of the ordinary courts, shall be submitted in Stockholm, Sweden.

During the proceedings before the Court of Appeal a second version of the arbitration clause, which was drawn from the English version, was produced, which read (in a re-translated English version) as follows:

---

[4]OLG Stuttgart, decision from 15 May 2006; file no. 5 U 21/06; [2006] IBR 1407.

> In the event of failure to reach amicable settlement, without recourse, legal action shall be
> taken before the ordinary court at Stockholm.

The High Court of Stuttgart granted the relief sought by the purchaser by relying on
the translation of the arbitration clause of the Russian translator arguing that is was
not sufficiently clear. It accordingly held that the seller was liable to refund the
advance payment which had received. Upon appeal of the seller the Court of Appeal
revised the decision and dismissed the claim. It held:

> The interpretation of contractual wording is a proper task of the court. This [rule] applies
> not only to not completely unambiguous and literally screwed up German texts but also to
> such in a foreign language. Hence, the intention of the Parties covered by the literal wording
> has to be ascertained also by means of teleological interpretation.

The court then studied dictionaries, took in consideration further relevant
circumstances (such as the fact that the Stockholm arbitration is one of the
internationally well known arbitration forums and that written communication
implied a common understanding of the relevant clause in favour of valid arbitration clause) and finally interpreted the aforementioned clause as it was: a valid
arbitration clause.

6.7 Unidroit Principles

The very nature of a contract is that it is a binding instrument. However, whether a
contract is binding or not depends on the proper law of the contract which must be
determined in accordance with the conflict of laws rules (see Chap. 2 in this book).
Even though it might be argued that the principles of contractual freedom and pacta
sunt servanda are recognised worldwide, the courts are usually not prepared to refer
to a non state body of law. For the first time the Rome I Regulation seems to allow
for a reference to a non state body of law (Recital 13). However, in daily practice it
may prove difficult to either determine or ascertain the proper law of the contract.
It is often the case that national or domestic law is not accessible. However, even
though FIDIC forms of contract provide for a detailed and carefully crafted set of
inter-related clauses, they do not cover every eventuality. Thus, there is a need for
complementary framework. It is therefore worthwhile to refer to the Unidroit
Principles of international commercial contracts (UP).

The UP represent a totally new approach to international trade law (Bonnell
2002, p. 335). First of all, on account of their scope which, contrary to that of all
existing international conventions including CISG, is not restricted to a particular
kind of transaction but covers the general part of contract law (Bonnell 2002,
p. 335). Further, and more importantly, the UP – prepared by a private group of
experts which, though acting under the auspices of a prestigious Institute such as
UNIDROIT, lacked any legislative power – do not aim to unify domestic law by
means of special legislation, but merely to "re-state" existing international contract
law (Bonnell 2002, p. 335). Finally, the decisive criterion in their preparation was

not just which rule had been adopted by the majority of countries ("common core approach"), but also which of the rules under consideration had the most persuasive value and/or appeared to be particularly well suited for cross-border transactions ("better rule approach") (Bonnell 2002, p. 335). In a summary UP are based on comparative law studies and express a common understanding of legal concepts worldwide, which exist in several languages, with commentaries.

Because of the complex nature of the construction process and the long-term character of such a mission usually the parties to a construction contract wish to specify the following issues in their contract:

- Conditions of Payment
- Time for Completion
- Taking Over and Discharge
- Remedy of Defects
- Defects Liability
- Clear risk allocation

The UP are applicable to commercial contracts, such as supply and exchange of goods and services as well as to investment and/or concession agreements or professional services contracts. However, the UP do not define any type of contract. Thus the contractor, the purchaser, the investor and the engineer are dealt in the same way. However the UP distinguish between the *duty to achieve a specific result* and the *duty of best efforts*. In determining whether a party owes the first or the second one, regard shall be had among other factors (Art. 5.1.5 UP):

(a) The way in which the obligation is expressed in the contract
(b) The contractual price and other terms of the contract
(c) The degree of risk normally involved in achieving the expected result
(d) The ability of the other party to influence the performance of the obligation

It seems that UP take regard "to the obligation incurred", will say that in a single contract obligations of *both types* may coexist.[5]

Where the parties to a contract have not agreed with respect to a term which is important for a determination of their rights and duties, a term which is appropriate in the circumstances shall be supplied (Art. 4.8(1) UP). In determining what is an appropriate term regard shall be had, among other factors (Art. 4.8(2) UP), to:

(a) The intention of the parties
(b) The nature and purpose of the contract
(c) Good faith and fair dealing
(d) Reasonableness

The contractual obligations of the parties may be express or implied (Art. 5.1.1 UP). Implied obligations stem from (Art. 5.1.2 UP):

(a) The nature and purpose of the contract

---

[5] UP Commentary, 132.

(b) Practices established between the parties and usages
(c) Good faith and fair dealing
(d) Reasonableness

Each party shall cooperate with the other party when such co-operation may reasonably be expected for the performance of that party's obligations (Art. 5.1.3 UP).

However, a UP-based *construction contract* remains quite a rudimental contract (for a more detailed analysis see Hök 2008, p. 115 et seq.). A simple construction contract based on UP will include the following items:

- Risk Allocation

  - No additional time, cost or profit for unforeseen weather conditions, ground conditions, etc., only for *hardship*

- Time Extension

  - Risk of time at large, because of lack of procedure for EOT

- Acceptance of the Works (Discharge)

  - No Tests at completion, no further defects correction period, no clear concept of substantial completion

- Payments

  - No interim payments allowed, no certification procedure, no evaluation procedure, no retention monies

- Performance within the time and with the quality fixed by the contract

  - However without any clear concept concerning EOT

- In the event of non-performance the Employer will be entitled to claim for

  - Remedying defects, damages, termination

- Possibility to adapt the contract with a view to restoring its equilibrium in the event of *hardship*
- Limitation Period for legal defects liability: 3 years unless otherwise ruled by contract

On the other hand the UP include a comprehensive set of rules which may fill gaps where FIDIC forms of contract would remain silent. Clause by clause commentaries will give guidance and help for interpretation.

References

Bonnell MJ (2002) The UNIDROIT principles of international commercial contracts and the harmonisation of international sales law. RJT 36:335
Bunni NG (2005) FIDIC forms of contract, 3rd edn. Blackwell, Oxford
Hewitt I (2005) Joint ventures, 3rd edn. Sweet & Maxwell, London

Hök G-S (2007) Zum Baugrundrisiko in Deutschland mit einem Blick ins Ausland und auf internationale Vertragsmuster. ZfBR 3, 10

Hök G-S (2008) FIDIC Verträge im Lichte der Unidroit Prinzipien als Vertragsstatut. ZfBR 115

Kus A, Markus J, Steding R (1999) FIDIC's new Silver Book under the German Standard Form Contracts Act. ICLR 538

Lloyd H (2007) Book review: understanding the new FIDIC Red Book. ICLR 503

Molineaux C (1997) Moving toward a Lex Mercatoria – A Lex Constructionis. J Int Arb 14:55

Putzier E (2002) Anpassung des Pauschalpreises bei Leistungsänderung. BauR 546, 549

Rosener W, Dorner G (2005) FIDIC, an analysis of international construction contracts. Kluwer, The Hague

Werner U, Pastor W (2008) Der Bauprozess, 12th edn. Werner, Köln

Chapter 7
FIDIC Contract Documents

7.1 FIDIC Rainbow

7.1.1 Overview

The FIDIC RED BOOK (Construction) is a contract form where the design is made by the Employer and the Contractor is paid on a measurement basis. Thus the Red Book follows the traditional procurement route of Design, Bid and Build. The Accepted Contract Amount is based on estimated quantities. The Contractor is paid for the actual quantities of work he carried out.

The FIDIC YELLOW BOOK (Plant) is a contract form where the design is carried out by the Contractor who shall be paid on lump sum basis. It is considered to be a well balanced contract form holding a fair balance between the interests of both parties to the contract.

The FIDIC SILVER BOOK (Turnkey) is a contract form where the design is carried out by the Contractor who shall be paid on a lump sum basis. The SILVER BOOK is envisaged for EPC/Turnkey projects and allocates most of the common risk to the Contractor. It is not intended for use where major unidentified risks are presumed or expected.

The FIDIC GREEN BOOK (Short Form) is intended for relatively small projects or works of a repetitive nature or short duration. The works are to be carried out according to the design provided by the Employer. FIDIC's Guidelines suggest that USD 500,000 and 6 months should be regarded as reasonable limits on the capital value and duration respectively.

The FIDIC Design, Build and Operate form (also referred to as the Gold Book) is a design and build contract form to which an operation and maintenance period has been added. This form joins the series of contract forms published by FIDIC since 1999 and was first presented at the FIDIC Annual Conference in Singapore in 2007. It has been followed by the First Edition, published in September 2008. The drafting work has been done by a special task group under the excellent chairmanship of Michael Mortimer-Hawkins with direct responsibility to the FIDIC

A.-V. Jaeger and G.-S. Hök, *FIDIC-A Guide for Practitioners*,
DOI 10.1007/978-3-642-02100-8_7, © Springer-Verlag Berlin Heidelberg 2010

Contracts Committee supported by special advisers, legal advisors, and reviewed by a number of reviewers worldwide. The Gold Book comprises a complex range of services. As the contract period is intended to continue for a period of more than 20 years it is critical that the parties to the contract attempt to co-operate throughout. The FIDIC DBO from provides a lump-sum price to be paid in instalments.

The FIDIC Form of Contract for Dredging and Reclamation Works (also referred to as the Blue Book) has been published in 2006. This new publication can be used for all types of dredging and reclamation work and ancillary construction with a variety of administrative arrangements. The works are to be carried out according to the design provided by the Employer. However, the FIDIC form can easily be altered into a contract that includes, or wholly comprises, contractor-designed works. The most essential part of a Blue Book contract is the description of the activity itself, the specifications, drawings and design of the work. The nature of dredging and reclamation works typically requires major dredging equipment. Thus there is a need for a particular risk allocation in order to protect the Contractor in the event of any additional mobilisation of such equipment.

For smaller contracts with a planned time for completion of less than 6 months and a contract amount of less than 500,000 USD, the so-called Green Book (Short Form of Contract) comes into play.

Depending on the contract form used, the FIDIC Books comprise the following services:

1. Step: Pre-tender duties such as scrutiny of Employer's documents and requirements site surveys and visits
2. Step: Pre-contract design
3. Step: Final design
4. Step: Completion of the works
5. Step: Remedy of defects
6. Post contractual liabilities
7. Operation an Maintenance Services

Which contract form will come into play depends on the Employer's decision and a consideration into his special interests. If the Employer is an experienced developer he will probably prefer to use the Red Book, especially if he intends to have an influence on the design process, as the Red Book allocates the design duties to the Employer. If the Employer is less experienced or not interested in exerting much influence on the design, he will probably prefer the application of the Yellow Book, where the design has to be made by the Contractor. The Silver Book will be appropriate if no major unknown risks are identified and the Employer wishes to have as much security in relation to price and time as possible.

Most of the FIDIC Books work with a person which, although not being a party to the contract, executes powers under this contract. Commonly referred to as the Engineer, this person is paid by the Employer and is nominated prior to the contract being awarded. The Engineer therefore is part of the Contractor's calculation.

Although the Engineer is both appointed and paid by the Employer, he carries out a role which presupposes a certain degree of impartiality and fairness imposed on him.

7.1.2 Balanced Forms of Contract

FIDIC Books are well known and recognised forms of contract. The reason for this is that all contract forms provide:

- Rules for the adaptation of the agreed contract amount
- Rules for extension of time for completion variation procedures

thus all contract forms – depending on their purpose in a more or less extensive way – are flexible management tools, requiring experienced and skilful staff working on behalf of not only the Contractor and the Employer but also the Engineer. Moreover as to the Engineer the contract forms require an independent and impartial person.

FIDIC forms of contract recognise that the successful completion of a project is a process which cannot be totally planned at an early stage, although they require great skill and care at pre-tender and tender stage.

FIDIC strongly recommends that the complete design or the Employer's Requirements shall be prepared by experienced engineers and architects in order to ensure that the intended purpose will be achieved and realised. The Contractor on the other side is to scrutinise the design or the Requirements before submitting his tender.

Although all these precautions are provided, no project can be realised on a green desk and under academic or perfect conditions. A lot of things may change or happen having an effect on the time for completion and the contract daily work of both parties to the contract and the engineer.

In order to counterbalance this uncertainty, FIDIC books dispose of a large arsenal of mechanisms such as:

- Instructions and variations
- Claims
- Suspension orders
- Proposals for variations
- Design changes

All members of the construction team must consequently and on a regular basis analyse progress of the works and all events, circumstances and factors affecting the price and time for completion. Sometimes the combination of some instruments which are available to overcome a particular situation may be practised and sometimes only one way out of the problem may be left.

For example it is not possible to combine acceleration orders with Variations (see Sub-Clauses 8.6 and 8.4 (a)). Thus it is either a Variation or an instruction based on Sub-Clause 8.6.

7.1.3 International Scope

FIDIC Contract forms are intended for worldwide use and to cover all kinds of work. However the international purpose of FIDIC Conditions is not really apparent from the point of view of Civil law lawyers. They would presume that they have a pure common law origin. However, common law lawyers would probably contest this opinion as there are some approaches which seem to have no common law origin.

In fact and notwithstanding the aforementioned discussion FIDIC Conditions require a certain knowledge of common law and common law based construction practice for perfect understanding of the Conditions. In relation to this, reference is made to the following key common law terms:

- Substantial completion
- Discharge
- Time is of the essence
- Time at large and liquidated damages
- Specific performance
- Breach of contract

Once these common law key principles of construction contracts have been explained, it is much easier to understand FIDIC contracts. However there are further issues which can give rise to misunderstandings.

Common law lawyers usually adopt the approach of defining the basic and fundamental contract terms and establishing their own proper contract world. Everything which they consider to be important is mentioned in and covered by the contract. Civil law lawyers by contrast rely on their Civil Codes which provide already a more or less specific contractual framework, which applies to the contract. Hence they normally focus on major aspects of the contract and the change of statutory provisions which they consider to be inappropriate.

Common law lawyers should be aware of the fact that this Civil law approach has a high degree of influence on the content of a FIDIC based contract. Civil Codes usually provide so-called complementary statutory rules which sometimes become complemented by non statutory rules which have been established by the courts by way of interpretation of the law. Thus a construction contract comprises a whole set of rules which are either mandatory or non mandatory. Non mandatory rules apply to the contract even though the parties probably would not have intended to include them in their contract if they had previously known them. Of course the parties to a contract can derogate from non mandatory rules but they have to do it by way of an express or implied term in the contract. If the contract remains silent as to the complementary rules they will still apply. Thus for example a German FIDIC based contract will include Sect. 631 et seq. German Civil Code whereas a French construction contract will include art. 1792 et seq. French Civil Code.

Another difficulty encountered by common law lawyers consists in the fact that Civil Codes usually contain different rules for different types of contract. The set of complementary or default rules which is applicable to a contract varies depending on the type of contract which is used. Hence under German law the answer to the question of whether an architect or engineer owes a duty of fitness for purpose or only a duty of skill and care will depend on the type of contract which is involved. Speaking in legal terms, the construction contract according to which a contractor owes the duty to carry out the works is clearly a contract for works and services (Werkvertrag) being subject to the rules of Sect. 631 et seq. German Civil Code. However German courts have held that in principle the contract according to which an architect or engineer carries out design, supervision and contract administration services must also be regarded as a contract for work and services.[1] Hence under a design and build contract the contractor owes an overall duty to carry out the design and works fit for purpose.

Additionally it is often the case that the governing law comprises fundamental risk allocation rules which are not easy to identify because most of the time they are not expressly mentioned in statutory law. German complementary terms of contract first of all often mirror a Leitmotiv by virtue of which the parties are not allowed to derogate through the use of standard terms of contract (see Sect. 307 German Civil Code). Secondly fundamental risk allocation rules may be included in some of the legal provisions. For example Sect. 645 German Civil Code contains the rule that the risk of differing site conditions is borne by the Employer. English law includes the rule according to which the Employer is only liable for those events which cause delay and cost which are within his power to control or are otherwise stated to be at his risk.[2] Another common law position on the apportionment of risk, in the absence of express terms to the contrary, is the following:[3]

> not to impose on one side all the perils of the transaction, or to emancipate one side from all chances of failure, but to make each party promise in law as much, at all events, as it must have been in the contemplation of both parties that he should be responsible for in respect of those perils or chances.

7.1.4 Interpretation

The contract is the law of the parties. It is drawn up to define what is required to be carried out in return for what payment. Thus the contract defines the duties and responsibilities to be undertaken by the parties to it. If the contract wording is either incomplete or ambiguous its terms must be interpreted. FIDIC contracts contain some guidance for interpretation. First of all reference has to be made to the definitions in Clause 1. All defined terms are written with a capital letter. Those terms which are used with capital letters shall be understood in the sense given to them by the definitions in Clause 1. However, a large number of FIDIC contract terms are not explicitly defined but are otherwise well known in common law jurisdictions. The meaning of some terms has been subject to much authority in England and is therefore not easy to translate. Examples of those terms are:

- *Reasonable:* The *reasonable man* or *reasonable person* standard is a widely used common law legal expression. The "reasonable person" is a hypothetical

---

[1] [82] BGHZ 100; BGH [2000] NJW 1196.
[2] See Fairweather & Co Ltd v. London Borough of Wandsworth (1988) 12 BLR 40.
[3] Moorcock, The (1889) 14 PD 64.

individual who is intended to represent the notion of an "average" man. The ability of this hypothetical individual to understand or treat matters is consulted in the process of making decisions of law. The test, "How would a reasonable person act under the same or similar circumstances" is a feature often used within contract law and tort law.

- *Fit for purpose:* means that the contractor is under a duty to achieve a specific result and that he not only liable for due skill and care.
- *Workmanship:* means that there is standard according to which the works have to be carried out.
- *Dispute:* is not just a word, which means that any difference can be brought before a court. Firstly a dispute must be constituted. The court will have to examine whether there is already a dispute in the legal sense of the word. There must for example be a claim which has been contested.

There is a strong presumption that English legal terms used in FIDIC contracts should be understood and used in the sense that the common law gives to them. Unfortunately it is quite often not easy to identify English legal terms and to distinguish them from non legal terms, especially for FIDIC users who have never had a great deal of previous experience with the Common Law.

Again, it must always be remembered that the FIDIC Conditions do not stand alone. They are embedded in the applicable law, the proper law of the contract. Hence the means and rules of interpretation vary from contract to contract, since as a rule the interpretation of contracts is governed by the proper law of the contract. The interpretation rules are not always the same and are seldom identical. Parties should be aware that there are substantial differences in the approach taken by different jurisdictions to the interpretation of contracts. Within a strict common law approach contracts shall be construed according to the plain and ordinary meaning of the words contained in it, without reference to extraneous circumstances such as prior negotiations or intentions of the parties. The "rule" that words must be given their ordinary and natural meaning means that the law does not easily accept that people have made linguistic mistakes, but on the other hand, if one would conclude from the background that something has gone wrong, the law will not attribute to the parties an intention which they plainly could not have had. The language cannot be read in a manner that "flaunts business common-sense".[4] However, English Judges do not, as under certain civil law systems, strive to give effect to the intentions of the parties. According to German law contracts have to be interpreted subject to the requirements of good faith, taking common usage into consideration. When interpreting a declaration of intent, the true intention is to be sought irrespective of the literal meaning of the declaration. Even though sect. 133 German Civil Code forbids a literal interpretation any interpretation has to be drawn from the literal meaning. Generally speaking, the common literal meaning is authoritative. Once having determined the literal meaning the interpreter shall then take into consideration the collateral circumstances. Hence he shall bear in mind the genesis

---

[4] Antaios Compania Naviera SA v. Salen Rederierna AB [1985] AC 191.

of the contractual relationship and the existing interests of the parties. In the event of doubt each interpretation shall come to a reasonable result. Thus German Courts are willing to look at past correspondence and conduct in order to ascertain the true intention of the parties and to reach a most reasonable result of interpretation having regard to the circumstances.

Finally Sub-Clause 1.2 gives some help to the parties and the Engineer.

7.2   Drafting a Contract

When drafting a contract with foreign elements a broad, philosophical difference in approach to contractual drafting has to be taken in mind. It is not simply that common law-derived contracts are usually longer and more detailed than civil law based contracts. It is more than that. Due to the fact that there is only a limited amount of statute law, common law practitioners will often attempt to create their own independent little contract world. The approach is to include statutes and case law in the terms of the contract if deemed useful or to circumvent it with great skill if considered a nuisance. Important terms will be defined and strictly used within the contract. Civil law practitioners on the other hand embed the contract into a grid of legal rules which consist of entire legal codifications. They will limit themselves to adjust the legal framework if possible. As a consequence contracts governed by civil law will be shorter than those governed by common law. Civil law practitioners will rely on implied terms and other provisions of the relevant codes (compare Hewitt 2005, note 20-13).

Typical features of a common law contract (Hill and King 2004):

- They are very long: a prominent corporate lawyer refers to "three pound acquisition agreement[s]".
- There is a great deal of explanation, qualification, and limitation in the language.
- There is a great deal of "legalese".
- The legalese is similar from agreement to agreement, but not exactly the same.
- More broadly, contracts of a particular type of transaction are similar in general coverage, but the specific language varies considerably from contract to contract.
- The initial drafts are relatively divergent, with, for instance, the buyer wanting extensive representations and the seller wanting to give many fewer, and highly qualified, representations; after a long series of negotiations, the parties end up in the middle.

An English style construction contract, like other commercial contracts, usually contains numerous obligations: some merely *administrative* or *part of the machinery*; some *preliminary* (e.g. the giving of notices and other conditions precedent); some ancillary and some are *substantive*. Non-compliance with those in the former categories either does not or is unlikely to give rise to claim for damages by the other party, not least because none will have been suffered , (or none discernible).

Failure to give a notice, if a condition precedent, will preclude a claim and avert a payment that might otherwise be made. Non-compliance may be beneficial not detrimental.[5]

Typical features of a German contract (Hill and King 2004):

- The agreements are much "lighter" – by some accounts, German agreements are one-half or two-thirds the size of otherwise comparable US agreements.
- There is much less explanation, qualification, and limitation in the language.
- There is much less legalese.
- The legalese is almost identical from contract to contract.
- Many provisions are quite similar from contract to contract.
- The initial drafts are far closer to one another than are the US drafts, with the parties ending up far closer to their starting positions.

The following comments on the drafting of international commercial contracts may be useful:

- Matters of principle, such as venue, applicable law, price, etc., should be discussed before starting the process of contract drafting. As any contract is embedded in a law system the draftsman should be aware of the fact that the applicable law can affect the contract. It therefore important to know at early stage which law will be applicable.
- It is helpful to use international soft law, such as the Unidroit Principles of International Commercial Contracts. The Unidroit Principles have been published by Unidroit at Rome, actually consisting of a more or less complete set of rules for all kind of contracts. As they are available in different languages they are very helpful when drafting a contract, because the understanding and content of each clause may be verified in different languages.
- It is useful to use standard clauses whenever possible because the other party will be familiar with it, which will help during negotiations and to save time. When using standard clauses or standard forms be reluctant to alter or change them. Ensure that the used standard clauses are coherent and remain coherent with the standard form when drafting Particular Conditions.
- In drafting clauses it is critical to use short sentences and sensible punctuation. Any wording should be clear and certain. Ambiguities in a clause are often construed by courts against the person who is trying to rely on it.
- If the draftsman uses a language other than his native language he should carefully verify the exact meaning of the used language, especially when the applicable law has been set in force in a different language. Sometimes the used terms have an exact legal meaning with which the draftsman is not familiar. Sometimes legal terms of the applicable law cannot be translated exactly into the ruling language.

---

[5] Masons (A Firm) v. WD King Ltd & Anor [2003] EWHC 3124 (TCC) (17 December 2003).

- Achieving the best result does not always mean to draft a contract which is heavily weighted in favour of one party. A reasonably balanced contract which covers all relevant points may be more appropriate.
- The draftsman should aim to use strictly identical wording. Any different wording will be interpreted by courts in a different way, because it will assume that different things are meant by different phrases. It is no mistake to repeat a sentence or words.
- Be vigilant for the impact of mandatory rules, which may be applicable. This may happen especially if the proper law of the contract is not the same as the local law of the site.
- Local legislation as to taxes, royalties, environment, currency transfer and employment should be taken into consideration.

7.3 General Observations as to the FIDIC Contract Documents

All FIDIC Books refer to definitions. Most definitions are those which are listed in Clause 1. However, the parties will also find definitions in other documents and even outside the contract. For example some of the FIDIC clauses refer to the Base date, which is defined in Sub-Clause 1.1.3.1 as being the date 28 days before the latest date for the submission of the tender. Some further definitions depend on the Letter of Tender, some on the Letter of Acceptance or the Contract Agreement and some on other contract documents, such as the Specifications and the Schedules.

The parties must also be aware of the fact that the General Conditions contain so-called fall-back clauses which need to be given effect by the parties. Care has therefore to be taken when completing the Appendix to Tender. Additionally, Sub-Clause 13.6 will only apply if a Daywork schedule has been included in the documents. Also the Sub-Clause 13.8 only applies if the adjustment data have been included in the Appendix to Tender. If parties fail to complete those data which are necessary for the application of fall back clauses, those clauses will not apply.

One of the most critical contract documents are the *Particular Conditions*, especially if they set aside provisions contained in the General Conditions and if they amend them. It is often the case that parties who are not familiar with the FIDIC risk allocation approach, the main FIDIC concepts, the underlying governing law, and the techniques on how to change and amend the FIDIC documents fail to put together a clear contract which is free from ambiguities and discrepancies. It is however critical for a contract to be clear and free from ambiguities and discrepancies. The clearer the contract is, the greater will be the parties' incentive to avoid or mitigate non-performance and disputes. If a contract is unclear, it will be very difficult to make rational decisions about avoiding or mitigating risks. Therefore it is strongly recommended to respect the following drafting general principles:

- Determine the applicable law and check the meaning of any terms and expressions in this context

- Avoid using any terms which have been translated into English without having cross checked their legal meaning
- Beware that FIDIC has adopted a number of Anglo-Saxon concepts, such as the principles of time at large, delay or liquidated damages, substantial performance, Engineer, etc.
- Remember that FIDIC defines many terms, which are capitalised and that a correct and careful application of defined terms is critical in order to avoid misunderstandings, ambiguities and discrepancies.
- Beware that FIDIC documents incorporate many cross references. Thus the deletion of a Sub-Clause may lead to complicated and time consuming disputes. For example, in Eastern Europe contractors encounter the problem that quite often Sub-Clause 20.2 to Sub-Clause 20.4 has been deleted, without having changed Sub-Clause 20.6. However Sub-Clause 20.6 presupposes that a DAB has decided upon the dispute before the dispute can be referred to arbitration.

Quite often the parties to a FIDIC contract ignore the Engineer's power to interpret the contract and to issue instructions in the event that discrepancies and ambiguities arise (see Sub-Clause 1.5 Red and Yellow Book and Sub-Clause 1.3 Green Book).

In addition FIDIC forms of contract are viewed as manuals that provide details of contract management tools. The Books contain mechanisms for prescribing and controlling the behaviour of the parties, in particular they require compliance with the reporting (see Sub-Clause 4.21) and communication rules (see Sub-Clause 1.3), the programming requirements (see Sub-Clause 8.3) and the claim procedures (see Sub-Clauses 3.5, 2.5 and 20.1). Reviewing and altering a FIDIC based contract means therefore not only to have a look on risk allocation rules and the obligations of the parties, but also on the management tools. Beware that the alteration of management rules may change the whole contractual system and can lead to unreasonable results. This will be the case if the Particular Conditions provide additional claims of the Employer without reference to Sub-Clause 2.5. Failure to do so may allow the Employer to withhold payments beyond the payment certificates which are issued by the Engineer.

7.4 Contract Documents Book by Book

7.4.1 Red Book

Assuming the traditional procurement route with the FIDIC *Red Book* 1999 edition standard form of contract and a bill of quantities then the contract documents in order of importance are as follows:

(a) The Contract Agreement (if any)
(b) The Letter of Acceptance

(c) The Letter of Tender
(d) The Particular Conditions
(e) These General Conditions
(f) The Specification
(g) The Drawings
(h) The Schedules and any other documents forming part of the Contract

The *Contract Agreement* (if any) as referred to in Sub-Clause 1.6, represents subject to the governing law, the legally binding agreement between the parties, which refers to all the documents which are incorporated into the contract. The *Letter of Acceptance* means the letter of formal acceptance as referred to in Sub-Clause 1.1.1.3. The *Letter of Tender* is defined in Sub-Clause 1.1.14, including the *Appendix to Tender* (see Sub-Clause 1.1.1.9) and covers important elements such as expected time for completion, access to the site, applicable law, ruling language, etc. The *Particular Conditions* as mentioned in Sub-Clause 1.5, which have to be drafted by the Employer according to the Guide for Preparation of Particular Conditions, cover important elements such as storage areas available to the Contractor, changes and amendments to the General Conditions, etc. The *Drawings* indicate the location, scope and design complexity of the works and show graphically the full extent of what is required to be constructed. They cannot readily represent quality – they therefore have cross-references to specification clauses which fully describe the expected quality of each element. The *Specification* details the quality required in the works. Quality may be specified by prescriptive or performance criteria. The *Schedules* may comprise a *Bill of Quantities*. *Bill of Quantities* means more or less a list of items giving brief identifying descriptions and estimated quantities of the work comprised in a Contract. This definition rightly infers that the bill should be brief and should not unnecessarily repeat information contained elsewhere on the drawings or the specification. Because of the uncertain nature of much of civil engineering work at the billing stage the quantities are correctly defined as "estimated", and in the majority of contracts the works will be remeasured on site to reflect the true quantities actually required. It should be noted that bills of quantities, while desirable, are not essential contract documents. However the other three documents are essential in order to fully detail what is contractually required.

7.4.2 Green Book

Assuming the traditional procurement route with the FIDIC *Green Book* 1999 edition standard form of contract then the contract documents in order of importance are as follows:

The Contract as referred to in Sub-Clause 1.1.1 represents the legally binding agreement between the parties. Pursuant to Sub-Clause 1.3 the documents forming the *Contract* are to be taken as mutually explanatory of one another. The priority of the documents shall be in accordance with the order as listed in the Appendix. The Appendix as included in the Book lists the documents as such:

(a) The Agreement
(b) Particular Conditions
(c) General Conditions
(d) The Specification
(e) The Drawings
(f) The Contractor's tendered design
(g) The Bill of quantities

According to Sub-Clause 1.1.1 Contract means the Agreement and the other documents listed in the Appendix, which is included in the Book. *Specification* means the document as listed in the Appendix, including Employer's requirements in respect of design to be carried out by the Contractor, if any, and any variation to such document. *Drawings* means the Employer's drawings of the Works as listed in the Appendix, and any Variation to such drawings.

7.4.3 Yellow Book

Assuming the Design and Build procurement route with the FIDIC *Yellow Book* 1999 edition standard form of contract and Employer's Requirements then the contract documents in order of importance are as follows:

(a) The Contract Agreement (if any)
(b) The Letter of Acceptance
(c) The Letter of Tender
(d) The Particular Conditions
(e) These General Conditions
(f) The Employer's Requirements
(g) The Schedules
(h) The Contractor's Proposal and any other documents forming part of the Contract

The *Contract Agreement* (if any) as referred to in Sub-Clause 1.6, represents subject to the governing law, the legally binding agreement between the parties, which refers to all the documents which are incorporated into the contract. The *Letter of Acceptance* means the letter of formal acceptance as referred to in Sub-Clause 1.1.1.3. The *Letter of Tender* is defined in Sub-Clause 1.1.1.4, including the *Appendix to Tender* (see Sub-Clause 1.1.1.9) and covers important elements such as expected time for completion, access to the site, applicable law, ruling language, etc. The *Particular Conditions* as mentioned in Sub-Clause 1.5, which have to be drafted by the Employer according to the Guide for the Preparation of Particular Conditions, cover important elements such as storage areas available to the Contractor, changes and amendments to the General Conditions, etc. The *Employer's*

Requirements outline and define the purpose, scope, and/or design and/or other technical criteria, for the Works (see Sub-Clause 1.1.1.5). The *Schedules* as referred to in Sub-Clause 1.1.1.6 mean the documents entitled schedules, completed by the Contractor and submitted with the Letter of Tender. They may include data, lists and schedules of payments and/or prices. The *Contractor's Proposal* means, according to the definition in Sub-Clause 1.1.1.7 the document entitled proposal, which the Contractor submits with the Letter of Tender and covers the Contractor's *preliminary design*.

The term *preliminary design* is not defined. Thus the question arises as to what is meant by preliminary design. Sure, it has to be developed from the Employer's Requirements. The issue is that there is no clear definition of what is meant by Employer's Requirements. In essence the Requirements set out what the Employer requires from the Contractor. According to Sub-Clause 1.1.1.5 the Employer's Requirements specify the purpose, scope, and/or design and/or other technical criteria for the Works. The FIDIC Contracts Guide explains that the overall design may comprise three stages, the conceptual design (incorporated in the Employer's Requirements), the preliminary design (incorporated in the Proposal) and the final design to be made once the contract has been awarded. Hence, in principle the Employer's Requirements should describe the principle and basic design of the project on a functional basis (i.e. performance specification) and specify the purpose, scope and/or design and/or other technical criteria for the Works. But they may comprise much more than that. RIBA suggests that the Employer's Requirements should comprise 1:1000 plans, sections and elevations, 1:500 site layout, including critical setting out data, site extent, landscape design, fire compartments and escape routes, engineering services, plant spaces, drainage, etc.

However, it could be said that the Employer's Requirements do not define the particular Works which have to be carried out by the Contractor, because this document specifies (only) the purpose, scope, and/or design and/or other technical criteria, for the Works. Thus the Employer's Requirements set out the *key requirements* and *constraints* for the Works and do not describe the Works in detail. *Works* mean the Permanent Works and the Temporary Works, or either of them as appropriate. Pursuant to Sub-Clause 4.1 the Contractor shall design, execute and complete the Works in accordance with the Contract. However, which particular works have to be carried out depends on the design of the Contractor and the scope of works included in his contract. At this critical point an issue may arise, if the Employer divides the whole project into different lots. In this event the Employer's Requirements must carefully define the interfaces, otherwise discrepancies and ambiguities will arise.

Example: Supposed that a design and build contract for a waste treatment plant was awarded to Contractor A, apart from the "civil works", which was awarded to Contractor B. What exactly this entails must as a consequence be cleared up.

Thus what the Contractor's proposal will have to include will depend on the degree of specification and the manner in which the Requirements are detailed. On the other hand it is not intended that the Contractor shall prepare a detailed design at tender stage without knowing whether the contract will be awarded to him or not.

It is therefore suggested that the preliminary design referred to in Sub-Clause 1.1.17 is something between an Outline Proposal according to Work Stage C of the RIBA Plan of Work for the procurement of the Contractor's Proposal and a detailed proposal as referred to in RIBA Work Stage D for a fully designed building project or even less than that. It is therefore strongly recommended that the instructions to tenderers indicate the extent of detail required. By doing this the Employer should take in consideration that the Contractor's Proposal becomes part of the contract documents whilst the final design remains under the full responsibility of the Contractor.

However, in accordance with Sub-Clause 1.5 the so-called Proposal, even though it has been developed from the Employer's Requirements, has lower priority than the Requirements. Thus in the event that the Contractor's Proposal includes details which deviate from the Requirements the Contractor must follow the Requirements instead of the Proposal. If the Contractor intends to follow his Proposal he must firstly request an instruction from the Engineer, who has the power to change the priority of documents. As it is suggested that an instruction which changes the priority of the contractual documents in a way that a document of lower priority overrules a document of higher priority constitutes a variation, the Engineer must carefully consider the consequences of such an instruction, in particular if he is under the duty to obtain prior approval from the Employer for any instructions which have an impact on the Contract Price.

7.4.4   Silver Book

Assuming the Design and Build procurement route with the FIDIC *Silver Book* 1999 edition standard form of contract and Employer's Requirements then the contract documents in order of importance are as follows:

(a) The Contract Agreement
(b) The Particular Conditions
(c) These General Conditions
(d) The Employer's Requirements
(e) The Tender and any other documents forming part of the Contract

The *Contract Agreement* as referred to in Sub-Clause 1.6, and being the main document under a Silver Book contract, represents subject to the governing law, the legally binding agreement between the parties, which refers to all the documents which are incorporated into the contract. There is in principle no *Letter of Acceptance*. The related definition has been deleted in the Silver Book. The *Tender* is defined in Sub-Clause 1.1.1.4. The so-called *Appendix to Tender* as referred to in Sub-Clause 1.1.1.9 Yellow Book, covering important elements such as expected time for completion, access to the site, applicable law, ruling language, etc., is missing in the Silver Book. It is suggested to include such data in the *Particular Conditions*. The *Particular Conditions* as mentioned in Sub-Clause 1.5, which have to be drafted by the Employer according to the Guide for the Preparation of Particular Conditions, cover additionally important elements such as storage areas available to the Contractor, changes and amendments to the General Conditions, etc. The *Employer's Requirements* outline and define the purpose, scope, and/or design and/or other technical criteria, for the Works (see Sub-Clause 1.1.1.3). *Schedules* as referred to in Sub-Clause 1.1.1.6 Yellow Book are not expressly defined in the Silver Book. However, they are important documents under the Silver Book as well and may include data, lists and schedules of payments and/or prices. Again, there is no definition for the *Contractor's Proposal* as referred to in Sub-Clause 1.1.1.7 Yellow Book. It is however suggested that the Contractor submits a preliminary design.

The term *preliminary design* is not defined. Thus the question arises as to what is meant by preliminary design. Sure, it has to be developed from the Employer's Requirements. The issue is that there is no clear definition of what is meant by Employer's Requirements. In essence the Requirements set out what the Employer requires from the Contractor. According to Sub-Clause 1.1.1.3 the Employer's Requirements specify the purpose, scope, and/or design and/or other technical criteria for the Works. The FIDIC Contracts Guide explains that the overall design may comprise three stages, the conceptual design (incorporated in the Employer's Requirements), the preliminary design (incorporated in the Proposal) and the final design to be made once the contract has been awarded. Hence, in principle the Employer's Requirements should describe the principle and basic design of the project on a functional basis (i.e. performance specification) and specify the purpose, scope and/or design and/or other technical criteria for the Works. But they may comprise much more than that. RIBA suggests that the Employer's Requirements should comprise 1:1000 plans, sections and elevations, 1:500 site layout, including critical setting out data, site extent, landscape design, fire compartments and escape routes, engineering services, plant spaces, drainage, etc.

However, as already mentioned for the Yellow Book, it could be said that the Employer's Requirements do not define the particular Works which have to be carried out by the Contractor, because this document specifies (only) the purpose, scope, and/or design and/or other technical criteria, for the Works. Thus the Employer's Requirements set out the *key requirements* and *constraints* for the Works and do not describe the Works in detail. *Works* mean the Permanent Works and the Temporary Works, or either of them as appropriate. Pursuant to Sub-Clause 4.1 the Contractor shall design, execute and complete the Works in accordance with the Contract. However, which particular works have to be carried out depends on the design of the Contractor and the scope of works included in his contract. At this critical point an issue may arise, if the Employer divides the whole project into different lots. In this event the Employer's Requirements must carefully define the interfaces, otherwise discrepancies and ambiguities will arise.

Making use of the Silver Book requires an acceptance of a special risk allocation concept which requires both discipline and instinct from the draftsman. FIDIC points out that the Conditions of Contract for EPC/Turnkey Projects (the Silver Book) are not suitable for use in the following circumstances:

- If there is insufficient time or information for tenderers to scrutinise and check the Employer's Requirements or for them to carry out their designs, risk assessment studies and estimating (taking particular account of Sub-Clauses 4.12 and 5.1).
- If construction will involve substantial work underground or work in other areas which tenderers cannot inspect.
- If the Employer intends to supervise closely or control the Contractor's work, or to review most of the construction drawings.
- If the amount of each interim payment is to be determined by an official or other intermediary.

In the event of doubt the parties are advised to use the Yellow Book which is a more balanced contract form although also requiring a substantial amount of skill and care from the Contractor at pre-tender stage.

7.4.5 Gold Book

Assuming the design, build and operate procurement route with the FIDIC *Gold Book* 2008 edition standard form of contract and Employer's Requirements then the contract documents in order of importance are as follows:

(a) The Contract Agreement (if any)
(b) The Letter of Acceptance
(c) The Letter of Tender
(d) The Particular Conditions – Part A (Contract Data)
(e) The Particular Conditions – Part B (Special Provisions)
(f) These General Conditions
(g) The Employer's Requirements
(h) The Schedules
(i) The Contractor's Proposal and any other documents forming part of the Contract

The *Contract Agreement* (if any) as referred to in Sub-Clauses 1.6 and 1.1.11, represents subject to the governing law, the legally binding agreement between the parties, which refers to all the documents which are incorporated into the contract. The *Letter of Acceptance* means the letter of formal acceptance as referred to in Sub-Clause 1.1.48. The *Letter of Tender* is defined in Sub-Clause 1.1.49. This document no longer includes an Appendix to Tender, which was replaced by the Contract Data as referred to in Sub-Clause 1.1.14. It covers important elements such as expected time for completion, access to the site, applicable law, ruling language, etc., and became part A of the Particular Conditions. The *Particular*

Conditions as mentioned in Sub-Clause 1.5, which have to be drafted by the Employer according to the Guide for the Preparation of Particular Conditions, cover additional important elements such as storage areas available to the Contractor, changes and amendments to the General Conditions, etc. The *Employer's Requirements* outline and define the purpose, scope, and/or design and/or other technical criteria, for the Works (see Sub-Clause 1.1.34). The *Schedules* as referred to in Sub-Clause 1.1.68 mean the documents entitled schedules, completed by the Contractor and submitted with the Letter of Tender. They may include data, lists and schedules of payments and/or prices. The *Contractor's Proposal* means, according to the definition in Sub-Clause 1.1.20 the document entitled proposal, which the Contractor submits with the Letter of Tender and covers the Contractor's *preliminary design*. The *Operating Licence* as mentioned in Sub-Clause 1.1.54 represents a licence referred to in Sub-Clause 1.7 by which the Employer grants a royalty-free licence to the Contractor to operate and maintain the Plant during the Operation Service.

7.5   Contract Documents Manual

7.5.1   *Contract Agreement*

Drafting of a Contract Agreement is not always essential. A FIDIC Yellow Book and a FIDIC Red Book contract become effective upon receiving the Letter of Acceptance. However, when preparing the Contract Agreement and its components as referred to in Sub-Clause 1.5 Silver Book the following aspects should be considered:

* The Contract comprises all documents which are listed in Sub-Clause 1.5 as the case may be modified by the Particular Conditions or the Contract Agreement.
* Under a Silver Book Contract the Particular Conditions replace the Appendix to Tender as referred to in the Yellow Book.
* The Employer's Requirements play a pre-dominant role, because they have to be scrutinised prior to submission of tender. Whilst the Yellow Book allows for additional scrutiny at a later stage (see Sub-Clause 1.9 and 5.1) the Silver Book remains silent as to this issue.

Whilst under a Silver Book contract a Contract Agreement constitutes an essential element of the Contract, a Contract referring to either the Red or Yellow Book becomes effective upon receiving of the Letter of Acceptance. However, if the Parties find it more appropriate to sign a Contract Agreement, they are free to do so. A model form for a Contract Agreement is included in each FIDIC Book.

7.5.2 *Particular Conditions*

The Particular Conditions shall cover all project details and particularities including any modifications of the General Conditions, except those to be specified in the Appendix to Tender. Under a Silver Book contract all details otherwise contained in the Appendix to Tender must be covered by the Particular Conditions. The Silver Book comprises a Guidance for the Preparation of Particular Conditions, to which reference is made. However, most of the data included in the Appendix to Tender of the Yellow Book form must also be inserted in the Particular Conditions of a Silver Book contract, as there are:

Sub-Clause 1.1.2.2	Employer's name and address	
Sub-Clause 1.1.2.3	Contractor's name and address	
Sub-Clause 1.1.3.3, 8.2	Time for completion of the works	
Sub-Clause 1.1.3.7, 11.1	Defects notification period	
Sub-Clause 1.1.5.6	Sections	
Sub-Clause 1.3	Electronic transmission systems	
Sub-Clause 1.4	Governing law	
Sub-Clause 1.4	Ruling language	
Sub-Clause 1.4	Language for communications	
Sub-Clause 2.1	Time for access to the Site	[*Should be fixed with regard to Sub-Clause 8.1: Notification of commencement date*]
Sub-Clause 3.5	Declaration of dissatisfaction by contractor	[*Can be changed, for example instead of 14 days 21 days*]
Sub-Clause 4.2	Amount of performance security	% of the accepted contract price, in the currencies and proportions in which the contract price is
Sub-Clause 4.4	Notice of subcontractors	
Sub-Clause 5.4	Technical standards	
Sub-Clause 6.5	Normal working hours	
Sub-Clause 8.7	Delay damages for the works	% of the final Contract Price per day, in the currencies and proportions in which the Contract Price is payable
Sub-Clause 8.7	Maximum amount of delay damages	% of the final Contract Price
Sub-Clause 13.6	Daywork	The work shall be evaluated in accordance with the Daywork Schedule reference to which is made
Sub-Clause 13.8	Adjustments for changes in cost	[*Insert adjustment data*]
Sub-Clause 14.2	Total advance payment	
Sub-Clause 14.2	Number and timing of instalments	
Sub-Clause 14.2	Currencies and proportions	
Sub-Clause 14.2	Start repayment of advance payment	

Sub-Clause 14.2	Repayment amortisation of advance payment	
Sub-Clause 14.3 (c)	Percentage of retention	
Sub-Clause 14.3 (c)	Limit of retention money	
Sub-Clause 14.9	Percentage of retention for each section (if any)	
Sub-Clause 14.3	Minimum amount of interim payment	
Sub-Clause 14.15	Currencies of payment	
Sub-Clause 17.6	Limitation of liability	
Clause 18	Periods for submission of insurance	
Sub-Clause 18.1	Employer's insurance	
Clause 18.2 (d)	Maximum amount of deductibles per occurrence for insurance of the employer's risks	
Sub-Clause 18.3	Minimum amount of third party insurance	
Sub-Clause 20.1	Claim notification delay	*[Can be changed, for example instead of 28 days 21 days]*
Sub-Clause 20.2	Number of members of DAB: The DAB shall be:	One sole Member/adjudicator *Or:* A DAB of three Members
Sub-Clause 20.3	Appointment (if not agreed) to be made by	The President of FIDIC or a person appointed by the President
Sub-Clause 20.6	Any disputes shall be settled by Arbitral Court of the International Chamber of Commerce according to the Rules of Arbitration of the International Chamber of Commerce	
Sub-Clause 20.6	Arbitration language	
Sub-Clause 20.6	Seat of arbitration	The seat of arbitration shall be [. . .]

Some of the above-mentioned items are optional, such as changes to Sub-Clause 3.5 or Sub-Clause 20.1. Some of them require data, because otherwise the related Sub-Clause will not apply (see Sub-Clause 4.2, 13.6, 14.2, 18.2(d), 18.3). Sub-Clause 13.8 Silver Book other than Sub-Clause 13.8 Yellow Book does not expressly mention what happens if the Particular Conditions do not contain data for the adjustment of the Contract Price. It is however suggested, that it will not apply if the parties fail to insert the relevant data.

Under a Red or Yellow Book contract, where specific project details are specified in the Appendix to Tender or under a Gold Book contract where such details are specified in the Contract Data, Particular Conditions may be used for the adjustment of the General Conditions, if appropriate or necessary. A Guidance for the Preparation of Particular Conditions being included in each FIDIC Book provides for additional model clauses and/or recommendations as to the adjustment of the General Conditions. If any civil law is the governing law, adjustments may be essential.

7.5.3   Employer's Requirements

Under a Silver Book or Yellow Book Contract as well as under a Gold Book Contract the Contractor is in principle responsible for all design, workmanship and sequence of the works. When completed, the Works shall be fit for the purposes for which the Works are intended as defined in the Contract (see Sub-Clause 4.1). It can be seen from the above provisions that the Contractor is under an obligation to complete the design and then to complete the Works in accordance with that completed design, so that at the end of the day the Contractor hands over the Works which comply with the Employers' Requirements and the Contractor's Proposals or Contractor's documents, as the case may be.

In other words, the underlying philosophy of the Yellow Book, Silver and Gold Book contract is that the Contractor is responsible for satisfying the Employer's Requirements, which must therefore be the principal document. In addition, under the Silver Book at Sub-Clause 5.1 the Contractor is deemed to have scrutinised, prior to Base Date, the Employer's Requirements. The Employer shall not be responsible for any error, inaccuracy or omission of any kind in the Employer's Requirements. In view of this added responsibility taken on by Contractors who design and build the works for a particular project, caution must be exercised from the outset. From the point of view of the Employer care must be taken that this clear risk allocation will be maintained, when preparing the tender documents, including the Employer's Requirements. Again, when drafting the documents care should be exercised to avoid any possible conflict with the other contract documents.

Employer's Requirements means the document entitled Employer's Requirements, as included in the Contract, and any additions and modifications to such document in accordance with the Contract. Such document specifies the purpose, scope, and/or design and/or other technical criteria, for the Works (Sub-Clause 1.1.1.5). The Employer's Requirements shall state the parts of the Works which are to be designed by the Contractor and the criteria which such designs must adhere to. Such criteria could comprise details of the cubes, dimensions, form, geometry, specifications, codes of practise, standards and environmental details. Care should be taken to not include method statements and to leave full responsibility as to the choice of methods with the Contractor. He shall then subject to Sub-Clause 8.3 lit. d provide a general description of the methods which he intends to adopt. The reason for this is to allow the Engineer or Employer as the case may be to check that the proposed methods of construction will not have a negative effect on the intended quality or purpose. The purpose of this document is to impose obligations on the Contractor. US courts have held that performance specifications dictate an ultimate result that a contractor must achieve, leaving the contractor with the discretion to determine the means to achieve that result.[6] However, if design specifications set forth in detail the materials that a contractor must use and the manner in which the contractor is to employ the materials under a particular

---

[6]Big Chief Drilling Co v. United States, 26 Cl. Ct. 1276 (1992).

contract, the contractor has virtually no discretion to deviate from these details, and must follow them like a road map.[7]

The Employer's Requirements are intended to specify the purpose, scope and/ or design and/or other criteria, for the Works. Under the Contract, the Contractor is required to execute the design and the Works in accordance with the Contract documents. They include these Requirements, the Schedules and the Proposal, with the Employer's Requirements having priority under Sub-Clause 1.5 of the Conditions of Contract. The project brief should define the site and the works which may require drawings to be included. All relevant criteria which are to govern the works including quality and performance requirements should be provided.

Under a Gold Book contract the Employer's Requirements include Operation Management Requirements. The operation of the plant has to be done in compliance with the Operation Management Requirements and the Operation Maintenance Plan. The Employer is only responsible for the delivery of any raw materials (Sub-Clause 10.4 Gold Book). During the Operation Service Period the Contractor shall achieve the production outputs required under the terms of the Contract (Sub-Clause 10.7 Gold Book). Failure to achieve the production outputs may lead to claims of the Employer and/or the Contractor subject to the independent audit. Any further detail as to the operational duty has to be put in the Employer's Requirements and in the Operation and Maintenance Plan.

Two contrasting approaches to contract strategy and drafting Employer's Requirements, applicable to high-quality commercial schemes and buildings with a lower technical content, illustrate the options available to the employer:

- Employer's Requirements drafted for projects where the contractor has limited influence over design development.
- Concise, functional requirements, with an indication of only critical areas of design.

Both, the Yellow Book and the Silver Book follow the second route. The Silver Book Guidance for the Preparation of Particular Conditions as well as the Yellow Book Guidance clearly indicate that the Employer's Requirements should specify the particular specifications for the completed Works on a functional basis, including detailed requirements on quality and scope.

It is critical to understand that under a FIDIC Yellow Book or Silver Book or even Gold Book contract the Employer's Requirements shall define the full range of works and design to be carried out by the Contractor against the agreed Contract Price, which is a lump sum price. Hence in principle the Contractor will have to complete a whole work. The contract includes the promise to provide everything indispensably necessary to complete the whole works, even though not expressly specified or wrongly stated in the tender documents. It is however sometimes a

---

[7] J.L. Simmons Co v. United States, 188 Ct. Cl. 684 (1969).

difficult question of construction to determine whether the contractor has promised to complete a whole work. If for example bills of quantities are incorporated in the contract or if drawings or descriptions comprise information with considerable precision it can be argued that the contract limits the obligation of the contractor to works expressly described in such bills of quantities, description or drawings (see Furst and Ramsley 2006, note 4-027).

Unfortunately too often the Employer carries out much detailed design work prior to tender which restricts the post award options available to the Contractor to develop the design, to choose the appropriate methods of workmanship and to plan the sequence and timing of each stage of work, although it is not unknown that FIDIC design and build forms work best when the Employer's Requirements are kept to the bare minimum of detail commensurate with achieving the Employer's aims, thereby affording the maximum degree of flexibility to the Contractor in complying with the contract. Excessive design work carried out by the Employer at pre-contract stage and too detailed Employer's Requirements can cause difficulties in determining the responsibilities of each of the parties once the contract has been awarded. In fact detailed Employer's Requirements give the Employer full control over design. Under this approach the design is completed to a high level of detail by or on behalf of the Employer before tender. In this event the Contractor's design contribution is generally limited to working drawings and completion of the design of some specialist packages. By this the design responsibility becomes re-shifted to the Employer. It must be emphasised that this full responsibility has a price. Each change to the Employer's Requirements constitutes a Variation under Clause 13, having an effect on both Time for Completion and on cost.

Thus great skill and care is required by the draftsman who prepares the project brief on behalf of the Employer when specifying the project requirements. The terminology used should not be too detailed in case it reduces the Contractor's design responsibility, which is not after all the intention.

However, it is critical that the Employer's Requirements document clearly communicates material standards, workmanship standards, performance standards, aesthetic intent and functional requirements. The Employer's Requirements needs to be responsive to this approach to describing the project, the designer's role and risk transfer to the Contractor. Where the design is complex, the emphasis is on transferring design, cost and programme risk to the Contractor.

The following recommendations should be followed:

- The Employer's requirements shall contain a comprehensive definition of the critical item to be developed, including a specification of the minimum critical item design and construction standards that have general applicability and are applicable to major classes of equipment
- The Employer's Requirements shall define in a comprehensive way which elements of design are prescriptive and which require completion by the Contractor
- The Employer's Requirements shall describe dimensional and cube limitations

- The Employer's Requirements shall state security criteria and health and safety criteria
- The Employer's Requirements shall contain specifications as necessary for particular materials and processes to be utilized in the design of any critical item.
- The Employer's Requirements shall specify the Contractor's Documents which must be submitted to the Employer for review and/or approval. If appropriate the review period shall be indicated.
- The Employer's Requirements should make no reference to the Tenderers, and should not specify actions which take place prior to award of the Contract.
- The Employer's Requirements must describe the process of delivery so they may need to go beyond a typical preliminaries document.
- The Employer's Requirements shall collate a comprehensive and consistent set of documentation.
- The Employer's Requirements should only permit information, which is relevant to the Contractor to be included therein, rather than all associated project documentation, which can create ambiguity.

Moreover under a Yellow Book contract the following items shall be specified in the Employer's Requirements:

2.1: Definition of conditions of access to the Site
4.20: Specification of Employer's Materials
4.6: Specification of co-ordination requirements
5.2: Documents to submit for review and approval
5.2: Delay for review and approval
5.1: Specification of experiences and qualifications of the designers
5.4 Specification of Technical Standards
5.5: Specification of training
5.6: Specification of as built drawings
5.7: Specification of maintenance manuals
6.1: Specification concerning personnel
9.1: Specification of testing procedures

Under a Gold Book contract the Employer's Requirements usually include *general descriptions, outline drawings, performance specifications, applicable codes of practice* and where necessary *detailed specifications, provisions of the Operation Service. The following items shall be specified in the Employer's Requirements:*

1.7 Operating Licence
1.12 Contractor's Use of Employer's Documents (Intellectual Property Rights)
1.14 Compliance with Laws (Permision being obtained by the Employer)
4.1 Contractor's General Obligations (Intended Purposes for which the Works are required)
4.5 Nominated Subcontractors
4.6 Co-operation

4.7 Setting Out
4.9 Quality Assurance
4.10 Site Data
4.18 Protection of the Environment
4.20 Employer's Equipment and Free-Issue Materials
4.21 Progress Reports
5.1 General Design Obligations (if Employer's Requirements include an outline
    design – clarification of suggestion or request)
5.2 Contractor's Documents
5.4 Technical Standards and Regulations
5.5 As-Built Drawings (5.6 Operation and Maintenance Manuals)
7.1 Manner of Execution
7.4 Testing
8.3 Programme
8.7 Handback Requirements
10.4 Delivery of Raw Materials
11.1 Testing of the Works (1.1.76 on Completion of Design-Build, 1.1.77 to
     Contract Completion)
11.9 Procedure for Tests Prior to Contract Completion
17.12 Risk of Infringement of Intellectual and Industrial Property Rights

A clear and careful distinction must be drawn between performance and prescriptive information, because in principle design specifications which set forth in detail the materials to be employed and the manner in which the work is to be performed put the Contractor under the obligation to follow them as one would a road map.[8] Whereas, performance specifications simply set forth an objective or end result to be achieved, and the Contractor may select the means of accomplishing the task. In the United States it is well-settled doctrine that when a government specification does not require a certain method of performance, the contractor is entitled to perform by its chosen manner or method,[9] where it is stated:

> [W]hen a contract prescribes the desired end but not the means of accomplishing that end, it is within the contractor's discretion to select the method by which the contract will be performed. A Government order rejecting the proposed method and requiring the contractor to perform in some other specified manner denies the contractor the opportunity to exercise a valid option as to the method of performance and changes the contract, justifying an equitable adjustment for additional costs incurred thereby.

The typical differences between performance criteria and prescription criteria to be alternatively included in the Employer's requirements are listed below in a comparative schedule:

---

[8] Big Chief Drilling Co v. United States, 26 Cl. Ct. 1276 (1992).
[9] See North Star Alaska Housing Corp v. United States, 30 Fed. Cl. 259, 285 (1993).

Specification type	Prescription
1. General remarks Performance criteria (results specification) It should be clearly indicated what is required, but not how to do it. Again limiting a contractor to specific materials, workmanship, parts, etc., should be avoided. Instead the Requirements can prohibit certain materials, processes, or parts when the Employer has certain quality, reliability, or safety concerns	Detailed Requirements include "how to" and specific design and method requirements. The Requirements should contain as many performance requirements as possible. However they shall not conflict with detail requirements
2. Specification type *Open specifications* (meaning to describe a result without naming a single supplier of goods or submitting a supply list) *Exclusive specifications* (meaning to prohibit classes of goods or methods of working prohibited) *Negative specifications* (implying acceptance of those items which are not expressly prohibited) *Manufacturers' specifications* shall be avoided because they are bound to be of the closed type	*Closed specifications* (meaning that the description will offer no alternative; it is absolute) *Restricted specifications* (meaning a statement of a range or type within which the contractor can choose to meet the specification requirements)
3. Performance criteria The Requirements should describe the capacity, performance or function of the plant or project and indicate the performance benchmarks of it. Examples may be the requirements for power consumption, chemical consumptions, raw material consumptions, noise levels, quality and quantity of final outputs	In addition the Requirements shall indicate in detail how to achieve the performance criteria
4. Design It is critical to respect the design responsibility of the contractor. Indication of "how to" or specific design requirements should be strictly avoided	The requirements should include "how to" and specific design requirements. It is common use to specify exact parts and components
5. Physical Characteristics Indicate only particulars to the extent necessary for interface, interoperability, environment in which the project or plant must operate, or human factors. Includes the following as applicable or as the case may be: overall dimension limits, cube limits, general standards which must be applied to the design or execution of the works	In addition the requirements should give specifics as to weight, size, dimensions, etc., for plant or project and component parts. Usually detailed design criteria are added

6. Interface Requirements	Interface requirements are critical for both types of Employer's Requirements. In particular if the Employer wishes to divide the works in lots, it is critical to clearly indicate and describe the interfaces in order to ensure interoperability and interchangeability	
7. Materials	The Requirements should not specify particular or specific materials; any choice and determination of materials should remain under the responsibility of the Contractor. If necessary or appropriate the Requirements may describe some material characteristic; e.g. average pumping rotation speed, fire resistance, life cycle, etc. It should be avoided to state detailed requirements except if unavoidable	The Requirements may include the specification of specific materials, usually in accordance with a specification or standard
8. Processes and methods	The Requirements should not indicate any requirements. If any, they should be unique and unavoidable	The Requirements often specify exact processes and detailed procedures to be followed by the Contractor in order to ensure the achievement of a specific result; for example, annealing, machining and finishing, soldering, tempering and welding procedures
9. Parts	The Requirements shall not require specific parts	The Requirements indicate which screws, fasteners, electronic piece parts, cables, fittings, sheet stock, etc., shall be used
10. Construction, Fabrication, and Assembly	The Requirements should only specify a minimum number of requirements	The Requirements describe the steps and methods involved or references procedures which must be followed; they also describe how individual components are assembled, connected or fixed
11. Operating Characteristics	None, except very general descriptions, if appropriate	The Requirements describe in detail how the plant shall work
12. Workmanship	The Requirements should only specify a minimum number of requirements	The Requirements specify standards, steps or procedures, as the case may be
13. Performance	The Requirements indicate performance characteristics in quantitative terms, e.g. output per hour in tons. In addition, the conditions (winter, summer, etc.) under which the requirements must be met should be indicated. Minimum values should be stated for each requirement, e.g. mean time between replacement	Quite often the Employer refers to a known reliable design

| 14. Maintainability | The Requirements shall specify quantitative maintainability criteria such as life cycle and probably maintenance cycles. It may also comprise mean and maximum downtime, mean and maximum repair time, mean time between maintenance actions, the ratio of maintenance hours to hours of operation, limits on the number of people and level of skill required for maintenance actions, or maintenance cost per hour of operation | The requirements often indicate how preventive maintainability requirements shall be met. Again, they often specify exact designs to accomplish and reduce maintenance efforts and cost. Again they often define the required or available staff and pre-determined replacement periods or sequences. They refer sometimes to requirements of maintenance operators |
| 15. Environmental Requirements | The requirements include requirements for humidity, temperature, shock, vibration, soundproofing, etc., and requirement to obtain evidence of failure or mechanical damage | No additional information required |

However, it is obvious that the Employer must at least be responsible for defining what he wants to procure, even if it is expressed in performance terms rather than in prescriptive terms, as with a technical specification. This is recognised by the Silver Book General Conditions in Sub-Clause 5.1 by providing that:

> However, the Employer shall be responsible for the correctness of the following portions of the Employer's Requirements:
>
> (a) Definition of intended purposes for the Works or any parts thereof
> (b) Criteria for testing/performance of completed Works
> (c) Any other portions which are stated as being the responsibility of the Employer

FIDIC itself recommends the following items to be included in the Employer's Requirements:

1.8 Number of copies of Contractor's Documents
1.13 Permissions being obtained by the Employer
2.1 Phased possession of foundations, structures, plant or means of access
4.1 Intended purposes for which the Works are required
4.6 Other contractors (and others) on the Site
4.7 Setting-out points, lines and levels of reference
4.14 Third parties (Yellow Book only)
4.18 Environmental constraints
4.19 Electricity, water, sewage, gas and other services available on the Site
4.20 Employer's Equipment and free-issue material
5.1 Criteria for design personnel
5.2 Contractor's Documents required, and whether for approval
5.4 Technical standards and building regulations
5.5 Operational training for the Employer's Personnel
5.6 As-built drawings and other records of the Works
5.7 Operation and maintenance manuals
6.6 Facilities for Personnel
7.2 Samples
7.3 Off-site inspection requirements (Silver Book only)
7.4 Testing during manufacture and/or construction
9.1 Tests on Completion
9.4 Damages for failure to pass Tests on Completion
12.1 Tests after Completion
12.4 Damages for failure to pass Tests after Completion
13.5 Provisional Sums (Yellow Book only)

It can be summarised that drafting the Employer's Requirements should be understood as an opportunity for the Employer to package a project in a way that optimises project progress. Preparing Employer's Requirements that meet the demands of project monitors, funders, future users with regard to audit trails and availability of warranties, saves time and effort further down the line.

By the way, it should be reiterated that FIDIC Silver Book at Sub-Clause 5.1 passes to the Contractor full responsibility for the accuracy and completeness of the Employer's Requirements. The Employer is expressly stated not to be responsible for any error, inaccuracy or omission in the Employer's Requirements. The Employer remains only responsible for the definition of the intended purpose of the Works and the criteria for testing/performance of completed Works. A less severe provision for responsibility for the Employer's Requirements is to be found at Sub-Clause 5.1 of the Yellow Book. This allows the Contractor within a specified period after Notice of the Commencement Date, to notify the Engineer of any error, fault or defect in the Employer's Requirements. The Engineer then decides whether to issue a variation. In this event the Contractor is entitled to extension of time (Sub-Clause 8.4) and adjustment of the Contract Price, unless the error was one which an experienced contractor would have discovered before submitting his Tender, had he used reasonable skill and care. The Silver Book therefore clearly envisages that the Contractor will carry out a rigorous check of the Employer's Requirements before submitting his tender and take the risk of any errors whether it is reasonable or not for the Contractor to identify the errors.

Hence the Contractor should be aware that where the Employer supplies any part, small or substantial, of the design, the terms of the Silver Book become little less than a required guarantee from the Contractor of the Employer's design for these parts (Huse 2002, p. 210; Wallace 1999, pp. 7–9). However, under the terms of Sub-Clause 5.1 lit (a) to (d) the Employer is responsible for the correctness of:

(a) Portions, data and information which are stated in the Contract as being immutable or the responsibility of the Employer
(b) Definitions of intended purposes of the Works or any parts thereof
(c) Criteria for the testing and performance of the completed Works
(d) Portions, data and information which cannot be verified by the Contractor except as otherwise stated in the Contract

Indeed, in particular paragraph (d) may be used by Contractors in order to avoid liability otherwise imposed by Sub-Clauses 4.10 and 4.12 (Huse 2002, p. 210). This paragraph was added due to pressure from Contractors (Corbett 2000, p. 269). But what does this subparagraph mean? It could be argued that it constitutes a warranty. But being responsible for something does not automatically mean to be liable for something. However, it follows from the wording of the paragraph that the Employer is not only responsible for the data but for its correctness. It is suggested that having responsibility for correctness means being under the obligation to provide correct data. It is therefore submitted that Sub-Clause 5.1 includes a warranty by the Employer to provide correct data. If he fails to do so he may become liable for breach of contract subject to the proper law of the contract. However, as Mr Corbett (2000, p. 269) has pointed out Sub-Clause 5.1 lit. (a) to (c) does not grant much of a relief to the Contractor because the purpose and performance criteria are unlikely to be "wrong". The issue of what cannot be verified by the Contractor can easily be overcome by giving enough time for of the purposes of scrutiny and verification. If however the Employer does not provide sufficient or reasonable time for the purposes of scrutiny and verification there will be a veritable risk for the Employer having not prepared correct data. The Contractor will then be protected against incorrect portions, data and information which could not be verified at tender stage when some allowance could be made irrespective of the date when the Contractor discovers the error, mistake or incorrectness (see Corbett 2000, p. 269). However the issue of what cannot be verified may be complex. The wording of lit. (d) does not give any guidance. Does the wording mean that the Contractor must show evidence that it was impossible to verify the relevant portions, data and information or will it be sufficient to show that he was simply unable to verify the portions, data and information to the extent what was practicable with regard to cost and time. It is suggested that the use of the terms "cannot be verified" implies the understanding that the Contractor was not in the position to carry out further investigations and scrutiny efforts irrespective of what was reasonable or practicable. According to Sub-Clause 4.10 Silver Book the Contractor shall be responsible not only for the interpretation of data which were made available to him but also to verify them. Other than under the Yellow Book the Contractor's responsibility of verification is not limited to what was practicable (taking account of cost and time). Even though he may not have much time for scrutiny and verification according to Sub-Clause 4.11 he will be deemed to have obtained all necessary information as to risks, contingencies and other circumstances which may influence or affect the Works. By consequence the escape clause in Sub-Clause 5.1 lit. (d) will only apply if the Contractor was not in the position to verify the relevant portions, data or information. This may include the argument that having regard to the subject matter of the obligation and the principle of good faith the expected efforts were manifestly disproportionate to the Employer's interest in performance (compare Section 275 paragraph 2 German Civil Code). Thus the circumstances of the case may excuse the Contractor, but the simple excuse that time was too short will not be a valid excuse as such. Following Mr. Corbett, it has been found that in practise many Employers, for example in the windmill industry, attempt to delete Sub-Clause 5.1 lit. (d).

7.5.4　Contractor's Proposal

The Tender Dossier issued to tenderers do not contain any document called a "Proposal". This document has to be prepared by each tenderer in accordance with the Instructions to Bidders and the Employer's Requirements. Clearly, the basic premise of the invitation to tender is to obtain acceptable and competitive tenders, each of which will include a Contractor's Proposal and shall detail how the Tenderer would execute the Works in accordance with the documents which form the Contract in order to satisfy the Requirements. In this respect, the Contractor's Proposal shall comply with the Employer's Requirements in the sense that the Works proposed therein shall comply with them.

According to Sub-Clause 1.1.1.7 Yellow Book the *Contractor's Proposal* means the document entitled proposal, which the Contractor submitted with the Letter of Tender, as included in the Contract. Such document shall include the Contractor's preliminary design, which is a statement of the design fundamentals (supported by drawings) together with a more or less detailed specification of the Works (see Trickey and Hackett 2001, note 8.1.7 as to JCT 1998 WCD).

Sub-Clause 1.1.1.7 Yellow Book does not appear in the Silver Book. However, it is intended that the Contractor submits a design proposal together with his tender, which will become included in the Contract according to Sub-Clause 1.5 lit. e.

According to Sub-Clause 1.1.20 Gold Book the Contractor's Proposal means the document entitled proposal, which the Contractor submitted with the Letter of Tender, as included in the Contract.

It is sometimes argued under the Yellow Book that the Employer accepts the Contractor's Proposal, which forms part of the contract and therefore takes precedence over the Employer's Requirements. However, this is not true, because it is free from doubt that Sub-Clause 1.5 makes the Employer's Requirements the prevailing determinant of all kind of design, standard of materials and workmanship.

If any part of the contractor's design does not comply with the Employer's Requirements, the Employer's Requirements will prevail. Any change to the Employer's Requirements provided by the Contractor for his design which is made at his request or to comply with other Requirements provided by the Employer is not a Variation. If the Contractor submits a proposal for a change to its design, then it has to submit the particulars under Sub-Clause 13.2 Silver Book for the Employer to accept or reject. Whether such a proposal, if accepted, constitutes a variation will depend on whether the proposal changes the Employer's Requirements. In principle this will be the case, if and when according to an instruction of the Employer or the Engineer, if any, a document of lower priority as referred to in Sub-Clause 1.5 must be obeyed (see Totterdill 2006, p. 94). But there is an issue. If the Contractor's Proposal in the sense of Sub-Clause 1.1.1.7 which becomes part of the contract does not comply with the Employer's Requirements, the latter still prevails. However, if in such a case the Employer or the Engineer decides that the Contractor should comply with his Proposal the question arises, whether this instruction constitutes a variation. It is arguable that this should be confirmed because the instruction changes the line of priority of the contract documents as referred to in Sub-Clause 1.5. However, instead it seems to be reasonable to apply Sub-Clause 5.1 by analogy, according to which Time for Completion shall not be extended and the Contract price shall not be adjusted if an experienced Contractor exercising due skill and care would have discovered the error, fault or other defect in the Employer's Requirements when examining the Site and the Employer's Requirements. Anyway the Contractor should have priced and made allowances for this change of the Employer's Requirements, of which he was already aware when submitting his tender.

All contractors should carefully consider who will finally assess their proposal. If the assessment panel is not composed of skilful and experienced members being incapable of understanding the technical details and to evaluate the economic values of the proposal, under competitive conditions it is not worth submitting an innovative and detailed technical proposal, because in most cases only the price will then be the decisive factor.

7.5.5 Payment Schedule

According to Sub-Clause 14.1 the Contractor is entitled to the payment of the Contract Price. According to common law and the entire contract principle ruled therein payment will only become due after completion of the Works.[10] The situation is similar in civil law (see Sect. 641 paragraph 1 German Civil Code).

The common law entire contract principle is "an essential and necessary sanction to discourage the deliberate breaking or abandonment of contracts, which would be absent if in such cases the builder was entitled to demand partial payment notwithstanding his own breach": see Wallace (1995, p. 476, 4.007).

The common law principles to be applied in relation to entire contracts and entire obligations were recently discussed in *GEC Marconi Systems Pty Ltd v. BHP Information Technology Pty Ltd* [2003] FCA 50 ; (2003) 128 FCR 1 at 164–165 by Finn J at [702]–[706] in the following terms:

1. An entire contract, or an entire obligation, is one in which, or in relation to which, the consideration for the payment of money or the rendering of some other counter performance is entire, indivisible and not severable: *Baltic Shipping Co v. Dillon*, [(1993) 176 CLR 344] at 350; *Steele v. Tardiani* (1946) 72 CLR 386 at 401; *Phillips v. Ellinson Brothers Pty Ltd* (1941) 65 CLR 221 at 233ff.

2. If a contract or an obligation is entire its complete performance is a condition precedent to payment or counter performance: Phillips v Ellinson Brothers Pty Ltd, above; *Hoenig v. Isaacs* [1952] 2 All ER 176 at 181; see Seddon and Ellinghaus (2007, para. 26.13). The court has no power to apportion the consideration which, in the case of money, is thus regarded as a "lump sum": see generally Beale (1999, vol. 1, para. 22–030, p. 704)

3. The question whether a contract or an obligation is entire or is, in contrast, divisible, is a question of construction: *Ownit Homes Pty Ltd v. Batchelor* [1983] 2 Qd R 124 Hoenig v Isaacs, above. While building contracts … have commonly been regarded, prima facie, as entire or "lump sum" contracts: see *Gilbert-Ash (Northern) Ltd v Modern Engineering (Bristol) Ltd* [1974] AC 689 at 717; Beale (1999, vol. 2, para. 37–139); and see Halsbury's Laws of Australia (1998, vol. 3(2), pp. 65–1255); such contracts commonly provide to the contrary by, for example, apportioning the consideration: e.g. *Walsh v. Kinnear* (1876) 14 SCR (NSW) 434; but *Hyundai Heavy Industries Co Ltd v. Papadopoulos* [1980] 1 WLR 1129 where the contract provided both for the payment of instalments and for their refund if the contract was cancelled in specified circumstances.

The large expenditure which builders and contractors have to incur in carrying out the works which they have undertaken to construct renders it usual for the contract to provide for payments on account of the price during the construction of the works. The manner in which these payments on account are regulated varies according to the terms of the contract.[11] Sometimes the several instalments become due on the completion of particular stages of the work … ; sometimes the interim

---

[10] Modern Engineering (Bristol) Ltd v. Gilbert-Ash Northern [1974] AC 689.

[11] Tan Hung Nguyen v. Luxury Design Homes [2004] NSWCA 178.

payments are to be not less than a fixed sum ... ; or, again, at fixed periods, irrespective of amount ... .[12]

By contrast according to German law (see Sect. 632a Civil Code) the Contractor may demand payments according to actual progress of performance from the Employer for coherently definable parts of the work or service part. This also applies to required materials or building components that are specially prepared or supplied.

According to Sub-Clause 14.4 FIDIC expects the parties of the contract to include a Schedule of Payments in the contract. If the parties fail to do so, the Contractor shall submit non-binding estimates of the payments which he expects to become due during each quarterly period. However it is advisable for the method and periodicity of payments to be agreed between the Employer and the Contractor when negotiating the fee structure. It should be noted, if payment is being made in arrears, that the Contractor's basic payment will need to be increased to cover the interest costs of carrying a negative cash flow. Usually the parties agree to an advance payment according to Sub-Clause 14.2 in order to avoid this problem.

The FIDIC Guidance for the preparation of Particular Conditions recommends that the Schedule of Payments could be in one of the following forms:

(a) An amount (or percentage of the estimated final Contract Price) could be entered for each month (or other period) during the Time for Completion, which can prove unreasonable if the Contractor's progress differs significantly from the expectation on which the Schedule was based.
(b) The Schedule could be based on actual progress achieved in executing the Works, which necessitates careful definition of the payment milestones.

Therein two contrasting approaches illustrate the options available to the parties:

- Milestone payments
- Periodic payments

Milestones governing payment have largely displaced the old measure and value system, arguably to avoid the risk of non-performance and are usually combined with lump sum price agreements.

Quite often it is possible to specify clear milestones or activities within a project (for example, excavations, foundations, 10 km of railways, plant commissioning, completion of defects notification period, etc.) and to arrange for payment to be made in instalments as those milestones are achieved. However, disagreements and disputes may arise when the work required for a payment milestone is not clearly defined. Moreover the following issues must be taken into consideration:

- If the identifiable milestones or activities are spaced out too widely, the finance charges incurred by the Contractor in carrying a negative cash flow for a long

---

[12]Tan Hung Nguyen v. Luxury Design Homes [2004] NSWCA 178.

period may be inappropriate and unreasonable. In this case, a mechanism for identifying and quantifying interim progress should be identified, making payments as the work progresses through those interim stages.

- Using a milestone payment schedule may result in payment for specific work not being made for extended periods of time – i.e. not for the work as performed, but for the milestone task as (substantially) completed. This can result in payments not being made until 6–9 months after work is performed.

Periodic payments are quite a common although not always appropriate feature. The recommended practice is for invoices to be issued monthly for the work undertaken during the period. Periodic invoices may also be used in conjunction with progress payments when the invoice is issued for all milestones completed and/or measured progress achieved during the period.

For major projects it may also be appropriate to identify Sections. By this it will be avoided that the Employer combines milestones with delay damages which is not intended by FIDIC and in principle in contradiction with the concept of time at large and claims with regard to time extension.

It is sometimes suggested to create a bonus system for early completion, which can be included in the Schedule for Payments. The bonus system should be linked to "Work Stages" and not withstanding any provisions in the agreement the payment of bonuses should be clearly regulated. For early completion of the amount of work stipulated for any of the milestones, the bonus at the rate of ½% of contract price per week of early completion, subject to a maximum of 5% of contract price may be considered. The detailed formulation of the clause may be prepared on the basis of legal advice.

Finally the parties may include additional payment procedures to be followed in the Schedule for Payments.

7.5.6 *Drawings*

It is not intended but quite usual for the Employer's Requirements to already contain drawings. Care should be taken to avoid constraints on the Contractor's design responsibility. In the event that the drawings which are included to the Employer's Requirements contain more than site maps and a rough outline design it may therefore be wise to include a disclaimer.

Under a Red Book contract drawings are essential. According to Sub-Clause 1.1.1.6 Drawings means the drawings of the Works, as included in the Contract, and any additional and modified drawings issued by the Employer in accordance with the Contract. If they are not included in the tender documents they shall be issued in a timely manner. Sub-Clause 1.9 of the Red Book entitles the Contractor to additional time and cost (plus profit) if he suffers delay and/or incurs cost as a result of failure of the Engineer to issue drawings within a time which is reasonable.

7.5.7 Specifications and Bills of Quantities

According to Sub-Clause 1.5 a Red Book contract includes Specifications and Schedules. As covered by Sub-Clause 1.1.1.10 the Bill of Quantities means the documents so named which are comprised in the Schedules. It is worthwhile to note that according to Sub-Clause 12.2 lit. b the method of measurement shall be in accordance with the Bill of Quantities or other applicable Schedules. In order to avoid debate and disputes it is strongly recommended to disclose the method used for the purposes of establishment of any Bills of Quantities.

In the Red Book it is significant that the Employer makes the design. Thus the Specifications and Bills of Quantities should enable the Contractor to offer a price covering the entire quantities. Employers should take into account that the Accepted Contract Amount is subject to measurement and that changes in quantities may affect the Contract Price. For precaution reference is made to Sub-Clause 12.3.

7.5.8 Further Documents (Gold Book)

It is significant for the Gold Book that it includes the Operation Service. Thus a Gold Book contract includes particular documents for the purposes of the Operation Service. According to Sub-Clause 1.7, together with the Letter of Acceptance, the Employer shall issue to the Contractor the Operating Licence. Further the Schedules include an Asset Replacement Schedule meaning the schedule referred to in Sub-Clause 14.5 prepared by the Contractor covering the identification and timing of asset replacements. As mentioned in the Notes on the Preparation of Tender Documents the tender documents should include details of schedules and other information required from tenderers. Furthermore it is worthwhile to mention the handback requirements. This type of document not being defined by the Contract but referred to in Sub-Clause 8.7 also forms part of the Employer's Requirements. It is designed to include the requirements as to the Works in case of handover of the Works after the date of expiry of the Operation Service. Finally the Operation Management Requirements and the Operation and Management Plan must be mentioned. Both are designed to specify the Operation Service. Whilst the Operation Management Requirements forms part of the Employer's Requirements the Operation and Maintenance Plan meaning the plan for operating and maintaining the facility shall be submitted by the Contractor, agreed with the Employer and included in the Contract.

A veritable new feature beyond the needs resulting from the new scope of services is the Financial Memorandum as referred to in Sub-Clause 1.1.43, meaning the document which details the Employer's financial arrangements and which is attached to or forms part of the Employer's Requirements. According to Sub-Clause 1.4 it is intended to give detailed information about the Employer's financial arrangements including the provision of the Asset Replacement fund.

7.5.9   Dispute Adjudication Agreement

Since the introduction of the FIDIC Orange Book (Conditions of Contract for Design-Build and Turnkey) in 1995 under the task group chair of Axel Jaeger all FIDIC Books comprise clauses concerning the resolution of disputes by a Dispute Adjudication Board. A special form of agreement is annexed to the Books, which must be executed. If the parties agree – as recommended by the Silver Book and the Yellow Book – to an ad hoc DAB, the Dispute Adjudication Agreement will have to be executed if a dispute arises. If the parties agree – what seems to be reasonable in order to ensure the benefit of the dispute avoiding function of the DAB – to a permanent DAB, the Dispute Adjudication Agreement shall be executed within reasonable time after the contract has been awarded or even before. The Red Book and the Gold Book already provide for a permanent DAB.

Again, at tender stage some preliminary steps as to dispute adjudication must be carried out. Either the Appendix to Tender or the Particular Conditions should indicate a list of eligible adjudicators and/or a nominating body in the event of failure to reach agreement as to the adjudicator(s).

7.5.10   Guarantees

In most cases the Employer will insist on obtaining a Performance Security as provided in Sub-Clause 4.2. FIDIC recommends special forms of Performance Securities in the Appendix to each Book. It is quite common for the Employer to require an on demand guarantee as proposed in Annex C of the Books. It is however recommended that a surety bond as referred to in Annex D should be used. On demand guarantees are quite a dangerous instrument due to the fact that in principle the beneficiary becomes entitled to call for payment despite lack of any reason or justification to do so, whereas a surety bond can only be drawn if and when a substantial claim exists which remains unsatisfied.

Moreover FIDIC proposes some other forms of securities, such as an Advance Payment Guarantee, a Retention Money Guarantee and a Payment Guarantee by Employer. All these documents are based on Uniform Rules for Demand Guarantees published by the International Chamber of Commerce, whereas the Surety Bond as referred to in Annex D is based on Uniform Rules for Contract Bonds published by the International Chamber of Commerce.

In international cases the issue often arises that the Employer does not accept or is not allowed to accept a guarantee or bond issued from a bank based abroad. In such cases the Contractor's home bank will issue a so-called indirect guarantee or bond, whereas another bank in the country of the Employer will issue a direct guarantee or bond. Care has to be taken that both instruments are congruent. The contractor must be aware of the fact that his bank will ask him for a deposit as security for repayment of the funds which will probably be drawn by the Employer.

The funds will be blocked until discharge from the obligations under the indirect guarantee. Subject to the terms of the agreement with the bank in most cases this requires the return of the original guarantee or bond document. It unfortunately happens sometimes that the foreign bank delays the return of the document unduly even though the direct guarantee or bond has not been drawn before its expiry date or even though the direct guarantee has been handed over to the foreign bank according to Sub-Clause 4.2. It is therefore recommended to include a special clause in the contract as follows:

> The Employer shall take full responsibility that any indirect guarantee or bond which has been issued for the purposes of Sub-Clause 4.2 shall be promptly returned to the issuing bank. The Employer shall indemnify and hold harmless the Contractor against all charges, losses and expenses in respect of any delay with regard to the return of the indirect guarantee.

7.6 Contract Preparation and Pitfalls

It is critical to underline that preparing the contract documents does not mean to make copies of existing schedules, bills of quantities, specifications and standard forms. Even though it may be helpful to review such existing forms, contract preparation means to shape an individual law for an individual project. Moreover existing standard forms assume that the parties using them have carefully scrutinised them and filled them out properly with full knowledge of what the standard form entails.

FIDIC standard forms are recommendations and recognise that particular adjustments are often appropriate. A careful reader of the FIDIC conditions will frequently find the wording "unless otherwise" agreed or stated. Whenever this wording has been used within the General Conditions the FIDIC Drafting Committee has supposed that adjustments or changes to the recommended wording can be either useful and appropriate or even necessary.

FIDIC standard forms shall be completed by stating and indicating the according data in either the Appendix to Tender or the Particular Conditions. Sometimes completion of data shall be done in Schedules and Appendices. Some of the Sub-Clauses within the General Conditions do not apply if the therein required data are omitted.

7.6.1 Technical Standards

Pursuant to Sub-Clause 4.5 the design, the Contractor's Documents, the execution and the completed Works shall comply with the Country's technical standards, building, construction and environmental Laws, Laws applicable to the product being produced from the Works, and other standards specified in the Employer's

Requirements, applicable to the Works, or defined by the applicable Laws. It is thus extremely important to carry out a local survey on existing technical standards in order to ensure compliance with them. In addition the Particular Conditions may specify supplemental standards or even replace local standards by other ones.

However there are examples of clauses which may lead to uncertainty and disputes, such as the following:

- Contractor will use European Codes and Iranian Codes where appropriate based on client approval.
- Every item of electrical equipment used in the electrical system shall comply with the relevant IEC, or equivalent standards.
- Power cables have to be in accordance with the respective IEC or DIN-VDE standards or other equivalent norms.

Such types of clauses are unclear. It is obvious that the parties have refrained from ascertaining the relevant rules and determining clear standards. Instead the parties would be advised to refrain from changing Sub-Clause 5.4.

While CE standards are principally used within the EU, third (non-EU) countries may have their own standards and it is up to the Contractor to check import requirements in each destination country. The English Institute of Building Control produced a series of individual country reviews of *building regulations and technical provisions* throughout Europe and the EFTA countries in 1993, which are updated periodically.

> *Examples:* As for technical standards for buildings in *Japan*, the Law prescribes "building code" and "zoning code". The building codes are technical standards for all buildings in order to ensure building safety with regards to structural strength, fire prevention devices, sanitation, etc. (Chapter II, Articles 19 to 41). The *United Arab Emirates* Authority for Standardisation and Metrology (ESMA), being responsible for setting UAE standards, has been preparing, approving, publishing, reviewing, modifying, issuing and adapting standards and technical regulations, and establishing a national measurement system (NMS) in the country. In the *Federation of Bosnia and Herzegovina*, a manual of technical and obligatory conditions for the construction, reconstruction, repair and adaptation of construction (building) units has been published by the Ministry of Physical Planning and Environment.

A periodical survey of local standards is critical because Sub-Clause 5.4 puts the Contractor under the obligation to comply with standards prevailing when the Works or Section are taken over by the Employer under Clause 10.

7.6.2   Delay Damages

The relevant rate of delay damages must be stated in the Appendix to Tender (Red Book and Yellow Book) or the Particular Conditions (Silver) as a rate per day of delay. In addition there is provision for stating a maximum amount of delay damages. The Appendix to Tender (Red and Yellow Book) requires a percentage of the Accepted Contract Amount to be stated for both the delay damages and the limit. Clause 14.15(b) (Red and Yellow) provides that damages shall be made in the currencies and proportions stated in the Appendix to Tender.

The figures of delay damages should be a reasonable estimate of the actual losses which will be incurred by the Employer. The term "delay damages" originates from English law, where delay damages or liquidated damages mean a "genuine pre-estimate of the creditor's probable or possible interest in the due performance of the principal obligation",[13] whether a sum is called penalty or damages.[14]

It is usually intended for the percentage delay damages to be calculated or estimated as the sum of:

(a) The anticipated average cost to the Employer of the extended period of the Engineer's supervision, plus
(b) The anticipated average benefit to the Employer of the completed Works, or (2) an amount roughly equivalent to the commercial cost of borrowing the Accepted Contract Amount from a local bank.

It should be noted that due to the nature of liquidated damages save for liquidated damages payable under this Sub-Clause 8.7, the failure by the Contractor to attain any milestone or other act, matter or thing by any date specified in the corresponding Appendix (Time Schedule) to the Contract Agreement and/or other program of work prepared shall not render the Contractor liable for any (further) loss or damage thereby suffered by the Employer. This nature is clearly shown in the requirements of Sub-Clause 8.7, according to which delay damages shall be the only damages due by the Contractor for default to comply with Time for Completion.

The nature of delay damages in the sense of Sub-Clause 8.7 is often misunderstood or becomes ignored, in particular in civil law countries. Civil law jurisdictions allow for penalty clauses (see Sect. 339 German Civil Code), which are commonly used. However, it must be noted that German law draws a clear difference between penalty clauses and liquidated damages.[15] Although there is some discussion about whether the beneficial of a liquidated damages clause is free to show evidence of a higher damage than originally estimated,[16] agreements as to liquidated damages are admissible and valid (see Palandt and Heinrichs 2009, Section 276, note 26). The argument which is sometimes used in Eastern European countries that delay damages subject to Sub-Clause 8.7 must be qualified as a penalty clause because there is a lack of an admissible and valid alternative, must therefore be rejected.

[13] Commissioner of Public Works v. Hills [1906] AC 368, at 375 to 376.
[14] See Alfred McAlpine Capital Projects Ltd v. Tilebox Ltd [2005] EWHC 281 (TCC).
[15] See BGH [1970] NJW 32.
[16] See OLG Schleswig [1985] DNotZ 310 and in the opposite direction LAG Düsseldorf [1973] DB 85.

According to common law authorities a claim for time extension may be dismissed, if the Contractor is already in culpable delay.[17] In Balfour the contractor argued that "the effect of the issue of variations during a period of culpable delay was to render time at large, leaving the contractor to complete within a reasonable time". This being the case, the Employer would lose his rights to levy liquidated damages. Mr Justice Colman did not agree with the contractor. He held that a variation issued during a period of culpable delay would not render time at large.

Under a FIDIC contract there seems to be a strong argument in favour of Balfour Beatty decision. It can be seen from the requirements in Sub-Clause 8.4 that extension of Time for Completion shall only be awarded for the purposes of Sub-Clause 10.1. If the Contractor already failed to comply with Sub-Clause 8.2 the risk of further delays caused by Employer's risks or by culpable actions of the Employer is clearly allocated to the Contractor. As the Contractor is already liable to pay Delay Damages, the argument of "time at large" plays no further role. One could also argue that this is a foreseeable risk to which the Contractor should have given allowance in advance. The Contractor may therefore consider it to be wise to include an additional clause which ensures that if the Employer causes delay by initiating a variation after passing Time for Completion he will be discharged from Delay Damages for this additional period.

7.6.3 Performance Damages

All FIDIC forms miss a provision for liquidated damages for failure to meet the performance criteria of the plant, for example, efficiency, input, output or availability. Instead Sub-Clause 9.4(b) provides that if the Works or a Section fails to pass the Tests on Completion and if this failure deprives the Employer of substantially the whole benefit of the Works or Section, then the Employer can reject the Works or Section and terminate the Contract as a whole or in respect of the major part which cannot be put to intended use.

Although failure to achieve the specified performance criteria is critical for the Employer, he may sometimes wish to stick to the contract. Both, the Contractor and the Employer may therefore probably wish to amend the contract and to add a liquidated damages clause. A measurable performance target is then required, because the measure of liquidated damages will depend on the relevant warranty. In order to establish the threshold for levy of liquidated damages the required performance benchmarks must be prescribed by measurable parameters. Moreover the procedures within which the Contractor shall show that he complies with the benchmark criteria should be stated.

---

[17] Balfour Beatty Building Ltd v. Chestermount Properties Ltd (1993) 62 BLR 12 in contradiction with Pickavance (2005, note 6.79).

However, if failure to comply with the requirements deprives the Employer of substantially the whole benefit of the Works or Section, the Employer may nevertheless wish to terminate the contract. It may then be useful to have stipulated a minimum level of performance required, in order to save the remedy of termination in favour of the Employer. If performance falls below the indicated minimum level the plant may be considered and agreed no longer to be a viable plant, the liquidated damages provision no longer an adequate remedy and the contractor's performance not to be performance at all. The Employer shall then no longer be bound to rely on the liquidated damages clause.

In order to be enforceable, performance liquidated damages must again be a genuine pre-estimate of the loss and damage that the Employer will suffer over the life of the project if the plant or facility does not achieve the specified performance warranties. Performance liquidated damages usually represent a net present value calculation of the revenue forgone over the intended life cycle of the project.

An additional clause as to performance liquidated damages may have the following wording:

> Contractor guarantees that the Works will meet the minimum performance guarantees as set forth below during the Tests on Completion.
>
> Contractor shall pay to the Employer the Performance Liquidated Damages as set forth below, to the extent that the Works does not meet the Performance Guarantees during the Test on Completion.
>
> The total aggregate Performance Liquidated Damages under the Contract shall not exceed [...] percent of the Contract Price.

7.6.4   Defects Notification Period

Subject to Clause 11 each FIDIC form of contract provides a so-called Defects Notification period which is defined in Sub-Clause 1.1.3.7 and should therefore not be confused with the legal defects liability period. Instead it means the period for notifying defects in the Works or Section under Sub-Clause 11.1 as stated in the Particular Conditions or the Appendix to Tender, as the case may be. The Particular Conditions should state the duration of this period, which is a special period of time during which the Contractor owes the duty to repair defects of all type and notwithstanding his own responsibility as to the defective issue (see Sub-Clause 11.2). Unless otherwise stated in the Particular Conditions/Appendix to Tender this period lasts over 365 days. Under FIDIC, the defects notification period is calculated from the date of completion of a Section or of the Works. The period can be extended if, following the issue of the Taking over Certificate, the Works, a Section of the Works or a major item of plant cannot be used for the purposes for which they are intended. Under FIDIC, the Defects Notification Period cannot be extended by more than 2 years. Each Section will be treated differently. Thus the Defects Notification Period for different Sections of the plant will not necessarily be aligned. However, it is common in some branches of the industry to have a Defects

Notification Period or extended maintenance warranty for anything up to 5 years. If this is a key issue for the Employer he should amend the Particular Conditions accordingly.

7.6.5 Retention Money

Retention Money is a defined term meaning the accumulated retention monies which the Employer retains under Sub-Clause 14.3 and pays under Sub-Clause 14.9. The percentage of deduction and the limit of Retention Monies must be stated in the Particular Conditions. The Contractor should take into consideration that the first half of the Retention Monies will be paid to him after Taking Over and the second half after the end of the Defects Notification Period as referred to above.

7.6.6 Sections

Sub-Clause 1.1.5.6 provides a very useful feature which is often overlooked, underestimated or simply confused with milestones. Whereas the provision for sectional completion entails the taking over of a defined Section, a milestone date sets out a completion date for a special part of the Works, commonly for the purpose of an interface, which is not at all the same thing.

By the definition of Sections within the Appendix to Tender or the Contract Data or the Particular Conditions (as the case may be) the parties of the contract will activate some special features of the General Conditions which are quite useful:

- Firstly the Contractor is entitled to a sectional taking over. According to Sub-Clause 10.1 the taking over procedure rules apply also to Sections. Thus the Contractor may apply for a Taking-Over Certificate for each Section.
- Secondly, once a sectional Taking-Over Certificate has been issued, subject to Sub-Clause 14.9 the Contractor is entitled to the first half of the Retention Monies.
- Thirdly the Contractor will be entitled to get the second half of the Retention Monies as soon as the relevant Defects Notification period has expired.

Although common law courts have not generally dismissed liquidated damages claims based on failure to comply with agreed milestone dates,[18] Sections should in particular be used if the Employer intends to define interim goals. It is not appropriate to agree to milestones in combination with delay damages. By contrast it is appropriate to agree to Sections. This ensures that time extension claims will be treated separately Section by Section, which is critical in order to avoid the

---

[18] See Philips Hong Kong Ltd v. Attorney General of Hong Kong (1990) 50 BLR 122.

argument of "time at large". If there is no effective system for the extension of time for each part of the works, the Employer must be cautious not to enter in "time at large". As a matter of fact there is no such effective system because according to Sub-Clause 8.4 extension for Time of Completion may only be granted if and to the extent that completion for the purposes of Sub-Clause 10.1 is or will be delayed.

However at a first view provisions for stating delay damages for each Section don't seem to be present in the FIDIC forms. But this is not true, because Sub-Clause 8.2 clearly requires the Contractor to complete the whole of the Works and each Section within the Time for Completion for the Works or Section. Once the Contractor has received the Taking-Over Certificate for a Section he is accordingly discharged from Delay Damages for this Section. Thus the delay damages as stated in the particular Conditions or the Appendix to Tender, as the case may be, apply either to the whole Works or to any defined Sections. Sub-Clause 8.4 clearly refers to Sub-Clause 10.1 and is therefore applicable to either the whole Works or to Sections as stated in the contract.

If Sections have been determined within the Particular Conditions or in the Appendix to Tender, sectional completion dates should be stated. If Sections have different importance to the Employer different Delay Damages rates can be fixed. It can be seen that Sections make the contract much more flexible and sometimes also more balanced.

For the avoidance of doubt Sections should not be confused with parts of the Works. According to Sub-Clause 10.2 the Employer is entitled to take over parts of the Works. The contractual framework as to Sections does not apply to the taking over of parts of the Permanent Works.

7.6.7   Taxes, Levies and Customs

It is important to be aware of which kind of tax contributions, levies and customs duties will have to be paid by the Contractor under the laws of the country where the site is located. Sub-Clause 14.1 states that the Contractor shall pay all taxes, duties and fees required to be paid by him under the Contract, and the Contract Price shall not be adjusted to cover s any of these costs. It is useful to find an additional clear wording as to all local duties. The below mentioned Sub-Clause can be used as a boilerplate.

14.1.1 All import duties and levies on the import of Goods and equipment under this Contract will be settled by the Employer.

14.1.2 All further taxes in connection with the execution of this Contract levied by the [Chinese Government] on the Employer in accordance with the tax laws in effect shall be borne by the Employer.

14.1.3 All taxes in connection with the execution of this Contract levied by the [Chinese Government] on the Contractor in accordance with the tax laws in effect and the "Agreement Between the Government of the [People's Republic of China] and Government of the Bidder's country for the Reciprocal Avoidance of Double Taxation and the Prevention of Fiscal Evasion with Respect to Taxes on Income and Property" shall be borne by the Contractor.

14.1.4 All taxes arising outside [of China] in connection with the execution of this Contract shall be borne by the Contractor.

A different and more detailed clause is recommended by FIDIC in the Guidance.

In addition, local laws may require from the Contractor to pay *social contributions* for own personnel and sub-contractors, which can often amount to considerable sums.

Examples: In accordance with the Law on Social Insurance of *Azerbaijan*, foreign nationals shall pay social contributions from Azerbaijani source income at a rate of 3%. Employers are responsible for withholding this contribution, paying it to the Budget and then reporting to the national authorities. Again, the employer is liable to pay social contributions at the rate of 22% of the accrued payroll fund. In *Romania* foreign citizens working in Romania on a work permit and under a labour contract registered with the Labour Office are required to pay the Romanian social contributions (except 1% unemployment contribution).

7.6.8 Copyright

Both the Yellow Book and the Silver Book provide three stipulations in relation to copyright and intellectual property rights. Sub-Clause 17.5 contains an indemnification rule in the event of copyright infringements. Sub-Clause 1.11 preserves the copyrights and intellectual property rights of the Employer. Sub-Clause 1.10 deals with copyrights and other intellectual property rights of the Contractor. Obviously design and build contracts often involve a considerable transfer of know how. In particular as with any process plant, the preservation of know-how is precious to the Contractor. Contractors shall supply the Contractor's Documents as referred to in Sub-Clause 1.1.6.1 which include not just the usual menu of drawings, manuals and calculations but also extends to "computer programs, other software and models". According to Sub-Clause 1.10 the Contractor shall retain the copyright and other intellectual property rights made by the Contractor. Software and programs may in fact be owned by third parties. As to this issue Sub-Clause 17.5 applies.

The extent of know-how transfer may give rise to some concerns from Contractors in that the drafting of clause 1.10 is not sufficiently tight to protect its intellectual property rights. Subject to Sub-Clause 1.10 the Employer is granted a "non-terminable, transferable non-exclusive royalty-free" licence to use Contractor's Documents including the right to copy, use, communicate and modify such documents. This licence is limited "for the purposes of completing, operating, maintaining, altering, adjusting, repairing and demolishing the Works", and this "throughout the actual or intended working life of the relevant parts of the work". The intention behind the drafting was clearly to limit such use to completing, modifying or altering the Works themselves. However, the circumstances may require more detailed provision.

Some Sub-Contractors and suppliers may be interested in preserving their rights through the inclusion of an express clause. It is therefore suggested to replace Sub-Clause 10.1 first sentence by a special clause concerning copyrights, such as:

> Without prejudice to Sub-Clause 1.10 the copyright and other intellectual property in all Contractor's Documents furnished to the Employer by the Contractor herein shall remain vested in the Contractor or, if they are furnished to the Employer directly or through or on behalf of the Contractor by any third party, including suppliers of materials and designers. The copyright in such documents shall remain vested in such third party.

7.6.9   Labour

It is not always necessary but can be useful nevertheless to amend a number of Sub-Clauses in order to take account of the circumstances and locality of the Works, covering such matters as permits and registration of expatriate employees; details of repatriation to place of recruitment; provision of temporary accommodation for employees; requirements in respect of accommodation for staff of Employer and Engineer; standards of accommodation to be provided; provision of access roads, hospital, school, power, water, drainage, fire services, refuse collection, communal buildings, shops, and telephones and particular maintenance of records of safety and health.

7.6.10   Handback Requirements (only Gold Book, DBO)

The connotation "handback requirements" as covered by Sub-Clause 8.7 seems to be harmless. According to Sub-Clause 8.7 the Contractor shall ensure that the Works comply with the handback requirements specified in the Employer's Requirements. Though FIDIC intended to discharge the Contractor from all post contractual defects liability, the exact opposite can be specified in the Employer's Requirements by including residual life requirements as to the Works.

In order to ensure that roads are handed over in an adequate condition for service that will not require major capital maintenance immediately following the end of the contract, Employers may wish to include specific clauses in the Contract regarding handback. A required residual life will then be specified for each element of the project road. For example, a requirement that at least 85% of the road pavement should have a 10-year residual life on handback may be included. Another example for specific handback requirements can be found in bridge projects. Though bridges have a design life of 120 years, it is usually considered necessary to demonstrate that most elements of these structures have a residual life of at least 30 years on handback.

FIDIC provides for a joint inspection not less than 2 years prior to the expiry date of the Operation Service Period in order to identify maintenance and replacement needs to satisfy the handback requirements and the possible remedial action that may be needed to achieve the required standard. If the Works fail to pass the Tests prior to Contract Completion the Employer may rely on Sub-Clause 11.12. Part of the payments otherwise due to the Contractor can be withheld and used to remedy defects if handback criteria are not met at expiry. This clearly follows from Sub-Clause 14.19.

7.7   Alteration of FIDIC Conditions

7.7.1   Guiding Principles

FIDIC strongly recommends that tender documents should be prepared by suitable qualified engineers who are familiar with the technical aspects of the required works and that a review by suitably qualified lawyers is advisable. Consideration must be given to the technical requirements, the suitable procurement method and the governing law. All FIDIC Books contain the warning advice that modifications to the FIDIC Conditions may be required in some legal jurisdictions. FIDIC also alerts that the FIDIC Conditions do not contain any limitation on the duration of legal liability (FIDIC Contracts Guide 2001, p. 203).

The guiding principles as to the drafting of Particular Conditions should be such which are mentioned in the FIDIC Books, in particular in the Notes for the Preparation of Tender Documents. From the point of view of a lawyer some pre-considerations must be given to the governing law. The governing contract law should be stated in the contract. However some legal questions which may arise will not directly be governed by the applicable contract law. Accidents on site will be governed by the lex loci commissi. Procedural questions and questions concerning the decisive private international law will be governed by the lex fori. It is therefore critical to fix the seat of arbitration. This will help to ensure that most of the questions as to the applicable law will be ascertainable in advance. The governing contract law itself covers all questions as to the validity of the contract, interpretation of the contract, available remedies for breach of contract and limitation periods.

7.7.2   Preparing Tender Documents – The FIDIC Contracts Guide –Guidance for the Preparation of Particular Conditions

The FIDIC Contract's Guide and the Notes on the Preparation of tender Documents will give considerable assistance and help to the parties to draft Particular Conditions where appropriate. However care has to be taken when doing so. The FIDIC Conditions contain a considerable number of definitions. Defined words, terms and expressions always begin with a capital letter when used in the General Conditions and the complementary documents. It is crucial to always have in mind the definitions and to use them carefully. When for example using the word "works" the draftsmen should take into consideration that "Works" means a different and defined thing. Furthermore all FIDIC Conditions contain a lot of cross references, which should be taken into consideration. It makes a great difference whether an additional claim of the Employer has to be notified according to clause 2.5 or not. Only by reference to clause 2.5 it is ensured that the Employer is not allowed to withhold payments out of the certification procedure which is ruled by the Conditions. Finally in particular non native English speakers should carefully check the legal meaning of any word which is inserted in the contract, if the ruling language is English. Under all circumstances it should be checked whether the expression used is suitable for the particular circumstances.

Any amendments to the contract should first be examined as to whether they are necessary or not. It often happens that the parties add milestone clauses to the contract, which are not suitable at all. FIDIC has chosen a proper approach as to milestones in order to ensure that time extensions can be determined and allocated. The FIDIC approach consists in the offer to the parties to agree to sections of work. Sections (see the definition in Sub-Clause 1.1.5.6 Silver Book) are dealt separately as to time and taking over. Thus by agreeing sections milestones become unnecessary.

On the other hand the parties to the contract must ensure that they respond to all requirements of the General Conditions to specify details. Some clauses of the general Conditions only apply if particulars have been additionally agreed. For example Sub-Clause 13.6 only applies if a Daywork schedule is included in the contract. Sub-Clause 14.2 only becomes effective if the amount of the advance payment is stated in the Particular Conditions.

As already mentioned all of the FIDIC Books contain a Guide on the Preparation of Particular Conditions. This guide already comprises sample clauses for the proper alteration of the contract. If appropriate the parties can for example easily change the FIDIC Red Book from a remeasurement contract into a lump sum contract. The Guide gives clear wording and guidance to the parties to do so.

7.7.3 Complementary Terms of Contract

At first sight, contracts mirror what the parties intend to agree. One of its main principles is said to be freedom of contract. However, the proper law of the contract is a host of very detailed rules on every possible aspect of contractual relationships. These rules apply to the contract even though the parties probably do not intend to be bound by them. But if the contract itself remains silent the parties to it incorporate those rules by reference to the proper law of the contract, whether this law was chosen by express or implied intention or whether it applies according to the conflict of laws rules which are applicable. According to the principle of freedom of contract the parties are free to set those rules aside in their contract and, once they have done so, these legal rules do not bind them. As a matter of fact, most contract rules which are contained in continental civil codes and in case law and statutes in the United Kingdom, can in principle be set aside by the parties, if they wish to do so. However it is often not that easy to identify those rules which become incorporated into a contract. Many of the rules deal with fundamental issues in a contractual relationship. For example, rules which allocate certain risks, or define the quality which is expected from a contractor or consultant, or rules which indicate reasons why a party may terminate the relationship, or determine the consequences of late delivery. If the parties have carefully identified such rules they are free to set them aside. In international commerce however it is often very difficult to identify all those rules and to set them aside, which is one source of misunderstandings and disputes.

However, some of the rules which are embedded in the proper of law of the contract are even not amenable to derogation by the parties. This set of rules is known as the mandatory law. It applies even though the parties have identified it and do not intend to be bound by it. One could think that the parties would be free to avoid this by agreeing to apply another different law. But sometimes even this is proved to be impossible because of either the so-called ordre public of the lex fori or the nature of the rule itself, which then is called loi de police or loi d'application immédiate. Whether a set of rules is mandatory or non mandatory must be decided on a case by case basis and subject to the applicable law.

It is beyond doubt, that French law draws a distinction between mandatory laws (*lois impératives*) and non-mandatory laws (*lois supplétives (de volonté), dispositives, interprétatives*). Non-mandatory rules are considered as a type of legislation with minor force: the rule of law has various degrees and non-mandatory rules have a lesser binding force than mandatory rules. As a matter of fact it is not always easy to identify the nature of a rule. However, recent statutes often explicitly say so when derogation is not allowed.

German law also draws a distinction between mandatory law (*zwingendes Recht*) and non-mandatory law (*dispositives, nachgiebiges, abdingbares, subsidiäres Recht*). The German legislator has provided non-mandatory rules for the most frequent and most typical contracts, such as sales contracts, contract for works, contract for services, loan contracts, etc. Mandatory rules are not very frequent but they do exist. For example according to Sect. 648a any agreement deviating from the provisions of subsections (1) to (5) of this provision is ineffective.

Both, French and German law provide rules which typical parties to typical contracts would opt for. Both jurisdictions have therefore defined typical contract types (nominate contracts) and so-called innominate contracts. The basic idea is that most contracts have some particular aspects in common, even though they are concluded by different parties, in different places with different preferences. The law should therefore provide rules which the typical parties to typical contracts would opt for. Whether or not they have the intention of opting for these rules is of no particular interest.

Compared to Civil law jurisdictions common law jurisdictions usually do not rely on complementary statutory rules because of the simple fact that none exist.

The traditional common law concept is "implied terms". In addition to the "express terms" of a contract, which can be established by means of contract interpretation, there may also exist so-called implied terms. Originally, these terms were always attributed to the intention of the parties. Later on, a distinction between terms implied "in fact", "in law", and "by custom" became recurrent.

For example the Institute of Electrical Engineer's Wiring Regulations 16th Edition at page 540, paragraph 414-01-02, provide:

> ...as far as reasonably practical, wiring should be so arranged or marked that it can be identified for inspection, testing, repair or alteration of installation.

But there is no clear cut between common law jurisdictions and civil law jurisdictions. For example German law not only refers to non mandatory law but fill up gaps through the concept of *ergänzende Vertragsauslegung* if and when a contract seems to be incomplete. Just like non-mandatory rules, and unlike ordinary interpretation, this is also a gap-filling feature. Thus, whereas ordinary interpretation is aimed at determining the meaning of the contract, *ergänzende Vertragsauslegung* aims at filling a gap in the contract.

The difference between common law systems and civil law systems leads to a radically different approach to contract analysis. Whereas a common law lawyer faced with a contract would firstly rely on the terms of the contract and then on the implied terms, a civil law lawyer would rely on the terms of the contract and itself and then on the complementary rules provided by the Civil Code for the type of contract which the parties have agreed on. Thus a civil law lawyer will ask the question "into what type of contract did the parties enter" whereas a common law lawyer will firstly question "to what the parties did agree". Common law layers should be aware of this different approach when identifying complementary mandatory and non mandatory contract terms with regard to contracts which are governed by civil law.

Example: Whether a designer under German law will be liable to carry out the design work according to the standard of fitness for purpose or the standard of due skill and care will only depend on the answer to the question of whether the contract is qualified as a service contract (*Dienstvertrag*: due skill and care) or a contract for work (*Werkvertrag*: fit for purpose).

7.7.4 Recommendations

It is strongly recommended to recognise and take into consideration that Sub-Clause 1.5 rules the priority of the contract documents. Hence it is critical to insert additional clauses in the appropriate document in order to avoid ambiguities and discrepancies which may be solved in disfavour of the party who is interested in the clause.

FIDIC recommends the use of the original English version of the FIDIC Books. This seems to be wise because any translation of the books is to some extent already an interpretation of the contract. The literal meaning of any word or expression may be translated correctly. But whether the translator was able to understand the correct legal meaning of the original wording and whether he was able to find a similar translation remains open, in particular if one of the parties of the contract does not practise English at all. In order to grasp the true meaning of the text (we understood this to be the meaning which the drafter of the conditions intended), one must not only have a deep intrinsic knowledge of the subject matter pertaining to the conditions but also of the legal system behind them. Whilst the available translations of the FIDIC Books have usually been made with due skill and care small discrepancies and ambiguous expressions can never be fully prevented. The extent to which translations may lead to different results in law can easily be verified when comparing court decisions from different states based on CISG or on European Regulations or Directives.

Any changes or additional clauses should be included in the Particular Conditions. It is common and good practice to establish a schedule which refers to the General Conditions and contains any changes or additions on a clause by clause basis. This makes it easy and less time consuming to check each change and addition with regard to each original clause. If a clause shall become deleted the draftsman should just enter the word "deleted" in the schedule.

7.7.5   Pitfalls and Issues

The Particular Conditions are prepared for the particular project and should include any changes or additional clauses which the parties have decided to include for adaptation of the local and project requirements.

One of the main pitfalls consists in ignoring the local requirements. If for example a local license is necessary for the supervision of the works commencement of the works will depend on the notification of a licensed person to the local authority. Delay and disruption are likely to be incurred. FIDIC defines that a day means a calendar day. The Contractor should therefore undertake any necessary investigations in order to establish all national holidays and religious celebrations which will prevent him from proceeding with the works. Additional cost may arise from local restrictions to import goods or to export currencies. The Contractor should always be aware of the fact that public authorities usually are bound to their approved budgets which sometimes even become used for purposes other than the payment of works. Thus any claims for additional payment may become needless because the Employer's funds are already spent. Great care should therefore be taken not to accept a contract for public works if it is already foreseeable that the accepted contract amount will be grossly exceeded.

It has happened that the parties to a contract could not agree on the applicable law, because both parties refused to accept the law of the other party. They finally agreed to apply a so-called neutral law, in this case Swiss law. Neither party was familiar with it. Both parties had ignored it during contract negotiations. Thus disputes were likely to arise and arose quite soon after the contract became effective.

In any case translations should be checked. It has happened that although a translation was more or less authentic it deviated from the English version at a critical point. By consequence when a dispute arose from the contract and the parties wanted to refer it to dispute adjudication the English version provided that the adjudicator should be nominated from the FIDIC President's list whilst the translation referred to the President of a national engineer's association. As both languages had been chosen to apply simultaneously two different chairmen of the DAB became appointed.

A further critical issue is the ruling language and the communication language. In a worst case scenario the parties agree to use English as ruling contract language, but allow daily communication in Chinese, which is the language of the financing institution, and Portuguese, which is the language of the country where the works have to be performed. By consequence instructions become issued in Chinese whilst the contractor practises only English. If a third language, for example Portuguese, is used in arbitration because the place of arbitration is Luanda in Angola any English and Portuguese communication and the English contact must be translated in the Portuguese language. It is obvious that such a result should be avoided.

The contractor should check the nominated engineer before submitting his tender. If for example the employer nominates a single natural person it may happen that this person is an employee of the employer or simply a functionary or public servant.

Pay-when-paid clauses are usually not welcome, and sometimes are even illegal, as is the case under English law. However they are quite useful and many contractors will try to have pay-when-paid clauses in their sub-contracts. The World Bank recently incorporated a clause in its Red Book harmonised version leading to the result that the contractor may refuse to accept a nominated sub-contractor if the sub-contract does not contain a pay-when-paid-clause. On the other hand contractors should be aware of the fact that the engineer will survey the payment of nominated sub-contractors. If the contractor fails to produce evidence of payments which have become due to the sub-contractor in accordance with payment certificates the employer may be entitled to pay direct to the subcontractor.

References

Beale HG (1999) Chitty on contracts, 28th edn. Sweet & Maxwell, London
Corbett EH (2000) FIDIC's New Rainbow 1st edition – an advance? ICLR 17:253
FIDIC Contracts Guide (2001) International Federation of Consulting Engineers, Geneva
Furst S, Ramsley V (2006) Keating on construction contracts, 8th edn. Sweet & Maxwell, London
Halsbury's Laws of Australia (1998) Building and Construction, vol 3(2). LexisNexis Butterworths, Sydney
Heinrichs H (2009) in: Palandt (ed) Commentary to BGB, 68th edn. C.H. Beck, München

Hewitt I (2005) Joint ventures, 3rd edn. Sweet & Maxwell, London

Hill CA, King C (2004) How do German contracts do as much with fewer Words? Chi-Kent L Rev 889. http://lawreview.kentlaw.edu/articles/79-3/Hill%20King.pdf

Huse JA (2002) Understanding and negotiating turnkey and EPC contracts, 2nd edn. Sweet & Maxwell, London

Pickavance K (2005) Delay and disruption, 3rd edn. LLP, London

Seddon NC, Ellinghaus MP (2007) Cheshire and Fifoot's law of contract, 8th Aust ed. LexisNexis, Sydney

Totterdill BW (2006) FIDIC user's guide, 2nd edn. Thomas Telford, London

Trickey G, Hackett M (2001) The presentation and settlement of contractor's claims, 2nd edn. Taylor & Francis, London

Wallace DIN (1995) Hudson's building and engineering contracts, 11th edn. Sweet & Maxwell, London

Wallace DIN (1999) Design-and-build: a no-no for owners. Const Eng L 4:7

Chapter 8
Employer's Duties

8.1 Introduction

The Employer's duties and obligations are quickly summarised. He shall grant access to the Site and possession of the Site, make arrangements for payments, pay the Contract Price, disclose Site data and co-operate with the Contractor to the extent provided by the Contract. He shall also compensate the Contractor for additional cost and disruption if a risk eventuates which is borne by the Employer.

8.2 Arrangement for Payments

As all contractors know, recovering payment after having completed the works can be an enormous headache, because they can seriously affect cash flow. It is therefore always advisable try to ensure that payment difficulties do not arise. Whilst it is, of course, impossible to avoid such concerns completely, FIDIC has included certain provisions in its contracts, which help to reduce exposure to non-payment and provide the Contractor with options to pursue should payment not be forthcoming.

One of those options can be found in Sub-Clause 2.4. Subject to Sub-Clause 2.4 the Employer shall submit, within 28 days after having received any request from the Contractor, reasonable evidence that financial arrangements have been put in place and are being maintained which will be enable the Employer to pay the Contract Price. There is authority for the view in a case from Trinidad and Tobago[1] that the mere fact that an Employer is wealthy is inadequate for the purposes of clause 2.4. Accordingly, mere evidence that the Employer, who was in this case the Government of Trinidad and Tobago, had very substantial funds did not by itself satisfy clause 2.4. In fact the Employer has to put in place financial arrangements which would enable him to pay which may require him that Cabinet approval becomes obtained.

---

[1] National Insurance Property Development Co Ltd v. NH International (Carribbean) Ltd, High Court of Justice Trinidad and Tobago-unreported.

A.-V. Jaeger and G.-S. Hök, *FIDIC-A Guide for Practitioners*,
DOI 10.1007/978-3-642-02100-8_8, © Springer-Verlag Berlin Heidelberg 2010

Another possibility is to provide for greater frequency of interim payments. This will not only help cash-flow but will help to avoid, or at least limit, exposure to non-payment.

A further option is to take security over payment as part of the contract. The Contractor may ask for example, that the Employer makes available a parent company guarantee, a payment guarantee, performance bonds, security cheques, establishing an escrow account, a standby letter of credit, etc. Indeed payment guarantees are recognised by FIDIC who added a form of payment guarantee to be issued by a bank in favour of the Employer as an annex to the Red and Yellow Books.

Finally rapid dispute resolution procedures in order to resolve disputes as to as quickly as possible may also ensure cash flow. It is therefore strongly regrettable that some Employers still try to delete Dispute Adjudication clauses, which on the hand ensure that payments are met under a certain control but do not suspend them too long, if already due.

Unfortunately retention of title provisions in the contract, whereby ownership of goods and materials does not pass to the client until the Contractor has been paid for them, are often useless, because they are not always recognised by the law of the country where the site is situated. However, it is the law of this country which is applicable in this respect, according to the world-wide accepted principle of lex rei sitae.

However, although all of these options are particularly worth trying, some jurisdictions provide for further assistance. According to German law the Contractor would be allowed to claim for registration of a charge against the land of the owner, if and when he is the main contractor (see Sect. 648 German Civil Code). In addition, subject to Sect. 648a German Civil Code each Contractor is entitled to claim for a bond as a security for payment of any future parts of the Contract Price. If the Employer fails to provide such a bond, the Contract becomes terminated by force of law.

Under the new FIDIC Gold Book Sub-Clause 2.4 has been slightly reviewed and reformulated. A new feature has been included which is the Financial Memorandum which means the document which details the Employer's financial arrangements. Without going to the roots of this new feature it is at least clear that the Contractor will have based his offer and its availability on this document. Thus any changes, alterations or misrepresentations as to the content of the Financial Memorandum will lead to serious consequences which may vary subject to the applicable law.

8.3   Duty to Pay

8.3.1   Introduction

According to Clause 14 the Employer shall pay the Contract Price to the Contractor. He shall not withhold any payments or set off against an amount certified in a Payment Certificate (Sub-Clause 2.5).

8.3.2   Contract Price

Depending on the FIDIC form of Contract used the price which is to be paid by the Employer (the Contract Price) is not yet fixed at the moment of contract execution. At this stage all that is known and agreed is that the Employer shall pay the Contract Price (Sub-Clause 14.1), which is either composed of the remeasured Accepted Contract Amount and any adjustments made under the rules of the Contract (Red Book) or composed by the lump sum Accepted Contract Amount as adjusted in accordance with the Contract (Yellow Book). Even under the Silver Book, where the parties agree to a Lump Sum Contract Price adjustments are not generally excluded. Thus all FIDIC Books do not provide for an overall lump sum price or fixed lump sum price, which is not intended to be adjusted in any way either by variation or remeasurement. Hence, all FIDIC Books reflect the idea that the Contractor should not be bound to carry out any additional or different work without any additional payment, although the Lump Sum Contract Price under a Silver Book Contract covers much more risks than the Contract Price under a Yellow Book Contract. However, the Contractor who accepts to carry out works under a Silver Book Contract takes the risk of changes in cost arising from his design and he shall be deemed to have obtained all necessary information as to risk, contingencies and other circumstances which may influence or affect the Works.

Under the Red Book the Accepted Contract Amount is nothing more than a price estimate. All of the Works, whether originally agreed or subsequently adjusted in accordance with the Contract, will be measured and evaluated according to Sub-Clause 12.3. Thus the Contractor does not take any risk of the design. In this respect it must be pointed out, that it is the Engineer who shall make the measurement (see Sub-Clause 12.1 Red Book).

8.3.3   Provisional Sums

The FIDIC Rainbow Edition contains a special feature with regard to the Contract Price. Subject to Sub-Clause 13.5 a Provisional Sum may be used in accordance with the Engineer's instruction, and the Contract Price shall be adjusted accordingly. According to Sub-Clause 1.1.4.10 "Provisional Sum" means a sum which is specified in the Contract as a provisional sum, for the execution of any part of the Works or for the supply of Plant, Materials or services under Sub-Clause 13.5. Provisional Sums may be for extras or for some items which cannot be precisely estimated, or for a sub-contract which has to be placed after the main contract is entered into (see Furst and Ramsley 2006, note 4-035). One could think that this wording is clear and unambiguous. However some questions may arise:

If Sub-Clause 13.5 is applied correctly, this will avoid the argument concerning whether a Contractor is entitled to an extension of time and additional cost for carrying out work, supplying Plant, Materials or services instructed against a

Provisional sum. If the Provisional sum is for defined items, there will be no entitlement to such claims. Hence, the Contractor is deemed to have made appropriate allowances elsewhere in his tender.

The use of the word "provisional" indicates that the parties do not expect that sum to be paid without adjustment of the Contract Price. Under a Yellow Book contract this understanding may lead to the question whether the Provisional Sum was included in the Accepted Contract Amount or not. Supposing the Provisional Sum is or was included therein the Provisional Sum must be deducted from the Accepted Contract Amount, if the Engineer does not instruct the Contractor to carry out works, supply Plant or Materials or carry out services to which the Provisional Sum relates. Unfortunately neither Sub-Clause 1.1.4.10 nor Sub-Clause 13.5 clearly indicate whether any Provisional Sums are included in the Accepted Contract Amount or not.

However, it is suggested that FIDIC uses the term of Provisional Sums in a manner meaning that Provisional Sums are by definition in these contract forms only payable at all if and to the extent that the Engineer or Employer so instructs. It is also suggested that FIDIC understands Provisional Sums as defined items for which, if used and instructed, the Contract Price shall be adjusted accordingly. Subject to Sub-Clause 14.1 Yellow Book the Contract Price shall be the lump sum Accepted Contract Amount subject to adjustments in accordance with the Contract. Thus Provisional Sums are intended to be used for additional works, supplies and/or services which are not yet part of the Accepted Contract Amount. Hence, the understanding is this: If Provisional Sums are used the Contract Price shall be adjusted accordingly. The Provisional sum is usually not included within the Accepted Contract Amount as an approximate guess. However, the precise meaning and effect of Provisional Sums depends on the terms of the individual contract.

In the recent English case of *Midland Expressway v. Carillion Construction & Others* [2006] EWCA Civ 936, Carillion contended that though it should be paid for work instructed against the provisional sums, nowhere in this clause was there a requirement to deduct the provisional sum itself. It therefore claimed an entitlement to payment for the work it carried out and, in addition, to be paid the entirety of the provisional sums entered into the contract. Lord Justice May, in the Court of Appeal, held that provisional sums were by definition in this contract only payable at all if and to the extent the employer so instructed. If instructed it was necessary to omit the provisional value and to substitute it with actual value.

However, the precise meaning and effect of Provisional Sums depends not only on the terms of the individual contract but again on the conditions under which it has been executed. If for example the instructions to bidders or the applicable procurement law indicate or provide that any Provisional Sums shall be included in the Accepted Contract Amount, the understanding of Provisional Sum will change completely. For example under German procurement law any defined provisional sums must be valued and assessed with their maximum amount.[2] According to

---

[2] See Procurement Chamber at the District Government Arnsberg, 28 January 2004; file no. VK 1 – 30/2003.

Sect 9 VOB/A provisional sums shall only exceptionally be included in the specifications or bill of quantities, because they are considered to stand in conflict with the requirement of an unambiguous and exhaustive specification or bill of quantity for the purposes of public procurement. In this context the Accepted Contract Amount as referred to in the FIDIC documents will include any Provisional Sums, which must be deducted from the Accepted Contract Amount in an amount corresponding to the amount which was included during the assessment of the bid, before the Contract Price shall be adjusted subject to Sub-Clause 13.5.

8.4 Duty to Co-operate

Subject to the governing law the Employer may be under a duty of good faith including an obligation to perform the contract in a manner consistent with good faith taking into account common usage (see Section 242 German Civil Code). Also according to French law agreements shall be performed in good faith (Art. 1134 Code Civil) and agreements are binding not only as to what is therein expressed, but also as to all the consequences which equity, usage or statute give to the obligation according to its nature (Art. 1135 Code Civil). Common law judges are more reluctant to rely on the term of good faith. They will therefore be happy to find express terms as to the duty of co-operation by the Employer. FIDIC has obviously included a spirit of good faith in the Contract to the extent which was necessary to ensure that the progress of the Works will not be adversely interfered with.

8.4.1 Access to the Site

Access to and possession of the Site is essential. A construction contract necessarily requires the owner to give the contractor such possession, occupation or use as is necessary to enable him to perform the Contract.[3] Rules relating to "possession" or "use" or "access" or "occupation" are therefore used in many contracts to describe the contractor's right to enter the site, occupy or use the site and carry out the specified works. Possession will usually involve such exclusive occupation and use of the site as required for performing the works. Thus according to Clause 2.1 the Employer shall give the Contractor possession of all parts of the Site at the times stated in the Appendix to Tender (Particular Conditions in the Silver Form). However, the Employer may withhold possession until the Performance Security has been received by him.

The FIDIC Conditions of contract comprise an elaborate code relating to the occupation, possession and handing over of the site (see Sub-Clause 2.1). These

---

[3]The London Borough of Hounslow v. Twickenham Gardens Development (1970) 78 BLR 89.

provisions are linked to the completion of the Works, the time for completion of the Works and the obligation to pay liquidated damages (Sub-Clause 8.7). In summary, FIDIC Conditions provide that the Contractor shall be given possession of the site on the date for possession (Sub-Clause 2.1), that that possession may not be exclusive to the Contractor (Sub-Clause 2.1) and that the Contractor is to complete the works on or before the completion date (Sub-Clauses 4.1 and 8.2). Time for completion may be extended if any of the contractually defined events giving rise to such an extension have occurred and have caused delay to completion (Sub-clause 8.4). Liquidated damages are payable if the completion date or the extended completion date is not met (Sub-clause 8.7). The relevant period for such payment is the period between the completion date and the date for completion (Sub-clause 8.7).

However, the meaning and extent of "possession" of the site, and the apportionment and allocation of risk for events that interfere with possession, will depend upon the express and implied terms of the contract. It is suggested that according to FIDIC Conditions the Contractor is granted exclusive possession of the Site and of the Works and retains exclusive possession until practical completion occurs unless the contract provides otherwise or subject to express reservations of the Employer.

It is the return of exclusive possession by the Contractor to the Employer which brings the working period of the contract to an end. Although the Works and each part of them are in the exclusive possession of either the Contractor or the Employer, a lesser form of physical presence on or within the Works that is defined as the use or occupation of the incomplete Works by the Employer is allowed notwithstanding the exclusive possession of the Works by the Contractor (Sub-clause 4.6). This presence by the Employer has no effect on the Contractor's exclusive possession of the Works, nor on the Contractor's obligations and entitlements with regard to liquidated damages, retention, defects liability, insurance, reinstatement or the preparation of a Statement at Completion. The Employer is, in effect a sub licensee to the Contractor who, otherwise, retains exclusive possession of the Works.

Thus, there are four relevant and separate types of possession and occupation to consider. The first is where the Contractor is granted non exclusive possession. The second is where the Contractor, whilst carrying out the Works, has exclusive possession of those Works. The third, following partial possession, is where the Employer takes back exclusive possession from the Contractor for that part of the Works. The fourth is where the Contractor retains exclusive possession but allows the Employer to use or occupy part or all of the site or the Works. This might be a useful differentiation for better consideration of the following situation:

If for example the contract specifies that the Employer is to give possession of any foundation, structure or plant, then he must do so in the time and manner stated in the Specification (see Cl. 4.6). In such a case the Contractor will be either granted non exclusive possession or partial possession. If the Contract is silent, it is suggested that then the possession of the foundation, structure or plant is required to be at such time as to allow the Contractor to proceed in accordance with the submitted programme. However, if the Employer fails to give possession at the appropriate time, the Contractor is entitled to an extension of time and payment of Cost and profit, subject to notice according to Cl. 20.1 and 2.1. He may also rely on Cl. 8.4 for any delay, impediment or prevention caused by or attributable to the Employer, the Employer's Personnel, or the Employer's other contractors on the Site (Fig. 8.1).

A German court has held that depending on the contract wording a contractor may withhold possession of the site until full payment of all services performed by him. The facts were as such: The contract provided a clause according to which the employer was not allowed to take possession of the site until full payment of the contractor. When the employer took possession after acceptance of the works he was held guilty of deprivation of possession. Thus the contractor could require possession to be restored by the employer who was in defective possession in relation to him.[4]

8.4.2   Permits, Licences or Approvals

Sub-Clause 2.2 provides for an obligation to assist the Contractor to obtain copies of the Laws of the Country and with any applications for permits, licences or approvals required by these Laws, which are not necessarily the same as stated in Appendix to Tender being the governing law of the Contract.

8.4.3   Duty to Minimise Delay

Each Party shall at all times use all reasonable endeavours to minimise any delay in the performance of the Contract as a result of Force Majeure. Unfortunately this duty is not an overriding duty, which would be viewed in a positive light because the success of the project will strongly depend on the co-operation of the Employer. However the Contractor may at all times rely on Sub-Clause 8.4 lit. e if and when he considers to be impeded in the performance of the Contract by the Employer.

8.4.4   Duty to Make Financial Arrangements

Sub-Clause 2.4 provides for a strong instrument in favour of the Contractor. Unfortunately the Contractor's use of the sub-clause may lead to interpretation issues.

FIDIC has not defined the connotation "reasonable evidence". Some authors simply presume that Contractors and Employers would wish to have more precise

---

[4]See OLG Braunschweig [2000] IBR 116 Schwenker.

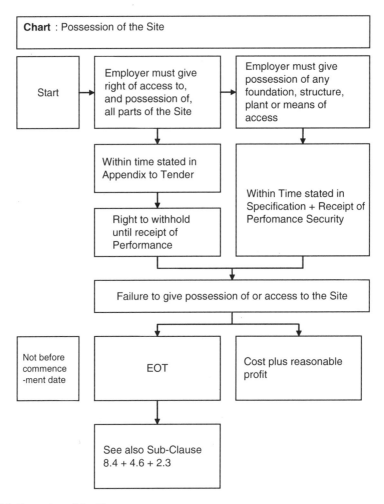

Fig. 8.1 Possession of the Site

guidelines than that and warn that the vagueness of "reasonable evidence", coupled with severe sanctions, where such is not provided for the Contractor's satisfaction, might engender much debate (Huse 2002, note 6-11; Corbett 1999, p. 41). It is of course desirable to rely only then on severe sanctions such as termination of the Contract if it is clear that all elements have been met. It is submitted that reasonable evidence does not mean conclusive evidence. However it means more than a mere allegation of fact. Thus the Employer should submit details and supporting evidence by which the Contractor may be allowed to believe that financial arrangements have been put in place and maintained. However, the means of evidence are manifold. Eligible evidence may for example consist of the production of a written instrument or witness statements. By contrast extrinsic and indirect evidence should only be accepted if the alleged fact justifies the strong presumption that financial arrangements have been put in place and maintained. An example for this may be a financial arrangement with a funding organisation. However, care must be taken in this respect. It is often the case that any extra cost caused by variations and unforeseen conditions may require the previous approval of the funding organisation before such funds are made available.

A second interpretation issue arises from the use of the connotation Contract Price (as estimated at that time). Once again the wording of Sub-Clause 2.4 is vague. The term Contract Price is subject to a definition. Pursuant to Sub-Clause 14.1 the Contract Price is the lump sum Accepted Contract Amount being subject to adjustments in accordance with the Contract. Claims and Variations shall be determined by the Engineer (Sub-Clause 3.5). Any determination is binding on the Parties of the Contract (Sub-Clause 3.5). Thus, once the Engineer has determined a Variation or a claim the Contract Price has already been adjusted. As a result an "estimate at that time" should be made prior to any determination. Hence the Contractor should be entitled to require the Employer to demonstrate financial arrangements after the issuance of any Variation even if there is not yet any determination of the Contract Price.

Moreover Sub-Clause 2.4 does not give precise guidelines for the interpretation of the word estimate. It remains therefore unclear as to who should provide the estimate (compare Totterdill 2006, p. 108) or probably better which are the estimation criteria. It seems to be clear that any over-estimation will be at the risk of the Contractor if he relies on it for the purposes of a termination notice. Thus it is strongly recommended to adopt a cautious approach in making use of Sub-Clause 2.4 with regard to an over-estimate.

There is finally authority for the view in a case from Trinidad and Tobago[5] that the Employer has to put in place financial arrangements which woud enable him to pay which may require him that Cabinet approval becomes obtained. He shall then show evidence for having obtained the approval.

8.4.5 Duty to Provide Information

Pursuant to Sub-Clause 4.10 the Employer shall make available to the Contractor all relevant data in the Employer's possession. This is obviously much less than what is required by German law, where by reference to Sect. 645 Civil Code the Employer is required to disclose all physical conditions of an unusual nature, which differ from those ordinarily found to exist and generally recognized as inherent in construction activities of the character provided for in the contract documents.

The phrase all relevant data in the Employer's possession is a very wide requirement which presumably includes all data acquired by the Employer

---

[5]National Insurance Property Development Co Ltd v. NH International (Carribbean) Ltd, High Court of Justice Trinidad und Tobago-unreported.

concerning the Site (Totterdill 2006, p. 132). However, if the contracting body is a State this requirement would probably be too wide. Supposing that the Ministry of Finance of a given State awards a contract to a Contractor for a building in a city of the relevant State, it cannot be argued that the Ministry knows what local authorities might know about the Site or that the Ministry is in possession of data which is in possession of the local authorities.

8.4.6 Estoppel

It is a common place that the law will not permit an unconscionable – or, more accurately, unconscientious – departure by one party from the subject matter of an assumption which has been adopted by the other party as the basis of some relationship, course of conduct, act or omission which would operate to that other party's detriment if the assumption be not adhered to for the purposes of the litigation. Thus in particular the Employer should carefully check whether his conduct departs from the subject matter of any assumption which the Contractor might have adopted. Usually the Contractor will assume that he will have the agreed Time for Completion in order to complete the Works, he will assume that during the Defects Notification Period he is allowed to remedy defects and that access to the Site will be given to him for those purposes. Again he will assume that the Engineer will act fairly and in a timely manner. Thus, even though the principle of good faith has not yet been generally adopted by Common law courts, failure to comply with the duty to cooperate may lead to serious disadvantages. German courts quite often refer to the duty of good faith and the duty to cooperate in particular when one of the parties is completely dishonest and/or stubborn.

8.5 Duty to Compensate

FIDIC standard terms of contract apportion and reallocate the risks that are attached to them through the operation of the contract provisions. To the extent FIDIC presumes that risk should be mitigated or reallocated by operation of compensation clauses the General Conditions provide for claims. Claim management will be discussed in detail in Chap. 21. However, some main duties to compensate shall be explained here:

1. Compensation for failure to grant access to or possession of the site
   According to Sub-Clause 2.1 the Employer shall give the Contractor right of access to, and possession of the Site within the time stated in the Appendix to Tender. If the Contractor suffers delay and/or incurs Cost as a result of a failure by the Employer to give any such right or possession within such time, the Contractor is entitled, subject to Sub-Clauses 2.1 and 20.1 to extension of Time for Completion and to payment of any such Cost plus reasonable profit.

2. Compensation of unforeseeable physical events

The Red, Yellow and Gold book follow a "traditional" foreseeability test when adverse physical conditions are encountered on site. Sub-Clause 4.10 requires the Employer to have made available all relevant data in his possession on sub-surface conditions, not later than 28 days prior to the submission of the tender. On the other hand Sub-Clause 4.10 requires the Contractor to make additional efforts in obtaining complementary data. According to Sub-Clause 4.11 lit. b the Contractor is deemed to have based the contract amount on such data. Thus in principle the Employer warrants the accuracy of the information he has provided and the Contractor is responsible for collecting additional data and for interpreting the data provided to him prior to tender.

If the Contractor encounters adverse physical conditions which he considers to have been Unforeseeable, (see Sub-Clause 1.1.6.8) the Contractor shall give notice to the Engineer as soon as practicable. If he suffers delay and/or incurs Cost due to these conditions he is entitled subject to Sub-Clauses 2.1 and 20.1 to extension of Time for Completion and to payment of any such Cost. Thus compensation will become due if the Contractor encounters adverse physical conditions which he considers to have been Unforeseeable. In order to avoid compensation to the maximum extent possible, according to Sub-Clause 4.10 the Contractor is deemed to have inspected and examined the Site and the surroundings and he is also deemed to have been satisfied before submitting the Tender as to all relevant matters, including the form and the nature of the Site and the hydrological conditions. Also he may only consider the conditions to have been unforeseeable in line with Sub-Clause 1.1.6.8, according to which Unforeseeable means not reasonably foreseeable by an experienced contractor by the date for submission of the Tender.

However two types of adverse physical conditions must be distinguished. The Contractor may encounter conditions at the Site which are (1) subsurface or otherwise concealed physical conditions which differ from those indicated in the contract documents or (2) unknown physical conditions of an unusual nature, which differ from those ordinarily found to exist and generally recognized as inherent in construction activities of the character provided for in the contract documents. Sub-Clauses 4.12 does not define the term "adverse". Thus it may be debated whether the Contractor can rely on Sub-Clause 4.12 to shift the risk to the Employer where an unforeseeable site condition is encountered, which is not an adverse physical condition. In particular under German law the Contractor may rely on unknown physical conditions of an unusual nature, which differ from those ordinarily found to exist and generally recognized as inherent in construction activities of the character provided for in the contract documents. However, whether English courts would recognise such an idea, must be left open to further discussion.

Also the question may arise whether a relevant condition is only a condition that existed at the time the contract was executed. Courts in the United States have been called upon to determine this very question.[6] In Olympus the contract contained a differing site conditions clause which provided, in relevant part:

(a) The Contractor [Olympus] shall promptly, and before the conditions are disturbed, give a written notice to the Contracting Officer of (1) subsurface or latent physical conditions at the site which differ materially from those indicated in this contract, or (2) unknown physical conditions at the site, of an unusual nature, which differ materially from those ordinarily encountered and generally recognized as inherent in the work of the character provided for in the contract.
(b) The Contracting Officer shall investigate the site conditions promptly after receiving the notice. If the conditions do materially so differ and cause an increase or decrease in the Contractor's cost of, or the time required for, performing any part of the work under this contract, whether or not changed as a result of the conditions, an equitable adjustment shall be made under this clause and the contract modified in writing accordingly.

On 18 April, Olympus received a Notice to Proceed from the Contracting Officer. One month later, Textron Lycoming, an independent government contractor that operated the plant, accidentally cut open an underground oil pipe while clearing a trench in a plant yard. Oil escaped from the pipe, contaminating the soil and preventing Olympus from paving the plant yard. Soon thereafter, Textron employees went on strike, picketing all entrances to the plant and preventing Olympus employees from accessing the plant yards for nearly two months. After the strike ended, Olympus spent one week assisting Textron's environmental contractor in the removal of the contaminated soil. On 2 August, Olympus resumed paving.

Olympus timely notified the Contracting Officer of both the contamination and strike delays and requested an equitable adjustment to the contract to provide a 69-day time extension and a price modification to account for Olympus's additional costs of $107,988.79. The Contracting Officer allowed the requested time extension, but granted a price increase of only $5,358, attributable solely to the contamination delay. Olympus rejected this proposal and submitted a claim to the Contracting Officer, demanding both additional costs and a final decision. After the Contracting Officer issued a final decision in which he rejected Olympus's claims, Olympus filed suit in the United States Court of Federal Claims seeking to recover all of its additional costs. The claim was dismissed.

The court[7] interpreted the clause to apply only to conditions existing when the contract was executed and it noted that neither the oil pipe break nor the strike locking the contractor off the site yet existed at the time the contractor signed the contract. Since those conditions arose during contract performance and did not exist when the contract was made, they did not qualify the contractor for relief under the differing site conditions clause. In addition to the temporal limitation, on which the

---

[6] Olympus Corp v. United States 98 F3d 1314 (Fed. Cir. 1996), 1317; John McShain Inc v. United States 375 F2d 829, 833 (Ct. Cl. 1967).
[7] Olympus Corp v. United States 98 F3d 1314, 1317 (Fed. Cir. 1996).

court based its decision, it was also clear that the clause applied only to "physical" conditions at the work site, not to actions of third-parties that deny the contractor access to the work site.

Although this decision can not be recognised as a rule of law and must be read in conjunction with the merits of the case and the contractual wording, it becomes obvious that Sub-Clause 4.12 should be carefully examined. Reference must be made to Sub-Clause 4.18 according to which the Contractor shall protect the environment, both on and off the Site. Further, according to Sub-Clause 4.22 the Contractor is responsible for keeping unauthorised persons off the Site. Finally Sub-Clause 4.23 puts the Contractor under the obligation to keep the Site free from all unnecessary obstruction and rubbish.

Also acts of Force Majeure are presumably not differing site conditions. Thus, groundwater at a higher level than is shown in the tender documents, which was caused by unusually heavy rain before submission of the Tender, is not an adverse site condition.

Whether the failure to actually make an inspection or examination will defeat any claim will also be an issue. It is submitted that such a failure will not defeat the claim, unless the condition would have been discovered in such a reasonable site inspection.[8]

Finally the use of the term "unforeseeable" may create difficulties in itself. The foreseeability concept is subject to fair criticism on the ground that uncertainty is introduced. Firstly the baseline of deemed knowledge is unclear. Secondly the base date must be determined which is the case in Sub-Clause 1.1.3.1. Thirdly the definition of "experienced contractor" may lead to much debate. However the concept as a whole is useful. If an event eventuates which is foreseeable, the defaulting party is considered as having assumed the risk of its realization. Contractors will frequently argue that "foreseeability" should attach even to events which would be very likely to occur in the circumstances, whilst Employers will rely on a more restrictive interpretation according to which it should apply only to very remote occurrences. In so far the standard of an experienced Contractor as referred to in Sub-Clause 1.1.6.8 is helpful. However, it may be argued that proof of foreseeability requires submission of statistical data. If an experienced Contractor would have done so, it will be a helpful argument. Finally under German law the term unforeseeable includes an element of fault or default which in principle is in line with the concept of an experienced contractor.

8.5.1 Compensation for Interference by Employer

The consequences of any interference to the Works or to progress of the Works caused by the Employer usually constitute a risk borne by the Employer. If such a

---

[8] Vann v. United States 420 F2d 968 (Ct. Cl. 1970).

risk eventuates it should be compensated. FIDIC is in line with this principle. Examples are Sub-Clauses 2.1, 7.4, 8.4 lit. e, 8.4 lit. a, etc. The main issue regarding such a compensation clause is whether the interference is already covered by the Contract. In many cases the Specifications, Employer's Requirements and other Contract documents provide for particular solutions. Quite often co-operation requirements are already specified within the documents which will otherwise result in a Variation in accordance with Sub-Clause 4.6. Additional testing requirements will be found in the Specifications or Employer's Requirements as well. However, if not, Sub-Clause 7.4 may be applicable. The Engineer may instruct acceleration in accordance with Sub-Clause 8.6 if the Contractor is late.

References

Corbett E (1999) FIDIC's new rainbow: an overview of the red, yellow, silver and green test editions. ICLR 39

Furst S, Ramsley V (2006) Keating on construction contracts, 8th edn. Sweet & Maxwell, London

Huse JA (2002) Understanding and negotiating turnkey and EPC contracts, 2nd edn. Sweet & Maxwell, London

Totterdill BW (2006) FIDIC user's guide, 2nd edn. Thomas Telford, London

Chapter 9
Contractor's Duties

9.1 Introduction

The Contractor promises to the Employer to complete the Works and to remedy any defects therein (Red Book). If the contract provides for the design by the Contractor (Yellow Book and Silver Book), then he will design the Works as well. The design, if any, and the completion of the Works including the remedying of defects shall be accomplished within Time for Completion. Moreover, if the contract provides for the operation of the Works by the Contractor (Gold Book), then he will also operate the Works.

9.1.1 Pre-contractual Duties

It is common sense that a contract is a legally binding instrument which creates obligations. However, prior to the execution of a contract the parties enter either into negotiations or are involved in a formal procurement procedure. At this stage the employer or client will disclose the project requirements combined with site data and other useful information in order to enable the contractor or consultant to submit an offer. Whether and to what extent already at this stage enforceable obligations between the parties as to the way in which they are to behave do exist is questionable (see Hök 2009, p. 23 et seq.). However FIDIC forms of contract clearly create retroactive obligations. According to Sub-Clause 4.10 the Contractor shall carry out inspections and examinations of the Site before submitting his tender. According to Sub-Clause 5.1 Yellow, Silver Book and Gold Book he shall also be deemed to have scrutinised the Employer's Requirements. If the Contractor encounters difficulties as a result of any errors, fault or defect in the Employer's Requirements which could have been disclosed by an experienced Contractor before submitting the Tender the Time for Completion and the Contract Price shall not be adjusted.

A.-V. Jaeger and G.-S. Hök, *FIDIC-A Guide for Practitioners*,
DOI 10.1007/978-3-642-02100-8_9, © Springer-Verlag Berlin Heidelberg 2010

9.1.2   Completion of the Works

The general duty of the Contractor consists in the obligation to complete the Works in compliance with the Contract. His responsibility for quality is therein embedded. The below mentioned features are in line with his contractual duty to provide the Works in accordance with the Contract. Additionally the General Conditions at Sub-Clause 7.1 put the Contractor under the obligation to carry out the manufacture of Plant, the production and manufacture of Materials, and all other execution of the Works in a manner specified in the Contract, in a proper workmanlike and careful manner, in accordance with recognised practise and with properly applied facilities, etc.

FIDIC contracts have always embedded with them particular features in order to ensure best quality. Since the 1999 FIDIC Edition has been published, quality is no longer defined by reference to the Engineers opinion or satisfaction. It is strictly defined and specified by the Contract itself. The current Rainbow Edition provides the following features:

- The Contractor shall remedy any defects in the Works (Sub-Clause 4.1).
- The Employer's Personnel has full access to all parts of the Site (Sub-Clause 7.3 lit. a).
- The Employer's Personnel is entitled to examine, inspect, measure and test the materials and workmanship (Sub-Clause 7.3 lit. b).
- The Engineer is entitled to carry out examinations, inspections, measurement or testing (Sub-Clause 7.3).
- The Contractor shall uncover work, which is covered, put out of sight, or packaged for storage or transport before giving notice that work was ready (Sub-Clause 7.3).
- The Engineer may attend any tests (Sub-Clause 7.4).
- The Engineer may reject any Plant, Materials or workmanship found to be defective (Sub-Clause 7.5).
- The Engineer may require Plant, Materials or workmanship to be retested (Sub-Clause 7.5).
- The Engineer may instruct the Contractor to remove from the Site and replace any Plant or Materials which is not in accordance with Contract (Sub-Clause 7.6 lit. a).
- The Engineer may instruct the Contractor to remove and re-execute any other work which is not in accordance with Contract (Sub-Clause 7.6 lit. b).
- The Engineer may instruct the Contractor to complete any outstanding work (Sub-Clause 11.1 lit. a).
- The Employer may give notice to the Contractor of defects or damage on ore before expiry of the Defects Notification period (Sub-Clause 11.1 lit. b).
- The Employer may give notice to the Contractor of any defective work which is not attributable to the Contractor (Sub-Clause 11.2).
- The Employer may fix a date, on or by which a defect or damage is to be remedied (Sub-Clause 11.4).

- The Employer may carry out remedial work by himself or by others (Sub-Clause 11.4 lit. a).
- The Employer may require the Engineer to agree or determine a reasonable deduction in the Contract Price (Sub-Clause 11.4 lit. b).
- The Employer may terminate the Contract if a defect or damage deprives him of substantially the whole benefit of eth Works or any major part of the Works (Sub-Clause 11.4 lit. c).
- The Contractor shall submit monthly progress reports which shall include photographs showing the status of manufacture and progress on the Site (Sub-Clause 4.21).
- The Contractor shall submit monthly progress reports which shall include copies of quality assurance documents, test results and certificates of materials (Sub-Clause 4.21).
- The Contractor shall submit all Contractor's Documents which are stated in the Particular Conditions for review and/or for approval (Sub-Clause 5.2).
- The Contractor shall correct any errors, omissions, ambiguities, inconsistencies, inadequacies or other defects found in the Contractor's Documents (Sub-Clause 5.8).

This quality framework is the contractual approach of quality assurance. The above mentioned features intend to ensure access to all parts of the works and compliance with the Contract. It is intended to avoid defects as early as possible and to deal with defects without recourse to legal proceedings. Prior to the issue of the Performance Certificate the Works shall be free of any defects.

9.1.3 Design

The Contractor may also assume the responsibility for the design. Design by the Contractor, if any, shall be fit for purpose (Sub-Clause 4.1) and in accordance with the Specifications (Red Book) or Employer's Requirements (Yellow Book, Silver Book, Gold Book), as the case may be. The design responsibility is subject to further consideration in Chap. 10.

9.1.4 Operation

Under the Gold Book the Contractor also assumes the responsibility for the operation of the Works. The Gold Book comprises an aggregate Contract Period, divided in a design and build period and an Operation Service Period, followed by a post contract liability period subject to the governing law (Figs. 9.1 and 9.2). At the end of each contractual period a certificate will be issued, so that each period will have an exact end and commencement date. A particularity of the DBO form may be

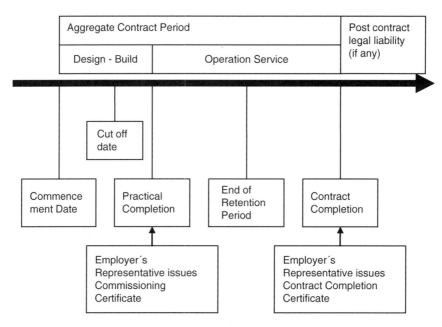

Fig. 9.1 DBO project development I

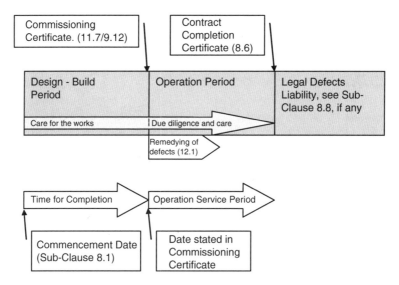

Fig. 9.2 DBO project development II

found in Sub-Clause 9.13. This clause represents a safeguard for the Employer if the Contractor fails to complete by the Cut-Off Date. If the Contractor is seriously late, the Employer is allowed to terminate the contract.

According to Sub-Clause 4.1 as soon as the works are completed, the Contractor shall enter into the last phase of the contract, which is the Operation Service Period, covered in detail in Clause 10. At the end of this period the Employer's Representative will issue the Contract Completion Certificate (Sub-Clauses 10.8, 8.6).

Unless otherwise stated in the Employer's Requirements, the Operation Service shall begin from the date stated in the Commissioning Certificate (Sub-Clause 10.2). During the Operation Service period the Contractor shall provide the Operation Service in compliance with the Operation Management Requirements (Sub-Clause 10.1) and the Operating Licence (see Sub-Clauses 1.7). The obligation of the Contractor to operate and to maintain the Plant shall cease at the end of the period stated in the Contract as the Operation Service Period (Cl. 10.8). But in fact the performance of the Contractor's obligations in respect of the Contract shall not be considered to have been completed until the Contract Completion Certificate has been signed by the Employer's Representative and issued to the Contractor (Sub-Clause 8.6). Moreover, and this is something which should not be ignored, Sub-Clause 8.8 makes clear that each Party shall remain liable for the fulfilment of any obligation which remains unperformed at the time of the issue of the Contract Completion Certificate. As neither Sub-Clause 8.6 nor Sub-Clause 8.8 include terms such as "final and binding", it is submitted that the issuing of the Contract Completion Certificate will not serve as final and conclusive proof as to the Contractor's satisfactory performance under the Contract. Hence in principle a post contractual defects liability period according to the applicable law (legal defects liability) can be attached to the defects liability period under the contract, but this issue is subject to further discussion below.

According to Sub-Clause 11.7 the Commissioning Certificate shall be deemed to constitute acceptance of the *Works*. However, in order to avoid premature conclusions Sub-Clause 11.7 should be read together with Sub-Clause 8.6 where it is ruled that only the Contract Completion Certificate shall be deemed to constitute acceptance of the "Contractor's completion of his obligations under the Contract" and that only following the issue of the Contract Completion Certificate shall the Employer be fully responsible for the care, safety, operation, servicing and maintenance of the Works. Finally Sub-Clause 17.5 provides that the Contractor takes full responsibility for the care of the Works from the Commencement Date until the Commissioning Certificate is issued and that he shall also be responsible for the care of the Permanent Works during the Operation Service Period.

However, at any time during the aggregate Contract Period the Employer's Representative may instruct the Contractor to remove from the Site and replace any Plant or Materials which are not in accordance with the Contract, remove and re-execute any other work which is not in accordance with the Contract and execute any work which is urgently required for the safety of he Works (Sub-Clause 7.6). In addition to that the Contractor remains liable to maintain the Plant until the Contract Completion Certificate has been issued (Sub-Clause 10.8). Moreover the Contractor is kept under an obligation to repair and make good any damage or defect occurring during the Operation Service Period (Sub-Clause 12.1 lit. b).

It follows from Sub-Clause 8.6 that only by means of the issue of the Contract Completion Certificate will the Employer be fully responsible for the care, safety, operation, servicing and maintenance of the Works. However, in principle and subject to Sub-Clause 8.8 the Employer remains able to sue the Contractor for defective works subject to the proper law of the contract.

It should be emphasised that the Contract Committee did not aim to deviate from the principle of substantial completion. Sub-Clause 11.5 mirrors the principle and keeps hold of it. Meanwhile Sub-Clause 9.12 does not at all envisage changing it. Whereas Sub-Clause 11.5 lists the conditions which must be met for the issue of the Commissioning Certificate Sub-Clause 9.12 only summarises all of the steps until substantial completion. Of course the Works must be fully designed and executed. But this must have been done in accordance with the Employer's Requirements and other relevant provisions of the contract, including Sub-Clause 11.5.

The objective of the Operation Service Period is that the Contractor operates the Plant and maintains it until the issue of the Contract Completion Certificate. The obligation to maintain and to operate is clearly expressed in Sub-Clause 4.1. In addition to that Sub-Clauses 14.18 and 14.19 presuppose that the Contractor maintains and replaces Plant and Material. For the purposes of the Operation Service Period FIDIC has established some new features:

Operation and Maintenance Plan: This document is subject to a definition in Sub-Clause 1.1.56 and means the plan for operating and maintaining the facility, submitted by the Contractor, and agreed and included in the Contract

Operation Management Requirements: This document is subject to a definition in Sub-Clause 1.1.55 and means the set of procedures and requirements, provided by the Employer, included in the Employer's Requirements for the proper implementation of the Operation Service

Operating Licence: This document is subject to a definition in Sub-Clause 1.1.54 and means the licence referred to in Sub-Clause 1.7. It is intended to grant the legal authorisation enabling the Contractor to operate and maintain the Works.

Operation and Maintenance Manuals: These documents shall be prepared by the Contractor who shall submit them to the Employer's Representative prior to the commencement of the Commissioning Period as provided for in Sub-Clause 5.6

Handback Requirements: The handback requirements are referred to in Sub-Clause 8.7 and are part of the Employer's Requirements

Sub-Clause 10.1 stipulates the Contractor's obligation to comply with the Operation Management Requirements and to follow the Operation and Maintenance Plan as submitted and agreed. The Operating Licence (see Sub-Clause 1.7) shall be issued together with the Letter of Acceptance and come in force upon the issue of the Commissioning Certificate. It seems however that FIDIC has put the main focus on the maintenance obligation of the Contractor rather than to specify any particular operation details. Thus details of the operation and maintenance service must be specified in the Operation Management Requirements, the Operation and Maintenance Plan and the according Manuals. The Operating Licence will only constitute the authorisation to enable the Contractor to run the Works.

Hence, the operation of the plant has to be carried out in compliance with the Operation Management Requirements and the Operation Maintenance Plan. The Employer is only responsible for the delivery of any raw materials (Sub-Clause 10.4). During the Operation Service Period the Contractor shall achieve the production outputs required under the terms of the Contract (Sub-Clause 10.7). Failure to achieve the production outputs may lead to claims of the Employer and/or the Contractor subject to the independent audit. Any further detail as to the operational duty has to be put in the Employer's Requirements and in the Operation and Maintenance Plan.

As to the maintenance of the Plant, FIDIC adopts quite a sophisticated approach. Again FIDIC has introduced some new features, such as the Asset Replacement Schedule (Sub-Clause 14.5), the Asset Replacement Fund (Sub-Clause 14.18) and the Maintenance Retention Fund (Sub-Clause 14.19).

Major items of Plant specified in the Asset Replacement Schedule may be replaced as foreseen in the Schedule and according to Sub-Clause 14.18, being mutually agreed under competition. All routine maintenance work, replacement of Plant and Materials with a life expectancy of less than 5 years and the provision of any spares between scheduled dates for major plant replacement as well as the replacement of Plant and Materials which are not identified in the Asset Replacement Schedule is included in the Contract Price (see Sub-Clause 14.18). In order to secure the maintenance required under the Contract the Maintenance Retention Fund shall be created by deducting 5% from the value of each Interim Payment during the Operation Service Period due to the Contractor but limited to an amount stated in the Contract Data (if any). According to Sub-Clause 12.1 lit. b the Contractor shall also be responsible for repairing and making good any damage or defect occurring the Operation Service Period. All that work shall be executed at the risk and cost of the Contractor except where it is attributable to any act by the Employer or his employees or agents or where it is as a result of an event that is covered under Clause 18. In such an event the work required to remedy any defect or damage shall be dealt as a variation upon notification of the Contractor. In so far FIDIC has slightly changed the wording of the Rainbow Edition, where the Employer was required to notify the Contractor in order to activate the variation process.

Not less than two years prior to the expiry date of the Operation Service Period the Employer's Representative and the Contractor shall carry out a joint inspection of the Works (Sub-Clause 11.8). As a result of the joint inspection the Contractor shall submit a report on the condition of the Works identifying maintenance works (excluding routine maintenance works and the correction of defects), replacement and other works required to be carried out to satisfy the handback requirements of the Operation and Maintenance Plan after the Contract Completion Date. This work shall be carried out over the remainder of the Operation Service Period at the Contractor's cost, unless the items to replace are specified in the Asset Replacement Schedule. Towards the end of the Operation Service Period tests prior to contract completion shall be carried out in accordance with the Employer's Requirements (Sub-Clause 11.9).

FIDIC has left open to mutual agreement any standard for the Tests prior to Contract Completion. It is submitted that the Employer is free to define this standard in the Employer's Requirements subject to further pre-contractual negotiations.

Subject to Sub-Clause 1.7 the Operating Licence shall give the authorisation to enable the Contractor to operate and maintain the Plant during the Operation Service. It is not intended that the Contractor operates and maintains the Plant in his vested interest. To the contrary he acts on behalf of the Employer. For precaution FIDIC has made clear that the Licence does not grant any title in land.

9.2 Quality and Defects

9.2.1 Overview

As already mentioned above FIDIC dedicates a whole set of provisions to quality. The Engineer has full power to reject defective works at any time during the course of the Works. The Contractor shall then promptly make good the defect and ensure that the rejected item complies with the Contract. If the Contractor fails to do so the Engineer may give instructions according to Sub-Clause 7.6. He may instruct the Contractor to:

(a) Remove from the Site and replace any Plant or Materials which are not in accordance with the Contract
(b) Remove and re-execute any other work which is not in accordance with the Contract
(c) Execute any work which is urgently required for the safety of the Works, whether because of an accident, unforeseeable event or otherwise

If the Contractor fails to comply with the instructions of the Engineer, the Employer shall be entitled to employ and pay other persons to carry out the work. Except to the extent that the Contractor would have been entitled to payment for the work, the Contractor shall subject to Sub-Clause 2.5 [Employer's Claims] pay to the Employer all costs arising from this failure.

9.2.2 Workmanlike Manner

Everything in this regard seems to be clear and straightforward. Irrespective of any legal approach as to defects the Contractor's liability will depend on the workmanlike manner in which the works must be carried out, the use of good and appropriate materials and goods and finally on the purposes of the project. The contract documents may specify workmanship, materials and determine the purposes.

As already mentioned all Works shall be carried out in a proper workmanlike and careful manner and in accordance with recognised practice. Whatever this standard may be remains open or subject to further specification by the Contract. Sub-Clause 7.1 does not refer to local standards of workmanship or recognised practice. Whether an internationally and globally recognised practice has been established must be doubted. However, the Contractor must comply with local laws and technical standards, which can be clearly seen in the requirements of Sub-Clauses 1.13 and 5.4 (Yellow Book and Silver Book). It is therefore suggested that Sub-Clause 7.1 refers also to local standards unless otherwise defined in the Particular Conditions. However, it happens that the parties to the contract ignore that the reference in Sub-Clause 8.3 to the programme includes method statements. According to Sub-Clause 8.3 the Contractor shall submit a programme including "a general description of the methods which the Contractor intends to adopt". The methods statement should identify the standards of workmanship which the Contractor intends to apply. It follows from this that the Contractor is not only under the duty to submit a time schedule but also quality related statements. The Engineer may reject the programme stating the extent to which it does not comply with the Contract. He may thus reject the programme not only for failure from the part of the Contractor to comply with time for completion but also for failure to comply with methods in accordance with the Contract. The related reasons for not accepting the programme may be as follows:

- The methods do not comply with the prescriptions in the Particular Conditions or Employer's Requirements.
- The methods which are stated in the programme are not practicable.
- The methods do not meet the local or otherwise specified standards of workmanship.
- The programme does not show the methods at all or insufficiently.
- The programme does not comply with express or implied constraints in the Contract.

Care must be exercised from the outset that the Contract ensures compliance with the required standards. Any constraints on methods subsequently introduced by the Engineer or Employer will probably lead into a Variation subject to Clause 13. Thus any special requirements as to the methods to be applied by the Contractor must already be clearly stated in the contract documents. However, the Contractor must be aware of the fact that, although the Employer's Personnel may rely on the actual programme until revised, the programme which was not rejected is not deemed to be accepted by the Engineer or the Employer. Failure to comply with the programming requirements under Sub-Clause 8.3 does not mean that the Contractor is allowed to stop work. If even the Engineer rejects a submitted programme for failure to comply with Sub-Clause 8.3 the Contractor is still bound to continue working. However, the lack of attention by the Contractor to his obligations with regard to Sub-Clause 8.3 results in the risk that the Engineer carries out his own assessment and issues instructions subject to Sub-Clause 8.6. Failure to comply with Sub-Clause 8.3 may also be one of the relevant circumstances to be taken in consideration under Sub-Clause 3.5.

However it must be noted that English courts are reluctant to judge the work in progress by the standards applicable to completed works, unless and until the contractor had said that, in his opinion, those works were indeed complete. To put the point another way, the Engineer should only be condemning a defect; if the work is not yet finished, it cannot fairly be said to be defective. It has been held in Oval[1] that:

> An employer such as the plaintiff expects that the contractor will proceed in a regular and diligent fashion with the performance of its obligations, but it does not expect initial perfection in on-site performance by all operatives engaged in the works at all times (see generally the well-known observations of Lord Diplock[2] with which I find myself in total agreement and respectfully follow) … It follows that, in my view, such temporary disconformities would not constitute either non-performance or non-observance of the terms of the construction contract.

9.2.3 Design Skills

As a matter of fact all obligations of the Contractor are more or less dependent on design skills. Even under the Red Book the Contractor assumes design responsibilities. It cannot be denied that the choice of materials and workmanship involves design responsibilities. Thus the dividing line between the Red Book and the Yellow Book is much finer than is commonly supposed. It is suggested that the Contractor's main obligation under the Red Book, which is the obligation to carry out the Works, undeniably includes design responsibilities. The difference between the Red and the Yellow Book lays in the extent to which design responsibilities are shifted to the Contractor.

9.2.4 Definition of the Term "Defect"

However the question may arise as to what a defect is. The meaning of the term "defect" is not defined by FIDIC conditions, neither for the purposes of the defects correction obligation under the contract, nor for the purposes of the post contractual legal liability, the latter being completely submitted to the discretion of the governing law. Hence its meaning is subject to determination by the applicable law. Unfortunately the exact characteristics of the contractor's liabilities for defects are inconsistent with one another throughout different jurisdictions.

---

[1] Oval (717) Ltd v. Aegon Insurance Co (UK) Ltd [1997] 54 Con LR 74.
[2] P and M Kaye Ltd v. Hosier and Dickinson Ltd [1972] 1 WLR 146.

According to Section 633 paragraph 2 German Civil Code:

the work or service is free from defects as to quality if it is of the agreed nature. To the
extent that the nature has not been agreed, the work or service is free from defects in quality

1. if it is suitable for the use presupposed by the contract, otherwise
2. if it is suitable for customary use and has a nature that is customary with works and
   services of the same type and that the customer may expect from that type of work.

If the contractor produces work different from the work ordered or work of a lesser
amount than that ordered, that is equivalent to a defect as to quality.

Section 633 Civil Code understands the term defect as a divergence from the
contractually agreed work programme. Defective work is understood as a subdivi-
sion of non performance. In principle the Works must be of the agreed nature,
alternatively of the commonly presupposed nature or else of the customary nature.
The courts usually assume that the Contractor has tacitly agreed to recognise the
"acknowledged technical rules" or the rules of profession. If the parties have
incorporated the VOB part C all of the DIN norms being part of it become part of
the contract. Usually the works must comply with these standards and norms.

In a recently settled case the Federal Supreme Court[3] has overruled the decisions
of the High Court of Munich II and the Court of Appeal of Munich who both had
dismissed a claim for defects by the owner against a technical firm having agreed to
execute the works for the heating of a house which was not connected with the
public electrical grid. Thus the heating system was to be connected with a co-
generation plant having been constructed by another company. After completion it
proved that the house's consumption of electricity was too low for the production of
sufficient waste heat by the co-generation plant. Thus there was not enough waste
heat in order to heat the house. Other than the High Court and the Court of Appeal
the Federal Supreme held that the heating system was not fit for the intended
purposes. Whilst the High Court and the Court of Appeal considered that the
heating system as such was fit to heat the house if there would have been enough
waste heat, the Federal Supreme Court assumed that the construction of the contract
must include all relevant characteristics of the works, which subject to the agreement shall constitute the result of the works, in order to ascertain the agreed nature
of the works. The result which is due by virtue of the contract shall be determined
by the purposes of the works according to the intentions of the parties. Hence the
works must meet the agreed and assumed purpose. If not the works are considered
to be defective. In the given case the agreed purpose of the works was to heat the
house which was not met. This was due to the insufficient production of waste heat
of the co-generation plant having been built by another company. However, in the
eyes of the Federal Supreme Court that was no valid defence because of the duty of
the technical firm to advise the owner.

French law seems to be much more sophisticated. The term "defect" may be
translated by "vice", "malfaçon", "défaut de conformité" or "désordre", each of

---

[3] BGH [2008] IBR 77 Veyer.

them having a particular meaning. According to Art. 1792-6 paragraph 2 French Civil Code the Contractor is under a warranty of perfect completion. The warranty of perfected completion, to which a contractor is held during a period of 1 year, after the approval of the works, extends to the repairs of all shortcomings indicated by the building owner, either through reservations mentioned in the memorandum of approval, or by way of written notice as to those revealed after the approval. In addition according to Art. 1792 Civil Code any builder of a work is liable as of right, towards the building owner or purchaser, for damages, even resulting from a defect of the ground, which imperil the strength of the building or which, affecting it in one of its constituent parts or one of its elements of equipment, render it unsuitable for its purposes. This is the famous French decennial liability. However the meaning of the term "defect" will be settled on case by case basis. As a rule a French Contractor owes a duty to achieve a result (obligation de résultat).[4] It has been held by French courts that the contractor was liable for plastering works even though it did not have any function of impermeability.[5] Non-conformity of the works will be assumed in comparison to the contractual stipulations (Caston 2000, note 4-90).

Apparently also under the common law the term "defect" is not a fundamental legal term. There must be a breach of contract. The existence of a defect means that there is a breach of contract by the contractor.[6] In general "breach" in relation to a contract means a failure, without legal justification, to perform an obligation under the contract as required by the contract. However, as Hudson (Wallace 1995, note 5.025) suggests, defective work can be described as work which fails to comply with the express descriptions or requirements of the contract, including very importantly any drawings or specifications, together with any implied terms as to its quality, workmanship, performance or design. By definition, therefore, defects are breaches of contract by the contractor (Wallace 1995, note 5.025). Hence as in Germany technical and contractual defects constitute breach. But it must be doubted that under common law the overall purposes of the works will be taken into consideration. This would not be in line with the speech of HHJ Seymour in *Tesco Stores*[7] where he held:

.. the law does not impose upon parties a contract which they have not made for themselves, any more than it imposes upon parties who have made a contract a term as an implied term which they have not themselves agreed just because the court considers that the term would be a beneficial addition to the contract.

Other than in Germany in England there is no legal background to come to the result that a contractor must comply with the "assumed purpose", unless there is an

---

[4] Cour de Cassation, 07.03.1968 D. 1970, 27.
[5] Cour de Cassation, 18.12.1996, arrêt no. 1987 D, see Caston (2000, note 3–8).
[6] Pearce & High Ltd v. Baxter & Anor [1999] EWCA Civ 789 (15 February 1999).
[7] Tesco Stores Ltd v. Costain Construction Ltd & Ors [2003] EWHC 1487 (TCC) (02 July 2003) relying on Lord Pearson in Trollope & Colls Ltd v. North West Metropolitan Regional Hospital Board [1973] 1 WLR 601, p. 609.

express contractual provision to this effect. However it can be summarised that common law implies the obligation on the Contractor to construct the works free from defects at final completion[8] and to use material and products which will be of merchantable quality and fit for their intended purpose.[9]

Thus, in an English construction contract there is usually a term, implied as a matter of law, that the Contractor would perform any construction work which it undertook under the contract in a good and workmanlike manner. That term is usually implied into a building contract which is silent as to the quality of the work to be undertaken.[10] If the Contractor's obligation includes a requirement for good workmanship the Contractor must carry out the work with all proper skill and care.[11] Only where the Employer makes known to the Contractor the particular purpose for which the Works shall be carried out and the work is of a kind which the Contractor holds himself out as performing, and the circumstances show that the Employer relied on the Contractor's skill and judgment in the matter, there is an implied warranty that the work as completed will be reasonably fit for the particular purpose.[12] At the latest since IBA v. EMI and BICC it is clear that under a contract for professional services, such as to design and build a structure, a term may be implied at common law that the finished structure will be reasonably fit for the client's purposes.[13] The English position has for example been pointed out in Tesco Stores Ltd v. Costain Construction Ltd & Ors[14] by HHJ Seymour who held: "It may be appropriate to imply into a construction contract a term that the structure to be erected will, when complete, be reasonably fit for its intended purpose, but that will only be so if and insofar as the structure is to be designed by the contractor". In light of the reasoning of House of Lords in Young & Marten[15] this obligation is absolute (Wallace 1995, note 4-072). In IBA v. EMI Electronics and BICC Construction Ltd, where an aerial television mast collapsed from two separate causes operating at the same time, Lord Scarman stated "I do not accept that the design obligation of the supplier of an article is to be equated with the obligation of a professional man in the practice of his profession", where EMI had sought to argue that where a design required the exercise of professional skill, the obligation was no more than to exercise the care and skill of an ordinary competent member of the profession.[16]

---

[8] Sealand of the Pacific v. Ocean Cement Ltd (1973) 33 DLR (3d) 625.

[9] Young & Marten Ltd v. McManus Childs [1969] 1 AC 454, HL.

[10] See, for example, Hancock v. B. W. Brazier (Anerley) Ltd [1966] 1 WLR 1317.

[11] Young & Marten Ltd v. McManus Childs [1969] 1 AC 454, HL.

[12] Furst and Ramsley (2006, note 3-060) relying on Greaves & Co. (Contractors) Ltd v. Baynham Meikle and Partners [1975] 1 WLR 1095, p. 1098.

[13] IBA v. EMI Electronics and BICC Construction Ltd (1980) 14 BLR 1, p. 9.

[14] [2003] EWHC 1487 (TCC) (02 July 2003).

[15] Young & Marten Ltd v. McManus Childs [1969] 1 AC 454, HL.

[16] (1980) 14 BLR 1, p. 47: The less important of the causes was negligent design by sub-contractors, but they were held liable on the basis that their negligence materially contributed to the collapse notwithstanding that Lord Fraser of Tullybelton considered that the other cause was "by far the more important".

The existence of the term in that type of case was explained by Lord Denning MR in *Greaves & Co. (Contractors) Ltd v. Baynham Meikle and Partners.*[17] However, it is clear from the decision of the Court of Appeal in *Lynch v. Thorne*[18] that there is no such implied term in a case in which the contractor undertakes to build to a particular specification already, at the date of the relevant contract, devised by or on behalf of the employer, and it must follow that there is no such implied term if the contractor agrees to build in accordance with plans or specifications to be produced in the future by others.[19] If there is no such implied term the Contractor the Contractor shall comply with due skill and care only. But this may include relying uncritically and without due precautions on an incorrect design supplied by the Employer where an ordinarily competent builder should have grave doubts about the design's correctness.[20] In the Australian case of *Onerati v. Phillips Constructions Pty Ltd (in liq)*,[21] the court held that faulty workmanship is a reference to the manner in which something was done, to fault on the part of a workman or workmen (referred to in Dorter 1999, p. 369).

9.2.5 Operation Service

If the Contractor assumes the responsibility for the operation of the Works, as is the case under the FIDIC Gold Book, again the question arises with which standard the Contractor shall comply. It is envisaged by the Contracts Committee that the Employer shall include the operation requirements in the Employer's Requirements. The Contractor shall then develop the Operation and Maintenance Plan from it. Finally the Contractor shall follow the requirements of the Operation and Maintenance Plan and the operation and maintenance manuals. In the event that the Contractor fails to achieve the production outputs required under the Contract and the cause of failure lies with the Contractor, he then shall take all steps necessary to restore the output to the levels required under the Contract. It is submitted that this implies only skill and care. However, according to Sub-Clause 12.1 the Contractor is responsible for repairing and making good any damage or defect occurring during the Operation Service Period. It is submitted that this implies a standard fit for the purposes.

---

[17] [1975] 1 WLR 1095, p. 1098.

[18] [1956] 1 WLR 303.

[19] Tesco Stores Ltd v. Costain Construction Ltd & Ors [2003] EWHC 1487 (TCC) (02 July 2003); in line with Lynch v. Thorne [1956] 1 WLR 303, at 311 (CA).

[20] Furst and Ramsley (2006, note 3-056) relying on Lindeberg v. Canning (1992) 62 BLR 147, where a plan incorrectly showed obviously load bearing walls as non-load-bearing.

[21] (1989) 16 NSWLR 730.

9.2.6   Final Remarks

In practice quality will depend on the quality of the contract documents. The pass mark is compliance with the contract rather than some other test, and one should start with interpreting the contract. Although the Engineer will have the authority to test quality and to give instructions the former wording that the Works shall be "to the satisfaction of the Engineer" has been abandoned by FIDIC. Thus it is critical to clearly specify the performance criteria and the intended purposes. Most disputes arise from ambiguous and incomplete specifications and/or Employer's Requirements. A qualified and skilful quality pre-determination will often avoid disputes. The performance criteria will constitute the basis for quality control by the Engineer. If he expects better quality than agreed his instructions will constitute a Variation. Once having acknowledged this principle there is a big incentive to prepare comprehensive and clear contract documents in order to avoid cost overruns.

The intended purposes of the Works may be expressly or implicitly defined by the contract. In most cases the intended purposes are not expressly defined. They must then be inferred from the contract wording. For example a TV mast should be able to withstand likely weather conditions in the area where it was built or a heating system should heat a house or a Railway bridge should bear the load of a train.

9.3   Time for Completion

9.3.1   Duty to Comply with Time for Completion

According to Sub-Clause 8.2 the Contractor shall complete the whole of the Works, and each Section (if any), within Time for Completion for the Works or Section. The Appendix to Tender must state the quantity of time representing Time for Completion, which may be extended according to Sub-Clause 8.4. It is strongly recommended to state the relevant Time for Completion in Days and not in "months" or "weeks". A Day is a defined term meaning a calendar day whilst the terms months and week are not defined and therefore open to discussion and varying interpretation by the Parties.

9.3.2   Programme

Supposing that a Contractor promised to carry out works under a FIDIC contract, Sub-Clause 8.3 requires the Contractor to submit a programme to the Engineer or Employer as the case may be subject to the applied FIDIC contract form.

The programme must show how the Contractor aims to satisfy the Employer's Requirements in accordance with the whole contract.

According to Sub-Clause 8.3 (Red and Yellow Forms) the Contractor must submit a "detailed time programme" to the Engineer within 28 days of the notice of the Commencement Date, whilst under the Silver Book it is sufficient to submit a "time programme". The term "detailed time programme" is not a defined term, but Sub-Clause 8.3 lists details which are to be included with any programme submitted. These requirements may be amplified or extended in the Particular Conditions.

All three of the FIDIC forms require the programme to include the order in which the Contractor intends to carry out the Works, anticipated timing of various stages of work and the sequence and timing of inspections and tests specified in the Contract. The programme shall include a supporting report which gives a general description of the methods which the Contractor intends to adopt, and the major stages, in the execution of the Works. The report must also give details of resources. The term "programme" is therefore not simply used in the sense of a list of activities and dates, nor just a Bar Chart, but includes the method statement and allocation of resources.

The description of the programme in Sub-Clause 8.3 specifies the form that the programme should take. There is a clear duty to submit a method statement, showing the order in which the Contractor intends to carry out the Works, including the anticipated timing of each major stage of the Works, which implies a duty to submit the programme in the form of logic links between activities. It is therefore not sufficient to submit a programme in the form of a bar chart, together with the supporting report.

The main role of the programme under the FIDIC forms is to monitor the progress of the works by comparison to actual progress with the programme. Sub-Clause 8.3 provides that unless the Engineer (or the Employer under the Silver Form) gives notice that a submitted programme does not comply with the contract, the Contractor is required to proceed in accordance with the programme, subject to his other obligations under the contract. The Employer's Personnel is expressly entitled to rely on the programme when planning their activities. Hence the Contractor is under the express obligation to follow the programme, although this obligation is subject to his other obligations. This role is clearly shown in the requirements of Sub-Clauses 8.3, 4.21(h) and 8.6:

- Sub-Clause 8.3, also referred to as an early warning duty (Totterdill 2006, p. 180), requires the Contractor to promptly give notice to the Engineer of specific probable future events or circumstances which may delay the execution of the work. Under the Red and Yellow Book forms, the Engineer may request the Contractor to submit an estimate of the anticipated effect.
- Sub-Clause 4.21 requires a comparison of actual and planned progress to be included in the monthly report, which must be read in context with Sub-Clause 8.6
- Sub-Clause 8.6 entitles the Employer (or Engineer) to instruct the submission of a revised programme in the event of too slow actual progress

- The Engineer may also require a proposal for a Variation under Sub-Clause 13.3 of the Red and Yellow Book forms, which by contrast, will bar him to proceed in accordance with Sub-Clause 8.6. The Contractor is then obliged to state reasons why he cannot comply, or make a submission which includes a programme for the proposed work and the necessary modifications to the programme.

Moreover the role of the programme is to provide a means of assessment as to the effects of identified future and actual events. In other words, the programme will be used to demonstrate whether any event will cause a delay to completion. This role is clearly shown in the requirements of Sub-Clauses 8.3 and 8.4.

9.3.3   Obligation to Proceed in Accordance with the Programme

The Contractor is under the continuous obligation to proceed in accordance with the (its) programme and to update the programme. By contrast the Employer has the right to terminate in the event of failure of the Contractor to follow the programme (see Sub-Clause 15.2) or to issue a request subject to Sub-Clause 8.6.

If actual progress is too slow to complete with Time for Completion and actual progress has fallen behind the current programme, the Employer (or the Engineer) may instruct the Contractor to submit a revised programme and supporting report describing the revised methods which the Contractor proposes to adopt in order to expedite progress and complete within the Time for Completion (Sub-Clause 8.6). Unless the Employer notifies otherwise, the Contractor shall adopt these revised methods, which may require increases in the working hours and/or in the numbers of Contractor's Personnel and/or Goods, at the risk and cost of the Contractor. However, if these revised methods cause the Employer to incur additional costs, the Contractor shall subject to Sub-Clause 2.5 pay these costs to the Employer, in addition to delay damages (if any) under Sub-Clause 8.7.

However the Employer's claim subject to Sub-Clause 8.6 requires an instruction by the Engineer (Red Book, Yellow Book) or the Employer (Silver Book). Thus, if the Contractor submits a revised programme according to Sub-Clause 8.3 because the previous one has become inconsistent with actual progress, which causes the Employer to incur additional costs, he will not be entitled to compensation of this cost. In this event the Employer may no longer rely on the previous programme, because there is a new one.

Thus, if the Contractor decides himself to submit a revised programme in order to comply with its primary obligation to complete the Works within Time for Completion, he does nothing else than to comply with its obligation under Sub-Clause 8.3 and he is not in breach of contract. The Employer will then not be entitled to claims for compensation. He may only rely on the programme as long as it prevails. By contrast, a Contractor who ignores that actual progress is too slow until the Employer instructs him to submit a revised programme in accordance with Sub-Clause 8.6 must bear additional cost incurred by the Employer.

Any additional instruction to accelerate may constitute a Variation. However, if the Contractor decides by himself to accelerate in order to comply with its programme and the requirements of Time for Completion, any additional cost will be borne by him.

9.3.4 Extension of Time

The entitlement to extension of Time for Completion under Sub-Clause 8.4 arises if completion "is or will be delayed" by the particular event. This means that a delay must be critical or better on the critical path. Programming involves therefore introducing the parameter of time into linked work activities (see Bunni 2005, p. 358). It is thus obvious that the programme under Sub-Clause 8.3 – as described above – shall provide a basis of assessment for compensation events according to Sub-Clauses 8.4 and 3.5 (Totterdill 2006, p. 178). For the means of a retrospective analysis, the programme will only be cogent evidence if it accurately and subsequently recorded actual progress. As the programme shall include logic links it also forms the basis for valuation of the entitlement in a prospective analysis.

References

Bunni NG (2005) FIDIC forms of contract, 3rd edn. Blackwell, Oxford
Caston A (2000) La responsabilité des constructeurs, 5th edn. Le Moniteur, Paris
Dorter J (1999) Performance. BCL 15:361
Furst S, Ramsley V (2006) Keating on construction contracts, 8th edn. Sweet & Maxwell, London
Hök G-S (2009) Relationship between FIDIC conditions and public procurement law – reliability of tender documents. ICLR 23
Totterdill BW (2006) FIDIC user's guide, 2nd edn. Thomas Telford, London
Wallace DIN (1995) Hudson's building and engineering contracts, 11th edn. Sweet & Maxwell, London

Chapter 10
Design Responsibility

The design responsibility is covered by Sub-Clause 4.1. Under a Yellow, Silver and Gold Book Clause 5 contains additional detailed provisions as to the Contractor's design responsibility. Again Sub-Clause 1.13 should not be ignored, according to which it falls upon the Employer to obtain any construction or zoning permit. However, the fact that the Red Book does not dedicate a Clause to design does not mean that Contractors will be completely exempted from all design responsibility.

10.1   Introduction

Under a traditional construction contract, where the design is made by or on behalf of the employer any feasibility studies, soil investigations and the design of the works will be prepared in more detail than under a design and build contract. If a design and build contract is used, the initial phase is that during which the Employer's Requirements are prepared. All steps which will be necessary for the preparation of the Employer's Requirements will be completed at the tender stage, because the Employer's Requirements are a necessary element of the tender documentation. The Contractor who wishes to participate at a bidding procedure or to enter in direct negotiations with the Employer will then start to prepare his so called proposal which usually comprises a preliminary design for inclusion in the tender. Thus the Contractor will be obliged to prepare an outline design or proposal taking into account the Employer's requirements without any counter obligation from the part of the Employer. Thus if no contract is eventually concluded, the Contractor will not be paid for this work. It is therefore understandable that the Contractor will be reluctant to incur excessive tendering costs if the likelihood of success seems low. Final design for the works will only be produced after the contract has been set in force.

Under a FIDIC Contract the term "design" is not a defined term. Sub-Clause 5.1 of the Yellow Book simply states that the Contractor is responsible for the design of the Works which he shall carry out. A more detailed idea of what design could

A.-V. Jaeger and G.-S. Hök, *FIDIC-A Guide for Practitioners*,
DOI 10.1007/978-3-642-02100-8_10, © Springer-Verlag Berlin Heidelberg 2010

constitute is given in the White Book Guide. However, even there no clear definition of design and design stages can be found. In fact it has proved practically
impossible to find a harmonised definition of design stages. Due to different
traditions, legal provisions and practise in the various countries worldwide no
clear detailed specification of design for international business exists. Instead
each project has its own particularities and requirements to be met. Thus FIDIC
has been reluctant to define the term design. However it has ruled in detail the
procedures for design carried out by the Contractor within the Yellow, the Silver
and the Gold Book. The design stages and procedures which have to be followed
according to the FIDIC Books are best explained through the use of flowcharts
(Fig. 10.1).

It must however be noted that the design does not include any design necessary
for zoning and building permissions. It is commonplace that Sub-Clause 1.13
allocates this risk and task to the Employer, who shall have obtained the permissions.

The normal design stages of an architect or engineer vary from country to
country. In Germany architects will have to provide the design being necessary
for obtaining the construction permit, also referred to as the approval design within
the German Architect and Engineer's Fee Scale Regulation. In countries where it is
sufficient to submit a building notice this part of the design work is superfluous. The
apportionment of design responsibilities may also vary. In those countries where
quantity surveyors usually take off quantities from drawings, prepare Bills of
Quantities and measure works in progress this type of work is done by them.

10.2   Employer's Design

If the contractual relationship is regulated on the basis of the Red Book, the design
shall be carried out by the Employer. The Contractor shall execute and complete the
Works designed by the Employer. But of course FIDIC is not naive and inexperi-
enced in this regard. Thus, even though the design is an Employer's task the
Contractor shall design the Works "to the extent specified" in the Contract. This
is often ignored by the Contractor who does not bear in mind that the Employer
expects him to carry out the designed Work by providing a lot of design input in its
largest sense. Some of the required input is expressly covered by Sub-Clause 7.1
according to which the Works must be carried out in a proper workmanlike manner
with properly equipped facilities and non hazardous Materials, which means that
the Contractor is responsible for choosing the appropriate materials and methods of
working. In addition Sub-Clause 8.3 lit. d provides that the Contractor shall include
methods statements in his Programme, which makes it clear that there is some
discretion as to the way of working. Again the Contractor is in charge of forecasting
the progress of the Works in detail by submitting the Programme in the manner
stated in Sub-Clause 8.3. Finally as to the manner of execution Sub-Clause 7.3 lit. a
refers to the whole Contract. Therein the Contractor will usually find a number of

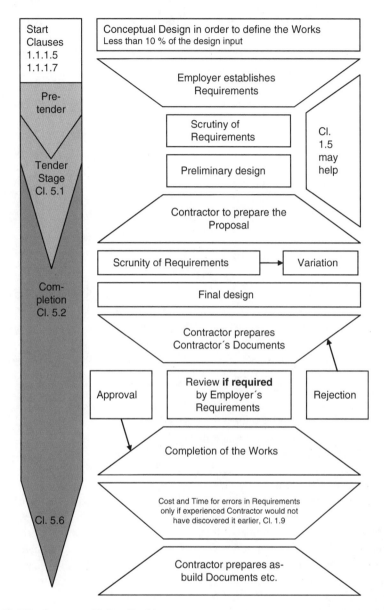

Fig. 10.1 Design stages (Yellow Book)

design requirements. The Contract documents may require to do all working, shop and erection drawings, associated trade literature, calculations, schedules, manuals and similar documents submitted by the Contractor to define some portion of the project work, also referred to as shop drawings. Quite often reinforcement and formwork design must also be done by the Contractor, in particular as to health and safety requirements. All this is important to know because according to Sub-Clause 4.1 lit. c the Contractor shall be responsible for his design, which, when completed, shall be fit for the intended purposes.

In fact, from a legal point of view the design requirement under a Red Book contract is an essential characteristic of any construction contract. If the Contractor becomes discharged from all design liability he will only carry out services under the supervision and superintendence of the Employer. He will then not be liable to achieve a specific result but only to comply with due skill and care. One could also say the Employer has hired services to be carried out (Civil law) or a man who carries out services (Common law).

10.3   Contractor's Design

The Contractor's design shall and will be based on the Employer's Requirements and Specifications which are incorporated in the Contract. Under the Yellow, Silver and Gold Book the Employer's Requirements must be met. According to Sub-Clause 1.5 the Contractor's Proposal has less priority than the Employer's Requirements. Thus even though the Employer has accepted the Proposal which becomes incorporated as part of the Contract, he may instruct the Contractor to strictly comply with the Requirements.

Sub-Clause 4.1 Yellow Book clearly states that the Works shall, when completed, be fit for the purposes for which the Works are intended as defined in the Contract. However, that does not automatically mean that the Contractor assumes an output guarantee. Some industries fear that "fit for purpose" means that all the wishes of the Employer must be met irrespective of whether the supporting conditions are met or not. For example the windmill industry often faces the requirement to design a windmill field which shall produce a clearly defined quantity of electricity. This may prove impossible if there is not enough wind in the designated area. Hence the windmill supplier will only be able to design a windmill field with a nominal output and not an effective output. This will meet the requirement fit for purpose. Of course the Employer may wish to take a step further. In such a case the Contractor will probably be liable to provide for much more windmills than it would have been necessary in order to achieve a nominal output.

In any case, the design responsibility includes all design services which are necessary for the completion of the Works. The Contract may specify design details, design stages and approval requirements. The Contractor shall then comply with all of them. Acting in compliance with all requirements may have an impact on time because design approvals will only be obtained within the time limits provided by the Contract (see Sub-Clause 5.2). A change of design requirements or method requirements is not allowed without prior approval by the Engineer. Any such changes may constitute a Variation.

10.4   Contractor's Design Liability

According to Sub-Clause 4.1, when completed the Works shall be fit for the intended purposes. Thus, if the Contractor assumes the responsibility for the design or for parts of the design it shall be fit for the intended purposes. Most Contractors will feel uncomfortable with this. However, some consulting engineers and Employers are unable to make the best of Sub-Clause 4.1. Unfortunately it is often the case that the intended purposes are not clearly defined or may even remain undefined. This happens for example if a project becomes divided in three lots. The overall concept is that each contractor shall design and complete a part of the Works. All three parts of the Works together will compose a factory or a waste water treatment plant or, a power station, etc. However, if the overall purpose is not indicated in the tender documents the works will be fit for the particular purpose of each contract. Supposing three contractors were to build a power station without a clear indication of the overall purpose. Thus at the end Contractor A will hand over a perfectly assembled generator, Contractor B will hand over a perfectly designed and completed control station and Contractor C will hand over a perfectly installed grid. However the beneficiary will not be able to sell any electricity because all three parts of the power station are neither linked to each other nor are compatible to be linked with each other.

Thus fit for purpose will not be achieved without in indication of a clear and unambiguous purpose. A Contractor will therefore carefully check the tender documents and identify the integral purpose. It may be more or less burdensome to achieve the intended result. Supposing the Contractor assumes the responsibility for the construction of a 20 megawatt windmill park the Works will not be fit for the intended purposes if he installs 20 wind turbine generators with a performance of one megawatt each. He will probably have to install many more windmill generators than firstly anticipated in order to achieve an average result of 20 megawatt despite any lack of wind for a couple of days per month or per year.

The above explanations are in line with English and German law. For example German courts have held:

The Employer envisaged awarding a contract for the waterproofing of two existing rolling shutter gates and the installation of two emergency hand drive systems in case of power cuts, and invited the Contractor to submit an offer. The Contractor submitted an offer which provided for the revision of the related ground areas and the supply and assembly of two hand wheels. When completed the Employer rejected acceptance of the Works because rain still entered in to some extent and the use of the emergency system proved to be very time consuming. The Contractor's claim for payment was dismissed by the court for reason of non performance.[1] The court held that the Employer's Requirements consisting of a functional description of the Works made the Contractor liable to design, execute and complete all works which were necessary in order to meet the requirements.

---

[1]LG Karlsruhe [2008] IBR 1108, annotation Neumann.

It was therefore not a valid defence to rely on the fact that the Contractor did not and could not become aware of the risk allocation that was inherent in the functional description of the Works.

The Contractor was to design and build a waste water treatment plant. The Employer's Requirements included a functional description of the Works, according to which the cells were to be encased in waterproof concrete of class B 35 in accordance with DIN 1045. After two years of operation a mud cell became defective due to corrosion. An expert ascertained that the corrosion resulted from missing coating of the inner surface of the cells. The Employer successfully claimed for damages because it was no good defence to argue that the Employer's Requirements did not mention the coating requirement.[2] As the Contractor was liable for fit for purpose he owed a duty to give advice to the Employer for any omission or error in the Employer's Requirements.

Thus, the phrase "when completed, the Works shall be fit for the intended purposes", means that the designer has to follow up the design until completion of the Works. If errors in the design become apparent the designer must develop an adjusted design which ensures that the design does not result in defective Works.[3] The designer must ensure that the Contractor will only carry out work which is in accordance with the Contract.[4]

English courts are reluctant to confirm a design responsibility if the Contractor's obligations are limited to the work shown in the contract drawings and bills. In Tesco Store HHJ Seymour held:[5]

> It may be appropriate to imply into a construction contract a term that the structure to be erected will, when complete, be reasonably fit for its intended purpose, but that will only be so if and insofar as the structure is to be designed by the contractor. The existence of the term in that type of case was explained by Lord Denning MR in Greaves & Co. (Contractors) Ltd. v. Baynham Meikle and Partners.[6] However, it is clear from the decision of the Court of Appeal in Lynch v. Thorne[7] that there is no such implied term in a case in which the contractor undertakes to build to a particular specification already, at the date of the relevant contract, devised by or on behalf of the employer, and it must follow that there is no such implied term if the contractor agrees to build in accordance with plans or specifications to be produced in the future by others.

Thus in Mowlem v. BICC, where the bills required "waterproof concrete" leaving the means of achieving the result unspecified and unpriced, it was held insufficient to make the Contractor responsible when the concrete leaked.[8] Thus where it is intended to make the Contractor fully responsible for the design, the Contract should include provision expressly making the Contractor responsible for the

---

[2]OLG Jena [2008] IBR 210, annotation Bolz.

[3]BGH [2002] BauR 1536.

[4]OLG Brandenburg [2007] IBR 315, annotation Löffelmann.

[5]Tesco Stores Ltd v. Costain Construction Ltd & Ors [2003] EWHC 1487 (TCC) (02 July 2003).

[6][1975] 1 WLR 1095, p. 1098.

[7][1956] 1 WLR 303.

[8]Mowlem v. BICC (1978) 3 Con LR 64.

design. However, if the Contractor in the course of his business agrees both to design and construct works, a term of fitness for purpose will be implied unless excluded by the express terms of the contract (Furst and Ramsley 2006, note 3-061). By contrast it has been observed on many occasions that those who provide professional services do not generally give an unqualified undertaking to produce the desired result. Thus in Greaves & Co. (Contractors) Ltd v. Baynham Meikle & Partners[9] Lord Denning M.R. held:

> Apply this to the employment of a professional man. The law does not usually imply a warranty that he will achieve the desired result, but only a term that he will use reasonable care and skill. The surgeon does not warrant that he will cure the patient. Nor does the solicitor warrant that he will win the case.

In Greaves & Co. (Contractors) Ltd v. Baynham Meikle & Partners consultant engineers were instructed to design a warehouse, the first floor of which, as they knew, was to be used for storing drums of oil that would be moved around by fork-lift trucks. The warehouse was built to the engineers' design but after a few months' use the first floor began to crack because it was not strong enough to bear the loads imposed on it. The main contractor, by whom the engineers had been employed, made a claim against them alleging that they had impliedly warranted that their design would produce a building fit for its intended use. Despite recognising that a professional man does not normally undertake an unqualified obligation to produce the desired result, the court held in that case that the exchanges between the parties were such as to give rise to an implied term that the warehouse as designed would be fit for the purpose for which it was required. In other words, the engineers assumed an unqualified obligation to produce a suitable design. In Platform Funding Ltd v. Bank of Scotland Plc[10] Lord Justice More-Bick pointed out, that a number of conclusions may be drawn from English precedents. He added:

> Perhaps the most obvious is that although there is a presumption that those who provide professional services normally do no more than undertake to exercise the degree of care and skill to be expected of a competent professional in the relevant field, there is nothing to prevent them from assuming an unqualified obligation in relation to particular aspects of their work. Whether a professional person has undertaken an unqualified obligation of any kind in any given case will depend on the terms of the contract under which he has agreed to provide his services.

Thus the very nature of the obligation on which the client relies may itself make it more or less likely that an obligation was intended to be qualified or unqualified, as the case may be.

Where the Contract is based upon the FIDIC forms of contract containing provisions dealing with conflict within and between the Employer's Requirements

---

[9][1975] 1 WLR 1095, p. 1100D.

[10]Platform Funding Ltd v. Bank of Scotland Plc (Formerly Halifax Plc) [2008] EWCA Civ 930 (31 July 2008).

and the Contractor's proposals, the Contractor is obliged within the agreed Accepted Contract Amount to design and construct everything shown in the Employer's Requirements and to carry out such further design work as would be necessary to develop the specific requirements.

10.5   Design Procedure

In the Yellow, Silver and Gold Book Sub-Clause 5.2 details the procedures and requirements for the production of the Contractor's Documents. Additional approval requirements may be provided by the Laws. The contractual periods for review and approval of design must be indicated in the Employer's Requirements, otherwise Sub-Clause 5.2 applies which provides for a review period of 21 days. In addition periods for review and approval of design shall be mirrored in the Programme. However, if the Employer's Requirements do not specify the documents which must be submitted for review or approval, no such review or approval is required. However, the Contractor shall always comply with construction permit requirements.

The Engineer may, within the review period, give notice to the Contractor that a Contractor's Document fails to meet the Requirements. The Document shall then be rectified, resubmitted and reviewed.

Until expiry of either the review period or the approval period the Contractor shall not carry out any Work. However if the Engineer fails to approve the design within the indicated period of time the Contractor's Document shall be deemed to have been approved by the Engineer. Neither an approval, nor a consent or any review shall relieve the Contractor from any obligation under the Contract (Fig. 10.2).

According to Sub-Clause 5.2 the Employer's Requirements shall describe Contractor's documents which are to be submitted to the Engineer for review and/or for approval. The Contractor shall not carry out parts of the Works until the Engineer has approved the documents. Thus the Contractor's programme must provide for sufficient review time. If the Engineer rejects any documents, the document shall be rectified, resubmitted and reviewed and if specified, approved. This may make it necessary to submit a revised programme.

However, the review procedure should not be misused for other purposes than those indicated in Sub-Clause 5.2. Sub-Clause 5.2 clearly states that the Engineer may reject design which fails to comply with the Contract. Whatever the Contract requires the Contractor to do may constitute a reason to reject. On the other hand the Contractor enjoys complete freedom to choose the materials and methods of working, unless the Contract sets out limits to this effect. The Engineer is therefore not allowed to reject design because he believes that the design includes materials or methods of working which should be replaced by better or more appropriate materials or methods of working, if the design is in full compliance with the Employer's Requirements. If the Contractor suffers delay as a result of such rejections, which are not justified by the Contract, it is submitted that he can rely

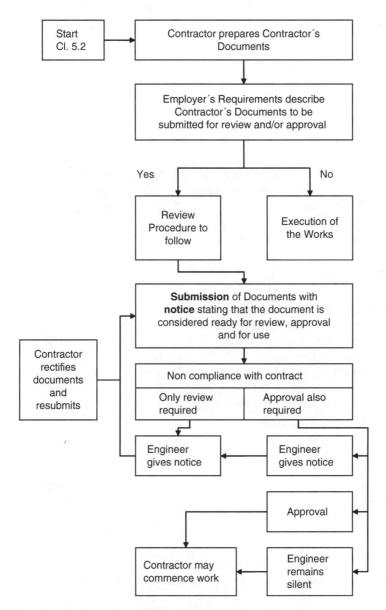

Fig. 10.2 Approval and review of design (Yellow Book)

on Sub-Clause 8.4 lit. e. A strong argument in favour of this interpretation stems from Sub-Clause 3.1. According to Sub-Clause 3.1 the Engineer is deemed to act on behalf of the Employer whenever he carries out duties or exercises authority, specified in or implied by the Contract. As the Contract allots the duty to review and approve the design to the Engineer Sub-Clause 3.1 is perfectly applicable.

10.6   Design Warranties

Under a FIDIC form of contract the Contractor warrants that he, his designers and design Subcontractors have the experience and capability necessary for the design. Also the Contractor shall ensure that the designers are available to attend discussions with the Engineer at all reasonable times, and this until the expiry date of the relevant Defects Notification Period. Notably sub-consultants will usually argue that they become discharged from all liability once they have submitted the design. Thus where it is intended to make the sub-consultant fully responsible for the design, the consultancy agreement should include a provision expressly making the sub-consultant responsible for the design until the expiry date of the relevant Defects Notification Period.

10.7   Design Update

Even though the Contractor has complied with all design obligations during the course of the Works he remains under a duty to update his design if new technical standards and regulations or even new legislation requires him to do so. The Works shall comply with technical standards, building, construction and environmental Laws. These Laws shall be those prevailing when the Works or Section are taken over by the Employer under Sub-Clause 10.1. Thus even if a few days before Taking-Over new technical standards come into force the Contractor shall reopen his design and submit a new design.

In practise once the Contractor becomes aware of new standards (being those which came into force after the Base date) he shall submit proposals for compliance. In the event that the Engineer determines that compliance is required, and the proposal for compliance constitutes a Variation then the Engineer shall initiate a Variation in accordance with Clause 13.

The Contractor must therefore take precaution and subsequently survey the development of legislation and technical standards. If he fails to do so, the Engineer will presumably refuse to issue the Taking-Over Certificate and the Contractor will be in danger of paying delay damages for the resulting delay.

At all times the Engineer may give instructions in order to change the design. Whether an instruction will constitute a Variation must be analysed on a case by case basis. Again the Contractor may also initiate Variations according to Sub-Clause 13.2. However, whilst an instruction may be given until the issue of the Performance Certificate, a Variation may only be initiated until the issue of the Taking-Over Certificate.

10.8 Deliverables

According to Sub-Clause 4.1 of the Yellow and Silver Book the Contractor shall provide the Plant and Contractor's Documents specified in the Contract. Pursuant to Sub-Clause 1.1.6.1 "Contractor's Documents" means the calculations, computer programs and other software, drawings, manuals, models and other documents of a technical nature (if any) supplied by the Contractor under the Contract; as described in Sub-Clause 5.2.

It is crucial to identify each development stage in detail and to specify the related services needed for the development. For each development stage drawings are required. Depending on the planning progress drawings with scales of 1:2,000, 1:1,000, 1:500, 1:200, 1:100 and finally 1:50, 1:20 or 1:1 have to be prepared. Shop drawings (in German: Werkstattzeichnungen), sectional drawings and crop drawings (in German: Schnitte) and finally as-build drawings are required. In particular if a Quantity Surveyor is involved he will need suitable drawings for measurement purposes (compare Sub-Clause 121. lit. b). Interfaces between all members of the construction team must be identified and precisely defined. For example Bills of Quantities and Specifications will be developed from the drawings and requirements. It is recommended to carefully scrutinise existing scopes of services, such as the RIBA stages of work or the ACE stages of work. Local usages, regulations and by-laws may require special or deepened services at stages where in other countries such kinds of services are either useless or not required.

Under all FIDIC Books the Contractor is required to submit as-built-drawings and operation and maintenance manuals prior to the commencement of the Test on Completion. Under the Red Book this obligation is subject to the design obligation of the Contractor whilst under the Yellow and Silver Book Sub-Clauses 5.6 and 5.7 clearly state unconditional obligations to submit as-built documents and manuals.

References

Furst S, Ramsley V (2006) Keating on construction contracts, 8th edn. Sweet & Maxwell, London

Chapter 11
Engineer

11.1 Introduction

In the Red Book and the Yellow Book, as well as in the Dredging and Reclamation
Form and the new Design, Build and Operate Form, a third party to the contract is
provided. Clause 3 of these forms, which are almost identical, deal with the powers
and obligations of the so-called Engineer (Yellow Book, Red Book, Blue Book) or
Employer's Representative (DBO Form). The Engineer (or Employer's Representative referred to in the DBO Form) does not feature in the Silver Book where Clause 3
deals with the Employer's Administration. However, the Employer's Representative
introduced by the Silver Book and the Green Book must also be fair and reasonable,
as required by Sub-Clause 3.5.

11.2 The Role and Function of the Engineer

On one hand the Engineer has a number of functions in which he acts, either
expressly or impliedly, as the agent of the Employer. On the other hand, both
parties to the contract agree, at the time of entering into the contract, that the
Engineer is to perform certain determination/certifier functions under the contract.
The Engineer (or Employer's Representative) is thus a very powerful person which
is also referred to as a decision-maker, a function which requires a certain degree of
impartiality and fairness from him.

In common law, generally, the role of the Engineer will be divided between
actions taken as the employer's agent and those involving a professional opinion.
In the latter case the role of the engineer is best explained in the decision Sutcliffe
v. Thackrath[1] as follows:

---

[1] Sutcliffe v. Thackrah [1974] AC 727, 737.

A.-V. Jaeger and G.-S. Hök, *FIDIC-A Guide for Practitioners*,
DOI 10.1007/978-3-642-02100-8_11, © Springer-Verlag Berlin Heidelberg 2010

> The building owner and the contractor make their contract on the understanding that in all such matters the Engineer will act in a fair and unbiased manner and it must therefore be implicit in the owner's contract with the Engineer that he shall not only exercise due care and skill but also reach such decisions fairly, holding balance between his client and the contractor.[2]

Sub-clause 3.5 of the Yellow and Red Book provides, that the engineer shall make a fair determination in accordance with the contract, taking due regard of all relevant circumstances (Fig. 11.1). If this clause is deleted, there may be some doubt whether the Contractor may invoke the impartiality of the contract administrator because there is no express contract clause ruling the impartiality of the contract administrator (see Glavinis 1993, note 500). However, it is suggested, that even though Sub-Clause 3.5 was deleted, the Contractor should start from the point that there is an implied term of impartiality in common law contracts. Thus a contract administrator who colludes with the employer instead of exercising independent judgment or who deliberately misapplies the contract will probably be liable to the contractor under a tort known as wrongful interference with contract.[3] The ICC arbitration court has held in a case concerning the replacement of an independent engineer by an engineer belonging to the service department of the employer (who was in fact a state), that this amounted to frustration of contract.[4] Thus the determinations of the engineer were not binding (Glavinis 1993, note 500). Hence this case provides strong indications to support the view that it is not acceptable for the employer and the engineer to stem from the same organisation. However, in this case the FIDIC conditions included an expressed clause of impartiality.

However, even if there is a clause stating that the Engineer must protect the Employer's interests and ensure that the Employer does not pay more than he should, the Engineer must act equitably towards the Contractor.[5]

Under no circumstances should the Contractor assume from the fact that the Engineer belongs to the Employer that the Engineer in its role as a contract administrator would act partially. On the contrary the Contractor should expect the Engineer to act independently and impartially according to his professional judgement, even though he was engaged by the Employer and will often act as his agent. There is no denying that the philosophy reflected in the FIDIC standard conditions is such that the contract administrator should answer the question whether he is the man of the employer by stating that his strength in supporting the employer does not depend upon being the man of the employer (see Glavinis 1993, note 501 footnote 374 citing Peter O. Miller). This reflects the common understanding that the Engineer should act fairly and with regard to all relevant

---

[2] Sutcliffe v. Thackrath [1974] AC 727.

[3] John Mowlem & Co plc v. Eagle Insurance Co Ltd (1992) 62 BLR 126.

[4] ICC Arbitral Court 1985, p. 67.

[5] ICC award no. 3790/1983, cited from Glavinis (1993, note 501).

circumstances which means that he shall make its decisions in accordance with the Contract and the applicable law but also with regard to technical requirements.

French courts have held that a clause according to which the parties to a contract empower the architect, who is in charge on behalf of the employer, to settle disputes is null and void.[6] However, as the function of the Engineer is not so widely illustrated in civil law systems it might be helpful for lawyers and engineers from those countries to be provided with some examples on exactly how common law judges understand the role of a contractual certifier and maker of determinations. The duties of certifiers and others with decision-making functions under construction contracts have been the subject of much authority in England and other common law jurisdictions.

In Perini Corporation v. Commonwealth of Australia [1969] 12 BLR 82, the plaintiff was contracted to build a mail exchange for the defendant. Under the building contract the director of works, an officer of the defendant, had functions as a certifier. At pp. 97–98 Macfarlan J. stated the following about the duties of a "director":

> I am satisfied that the director of works was not an arbitrator and indeed, unless I am mistaken, this argument was not strongly pressed by learned counsel for the plaintiff. However, the argument that he was a servant and in the alternative that he was a certifier was developed in detail. The decisions of the courts extending back over many years show that in many agreements there are concluded provisions of the same general character as in clause 35. These characteristics appear most notably, and perhaps most frequently, in agreements which have been made for the construction of public works or where one party is a local governing body. The characteristic of them is that there is a person appointed on behalf of the government or semi-government body to supervise the execution of the contract on behalf of his employer. He is generally a senior engineer or a director of works or a principal architect or some other officer who, because of his technical qualifications and experience, is competent to undertake that work. He is, as I have said, an employee of the body on whose behalf he undertakes this work but, in addition, the same cases show that he is commonly charged with a duty either of resolving disputes between the contractor and the body which employs him or in certifying as to the quality of work done or the whole or part of the cost of doing that work. In my opinion the cases make plain that throughout the period or performance of all these duties the senior officer remains an employee of the government or semi-government body but that, in addition, while he continues as such an employee he becomes vested with duties which oblige him to act fairly and justly and with skill to both parties to the contract. The essence of such a relationship, in my opinion, is that the parties by the contract have agreed that this officer shall hold these dual functions and they have agreed to accept his certificate or opinion on the matters which he is required to decide.

At p. 107 Macfarlan J. added this comment:

> I have already held that the duty of director when acting as certifier was to act independently and in the exercise of his own volition according to the exigencies of a particular application.

---

[6]Cour de Cassation (commerciale), 09.03.1965, Bull.civ. IV no. 175.

In London Borough of Hounslow v. Twickenham Garden Developments Ltd. [1971] 1 Ch 233, Mr. Justice Megarry reviewed the duties of certifiers under building contracts. At pp. 259–260 he held:

> It seems to me that under a building contract the architect has to discharge a large number of functions, both great and small, which call for the exercise of his skilled professional judgment. He must throughout retain his independence in exercising that judgment: but provided he does this I do not think that, unless the contract so provides, he need go further and observe the rules of natural justice, giving due notice of all complaints and affording both parties a hearing. His position as an expert and the wide range of matters that he has to decide point against any such requirement: and an attempt to divide the trivial from the important, with natural justice applying only to the latter, would be of almost insuperable difficulty. It is the position of independence and skill that affords the parties the proper safeguards and not the imposition of rules requiring something in the nature of a hearing.

Let us now move on 14 years to Beaufort Developments (NI) Ltd v. Gilbert Ash (NI) Ltd [1999] 1 AC 266. This is the well known case in which the House of Lords overruled Northern Regional Health Authority v. Derek Crouch Construction Co Ltd [1984] QB 644. The House of Lords held that the court had the inherent power to open up, review and revise architects' certificates under the JCT standard form of building contract. Lord Hoffmann, in a speech with which Lord Lloyd agreed, held at pp. 275–276:

> If the certificates are not conclusive what purpose do they serve? If one considers the practicalities of the construction of a building or other works, it seems to me that parties could reasonably have intended that they should have what might be called a provisional validity. Construction contracts may involve substantial work and expenditure over a lengthy period. It is important to have machinery by which the rights and duties of the parties at any given moment can at least provisionally be determined with some precision. This machinery is provided by architect certificates. If they are not challenged as inconsistent with the contractual terms which the parties have agreed, they will determine such matters as when interim payments or due or completion must take place. This is something which the parties need to know. No doubt in most cases there will be no challenge. On the other hand, to make the certificate conclusive could easily cause injustice. It may have been given when the knowledge of the architect about the state of the work or the effect of external causes was incomplete. Furthermore, the architect is the agent of the employer. He is a professional man but can hardly be called independent. One would not readily assume that the contractor would submit himself to be bound by his decisions subject only to a challenge on the grounds of bad faith or excess of power. It must be said that there are instances in the nineteenth century and the early part of this one in which contracts were construed as doing precisely this. There are also contracts which provided that in case of dispute the architect was to be the arbitrator. But the notion of what amounted to a conflict of interest was not then as well understood as it is now. And of course the inclusion of such clauses is a matter for negotiation between the parties or, in a standard form, the two sides of the industry, so that what is acceptable will to some extent depend upon the bargaining strength of one side or the other. At all events, I think that today one should require very clear words before construing a contract as giving an architect such powers.

Finally, in Scheldebouw BV v. St. James Homes (Grosvenor Dock) Ltd [2006] EWHC 89 (TCC) (16 January 2006) HHJ Jackson summarised the legal situation as follows:

Three propositions emerge from the authorities concerning the position of the decision-maker:

(1) The precise role and duties of the decision-maker will be determined by the terms of the contract under which he is required to act.
(2) Generally the decision-maker is not, and cannot be regarded as, independent of the employer.
(3) When performing his decision-making function, the decision-maker is required to act in a manner which has variously been described as independent, impartial, fair and honest. These concepts are overlapping but not synonymous. They connote that the decision-maker must use his professional skills and his best endeavours to reach the right decision, as opposed to a decision which favours the interests of the employer.

Again, HHJ Jackson added:

The fact that the construction manager acts in conjunction with other professionals when performing his decision-making function does not water down his legal duty. When performing that function, it is the construction manager's duty to act in a manner which is independent, impartial, fair and honest. In other words, he must use his professional skills and his best endeavours to reach the right decision, as opposed to a decision which favours the interests of the employer.

It must be added that for example according to Article 246 of the UAE Federal Law No 5 of 1985 (the Civil Code) and according to Sect. 242 German Civil Code contracts must be performed in a manner consistent with the requirements of *good faith*. Obviously, this applies to the parties to the contract, namely the employer and the contractor, but it also applies to the person who has the power to determine extensions of Time for Completion and to certify payments, such as the Engineer, for example, under the 1999 edition of FIDIC's Books.

There is therefore a strong contractual argument that if the Engineer does not act fairly towards the Contractor, this constitutes a breach of contract by the Employer. It is suggested that breach of contract can result either through an act or an omission of the Employer and that the Employer *shall ensure* that at all times there is an Engineer and that in the exercise of the functions of the Engineer under the Contract, the Engineer acts in a timely manner with due regard to all relevant circumstances and that he acts honestly and fairly.

In civil law countries such a powerful person, who is a third party to the contract but derivates its powers from the contract between the parties, is more or less unknown. Of course, the Employer usually takes advice from an architect or engineer and often he would become appointed as a supervisor and/or contract manager. But there is no agreement on the powers and duties of this person, which usually is simply appointed as an agent of the Employer with powers on behalf of the Employer. This is not the same as an Engineer under the FIDIC Contracts, where the parties promise to each other that the Engineer shall have the duties and powers arising from the Contract itself, and where, for example, the entitlement of the Contractor to payments depends on the issue of payment certificates.

Thus the Engineer is not only an agent of the Employer who exercises the rights and duties of the Employer. It seems therefore not to be appropriate to apply Sect. 315 German Civil Code, because this would not mirror a true picture of the

Engineer (Mallmann 2002, p. 106.). However, Sect. 317 German Civil Code provides that, where specification of performance is left to a third party, in case of doubt, it must be assumed that the specification must be determined with equitable discretion. In principle this kind of determination leads to an amendment of the contract, which is finally binding on the parties, unless it is manifestly inequitable. However it is not a common understanding that this person must be unbiased and impartial. Nor is he under a duty to follow procedural rules. It is therefore suggested that Sections 317, 319 German Civil Code should not apply to the Engineer. By consequence under German law the Engineer remains somewhat atypical, which is not surprising in light of its common law origin (see Mallmann 2002, p. 108 et seq.).

Moreover the FIDIC based Engineer, although not being allowed to amend the contract, has powers to instruct Variations (see Sub-Clauses 3.1, 13.1). Unfortunately it is often the case for Employers and their consultants to attempt to limit the powers of the Engineer under an express condition of prior approval by the Employer. If the Employer wishes to do so, he shall include such restrictions in the Particular Conditions.

Care must be had in this respect since this kind of restriction or constraint must be disclosed and agreed by the Contractor. Thus hidden constraints and restrictions are not binding on the Contractor and must therefore not be accepted by him. However, if the construction contract discloses such constraints, they will be binding on the Contractor. Increasingly the following clauses are to be found in FIDIC Contracts:

> The Engineer shall obtain the specific approval of the Employer before taking action under the following Sub-Clauses of these Conditions:
>
> (a) Sub-Clause 10.1: Specific approval of the Employer is required before issuing any Taking-Over Certificate.
> (b) Sub-Clause 11.9: Specific approval of the Employer is required before issuing the Performance Certificate.
> (c) Sub-Clause 13.1: Specific approval of the Employer is required before instructing or approving any Variation that would cause the Contract Price to exceed the Accepted Contract Amount or any contract amount subsequently agreed upon by the Employer and the Contractor in addenda to the Contract.

However, an Employer who puts his Engineer under such further constraints other than those already stipulated in the Red Book, Yellow Book and the so-called Dredging Form must know that he will *not* escape from his duties under the contract. All the duties under the contract are maintained even though the powers of the Engineer are limited. Hence, the Engineer will still be obliged to make fair determinations and certificates and he shall continue to give instructions and all contractual remedies and claims continue to exist. Thus, the aforementioned constraints will put the Employer under strong pressure to comply with the time limits, which are set out in a FIDIC Contract. Again, he must himself take regard of all circumstances and reach decisions in a timely manner. Thus in principle all the aforementioned constraints do not substantially change the contract but they lead to significantly more administrative work. In summary they are nothing more than the expression of distrust against the Engineer, who in principle should have the full confidence of the Employer.

Regrettably the role of the Engineer seems increasingly to be misunderstood on another field. He is not intended to be only a mere contract administrator with limited engineering skills and experiences. Much to the contrary, he is intended to be an engineer with complete engineering skills and experiences having also a good understanding of the contract and the required contract administration procedures. Thus he should be able to determine new rates under a Red Book contract (see Sub-Clause 12.2) or to agree or determine adjustments to the Contract Price under a Yellow Book contract. He should also be capable to review and/or approve the Contractor's design against the Employer's Requirements as the case may be. Again he should be able to foresee all legal, commercial and technical consequences of any instructions, in particular those leading to variations. FIDIC does not only require from the parties to enable the Engineer to do his work. Instead they are required to follow the contract's procedural rules. In this context FIDIC expects the Engineer to be a sufficiently experienced and skilled person in order to satisfy all the requirements of the contract. If for example the Engineer instructs a variation he should already have in mind its consequences and be prepared for the Contractor to presumably ask for an adjustment of the Contract Price and/or extension of Time for Completion. The FIDIC Conditions will then give him guidance for the evaluation of the Variation. According to the Yellow Book the adjustment shall include reasonable profit. Well, this will mean nothing else than this: Firstly, the Contractor is entitled to additional cost as referred to in Sub-clause 1.1.4.3. Secondly the Contractor is entitled to reasonable profit. Cost means all expenditure reasonably incurred by the Contractor. Thus the Engineer has to verify actual cost based on open market prices, taking in consideration all relevant circumstances, including shipping cost, urgency, quality and quantities. He will then add reasonable profit and may in so far rely on data provided by the Contractor but also on other available data and his proper experience within the industry.

11.3 Determinations

Whenever the General Conditions provide that the Engineer shall proceed in accordance with Sub-Clause 3.5 to determine any matter, the Engineer shall make a fair determination in accordance with the Contract, taking due regard of all relevant circumstances. To act in accordance with the Contract means to comply with the Contract. The Engineer shall act as decision maker and is therefore required to determine the law. Thus any determination must be in accordance with the Contract and the therein referred law. Sub-Clause 3.5 does not confer discretional or arbitrary powers to the Engineer.

The Engineer shall make determinations as to claims, new rates (Red Book only) and as to the evaluation of variations. However the Engineer is not allowed to amend the Contract or to relieve any Party of any duties, obligations or

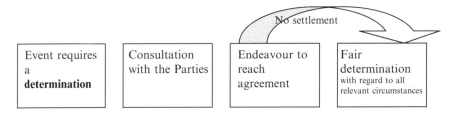

Fig. 11.1 Determination

responsibilities. Though a determination is binding on the Parties it does not create new duties or obligations.

11.4 Constraints and Restrictions on the Engineer

The Engineer as referred to in Clause 3 FIDIC Conditions is obviously a suitable and useful supporting feature. The fact that he is paid by the Employer and bound to him by a particular contract should not be overestimated. It is up to the Employer to appoint a skilful and experienced Engineer who is able to exercise the role of the Engineer in a way which ensures a successful project development. By imposing constraints and restrictions on the Engineer the Employer expresses more or less that he does not believe in the skills of his Engineer and that moreover he does not expect his Engineer to exercise his powers with care. Some Employers, in particular public authorities, argue that they have to comply with budgets and that any adjustment of the Contract price must remain under the direct control of the Employer, which justifies any constraints and restrictions on the Engineer's powers. In doing so, they ignore the fact that by using a FIDIC document they already accept that the project shall be realised in a fair and balanced manner. All the claims and variations clauses which are included in the FIDIC documents are nothing more than a mirror of a fair and balanced contract form. Thus, when preparing the budgets it must be kept in mind that the Accepted Contract Amount as referred to in Sub-clause 1.1.4.1 is only a snapshot, which mirrors the estimated costs at the submission date, and that there is a clear connection between the quality of the tender documents and the Contract Price.

It is in this context that the role of the Engineer must be understood. All of his powers are based on and arising from the contract. Again it is clearly stated that the Engineer is not allowed to amend the contract (see Sub-clause 3.1). He is also not allowed to relieve either Party to the contract of any duties, obligations or responsibilities under the Contract. In particular any approval, check, certificate, consent, examination, inspection, instruction, notice, proposal, request, test, or similar act shall not relieve the Contractor from any responsibility he has under the Contract

(Sub-clauses 3.1, 7.3). Thus the Engineer never changes the contract or deviates from that which has been agreed by the parties.

11.5 Powers of the Engineer

Anyway, the Engineer (or Employer's Representative) has many powers, which may be summarised as such:

- The Engineer is responsible of the kick-off, because he must notify the Commencement date (Sub-Clause 8.1).
- The Engineer may reject any submitted programme (Sub-clause 8.3).
- The Engineer participates at the tests and is allowed to reject any Plant, Materials or workmanship (Sub-Clause 7.5).
- The Engineer inspects the Works (Sub-Clause 7.3).
- The Engineers shall measure the Works (Sub-Clause 12.1 Red Book).
- The Engineer shall determine new rates (Sub-Clause 12.3 Red Book).
- The Engineer shall evaluate and determine variations (Sub-Clause 13.3).
- The Engineer shall review and approve the design, if so specified (Sub-clause 5.2 Yellow Book).
- The Engineer shall certify payments (Clause 14).
- The Engineer shall issue Taking-Over Certificates, Performance Certificates (Sub-clauses 10.1, 11.9).
- The Employer's Representative shall issue Commissioning Certificates (Gold Book).
- The Engineer shall approve or disapprove and determine claims (Sub-Clause 3.5).
- The Engineer shall give instructions (Sub-Clause 3.1, 1.5, 13.1).
- The Engineer shall request proposals (Sub-Clause 13.3).

Also the FIDIC Dredging Form (Blue Book) gives the Engineer several duties and authorities such as approval of contractor's design, the authority to instruct variations to the Contractor, the issuing of Taking Over Certificates and the certification of payments.

To which extent the Engineer is responsible of advising the Employer (his client) is subject to the applicable law and the contract between the Employer and the Engineer, for example a White Book Agreement. However, as he is under an obligation to carry out his services in a fair and unbiased manner he should disclose any relevant circumstances which may have an impact on his actions. Thus he will not be allowed to reject any claims without giving particulars or reasons. Again he is also under the duty not to withhold and to delay any approvals, certificates, consents and determinations (Sub-clause 1.3). By the way, there is no express duty not to withhold or to delay instructions. But reference has to be made to Sub-clause 19.3, according to which both Parties shall at all times use all reasonable endeavours to minimise any delay in the performance of the Contract as a result of Force

Majeure. It is suggested that this includes an implicit duty to give instructions in a timely manner.

11.6   Instructions

Instructions deserve closer attention. They are like a sword, in that their use may be necessary but have the ability of causing disastrous consequences. Although the use of instructions is usually not mandatory sometimes it may turn out to be. According to Sub-Clause 1.5 the Engineer shall give instructions and clarifications if there is any ambiguity or discrepancy in the Contract documents. It is often the case that the issuing of an instruction is avoidable. According to Sub-Clause 13.3 the Engineer may request a proposal instead of giving an instruction. This will enable him to check all of the consequences of the intended Variation. Whilst Sub-Clause 4.12 gives the Engineer the power to instruct a Variation he may nevertheless remain silent because the Contractor is already under the obligation to overcome the issue. In any event Engineers are well advised to carefully check all of the consequences of an instruction which will be immediately binding on the Contractor and he should use this "sword" only with the utmost reluctance and caution. An instruction may cause additional cost, delay and disruption. Delay may cause additional risk such as increasing prices and varied currency rates. Financial requirements may be affected, etc. According to Sub-Clause 3.3 any instruction may constitute a Variation. Thus before giving an instruction the Engineer should check whether the intended instruction changes the Works or the Employer's Requirements. This may prove difficult and time-consuming. However it is necessary in order to avoid debate and disputes. If the Engineer's powers are made subject to restrictions he should be aware of the fact that such restrictions do not compromise the validity of any instruction being issued without prior consent or approval by the Employer. Sub-Clause 3.1 takes care of this. Whenever the Engineer exercises a power or authority under the Contract for which the Employer's approval is required, then (for the purposes of the Contract) the Employer shall be deemed to have given approval. The meaning of "for the purposes of the Contract" is such that the Engineer is in breach of his agreement with the Client.

11.7   White Book

In practice Employers and Consultants often make their contract by reference to the Conditions of the Client – Consultant Model Services Agreement also referred to as the FIDIC White Book. The terms of the Client Consultant Model Services Agreement (The White Book), being available in a 4th edition 2006, have been prepared by FIDIC and are recommended for general use for the purposes of pre-investment and feasibility studies, designs and administration of construction and project management, where proposals for such services are invited on an international basis. They are equally adaptable for domestic agreements. The White Book is in particular suitable for use with the FIDIC Red and Yellow Book according to which an Engineer shall be appointed by the Employer who shall administer the Contract.

11.7.1   Overview

The White Book comprises an Agreement form, General Conditions and Particular Conditions and Appendices. The Particular Conditions must be specially drafted to suit each individual Agreement and type of Service. That part of the text of the Particular Conditions which must be completed is printed on pages which should be completed for incorporation with additional clauses. FIDIC intends to publish an updated White Book Guide which includes comments on clauses in the Model Services Agreement and notes towards the preparation of Appendices 1 [Scope of Services], 2 [Personnel, Equipment, Facilities and Services of Others to be Provided by the Client], 3 [Remuneration and Payment] and 4 [Time Schedule for Services].

The General Conditions comprise eight clauses with Sub-Clauses, covering general aspects, Client's duties, Consultant's duties, commencement, completion, variation and termination, payments, liabilities, insurance and disputes.

11.7.2   Cooperation

If the Services are impeded or delayed by the Client or his contractors so as to increase the scope, cost or duration of Consultant's Services the Consultant shall inform the Client hereof together with a breakdown of probable effects. The Client shall give to the Consultant free of cost all information which may pertain to the Services which the Client is able to obtain. This could involve any one or more of the following:

- Design or information supplied by the Client and/or other persons involved in the project
- Consent to proceed to the next stage from the Client or on behalf of the Client
- Result of works and services provided by others, for example expertises made by experts

Thus Consultants will have to ensure that the Client is informed about probable future events and requirements in good time. The Client will then have to ensure to provide such information in a timely manner in order to avoid impediments of and interference with the Services.

11.7.3 Liability

As required by Sub-Clause 3.3.1 White Book the Consultant shall have no other responsibility than to exercise reasonable skill, care and diligence in the performance of his obligations under the Agreement. The standard of "reasonable skill, care and diligence" is conventional for professional consultant firms in common law countries and it is the standard against which the PI insurance industry within common law countries usually provides cover. In English law the designer's design must be such that those who are responsible for implementing it, and those who are responsible for supervising that implementation, can do so by the exercise of the skill and care ordinarily to be expected of them.[7] In Equitable Debenture Assets Corporation Ltd v. William Moss Group[8] His Honour Judge Newey QC at p. 21 said:

> I think that if implementation of part of a design requires work to be carried out on site, the designer should ensure that the work can be performed by those likely to be employed to do it, in the conditions which can be foreseen, by the exercise of the care and skill ordinarily to be expected of them. If the work would demand exceptional skill, and particularly if it would have to performed partly from scaffolding and often in windy conditions, then the design will lack what the experts in evidence described as "buildability".
>
> Similarly, I think that if a design requires work to be carried out on site in such a way that those whose duty it is to supervise it and/or check that it has been done will encounter great difficulty in doing so, then the design will again be defective. It may perhaps be described as lacking "supervisability".
>
> In my view, applications of sealant in accordance with the design were possible in this case. A person with Mr Plough's experience, acting carefully and with determination, could no doubt have carried them out correctly. However, I think that ordinary fitters, even if they were not, as described by Mr Rae on 22 December 1979, "getting through the job as quickly as possible", could not have been expected, or relied upon, especially in view of working conditions, to do the job properly. It follows that in my opinion the design did not meet the requirements of "buildability".

However, according to German law design services must be fit for the purposes, so that the General Conditions should be adapted accordingly. Under French law it should be carefully verified whether the consultant shall perform the services with best efforts (obligations de moyens) or fit for the intended purposes (obligation de résultat). Moreover some of the Consultant's obligations should, of course, be

[7]Department of National Heritage v. Steensen Varming Mulchay, Balfour Beatty Ltd, Laing Management Ltd [1998] EWHC Technology 305 (30 July 1998).
[8]Equitable Debenture Assets Corporation Ltd v. William Moss Group Ltd (1984) Con LR 1.

understood as absolute obligations, such as the duty not to commit bribery acts, the duty to commence the services, the duty to provide for PI-insurance cover and to maintain it during the whole service period.

According to Sub-Clause 6.6.1 the Consultant shall only be liable to pay compensation to the Client arising out of or in connection with this Agreement if a breach of Clause 3.3.1 is established against him. This is clearly a limitation of liability. However the extent of limitation remains open to discussion. If, despite his reasonable efforts, the Consultant is unable to provide sufficient numbers of qualified personnel for the project, it seems reasonable that the Client should, after giving notice, be in a position give a notice of termination subject to Sub-Clause 4.6.2. Whether the Client may also recover from the Consultant the additional costs the Client incurs in having the Services completed by a new firm, depends on the applicable law. However, the Client may wish to add substantial amendments in the Particular Conditions in order to ensure that he may recover such additional cost.

Sub-Clause 6.3 provides for maximum amount of compensation payable by either party to the other in respect of liability under Sub-Clause 6.1. The amount shall be stated in the Particular Conditions.

11.7.4   Scope of Services

As the scope of services for consultancy services varies from country to country and from project to project FIDIC did not publish typical scopes of services with work stages and work descriptions. However, the Association of Consulting Engineers (ACE), UK, has published Conditions of Engagement that include draft scopes of services which may serve as a further guide to the completion of Appendix 1. Reference can also be made to the German fee schedule including detailed descriptions of services for architects and engineers.

Skill and care should be taken when drafting the scope of services (Appendix 1). The drafters should be familiar with the country of the assignment and the sector into which the assignment fits. Consultants and Clients often completely ignore that the scope of services may vary from country to country. Construction projects are complex missions which must meet multiple legal requirements. The existing legal requirements cover various aspects, such as the need for a construction permit in accordance with domestic building regulations and zoning law, the appointment of a commission composed by representatives of the Contractor the Employer and the local authorities for the purpose of reception of the Works or simply the need for special licences to be obtained by the members of the construction team. Local laws also usually have great influence on the scope of services of consultants. In some countries particular services may be superfluous whilst in other countries this type of service is mandatory.

11.7.5 Payments

Though in most countries fees are subject to mutual agreement, some countries such as Germany have set in force special laws and regulations limiting contractual freedom. In Germany a special fee schedule (in short HOAI) exists which according to the German Supreme Court is mandatory for construction projects situated within the territory of Germany.[9] Despite this the White Book provides for a payments related to normal services, additional services and exceptional services. Details shall be fixed in Appendix 3. Moreover, Clients need to be aware that Sub-Clause 4.3.3 suggests that the Client has no right to require his Consultant to carry out varied services unless and until the fees associated with the change have been approved or agreed. This suggests that if the Consultant is unwilling to carry out the varied services he can, within the limits of the principle of good faith, if applicable, present an unfeasibly high fee, safe in the knowledge that the Client will reject it. In other words, there is no clear requirement for the Consultant to undertake any varied services, unless he agrees to do so. Whether this is workable in practice could be doubted. Clients may therefore wish to change this. However as to other additional or exceptional services, Sub-Clause 4.8 and Sub-Clause 4.4 do not refer to Sub-Clause 4.3.3. This suggests that if circumstances arise for which neither the Client nor the Consultant are responsible and which make it irresponsible or impossible for the Consultant to perform in whole or in part the Services in accordance with the Agreement or if the Services are impeded or delayed by the Client or his contractors, payment of additional and exceptional services do not depend on prior agreement by the Parties to the Agreement.

Pursuant to Sub-Clause 5.6 except where the Agreement provides for lump sum payments the Client can require for a reputable firm of accountants nominated by him to audit any amount claimed by the Consultant.

Retentions sometimes appear in bespoke consultancy agreements. The White Book does not provide for retention monies. However, public procurement law may require to add clauses providing for retention monies, for example in Algeria.

11.7.6 Changed Circumstances

In the event of changed circumstances Sub-Clause 4.5 provides for certain precautions to be taken. The Sub-Clause says: "If circumstances arise for which neither the Client nor the Consultant is responsible and which make it

---

[9] BGH [2003] ZfBR 367; Hök (2003, p. 76).

irresponsible or impossible for the Consultant to perform in whole or in part the Services in accordance with the Agreement, he shall promptly dispatch a notice to the Client". Civil law practitioners may presumably give answers whether "irresponsible" or "impossible" means unfeasibly expensive, economically impracticable, physically impossible, likely to endanger life and limb, a potential breach of national security, etc. by reference to their Civil Codes, whilst common law lawyers would prefer to eliminate vagueness of the clause by adding clear answers.

11.7.7 Intellectual Property

Intellectual property is covered by Sub-Clause 1.7. The Consultant retains design rights and other intellectual property rights and copyrights of all documents prepared by him. The Client shall be entitled to use them only for the Project and the purpose for which they are intended. The provisions need to be checked. Some employers do insist to be vested in the rights of the consultant such as public bodies. This may prove to be impossible subject to the intellectual property law which is applicable. According to German copyright law the author cannot assign the copyright but only grant licences on it.

11.7.8 Disputes

The White Book provides for a three stage dispute resolution system (Fig. 11.2). If a dispute arises out of or in connection with the Agreement the Parties shall first attempt to settle it by negotiation. In the event of failure to reach an agreement the Parties shall attempt to agree on a neutral mediator and mediation shall be initiated then by written notice requesting a start to the mediation. If the mediator fails to settle the dispute the Parties may refer the dispute to arbitration. Neither Party may commence any arbitration of any dispute relating to the Agreement until it has attempted to settle the dispute with the other Party by mediation. However, arbitration may be commenced if the dispute has not been settled within 90 days of giving the notice requesting start of mediation according to Sub-Clause 8.2.2.

Payments shall only be withheld upon previous notice by the Client of his intention to withhold payment with reasons no later than four days prior to the date on which the payment becomes due. If no such notice of intention to withhold payment is given then the Consultant shall have an enforceable contractual right to such payment. The remainder of the invoice shall not be delayed. In the event of any delay as to payments the Consultant is entitled to either suspend performance or to terminate the Agreement.

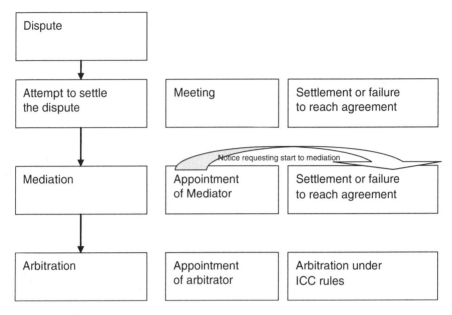

Fig. 11.2 Dispute resolution (White Book)

References

Glavinis P (1993) Le contrat international de construction. GLN Joly, Paris

Hök G.-S (2003) HOAI: Preisbindung im Geschäft mit Auslandsberührung. BauR 76

Mallmann RA (2002) Bau- und Anlagenbauverträge nach FIDIC Standardbedingungen. C. H. Beck, München

Chapter 12
Time for Completion

12.1 Introduction

The FIDIC concept of Time for Completion is based on Clause 8 FIDIC Conditions. According to this concept the parties agree on a period of time for completion, which is usually indicated in the Appendix to Tender (Yellow Book, Red Book), in the Particular Conditions (Silver Book) or the Contract Data (Gold Book). Time for completion starts when the Engineer has notified the Commencement Date, which he shall do within 42 days after the Contract has been executed by a seven days' notice (14 days under the Gold Book). Subject to Sub-Clause 1.1.3.3 Time for Completion means the time for completing the Works or a Section (as the case may be) under Sub-Clause 8.2, as stated in the Appendix to Tender or the Particular Conditions (with any extension under Sub-Clause 8.4, calculated from the Commencement Date). According to Sub-Clause 8.2 the Contractor shall complete the whole of the Works within the Time for Completion for the Works including completing all work which is stated in the Contract as being required for the Works or Section to be considered to be completed for the purposes of taking-over under Sub-Clause 10.1. In other words, the Contractor complies with the requirements for Time for Completion if he completes the Works within Time for Completion until the issue of the Taking Over Certificate.

Unless agreed otherwise, failure to comply with Time for Completion will usually lead to the entitlement of delay damages pursuant to Sub-Clause 8.7. However if and when the Contractor is prevented from carrying out the works or if the Employer causes delay to the progress with effect to Time for Completion the Contractor is entitled to claim for extension of time (EOT) (Fig. 12.1).

A.-V. Jaeger and G.-S. Hök, *FIDIC-A Guide for Practitioners*,
DOI 10.1007/978-3-642-02100-8_12, © Springer-Verlag Berlin Heidelberg 2010

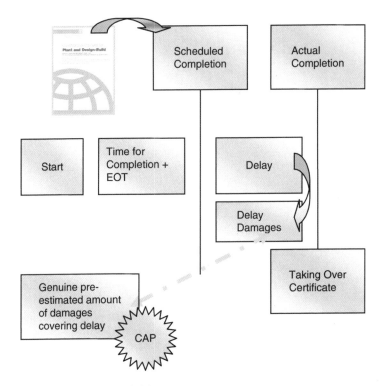

Fig. 12.1 Time for completion and delay

12.2 The English Concept of Time for Completion

The above outlined concept has been adopted from English law, where time remains only of the essence if and when the contract provides for time extension claims for those events attributable to the employer, which cause delay and disruption. Failure to provide such claims leads to time at large, which will mean that the Employer looses his entitlement to delay damages. Thus EOT claims release the Contractor from his liability for delay damages and protect the Employer against the loss of his entitlement to delay damages in the event that the Contractor fails to comply with Time for Completion.

This English concept includes the presumption that there is an effective contractual system for time extension, including that the Engineer grants EOT in accordance with the contract whenever an EOT claim becomes notified by the Contractor. Failure to comply with the contractual system of EOT management rules may also lead to *time at large*.

Thus under English law the parties conclude their contract with the understanding that the Contractor's liability for delay damages is based on a concept which releases the Contractor from this liability to the extent which is ruled by the contract. However if the Contractor himself fails to comply with the contract management rules extension of time will not be granted (see Sub-Clause 20.1 FIDIC Conditions) and his liability for delay damages continues to exist even though the Employer causes delay to Time for Completion. This has been subject to some degree of criticism. The legal basis for this critique is the Australian decision in *Gaymark Investments Pty Ltd v. Walter Construction Group Ltd.*[1] However, the correctness of the *Gaymark* decision has been a matter of some debate. HHJ Jackson has summarised this discussion as follows:[2]

> The editors of Keating on Building Contracts (8th edition 2006) note, that there is no English authority on the matter but incline to the view that *Gaymark* was correctly decided (see paragraph 9-025). The editor of Hudson on Building Contracts, the late Ian Duncan Wallace QC, argues that *Gaymark* was wrongly decided (see paragraph 10.026 of the first supplement to the 11th edition of Hudson). Professor Wallace (a formidable commentator on construction law, who is now sadly missed) also wrote a trenchant article on this subject. See "Prevention and Liquidated Damages: a Theory Too Far" (2002) 18 Building and Construction Law, 82. In that article Professor Wallace refers to the *Turner* case, which I have previously mentioned, and certain other authorities. He points out the useful practical purpose which contractual provisions requiring a contractor to give notice of delay serve. Professor Wallace argues that both the arbitrator and the judge came to the wrong conclusion in *Gaymark*. In Professor Wallace's view, *Gaymark* extends the prevention theory too far.

In *Peninsula Balmain Pty Ltd v. Abigroup Contractors Pty Ltd*[3] declined to follow the *Gaymark* ruling and preferred the reasoning of Professor Wallace. Hodgson JA gave the leading judgment with which other members of the court agreed. At paragraph 78 Hodgson JA held the following:

> "I accept that, in the absence of the Superintendent's power to extend time, even if a claim had not been made within time, Abigroup would be precluded from the benefit of an extension of time and liable for liquidated damages, even if delay had been caused by variations required by Peninsula and thus within the so-called 'prevention principle'. I think this does follow from the two *Turner* cases and the article by Mr. Wallace referred to by Mr. Rudge".

A year after *Peninsula*, the Second Division of the Inner House of the Court of Session gave judgment in *City Inn Ltd v. Shepard Construction Ltd*,[4] where the court held that the contractor could not obtain an extension of time if it did not comply with that provision (see paragraph 23 of the Opinion of the court).

Finally HHJ Jackson held the following:

> I am bound to say that I see considerable force in Professor Wallace' criticisms of *Gaymark*. I also see considerable force in the reasoning of the Australian courts in *Turner* and in

---

[1] [1999] NTSC 143; (2005) 21 Const. LJ 71.

[2] See Multiplex Constructions (UK) Ltd v. Honeywell Control Systems Ltd (No. 2) [2007] EWHC 447 (TCC).

[3] [2002] NSWCA 211, the New South Wales Court of Appeal.

[4] [2003] SLT 885.

Peninsula and in the reasoning of the Inner House in *City Inn*. Whatever may be the law of the Northern Territory of Australia, I have considerable doubt that *Gaymark* represents the law of England. Contractual terms requiring a contractor to give prompt notice of delay serve a valuable purpose; such notice enables matters to be investigated while they are still current. Furthermore, such notice sometimes gives the employer the opportunity to withdraw instructions when the financial consequences become apparent. If *Gaymark* is good law, then a contractor could disregard with impunity any provision making proper notice a condition precedent. At his option the contractor could set time at large.

HHJ Jackson therefore upheld the old position, that if the facts are that it was possible to comply with claim procedure rules but the contractor simply failed to do so (whether deliberately or not), then those facts do not set time at large. Thus Honeywell was not entitled to the relief of delay damages which it sought in respect of the *Gaymark* point.[5]

This concept includes the understanding that delay damages are meant as a genuine pre-estimated lump sum for failure to comply with time for completion.[6] Delay damages, which are also referred to as liquidated damages, should therefore not be confused with so-called penalties, which, it is noteworthy to state, are not admissible under English law.

The whole concept leads to a number of conclusions, summarised as follows:

- Firstly delay damages must in principle be understood as a limitation of liability for delay.
- Secondly there is no space for so-called milestone damages, which are often encountered by Contractors. Milestone provisions in FIDIC contracts should be avoided. They do not fit within the structure of FIDIC Conditions, because it is not possible to apply the concept of EOT to them. Instead FIDIC Conditions recommend so-called Sections, which must be agreed by the parties and which are compatible with the concept of EOT. Remember in this regard that EOT creates a win-win situation, through which the Employer is protected against the loss of delay damages and the Contractor becomes released from liability for delay damages. As complementary milestone provisions are not compatible with this system it is suggested that they lead to time at large.
- Thirdly delay damages do not fall under national legislation concerning penalties. They have nothing to do with the compensation for a time overrun. By contrast they include a promise to pay a certain amount of money for non compliance with this particular agreement only.
- Fourthly, if and when delay damages are related to milestones they become due even though the Contractor complies with Time for Completion. In this respect it should be taken into consideration that according to FIDIC Conditions the Contractor has to submit and maintain a programme (see Sub-clause 8.3) according to which he shall proceed to carry out the Works. This means that

---

[5] Multiplex Constructions (UK) Ltd v. Honeywell Control Systems Ltd (No. 2) [2007] EWHC 447 (TCC).
[6] Alfred McAlpine Capital Projects Ltd v. Tilebox Ltd [2005] BLR 271 TCC.

the Contractor has absolute discretion as to how the work is planned and performed. Milestone agreements are therefore in contradiction to the whole concept of the contract and include constraints on the ability of the Contractor to carry out the works in accordance with the contract.

It is noteworthy to mention that the concept of time is of the essence slightly varies from common law jurisdiction to common law jurisdiction. In India the contract shall be read and construed against the background of Sections 55 and 63 of the Contract Act. This has led the Supreme Court of India to the proposition that "it cannot be disputed that question whether or not time was of the essence of the contract would essentially be a question of the intention of the parties to be gathered from the terms of the contract"[7]. In Hind[8] the Supreme Court therfore held that it will be clear from the law that even where the parties have expressly provided that time is of the essence of the contract such a stipulation will have to be read along with other provisions of the contract and such other provisions may, on construction of the contract, exclude the inference that the completion of the work by a particuar date was intended to be fundamental, for instance, if the contract were to include causes providing for extension of time in certain contingencies or for payment of fine or penalty for every day or week the work undertaken remains unfinished on the expiry of the time provided in the contract such clauses would be construed as rendering ineffective the express provision relating to the time being of the essence of contract. Also where parties of the contract commit defaults in performance of the contract and grants extension after extension to the contractor to complete the works, time cannot be considered to be of the essence[9]. If time is not of the essence the contract is not voidable though the Employer, in line with the second paragraph of Section 55 of the Contracts Act, may recover delay damages in the event that the Contractor fails to complete the Works within Time for Completion (Patil, p. 378). It needs to be emphasised that any extension shall be given in accordance with the contract and that delay damages must be fixed soon after the due date. Failure to do so may amount to waiver of the right to fix compension[10]. If time is of the essence the Employer may terminate the contract immediately after the time limit is over. As an alternative he may keep the contract alive and grant time extension. However he shall then give a notice of his intention to recover damages at the time the extension is granted (Patil, p. 348). By the way, the Supreme Court has also held that a clause according to which the Contractor is

---

[7] Hind Construction Contractors v. The State of Maharashtra [1979] AIR 720, 1979 (2) SCR1147, 1979 (2) SCC 70.

[8] Hind Construction Contractors v. The State of Maharashtra [1979] AIR 720, 1979 (2) SCR1147, 1979 (2) SCC 70; see also Shambhulal Pannalal, Secretary of State [1940] AIR Sind I.

[9] Mohinder Singh and Co v. Executive Engineer, CPWD, [1971] AIR J&K 130.

[10] State of Rajasthan v. Chandra Mehan [1971] AIR, Raj. 229.

only entitled to recover extension of Time for Completion excludes all remedies as to additional money[11].

12.3   Civil Law Approach

Under Civil law the Employer will not be entitled to liquidated damages if by his act or omission he prevented the Contractor from completing the contract by the agreed date. It could therefore be argued that the concept of time being of the essence and time at large is a pure common law concept which does not fit with Civil law jurisdictions, where time extension is usually not claim based and not put under claim management rules. This concept usually leads to time-consuming discussions about the release from penalties at the end of each project on a case by case level, which means that the parties will discuss each event through which the Contractor was prevented from performing the contract in order to reduce the total time overrun. However this system allows milestone agreements, which are quite often used. The following German cases illustrate the dangers of this system:

- The parties to the contract had agreed to a delay penalty of 0.1% of the whole contract amount per day up to a cap of 10% of the whole contract amount. The penalties were due for failure to complete the whole of the works within time for completion. It remained undisputed that the contractor was late for about 14 months. However during the course of the works the parties had agreed to sectional completion dates for different parts of the works. No new date for completion for the whole of the works was fixed. It was unclear whether the parties wanted to put the sectional completion dates under the penalty clause. The employer was not able to show evidence for this. The court held that due to the change of the completion dates the whole system for time for completion was disturbed. Hence it held that the employer was no longer entitled to penalties.[12]
- The contractor promised by a turn key contract to complete the works according to a time schedule according to which the works should be completed on 30 April 1994. In the event of failure to complete the works according to the time schedule the contractor owed a penalty of 10,000 DM per day up to a cap of 10% of the contract amount. After the commencement date the employer instructed a considerable number of variations to the design. Not earlier than in January 1994 the contractor was able to submit a final programme. He then gave notice that he could no longer comply with the agreed completion date. The court held that the original time schedule vitiated without any possibility to amend or update the

---

[11] Ramnath International Construction Pvt. Ltd v. Union of India 2007 AIR 509, 2006 (10) Suppl. SCR 570, 2007 (2) SCC4 53, 2006 (14) SCALE 49.
[12] OLG Celle [2000] IBR 245.

original time schedule and that the delay was not attributable to the contractor. In such a case, the court added, a penalty clause vitiates as well.[13]

- The contractor had agreed to complete the works within seven months. Various delays and disruptions occurred. The construction permission was handed over late, the employer instructed variations and the local authorities required some additional fire protection items. Upon the merits of the case the delays were attributable to the employer. The Federal Supreme Court held that the penalty clause vitiated.[14]

- According to the standard terms of a contract non compliance with time for completion and all milestone dates was covered by a penalty clause. The penalties amounted to a percentage of the whole contract amount for both, the milestone dates and time for completion for the whole of the works. The court held that it was unreasonable and void to put the contractor under the obligation to pay penalties for non compliance with milestone dates and again for failure to comply with time for completion for the whole of the works. In addition the court argued that the penalties at the milestone dates were unreasonably high.[15]

It can be summarised that in principle it is possible to agree to penalties for both milestone dates and completion dates, as long as this is done separately and without ambiguity.[16] Penalty clauses, which do not clearly indicate whether the cap applies to the whole of all of the penalties or to each kind of penalty, are void. Thus the Court of Appeal Koblenz (Germany) held the following clause to be invalid:[17]

> The contractor shall pay for failure to complete the works until the final completion date a penalty of 0.5% of the contract price per calendar day, at the maximum 20 days, for each day of delay. This clause applies also to milestone dates. The whole amount of penalties is limited to the maximum of 10% of the contract price.

Moreover the Court of Appeal of Hamm (Germany) declared a penalty clause void which allowed to claim for penalties for failure to meet the milestone dates up to the agreed cap independent from the fact whether the contractor would comply with time for completion for the whole of the works or not.[18]

However we would not agree with the argument that the common law concept of time for completion does not fit with Civil law. Common law shows very clearly that the principles of time at large are based on the prevention principle, which is also a well-known principle under Civil law. Thus making time of the essence means to provide for a contractual mechanism allowing for time extension in the

---

[13] OLG Hamm [1996] IBR 509.

[14] BGH [1993] IBR 368.

[15] OLG [2002] IBR 542.

[16] See Schulze-Hagen [2001] IBR 165.

[17] OLG Koblenz [2000] IBR 535.

[18] OLG Hamm [2000] IBR 489.

event of any act of prevention by or on behalf of the Employer. If not, liquidated or delay damages become invalid. Thus what makes the difference is that under FIDIC terms of contract and its Common law approach all or purportedly all acts of prevention and/or interference must be anticipated by the parties to the Contract in order to ensure that Contractor will not be put under a liability for failure to comply with the agreed Time for Completion if and when the delay has been caused by the Employer.

Thus if the parties convene that the Contractor shall carry out the Works within Time for Completion according to a programme which he is required to submit, then he should not be put under further constraints. Any further constraints such as milestones will have an impact on the contractual risk allocation, because the Contractor is no longer free to decide in which way he will satisfy his obligations. On the other hand if there is the common understanding of the parties to comply with Time for Completion according to the principles of a FIDIC contract the concept of time at large will be inherent to the contract. If the Employer is not satisfied with this system he should accept the consequences of his dissatisfaction, which means that he looses delay damages for non compliance with Time for Completion.

From a purely legal point of view, it could be argued that the parties accept either a system as a whole or they create a new one. In our eyes the FIDIC concept of Time for Completion is condition precedent of the contract. On the one hand the Contractor is free to carry out the Works in accordance with his programme combined with the entitlement to EOT as foreseen in the Conditions. On the other hand the Employer will be entitled to delay damages, if the Contractor fails to comply with his obligations subject to EOT entitlements as the case may be. Milestones will alter the contract and turn it into something completely different. The Contractor then obliges himself to comply with a pre-determined programme without any responsibility for the progress of the Works as a whole. And this presumably leads to the foreclosure of delay damages for time overrun concerning the overall project.

The mere fact that FIDIC recommends an option to agree to Sections shows that there is an alternative which fits with the concept of time for completion which is inherent to the contract. The parties to a FIDIC contract are strongly recommended to opt either for Sections or to maintain the concept of full and absolute discretion as to how the Works are planned and carried by the Contractor.

Finally a common misunderstanding should be clarified. Most contractors argue that an event warranting time extension entitles the contractor to extra money. This is wrong. From a legal point of view an extension of time has only one effect. Under FIDIC it adjusts time for completion and in doing so it defers the date from which the Contractor becomes liable to pay delay damages to the Employer. Whether the Contractor is entitled to additional further cost or cost and reasonable profit depends on the nature of the event and must be ascertained after the event has occurred. Only if and when the contract or the governing law provides for an entitlement to extra cost may the Contractor give notice of a complementary cost claim.

12.4   Time Control

One of the underlying principles of all FIDIC forms of contract is the avoidance and reduction of the amount of change that occurs on construction projects. On the other hand FIDIC recognises that change is inevitable, even though many changes can generally be avoided through good planning. Once having accepted that changes are inevitable a management tool for time survey and time management is necessary. This is the reason why FIDIC requires the Contractor to provide a Programme. The Programme is one of the most important tools for the Engineer and the parties to the contract during the whole course of the Works.

The Programme as referred to in Sub-Clause 8.3 is far more than a simple bar chart. It shows the intended order and duration of all activities which are necessary in order to complete the Works. It shall also include all resources needed for each activity. It is a management tool which must be updated regularly.

According to Sub-Clause 8.3 the Contractor shall submit a Programme within 28 days after the Commencement date. It is submitted to the Engineer who may reject it within 21 days after having received it. By doing so he must state the extent to which it does not comply with the Contract. If the Engineer remains silent, the Contractor shall proceed in accordance with the Programme. As soon as the Programme is inconsistent with actual progress or with the Contractor's obligations the Contractor shall submit a revised Programme. Thus the Programme does not become accepted by the Employer, but it is nevertheless binding on the Contractor.

Each Programme shall include the following information:

(a) The order in which the Contractor intends to carry out the Works, including the anticipated timing of each stage of design (if any), Contractor's Documents, procurement, manufacture, inspection, delivery to Site, construction, erection, testing, commissioning and trial operation
(b) The periods for reviews under Sub-Clause 5.2 [*Contractor's Documents*] and for any other submissions, approvals and consents specified in the Employer's Requirements – each of these stages for work by each nominated Subcontractor (as defined in Clause 5 [*Nominated Subcontractors*])
(c) The sequence and timing of inspections and tests specified in the Contract
(d) A supporting report which includes:

   (1) A general description of the methods which the Contractor intends to adopt, and of the major stages, in the execution of the Works
   (2) Details showing the Contractor's reasonable estimate of the number of each class of Contractor's Personnel and of each type of Contractor's Equipment, required on the Site for each major stage

Thus the Programme includes full information about the anticipated timing of each stage of work, including details about delivery of material and goods, procurement, design, testing, etc. There is therefore a strong incentive to go through the exercise of forecasting all stages of work, which are necessary to complete the Works.

The Programme enables the Engineer to assess claims for Time extension and to instruct acceleration, if necessary.

The Programme has to show the Commencement date and the anticipated date for completion. If the Contractor encounters difficulties which result in delay or disruption then there are two possibilities. Either he encounters a difficulty which is at his risk, in which case he has to revise the Programme and to show how he plans to recover the delay, or else he suffers delay from an event which is at the risk of the Employer. He is then entitled to claim for Time extension. Once Time extension has been granted, he shall submit a revised Programme showing the new date for completion. In any case the Contractor shall submit a revised Programme as soon as the Programme becomes inconsistent with actual progress or with the Contractor's obligations. However there is no requirement for a regular and subsequent update of the Programme. As long as the Programme is consistent with actual progress and with the Contractor's obligations it can be maintained. But if actual progress is too slow or if progress has fallen behind the current Programme the Engineer may instruct the Contractor to submit a revised Programme in accordance with Sub-Clause 8.6. However he shall not do so if the delay is caused as a result of an event listed in Sub-Clause 8.4. In so far it is common understanding that Sub-Clause 8.6 applies if and when the Contractor has failed to give notice of a claim arising from an event listed in Sub-Clause 8.4.

It is critical to know whether the Contract provides constraints on how the Contractor performs the work. If so, the Contractor shall then reflect these constraints in his planning of the order and timing of the Works. However, if the Employer or the Engineer introduces new constraints during the course of the Works, this will be considered to be a change to the Works or the Employer's requirements and thus constitute a variation.

In any case the Engineer has the duty to review and the power to reject the Programme once it has been submitted by the Contractor. However, he should not reject the Programme for other reasons than non compliance with the Contract. As the responsibility for scheduling the works lays with the Contractor the Engineer should not put further constraints on the Contractor. Thus its means of control is in principle limited to the following questions:

- Does the Programme comply with all contractual obligations?
- Does the Programme comply with milestones, or restraints on working hours or methods?
- Does the Programme comply with approval requirements as to the design?
- Does the Programme comply with current determinations, instructions, etc.?
- Is the entire scope of the work represented?
- Are there any obvious errors in the programme related to the sequence or timing of the works?
- Does the Programme comply with actual progress?
- Does the Programme comply with testing requirements?

However he should not ask whether any activity durations are questionably too long, or too short for the scope of work they represent unless it becomes obvious that the Works will not be completed within Time for Completion. The Engineer should be aware of the fact that any instructions may constitute a Variation.

12.5   Extension of Time

There are two propositions: (1) If one finds in the contract the time limited within which the Contractor is to do this work that means not only that he is to do it within that time, but it means also that he is to have that time within which to do it. (2) When parties agree that a contract is to be implemented by a fixed date, conduct by the Employer which is already authorised by the contract (e.g. issuing variation orders in accordance with Clause 13) surely cannot alter or nullify the agreed Time for Completion.

It is also for the aforementioned reasons that building contracts nowadays almost invariably contain express provisions making allowance for extensions of time. However, when the conduct of the Employer is unlawful (and constitutes a breach of contract) the position may be that a debtor is generally excused from performing an obligation on time if his creditor wrongfully prevented him from doing so, in particular if the decision about extra time rests with the Employer who then becomes arbiter of, and gains an advantage from, his own – wrong. It is for this reason that Sub-Clause 8.4 provides for extension of Time for Completion not only in the event of additional or changed work but also in the event of acts of unlawful prevention and subject to further determination by the Engineer.

Apart from Sub-Clause 8.4 various other Sub-Clauses provide for extension of Time for Completion. A careful Contractor will inter alia identify the following events which may cause an entitlement to additional time:

- Delayed drawings (Red Book only) (Sub-Clause 1.9)
- Lack of access to and possession of the Site (Sub-Clause 2.1)
- Adverse physical conditions (Sub-Clause 4.12)
- Fossils (Sub-Clause 4.24)
- Delayed tests (Sub-Clause 7.4)
- Interference with Tests on Completion (Sub-Clause 10.3)
- Changes in legislation (Sub-Clause 13.7)

12.6   Concurrent Delay

Delay and disruption occur almost inevitably. According to Sub-Clause 4.21 the Contractor must compare actual progress and planned progress showing details of any event or circumstance which may jeopardise completion. Unfortunately it is often the case that concurrent causes of delay occur. This is the case if delay occurs when Contractor and Employer have both caused independent delays. In other words, a concurrent delay appears when two or more causes of delay overlap.

It is however critical to note that it is the overlapping of the causes of the delays not the overlapping of the delays themselves. Ignoring this distinction will lead to confusion and sometimes disputes. If the contract is silent on the issue of concurrent delay, as is the case under FIDIC, the parties often assume that the silence operates to their benefit. The existing and conflicting case law makes it difficult to determine who, in a particular factual scenario, is correct. Whilst a single cause of delay usually presents no problem when dealing with extension of time claims, it is thus obviously different for delay caused by multiple reasons. This situation presents more difficulties to decide whether the Contractor is entitled to extension for Time of Completion. Usually the situation is as follows (Figs. 12.2–12.5):

Situation 1: Overlapping Events

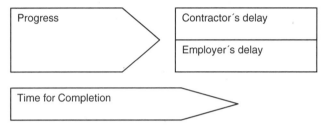

Fig. 12.2 Concurrent delay I

Situation 2: Combined Events

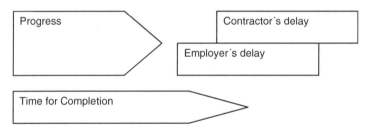

Fig. 12.3 Concurrent delay II

Situation 3: Employer's Delay is dominant

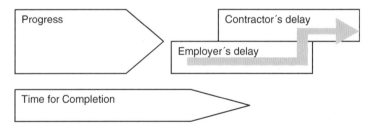

Fig. 12.4 Concurrent delay III

Situation 4: Contractor's Delay is dominant

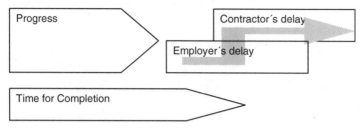

Fig. 12.5 Concurrent delay IV

Some standard forms attempt to address the concurrent delay issue by particular clauses, such as the Australian AS2124-1992 form of contract, at Sub-Clause 35.5:

> Where more than one event causes concurrent delays and the cause of at least one of those events, but not all of them, is not a cause referred to in the preceding paragraph, then to the extent that the delays are concurrent, the Contractor shall not be entitled to an extension of time for Practical Completion.

This clause clearly deprives the contractor from extension of time for a concurrent delay, being far away from providing a balanced approach to the issue.

The similar Utah standard terms for construction include the following Sub-Clause 4.7.14:[19] *Notwithstanding any other provision of these General Conditions, to the extent a non-compensable delay occurs at the same time as a compensable delay, the DFCM shall not be responsible for any compensation for the period of the non-compensable delay.*

12.6.1 Common Law

The effect of provisions as to time for completion was set out by Lord Fraser of Tullybelton in *Percy Bilton Ltd v. Greater London Council*:[20]

- The general rule is that the main contractor is bound to complete the work by the date for completion stated in the contract. If he fails to do so, he will be liable for liquidated damages to the employer.
- That is subject to the exception that the employer is not entitled to liquidated damages if by his acts or omissions he has prevented the main contractor from completing his work by completion date....
- These general rules may be amended by the express terms of the contract.

---

[19] Pursuant to UCA 63-56-601 and Utah Administrative Code Rule R23-1-60.
[20] [1982] 1 WLR 794, at 801.

The following terms may affect the general rule: Where completion is delayed (a) by force majeure, or (b) by reason of any exceptionally adverse weather or (c) by reason of unforeseeable physical conditions or (d) by any prevention caused by or attributable to the Employer, the Engineer is bound to make a fair extension of Time for Completion of the work. Without those express provisions, the Contractor would be left to take the risk of delay caused by force majeure or exceptionally adverse weather, etc., under the general rule.

Colman J.'s speech in *Balfour Beatty Building Ltd v. Chestermount Properties Ltd*,[21] summarises the following:

"[I]t is right to examine the underlying contractual purpose of the completion date/extension of time/liquidated damages regime. At the foundation of this code is the obligation of the contractor to complete the works within the contractual period terminating at the completion date and on failure to do so to pay liquidated charges for the period of time by which practical completion exceeds the completion date. But superimposed on this regime is a system of allocation of risk. If events occur which are non-contractor's risk events and those events caused the progress of the works to be delayed, in as much as such delay would otherwise cause the contractor to become liable for liquidated damages or for more liquidated damages, the contract provides for the completion date to be prospectively or, under clause 25.3.3, retrospectively, adjusted in order to reflect the period of delay so caused and thereby reduce pro tanto the amount of liquidated damages payable by the contractor. Likewise, if the works are reduced by an omission instructed by the architect it may be fair and reasonable to *reduce* the contract period for completion prospectively or retrospectively and therefore to advance the completion date. In view of the inherent difficulties in predicting with precision the impact on the progress of the works of non-contractor's risk events, particularly when operating simultaneously with contractor's risk events the architect is given a power of retrospective adjustment of the completion date. The underlying objective is to arrive at the aggregate period of time within which the contract works as ultimately defined ought to have been completed having regard to the incidence of non-contractor's risk events and to calculate the excess time if any, over that period, which the contractor took to complete the works. In essence, the architect is concerned to arrive at an aggregate period for completion of the contractual works, having regard to the occurrence of non-contractor's risk events and to calculate the extent to which the completion of the works has exceeded that period".

Further authority on the application of such clauses is found in *Henry Boot Construction (UK) Ltd v. Malmaison Hotel (Manchester) Ltd.*[22] In that case Dyson J., after referring to the analysis of Colman J. in *Balfour Beatty*, continued:

"13. [I]t is agreed that if there are two concurrent causes of delay, one of which is a relevant event, and the other is not, then the contractor is entitled to an extension of time for the period of delay caused by the relevant event notwithstanding the

---

[21] (1993) 62 BLR 1, at 25 (concerning a JCT contract).

[22] (1999) 70 Con LR 32.

concurrent effect of the other event. Thus, to take a simple example, if no work is possible on a site for a week not only because of exceptionally inclement weather (a relevant event), but also because the contractor has a shortage of labour (not a relevant event), and if the failure to work during that week is likely to delay the works beyond the completion date by one week, then if he considers it fair and reasonable to do so, the architect is required to grant an extension of time of one week. He cannot refuse to do so on the grounds that the delay would have occurred in any event by reason of the shortage of labour.

15 It seems to me that it is a question of fact in any given case whether a relevant event has caused or is likely to caused delay to the works beyond the completion date in the sense described by Colman J. in the *Balfour Beatty* case. In the present case, the [employer] has... both a negative and a positive defence to the [extension of time] claim. The negative defence amounts to saying that the variations and late information, etc., relied on by the claimant did not cause any delay because the activities were not on the critical path, and on that account did not cause delay. The positive defence is that the true cause of the delay was other matters, which were not relevant events, and for which the contractor was responsible. In my view the respondent is entitled to advance these other matters by way of defence to the [extension of time] claim. It is entitled to say (a) the alleged relevant event was not likely to or did not cause delay, e.g. because the items of work affected were not on the critical path, and (b) the true cause of the admitted delay in respect of which the claim for an extension of time is advanced was something else. The positive case in (b) supports and fortifies the denial in (a). The respondent could limit its defence to the claim by relying on (a), but in my view there is nothing in cl. 25 which obliges it to do so. Likewise, when considering the matter under the contract, the architect may feel that he can decide the issue on a limited basis, or he may feel that he needs to go further, and consider whether a provisional view reached on the basis of one set of facts is supported by findings on other issues. It is impossible to lay down hard and fast rules. In my judgment, it is incorrect to say that, as a matter of construction of clause 25, when deciding whether a relevant event is likely to cause or has caused delay, the architect may not consider the impact on progress and completion of other events".

Dyson J.'s opinion in *Henry Boot Construction (UK) Ltd v. Malmaison Hotel (Manchester) Ltd* was considered by Judge Richard Seymour QC in *Royal Brompton Hospital NHS Trust v. Hammond (No 7)*, (2001) 76 Con LR 148, at paragraph 31. In *City Inn Ltd v. Shepherd Construction Ltd* [2007] CSOH 190 (30 November 2007) Lord Drummond Young has considered this speech in the following words:

"In that passage Judge Seymour gave a further explanation of what is meant by "events operating concurrently". He drew a distinction between on one hand a case where work has been delayed through a shortage of labour and a relevant event then occurs and on the other hand a case where works are proceeding regularly when both a relevant event and a shortage of labour occur, more or less simultaneously. Judge Seymour considered that Dyson J. had only been concerned with the latter situation, and not with the former; in the former situation the relevant event had no effect upon the completion date. I have some difficulty with this distinction.

It seems to turn upon the question whether the shortage of labour and the relevant event occurred simultaneously; or at least it assumes that the shortage of labour did not significantly predate the relevant event. That, however, seems to me to be an arbitrary criterion. It should not matter whether the shortage of labour developed, for example, two days before or two days after the start of a substantial period of inclement weather; in either case the two matters operate concurrently to delay completion of the works. In my opinion both of these cases should be treated as involving concurrent causes, and they should be dealt with in the way indicated in clause 25.3.1 by granting such extension as the architect considers fair and reasonable".

Lord Young continued to say: It is in any event clear from older authority that the fact that delay has been caused by matters for which the contractor is responsible will not deprive the contractor of his right to claim an extension of time for delay caused by a relevant event. That is essentially the ratio of *Wells v. Army and Navy Co-operative Society*, 1903, 86 LT 764. A more modern statement of this principle is found in *S.M.K. Cabinets v. Hili Modern Electrics Pty Ltd*, [1984] VR 391, a decision of the Supreme Court of Victoria. In that case, Brooking J., whose opinion was upheld by the other judges of the court, stated (at 398):

"The sole remaining matter is that of the soundness of the ground on which the arbitrator in fact rejected the defence of prevention [that is, acts of the employer that prevent the contractor from completing on time]. He evidently considered that where acts or omissions of a proprietor do in fact substantially delay completion, the proprietor nonetheless cannot be sent to have prevented the contractor from completing by the relevant date unless the contractor would have been able to complete by that date had it not been for the supposed prevention.... But it has been accepted for more than one hundred years that this is not the law. The cases are all one way".

Cases were then cited from Australia, England, New Zealand and Canada; these included *Wells*. In relation to *Wells*, Brooking J. said (at 399):

"The principle of the decision is not as clear as one would wish, but appears to be that if the supposed prevention was such as would in ordinary circumstances have made it impossible for the contractor to complete in time, then prevention has in law occurred, notwithstanding that the contractor may in fact have disabled himself by his own delays from completing by the due date".

12.6.2 Civil Law

Under German law the legal situation seems to be as follows:

In most cases the parties to the contract agree on a deadline and/or milestones. It is often the case that the contract documents comprise a work programme or working schedule. Again it is not uncommon to agree on penalty clauses for non compliance with time for completion, which in principle are valid clauses, whilst in practise they are often ineffective according to the well known "main rouge" principle applicable to standard terms of contract. This is clearly illustrated by a recent decision of the Federal Supreme Court, which held:[23]

> A penalty clause in standard terms of a construction contract stipulating the following is void: *Time for Completion is absolute and shall not be extended in the event of adverse climatic conditions. In the event of failure to comply with Time for Completion the Contractor shall pay to the Employer 0.3% of the contract amount per day to the maximum of 10% of the contract price.*

However, once the parties to the contract have agreed on a deadline with according penalties the contractor will fall in breach of contract if he fails to comply with the agreed deadline. The employer is then entitled to the payment of the agreed penalties.

If the contractor is prevented from performing the contract he may give notice of the event or circumstance. If the delay is caused by circumstances which belong to the risks which are allocated to the employer the delay will be excused, which is considered to constitute a defence against penalty claims. In addition the contractor will be entitled to a claim for loss of productivity. But there is no clear and systematic approach. Case law prevails:

Abuse of rights case: The contractor had promised to complete the works within the summer school holidays. The contract contained a penalty clause according to which penalties were due for failure to comply with time for completion. The contractor failed to complete the works within the school holidays. Hence the employer refused to pay the final invoice. At court the contractor showed evidence that the delay was caused by the employer who failed to hand over drawings in a timely manner and instructed numerous variations. Thus the court held that it was an abuse of rights to rely on the penalty clause.[24]

Loss of productivity case: A contractor was contracted to complete the civil works for a health care centre. Time for completion, milestone dates and particular milestone for the handing over of the approved design had been agreed. The design was not handed over in a timely manner. The contractor incurred delay. Due to acceleration measures the contractor completed the works within time for completion but incurred additional cost. The Federal Supreme Court held that the contractor did not avert the delay in sufficient detail. The court pointed out that it was necessary to show each delay in a detailed manner. It explained that it is necessary to describe each event and its impact on progress of the works. The contractor has to consider whether he could overcome the delay or its effects on time for completion.[25]

Independent claim for extension of time case: A general contractor claimed for extension of time. The employer failed to provide a valid construction permission. The local authorities issued a suspension order. Parts of the works had to be demolished and reconstructed. It became impossible to complete the works within

---

[23] 6 December 2007; file no. VII ZR 28/07.

[24] OLG Zweibrücken [2006] IBR 246.

[25] BGH [2002] IBR 354; BGH [2005] IBR 246.

254   12 Time for Completion

the original time for completion. Thus the contractor claimed for extension of time. The claim was rejected for procedural reasons. In summary the court held that according to Sect. 6 VOB/B extension of time for completion becomes granted automatically without any need to go to court for this particular issue. As a rule extension for time for completion should be discussed as part of a claim for loss of productivity or as a defence against penalties.[26]

Under English law the Contractor must compare actual progress and planned progress showing details of any events or circumstances which have jeopardised completion. Each "hindrance", its beginning and its end must be shown in detail. This requires the production of bar charts or network plans and a comparison of actual and planned progress. The contractor must contend and prove the causal connection between each event and circumstance and delay. In the event of concurrent delays it must be shown that the relevant event has nevertheless caused delay on time for completion. According to Sect. 6 no. 6 VOB/B a claim for loss of productivity will be given if the following conditions are met (Werner and Pastor 2008, note 1821):

- The contractor has effectively been prevented from performing the works or parts of it.
- This prevention has caused delay.
- The event has been notified promptly.
- The delay is attributable to the employer.
- The delay has caused loss of productivity.

If both, contractor and employer have caused the same delay by different reasons Sect. 254(1) Civil Code applies,[27] which reads as follows:

(1) Where culpability on the part of the aggrieved party contributed to the liability in damages as well as the extent of compensation to be paid depend on the circumstances, in particular to what extent the damage was caused mainly by the one party or the other one.

The consequences must then be estimated according to Sect. 287 Civil Procedure Code giving the court discretion to decide on the matter (Kappellmann and Schiffers 2006, note 1354).

12.6.3 FIDIC

In daily practice the various causes of delay and disruption are likely to interact in a complex manner; shortages of labour will rarely be total; some work may be possible despite exceptionally adverse weather; and the degree to which work is affected by each of these events may vary from day to day. Other more complex situations can easily be imagined, such as flawed design by the employer and concurrent flawed workmanship by the contractor.

---

[26]KG Berlin [2003] IBR 67, further appeal to the Federal Court of Justice dismissed.
[27]BGH [1993] BauR 600, at 603.

What is required by Sub-Clause 8.4 is that the Engineer should exercise his judgment to determine the extent to which completion has been delayed by the relevant events. According to Sub-Clause 3.5 the Engineer must make a fair determination having regard to all relevant circumstances. Where there is true concurrency between a relevant event and a Contractor default, in the sense that both existed simultaneously, regardless of which started first, it may be appropriate to apportion responsibility for the delay between the two causes; obviously, however, the basis for such apportionment must be fair and reasonable. Precisely what is fair and reasonable is likely to turn on the exact circumstances of the particular case.

As already mentioned above under FIDIC the determination of the extension of time subject to Sub-Clause 3.5 shall be fair having due regard to all relevant circumstances. It is suggested that this requires account to be taken of the steps which could reasonably have been taken by the Contractor to mitigate the delay. One of these steps can be identified in Sub-Clause 8.3 according to which the Contractor shall give notice of all probable future events or circumstances which may delay execution of the Works. Under the Gold Book the advanced warning policy is covered by Sub-Clause 8.4 of the Gold Book.

As discussed delay for which the Contractor is responsible will not preclude an extension of time based on an event, which in principle entitles the Contractor to an extension of the Time for Completion. Thus the critical question will frequently, perhaps usually, be how long an extension is justified by the relevant event. FIDIC does not give any clear guidelines as to this issue but offers some support. However according to Sub-Clause 8.3 the Contractor shall provide a programme showing each activity with clear dates, which means with a start date and an end date for each activity. Thus as a first step the Engineer will have to verify which activity has become delayed. If two concurrent causes occur, each of them having an impact on Time for Completion (e.g. flawed design by or on behalf of the Employer and flawed workmanship by the Contractor) the Engineer will be spoilt for choice. He may either rely on the dominant cause doctrine or make a fair decision with regard to all relevant circumstances. According to German law he would estimate the effective delay upon all relevant facts which were presented to him, taking account of the principles laid down in Sect. 254 Civil Code.

However, the impact of the proper law of contract on the assessment of time extension claims remains unclear. Neither under English law nor under German law does the use of the critical path method seem to be a legal requirement. Case law in Germany and England seems mainly to be based on contract interpretation, thus the results depend on the contract wording. On the other hand the principles of contributory negligence and mitigation of loss are pure legal principles which apply subject to the applicable law only.

As a prerequisite to bringing a claim the Contractor is to provide full supporting details of his application within 42 days of the occurrence of the delaying event. In practice, this will be difficult for the Contractor. The basic requirement is to give particulars supporting the claim. In the event of concurrent causes of delay, a period of delay should be attributed to each cause. The Contractor then needs to show which delay, if any, caused more overall delay.

12.7   SCL

Fortunately the English Society of Construction Law has published some helpful guidance as to the issue. The so-called SCL Delay and Disruption Protocol states that where Contractor delay to Completion occurs concurrently with Employer delay to Completion, the Contractor's concurrent delay should not reduce any EOT due. Reference is made to the SCL protocol for further information.

However it can be summarised that true concurrent delay is the occurrence of two or more delay events at the same time, one an Employer Risk Event, the other a Contractor Risk Event. The effects of both events are felt at the same time. Now, the suggestion in the SCL Protocol is that the Contractor shall obtain the extension of time but he shall only be entitled to any extra costs incurred as a specific consequence of the employer-caused delay.

12.8   Liquidated Damages and Penalties

As time and quality are often of the essence the parties to a contract may wish to ensure compensation for non compliance. A way in which liability for delay or quality is often ruled is by reference to a liquidated damages clause. Such a clause imposes an obligation upon one party to a contract to pay to the other a fixed sum of money in the event of the parties' breach. At common law such a clause must fix a genuine pre-estimate of the loss that would be suffered by the aggrieved party in the event of breach. If the defendant can show that the sum in question is not a genuine pre-estimate of loss, there is a risk that the courts will regard it as an invalid penalty. At civil law the courts will probably adjust the fixed amount, if it seems to be unreasonable high.

12.8.1   Validity of Liquidated Damages Clauses

The German Federal Court of Justice has recently held:[28]

> A penalty clause in standard terms of a construction contract stipulating the following is void:
>
> Time for Completion is absolute and shall not be extended in the event of adverse climatic conditions. In the event of failure to comply with Time for Completion the Contractor shall pay to the Employer 0.3% of the contract amount per day to the maximum of 10% of the contract price.

Under common law in order for the liquidated damages to be enforceable, they must be a reasonable forecast of the likely or actual damages if a delay occurs and

---

[28] 6 December 2007; file no. VII ZR 28/07.

not disproportionate to the presumed loss or injury to the non-breaching party.[29] If the forecast of damages prior to contract performance was unreasonable and excessive, then the courts and boards will consider these damages to be a penalty and, hence, unenforceable.[30]

A recent case illustrates another issue. Braes of Doune Wind Farm v. Alfred McAlpine Business Services[31] concerned two applications in relation to the First Award of an arbitrator concerning an EPC (Engineering, Procurement and Construction) Contract 2005 between Braes of Doune Wind Farm (Scotland) Ltd as Employer and Alfred McAlpine Business Services Ltd as Contractor, whereby the Contractor undertook to carry out works in connection with the provision of 36 wind turbine generators (the "WTGs") at a site some 18 km from Stirling in Scotland. The EPC contract was adapted from the FIDIC "Silver Book" used for EPC contracts and was governed by English law and conferred exclusive jurisdiction on the English Courts, subject to arbitration with the Construction Industry Model Arbitration ("CIMA") Rules.

A dispute arose between the parties as to Braes' entitlement to delay damages. The dispute was referred to arbitration in accordance with the arbitration agreement contained in the EPC contract. The arbitration agreement provided that the seat of arbitration would be Glasgow, Scotland and that any reference to "arbitration" in the Contract was deemed to be a reference to "arbitration" within the meaning of the Arbitration Act 1996.

The arbitrator held that the delay damages provisions within the EPC contract were insufficiently certain and accordingly unenforceable. He found that there was no entitlement to withhold or set off against sums otherwise due to McAlpine and issued an award in favour of McAlpine.

Braes applied for leave to appeal against this award upon a question of law whilst the McAlpine sought in effect a declaration that this Court had no jurisdiction to entertain such an application and for leave to enforce the award.

The relevant issues were whether (1) the English courts had jurisdiction to hear an application by either party under section 69 of the Arbitration Act 1996 (English law), which permits and requires a court to hear applications for leave to appeal and (2) to grant Braes' appeal in relation to the interpretation of the liquidated damages.

Akenhead J found that the arbitrator's decision was not obviously wrong. Therefore the application for leave to appeal failed and Alfred McAlpine was entitled to enforce the award. The court held that the most convincing argument advanced by the arbitrator for the Contractor was that the liquidated damages clause could well impose a liquidated damages liability on the Contractor in respect of

---

[29] Mitchell Engineering & Construction Co, Inc, ENG BCA No. 3785, 89-2 BCA 21, 753.

[30] Engineered Electric, ENG BCA No. 4944, 84-2 BCA 17, 316.

[31] Breas of Doune Wind Farm (Scotland) Ltd v. Alfred McAlpine Business Services Ltd [2008] EWHC 426 (TCC) per Akenhead J.

delays to individual wind turbines caused by the Wind Turbine Contractor. In fact it could be summarised:

A. The extension of time clause (Clause 8.4) did allow the Contractor extensions to the extent that overall or critical delay was caused by the Wind Turbine Contractor.
B. There was no provision in the contract for sectional completion of the Works. Thus, until all 36 WTGs were complete and fully connected into the (Contractor's) Works, the Works could not be completed.
C. However, if overall or critical delay was caused by the Contractor but individual WTGs were delayed by the default of the Wind Turbine Contractor, there was no provision to alleviate the imposition of liquidated damages on the Contractor.
D. As each WTG accounted for 2 MW and each megawatt accounted for £642 or £385 (depending upon the time of year) by way of liquidated damages per day of unavailability, the Contractor could end up paying liquidated damages for delays caused by the Wind Turbine Contractor's defaults in completing their work on the turbines even though the parties had agreed that for critical or overall delay the Contractor was not responsible.
E. Because it was clearly intended that the Contractor was not as such to be responsible for the defaults of the Wind Turbine Contractor or at least those which good co-ordination by the Contractor would have avoided, the parties nonetheless agreed a liquidated damages clause which would impose such damages upon the Contractor in certain foreseeable circumstances.
F. In those circumstances, there is in law a penalty which English Law will not enforce.

12.8.2   Delay Damages

Unless agreed otherwise, failure to comply with Time for Completion will usually lead to the entitlement of delay damages according to Sub-Clause 8.7. If the Contractor fails to comply with Sub-Clause 8.2, the Contractor shall subject to Sub-Clause 2.5 pay delay damages to the Employer for his default. The Appendix to Tender must state the daily amount and the maximum total amount of the damages due from the Contractor to the Employer for failure to complete the Works within the agreed Time for Completion. The figures must be given as percentages of the Final Contract Price and shall represent a reasonable estimate of the actual losses which will be incurred by the Employer. The Employer is strongly recommended to prepare such an estimate at tender stage in order to be prepared against the Contractor's argument that the agreed delay damages are in fact in the nature of a penalty. For the purposes of delay damages Time for Completion must be determinable. Thus a clear commencement date and the amount of days available for completion shall be fixed. Also the Engineer and the parties must know in advance the criteria for the assessment of the delay overrun.

Under a FIDIC contract delay is the time overrun compared with the current Time for Completion (as extended subject to the provisions of the Contract) until the issue of the Taking-Over Certificate. The same applies to Sections.

12.8.3 Milestone Damages

If a Contract links milestones with delay damages care must be taken that time does not become at large. It is beyond doubt that FIDIC has anticipated the wish to ensure that not even the Works as a whole but that also parts thereof become completed in time if this seems to be appropriate or necessary. However FIDIC has carefully adopted the English approach including its requirements as to delay damages in the event of milestones. It is therefore possible to define Sections which may be completed as an independent part of the Works. If the Contract provides for Sections it is easily possible to determine the respective Delay damages. However if the parties ignore the possibility to agree Sections but the Works are to be completed according to milestone dates difficulties will arise because then the Contract does not provide for effective provisions for extension of time for those particular activities and no feature exists to release the Contractor from its liability for Delay Damages.

References

Kappellmann K, Schiffers K-H (2006) Vergütung, Nachträge und Behinderungsfolgen beim Bauvertrag, vol. 1, 5th Edition. Werner, Köln
Patil (2005) Building and Engineering Contracts, 5th Edition, Patil, Pune
Werner U, Pastor W (2008) Der Bauprozess, 12th Edition. Werner, Köln

Chapter 13
Variations

When parties agree that a contract is to be implemented by a fixed date and by using specified methods, conduct by the employer which is authorised by the contract (e.g. issuing Variation orders, ordering extra work) surely cannot alter or nullify the agreed date for completion or other mutually agreed stipulations of the Contract. It is for that very reason that building contracts nowadays almost invariably contain express provisions making allowance for Variations.

Under a FIDIC contract Variations are covered by Clause 13. The Clause covers both the authority of the Engineer and the Employer as well as the procedures for work being added, omitted, or changed from the original contract, either by initiative of the Contractor (Value Engineering) or the initiative of the Engineer. Also the effects of any Variation order on time and money are expressly stipulated.

The Engineer's power to issue instructions which constitute a Variation is often conditional on prior approval by the Employer. However, if there is any such restriction which must have been disclosed in the Particular Conditions and the Engineer issues an instruction which constitutes a Variation, the Contractor may rely on it, because according to Sub-Clause 3.1, whenever the Engineer exercises a specified authority for which the Employer's approval is required, then the Employer shall be deemed to have given his approval.

13.1 Introduction

13.1.1 Variations in General

The so called scope of the works, once defined within the contract, including the Employer's Requirements, Specifications, Drawings and Bills of Quantities, may require various alterations to successfully adapt to circumstances and events which were not foreseen in detail. Typically construction contracts provide so called variation clauses allowing the employer to unilaterally change the scope, sequence,

A.-V. Jaeger and G.-S. Hök, *FIDIC-A Guide for Practitioners*,
DOI 10.1007/978-3-642-02100-8_13, © Springer-Verlag Berlin Heidelberg 2010

method or design of the works. By this means the contract is able to respond to the practical needs of all kinds of projects. In fact, variations to the works are almost inevitable, because of the fact that events and circumstances arise which may be beyond the control of the parties albeit also being caused by them. Thus the reasons for variations can be manifold. Several groups of reasons can be characterised:

- Changed conditions and circumstances
  - Examples: weather, legal conditions, etc., floods, earthquakes
- Erroneous presumptions or different conditions from those which were anticipated by both parties
  - Examples: unforeseen subsoil conditions
- Changed quantities
  - Examples: Due to changes in quantities progress of the works is too slow, for example if the volume of concrete requires overtime, the volume of reclamation work requires overtime
- Technical innovations
  - Examples: A new product line is available which decreases maintenance cost or makes it possible to complete the works earlier than expected
- Changed requirements of the employer:
  - Examples: The intended user of the building wishes extras to be incorporated into the project
- Errors or defects of a technical nature within the Contract documents
- Co-operation with other contractors and staff of the Employer

13.1.2 Contract Clauses

As a rule a contract is legally binding on the parties to it. Changes to the contract would necessitate a new contract being drawn up if changes to the works had to be made during the course of the works. Thus most contract forms used in the construction industry allow for variations or changes to the works and the design of the works, because there must be a basis from which a variation instruction can arise. Such allowance needs to be crystallised by an instruction or order of the employer or third person, to which the contract gives the power to do so. As Variations may affect not only the works or their design but also the Contractor's costs and profit, both the consequences of a variation to the Contractor and those to the Employer have to be fixed by the variation order. Thus standard contract forms usually provide rules which specify the effects of a variation order on the parties. In principle such clauses will give rise to claims for additional payment and/or extension of time. Under a FIDIC form of contract the variation valuation procedure as described in Sub-Clause 13.3 applies to cost and profit and an extension of time claim can be submitted to the Engineer subject to Sub-Clause 8.4.

Usually the contracts define the procedures and requirements whereby variations might be initiated and processed:

- Under contracts based on the common law the engineer typically has the authority to initiate variations by giving instructions to the contractor. The contractor will then have to consider whether he is entitled to claims for additional payment or whether the contract provides a valuation procedure which has to be implied anyway.
- Under contracts based on the civil law, the employer himself is usually authorised to instruct changes to the works. Thus according to Sect. 1 no. 3 and no. 4 VOB/B the employer has the right to instruct changes to the design and to order additional work. If such change alters the basis of the price for work, which is within the scope of the works, according to Sect. 2 No. 5 VOB/B a new price must be agreed by taking into consideration the higher and lower cost compared with the tender price. As to additional work the procedure is slightly different, because the Contractor must firstly and in any event before starting to perform the additional work, warn the Employer that he will claim for special payment in respect of the additional work (compare Sect. 2 no. 6 VOB/B). Otherwise his claim for additional payment will lapse.

13.1.3   Extent of Change Allowance Rules

However the question arises as to what extent the allowance for changes can be used by or on behalf of the employer or to what extent such clauses are binding on the contractor. The answer depends on the contract and an interpretation of it.

It could be argued that a contractor, especially when the employer is to deliver the design, is only expected to carry out specified work, which as whole becomes the intended building or plant. The foundations, walls and roof are all constitutive elements of the house, but the contractor is only responsible for carrying out, excavation work, brick laying work and tiling work of a pre-defined kind, nature and quantity, which normally is listed in bills of quantities and depicted in drawings. It could also be argued that the contractor has to build a house, composed of foundations, walls and a roof. If the works must be fit for (the intended) purpose, there must be common goal or target to be achieved at the end of the efforts of both parties. If not the contractor might carry out the work specified in the bills of quantities and the drawings, and nothing more. If and when the pre-estimated quantities are met, he could stop the work. In the worst case a torso building will be the result.

Thus, in principle any construction contract, by which the parties intend to construct a plant, building or tunnel, binds the contractor to do more than to carry out the works which are specified in any bills of quantities and drawings. In this event the data stated in the bills of quantities does not specify the scope of the works. By contrast they only quantify the expected quantities for later measurement or for calculation purposes. In this sense bills of quantities are nothing more than a method used to calculate or estimate the cost of the building. Under a measurement contract the final quantities will become measured at completion and be paid according to the agreed unit rates. Under a design & build contract the parties to it assume the risk of an erroneous estimation of the quantities listed in any bill of quantity. In both cases the scope of the works or services must therefore be identified in a different way than by relying on bills of quantities.

One of the grave errors in German law is the distinction between changes to the scope of the works and the instruction of additional work. This leads to the misleading understanding that the employer is allowed to instruct anything radically different from the original contract. However, this not true because according to Sect. 631 paragraph 1 BGB the contractor is bound to produce the work promised. The term "work" means the result of all the works and of all kind of works which have to be done in order to achieve the result. According to Sect. 1 no. 4 sentence 1 VOB/B the employer has only the right to subsequently instruct additional work, which is necessary to perform the contractual work (in the above mentioned sense). Thus in fact the employer is not allowed to instruct anything different from the original scope of the contract. By this he has to respect the limits of the contracts, which are defined by the scope of the works.

However, the question of what exactly this entails still remains open. In fact any builder assumes the task of achieving a target. Anything which has to be done in order to achieve the target must be done. Thus no exact quantities and items and specified methods of works can be pre-defined at tender stage. There is a dynamic working process within which specifications and instructions are sometimes inevitable. This does not mean that the employer already instructs a variation. Only if and when he changes the scope of works a variation order becomes apparent.

13.1.4 Change Orders

A different question is whether an order or instruction is a pure site instruction without any effect on the scope of services or works. Often, a site instruction is not defined in the conditions of contract. Variation orders tend to be more formal than site instructions, which can be issued in writing within a few hours of the event or verbal instruction. Variation orders tend to include the financial and time effects of an instruction and tend to be signed on behalf of the Client or Employer by the Supervisor, Engineer, Project Manager or similar person. But this is a very formal approach to the problem, which is not always suitable to give the right answers. In fact the test must be whether the instruction is inherent in the scope of works which has been agreed by the parties.

Example: The drawings show that boreholes must be made for tubes and pipes. The contractor is accustomed to firstly erect the walls and consequently perforating the boreholes. This is time consuming. The Engineer wants the contractor to provide block-outs. This is a pure site instruction subject to further consideration on the merits.

If not, it is more than this, it is a variation order.

Example: The drawings do not show any boreholes where the Engineer would want them to be present. Although they are necessary for the works, the additional boreholes are not within the scope of the works.

However, there is an inherent risk that an instruction may constitute a variation. Hence an Engineer or Contract Administrator will usually be reluctant to give instructions, especially in view to assisting a contractor with a difficulty which otherwise would be his contractual obligation to surmount by whatever methods he might choose to adopt. Although in that kind of situation the employer may strictly rely on the contract which states that any instruction of the Engineer which complies with the formal requirements of a variation instruction can constitute a variation. Such difficulties may be avoided by the Engineer through the use of clear language, stating that his instruction is not intended to constitute an order under the respective variation clause.

13.1.5 Control

It is obvious that changes to the works must be under the control of the contract. The parties to a contract usually do not expect to be bound to something which they do not know and which they cannot afford or realise.

Example: A craftsman agrees to paint a wall subject to variations by the employer. The employer instructs the craftsman to use specific methods and techniques of the middle ages. This is something which the craftsman cannot afford. Only a specialised restorer would be able to do so. Thus the variation is not binding on the craftsman.

It is common understanding that a contract must be complete in its terms, although the parties may leave an essential term to be settled by specified means outside the contract, for example by means of a third person (expert, adjudicator or arbitrator) to determine the term. By contrast no agreement exists if it what terms the parties have agreed on remain uncertain. As agreements should normally be interpreted in the sense to give them effect, variation clauses should be construed in the sense that they are only binding on the contractor if they are considered necessary for the completion of the Works or at the maximum that may be desirable to improve the functioning of the Works. Such variations may include (Ashworth 1998, p. 229):

- Additions
- Omissions
- Substitutions

- Alterations
- Changes in quality, quantity, form, character, kind, position, dimension, level, line
- Changes in specified sequence of works and method of timing

13.1.6 Consequences

It is not at all surprising that variations usually affect price and time for completion. The extent to which the agreement in terms of price and time for completion will be affected by variation orders is commonly stipulated in detail by the contract. In practice variations have some effect on the progress of the works and the method of executing the work. They may also cause increases and decreases to cost.

Most standard forms of contract including FIDIC forms of contract distinguish between the effects of variations upon time and cost and provide different rules for claims as to extension of time and cost. In line with this as to the Contract Price Sub-Clause 13.3 refers either to Clause 12 Red Book or directly to Sub-Clause 3.5 (Yellow Book, Silver Book). AS to the effect upon time Sub-Clause 8.4 lit. a provides for an entitlement to extension of Time for Completion.

Thus. in principle variation instructions which affect Time for Completion entitle the Contractor to additional Time for Completion according to Sub-Clause 8.4 FIDIC Books.

However, as to the cost related effects of variations, the situation is almost more complicated. The FIDIC Yellow Book for example allows for additional payment only if the Engineer instructs a variation to the Employer's Requirements or the Works. Employers will therefore usually refrain from detailing the Employer's Requirements too much and instead will only define core goals and targets. Everything which is within those core goals and targets must be done, even though the Engineer may give detailed instructions. However, if an instruction alters the Employer's Requirements or the Works the Contractor will be entitled to price adjustments including reasonable profit. By contrast under the FIDIC Red Book the entitlement to reasonable profit is not expressly mentioned. According to Sub-Clause 13.3 each variation shall be evaluated in accordance with Clause 12.

Sub-Clause 8.4 clearly states that any entitlement to extension of Time for Completion shall be subject to a claim in accordance with Sub-Clause 20.1. As to the cost related effects there is no such express reference to Sub-Clause 20.1. It can be argued that Sub-Clause 20.1 itself provides that any entitlement to additional time or money shall be subject to a prior notice within the therein stipulated time limits. However this argument conflicts with Sub-Clause 13.3 Red Book which merely states that each Variation shall be evaluated. Instead the Yellow Book directly refers to Sub-Clause 3.5 and therefore puts the Engineer or Employer under the duty to evaluate and determine the cost effects. It is therefore submitted that any cost effects are not time barred. Cost effects which result from a Variation must be determined ex officio without further efforts of the Contractor. This is in line with Sub-Clause 13.3 of the Yellow Book according to which the adjustments shall include reasonable profit taking account of the Contractor's submissions under Sub-Clause 13.2.

It follows from the wording in Sub-Clause 13.3 that except in relation to the matters extraneous to the valuation process, there is no need to wait for a substantiation of a claim as referred to in Sub-Clause 20.1. Instead the Engineer shall proceed in accordance with Sub-Clause 3.5 without any intermediate step.

Any further constraints on this entitlement also conflict with the very nature of a construction contract. The fact that Variations are authorised by the contract does not mean that the principle of reciprocity has been waived. The Contractor has accepted to carry out the Works in consideration of the Accepted Contract Amount. However he has not accepted the risk of additional or altered work though the Accepted Contract Amount rests unmodified. Instead Clause 13 provides its own machinery for the ascertainment of the valuation of variations and adjustments to the Contract Price. Upon instructing a Variation, the Engineer shall either proceed in accordance with Sub-Clause 3.5 to agree or determine adjustments of the Contract Price (Yellow Book) or he shall proceed in accordance with Clause 12 (Red Book) to measure and evaluate the Variation. Sub-Clause 3.5 makes clear that it is for the Engineer to identify a reasonable rate and to come to a fair determination with regard to all relevant circumstances. The Engineer is not relieved of his duty by the failure of the Contractor to give notice or to give notice promptly. He must consider independently in the light of his own knowledge of the Contractor's efforts and of the progress of the Works and of his knowledge of other matters affecting or likely to affect the Contract Price. If necessary he must make his own inquiries, whether from the Contractor or others. In so far as Variations are concerned the contractual machinery as to price adjustments is close and reference to Sub-Clause 20.1 has been waived or omitted.

13.1.7   Remarks

Unfortunately there is no self-contained system as to changes to the scope of works. From a lawyer's point of view it is not strictly logical that some changes to the works do not lead to the variation procedures.

Examples:

- In the event of Force Majeure for example, the contractor must change sequence of the works and afford additional cost in order to overcome the situation. But sub-clause 19.4 FIDIC Books entitles the contractor only to additional cost without any added profit.
- In the event of exceptionally adverse climatic conditions progress of the works and the cost situation will be affected. However, he will only be entitled to extension of time according to sub-clause 8.4 and not automatically to additional

cost and reasonable profit. This is only the case if the event constitutes at the same time an event which falls under sub-clause 17.3 or sub-clause 19.1. In both these cases the contractor is entitled to additional payment but only if and when an experienced contractor couldn't have foreseen the event (compare sub-clause 17.3 h and sub-clauses 19.1, 19.4).

- If the employer is not able to grant possession of the site within the time provided by the contract, the contractor may claim for extension of time, cost and reasonable profit (see sub-clause 2.1). However, in this situation the contractor is entitled to additional payment only if he notifies a claim within the time bar of sub-clause 20.1, whereas under the variation procedure it would be needless to do so.

However if the parties have clearly allocated the contractual risks their wishes should be respected.[1] All situations which are already covered by a specific clause within the contract documents escape from the scope of the variation clause. According to Sub-Clause 4.1 the Contractor shall design, execute and complete the Works in accordance with the Contract. This means according to Sub-Clause 4.12 Red Book that if the Contractor encounters adverse physical conditions he shall continue working, using such proper and reasonable measures as are appropriate for the physical conditions in question. Only if and to the extent that he encounters unforeseeable physical conditions will he be entitled to an extension of Time for Completion and payment of additional Cost. There is no need for a variation although Sub-Clause 4.12 does not exclude the possibility of a variation.

13.2   Variations Under FIDIC

FIDIC empowers the Engineer to initiate variations either by instruction (Sub-Clause 3.3) or by a request for the Contractor to submit a proposal (Sub-Clause 13.1). An instruction can be issued at any time to the extent that it is necessary for the execution of the Works (Sub-Clause 3.3). However, FIDIC limits the power of the Engineer to give an instruction which constitutes a Variation until the Engineer has issued the Taking-Over Certificate. No Variation can be initiated after the issue of the Taking-Over Certificate.

In order to avoid non intended variation orders or variation orders without having a full appraisal of its consequences, the Engineer will usually request a proposal from the Contractor (Sub-Clause 13.3). The latter will then respond in writing as soon as practicable, either by giving reasons why he cannot comply or by submitting a detailed proposal in accordance with Sub-Clause 13.3. Such kind of proposal will not constitute a firm offer to carry out the variation. Thus the Engineer will not accept an offer but simply give the instruction to execute the proposed

---

[1] Pacific Associates v. Baxter [1990] 1 QB 993 at 1010, confirmed by the House of Lords in White v. Jones [1995] 2 AC 257.

variation. If instructed, payment will be made either by measurement and evaluation (Red Book) and subsequent determination (Red Book) or by further determination according to Sub-Clause 3.5 (Yellow Book). Moreover extension of Time for Completion would be determined under the procedures at Sub-Clause 20.1, 3.5 and subject to Sub-Clause 8.4.

The Contractor is bound to execute each variation, unless he promptly gives reasons with supporting particulars stating the grounds for which he is not willing to do so. However the contract gives little scope for excuses. The extent to which variations are admissible is covered in Sub-Clause 13.1. The Engineer is not permitted to omit work in order to have it done by others. He is also not permitted to amend the contract. Thus variations must not differ radically from what the Contractor has already promised to do.

According to Sub-Clause 13.2 the Contractor is also entitled to initiate variations on special grounds. This kind of variation has been named Value Engineering. The types of variations which fall under Sub-Clause 13.2 are clearly defined in Sub-Clause 13.2. However, if the Engineer approves a proposal of the Contractor which did not meet the requirements of Sub-Clause 13.2 this will nevertheless constitute a Variation order. But only if the requirements of Sub-Clause 13.2 are met, will the Contractor be entitled to an additional fee pursuant to Sub-Clause 13.2 lit. c of the Red Book.

For both the parties to the contract and the Engineer, it is critical to know whether an instruction from the Engineer should be treated as a variation or a simple site instruction (compare Sub-Clause 3.3 where it is said, that if an instruction constitutes a Variation, Clause 13 applies).

Under the terms of a FIDIC contract the Engineer is required to give instructions for a number of different purposes. He may instruct to make good defects, to recover work and to test work. According to Sub-clause 1.5 he is entitled to issue instructions if an ambiguity or discrepancy is found in the documents. If any of his instructions change the order of priority of the documents which is ruled in Sub-clause 1.5 it is suggested that the instruction according to which a document of less priority overrules a document of higher priority should constitute a Variation. Some of his instructions may have the nature of a Variation, some remain simple site instructions without any impact on time and money. Some of those instructions deemed to constitute a Variation, would include an instruction under Sub-Clause 4.6 (instructions to allow opportunities for carrying out work to the Employer's Personnel, any other contractors or personnel of any legally constituted public authority) or one under Sub-Clause 11.2 (instruction to remedy defects which are not attributable to the Contractor). Others may constitute a Variation according to Sub-Clause 1.1.6.9 Red and Yellow Book, Sub-Clause 1.1.6.8 Silver Book or Sub-Clause 1.1.81 Gold Book (Fig. 13.1).

A "Variation" in this context is a very specific item. It is defined:

- (Sub-Clause 1.1.6.9 Yellow Book) as any "change to the Employer's Requirements or the Works"
- (Sub-Clause 1.1.6.9 Red Book) as any "change to the Works"

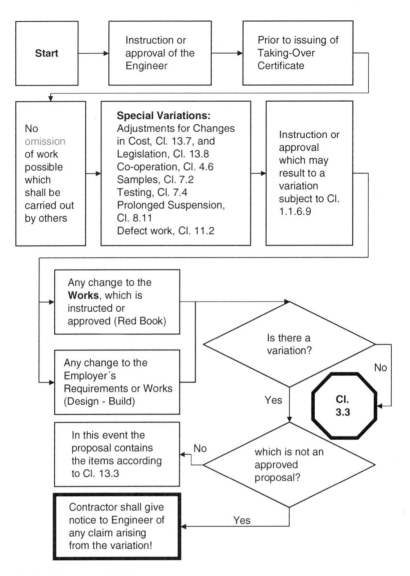

Fig. 13.1 Variations (meaning I)

- (Sub-Clause 1.1.6.8 Silver Book) as any "change to the Employer's Requirements or the Works"
- (Sub-Clause 1.1.81 Gold Book) as any "change to the Employer's Requirements
  or the Works"

which is, in each of the cases, instructed or approved as a variation under Clause 13.
It is thus something which is instituted by the Engineer or Employer by way of an
"instruction". An "instruction" is not a defined term.

The reason for the above mentioned terms seems to be clear. It is to define the precise circumstances in which the Contractor may or may not be paid for additional work, which will be evaluated subject to Sub-Clause 13.3 and determined subject to Sub-Clause 3.5. It gives to the Engineer and/or Employer a power to instruct or to approve additional work and, if that power is exercised in terms of the contract by written "instruction" or "approval", the Contractor will come under an obligation to carry out that work but will have a corresponding right to payment for it. The Engineer or Employer can not instruct something beyond the general scope of the Works. Under and in terms of the contract, if there is no formal "instructed" or "approved" variation, there is no obligation on the part of the Contractor to carry out any additional work but conversely there is no right to payment if he chooses to carry out such work.

On the other hand an instruction is a binding instrument. The Contractor will have to execute each instruction which has been given to him. He will also have to verify whether such an instruction constitutes a Variation. If so, Clause 13 applies. Whether the Engineer specifically uses the term Variation or not is not conclusive. Where a document contains a legal term of art the court should give it its technical meaning in law, unless there is something in the context to displace the presumption that it was intended to carry its technical meaning (Lewison 2004, note 5.08). It is therefore submitted that the use of the term "Variation" may give rise to the conclusion that the Engineer intended to give a Variation order. Also there is an English rule stating that where an instrument uses a legal term of art, it is presumed in the absence of clear indications to the contrary, that the term of art is being used in its correct legal sense, even if there are indications that the drafter misunderstood the law.[2] Again in German law the use of a term of art among professionals constitutes the presumption in presence of clear indications that the term has been used in its technical sense (Bamberger et al. 2008, Section 133, note 23). However, as Variation is a term which has been defined by the Contract, the Contractor cannot presume that the Engineer gives Variation orders beyond the authorities which have been confined to him.

13.2.1 Yellow, Silver and Gold Book

However, the variation clauses must be construed in the context of the contract as a whole, on an objective basis and in such a way as to produce a commercially sensible result. If the parties' contract is a lump sum contract it is this type of contract which was intended to be concluded. That fact is central to the nature of the contract, as it affects the fundamental basis of the price payable for the contract works. Obviously a lump sum construction contract is normally subject to provision for variations and additional work, and FIDIC contracts are no exception.

---

[2]I.R.C. v. Williams [1969] 1 WLR 1197.

Nevertheless, it is clear that a lump sum contract is not a remeasurement contract, in particular if a design and build contract standard form is in use. Under a design and build lump sum contract the courts usually infer a promise on the part of the Contractor to provide everything indispensable necessary to complete the whole of the Works (Furst and Ramsley 2006, note 4.024). In particular work carried out in a manner directed by the Engineer, where the contract set out no specific method of carrying out particular operations necessary to complete the works but provided that the works should be carried out under the Engineer's directions and the best manner to his satisfaction, is no additional work for which the contractor can claim additional money.[3]

It is thus suggested that all of the FIDIC forms of contract refer to the term "Works" with the meaning of "scope of the works" or the "whole of the Works". Sub-Clause 1.1.5.8 (definition of the term "Works") gives no further guidance in this matter. However, if the term "Works" comprises the whole of the works the meaning of Sub-Clause 13.1 lit. e Red Book becomes questionable, where it is stated that a variation may include any additional work, Plant, Material or services "necessary for the permanent Works".

Moreover the meaning of a change to the Employer's Requirements is unclear, in particular if the Works are widely defined, for example by a functional description. The question then arises whether any instruction which does not change the functional requirements remains unpaid or whether there is an implied term according to which any instruction which may affect the Contract Price, Time for Completion and/or the design responsibility of the Contractor constitutes a Variation. This would apparently not be the case if the Works should be carried out under the Engineer's directions and the best manner to his satisfaction. The former Red Book (Edition 1987) provided the following wording at Sub-Clause 13.1:

> Unless it is legally or physically impossible, the Contractor shall execute and complete the Works and remedy any defects therein in strict accordance with the Contract *to the satisfaction of the Engineer*.

This wording has been deleted in the 1999 edition. But the Engineer is still authorised to issue instructions at any time. Whether such an instruction constitutes a variation or not must be decided in accordance with Clause 13 (see Sub-Clause 3.3). Two conclusions are admitted. Firstly an instruction is not automatically a variation. Secondly an instruction constitutes a variation subject to Clause 13 and to Sub-Clause 1.1.6.9 (or 1.1.6.8 Silver Book or 1.1.81 Gold Book as the case may be). Moreover it follows from Sub-Clause 13.1 that an instruction will only constitute a variation if it has been issued prior to issuing of the Taking Over Certificate or under a Gold Book contract prior to the issue of the Commissioning Certificate.

However it is arguable that under the Yellow, Silver and Gold Book an instruction, which specifies or determines the method of working, a detail of the Works or the timely manner in which the Works shall be carried out, does not constitute

---

[3] Neodox Ltd v. Borough of Swinton and Pendlebury (1958) 5 BLR 38.

a Variation, to the extent that it leaves the Employer's Requirements as such unchanged, because this is inherent to the contract and already covered by Sub-Clause 3.3. This would reduce the scope of application of Clause 13 to a minimum. On the other hand it seems that there are some strong arguments to the contrary:

- According to Sub-Clause 8.4 lit. a (Sub-Clause 9.3 Gold Book) the timely effects of a change shall lead into an entitlement to extension of Time for Completion.
- According to Sub-Clause 5.1 the Contractor has the full responsibility for the design.
- Sub-Clause 8.3 presumes that the Contractor is responsible for the choice of the methods he intends to apply and the determination of the order in which the Contractor intends to carry out the Works
- According to Sub-Clause 4.11 the Contractor has satisfied himself as to the correctness and sufficiency of the Accepted Contract Amount.

In summary the Contractor has made his offer with the understanding that his price covers the Works (the whole of it) as assumed, designed, planned and to be carried out with the methods and in the order to be determined by him. Any change as to the methods of working, the order of the works and the design is thus not included in his price. It is therefore suggested that under a Yellow, Silver and Gold Book contract with a widely defined scope of works an instruction constitutes a Variation if:

- it affects the methods of working.
- it affects the Contract Price.
- it affects Time for Completion.

even though the requirements as stated in the functional description of the works remain unchanged, unless the additional or extra work is already included in the scope of the works and it could be expected from the Contractor to make allowances for it. However, the difficulties in determining in any particular situation whether an instruction affects the Contract price and/or Time for Completion are considerable. It is suggested that the Contractor will have the burden of proof of showing that an instruction affects the Contract Price. He will have to establish that the instruction requires him to do something, which is different to his design, planning and methods and which is more expensive or burdensome than what is expected from him.

If the Employer's Requirements are very detailed any change to them can easily be ascertained.

13.2.2   Red Book

The Red Book contains a much more sophisticated definition of the term "variation" than the Yellow, Silver Book and Gold Book, although Sub-Clause 1.1.6.9 seems to be unambiguous and at a first view comprehensive. However Sub-Clause 13.1 states that each Variation may include the matters referred to in lit. a to lit. f.

According to Sub-Clause 13.1 lit. e a Variation may include any additional work, Plant, Material or services *necessary for the Permanent Works*. The meaning of this

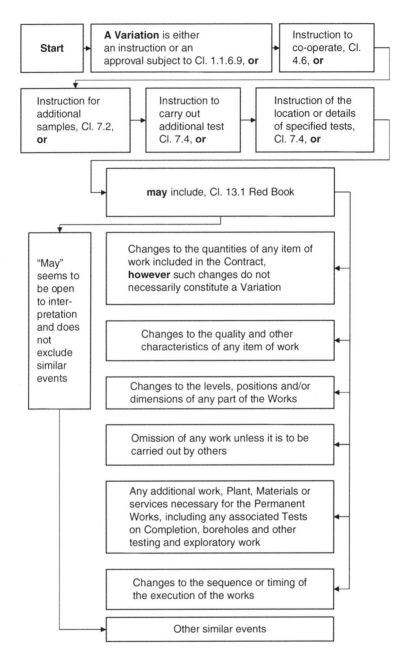

Fig. 13.2 Variations (meaning II)

is unclear because according to Sub-Clause 4.1 the Contractor is already liable to complete the Works (Fig. 13.2).

Again, the variation clause must be construed in the context of the contract as a whole, on an objective basis and in such a way as to produce a commercially sensible result. Subject to Sub-Clause 4.1 the Contractor shall execute a "whole work", including all goods and services. As has been stated by Mr. Totterdill the requirement to execute and complete can give an obligation to complete any item of work which is necessary for total completion of the Works, but which not may have been shown in detail on the Drawings (Totterdill 2006, p. 122). If what has been stated above is true, any instruction to carry out works which are necessary for the Permanent Works is already covered by Sub-Clause 4.1. There is no need to include such kind of additional work in a Variation. However it could be argued that Sub-Clause 13.1 means that any instruction concerning work which is not shown in detail in the Specifications or Drawings constitutes a Variation. We would dismiss this argument for the following reasons:

Variations can only be made to the contract within the limits which the parties themselves have agreed.[4] A construction contract notwithstanding its applicable pricing system is a contract for the delivery of goods and services for a price payable by instalments as the goods are delivered and the work is done. Having these principles in mind Sub-Clause 13.1 lit. e should be understood with the meaning that a Variation shall have a connection with the contract whilst it should not be ignored that the Contractor owes a duty to complete the whole of the works with the meaning of "scope of the works". Thus anything in between of both limits constitutes a Variation, including but not limited to changes to the quantities, changes to the quality and changes to the sequence or timing of the execution of the Works. However, it is submitted that the term "necessary" makes clear that in case of a Variation everything to be done shall be included.

Apart form these critical issues the following remarks seem to be noteworthy:

According to Sub-clause 4.6 the Contractor shall allow appropriate opportunities for carrying out work to Employer's personnel, any other contractors employed by the Employer and the personnel of any legally constituted public authorities. Upon any instruction to do so the Contractor may rely on the variation procedure and may claim for additional time subject to Sub-clause 8.4.

Beware that any Variation may lead to EOT claims under Sub-clause 8.4. If the Contractor incurs any cost as a result of a variation he will be entitled to payment according to the Variation valuation procedure rules in Sub-clause 13.3. Variations do not lead to claims for additional payments. Thus there is no time bar for adjustments as to costs and reasonable profit, if and when an instruction constitutes a Variation.

Under the Red Book variations instructed by Engineer are valued at contract rates where applicable and reasonable or, failing that, rates agreed upon between Employer's Engineer and Contractor (Sub-Clause 12.3). In the event of

---

[4]Beaufort Developments (NI) Ltd v. Gilbert-Ash (NI) Ltd and Others [1998] 2 All ER 778, 798j.

disagreement, the Engineer fixes new rates. The Engineer may elect to have varied
work performed on daywork basis (Sub-Clause 13.6).

13.3   Variation Procedure

According to Sub-Clause 13.3 Variations can be instructed or approved, although
the wording of Sub-Clause 13.3 Yellow Book is slightly different from that in Sub-
Clause 13.3 Red Book. However this wording gives rise to some remarks.

If there is any instruction which constitutes a Variation a detailed procedure
must be followed. Upon receiving any such instruction the Contractor shall
promptly give notice to the Engineer stating any objections as covered by Sub-
Clause 13.1. The Engineer shall then cancel, confirm or carry the instruction. However if the Contractor accepts the instruction unconditionally he shall
execute it.

Under a Red Book contract the Engineer shall then evaluate the Variation in
accordance with Clause 12. If the Contractor suffers delay as a result of the
Variation he may proceed in accordance with Sub-Clauses 8.4 lit. a and 20.1
(Fig. 13.3).

Under a Yellow, Silver or Gold Book contract either the Engineer or the
Employer's Representative shall proceed in accordance with Sub-Clause 3.5 to
agree or determine adjustments of the Contract Price.

However, if the Engineer (Red and Yellow Book) or the Employer's Representative (Gold Book) has requested a proposal, prior to instructing a Variation, the
Contractor shall respond in writing, either by giving reasons why he cannot comply
(if this is the case) or by submitting the information as specified in Sub-Clause 13.3
(Fig. 13.4).

Any such proposal will not constitute a firm offer which can be accepted by the
Engineer. It is submitted, that according to Sub-Clause 13.3 para. 1 the Engineer
is only empowered to kick off a Variation by means of an instruction, even though
he has requested a proposal. However, according to Sub-Clause 13.3 para. 2, after
receiving a proposal, he shall respond with approval, disapproval or comments.
Whether any such approval constitutes an instruction to proceed or not, will
depend on the wording of the approval. Pursuant to Sub-Clause 3.1 lit. c any
approval by the Engineer shall not relieve the Contractor from any responsibility
he has under the Contract. Thus a mere approval of a proposal which has been
made upon request as covered by Sub-Clause 13.3 should not relieve the
Contractor from complying with the Contract. Instead it must be clear from the
wording used by the Engineer that the Engineer does not only approve
the Variation but that he gives an instruction to proceed in accordance with the
approved design. There must be the intention to kick off a Variation with which
the Contractor shall comply in accordance with Sub-Clause 3.3. Any resulting
consequences as to the Contract Price shall then be determined in accordance with
Sub-Clause 3.5.

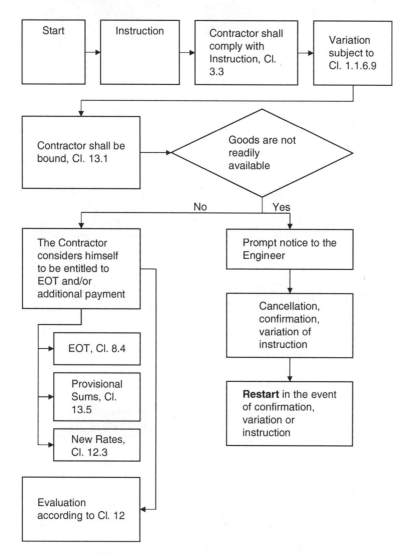

Fig. 13.3 Variation instruction procedure (Red Book)

It follows from this that Variations and in particular its effects on the Contract price and Time for Completion cannot be agreed by the Engineer or Employer's Representative by approving a proposal unless otherwise agreed between the Employer and the Contractor. This is in line with Sub-Clause 3.1, according to which the Engineer is not allowed to amend the Contract. A requested proposal will merely disclose the future impact on the programme and on the Contract Price which helps the Engineer to consider whether he should give an instruction. Usually the proposal will then serve as the basis for any further consultation

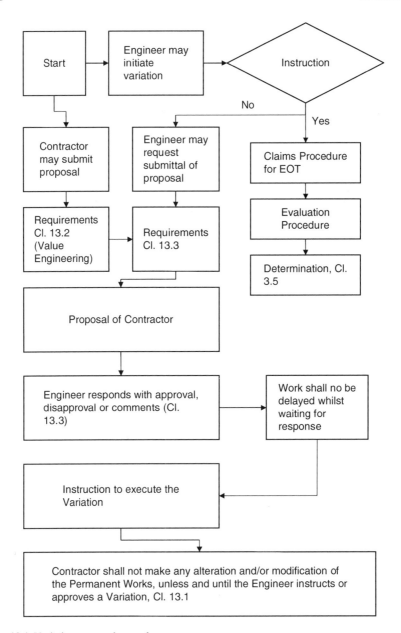

Fig. 13.4 Variation proposal procedure

with the Parties and subsequent negotiations. However, this is a process covered by Sub-Clause 3.5, according to which the Engineer shall consult with the Parties in the endeavour to reach an agreement. He shall not by himself agree any proposals.

13.4   Avoidance of Variations

The right to give instructions which constitute a Variation is an extraordinary right. It must be used with due skill and care. If common law governs the Contract, in principle this right is confined to the Engineer in order to safeguard the Employer's entitlement to delay damages in the event that the Employer must interfere. This may be necessary or desirable for various reasons. However, if the Employer interferes he would cause disruption and/or delay, thus preventing the Contractor to comply with Time for Completion. Under Common law this would lead to time "at large" leaving the Employer without the safeguard of delay damages for late completion. In Civil law the concept of time at large is not a common concept. However, even civil law construction contracts usually provide for a variation clause. The rationale behind this is that the Employer may wish to adjust the scope of works by unilateral instructions, which requires a contractual power to do so.

Thus Variation clauses grant unilateral freedom of scope. Sub-Clause 3.3 expressly states that the Contractor is bound to instructions of the Engineer, even though an instruction may constitute a Variation. Any instruction to proceed should focus the Engineer's attention on the fact that he initiates binding effects which may have financial and other consequences. This is clearly expressed in Sub-Clauses 13.3 and 8.4 (Sub-Clause 9.3 Gold Book).

Unfortunately most instructions issued by the Engineer or Employer's Representative are prepared in a deficient manner or are ill-conceived. Sometimes they are even not necessary as would be the case in the event of unforeseeable physical conditions (see Sub-Clause 4.12). However, an instruction may bring in operation the whole contractual machinery. It may cause EOT claims and cost claims as well as price adjustments.

The precise content of an instruction should vary depending on the type of works and the intended effects. The latter depend on the specification of the Works and/or the Employer's Requirements, if any. Thus it is critical to carefully study the Specifications, Bills of Quantities and Employer's Requirements and to clearly identify the scope of the Works, method requirements, time requirements, quality requirements, quantities, rates, and other detailed determinations. An instruction which constitutes a Variation is binding and not revisable or revocable, even though its effects and consequences are technically or economically disastrous.

The avoidance of Variations starts at the outset. This means that carefully prepared Specifications, Bills of Quantities and Employer's Requirements will avoid ambiguity and discrepancies. If ambiguities and discrepancies appear the Engineer shall give instructions and clarifications (Sub-Clause 1.5), which are likely to constitute a Variation. Clear and unambiguous Contract documents are also self explanatory as a consequence of which the Contractor will not need any support from the Engineer. Conversely, unclear and ambiguous Contract documents will lead to misunderstandings and omissions. As a result instructions will be issued which may constitute a Variation.

A considerable number of instructions are avoidable if the Contract documents are well prepared. Testing requirements, method requirements, quality requirements, interface requirements, cooperation requirements can be perfectly

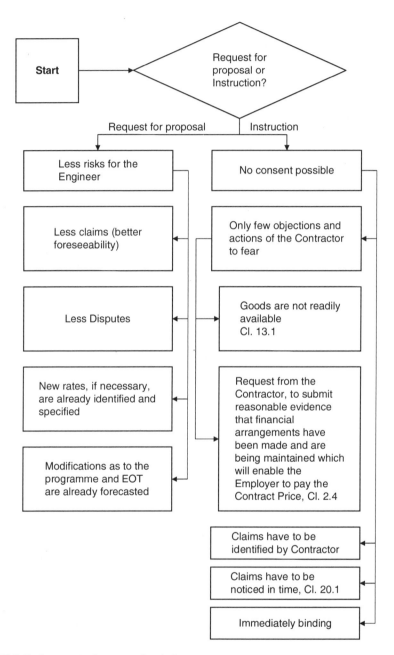

Fig. 13.5 Preferences in the event of variations

determined within the Contract documents. There will then be no further need for instructions. In the event of failure to provide such requirements, the Engineer will have to instruct tests, cooperation requirements, method instructions, etc. All of them are likely to constitute a Variation.

Finally it should be taken in account that the Contractor enjoys some freedom, including the freedom of choice concerning methods, materials and staff. Also he is responsible for the programme according to Sub-Clause 8.3. If the Engineer interferes with these freedoms he is likely to instruct a Variation. He should therefore carefully check whether it is really necessary to give an instruction or not. In the event of doubt he would be advised to request for a proposal according to Sub-Clause 13.3 (Fig. 13.5).

References

Ashworth A (1998) Civil Engineering contractual procedures. Addison Wesley Longman, Essex
Furst S, Ramsley V (2006) Keating on construction contracts, 8th edn. Sweet & Maxwell, London
Lewison K (2004) The interpretation of contracts, 3rd edn. Sweet & Maxwell, London
Totterdill BW (2006) FIDIC user's guide, 2nd edn. Thomas Telford, London
Wendtland H (2008) in: Bamberger, Roth (eds) Commentary to BGB, 2nd edn. C.H. Beck, München

Chapter 14
Tests

14.1 Introduction

All FIDIC Books provide detailed testing procedures. Tests are carried out by the Contractor except the Tests after Completion, if any, which are carried out by the Employer.

Both FIDIC Silver and Yellow Books provide for a three-stage commissioning procedure before the issue of the Taking-Over Certificate (Tests on Completion):

- Pre-commissioning tests, including "dry" functional tests
- Commissioning tests, including operational tests to demonstrate that the Works or relevant section operate safely, as specified and under all operating conditions
- Trial operation to demonstrate that the Works or section perform reliably and in accordance with the Contract

The Gold Book provides for Tests on Completion of Design – Build in accordance with Sub-Clause 7.4. Unless otherwise stated in the Particular Conditions, the Tests on Completion shall be carried out in the following sequence:

- Pre-commissioning tests, including appropriate inspections and functional tests (dry or cold)
- Commissioning tests, including operational tests
- Trial operation

Sub-Clause 7.4 provides the procedures for tests specified in the Contract documents and complementary tests instructed under Clause 13. Tests on Completion are ruled in Clause 9 which refers back to Sub-Clause 7.4. Tests after Completion are covered by Clause 12 Yellow Book (Silver Book). Thus Sub-Clause 7.4 will apply to all tests specified in the Contract, other than the Tests after Completion, if any.

The testing results of all Tests before the issue of the Taking-Over Certificate shall be reported and communicated to the Engineer who will then either endorse the test certificate or reject the test results. A detailed testing procedure is ruled in Sub-Clauses 7.4, 7.5 and Clause 9.

A.-V. Jaeger and G.-S. Hök, *FIDIC-A Guide for Practitioners*,
DOI 10.1007/978-3-642-02100-8_14, © Springer-Verlag Berlin Heidelberg 2010

Tests have to be carried out on completion, after commissioning and at all times which the Engineer considers necessary to instruct additional tests, even after having issued the Taking-Over Certificate.

The Engineer may at any time instruct additional tests (sub-clause 7.4). However, if the Contractor suffers delay and/or incurs cost he may be entitled to additional payment and extension of Time for completion.

More important than the test procedures which are included in the FIDIC Books is that the Employer's Requirements clearly indicate the requirements which have to be met.

14.2   Tests Until Completion

The Specifications and/or Bills of Quantities and/or Employer's Requirements may provide for particular tests to be carried out. Moreover the Engineer may instruct additional tests at all times. He may also vary the locations or details of specified tests. However, if the Engineer varies the locations or details of specified tests and/ or instructs additional tests Clause 13 applies, unless the varied and additional tests show that the tested plant, Materials or workmanship is not accordance with the Contract.

In the event that the Engineer instructs any additional tests the Contractor should give notice of a claim for extension of Time for Completion in order to ensure his compliance with Sub-Clause 20.1 and 8.4 lit. a. If the tests consequently show that the plant, Material or workmanship are not in accordance with the contract the claim will be dismissed.

The Contractor shall forward certified test reports to the Engineer. The Engineer shall then either endorse the Contractor's test certificate, or issue a certificate to him, to that effect. This seems to be superfluous if the Engineer did not attend the tests.

14.3   Tests on Completion

According to Sub-Clause 8.2 the Contractor shall complete the Works including achieving the passing of the Tests on Completion, which means that the Contractor shall first complete and then test the Works, and all of it within Time for Completion (Fig. 14.1). Tests on Completion shall be carried out in accordance with Clause 9, which refers back to Sub-Clause 7.4. The Works may be tested and retested if necessary. Test on Completion shall be carried out when the Work is ready to carry out each of the Tests on Completion.

Additional testing requirements may be found in the Employer's Requirements. Therein Tests on Completion should be tailored to the plant being built. It is the

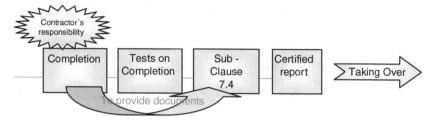

Fig. 14.1 Tests on completion

purpose of these tests to show that the Works are in accordance with the Employer's Requirements and that the plant operates to the standards specified in the Contract. It is obviously in the interests of both parties to ensure that testing criteria are drafted in a clear and precise way and that a pass or fail is objectively provable.

The Tests on Completion cannot be carried out until the Contractor has submitted the documents (for example: as-built drawings) and operation and maintenance manuals to Engineer as stated in Sub-Clause 4.1 lit d Red Book or Sub-Clauses 5.6 and 5.7 Yellow Book. The submission of these documents is a condition precedent. It is therefore in the interests of the Contractor to prepare as-built drawings and manuals as soon as possible. Even though the Works may be completed and ready for the tests, they cannot be carried out and the Taking Over Certificate cannot be issued until the Contractor has complied with his obligation to provide the Engineer with the said documents.

The Contractor shall then give 21-days-notice to the Engineer of the date when he will be ready to carry out the Tests on Completion. This requirement will ensure that the Engineer may arrange for any specialist engineers to attend and for the Employer to make any necessary arrangements (Totterdill 2006, p. 190).

Under the Yellow Book the Tests on Completion are a sequence of pre-commissioning tests, commissioning tests and trial operation, together with the performance tests which will be carried out during trial operation (Totterdill 2006, p. 191).

Finally the Contractor shall forward certified test reports to the Engineer. According to Sub-Clause 7.4 which applies by reference the Engineer shall then either endorse the Contractor's test certificate, or issue a certificate to him, to that effect.

However, the legal significance of passing Tests on Completion is sometimes misunderstood. Passing Tests on Completion does not mean that:

- Risk in the Works passes to the Employer (i.e. insurance).
- Liability for delay damages ceases for the Contractor.
- Defects liability period starts.

All three effects will only take place once the Engineer has issued the Taking-Over Certificate.

14.4 Tests After Completion

Tests after Completion are covered by Clause 12 Yellow Book (Fig. 14.2). They allow guaranteed performance to be demonstrated and tested under normal operating conditions and also for performance liquidated damages in the event of failure. Sub-Clause 12.1 provides for the testing procedures. Retesting of the Works or Sections is covered by Sub-Clause 12.3.

To the contrary of the procedures under Clauses 7 and 9 the Tests after Completion shall be carried out by the Employer, who is in charge of providing all the Materials, services and staff required to carry out the tests.

Test after Completion will be initiated by the Employer who shall give the Contractor 21-days-notice of the date after which the Tests after Completion will be carried out. Unless otherwise agreed the tests shall be carried out within 14 days after this date.

Tests after Completion must comply with the manuals supplied by the Contractor under Sub-Clause 5.7 and such guidance as the Contractor may be required to give during the course of the tests. Further requirements for the tests may be stipulated in the Employer's Requirements and will usually be specified in the Contractor's Proposal.

14.5 Tests During the Defects Notification Period

According to Sub-Clause 11.6 the Engineer may require the repetition of any of the tests described in the Contract, if the remedying of any defect or damage in line with Sub-Clause 11.1 may affect the performance of the Works. Such tests may be initiated by the Engineer by notice, which shall be made within 28 days after the defect or damage is remedied.

Sub-Clause 11.6 refers to Sub-Clause 11.2 which as such further refers to Clause 13. Thus if any damage or defect occurs which is not attributable to the Contractor the instruction of further tests will lead to a Variation.

14.6 Delayed Tests

Failure to pass the Tests on Completion themselves may lead to delay as a result of rejection of the Works by the Employer. In this event the Contractor must promptly remedy the defects. The Employer can instruct further repetition of tests and if

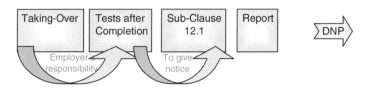

Fig. 14.2 Tests after completion

failure deprives the Employer of substantially the whole of the benefit of the Works or relevant Section, he can terminate. Moreover the Employer does have an option to take over and reduce the Contract Price to reflect the reduced value of the works.

However if the Employer causes delay the Contractor may be entitled to claims according to Sub-Clause 7.4, 9.2 and 10.3. If the Employer unduly delays:

- Any tests specified in the Contract or instructed in accordance with the Contract Sub-Clause 7.4 applies.
- The Tests on Completion Sub-Clause 7.4 and 10.3 apply (Sub-Clause 9.2).

14.7   ISO Standard

The ISO 9000 series of standards (ISO 9001, 9002, 9003) state the requirements for a quality management system which covers processes. It is applicable to a wide range of organisations, including but not exclusive to production, testing, research and inspection activities.[1] The application of ISO 9001 can be used for contractual or certification purposes.

The main areas of difference between the ISO 9001, 9002 and 9003 standards relate to the areas of competence which are covered under the various standards. Thus ISO 9001 covers design, development, production, installation and servicing and ISO 9003 covers final inspection and test areas (ISO 9001:1994 Introduction). ISO 9002 would "nest inside" ISO 9001 because its scope is limited with regard to areas of competence.

Under ISO 9001, a process can be an action such as carrying out a test, or an inspection, or producing a report. The intention of the quality control system is to provide control over various activities which may interact. For example, a request for analysis and the subsequent required activities may include:

1. Receipt of request: check requirements (methods, timescales, availability of personnel) can be met, acknowledge receipt of request, log request on system
2. Receipt of samples: log samples on system, pass to relevant personnel or laboratory
3. Check equipment is in calibration
4. Analyse sample in duplicate, check results against calibration data
5. Report results

The rationale behind the process approach is given in the Introduction section of ISO 9001: 2000 paragraphs 0.1–0.4.

---

[1] AIC Ltd v. Its Testing Services (UK) Ltd [2005] EWHC 2122 (Comm) (07 October 2005).

14.8 Tailoring Test Procedures

In some cases, the Employer does not want to wait to take over the plant only after it is tested, commissioned, performance-tested and ready for start-up. Instead he will in fact be an experienced operator of the plant, who therefore wants his own workforce operating the plant as soon as practicable. In this case the Employer is recommended to tailor particular testing procedures taking in consideration sectional tests and its effects.

References

Totterdill BW (2006) FIDIC user's guide. 2nd ed. London: Thomas Telford

Chapter 15
Certificates

15.1 Introduction

Certificates are a critical issue. The Contractor will only be paid after having obtained a Payment Certificate. Care of the Works will only pass to the Employer upon the issue of the Taking-Over Certificate. The post contractual legal liability will only start upon the issue of the Performance Certificate. According to Sub-Clause 14.14 the Employer shall not be liable for any matter except to the extent that the Contractor shall have included an amount expressly for it in the Final Statement. The first half of the Retention Monies will only become due after the Taking-Over Certificate is issued by the Engineer. The Contractor may only submit a final statement after having received the Performance Certificate (Fig. 15.1).

On the other hand the importance of certificates shall not be overestimated because any certificate shall not relieve the Contractor from any responsibility he has under the Contract (Sub-Clause 3.1 lit. c). For civil law practitioners it seems to be worthwhile to underline that subject to common law certificates only have the meaning attributed to them by the contract itself and that they do not show evidence for acceptance of the Works according to civil law except if all elements of acceptance have been met which must be verified case by case. Thus if the applicable law, for example Romanian law, provides for a two step procedure for acceptance of the Works, the exact point when final acceptance of the Works happens must be carefully examined in order to identify the starting point for the legal defects liability.

15.2 Taking Over

The date on which the Engineer issues the Taking-Over Certificate is taken to be Completion (Sub-Clauses 10.1, 8.2). When this occurs, several significant events occur. The defects notification period starts (Sub-Clause 1.1.3.7), half the retention

A.-V. Jaeger and G.-S. Hök, *FIDIC-A Guide for Practitioners*,
DOI 10.1007/978-3-642-02100-8_15, © Springer-Verlag Berlin Heidelberg 2010

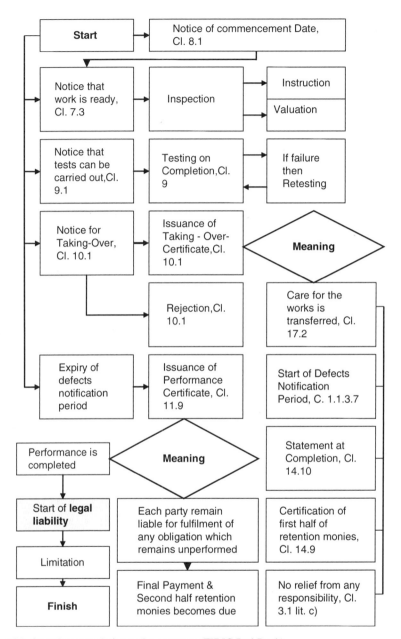

Fig. 15.1 Overview completion and acceptance (FIDIC Red Book)

fund becomes payable (Sub-Clause 14.9), the liability to pay liquidated damages ceases, the Contractor's obligation to reinstate the works if these are damaged by any but the excepted risks ceases (Sub-Clause 17.2, 18) and the period within which the Statement at Completion must be submitted by the Contractor starts to run (Sub-Clause 14.10).

However Taking Over according to FIDIC Conditions must not be confused with "reception" or "acceptance" of the Works according to French or German legislation. According to German and French law only acceptance of the Works by the employer discharges the contractor from his obligation to carry out the Works. Thus in principle the contractor remains liable to perform the Works and he is not released from care for the Works until the employer declares acceptance of the Works. According to German law acceptance is a declaration by the employer to the contractor that the latter has substantially completed the agreed Works in compliance with the contract.[1] This declaration covers both the Works themselves and compliance with time for completion. If the Employer does not make any reservations as to apparent defects or non compliance with time for completion any claims for liquidated or delay damages according to Sub-Clause 8.7 FIDIC Conditions and any claims based on apparent defective works will be foreclosed. One main effect of acceptance of the Works is that the post contractual legal liability period starts to run. As under German law specific performance is a legal remedy usually no additional defects notification period is necessary. The Employer is allowed to claim for the remedying of any defects which occur after acceptance of the works. This is the reason why it is not uncommon for civil law lawyers to misunderstand the nature of the defects notification period which is ruled in Clause 11 FIDIC Conditions. They often assume that the Defects Notification Period replaces the legal defects liability according to their own law, which is obviously wrong. The defects notification period is an additional period of time during which the duty to perform the Contract continues to exist. This can clearly be seen in Sub-Clauses 11.1 and 11.2. According to these Sub-Clauses the Contractor is still under the obligation to carry out any work which becomes instructed by the Employer, to the extent that a defect occurs which is not attributable to the Contractor.

However, according to FIDIC Conditions, except if the works fail to pass the tests the Engineer shall issue the Taking Over Certificate on request of the Contractor, when the Works have been completed in accordance with the contract. Once the Taking Over certificate has been issued responsibility for care of the works passes to the Employer (Sub-Clause 17.2).

Parts of the Works may be taken over subject to Sub-Clause 10.2.

15.3 Performance

Only the issue of the Performance Certificate shall be deemed to constitute *acceptance of the works*. By consequence and with regard to Sub-Clause 11.10 any legal defects liability will only start after the issue of the Performance Certificate. This

---

[1] BGH [1970] NJW 421.

will be the case after expiration of the so-called Defects Notification Period, during which the Contractor is obliged to remedy any defect, whether attributable to him or not. This complementary obligation is due to the fact that under common law specific performance is the exception rather than the rule. Thus only after having remedied any defects during the defects notification period acceptance of the works will happen and the Contractor will be discharged from the obligation to complete the Works. The Performance Certificate may be withheld until all defects which have been notified to the Contractor according to Clause 11 have been made good. Care has to be taken under civil law to make a reservation as to all defects which occurred after the expiration of the Defects Notification Period in order to save all legal remedies as to such defects.

15.4   Payments

15.4.1   Introduction

Depending on the contract form used the Contract Price as referred to in Sub-Clause 14.1 will be paid as a lump sum in instalments or as a price based on measurements paid according to the work progress in interim payments.

The Red Book is a so called measurement contract, which requires a measurement procedure, which is explained below. Beware that the Engineer is in charge of taking and preparing measurements. The procedure to follow is:

- The Engineer decides whenever appropriate that he requires a part of the Works to be measured.
- The Contractor attends and assists the Engineer.
- If the Contractor fails to attend, the measurements are deemed to be accurate and to be accepted by the Contractor.

The Yellow Book and the Silver Book are so called lump sum contracts. However, in principle both forms allow for price adjustments.

Under the Red Book and the Yellow Book all payments shall be certified by the Engineer. Only where there is no Engineer (or Employer's Representative as under the FIDIC DBO form) no certificates will be issued. The procedure according to which payments are certified is ruled in clause 14 (Figs. 15.2–15.7). Payments shall be certified in Interim Payment Certificates and a Final Payment Certificate.

As a rule according to all FIDIC forms of Contract the Employer shall pay to the Contractor the whole Contract Price as referred to in Sub-Clause 14.1. However, under some circumstances the Contract may become terminated before the Taking Over Certificate has been issued. When the Contract becomes terminated, in principle the Contractor shall be entitled to payment for all work he already carried out in accordance with the Contract. In addition he shall be entitled to recover loss and cost, if the reason for termination is not attributable to him.

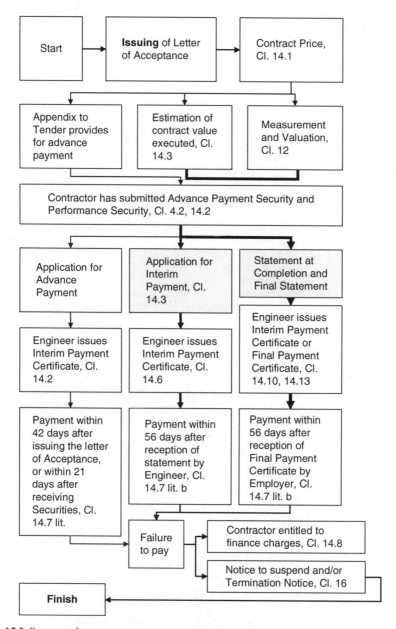

Fig. 15.2 Payments I

However only after a notice of termination under Sub-Clause 16.2 [Termination by Contractor] the Contractor is entitled to the amount of any loss of profit or other loss or damage sustained by the Contractor as a result of this termination.

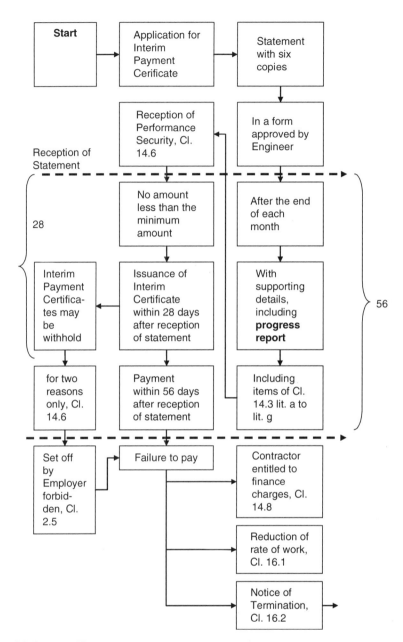

Fig. 15.3 Payments II

By contrast in the event of termination by convenience (Sub-Clause 15.5) and termination as a result of Force Majeure (Sub-Clause 19.6) the Contractor is only entitled to payment for those parts of the works which, due to termination will no

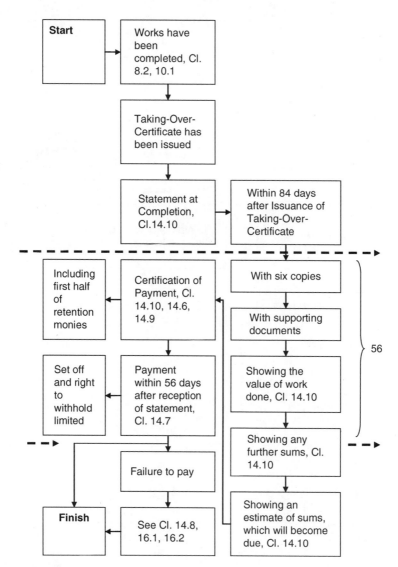

Fig. 15.4 Payments III

longer be carried out, to the extent that he incurred cost or liability which in the circumstances was reasonably incurred by him in the expectation of completing the Works. Thus in both these cases the Contractor is not entitled to reasonable profit as this is the case under Sub-Clause 16.4. The reason for this is that FIDIC considers both termination by convenience and termination a result of Force Majeure not to constitute a breach of contract.

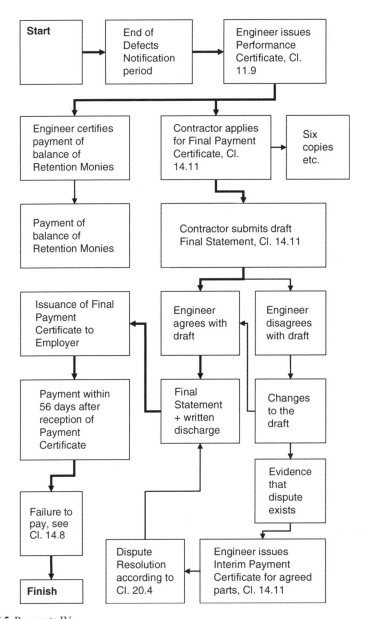

Fig. 15.5 Payments IV

15.4.2 *Measurement*

Where under the Red Book or the Green Book the Works must be measured for evaluation, it is quite useful to know in advance which method of measurement

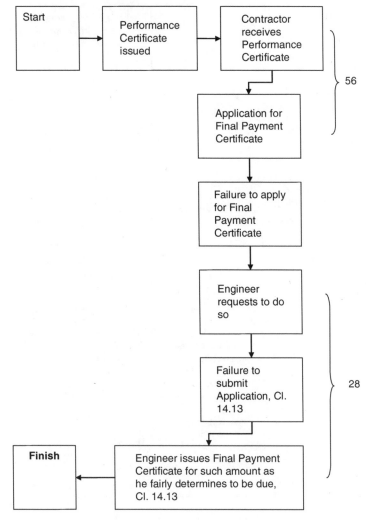

Fig. 15.6 Payments V

applies. Sub-Clause 12.2 does not refer to any standard method of measurement but measurement shall be in accordance with the Bill of Quantities or other applicable Schedules. However having more precise arrangements for measurement in place may avoid disputes. It is thus recommended to indicate either the method of measurement which has been used for the measurement of the quantities which are included in the Bills of Quantities or to indicate the method of measurement which will be used for measurement. This is a critical point, because measurement methods may heavily influence the Contract Price.

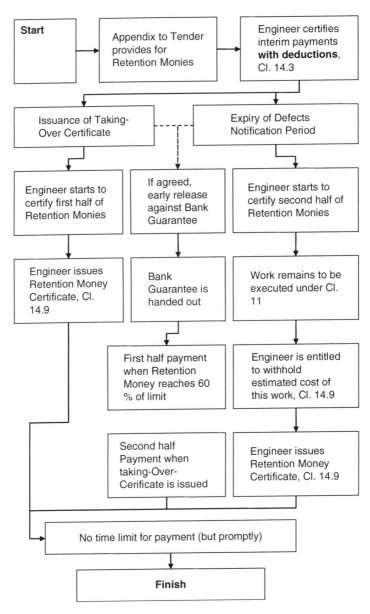

Fig. 15.7 Payments VI

Reference can be made to the Standard Method of Measurement of Building Works 7th Edition (SMM7) by the Royal Institution of Chartered Surveyors, which according to the 2003 RICS survey report is in use for example in the United Arab Emirates. It is often the case that domestic measurement methods also exist. A familiarity which such measurement methods is strongly recommended.

15.4.3   Valuation

Valuation procedures are not only necessary for measurement contracts such as the FIDIC Red Book, albeit them being critical in that setting because all amounts due under such a Red Book contract must be evaluated. Valuation procedures are however also needed in the event of contract termination before completion of the Works has been achieved.

According to Sub-Clause 12.3 Red Book the Engineer shall proceed in accordance with Sub-Clause 3.5 to agree or determine the Contract Price by evaluating each item of work. The procedure as such is self explanatory. It is therefore only referred to Sub-Clause 12.3.

Under the Red Book variations instructed by Engineer are valued at contract rates where applicable and reasonable or, failing that, rates agreed upon between Employer's Engineer and Contractor (Sub-Clause 12.3). In the event of disagreement, the Engineer fixes new rates. The Engineer may elect to have varied work performed on daywork basis (Sub-Clause 13.6).

All FIDIC Books contain a particular Sub-Clause for the evaluation of work in the event of termination subject to Sub-Clause 15.2. Valuation at Date of Termination has to be carried out in accordance with Sub-Clause 15.3. In the event that the Employer has given a notice of termination under Sub-Clause 15.2 the Engineer shall proceed in accordance with Sub-Clause 3.5 to agree or determine the value of the Works, etc., for work executed in accordance with the Contract.

Valuation in the event of termination due to grounds other than those ruled in Sub-Clause 15.2 is made by reference to Sub-Clause 19.6, if:

- The Contractor has terminated the Contract in accordance with Sub-Clause 16.2.
- The termination is based on Sub-Clause 10.6.
- The Employer has terminated the Contract by convenience subject to Sub-Clause 15.5.

Upon such termination, the Engineer shall determine the value of the work done.

15.4.4   Payment Procedures

All FIDIC Books set out very clearly how and when payments must be made. They provide a whole set of rules concerning the conditions and procedures under which payments shall be effectuated. Although the timetables for payment are self explanatory the procedures must be explained, in particular for the benefit of those who are not familiar with common law practice.

It is a common feature of construction contracts to provide for an independent third party to issue certificates indicating particular events and usually embodying administrative decisions. This kind of certificate is merely a manifestation of the parties' private agreement and its effect is no more than what the parties have agreed on (Uff 2005, p. 279). Thus the function of any certificate is usually to record events. The English position is probably well described as such:

If an amount has been certified in accordance with Sub-Clause 14.6 it becomes payable under the provisions of the Contract. In principle there is no effective defence against a certified amount. All counter claims of the Employer shall be determined and included as a deduction in the Contract Price and Payment Certificates, except those under Sub-Clauses 4.19 and 4.20.

According to FIDIC contracts all payments shall be certified, except those under a FIDIC Silver Book contract, where Sub-Clause 14.6 rules a different procedure. However, under the Red Book and the Yellow Book, the Engineer shall issue either an Interim Payment Certificate in accordance with Sub-Clause 14.6 or a Final Payment Certificate in accordance with Sub-Clause 14.11. Thus no payment will be made if no certificate has been issued. Conversely, no payments shall be withheld which have been certified (see Sub-Clause 2.5), except in relation to those payments which correspond to an amount which is due by virtue of Sub-Clauses 4.19 and 4.20. Payment Certificates shall not be withheld for reasons other than those stated in Sub-Clause 14.6.

The Engineer shall not certify a payment until the Employer has received and approved the Performance Security (Sub-Clause 14.6). Again, he is not bound to issue any Interim Payment Certificate in an amount which would be less than the minimum amount of Interim Payment Certificates stated in Appendix to Tender. Finally an Interim Payment Certificate shall not be withheld for any other reason than for the cost of rectification or replacement of any defective work or for work which the Contractor failed to carry out. What is meant by failure to perform an obligation is subject to interpretation by the Engineer. In fact, Sub-Clause 14.6 allows the Engineer to withhold an Interim Payment Certificate if the Contractor fails to perform an obligation. In this event the Engineer must evaluate the unperformed obligation and may refuse to certify the related amount.

The following is a breakdown of the payment procedure as outlined in Clause 14. The procedures apply to all forms of Certificates and Payments, including the Advance payment, Retention Monies, etc:

- The procedure starts with an application for Payment according to Sub-Clauses 14.3, 14.10, 14.11:

  - As the case may be the Contractor submits either a statement to the Engineer after the end of each month (or according to the payment Schedule), in a form approved by the Engineer, or he submits a draft final statement followed by an agreed final statement, in a form approved by the Engineer.
  - The statement shows in detail the amounts to which the Contractor considers himself to be entitled to, together with supporting documents.
  - The statement shall include all documents and items listed in Sub-Clause 14.3, 14.10 or 14.11 as the case may be.

- The Engineer shall then issue a Payment Certificate according to Sub-Clauses 14.6 or 14.13:

- The Engineer verifies whether all preconditions have been met, such as reception of the Performance security, Advance Payment Security, etc.
- As the case may be the Engineer verifies whether the amount to be certified is not less than the minimum amount stated in the Appendix to Tender.
- As the case may be the Engineer requests more information (Final Payment Certificate only).
- As the case may be the Engineer verifies whether the Contractor has submitted a written discharge in accordance with Sub-Clause 14.12.
- The Engineer makes an assessment in accordance with Sub-Clauses 14.6 or 14.13.
- The Engineer issues the Payment Certificate, either in the form of an Interim Payment Certificate or in the form of a Final Payment Certificate.

As the Engineer shall not withhold any Payment Certificates for any reasons other than those stated in Clause 14, he shall always certify the agreed parts of the Contract Price. If a dispute arises it shall be settled in accordance with Sub-Clauses 20.4, 20.5 or 20.6. Once the disputes have been settled, either a further interim statement or a final statement shall be submitted to the Engineer, as the case may be.

The period for assessment depends on the Certificate which is concerned. Interim Payment Certificates shall be issued within 28 days after receipt of a Statement with supporting documents. The last Interim Payment Certificate to be issued is the one following the Statement on Completion.

However, the procedure for a Final Payment Certificate is a little more complicated. The Engineer shall firstly reach an agreement with the Contractor. Once an agreement has been reached, the Contractor submits an agreed Final Statement. Within 28 days after having received the Final Statement and written discharge in accordance with Sub-Clause 14.12 the Engineer shall issue, to the Employer the Final Payment Certificate.

If the Contractor fails to apply for a Final Payment Certificate in accordance with Sub-Clauses 14.11 and 14.12, the Engineer shall request the Contractor to do so. If the Contractor then remains silent for more than 28 days, the Engineer shall issue the Final Payment Certificate as he fairly determines to be due. Sub-Clause 14.13 does not refer to Sub-Clause 3.5. Thus it is not necessary to consult each party in an endeavour to reach an agreement.

According to Sub-Clause 14.14 the Employer shall not be liable to the Contractor for any matter or thing under or in connection with the Contract or execution of the Works, except to the extent that the Contractor shall have included an amount expressly for it in his Statements. It is thus critical to carefully examine the actual situation before submitting the Statement at Completion or the Final Statement, in particular if disputes have arisen under or in connection with the Contract. Beware that the Contractor must then state all future cost of Dispute Adjudication and Arbitration in his Statements. However, whether Sub-Clause 14.14 applies in the event that the Contractor fails to submit an application for Final Payment and a written discharge is open to discussion. It is suggested that this not the case because

Sub-Clause 14.14 is a severe sanction against the Contractor for failure to comply with the procedures in Sub-Clauses 14.11 and 14.10, to the extent that the Contractor submits the Statements. If he fails to apply for a Final Payment Certificate there is already a particular sanction which does not expressly include the sanctions ruled in Sub-Clause 14.14. Thus the Engineer is strongly recommended to encourage the Contractor to comply with Sub-Clauses 14.11 and 14.12 before making a fair determination according to Sub-Clause 14.13 last sentence.

Payment after Termination is subject to Sub-Clause 15.4, Sub-Clause 16.4 and 19.6.

In Sub-Clause 15.4 no reference is made to Clause 14. Thus it appears that Sub-Clause 15.3 replaces Clause 14 in the event of a notice of termination by the Employer based on Sub-Clause 15.2. The Engineer will have to make a fair determination instead of a Payment Certificate. No written discharge in accordance with Sub-Clause 14.12 is required from the Contractor and Sub-Clause 14.14 will not apply. However, the Employer shall only pay the balance to the Contractor after recovering cost and losses as detailed in Sub-Clause 15.4. This means that the Employer may firstly:

(a) Proceed in accordance with Sub-Clause 2.5 [*Employer's Claims*]
(b) Withhold further payments to the Contractor until the costs of design, execution, completion and remedying of any defects, damages for delay in completion (if any), and all other costs incurred by the Employer, have been established
(c) Recover from the Contractor any losses and damages incurred by the Employer and any extra costs of completing the Works, after allowing for any sum due to the Contractor under Sub-Clause 15.3 [*Valuation at Date of Termination*]

How to proceed with regard to Retention Monies remains open or is subject to further agreement.

Upon termination in accordance with Sub-Clauses 19.6, 15.5 or 16.2 the Engineer shall issue a Payment Certificate which shall include:

(a) The amounts payable for any work carried out for which a price is stated in the Contract.
(b) The Cost of Plant and Materials ordered for the Works which have been delivered to the Contractor, or of which the Contractor is liable to accept delivery: these Plant and Materials shall become the property of (and be at the risk of) the Employer when paid for by the Employer, and the Contractor shall place the same at the Employer's disposal.
(c) Any other Cost or liability which in the circumstances was reasonably incurred by the Contractor in the expectation of completing the Works.
(d) The Cost of removal of Temporary Works and Contractor's Equipment from the Site and the return of these items to the Contractor's works in his country (or to any other destination at no greater cost).
(e) The Cost of repatriation of the Contractor's staff and labour employed wholly in connection with the Works at the date of termination.

15.4.5 Payment Delays

Payments shall be made on the basis of Payment Certificates. According to Sub-Clause 14.7 the Employer shall pay to the Contractor:

(a) The first instalment of the advance payment within 42 days after issuing the Letter of Acceptance or within 21 days after receiving the documents in accordance with Sub-Clause 4.2 [*Performance Security*] and Sub-Clause 14.2 [*Advance Payment*], whichever is later.

(b) The amount certified in each Interim Payment Certificate within 56 days after the Engineer has received the Statement and supporting documents; and (c) the amount certified in the Final Payment Certificate within 56 days after the Employer has received this Payment Certificate.

As may be seen from this Sub-Clause, payments must be made within strictly defined delays. For all Interim Payments the 56 days period starts after the Engineer receives the Contractor's Statement with supporting documents. As previously mentioned the Engineer shall issue an Interim Payment Certificate within 28 days after receiving the Contractor's Statement with supporting documents. As the expiry of the delay for interim payments does not depend on the issue of the Interim Payment Certificate the Employer bears the risk of late certification by the Engineer. If and when the Engineer is late, the Employer is not entitled to rely on the fact that all payments only become due as soon as a Payment Certificate has been issued. However as to the Final Payment the 56 days period starts when the Employer receives the Final Payment Certificate.

15.4.6 Late Payment

So what are the avenues to pursue when payment is delayed and there is no sign of it being effectuated? A Contractor in these circumstances is allowed to rely upon any rights to suspend the works or terminate the contract. Sub-Clauses 16.1 and 16.2 deal with these aspects. According to Sub-Clause 16.1 the Contractor may suspend work or reduce the rate of work unless he has received payment. A further remedy is ruled by Sub-Clause 16.2 according to which the Contractor is entitled to terminate the Contract in the event of sustainable non payment. Additionally the Contractor may claim for financial charges (Sub-Clause 14.8), Time extension (Sub-Clause 16.1) and finally cost plus reasonable profit (Sub-Clause 16.1). Neither of these options should be taken lightly as the consequences of exercising such "rights" wrongly can be particularly severe.

Depending on the merits of the case suspension of work and termination of contract can be interpreted as wrongful or become reinterpreted as an action which is different from that which is intended to be relied on. It will often be discussed whether a wrongful notice of termination can be understood as unconditioned refusal to continue the work, which may amount to saying "I will not perform the contract". In this case the other party to the contract may argue that it will treat the defaulting party as having put an end to the contract without prejudice to the right to sue for damages. In common law this situation is called repudiation.

In order to avoid such kind of discussion a party who intends to rely on the above mentioned remedies must ensure that all conditions for the exercise of the remedy are met, including all procedural requirements which are specified in the Contract.

15.4.7 Retention Monies

Sub-Clauses 14.3 and 14.9 of the General Conditions provide for the Engineer to deduct retention monies at the rate stated in the Appendix to Tender from interim payments; for one half of those retention monies to be released on taking-over; and for the balance to be promptly released following the expiry of the Defects Notification Period. The Parties may wish to add a clause by which the Contractor elects the option to provide a retention bond in lieu of the retention monies, as such:

> In the event that the Contractor elects the option to provide to the Employer a Retention Bond in lieu of the Retention, the Contractor shall procure and deliver to the Employer a Retention Bond for an amount equivalent to 5% of the actual Contract Price as certified by the Engineer, reducing to 2.5% of the actual Contract Price at Taking-Over ... and following receipt of the Retention Bond ...the Retention deducted by the Contractor from payments shall be paid to the Contractor.

A more sophisticated clause for release of retention may be found in the Guidance for the Preparation of Particular Conditions. A related model form for a Retention Money Guarantee is included in each FIDIC book.

15.5   Disputes

If there is a dispute as to the Engineer's "fair determination" forming the basis of the provisional certification, that dispute must be referred to a DAB. The DAB's decision, which is provisionally binding, if different from the provisional certification, takes effect as a revision of it. However the Contractor should always carefully check whether a dispute has arisen. An Employer can always argue that the Engineer may in any Interim Payment Certificate make corrections or modifications that should properly be made to any previous Payment Certificate (Sub-Clause 14.6).

References

Uff J (2005) Construction law, 9th ed. Sweet & Maxwell, London

Chapter 16
Defects Notification Period and (Post Contractual) Defects Liability

16.1 Introduction

The so-called Defects Notification Period as defined in Sub-Clause 1.1.3.7 is often both misunderstood and misinterpreted by civil law practitioners. The Defects Notification Period which is ruled in Clause 11 FIDIC Conditions covers a need which arises from the fact that at common law the only remedy for breach of contract is damages. Thus if a defect occurs either before or after the issue of the Taking-Over Certificate a common law judge is usually not empowered to grant specific performance. This has been considered to be inappropriate for construction projects where the performing contractor is usually most able and capable of remedying the defect. Thus common law construction contracts normally provide for an additional period of time during which the Contractor is obliged to remedy defects. The Defects Notification Period as ruled in Clause 11 of all of the FIDIC Books is thus an additional period of time during which the duty to perform the Contract continues to exist. This can clearly be seen in Sub-Clauses 11.1 and 11.2. According to these Sub-Clauses the Contractor is still under the obligation to carry out any work which becomes instructed by the Engineer or Employer, to the extent that a defect occurs which is or is not attributable to the Contractor. Instead civil law practitioners often assume that the Defects Notification Period replaces the legal defects liability according to their law, which is an incorrect assumption. The legal defects liability only starts after acceptance of the Works which will happen when the Engineer issues the Performance Certificate (Fig. 16.1).

16.2 Duration of the Defects Notification Period

The duration of the Defects Notification Period is stated in the Appendix to Tender or the Particular Conditions as the case may be. It is subject to extension according to Sub-Clause 11.3. It ends automatically after the expiry of the

A.-V. Jaeger and G.-S. Hök, *FIDIC-A Guide for Practitioners*,
DOI 10.1007/978-3-642-02100-8_16, © Springer-Verlag Berlin Heidelberg 2010

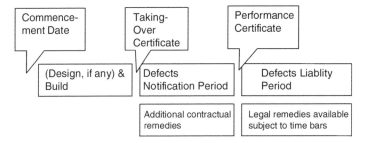

Fig 16.1 Defects notification period

fixed period of time, even though the Performance Certificate is not yet issued. It may therefore happen that defects occur after the expiry of the Defects Notification Period. In this event Sub-Clause 11.1 does not apply any more. The Contractor will then be in breach of contract subject to the applicable law. Care must be taken by the Engineer when issuing the Performance Certificate even when defects have occurred after the end of the Defects Notification Period due to the fact that issuing the Performance Certificate constitutes acceptance of the Works which may relieve the Contractor from his legal duties subject to the governing law.

16.3   Duty to Remedy and to Search

As has been mentioned above, the Contractor remains under a duty to remedy defects despite the fact that the Engineer has already issued the Taking-Over-Certificate. However, this duty is much larger than probably understood at first sight. In fact the Contractor shall remedy defects notwithstanding any causality on his part. Even though defective work is not attributable to him, he shall make it good. It follows from Sub-Clause 11.2 that the Contractor shall complete all outstanding work (work which is outstanding on the date stated in the Taking-Over Certificate) and execute all work required to remedy defects or damage as may be notified by (or on behalf of) the Employer on or before the expiry date of the Defects Notification Period for the Works or Section. Sub-Clause 11.2 makes it clear that the duty to remedy notified defects even covers defective work which is not attributable to the Contractor, because if and when the defect is attributable to any cause other than stipulated in Sub-Clause 11.2 lit. a to c, Sub-Clause 13.3 shall apply.

However there is a further issue. If and to the extent that such work is attributable to any other cause, the Contractor shall be notified promptly by the Employer, and Sub-Clause 13.3 shall apply. But what happens if the Employer refrains from giving a prompt notice according to Sub-Clause 11.2 last paragraph? It could be argued from the wording that Sub-Clause 13.3 will then not apply. It is however suggested that Sub-Clause 11.2 should be read in such a way that Sub-Clause 13.3 applies even though the Employer refuses to give notice, because it does not clearly follow from the wording that the application of Sub-Clause 13.3 shall depend on prior notice and it does not make any sense to expect the Contractor to remedy a defect without compensation if it is not attributable to him.

According to Sub-Clause 11.8 the Contractor is also under a duty to search for the cause of any defect. After the Employer has given notice of a defect to the Contractor, the Engineer may require the Contractor to search for its cause, doing so under the direction of the Engineer. Thus the Engineer may instruct the Contractor to investigate the problem. The cost of such search plus reasonable profit shall be agreed or determined by the Engineer in accordance with Sub-Clause 3.5 if the defect is not attributable to the Contractor. However if the Contractor must remedy the defect at his cost, the additional cost incurred as a result of instructions according to Sub-Clause 11.8 will be balanced in favour of the Contractor.

Sub-Clause 11.2 and 11.8 are not clearly linked to each other. Thus the Contractor is not bound to carry out a search without being required by the Engineer to do so, but he is nevertheless obliged to make good the defect. However he shall always be paid for any search if the cause of the defect is not attributable to him.

16.4 Meaning of the Duty to Remedy

The signification of the duty to remedy defects prior to the issue of the Taking-Over Certificate and also prior to the issue of the Performance Certificate has been discussed in detail by English courts. The authorities have made it plain that, at most, the denial of a right to make good defects affects the measure of the loss and nothing else.[1] However reference must also be made to the words of Mr Recorder Reese QC in Oval (717) Ltd v. Aegon Insurance Co (UK) Ltd[2] when he stated:

> An employer such as the plaintiff expects that the contractor will proceed in a regular and diligent fashion with the performance of its obligations, but it does not expect initial perfection in on-site performance by all operatives engaged in the works at all times (see generally the well-known observations of Lord Diplock in P and M Kaye Ltd v. Hosier and Dickinson Ltd[3] with which I find myself in total agreement and respectfully follow) ... It follows that, in my view, such temporary disconformities would not constitute either non-performance or non-observance of the terms of the construction contract.

---

[1]Tombs v. Wilson Connolly Ltd [2004] EWHC 2809 (TCC) (09 November 2004) relying on Pearce & High Ltd v. Baxter [1999] BLR 101 and the earlier, careful Judgment of His Honour Judge Stannard in William Tomkinson v. Parochial Church Council of St. Michael [1990] CLJ 319.

[2][1997] 54 Con LR 74.

[3][1972] 1 WLR 146.

Accordingly it has been held that if an item has been left incomplete when a contract comes prematurely to an end, the question is whether it is something which the contractor (or the architect) might fairly have regarded as work in progress, or whether it is something which should properly have been treated as complete.[4]

It is also worth referring to the words of Lord Justice Diplock in P and M Kaye v. Hosier:[5]

> At common law a party to a contract is entitled to recover from the other party consequential damage of this kind resulting from that other party's breach of the contract, unless by the terms of the contract itself he has agreed that such damage shall not be recoverable. In the absence of express words in the contract a court should hesitate to hold that a party had surrendered any of his common law rights to damages for its breach, though it is not impossible for this to be a *necessary* implication from other provisions of the contract.
>
> I can read no such *necessary* implication into condition 15 or any other condition of the R.I.B.A. contract. Condition 15 imposes upon the contractor a liability to mitigate the damage caused by his breach by making good the defects of construction at his own expense. It confers upon him a corresponding right to do so. It is a necessary implication from this that the employer cannot, as he otherwise could, recover as damages from the contractor the difference between the value of the works if they had been constructed in conformity with the contractor and their value in their defective condition, without first giving to the contractor the opportunity of making good the defects. The obverse of this coin is that the contractor is under an obligation to remedy the defects in accordance with the architect's instructions. If he does not do so, the employer can recover as damages the cost of remedying the defects, even though this cost is greater than the diminution in value of the works as a result of the unremedied defects.

However *Aegon* and *P and M Kaye* seem to be in contradiction with *Pearce and High Ltd v. Baxter.*[6] In *Pearce* the contractor's obligation was "with due diligence and in a good and workmanlike manner [to] carry out and complete the works in accordance with the Contract Documents using materials and workmanship of the quality and standards therein specified" (clause 1.1). When the Architect issues his certificate of practical completion (clause 2.4), the contractor leaves the site. He has, apart from the case of special arrangements, no more work to do. Clause 2.5 then provides for "defects ... or other faults" which appear during the defects liability period which follows. The only express provisions that these "shall be made good by the Contractor entirely at his own cost unless the Architect shall otherwise instruct". Lord Justice Evans[7] agreed that this obligation cannot be enforced against the contractor unless he is first given notice of the defect, whether by the employers or by the Architect on their behalf. He continued stating:

> The giving of notice can therefore be regarded as a condition precedent to the employer's right to require compliance with the clause, though different considerations might arise if the contractor became aware of the defects from some other source. It seems to me that

---

[4] McGlinn v. Waltham Contractors Ltd [2007] EWHC 149 (TCC) (21 February 2007) relying on Oval v. Aegon and M Kaye Ltd v. Hosier as cited before.

[5] [1972] 1 WLR 146.

[6] Pearce & High Ltd v. Baxter & Anor [1999] EWCA Civ 789 (15 February 1999).

[7] Pearce & High Ltd v. Baxter & Anor [1999] EWCA Civ 789 (15 February 1999).

"defects [etc.] which appear" during the period has to be read objectively, as a description of those defects to which the clause applies. The defect must become apparent, meaning become patent rather than remain latent, during the notice period, regardless of whether any particular person has actual knowledge of it.

Moreover Lord Justice Evans agreed that clause 2.5 can be regarded as giving the contractor a right to make good the defects at his own expense, and a licence to enter the property for that purpose. However he then said according to common law breach gives the employer, subject to the contract terms, a right to recover damages, but it would have no right to require the contractor to rectify the defect, apart from the theoretical and speculative possibility that in certain circumstances the Court might order specific performance of the contractor's obligation which had been broken. Hence Lord Justice Evans argued that in the given case Clause 2.5 gives the employer an express right to require the contractor to return, as well as to the contractor himself the right to return and repair the defect himself, if he is willing to do so. But he could not find any words of exclusion, yet the effect of the clause, if the judgment is correct, was that the employer's right to damages in respect of the cost of repairs is lost for all time. This was something with which he could not agree without express words or by a clear and strong implication from the express words used.

Lord Justice Evans finally relied on H.H. Judge Stannard in William Tomkinson v. St Michael's P.C.C.,[8] who held as follows:

Where [the defects] are not remedied by the contractor within the construction period, there is nothing in the wording of clause 2.5 to suggest that it is intended to exclude the employer's ordinary right to damages for breach of contract, including the right to recover the cost of remedying defective workmanship. It requires very clear words to debar a building owner from exercising his ordinary rights of suing if the work done is not in accordance with the contract – *per* Edmund Davies L.J. in *Billyack v. Leyland Construction Company Ltd.*[9] In construing such a contract, one starts with the presumption that neither party intends to abandon any remedies for its breach arising by operation of law, and clear express words must be used in order to rebut this presumption – *per* Lord Diplock in *Gilbert-Ash (Northern) Ltd v. Modern Engineering (Bristol) Ltd.*[10] In my judgment clause 2.5 is not such a provision exempting the contractor from liability, except in so far as it is part of an overall contractual scheme which, in the specific situation postulated by Lord Diplock, leads to the construction that nominal damages are irrecoverable. Otherwise the true function of clause 2.5 is in my judgment firstly to confer a remedy for defective works on the employer, i.e. the right to require the contractor to make them good. Such a provision is generally to be regarded as providing an additional remedy for the employer, and not as releasing the contractor from his ordinary liability to pay damages for defective works : *Hancock v. B.W. Brazier (Anerley) Ltd.*[11] Secondly, clause 2.5 confers on the contractor a

---

[8] [1990] CLJ 319.

[9] [1968] 1 All ER 783 at p. 787 E-F.

[10] [1974] AC 689 at p. 717H.

[11] [1966] 2 All ER 901 per Lord Denning M.R. at p.904F-I Adams v. Richardson and Starling Ltd (1969) 2 All ER 1221.

licence to return to the site after practical completion for the purpose of remedying defects :
H.W. Nevill (Sunblest) Ltd v. William Press and Son Ltd.[12] Thirdly, clause 2.5 is concerned
with the mitigation of loss, in that it confers on the contractor a right to reduce the cost of
remedial works by undertaking them himself. Effect is given to this last aspect of the clause
if the damages recoverable by the employer for his outlay in correcting defects in the works
are limited to such sum as represents the cost which the contractor would have I incurred if
he had been called on to remedy the defects. (p. 326)

Lord Justice Evans then turned to the speech of Lord Diplock Kaye v. Hosier
and held:

In my judgment, Lord Diplock was concerned with the measure of damages which the
employer is entitled to recover, rather than with the right to recover damages in respect of
the contractor's original breach. The latter remains as regards consequential damages, and
so it is not altogether excluded. As regards damages for loss directly caused, different
measures are possible, including diminution in value of the property by reason of the defect,
or the cost of repairs by a third party, and on the construction of clause 2.5 which I favour,
the lower amount which represents the cost of repairs to the contractor if he had remedied
the defects himself. Lord Diplock, in my respectful judgment, recognised that the measure
of damages may be affected by the clause, but he nowhere stated that the right to recover
direct damages was altogether excluded. Had he done so, it would have been inconsistent
with his express reminder that only an express term or a necessary implication from the
contractual provisions could be effective to do so

It must remain open to discussion by common law lawyers whether Lord Justice
Diplock's speech in Kaye v. Hosier has more authority than the one of Lord Justice
Evans. But the discussion clearly brings to light a legal issue as to the interpretation
of Sub-Clauses 7.5, 7.6 and 11.1.

It is suggested that under FIDIC forms of contract the fact that the Contractor
shall make good all manner of defects irrespective of the question whether the
relevant defect is attributable to him or not, must be understood in the sense that all
of the Works are still under progress until the Performance Certificate is issued.
Again, under civil law the remedies resulting from Sub-Clauses 7.5, 7.6, 11.1 and
11.4 will be understood having the nature of exclusive remedies without prejudice
to those which arise from the proper law of the contract after the issue of the
Performance Certificate. Although for example under German law the legal remedies in Sections 633 et seq. Civil Code in principle apply also to defects occurring
before acceptance of the works by the Employer according to Section 640 Civil
Code (Boldt 2004, note 241), nothing prevents the parties from replacing this
regime by another prior to acceptance of the works.

The issue of the Performance Certificate does not terminate the Contractor's
obligation for damages arising out of defective work claims.[13] In interpreting a
contract the starting point is the presumption that neither party intended to abandon
any remedies for breach of contract arising by operation of law. Clear express words

---

[12] (1981) 20 BLR 78 at p. 87.

[13] Alucraft Pty Ltd v. Grocon Ltd (no. 2) [1996] 2 VR 386.

must be used in order to rebut this presumption.[14] Thus the issue of the Performance Certificate is no conclusive evidence that the Contractor has completed the Works and made good all defects therein in all respects in accordance with his obligations under the contract unless in the clearest words. US courts have held that it seems more reasonable to interpret the provision requiring correction of defects appearing within a year as constituting a specific contractual liability that would be covered by a guarantee bond which would cease to be in effect long before the end of the period established by the statute of limitations. According to them such kind of clause is an added guarantee, inserted in the contract to extend rather than limit the contractor's liability for faulty construction.[15] Thus the legal defects liability starts running when the Performance Certificate has been issued. This will be in line with the presumed German position, in particular because of the clear FIDIC statement in the Contracts Guide (FIDIC 2001, p. 203) according to which FIDIC did not intend to interfere with legal remedies and at least because of the clear wording in Sub-Clause 11.9 according to which only the issue of the Performance Certificate "shall be deemed to constitute acceptance of the Works".

The amount, up to which damages can be claimed depend upon the test which has been applied in the House of Lords' decision in *Ruxley Electronics and Construction Ltd v. Forsyth*.[16] Following Ruxley, under common law the following applies:

1. The question of whether you will be allowed the cost of the remedial works claimed should be answered according to whether remedial cost would be so wholly disproportionate to its benefit as to make it unreasonable.
2. If it is so disproportionate, you may be entitled to recover on the basis of diminution of value, if there has been any.
3. Damages are not limited to only diminution of value or reinstatement. There may be a middle figure to reflect loss of amenity or inconvenience through the claimant not having received what he wanted and what he contracted for.

The extent, to which other jurisdictions grant damages in the event of defective work, must be ascertained on a case by case basis. According to German law (Sect. 635 Civil Code) the Employer is entitled to require the remedy of defects. If appropriate this may include the re-construction of the defective work. The Contractor must bear the necessary expenditure for cure, including without limitation the costs of carriage, transport, labour and material. However, without prejudice to Section 275(2) and (3) Civil Code, the Contractor may refuse cure if it is only possible at disproportionate cost. In the event that the Contractor fails to

---

[14] Gilbert-Ash (Northern) Ltd v. Modern Engineering (Bristol) Ltd [1974] AC 689 at 717 per Lord Diplock.

[15] Burton-Dixie Corporation v. Timothy McCarthy Construction Company 436 F.2d 405 (5th Cir. 1971).

[16] [1996] AC 344.

comply with Section 645 Civil Code the Employer may carry out the works himself and claim reimbursement for the necessary expenditure.

In any case remedies for defective work are usually time barred subject to the proper law of the contract. Limitation periods vary from country to country and must be ascertained on case by case basis. Whether legal limitation periods can be prolonged or shortened is a matter of law.

In Germany the limitation period for remedies concerning defective work is 2 years.[17] If a building or similar construction is concerned the limitation period is 5 years.[18] Under Polish law the limitation period is in principle 2 years.[19] French law provides for a more sophisticated system.[20] The limitation period of the warranty of perfect performance is 1 year. Some parts of the works may fall under a two year's warranty. Finally the so-called decennial liability lasts for ten years. In some countries the decennial liability is even longer than that, for example in Romania, where the decennial liability covers the whole life cycle of the building.

16.5   Removal of Defective Work

According to Sub-Clause 11.5 defective work can be removed from the Site, if it cannot be remedied expeditiously on the Site. Prior consent of the Employer is however required. But it is in the Contractor's best interests to carry out the work on the Site because otherwise the Employer may ask the Contractor to increase the Performance Security by the full replacement cost of the items to be removed.

16.6   Failure to Remedy defects

If the Contractor fails to remedy any occurring defects the Employer shall first fix a date, on or by which the defect or damage is to be remedied. The Employer shall give reasonable notice of this date. If the Contractor still fails to remedy the defect by this notified date, the Employer has the choice of three options. He may carry out the work himself or by others at the cost of the Contractor, he may require the Engineer to agree or determine a reasonable reduction in the Contract Price or alternatively he may terminate the Contract altogether; the latter only if the defect or damage deprives the Employer of substantially the whole benefit of the Works or any major part of the Works. Unlike Mr. Totterdill (2006, p. 205) we would not

---

[17] Section 634a German Civil Code.

[18] Ibid.

[19] Art. 646 Polish Civil Code.

[20] Art. 2270, 1792 et seq. French Civil Code.

expect the Employer to discuss his preference with the Contractor before taking any action. Sub-Clause 11.4 clearly states what has to be done before taking action. There is no further need to discuss the issue with the Contractor who is already in breach of contract not only because he failed to remedy the defect but also because he did not comply with the date which was fixed by reasonable notice.

16.7 Extension of the Defects Notification Period

Pursuant to Sub-Clause 11.3 the Employer is entitled to an extension of the Defects Notification Period. The entitlement shall be enforced subject to the procedure in Sub-Clause 2.5. Thus the Employer shall give notice to the Contractor of his claim for extension of the Defects Notification Period. The Defects Notification Period shall not be extended by more than 2 years. Employers who wish to include a longer Defects Notification Period, are advised to alter Sub-Clause 11.3. Otherwise the Defects Notification Period will expire after two years calculated from the date which is stated in the Taking-Over Certificate. This may prove wise if major items of work are susceptible to defects.

16.8 Legal Liability

FIDIC Books do not at all regulate post contract liability issues. By consequence after issuing the Performance Certificate all questions as to defects liability are exclusively governed by the applicable contract law (compare Sub-Clause 1.4), the proper law of the contract. Any provisions of the governing law concerning defect liability must therefore be respected, including limitation rules.

16.8.1 Normal Liability

In all countries breach of contract causes liability. However, whether there is breach of contract depends on the proper law of the contract. Also the extent to which defective work gives rise to a claim for damages varies from country to country. Under Common law damages are in most circumstances the only remedy for breach of contract. Civil law is much more sophisticated, because according to civil law specific performance is a common relief.

Usually there is breach of contract if the performed work is not in accordance with the Contract. Sometimes work which is in accordance with the Contract appears to be useless or use of it is less effective or more limited than expected or foreseeable. This may the result of different reasons. Design made by or on behalf of the Employer may be defective or inappropriate. Materials used may prove to be inappropriate, even if they have been sold for the required purposes, etc. Contractors are usually expected to have particular experiences and skills. Consequently they owe a duty of care, which may imply a duty to warn. Thus contractors have been held liable for failure to warn of design defects.

According to Sub-Clause 1.8 the Parties shall give prompt notice to each other if they become aware of an error or defect of a technical nature in a document which was prepared for use executing the Works. Sub-Clauses 1.9 and 5.1 of the Yellow Book impose on the Contractor a duty to disclose errors in the Employer's Requirements. Thus FIDIC puts the Contractor under an express duty to warn.

16.8.2   Decennial Liability

In some countries, inspired by French legislation, the so-called post contract liability comprises a very strict form of liability for structural works and structural design. French law provides a strict liability for structural elements over a period of 10 years. Contractors, architects and engineers must provide insurance cover for the whole period. The legal wording of the French decennial liability reads as follows:

> Art. 1792 Civil Code
> Any builder of a work is liable as of right, towards the building owner or purchaser, for damages, even resulting from a defect of the ground, which imperil the strength of the building or which, affecting it in one of its constituent parts or one of its elements of equipment, render it unsuitable for its purposes.
> Such liability does not take place where the builder proves that the damages were occasioned by an extraneous event.

Additionally Art. 1792-4-1 French Civil Code provides:

> Any natural or juridical person who may be liable under Articles 1792 to 1792-4 of this Code is discharged from the liabilities and warranties by which they are weighed down in application of Articles 1792 to 1792-2, after ten years from the approval of the works or, in application of Article 1792-3, on the expiry of the period referred to in this Article.

All countries which have adopted French legislation such as Belgium and Luxemburg have similar statutory regulations. However structural sustainability is a very important requirement not only in France, Belgium and Luxemburg. Therefore many other countries have adopted French decennial liability regulations, such as Algeria (art. 554 Civil Code), Angola, Cameroun (art. 1792 Civil Code, French jurisdiction), Chile (art. 2003-3 Codigo Civil), Egypt, Malta, Morocco, Portugal, Romania (art. 1483 Civil Code), Spain, Tunisia, United Arab Emirates (art. 880 Civil Code), among others. It seems that all these regulations belong to public policy and are compulsory.

It is important to be aware of decennial liability legislation for two main reasons. Firstly compulsory insurance may be required. The premiums for decennial liability insurance are usually very high. In addition to these premiums, costs for the so-called technical control by an authorised consultant company have to be considered. Secondly decennial liability may last very long, sometimes during the whole life cycle of the construction, and it is nearly impossible to escape from it. Especially in those countries where earthquakes are frequent decennial liability comprises a considerable risk for the insurer and the contractor.

It is finally worthwhile noting that decennial liability includes liability resulting from a defect of the ground. Thus Contractors coming from civil law countries where so-called ground risks would usually be borne by the Employer (as is the case in Germany and Austria, but also in Turkey) must take care to design and complete the Works in strict compliance with not only contractual requirements but also in strict compliance with the legal requirements of the decennial liability.

References

Boldt A (2004) Der neue Bauvertrag, 2nd edn. Carl Heyemanns, Köln
FIDIC (2001) FIDIC contracts guide. Geneva
Totterdill BW (2006) FIDIC user's guide, 2nd edn. Thomas Telford, London

Chapter 17
Termination

17.1 Introduction

Construction contracts may be brought to an end in a number of ways. The most common way by which a contract is ended is by the performance by the parties of their respective obligations under that contract. The promises are performed and the contractual obligations are satisfied. However there are circumstances in which a contract must be brought to an end before the respective obligations are discharged. Various grounds to give a termination notice may exist, such as:

- Funds are unavailable for continued performance, for example as a result of a Variation or a serious increase in quantity.
- Financial arrangements have not been made or become changed.
- Calculation error becomes obvious.
- Unforeseen risk eventuates, for example adverse climatic conditions or unexpected sub-soil conditions.
- Works are no longer needed.
- Changes in legislation or legal requirements.
- Quantity of the Works have been reduced or have been increased.
- Change in requirements beyond contractor's capability or expertise.
- Radical increase in the scope of Works.
- Radical increase of cost.
- Impossibility or impracticability of performance.
- Substantial Breach of Contract, such as:

  - Refusal to perform.
  - Prohibited activity is required.
  - Poor performance.
  - Delayed performance.
  - Failure to comply with material contract term/condition.
  - Abandonment of work.

A.-V. Jaeger and G.-S. Hök, *FIDIC-A Guide for Practitioners*,
DOI 10.1007/978-3-642-02100-8_17, © Springer-Verlag Berlin Heidelberg 2010

The need for the right to terminate a contract is generally recognised by FIDIC. Under a FIDIC form of contract the provisions for the Employer to determine or terminate the Contract are set out in Clause 15. Termination by the Contractor is covered by Clause 16. Also the FIDIC forms of contract contain provisions at Clause 19 for termination by the Employer or the Contractor in the event that certain specified circumstances, which are outside the control of the parties, have lead to the suspension of progress of the Works for the relevant period of time stated in the Contract. However, whether under the applicable law all types of provision found in Clauses 15, 16 and 19 would generally be recognised and upheld must be verified on a case by case basis, because in principle this right is an exception from the rule of pacta sunt servanda. Clauses 15 and 16 deal with both, the right to terminate the Contract for failure of the other party to comply with the Contract and the right to terminate for other reasons including the right to terminate the Contract for convenience.

The other question is how much will a termination cost. The answer depends on the termination clauses of the contract and the governing law. Under a FIDIC form of contract, there are clauses stating the grounds and procedures for termination. In addition the parties have to rely on general contract law. Termination is obviously one of the most serious provisions in a construction contract. Before advising about a termination, an advisor must be familiar with the entire contract, scrutinise particularly any clauses relating to termination, examine the clauses relating to any dispute underlying the reasons for termination, be familiar with the facts which justify a termination and evaluate how the dispute between the employer and contractor will be adjudicated.

Whether a termination is justified or not depends on the underlying facts. However, quite often the law must be determined. Thus it depends on the interpretation of the contract and the law whether there will be a valid termination notice or not. It may happen that either the contractor or the employer have good reason to terminate the contract, but the contract may not provide the possibility of terminating the contract for this particular reason. If this is the case the party concerned will try to find an alternative. This may prove difficult and dangerous. In any case a careful analysis of the situation will then be necessary. Prior to any termination the cost pursuant to the termination should be evaluated. Cost can be incurred on various levels and for various reasons, such as:

- Cost for plant and material ordered for the Works, for which the contractor is liable to accept delivery
- Inventory costs
- Repatriation cost
- Demobilization cost
- Cost for removal of temporary works
- Subcontractor settlement costs
- Settlement proposal preparation costs
- Cost or liability which was incurred in the expectation of the completing of the Works

Usually under a termination for default, the employer is not liable for the contractor's costs on undelivered work and is entitled to the repayment of advance and progress payments, if any, applicable to undelivered work. It depends on the contract whether the employer may elect to require the contractor to transfer title and deliver to the employer completed supplies and manufacturing materials, as directed by the Engineer. It is common practice that the employer shall pay the contractor the contract price for any completed works.

17.2   Termination for Convenience

The right to terminate a contract for convenience is not a common feature in all jurisdictions. Under common law both parties will be bound by the Contract until discharge, which will mean substantial performance of all contractual obligations. According to the common law this kind of right is therefore an exceptional right, which must be embodied in the Contract. No further consequences other than those ruled by the Contract will result from making use of the right. By contrast civil law jurisdictions commonly recognise a general right for termination for convenience. However if the parties make use of this right they can only do so under the constraints imposed by the law. This means that usually, if the Employer gives notice of his intention to terminate the Contract for convenience, the Contractor shall be entitled to the payment of the Contract Price with deduction of the saved expenditure. This is the case for example according to German law (see Sect. 649 Civil Code). Thus employers originating from common law countries may be faced with claims which do not result directly from the Contract but occur in connection with the Contract. Common law employers are therefore strongly recommended to carefully scrutinise the applicable law to discover whether they will find therein mandatory rules which apply in the event of termination by convenience.

However, Sub-Clause 15.5 entitles the Employer to terminate the contract for convenience, but he shall not terminate the Contract in order to execute or operate the Works (to the extent specified in the Contract).

17.3   Termination with Good Cause

Both Parties may terminate the Contract, if their counterpart fails to comply with the Contract. The reasons for termination are clearly indicated in Sub-Clauses 15.2 and 16.2. Sub-Clause 15.2 lists all the reasons which would entitle the Employer to terminate the Contract whilst Sub-Clause 16.2 lists all the reasons which would entitle the Contractor to do so.

The Contractor is entitled to terminate the Contract if:

- He does not receive reasonable evidence in accordance with Sub-Clause 2.4 within 42 days after giving notice under Sub-Clause 16.1.

- The Engineer fails, within 56 days after receiving a Statement ... to issue the relevant Payment Certificate.
- He does not receive the amount due under an Interim Payment Certificate.
- The Employer substantially fails to perform his obligations.
- The Employer fails to comply with Sub-Clause 1.6 or Sub-Clause 1.7.
- A prolonged suspension affects the Works.
- The Employer becomes bankrupt or insolvent or similar.

The Employer is entitled to terminate the Contract if:

- The Contractor fails to submit a Performance Security to comply with a notice to correct under Sub-Clause 15.1.
- The Contractor abandons the Works or otherwise plainly demonstrates the intention not to continue performance of his obligations under the Contract.
- The Contractor without reasonable excuse fails to proceed with the Works in accordance with Clause 8, or to comply with a notice issued under Sub-Clause 7.5 or Sub-Clause 7.6, within 28 days after receiving it.
- The Contractor subcontracts the whole of the Works or assigns the Contract without the required agreement.
- The Contractor becomes bankrupt or insolvent, or similar.
- The Contractor gives or offers to give (directly or indirectly) to any person any bribe, gift, gratuity, commission or other thing of value, as an inducement or reward.

The question may arise of whether any misconduct by the Engineer would fall under Sub-Clause 16.2 lit. d. The Engineer is not a party to the Contract and only if the Employer fails to perform his obligations under the Contract does the entitlement to terminate arise. Thus the question arises whether any misconduct of the Engineer constitutes breach of contract by the Employer. As is clearly stated in Sub-Clause 3.1 lit. a the Engineer is deemed to act for the Employer. In addition he will be appointed and paid by the Employer. Hence the Employer bears the responsibility of supervising the Engineer and to making him working in accordance to the Contract. Accordingly he must be deemed to fail to perform his obligations under the Contract if he does not ensure that the Engineer complies with its duties. As to its role as a payment certifier this is expressly ruled in Sub-Clause 16.2 lit. b. Thus if the Engineer fails to issue a Payment Certificate within 56 days after having received a Statement and supporting documents, the entitlement to terminate is given.

17.4   Notice

It is a common feature of good faith that any termination notice based on failure to comply with the Contract should be subject to a prior notice of such intention in case of continuous breach of contract. Such a notice may be all that is needed to encourage the other party to fulfil its obligations in that regard. It is therefore suggested that Sub-Clause 15.1 must be read and understood in the sense that the Engineer *shall* require the Contractor to make good the failure and to remedy it within a specified reasonable time instead of that the Engineer *may* do so, which is the literal wording of the Sub-Clause. Sub-Clause 16.1 shall be read in the same way meaning that the Contractor shall give notice of a failure to comply with payment requirements before giving a termination notice.

In any case both parties to the Contract are well advised to never take any action leading to possible termination lightly as the consequences of wrongful termination can be devastating.

Under common law, in principle a wrongful termination will not terminate the contract unless the other party accepts the breach as having this effect. The usual remedy for wrongful termination will be an action for damages. However, the claimant's unlawful purported determination may constitute a repudiatory breach of the contract that the defendant has no option but to accept. To the contrary, under German law a wrongful termination may be reinterpreted as a termination for convenience in accordance with Sect. 649 German Civil Code. Thus what happens if the Employer expressly relies on Sub-Clause 15.2 and it proves that the Contractor was not in breach of contract? Can the notice then be understood as a termination for convenience? According to German law this may prove successful. According to English law an unlawful purported termination notice may constitute repudiation and result in a claim for damages. It may also be argued that a purported unlawful termination may by itself constitute a breach of contract which meets the requirements of Sub-Clause 16.2.

17.5 Particular Reasons for Termination

It may prove impossible to perform the Contract due to acts of god and Force Majeure. However FIDIC does not allow the parties to abandon the Contract unless it proves effectively impossible to perform the Contract. Thus only if the execution of substantially all the Works in progress is prevented for a continuous period of 84 days by reason of Force Majeure of which notice has been given under Sub-Clause 19.2, or for multiple periods which total more than 140 days due to the same notified Force Majeure, either Party may give notice to the other Party of termination of the Contract.

17.6 Consequences of Termination

Upon termination the consequences of termination must be determined and settled.

17.6.1 *Works*

Once a notice of termination takes effect the Contractor shall leave the Site. If the Contractor has given a notice of termination he shall then also hand over the Contractor's documents, Plant, Materials and other work, for which the Contractor has received payment and remove all other goods from the Site (Sub-Clause 16.3). The rules in the event of a termination for convenience are the same as those for a notice of termination for the Contractor. However, if the Employer has given a notice of termination in accordance with Sub-Clause 15.2 the Contractor shall also deliver any required Goods and other design documents made by or for him, to the Engineer. After completion of the Works the Employer shall give notice to the Contractor that the Contractor's Equipment and Temporary Works will be released to the Contractor at or near the Site, who shall then promptly remove it at his risk and cost.

17.6.2 *Payments*

As to subsequent payments FIDIC provides for different consequences of termination. However, upon each termination of the Contract the Engineer (Red Book, Yellow Book) or the Employer's Representative (Gold Book) shall proceed in accordance with Sub-Clause 3.5 to agree or determine the value of the Works (Sub-Clauses 15.3, 19.6).

Typically, a common law termination for convenience clause will oblige the terminating party to pay the terminated contractor for the work performed and perhaps some costs associated with the contractor's need to terminate subcontracts or supply agreements. Quite often any liability for compensation of loss of profit for the uncompleted Works is expressly barred. Under FIDIC forms of contract the Contractor will be entitled to the amounts stated in Sub-Clause 19.6 including the amounts payable for any work carried out for which a price is stated in the Contract, the Cost of Plant and ordered for the Works which have been delivered to the Contractor, or of which the Contractor is liable to accept delivery, any other Cost or liability which in the circumstances was reasonably incurred by the Contractor in the expectation of completing the Works, the Cost of removal of Temporary Works and Contractor's Equipment from the Site and the return of these items to the Contractor's works in his country (or to any other destination at no greater cost) and the Cost of repatriation of the Contractor's staff and labour employed wholly in connection with the Works at the date of termination. Additionally entitlements may result from the governing law.

Upon a notice of termination by the Employer under Sub-Clause 15.2, Sub-Clause 15.4 applies. If a notice of termination under Sub-Clause 15.2 has taken effect, the Employer may proceed in accordance with Sub-Clause 2.5 [*Employer's Claims*], withhold further payments to the Contractor until the costs of design, execution, completion and remedying of any defects, damages for delay in completion (if any), and all other costs incurred by the Employer, have been established, and/or recover from the Contractor any losses and damages incurred by the Employer and any extra costs of completing the Works, after allowing for any sum due to the Contractor under Sub-Clause 15.3 [*Valuation at Date of Termination*]. After recovering any such losses, damages and extra costs, the Employer shall pay any balance to the Contractor.

Furthermore, upon a notice of termination by the Contractor under Sub-Clause 16.2 the Contractor is entitled to payment in accordance with Sub-Clause 19.6 and to additional payment of any loss of profit or other loss or damage sustained by the Contractor as a result of this termination (Sub-Clause 16.4). Also the Employer shall promptly return the Performance Security.

Finally, upon termination by either Party under Sub-Clause 19.6 by reason of Force Majeure the Engineer is required to certify the amounts payable for any work carried out for which a price is stated in the Contract, the Cost of Plant and ordered for the Works which have been delivered to the Contractor, or of which the Contractor is liable to accept delivery, any other Cost or liability which in the circumstances was reasonably incurred by the Contractor in the expectation of completing the Works, the Cost of removal of Temporary Works and Contractor's

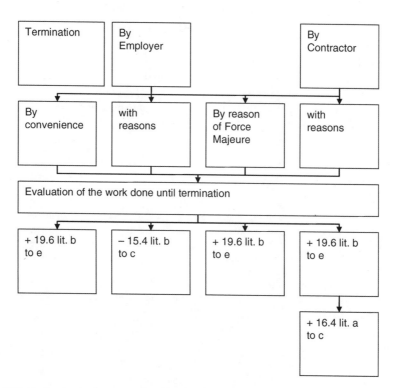

Fig. 17.1 Evaluation in the event of termination

Equipment from the Site and the return of these items to the Contractor's works in his country (or to any other destination at no greater cost) and the Cost of repatriation of the Contractor's staff and labour employed wholly in connection with the Works at the date of termination (Fig. 17.1).

It can be summarised that in principle the Contractor is always entitled to payment for the value of all work carried out to the date of termination, less any payments on account previously made. Pursuant to Sub-Clauses 19.6 and 15.3, upon termination, the Engineer shall determine the value of the work done and issue a Payment Certificate. It is thus critical that the Engineer or Employer's Representative immediately carries out any measurement of work after a notice of termination has taken effect. Unfortunately this may prove difficult for different reasons. Quite often this type of service is much more onerous than the normal evaluation of the Works. Also the Employer is not at all interested in making any further payments to the Contractor. Thus the issue may arise that the Engineer delays measurement or refuses to carry out the measurement work. In this event the only way out is to refer a dispute to the DAB.

17.7   Termination Agreements

The right of a party to terminate the Contract almost inevitably leads to considerable debate and dispute if acted upon. Standard business terms such as FIDIC forms of contract provide for standard solutions based on experiences. However, if a notice of termination seems to be appropriate, particular needs and interests may become apparent or can be foreseen. Thus the Parties may wish to come to an amicable settlement and to cancel their contract under agreed terms in order to avoid disputes and related costs. Such an agreement should include the following items:

BE IT HEREBY KNOWN THAT, and have previously entered into a Contract dated (month & day), (year);
    AND
WHEREAS, both parties desire to terminate the agreement:
NOW, both Parties agree to be bound by the following terms and conditions:
FIRST The above mentioned Contract shall cease on and as of (month & day), (year).
SECOND Both Parties agree to mutually release and discharge one another of any liability with regard to (said Contract or to the following obligations arising from the Contract [to be specified]).
THIRD In all other respects said Contract shall continue in full force and effect.
FOURTH Both parties do hereby set and affix their hand in agreement this day of (month & year).

Chapter 18
Discharge, Frustration and Force Majeure

Fortunately in most cases the Contractor performs the contract. He will then be released from his contractual obligations. Section 362 German Civil Code accordingly provides that the obligation is extinguished if the performance owed is effected to the obligee. Also under Common law performance of contractual obligations discharges the contract. However, the occurrence of unforeseen conditions, circumstances and events may have an impact on the performance. It is therefore critical to know:

- Who bears or has borne the risk which may eventuate
- The rights and obligations which stem from the occurrence of any risk
- The procedures under which such rights may be prosecuted
- Whether there is any to duty to mitigate risk

18.1 Risk and Risk Allocation

Any construction contract goes along with risk. A spectrum of risk matrices may be identified as being common to most, if not all, construction projects. It appears that one of the major differences between Civil law and Common law is the approach taken in respect of risk allocation. Whilst in Common law countries risk is allocated by the terms of the contract, in Civil law countries it is allocated by the Civil Code. The parties to the contract may then adjust the given risk allocation by the terms of the contract within the limits provided by law. Thus in Civil law countries risk allocation and risk allocation methods are not really a hot topic. Instead it is necessary to identify the risk allocation approach of each section of the Code before entering into adjustment discussions.

For example in German law most of the risks are allocated using the concept of charge of risk, which includes the concepts of "Leistungsgefahr" and "Vergütungsgefahr". Leistungsgefahr means the "risk of non-performance" or probably better explained "the risk of having to perform the contract once more until the risk has

A.-V. Jaeger and G.-S. Hök, *FIDIC-A Guide for Practitioners*,
DOI 10.1007/978-3-642-02100-8_18, © Springer-Verlag Berlin Heidelberg 2010

become shifted to the employer", whilst Vergütungsgefahr means the "risk of non-payment" or in other words the "risk to perform the counter obligation although the entitlement to performance does not exist any more". German law deals with the passing of such risk from the contractor to the employer. According to Sect. 644 German Civil Code the contractor assumes the risk of non-performance until acceptance of the works by the employer. He also assumes the risk of non-payment until acceptance of the works by the employer. However, if the employer delays acceptance of the work even though the entitlement to hand-over the works has become due (Sect. 293 German Civil Code) the risk of non-payment may become shifted to the employer (Sect. 644 para. 1(2) German Civil Code). Further according to Sect. 645 German Civil Code, if, prior to acceptance of the works, the works have been destroyed or have deteriorated or cannot be completed because of a defect in materials supplied by the employer or because of an instruction given by him and if no circumstance has contributed to this for which the contractor is liable, then the contractor is entitled to payment which corresponds to the work performed as well as to reimbursement of those expenses which are not included in the remuneration. Also German courts have derived from Sect. 645 German Civil Code that the risk of unforeseen site conditions is borne by the employer because the site is considered to be a material supplied by the employer. Any deviation from this risk allocation approach within standard business terms usually constitutes an unreasonable disadvantage for the contracting party contrary to the principles of good faith. Such provisions are ineffective.

Under common law it is important to emphasise that risk allocation follows the rules of the contract without any constraints or restrictions. In most construction contracts risks are allocated using the concept of control of risks although it seems that there is no related general rule.

However risk allocation through the operation of the governing law and the contract terms is quite an important task because risk allocation is very closely linked to the responsibility to overcome it if it eventuates. Again responsibility is linked very closely to liability, because liability usually follows and flows from risk allocation (Bunni 2009, p. 7). Any rights and obligations of the parties stem from the allocation of risks (Bunni 2009, p. 5).

Meanwhile a second aspect of risk assessment and risk allocation should not be underestimated. Identified risk can either be priced or insured. Unidentified risk is neither priced nor insured. Thus risk assessment takes priority over risk allocation. However, only when the allocation or reallocation of risk is linked to claims or remedies, there is no risk as to the price for the works. Hence risk assessment must include the identification of claims and remedies. It should also include the identification of all claim management requirements, such as notice requirements, delays and documentation requirements.

Finally despite any risk allocation by virtue of the contract, risk must be managed. If a risk eventuates it may cause expenses, damages or loss. It is usually in the interest of both parties to the contract to mitigate risk and damages. Risk management should therefore include efforts to mitigate risks of all kind. This can be done in various ways. FIDIC provides for early warnings (Sub-Clause 8.3), duties to mitigate in the event of Force Majeure (Sub-Clause 19.3) and a sophisticated set of notice requirements.

18.2   Normal Discharge

Knowing the exact point in time when discharge of contractual obligations have been achieved is the focal point of everyone's attention from the very early stages of a project. Despite this intense focus, much debate about whether discharge is actually achieved on a given date abounds across the whole construction industry. These debates often turn into disputes for no reason other than the Parties were not very clear on what they meant by "discharge" when they signed the construction contract. Apparently two legal concepts of discharge do exist. Civil law and Common law have adopted different solutions. A common feature of both concepts is that in a contract to erect buildings on the defendant's land for a lump sum, the builder can recover nothing on the contract before the work is completed. Apart from this both systems are completely different.

Under Common law a person who performs a contract in accordance with its terms is discharged from any further obligations. The question here was whether in a contract for work and labour for a lump sum payable on completion the Employer can repudiate liability under the contract on the ground that the work though "finished" or "done" is in some respects not in accordance with the contract. In Hoenig v. Isaacs[1] Lord Justice Denning said:

> When a contract provides for a specific sum to be paid on completion of specified work, the Courts lean against a construction of the contract which would deprive the contractor of any payment at all simply because there are some defects or omissions. The promise to complete the work is therefore construed as a term of the contract, but not as a condition. It is not every breach of that term which absolves the employer from his promise to pay the price, but only a breach which goes to the root of the contract, such as an abandonment of the work when it is only half done. Unless the breach does go to the root of the matter, the employer cannot resist payment of the price. He must pay it and bring a cross-claim for the defects and omissions, or alternatively set them up in diminution of the price. The measure is the amount which the work is worth less by reason of the defects and omissions, and is usually calculated by the cost of making them good.

Lord Justice Romer added:

> In certain cases it is right that the rigid rule for which the Defendant contends should be applied; for example, if a man tells a contractor to build a 10 ft. wall for him in his garden and agrees to pay £X for it, it would not be right that he should be held liable for any part of the contract price if the contractor builds the wall to 2 ft. and then renounces further performance of the contract, or builds the wall of a totally different material from that which was ordered or builds it at the wrong end of the garden. The work contracted for has not been done and the corresponding obligation to pay consequently never arises. But when

---

[1] Hoenig v. Isaacs [1952] EWCA Civ 6 (13 February 1952).

a, man fully performs his contract in the sense that he supplies all that he agreed to supply but what he supplies is subject to defects of so minor a character that he can be said to have substantially performed his promise, it is in my judgment far more equitable to apply the *Dakin v. Lee* principle than to deprive him wholly of his contractual rights and relegate him to such remedy (if any) as he may have on a quantum meruit; nor, in my judgment, are we compelled to a contrary view (having regard to the nature and terms of the agreement and the Official Referee's finding) by any of the cases in the books.

Thus if a Contractor has substantially completed the Works in accordance with the Contract he is discharged from any further obligations. Unless the breach goes to the root of the matter, the employer cannot resist payment of the price. He must pay it and bring a cross-claim for the defects and omissions, or alternatively set them up in diminution of the price. However, despite the significance of substantial completion to employers, contractors and subcontractors alike, it is quite apparent that very little attention is paid to the actual definition of substantial completion used in a construction contract, or the unique circumstances of a particular project. Complete or partial occupancy or use of the Works may thus lead to much debate. From a more practical point of view the concept of discharge and substantial completion is covered by contractual provisions which provide for the issue of certificates by a third party to the contract, such as an Engineer, Project Manager or Employer's Representative. However, the purpose of such certificates is not to release the contractor but to permit the employer to take possession of the Works and to allow the contractor to leave the site (Uff 2005, p. 307). Certificates usually only serve the function of recording facts but depending on their wording, they may be conclusive as to what they purport to certify (Uff 2005, 279).

Under Civil law the concept of reception or acceptance of the Works prevails.

According to Sect. 640 German Civil Code the Employer is obliged to accept the work produced in accordance with the contract save where the nature of the work precludes such acceptance. Acceptance may not be refused on account of insubstantial defects. Acceptance means a declaration by which the employer accepts that the contractor has substantially performed the works in accordance with the contract.[2] Acceptance may be explicit, implied or fictional. It covers the performance of all obligations arising from or out of the Contract and it is followed by three major consequences: (1) it represents the commencement of the legal defects liability, (2) it shifts the risk of loss of the Works and damage to the Works to the Employer and (3) the contract price becomes due. Also acceptance of defective works constitutes a waiver and the burden of proof for any defects becoming apparent after acceptance of the Works lies with the Employer. This explains why it is critical to expressly reserve any existing rights to claim for the remedy of defects, pay damages or liquidated damages. In the event of failure to make such a reservation acceptance constitutes a waiver.

According to art. 1792-6 French Civil Code acceptance is the act by which the building owner declares that he accepts the work with or without reservation.

[2]BGH [1970] NJW 421.

It occurs at the suit of the first requesting party, either amicably or, failing which, judicially. In any case, it shall be pronounced adversarily. The French Cour de Cassation insists on the fact that acceptance means approval of the performed works rather than mere delivery of the Works.[3] Acceptance may be explicit, implied or judicial. Acceptance without reservation constitutes a waiver by which all liability ceases to exist.[4] Since 1978 the French Civil Code imposes a concept of "unique acceptance". Until 1978 French law provided for a two stage acceptance consisting of a provisional acceptance with defects still to be implied and a final acceptance. In Belgium, Cameroon and Romania, where the French Civil Code has been adopted, this former concept still prevails.

This different approach as to discharge and completion of the Works may lead to confusion. German, French and Romanian practitioners are likely to misunderstand the meaning of the Taking-Over Certificate and the Performance Certificate as referred to in Sub-Clauses 10.1 and 11.9 of the 1999 FIDIC Rainbow Edition or the Commissioning Certificate and the Contract Completion Certificate as referred to in the FIDIC Gold Book.

The difficulty in determining the meaning of the aforementioned certificates can have enormous consequences. Delay damages, payments, releases of retainage and start of the Defects Notification Period are clearly tied to the issue of the Taking-Over and the Performance Certificate. However, the effects of acceptance of the Works as referred to in civil law jurisdictions must also be tied to the issue of the certificates. And this may prove difficult due to the conceptual differences in civil law. As a result, a lot of uncertainty as to the commencement and the length of the (post contractual) legal defects liability period may arise. It is therefore critical that the parties to the contract understand that the 1999 FIDIC Rainbow edition's Taking-Over Certificate does not constitute "acceptance of the Works" as referred to in German and French law. Only the issue of the Performance Certificate will constitute acceptance of the Works as it is clearly mentioned in Sub-Clause 11.9. Under Romanian law the Taking-Over Certificate will constitute provisional acceptance as provided by Law 10/1995 and GD 273/1994. Similar provisions apply in Algeria and in Cameroon.

18.3   Rebus Sic Stantibus

Performance of the Contract may sometimes become more onerous or impossible, whether temporarily or permanently. If an event occurs which prevents the Contractor temporarily or permanently from performing the Contract or if performance becomes more onerous than expected or foreseen by the Contractor the question arises whether the parties to the Contract will nevertheless be bound to perform the

---

[3] Cour de Cassation, 8.10.1974, file no. 73-12.347, Bull.civ. III no. 337.
[4] Cour de Cassation, 20.1.1982, file no. 80-16.415, Bull.civ. III no. 20.

Contract. In principle the rule of *pacta sunt servanda* applies according to which English courts have continuously held that a party is not absolved simply because performance becomes difficult or even impossible.[5] However a second principle in law referred to as *rebus sic stantibus* has to be mentioned. According to Mr. Molineaux this principle is considered by some commentators to be a sort of contrariety to *pacta sunt servanda*. However he considers that it is "really in healthy tension, an attenuation, covering all of the substantial varieties among different national systems of excuse concepts or varieties of relief from an unjust application of *pacta sunt servanda*". Mr. Molineaux continues to say that "lumping together related but not identical concepts, this includes *imprévision*, frustration, *Wegfall der Geschäftsgrundlage* and *force majeure*". In fact, for construction, this principle is not to be applied casually but only in extreme situations, since the foreseeable risks are presumably anticipated by contractor pricing (see Molineaux 1997, p. 55 et seq.) However, it seems that there is no commonly recognised principle which applies to such cases. French courts usually dismiss claims based on the principle of imprévision unless there is what they call *bouleversement de l'économie du contract*. English courts usually hold that contracts are not frustrated by the work proving more difficult or costly than could have been anticipated, unless the difficulty arises from some change of circumstances or supervening event (see Uff 2005, p. 200). By contrast German courts may rely on the principle of rebus sic stantibus, which has been recently expressly incorporated in the Civil Code (see Sect. 313 sentence 1 Civil Code). Also Islamic courts may rely on the principle of rebus sic stantibus (see art. 147 Civil Code Egypt).

18.4   Force Majeure

Some events or circumstances are considered being typically beyond the control of the parties. However, as a general rule at Common law contractual obligations are regarded as absolute. Thus a party is not relieved form its contractual liability because performance becomes difficult or even impossible. However, a contract may be frustrated and thereby automatically discharged. Examples of situations which have constituted frustration are a building in which the contractor is to carry out work is accidentally destroyed or government action which prevents performance of contract for a substantial period (see Uff 2005, p. 199).

In any event, the English doctrine of commercial frustration prospectively operates: the question of discharge is to be determined by reference to the time of the occurrence of the allegedly frustrating event.[6] However, it is a matter of speculation how long a prospective delay would be regarded as sufficient

---

[5] Thorn v. London Corporation (1876) 1 App Cas 120; see Uff (2005, p. 200).
[6] Total Gas Marketing Ltd v. ARCO British Ltd and Others [1998] UKHL 22 (20 May 1998).

to bring the contract to an end by operation of law. The judge would have to make a value judgment. The result would be uncertainty and unpredictability. Under Common law a party to a contract can excuse himself by showing that the event was owing to the plaintiff's default; or perhaps that the event was the consequence of *vis major*, or the act of god. To be an act of god an occurrence must be such that it:[7]

(1) Is the consequence of natural causes exclusively
(2) Is of an extraordinary nature
(3) Could not be anticipated or provided against by the defendant

However, this is a very narrow definition. All man-made events, such as war, or strike are not covered by it.

Most contracts for overseas supplies and services therefore contain particular stipulations concerning events which are beyond the control of the parties and which could not be expected to occur by the parties. Again, all FIDIC Forms of contract contain such a rule. The 1999 Rainbow Edition comprises Clause 19 which provides for detailed rules as to an event:

(a) Which is beyond a Party's control
(b) Which such Party could not reasonably have provided against before entering into the Contract
(c) Which, having arisen, such Party could not reasonably have avoided or overcome
(d) Which is not substantially attributable to the other Party

Sub-Clause 19.1 includes a list of typical Force Majeure events. However, whether an event constitutes a Force Majeure event must be determined in accordance with the applicable or governing law. The connotation Force Majeure is unfortunately a false friend. Art. 1148 of the French Civil Code uses the connotation by providing: "There is no occasion for any damages where a debtor was prevented from transferring or from doing that to which he was bound, or did what was forbidden to him, by reason of force majeure or of a fortuitous event". French courts have construed art. 1148 French Civil Code by saying that Force Majeure covers events which make performance impossible but that it does not cover events which make performance more onerous.[8] Quite often the German legal connotation "höhere Gewalt" becomes translated by Force Majeure although the meaning of "höhere Gewalt" is slightly different form its meaning in French law. FIDIC therefore has decided to refrain from using the connotation Force Majeure. Instead Clause 18 of the FIDIC Gold Book uses now the connotation Exceptional Risk. A reliable definition of Force Majeure was by the way introduced by Unidroit in its Uniform Principles of international commercial contracts (UP) which may be used to

---

[7] Superquinn Ltd v. Bray U.D.C. [1998] IEHC 28; [1998] 3 IR 542 (18 February 1998).
[8] Cour de Cassation, 04.08.1915, DP 1916, 1, 22.

interpret or supplement international uniform law instruments. UP Art. 7.1.7 UP reads as follows:

(1) Non-performance by a party is excused if that party proves that the non-performance was due to an impediment beyond its control and that it could not reasonably be expected to have taken the impediment into account at the time of the conclusion of the contract or to have avoided or overcome it or its consequences.

(2) When the impediment is only temporary, the excuse shall have effect for such period as is reasonable having regard to the effect of the impediment on the performance of the contract.

(3) The party who fails to perform must give notice to the other party of the impediment and its effect on its ability to perform. If the notice is not received by the other party within a reasonable time after the party who fails to perform knew or ought to have known of the impediment, it is liable for damages resulting from such nonreceipt.

(4) Nothing in this article prevents a party from exercising a right to terminate the contract or to withhold performance or request interest on money due.

However, if the Contractor is prevented from performing any of his obligations under the Contract through Force Majeure he shall be entitled, subject to Sub-Clause 20.1 to:

(a) An extension of time for any such delay, if completion is or will be delayed, under Sub-Clause 8.4 [*Extension of Time for Completion*].

(b) If the event or circumstance is of the kind described in sub-paragraphs (i)–(iv) of Sub-Clause 19.1 [*Definition of Force Majeure*] and, in the case of subparagraphs (ii)–(iv), occurs in the Country, payment of any such Cost.

Only if the execution of substantially all the Works in progress is prevented for a continuous period of 84 days by reason of Force Majeure of which notice has been given under Sub-Clause 19.2, or for multiple periods which total more than 140 days due to the same notified Force Majeure, then either Party may give to the other Party a notice of termination of the Contract. Thus FIDIC has chosen a two-step approach. As a first step the Contract becomes partially amended by virtue of claims. As a second step the parties to the Contract may give notice of termination of the Contract. However there is no general rule providing that adaptation of the contract may be claimed, as this is the case under Sect. 313 German Civil Code. But according to Sub-Clause 19.4 the Contractor may be excused from performing the Contract within the limits set out in the claim procedure rules. Consideration must be given to the fact that there is two-step procedure to be followed. According to Sub-Clause 19.2 the Contractor shall give notice of a Force Majeure event within 14 days. If he suffers delay and/or incurs Cost by reason of such Force Majeure he shall then give notice in accordance with Sub-Clause 20.1 of a claim subject to Sub-Clause 19.4.

Regrettably the extent to which the Contractor shall be entitled to extension of time and payment of additional cost subject to Sub-Clause 19.4 remains ambiguous.

The issue lies in the restrictive wording "is prevented from performing any of his obligations". If the Contractor is only entitled to claims to the extent and in so far as he is "prevented from performing any of his obligations" any (indirect) claim for additional time and cost resulting from consequences of a Force Majeure event must be dismissed. On the other hand Sub-Clause 19.4 refers to delay and/or Cost "by reason" of such Force Majeure. It could be argued that this includes any indirect consequences of Force Majeure such as the time needed for the reconstruction of temporary work, which has been demolished by an event, which constitutes a Force Majeure event. However this is not a strong argument, because of the limited scope of application of Clause 19, which in principle deals only with the prevention. This can be clearly contrasted with Sub-Clause 19.2 which states that the Party shall, having given notice, be excused performing of such obligations for so long as such Force Majeure prevents it from performing them. If the result of a Force Majeure event is that the temporary works have been demolished or damaged and the event itself has ceased to influence the progress, the Contractor is no longer prevented from carrying out the work. The fact that he has to carry out the work once again, is not mentioned in Sub-Clause 19.2 and 19.4. It is therefore suggested that in this case Sub-Clauses 17.4 and 17.3 exclusively apply, because the wording of Clause 19 covers only consequences of Force Majeure which directly affect progress of the Works, whereas Clause 17 deals with the risk of care for the Works. Most of the Employer's risks listed in Sub-Clause 17.3 are identical with the Force Majeure events listed in Sub-Clause 19.1.

References

Bunni NG (2009) The four criteria of risk allocation in construction contracts. ICLR 4
Molineaux C (1997) Moving toward a Lex Mercatoria – A Lex Constructionis. J Int Arb 14:55
Uff J (2005) Construction law, 9th edn. Sweet & Maxwell, London

Chapter 19
Risk, Insurance and Exceptional Risk

19.1 Introduction

It is common knowledge that risk means the likelihood of a specific event or circumstance combined with the consequences that will follow when this event eventuates. In most cases it is something which the parties do not expect to occur either deliberately or innocently. It depends on the particular case whether the parties have made allowance for risk or not. It is imperative for any contract for the execution of works to deal with risk. The options are manifold. The parties may ignore the risk or they may make allowances for it. However in any case the risk must be allocated to the parties. Allocation of risk may be implicit or express. Entering into a construction contract usually means to assume risk. Which one is either a matter of law or a matter of fact. If the contract itself does not contain any risk apportionment rules the law will be decisive. Thus a legal and contractual risk assessment is strongly recommended. It is critical to understand that foreign courts may have a different approach as to risk allocation. German courts are ready to interfere with contractual risk allocation whereas common law courts are more reluctant to disrupt or displace the agreed equilibrium of rights and obligations (see Bailey 2007, p. 399).

Risks faced may include:

- That the works will be completed late, including exposure to damages, penalties and costs in the event of delays in completion of the works
- That the works will be completed inadequately
- That the works become more onerous than expected
- Land acquisition risk
- Increasing cost in operating, e.g. increased labour costs;
- Design and construction defects impacting upon the operation of the completed project
- Deficiencies in other infrastructure or services upon which the successful operation of the project depends, e.g. feeder roads are not constructed or urban development does not proceed as anticipated

A.-V. Jaeger and G.-S. Hök, *FIDIC-A Guide for Practitioners*,
DOI 10.1007/978-3-642-02100-8_19, © Springer-Verlag Berlin Heidelberg 2010

- Political risk, e.g. change in priorities of governments and lack of funding
- Political support necessary to promote the success of the project
- Design risk
- Site conditions might be encountered which are different to those which were expected, and the consequences of unanticipated conditions (including contamination risk, native titles)
- Latent defects
- Site supervision and site superintendence
- Risks arising from Subcontractors, in particular direct claims of Subcontractors based on statute law (such as in Poland and France)
- Management risks
- Continuity of cash-flow
- Special risks arising from bank securities
- Damages resulting from third parties
- Damages to third parties, e.g. neighbours
- Consequences of the default, or failure of a consortium partner
- Ability to rectify defects after Taking-Over
- Consequential losses
- Litigation risk
- Currency rate risk and currency export restrictions

Risk must be adequately managed. Risk management means to identify and demonstrate the systems the Contractor intends on using to manage and control the construction process with regard to the requirements of the Contract and also with regard to identifying that the Contractor is working to current accepted best practice. FIDIC contracts have mechanisms in place to take care of this. Sub-Clause 4.9 requires the implementation of a quality assurance system. Moreover according to Sub-Clause 4.8 the Contractor shall comply with safety procedures.

It is strongly recommended to carry out a risk assessment prior to the submission of an offer. Risk assessment means to carry out a formalised process of identifying hazards and evaluating their consequence and probability of occurrence in order to develop strategies as appropriate for preventative and contingent actions. Risk management must include a complete risk assessment which should be started on the basis of legal background. This is in principle the proper law of the contract but includes tort law issues.

19.2   Legal Risk Allocation

The common law position as to the apportionment of risk, in the absence of express terms to the contrary, was stated in The Moorcock.[1] According to The Moorcock a contract shall operate so as "not to impose on one side all the perils of the

---

[1] Moorcock, The (1889) 14 PD 64.

transaction, or to emancipate one side from all chance of failure, but to make each party promise in law as much, at all events, as it must have been in the contemplation of both parties that he should be responsible for in respect of those perils or chances". In civil law countries quite often the "Leitmotiv" of the legislator replaces a general approach, in particular where the relevant Civil Code provides for special types of contract, as is the case in Germany, France and Poland. Thus in these countries a case-by-case study seems to be necessary in order to identify the legal risk allocation approach. Under German law a contractor is under the obligation to erect and deliver the individual works as defined in the contract in consideration of a remuneration. German courts currently proceed on the assumption that the contract for works between the parties is a contract of services (Werkvertrag). According to its nature the contract for services includes a promise of the contractor to achieve a specific result. Loss or damage to the works which occurs prior to handing over according to Sect. 640 German Civil Code is borne by the contractor. The so-called ground risk, in general meaning the risk of site conditions which are different to those indicated in the tender documents, is allocated to the employer. Risks which are beyond the control of the contractor are dealt with according to Sect. 313 German Civil Code, according to which adaptation of the contract may be claimed "having regard to all the circumstances of the specific case, in particular the contractual or statutory allocation of risk", "if circumstances upon which a contract was based have materially changed after the conclusion of the contract and if the parties would not have concluded the contract or would have done so upon different terms if they had foreseen that change" and if "it cannot reasonably be expected that a party should continue to be bound by the contract in its unaltered form". Under French law a contract for works usually has the nature of a contract for the hire of services (see Art. 1787 et seq. Code Civil). Whether the contractor promises to achieve a specific result or whether he is only liable for skill and care depends on the particular merits of the case. Usually contractors are under the obligation to achieve a specific result (obligation de résultat)[2] whereas engineers and architects are often only liable for skill and care (obligation de moyens).[3] Thus a contractor shall in principle complete the works free from defects and within the agreed time.[4] The design of an engineer or architect must be skilful but not fit for the intended purposes.

Under French law the cause of action is contractual if the damage results from breach of contract, which is either non-performance or improper performance of the contractual obligations. All contractual obligations must be performed with good faith.

Contractors, architects and engineers usually are under a split contractual liability. Until "reception" of the works French common law applies. After reception of the works special legal guarantees come into play, which are known as the

---

[2] Cour de Cassation, 08.11.2005, RD. Imm. 2006, 55 annotation Malinvaud.
[3] Cour de Cassation, 22.06.2004.
[4] Cour de Cassation, 13.09.2005.

guarantee of perfect completion (art. 1792-6 Civil Code), the guarantee of good running (art. 1792-3 Civil Code) and the so-called decennial liability (art. 1792 Civil Code).

French common law entitles the employer to request the removal or remedy of damage to the works resulting from non performance or wrongful performance of the contract. Moreover French common law provides for specific duties, such as a duty to warn and a duty to advise. To the extent that French common law applies it is critical to ascertain the nature of the relevant duty, which may consist in a duty of care (obligation de moyens) or a duty to achieve a specific result (obligation de résultat).

French courts do not accept an "obligation de résultat" from the part of the Contractor as such. In each case the courts have to examine whether the Contractor actually has taken the burden of such a kind of obligation. Usually, if the Contractor undertakes to complete the works within an agreed time for completion, he will only escape from its liability for failure to comply with time for completion if he proves that the delay was caused by an event which was not attributable to him.[5] He will again be bound to achieve a specific result if he promises to carry out the works in accordance with the contract and the applicable laws.[6] By contrast an architect will usually only be held liable for an "obligation de moyens"[7] although the courts have pronounced various opinions and in some cases also admit an "obligation de résultat".[8] The frontiers of differentiation are fluid. There is no systematic approach.

In principle the contractor is discharged from all common law liability at the date of acceptance of the works by the employer. Acceptance of the works by the employer constitutes reception of the works. On the date of reception the legal guarantees start running. According to Art. 1792 Civil Code the Works must be handed over free from defects. However if defects become apparent, contractors, architects and engineers are liable for breach of the guarantee of perfect completion of the works (garantie de parfait achèvement). In addition a guarantee of good running (bon fonctionnement) also exists and finally the so-called decennial guarantee completes the post reception triple guarantee under French law.

The French approach as to the ground risk is twofold. If the contractor promises to build something against a lump sum price this will be binding on him. The fact that he did not make allowance for unforeseen events or circumstances does not constitute any right to claim for a price adjustment or a re-negotiation of the contract. The contractor is obliged to make allowance in his price for all work which may become necessary to complete the works in a good workmanlike

[5] Cour de Cassation, 28.01.1998, RD imm 1998, 265.

[6] SA Prisunic v. SA Services Installations Frigorifiques, Court of Appeal Paris, 08.01.1999, RD imm. 1999, 261.

[7] Cour de Cassation, 11.06.1985, JCP (G) 1985 IV, 295; Cour de Cassation, 03.10.2001, RD. Imm. 2001, 498 annotation B. Boubli and Périnet-Marquet; Cour de Cassation, 16.02.2005, Mon TP 2005, 104.

[8] Cour de Cassation, 19.03.1986, no. 84-17.424.

manner.[9] However the Cour de Cassation has held that if the employer omits a work item in the tender documents which was necessary for the works, the claim for extra payment does not constitute a request for a price review but otherwise a remedy for cure of a manifest error resulting from the employer's non-compliance with his duty to verify the tender documents.[10] By contrast the so-called decennial liability includes the liability for defects in the ground.

In the words of Prof. Abraham, risk should be allocated as such (Abrahamson 1984, p. 241):

[A] party should bear a construction risk where:

1. It is in his control, i.e. if it comes about it will be due to wilful misconduct or lack of reasonable efficiency or care; or
2. He can transfer the risk by insurance and allow for the premium in settling his charges to the other party ... and it is most economically beneficial and practical for the risk to be dealt with in that way; or
3. The preponderant economic benefit of running the risk accrues to him; or
4. To place the risk on him is in the interests of efficiency (which includes planning, incentive, innovation) and the long term health of the construction industry on which that depends; or
5. If the risk eventuates, the loss falls on him in the first instance, and it is not practicable or there is no reason under the above four principles to cause expense and uncertainty, and possibly make mistakes in trying to transfer the loss to another.

19.3   Risk Assessment

19.3.1   Overview

The key areas for the evaluation of risk and risk apportionment in the FIDIC sets of Conditions are:

- The allocation of risks for damage to the Works (care for the Works) and the corresponding insurance provisions
- The clauses regulating unforeseeability
- The clauses regulating changes in cost
- The clauses regulating changes of technical standards and laws
- The clauses containing an excuse for non performance
- The clauses dealing with errors in Employer's documents

Most of the risk allocation rules within the FIDIC documents do not expressly deal with risk allocation, but they nevertheless do exist. All FIDIC forms of contract

---

[9]Cour de Cassation, 17.11.1999, Rd imm. 2000, 52.
[10]Cour de Cassation, 15.01.2003, Rd imm. 2003, 259.

state clearly that the Contractor assumes the responsibility for the execution and completion of the Works and the remedy of any defects. Under the Gold Book the Contractor also assumes the responsibility for the operation of the plant or facility. In return the Employer shall pay the Contract Price to the Contractor. The extent to which the responsibility of the Contractor includes extra cost arising from unexpected events or circumstances must be carefully ascertained (Bailey 2007, p. 403 et seq.). The Employer on the other side will be interested in knowing under which conditions he will be liable to pay the agreed price although the works have become demolished or damaged and to which extent he may be liable for extra cost in the event of unforeseen circumstances.

There are only few express risk allocation provisions within a FIDIC contract.

19.3.2 Employer's Risk

Although Sub-Clause 17.3 deals with Employer's Risk, it does not contain a general risk allocation rule. Instead Sub-Clause 17.3 applies in conjunction with the risk allocation rule in Sub-Clause 17.2 according to which the Contractor assumes the responsibility for care of the works. However if an event or circumstance listed in Sub-Clause 17.3 occurs the Contractor may rely on Sub-Clause 17.4 for compensation of any loss or damage resulting from such an event or circumstance. Undoubtedly there is a significant overlap between the Employer's Risk and the definition of Force Majeure in Clause 19. Nevertheless each of both these clauses has a proper scope of application. Sub-Clause 19.4 grants claims as to extension of Time for Completion and in some particular cases claims as to additional cost. Sub-Clause 17.4 grants also additional profit, if the event falls within Sub-Clause 17.3 lit. f and g. Moreover Sub-Clause 19.4 deals with the Contractor's prevention from performing whilst Sub-Clause 17.4 deals with the loss and damage to the Works by consequence of any event listed in Sub-Clause 17.3. In any case Sub-Clause 17.2 contains a clear risk allocation rule in favour of the Employer. Hence in principle the Contractor will be liable to reconstruct the whole of the Works if they become demolished by a fortuitous event before the issue of the Taking-Over Certificate. However if the Employer uses any part of the Works before the Taking-Over Certificate is issued the part which is used shall be deemed to have been taken over as from the date on which it is used (see Sub-Clause 10.2). In this event Sub-Clause 17.2 applies and the risk of damage to the Works becomes shifted to the Employer who will then have to pay for it.

19.3.3 Care for the Works

According to Sub-clause 17.2 the Contractor is responsible for care of the Works during construction, plus any outstanding Works that Contractor undertakes to finish during the defects notification period (see Sub-clause 11.1), excluding loss or damage caused by specified excepted risks (Sub-Clauses 17.3). All risk insurance is required (Sub-clause 18.2).

Thus Sub-Clause 17.2 allocates the risk of care for the works to the Contractor. This responsibility becomes shifted to the Employer at the date stated in the Taking-Over Certificate. However the Contractor should be aware of the fact that according to Sub-Clause 17.2 the burden of care for the works remains on him for any work to be carried out under Clause 11. Thus in fact the Contractor remains partially responsible for care for the works until the issue of the Performance Certificate. This is mirrored in Sub-Clause 18.2. However if and when the Works have been taken over there is a strong defence of the Contractor against any claim for loss or turnover or revenue caused by third party damage to the Works.

The expression care for the works presumably covers an issue which is precisely ruled in Civil law jurisdictions. According to German law the Contractor bears the risk (of accidental damage to the Works or demolition of the Works) until the work is "accepted". If the Employer is late in acceptance then risk passes to him (Sect. 644 paragraph 1 German Civil Code). Thus using the expression "care for the works" may lead to misunderstandings. According to civil law understanding FIDIC has undocked the risk shifting for care for the works from "acceptance of the Works". The latter will happen when the Engineer issues the Performance Certificate.

This very clear analysis makes it necessary to discuss in more detail what happens under the new Gold Book. Under the Gold Book the term "care for the Works" has been used twofold. It is free from doubt, that until the issue of the Commissioning Certificate the risk of care for the works is borne by the Contractor. This means that he will be liable to reconstruct everything which has been damaged or demolished before the Commissioning Certificate is issued. However, according to Sub-clause 17.5 paragraph 2 Gold Book the Contractor is also responsible for the care of the Permanent Works during the whole Operation Service. By using the expression care for the Works twofold the risk of mis- understandings appears in particular under Civil law, because therein care for the works means the risk of accidental damage to the Works. Well, the relevant Sub-clause of the Gold Book states that in so far the responsibility for care for the works shall be in accordance with the Licence Agreement pursuant to Sub-clause 1.7. The issue now is whether that means that the parties are free to define the content of the risk for care for the Works during the operation Service? All interpretation of the term must start from the wording of the Gold Book. Sub-clause 11.7 clearly states that the Commissioning Certificate shall be deemed to constitute acceptance of the Works. It is suggested that under German law this means that there is acceptance of the Works at the moment when the Commissioning Certificate is issued by the Employer's Representative. By consequence under German law, once the Contractor has received the Commissioning Certificate the risk for care for the Works has passed to the Employer. But will the risk be shifted back to Contractor by virtue of Sub-clause 17.5 Gold Book? There is no clear answer in relation to this. It seems however to be unreasonable to shift the risk back to the Contractor, who is not the owner of the Works and who is not the economic beneficiary of the Works. On the other hand the Contractor will be under the duty not only to maintain and operate the Works but also to replace major items of the Works, which will mean that he is under a continuing duty to carry out works. However, it arises from Sub-clauses 19.2 and 19.3 that apparently FIDIC does not expect for the Contractor to hold on being responsible for care for the works in the sense of the risk of accidental damage to the Works during the Operation Service, because there is no longer an obligation to provide insurance cover in so far. Thus it is suggested that the FIDIC wording care for the Works during the operation Service includes only a duty to take care for the Works as a prudent administrator. This will mean that the Contractor shall be responsible to take all necessary steps to protect and maintain the Permanent Works. This involves a duty of best efforts. In other words and by reference to article 5.1.4 Unidroit Principles the Contractor will then be bound to make such efforts as would be made by a reasonable person of the same kind in the same circumstances.

19.3.4   Sub-contractor's Risk

Sub-Clause 4.4 relates to faults by subcontractors. The Contractor shall be responsible for the acts or defaults of any Subcontractor, his agents or employees, as if there were the acts or defaults of the Contractor. The rationale behind this Sub-Clause is to include insurance cover for such kind of issues in the contractor's all risk insurance (CAR) policy.

19.3.5   Fencing, Lighting and Guarding

Sub-Clause 4.8 details the Contractor's obligation to provide fencing, lighting, guarding and watching of the Works. The insurer may rely on this Sub-Clause whenever a site survey discloses that safety procedures are inadequate.

19.3.6   Misinterpretation of Data

Sub-Clause 4.10 allocates the risk of any misinterpretation of site data to the Contractor and deems the Contractor to have informed himself as to all relevant risk. This means for the insurer that all risk aspects mentioned in the Sub-Clause 4.10 as being the Contractor's responsibility must be included in the CAR policy.

19.3.7   Bodily Injury

Sub-Clause 17.1 sets out the Contractor's responsibility in relation to bodily injury, sickness, disease or death, of any person and damage or loss of any property. These indemnities must be considered in conjunction with the insurance provisions in Sub-Clause 18.3. Sub-Clause 18.3 clearly indicates which liabilities may be excluded from the insurance cover.

19.3.8   Caps

Some risks are capped. According to Sub-Clause 17.6 the maximum amount of damages shall not exceed the sum stated in the Particular Conditions or as the case may be the accepted contract amount. The liability for indirect or consequential losses is excluded subject to the exceptions ruled in Sub-Clause 17.6. The amount of delay damages which become due for time overrun according to Sub-Clause 8.7 shall not exceed the maximum amount of delay damages stated in the Appendix to Tender. A number of English cases support the proposition that liquidated damages will normally be the Employer's sole and exclusive remedy for delay of any kind to practical completion.[11] If German or Polish law governs the contract the courts are likely to misunderstand the delay damages clause and to apply penalty law. By consequence they tend to ignore the cap which is inherent to delay damages clauses. On the other hand they are likely to reduce the agreed amount of delay damages if they think it is unreasonable or inadequate.

In any case, all types of limitation clauses must be read in conjunction with the proper law of the contract. It should be noted that according to Sect. 639 German Civil Code the Contractor may not rely on an agreement by which the Employer's rights in respect of a defect are excluded or restricted to the extent that he fraudulently concealed the defect or if he has guaranteed the nature of the work. In principle Sect. 639 BGB can apply to all forms of contractual guarantees.

Since a recent adaptation of Sect. 639 BGB it seems to be possible to create a proper system of liability. Until the reform Section 639 read as follows:

> The contractor may not rely on an agreement by which the customer's rights in respect of a defect are excluded or restricted *if* he fraudulently concealed the defect or *if* he has guaranteed the nature of the work.

---

[11] Including Pigott Foundations Ltd v. Shepherd Construction Ltd (1993) 67 BLR 48 (pp. 67G–68E); Temloc Ltd v. Errill Properties Ltd (1987) 39 BLR 30 (pp. 38–39); Peak Construction (Liverpool) Ltd v. McKinney Foundations Ltd (1970) 1 BLR 114, p. 121.

It now reads:

> The contractor may not rely on an agreement by which the customer's rights in respect of a defect are excluded or restricted *as far as* he fraudulently concealed the defect or *as far as* he has guaranteed the nature of the work.

Thus the Contractor is allowed to guarantee a specific result and to limit his liability in relation to it. Thus in principle the cap according to Sub-Clause 17.6 may apply. But it should be carefully examined to which extent Sub-Clause 17.6 applies if the Contractor promises complying with specific warranties or conditions.

19.4   Insurance

FIDIC presupposes that risk exists and should be covered by insurance, to the extent that is possible. It is in this context that Clause 17 and 18 should be read together. However insurance cover is only available for *insurable risk*, which is a risk depending on fortuity, which means that the event or circumstance has to be sudden and accidental and that comprehensive data for the purposes of premium calculation do exist. Obviously some of the risk which is inherent to a construction contract does not depend on fortuity. It is then not insurable. Thus differing ground conditions (see Sub-Clause 4.12) and unusual climatic conditions (see Sub-Clause 8.4) which may have a critical impact on the successful completion of the works are dealt with separately in FIDIC contracts. This type of risk is also referred to as speculative risk.

In principle speculative risks are not unforeseeable. An experienced Contractor should be able to foresee most of the current risks. The question is whether he should also make allowance for the event that the risk occurs. Unforeseeability is dealt with in Sub-Clause 1.1.6.8. According to Sub-Clause 1.1.6.8 unforeseeable means not reasonably foreseeable by an experienced contractor by the date for submission of the Tender. The General Conditions refer to the term unforeseeable as defined in Sub-Clause 1.1.6.8 in several Sub-Clauses, such as:

- Sub-Clause 4.6: Unforeseeable cost
- Sub-Clause 4.12: Unforeseeable physical conditions
- Sub-Clause 8.4: Unforeseeable shortages in the availability of personnel or goods
- Sub-Clause 8.5: Unforeseeable delay or disruption
- Sub-Clause 17.3: Unforeseeable operation of forces of nature

It is however an erroneous assumption that site investigations lay only in the interest of the Parties to the contract. Most insurers will expect Site and ground investigations to be carried out by or on behalf of the Client (ITIG 2006, p. 10). They should be phased appropriate to the pertaining physical and geological environments and be so designed and planned to:

(a) Identify, so far as reasonably practicable, artificial (man-made) and natural (geological/hydrogeological) hazards (including gases such as methane, radon)

and hence enable consequent risks to be assessed (which influence the design and construction of the project, including those that affect third parties)
(b) Provide sufficient information on pertaining site conditions, ground (including artificial and natural ground) and groundwater conditions, previous history of the project site including any constraints of an engineering significance relevant to the works to be carried out (such as mining/mineral extraction, contamination) in order to enable realistic and reliable assessments of different tunnelling methodologies (including temporary and permanent support/lining requirements and health and safety issues) to be made in terms of technical viability, cost, programme and impact to third parties
(c) Enable the financial and technical viability of the project to be confirmed from preliminary design studies
(d) Enable alignment options to be compared and the feasibility of the options in terms of cost, programme and Constructability to be evaluated

Most construction contracts for major works in general use comprise provisions relating to the obtaining of insurance and direct by whom insurance is to be obtained. Sub-Clause 18.2 et seq. are an example of this. In some countries additional requirements for insurance cover do exist. There is a strong presumption for the fact that an existing so-called decennial liability must be insured by the Contractor. This French type of liability has been adopted by a considerable number of jurisdictions worldwide, including Angola, Algeria, Belgium, Egypt, Luxemburg, Malta, Morocco, Tunisia, Romania, United Arab Emirates, etc. As a matter of fact insurance cover must be obtained for example in Algeria, Egypt, Belgium and France. FIDIC strongly recommends consulting an insurance expert prior to the conclusion of the contract. It is worth noting that the decennial liability insurance must be obtained before the Commencement Date. It is sometimes very difficult to obtain such insurance cover. Late efforts to obtain such an insurance policy may delay the commencement of the works at the risk of the Contractor.

All members of the construction team should attempt to cover risk by insurance to any extent possible. This is in line with FIDIC policy.

According to Sub-Clause 18.2(a) unless otherwise stated in the Particular Conditions, the insurance for the Works shall be effected and maintained by the *Contractor* as the insuring party and shall cover all loss and damage from any cause not listed in sub-clause 17.3 (Sub-Clause 18.2(c)). By consequence under the Red Book the Employer's design risk in the sense of 17.3(g) Red Book is not covered by the Contractor's insurance, whereas under the Silver and Yellow Book the Contractor shall obtain insurance cover for the complete design risk. Hence, if a Red Book contract includes some design by the Contractor then Sub-Clause 18.2 Red Book should be amended in the Particular Conditions to follow the Yellow Book requirement (Totterdill 2006, p. 278).

In addition contractors will provide insurance cover against damage to property or personal injury to third parties arising from construction activities on and off the site.

An obvious and insurable risk for professional consultants is that their design, drawings, or advice may prove inadequate and/or negligent. This type of risk will usually be covered by a Professional Indemnity Policy (PI), being a continuing annual policy which covers the professional against liability, such liability usually arising from negligence. Care must however be taken, whether such type of insurance covers the whole of the design risk because of the fact that in civil law countries the designer is most often liable for a design which is fit for the purposes.[12] Hence he is liable for defective work. For example in Germany the courts have continuously held that a contract for architectural services has the predominant nature of a contract for works.[13] If the mistaken design or the inadequate site supervision of the architect leads to defective work he will be liable for this.[14] In practice most breaches of design and supervision duties only become apparent after completion of the Works. By consequence it is a particular feature of a German PI insurance that the insurer must indemnify all damages resulting from breach of contract notwithstanding of the fact when a damage occurs. The relevant event is the first wrongful act or omission of the architect or engineer which has caused the damage. Insurance cover includes compensation for all cost necessary for rectifying the damage including all expenditure which is necessary to demolish and rebuild the defective part of the building (see, for more details, Mütze et al. 2007, p. 131 et seq.).

Usually Contractors will cover the following insurable risks:

- The Works under construction
- Materials for the project stored on-site and off-site
- Temporary structures (temporary Works)
- Hired plant and equipment
- Contractor's plant and equipment (although in some cases this is insured separately under Contractor's Constructional Plant insurance)
- Design by the Contractor to the extent specified in the Contract (see Sub-Clause 4.1)

The second paragraph of Sub-Clause 18.1 requires a meeting between the Employer and the Contractor in order to agree the terms of insurance prior to the issue of the letter of acceptance. This is a critical point, which should not be ignored. However it is desirable that the terms and issues of insurance are clearly identified before the Base Date.

---

[12] BGH [2001] NJW 1276.
[13] [82] BGHZ 100.
[14] OLG Jena [1998] IBR 491.

19.5   Contractor's All Risk Insurance

A "CAR" policy may be effected by the Employer or by the Contractor engaged for the work and can include all subcontractors. A CAR policy typically covers loss or damage to property in which the insured has an insurable interest. The material damage policy covers loss or damage to the property specified in the insurance contract. Damage to the Works may include machinery and electrical plant. Usually cover may be provided for the contract works (permanent and temporary works), construction plant, plant erection, goods in transit and damage to employees' property. The CAR policy terminates when the completed Works are handed over or any completed part is taken over or put into service. In respect of construction plant and the like, cover ends when such equipment is removed from the site. The CAR policy can be extended to a so-called "maintenance period", which usually lasts 12 months. The maintenance cover is for physical loss or damage to the Works occurring during the maintenance period stipulated in the provisions of the clauses in the contract relating to the Works. For the avoidance of misunderstandings, under FIDIC contracts the so-called maintenance period means the Defects Notification Period being ruled in detail in Clause 11.

Under FIDIC contracts the insurance cover shall be for not less than the full replacement value, including delivery to the Site. This should be the basis for arriving at the policy amount which should be subsequently reviewed during the policy period to ascertain its adequacy.

A CAR policy usually covers insurance interests for the loss or damage of a property while under construction and during the Defects notification period of the contract during which the Contractor has a duty to correct faults and defects that come to light. Cover can be extended to cover third party liability. It comprises an all-risk policy (subject to policy conditions). The insured items are those which are identified in the policy. As a rule the insured items (Works including material to be used in performing the contract, construction plant and equipment) are covered against any unforeseen and sudden physical loss or damage from any cause not excluded. The insured party is indemnified against all sums for which he is legally liable to pay as damages for accidental death or bodily injury to third parties or accidental damage to third party property arising out of performance of the contract. Loss damage or liability arising in the course of any operation carried out by the insured party for the purpose of complying with obligations during the Defects notification period is covered.

Besides, a number of specific issues should be taken into consideration: (1) A proper CAR policy would require for the insured sum to be adjusted at the end of the project by the jointly insured parties. All claims and adjustments will become added according to the value of the Payment Certificates issued, which will lead to the payment of an additional premium. Even though an automatic increase clause may be agreed in order to ensure adequate insurance cover the Contractor remains under the duty to eventually declare the final value of the works and paying the adjusted premium. (2) Most insurers will insist on applying deductibles.

If so, the insurance contract stipulates a deductible (excess) being a part of the loss amount not indemnified by the insurer. The rationale of the deductible is that it relieves the insurer from settlement of smaller claims and provides for settlement of major claims. (3) Normal CAR cover does not extend to the cost of debris removal. The removal of debris must be indicated and insured separately. This is a small sum which should be fixed by the Engineer or the Employers Representative at tender stage for the purposes of obtaining insurance cover. (4) In addition insurers will often insist on specific exclusions. Sub-Clause 18.2(e) permits such kind of exclusions.

Sub-Clause 17.1 contains an indemnity granted by the Contractor in favour of the Employer for claims for injury, death or third party property damage to the extent that the Employer is not responsible for that loss or damage (or to the extent not otherwise accepted). The relationship between indemnity and insurance provisions in a construction contract was considered in some detail by the Full Court of the Supreme Court of Western Australia in the *Speno* case.[15] The simple message to be taken away from the *Speno* case, which is of particular importance to contractors, is that one should not assume that an employer will not be able to enforce an indemnity clause against a contractor simply because the contract obliges the contractor to procure insurance that may cover the same events as are covered by the indemnity.

Although the CAR policy offers wide protection in the fields of engineering and environmental perils some risks are excluded from the insurance cover. There is a set of standard exclusions listed below:

- War, hostilities, civil commotion, riot or strike
- Nuclear reaction, nuclear radiation or radioactive contamination
- Wilful, intentional, careless, fraudulent, criminal actions or omissions of the insured or their representatives
- Total or partial cessation of work
- Faults in design, materials, bad casting and bad workmanship

It is critical for the wording of the CAR policy to follow as closely as possible the limitation upon the Contractor's liability. Under English law the exclusion in respect of a damage or risk will apply where the event excluded is to be regarded as the effective or dominant cause. In Wayne Tank v. Employers Liability the insurer relied on the following clause:

> the company will not indemnify the insured in respect of liability consequent upon … damage caused by the nature or condition of any goods … sold or supplied by or on behalf of the insured.

In fact the supplier supplied a pipe intended to carry hot wax, which was unsuitable for that purpose, coupled with a thermostat which did not work. The factory owner made the pipe run and the factory burnt down. The Court held that the supplier

---

[15] Speno Rail Maintenance Australia v. Hamersley Iron Pty Ltd [2000] WASCA 408.

could not rely on the defence that the factory owner had left the pipe in operation and unattended, before it had been tested. It was held that the dominant cause of damage was the dangerous installation of the pipe which was likely to melt under heat. Thus the cause of loss fell under the exclusion clause.[16]

In addition liquidated or delay damages being mutually accepted by the Contractor are generally excluded from the policy cover. Again wilful act or negligence will not be within the policy cover. Some specifications as to the exclusion of faults in design and workmanship seem to be worthy. Usually the defective part of work itself is excluded from the policy cover. However insurers are prepared to grant insurance cover for fortuitous damage to sound parts of the works caused by defective material or workmanship. However the insured person is well advised to carefully check the policy as to the extent of such cover.

Typically, a CAR policy will stipulate a limit of liability for each "occurrence". Generally, an "occurrence" is physical loss or damage to the works. As mentioned above, there is usually an excess or deductible for each occurrence. It is obvious that this can lead to disputes over what exactly constituted the "occurrence".

A typical CAR claim will be composed by three damage headings: (1) direct loss (the costs to repair); (2) prolongation costs to the employer; and (3) the prolongation or extended general conditions costs to the contractor and subcontractors. The third one may fall under the exclusion clause for "consequential loss". The meaning of "consequential loss" varies according to the context, but generally "consequential loss" refers to loss beyond the normal measure and includes such things as loss of profits and expenses caused indirectly by the event. Generally, such losses are not covered by the policy in the absence of express words.

Quite often larger projects require an *extension* of the normal CAR insurance cover. In this event the policy needs to be adapted with specific extensions.

It should be noted that insurers require the production of deliverables including site data and reports, methods statements, a risk assessment, etc. It is also worth to note that when a term in a policy is stipulated to be a condition precedent to the liability of the insurer, the condition has to be strictly complied with by the insured before the insured is entitled to bring a claim on the policy. This proposition is illustrated in the case of Chong Kok Hwa v. Taisho Marine & Fire Insurance Co Ltd.[17] In that case the court held that when a term in an insurance policy was stipulated to be a condition precedent to the liability of the insurer, the insurer was not liable under the policy unless the term has been strictly complied with by the insured. Thus the insured person should strictly comply with the terms of the policy. In Putra Perdana Construction Sdn Bhd v. AMI Insurance Bhd[18] the contractor was in breach of the condition to dispose waste and inflammable materials. Bad housekeeping prevented the fire brigades to carry out fire fighting effectively.

---

[16]Wayne Tank & Pump Co Ltd v. Employers Liability [1974] 1 QB 57.

[17][1977] 1 MLJ 244.

[18]Putra Perdana Construction Sdn Bhd v. AMI Insurance Bhd [2004] Part 4 Case 14 [HCM].

Hence the court dismissed the indemnity claim of the contractor for breach of conditions of the insurance contract.

19.6 Uninsurable Risk

Finally a set of special risks also know as Force Majeure events are usually not insurable. Sub-Clause 19.1 refers to such exceptional events or circumstances. This means an event or circumstance:

(a) Which is beyond a Party's control
(b) Which such Party could not reasonably have provided against before entering into the Contract
(c) Which, having arisen, such Party could not reasonably have avoided or overcome
(d) Which is not substantially attributable to the other Party

In so far non performance is excused without reference to the term of unforeseeability. Thus even though a Force Majeure event may be foreseeable in the sense of Sub-Clause 1.1.6.8, FIDIC excuses non performance if the event is beyond the control of the parties and none of them could reasonably have avoided or overcome it. This mirrors that there is a difference between those events and circumstances which can be overcome and avoided and those which are inevitable. However, if they are avoidable the question remains whether it is reasonable to put the burden of the risk on the Contractor or on the Employer. In principle the parties should bear the risk which they can best overcome and handle. If none of the parties can overcome or handle it, the risk becomes partially mitigated according to Clause 19. If the parties can overcome and handle it, the question arises again which of the parties should make allowance for it.

It is worthy to note that there is duty of mitigation according to Sub-Clause 19.3. Both parties shall use all reasonable endeavours to minimise any delay in the performance of the Contract as a result of Force Majeure. This must be read in conjunction with Sub-Clause 8.3 and the early warning rule contained therein.

References

Abrahamson M (1984) Risk management. ICLR 2:241
Bailey J (2007) What lies beneath. ICLR 394
ITIG (2006) Code of practise for risk management of tunnel works. The International Tunnelling Insurance Group
Mütze M, Senff T, Möller JC (2007) Real estate investments in Germany. Springer, Berlin
Totterdill BW (2006) FIDIC user's guide, 2nd edn. Thomas Telford, London

Chapter 20
Bonds, Guarantees, Letters of Credit

20.1 Introduction

In international commercial affairs it is quite common to use special forms of securities in order to ensure payment or performance of contracts. Most international real estate sales, developments contracts and electrical and mechanical plant projects are accompanied by the issue of such securities. Being familiar with all forms of bank securities is an essential requirement of international business. Strictly defined a security is an interest in property which secures the performance of an obligation to pay, to undertake something or to refrain from doing something. In the international context all three kinds of securities appear, including:

- A security, which ensures the repayment of a loan or advance payment or simply a security ensuring payment of the agreed price for services or delivery of goods
- A security, which secures that a bidder does not revoke his offer until the submission date
- A security by which performance of the works is guaranteed

Usually a bank or financial institution is involved in such kind of transactions. By consequence trade finance transactions usually create a tripartite relationship between the parties to a main contract, for example a construction contract for works between the employer and the contractor, for which a bank may grant security.

Once again the comparison between the English way of life and the one in civil law countries leads into difficulties. Whereas in common law countries contractual freedom is the rule, civil law countries provide a number of types of legal securities which can not be ignored in international practice. Whenever a debtor owes money to a creditor, the question arises how payment of the debt can be ensured. Everywhere in the world usually a third party, the guarantor, promises to pay the debt of the main debtor to the creditor, if the main debtor is unable or unwilling to pay the main debt by himself. The difference is the way in which such kind of transaction is ruled.

A.-V. Jaeger and G.-S. Hök, *FIDIC-A Guide for Practitioners*,
DOI 10.1007/978-3-642-02100-8_20, © Springer-Verlag Berlin Heidelberg 2010

20.2   Civil Law Security Types

Under French or German law the contract by which the guarantor undertakes it to pay the debt of the main debtor is ruled by law (sect. 765 et seq. German Civil Code, art. 2288 et seq. Code Civil). The main and common feature of a German *Bürgschaft* and a French "cautionnement" is that it is said "accessory" (sect. 767 German Civil Code; Art. 2289, 2290 Code Civil), which means that its origin, its existence and its discharge totally depends upon the main debt. This distinguishes the German *Bürgschaft* and a French "cautionnement" from other tangible securities such as the guarantee (German and French: *Garantie*). The consequences of the accessory principle are *as* follows. Any modification of the main debt, caused for example by delay or breach of contract, has a direct impact on the *Bürgschaft*. Discharge of the main debt is followed by discharge of the *Bürgschaft* or *cautionnement*. The accessory principle *also applies to* the *assignment* of the main debt from the creditor to a fourth party. By way of the assignment of the main debt, the *Bürgschaft* like all other accessory securities, is automatically transferred to the new creditor (sect. 412, 401 German Civil Code). On the other hand this leads to the conclusion that the guarantor can use defences arising from the main contract, such as retention rights and non-performance by the main debtor, in order to defend himself against the creditor, even if the main debtor has waived these defences (sect. 768 ph. 2 German Civil Code).

The difference between a guarantee and a Bürgschaft is that unlike the *Bürgschaft* the guarantee (German and French: *Garantie)* is completely independent from the main debt. The *Garantie* is not accessory in the above mentioned sense. However, *Bürgschaft* and *Garantie* have in common to secure the performance of the main debtor if he fails to perform, which is the difference between these instruments and the third type of personal security, the *kumulativer Schuldbeitritt*, which is the entry of a third party in the main contract as a joint debtor. In both countries, Germany and France, the guarantee has traditionally not been ruled by law as a special type of security. The French legislator however has recently set in force a set of rules concerning the independent guarantee. According to art. 2321 Civil Code an independent guarantee is an undertaking by which the guarantor binds himself, in consideration of a debt subscribed by a third party, to pay a sum either on first demand or subject to terms agreed upon. It is independent because a guarantor may set up no defence depending on the guaranteed obligation. Unless otherwise agreed, that security does not follow the guaranteed obligation. There is only one defence against the beneficiary of an independent guarantee. According to the law a guarantor is not bound in case of patent abuse or fraud of the beneficiary or of collusion of the latter with the principal.

20.3   Common Law Types

In common law guarantees (sometimes also known as bonds) are the undertaking of a third party, which is usually a bank, to pay a beneficiary, independent of the underlying contract (main or principal contract) between the customer of the bank (principal obligor) and the beneficiary. In compliance with the terms and conditions of the guarantee the bank is to pay beneficiary. It depends on the terms of the guarantee whether it is an on demand guarantee or a conditional guarantee. There are different classes of guarantees:

- On demand guarantees or bond
- Conditional guarantees or bond
- Conditional on-default guarantee or bond

The on demand guarantee (or bond), in the strictest sense, is a deed which is independent of the underlying contract, for example a construction contract. On demand guarantees, which overseas beneficiaries often insist on, can be called whenever the beneficiary presents a written demand.

A conditional guarantee can be called accompanied by a written statement in good faith, that damages have arisen under the underlying contract, for example the construction contract. Thus the client, subject to issues of fraud, needs only to comply with the formalities and procedures stated in the bond for the draft call to be valid.

A conditional on default guarantee, which is commonly also referred to as a performance guarantee, finally, creates a secondary liability which is dependent upon the contractor's liability. A valid draft on the guarantee can only be made once such liability arises. Thus a valid draft call must show some default by the other party of the underlying contract.

The distinction between the different forms of guarantees and bonds is critical, but not always easy to make and often leads to time consuming discussions. Depending on the nature of a guarantee or bond the range of defences of the guarantor can be broad or narrow. Independent on demand guarantees exclude any form of defence.

In some common law jurisdictions so called Standby Letters of Credit (Standby L/Cs) are often used instead of guarantees and bonds, which cover more or less the same classes and number of different transactions than guarantees and bonds.

20.4 Letters of Credit

A further instrument has to be shortly discussed which combines payment security with the payment function of the instrument. This form of security is usually referred to as *letter of credit*. Letter of Credit is abbreviated as an *LC* or *L/C*, and often is referred to as a *documentary credit*, abbreviated as *DC or D/C*, *documentary letter of credit*, or simply as *credit* (as in the ICC UCP 500 and UCP 600). The UCP 500 or 600 will usually be incorporated into the letter of credit by reference. The most secure form of a letter of credit is an irrevocable, divisible, negotiable and on demand letter of credit. It should contain a clause for prolongation of the expiry date, in particular for development projects, where time for completion is often subject to extension for reasons which are not attributable to the contractor.

In the majority of cases a *letter of credit* is a document issued by a financial institution which usually provides a payment undertaking to a beneficiary against presentation of complying documents as stated in the letter of credit. In practice a second bank, which is the home bank of the beneficiary, often issues a confirmation upon the letter of credit, which ensures direct payment out of the letter of credit in the home country of the exporting company. Confirmation by a home bank is essential, if the issuing bank comes from a country where the export of currencies is subject to control and prior permission or approval.

On request to the issuing bank or confirming bank, if any, within the expiry date of the LC, accompanied by complying documents, the issuing bank or confirming bank, if any, shall honour irrespective of any instructions from the applicant to the contrary. A basic principle is that a bank's undertaking on a letter of credit is separate from any underlying contract. Consequently the bank's undertaking is not subject to any defence which is not mentioned in the letter itself. Therefore care and diligence has to be taken when drafting the conditions under which drafts can be called. In international development affairs it is for example critical to specify the documents to be issued by either the employer or a so called certifier or engineer which have to be presented to the issuing bank.

20.5   FIDIC

FIDIC users will find a complete set of guarantee forms in each FIDIC book.

20.5.1   Performance Security

Subject to Sub-Clause 4.2 the Contractor has to provide a Performance Security, either as a Performance Bond (Annex D) or as an on Demand Guarantee (Annex C). The intention behind this security is to have the financial responsibility of the surety standing behind the contractor's completion obligations. However, not all performance securities are created equal. Some bonds (i.e. "completion securities") require that the surety for the defaulted contractor must complete the work. Other securities (i.e. "indemnity securities") simply require that the surety indemnify the party exercising a termination right for all costs flowing from the contractor default. Other security forms are woefully silent on exactly what is expected of the performance bond surety in the event of a default. Thus it is critical to pay as much attention to the language of the performance bond as to the language of any significant contract. The FIDIC model forms of securities require that the surety indemnify the employer for the consequences of default or breach of contract. Sub-Clause 4.2 clearly states the conditions under which the Employer is entitled to make a claim under the Performance Security.

In accordance with Sub-Clause 4.2 the Employer is entitled to call the Performance Security in the event of:

(a) Failure by the Contractor to extend the validity of the Performance Security as described in the preceding paragraph, in which event the Employer may claim the full amount of the Performance Security

(b) Failure by the Contractor to pay the Employer an amount due, as either agreed by the Contractor or determined under Sub-Clause 2.5 [*Employer's Claims*] or Clause 20 [*Claims, Disputes and Arbitration*], within 42 days after this agreement or determination

(c) Failure by the Contractor to remedy a default within 42 days after receiving the Employer's notice requiring the default to be remedied

(d) Circumstances which entitle the Employer to termination under Sub-Clause 15.2 [*Termination by Employer*], irrespective of whether notice of termination has been given

Any claim by the Employer under the Performance Security must follow the procedures of Sub-Clause 2.5. It is worth to note that, in some jurisdictions, the law may limit the Performance Security surety's liability with respect to certain types of damages. For example, in Florida, a performance bond ordinarily will not cover delay damages, unless the bond, on its face, identifies delay damages as within the scope of the bond's protection. In *Larkin*,[1] the Florida Supreme Court held that a performance bond surety could not be held liable for delay damages due to a contractor's default absent language in the bond specifically providing coverage for delay damages. Thus it is critical to carefully scrutinise the extent of liability under the Performance Security, in particular because Sub-Clause 4.2 includes an indemnity to the Contractor if the Employer was not entitled to make the claim.

20.5.2   Advance Payment Security

Subject to Sub-Clause 14.2 the Contractor is obliged to submit a guarantee in accordance with the Sub-Clause, if an advance payment has been agreed. Unless the Employer receives this guarantee, Sub-Clause 14.2 shall not apply. A model form for an Advance Payment Guarantee is included in each FIDIC book (see Annex E). The Advance Payment Guarantee shall be maintained until full and complete reimbursement of the advance payment. It is worth to note that the repayment of the advance payment will start when the certified interim payments exceed 10% of the Accepted Contract Amount. The reimbursement rate shall be 25% of the amount of each Payment Certificate. The Guidance for the Preparation of the Particular Conditions states that these figures were calculated on the assumption that the total advance payment is less than 22% of the Accepted Contract Amount. Any outstanding balance will immediately become due on the issue of the Taking-Over Certificate for the Works or prior to termination under Clauses 15, 16 or 19.

---

[1] American Home Assurance Co v. Larkin General Hospital, 593 So.2d 195 (Fla. 1992).

20.6   Conclusion

From a lawyer's point of view, the differences between civil law and common law are not as big as it could be envisaged. The main difference is probably that civil law courts usually will attempt to construe any tangible security as a *Bürgschaft* or *cautionnement* (suretyship), if and when the wording of the security shows any lien between the main debt and the security (principle of strict accessory). In practice in both jurisdictions care has to be taken when drafting a security. Were one instructed to do so, it would be helpful to rely on international standards, which make sure that the appropriate and envisaged form of security becomes issued. In practice it is common to refer to the available ICC standards, such as:

- Demand Guarantees become issued under the *Uniform Rules for Demand Guarantees* (URDG) as set out in International Chamber of Commerce (ICC) publication 458.
- Documentary credits are usually based on *Uniform Customs and Practices for Documentary Credits,* also referred to as *Letters of Credit* (ICC Publication 600).
- Standby letters of credit are governed by *International Standby Practices ISP98* (ICC publication 590).
- *Uniform Rules for Contract Bonds* (ICC publication 524) govern "accessory" guarantees.
- *Uniform Rules for Contract Guarantees* (ICC publication 325) have been published for guarantees of a hybrid nature which combine characteristics of independent undertakings and accessory undertaking.

It is submitted to note that *The United Nations Convention on Independent Guarantees and Stand-By Letters of Credit*, which applies to demand guarantees, in fact comprises legislative rules, primary aimed at adoption by individual states. The Convention does not offer any contractual rules to be chosen by the parties to a particular guarantee or counter-guarantee.

In any case a bond is a contract, and, therefore, a bond (or Performance Security) is subject to the general law of contracts.[2] The intent of the parties to the contract should govern the construction of a contract.[3] To determine the intent of the parties, a court should consider the language in the contract, the subject matter of the contract, and the object and purpose of the contract.[4] In Crabtree, the court held that a surety on a bond does not undertake to do more than that expressed in the bond, and has the right to stand upon the strict terms of the obligation as to his liability thereon.[5]

---

[2] Crabtree v. Aetna Cas & Sur Co, 438 So.2d 102 (Fla. 1st DCA 1983).

[3] Underwood v. Underwood, 64 So.2d 281 (Fla. 1953).

[4] Clark v. Clark, 79 So.2d 426 (Fla. 1955).

[5] Crabtree v. Aetna Cas & Sur Co, 438 So.2d 102 at 105 (Fla. 1st DCA 1983).

Chapter 21
Claim Management

21.1 Introduction

The term "Claim" is not a defined term in the FIDIC books, despite it being regularly used by FIDIC. However this is only half the truth. Pursuant to Sect. 194 German Civil Code "claim" means the right to require another person to do or to refrain from doing an act. According to Mr. Bunni a claim means an assertion of a right to money, property, or to a remedy (Bunni 2005, p. 293). Thus in a FIDIC contract the term claim means something in between the mere assertion for additional monies or for extension of Time for Completion and an actual entitlement to additional monies or for extension of Time for Completion. A claim arising out of or in connection with the Contract relates to a remedy which is not designated in the Contract. It may arise out of the proper law of the contract (for example a remedy for breach of contract). Also it may have its legal basis in the applicable tort law (for example in the event of misrepresentation) or it may arise out of the principles of unjust enrichment or out of quantum meruit. FIDIC does not deal with such claims. However it also does not limit or exclude reliance on extra contractual claims based in law.

The focus of FIDIC lies in two other fields. FIDIC forms of contract include a fair risk allocation. As a result of the risk apportionment claims have been designated in the Contract. Also FIDIC gives clear guidelines for the prosecution of claims arising out of, and in connection with the Contract (Fig. 21.1).

However, Contractors most notably will consider FIDIC claim procedures to be somewhat burdensome and sometimes unfair as they impose tough obligations upon the Contractor to give notice and subsequently provide particulars where something for which the Contractor is not responsible has caused, or is likely to cause, cost or delay. It is true to say that the Contractor's entitlement to an extension of Time for Completion or additional payment is conditional upon its compliance with the claim requirements, such a requirement being known as a "condition precedent". Thus non compliance with claim requirements leads to the lapse of the claim, even though the Employer is obviously aware of the fact that he has

A.-V. Jaeger and G.-S. Hök, *FIDIC-A Guide for Practitioners*,
DOI 10.1007/978-3-642-02100-8_21, © Springer-Verlag Berlin Heidelberg 2010

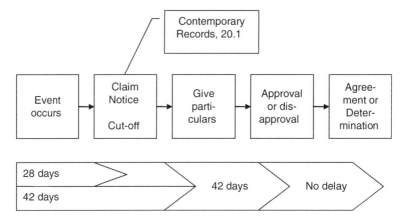

Fig. 21.1 Gold Book claim procedure I

caused disruption and additional cost. The traditional common law position as to notice requirements is that:[1]

> If the Builder, having a right to claim an extension of time fails to do so, it cannot claim that the act of prevention which would have entitled it to an extension of time for Practical Completion resulted in its inability to complete by that time. A party to a contract cannot rely upon preventing the contract of the other party where it failed to exercise a contractual right which would have negated the effect of that preventing conduct.

The legal basis for a more Contractor friendly position is the Australian decision in Gaymark v. Walter Construction Group,[2] where it was held that strict compliance with notice requirements "would result in an entirely unmeritorious award of liquidated damages for delays of its own making". The court continued to say, that "in the absence of such strict compliance there is no provision for an extension of time ..." allowing for extension of Time for Completion. The court then concluded that this would constitute time at large, which meant that the entitlement of the Employer to delay damages was lapsed. In Multiplex v. Honeywell the court rejected these arguments.[3] HHJ Jackson obiter said:

> Contractual terms requiring a contractor to give prompt notice of delay serve a valuable purpose; such notice enables matters to be investigated while they are still current. Furthermore, such notice sometimes gives the employer the opportunity to withdraw

---

[1] Turner Corporation Ltd (Receiver and Manager Appointed) v. Austotel Pty Ltd (2 June 1994); (1997) 13 BCL 378 at 12 by Cole J.

[2] Gaymark Investments Pty Ltd v. Walter Construction Group Ltd [1999] NTSC 143; (2005) 21 Const LJ 71.

[3] Multiplex Constructions (UK) Ltd. v. Honeywell Control Systems Ltd [2007] EWHC 447 (TCC), confirmed by Steria Ltd v. Sigma Wireless Communications Ltd [2007] EWHC 3454 (TCC) (15 November 2007).

instructions when the financial consequences become apparent. If *Gaymark* is good law, then a contractor could disregard with impunity any provision making proper notice a condition precedent. At his option the contractor could set time at large.

Under FIDIC terms of contract it should be taken in account that the claim procedures are part of a balanced risk allocation. One reason for time bars and other procedural restrictions lies in the fact that a claim notice enables matters to be investigated while they are contemporary. A second reason is that it gives the Engineer the opportunity to withdraw or to give instructions when the financial and timely consequences of a claim event become apparent. Also a determination can be made without undue delay. This leads to certainty and avoids prolonged disputes at the end of the project.

Incidentally, similar restrictions may be found in the French General Conditions for works referred to as AF P 03-001, according to which the Contractor may be entitled to additional payment if he carries out additional work which is technically justified or work which is urgent, if he gives notice of it on the same day. This seems to be a valid clause under French law,[4] although the French Cour de Cassation has also held that the Conditions AFNOR do not override art. 1793 French Civil Code.[5] Also the German Sect. 2 no. 6 of the General Terms and Conditions for the Execution of Public Work Contracts (VOB/B) includes a provision which imposes on the Contractor the duty to give notice of any additional work which was not within the scope of the works before he starts working. German courts have held that the notice requirement constitutes a condition precedent of a claim.[6]

Before entering into a more detailed discussion of claims and claim procedures it is worth to explain the concept of working:

1. Claim management is partially legal work

- Lawyers are used to think in actions.
- A cause of action (also referred to as a claim) is divided into discrete elements, all of which must be alleged and proved to present a winning case:

  - A cause of action generally encompasses both the legal theory (e.g. a contract providing for payment or the legal wrong the plaintiff claims to have suffered or other forms of breach of contract by the Contractor) and the remedy (the relief a court is asked to grant, e.g. payment of the Contract Price or damages).

Example: The Contractor considers to be entitled to additional payment because he encountered adverse physical conditions. According to Sub-Clause 4.12 the cause of action consists of the following elements: (1) Unforeseeable physical conditions, (2) notice of it, (3) claim notice in accordance with Sub-Clause 20.1, (4) the Contractor incurred additional Cost. The remedy is: payment of Cost.

---

[4]Cour de Cassation, 15.11.1972, Bull.civ. III no. 611, file number 71-11.651.

[5]Cour de Cassation, 11.05.2006, file number 04-18.092.

[6]BGH [1996] BauR 542; OLG Düsseldorf [1989] BauR 483, 485.

2. Identify a cause of action

- A cause of action is the legal ground or claim with which a party can file a lawsuit to find remedy or satisfaction of his claim:
- In other words there must be a legal relationship in between the appellant and the defendant creating a cause of action, which implies the right to bring a legal action.
- The legal work consists in:

    – Identifying a remedy to be sought and the related cause of action.
    – Ascertaining the set of facts sufficient to justify the identified right to sue.

- Beware: It is often the case that the facts or circumstances that entitle a person to seek judicial relief may create multiple causes of action!
- Beware: Procedural rules, such as Sub-Clause 20.1, do not constitute a cause of action and belong to the elements, all of which must be alleged and proved to present a winning case!

Example: The Contractor considers to be entitled to additional payment because he encountered adverse physical conditions. He identifies two causes of action: Sub-Clause 4.12 and misrepresentation.

3. Step-by-step approach

- Identify the event which causes cost and/or delay (Identification of the problem)
- Search for a legal or contractual cause of action:

    – Take in consideration all of the relevant and probably relevant causes of actions

- Test: Ask whether the event or circumstances meet the requirements of each cause of action/or at least of one cause of action
- Identify those claims which may have a legal background as a result of the previous test
- Check complaints or objections (defences) of the other party and own misbehaviour:

    – Beware that all defences are allowed!

This means: If the Contractor incurs for example cost or suffers a delay as a result of unforeseeable physical conditions, he should firstly identify the relevant Sub-Clause, which is Sub-Clause 4.12. Sub-Clause 4.12 is relevant because it entitles the Contractor to extension of time and additional costs. The test is then, whether the Contractor encountered Unforeseeable physical conditions. All elements of Sub-Clause 4.12 must be met, which are:

- Physical conditions (climatic conditions are not covered)
- Relevant physical conditions must have been Unforeseeable (Unforeseeable is a defined term)
- Previous notice is required, which should have been given as soon as practicable

- Claim notice is required according to Sub-Clause 20.1 and 1.3
- Review of other physical conditions in similar parts of the Works is required
- Cost is a defined term (Sub-Clause 1.1.4.3)
- As to EOT Sub-Clause 8.4 must be taken in account

Example: Unforeseeable physical conditions

If all claim requirements or elements are met the Engineer shall make a fair determination in accordance with Sub-Clause 3.5. By doing so he will take due regard to all relevant circumstances including any arguments and objections of the Employer. The Employer may present various arguments and objections, such as but not limited to:

- The relevant activity does not lie on the critical path (no EOT).
- The relevant circumstances were subject of a previous determination.
- The claim notice was late.
- The preliminary notice was late.
- An experienced Contractor could have foreseen the encountered physical conditions.
- etc.

21.2   Procedural Rules

As has been confirmed by Judge Sanders in *Attorney General for the Falkland Islands v. Gordon Forbes Construction (Falklands) Ltd*, Falkland Islands Supreme Court 14 March 2003,[7] FIDIC contracts are aimed at the early resolution of any queries at the time when the claim arises, with the likelihood that plant, manpower and witnesses are still on site. Thus claims have to be pursued in a detailed procedure provided by the FIDIC contracts.

Sample: Early warning notice
To Engineer, if a future probable event or circumstance occurs
This letter is suitable for use with all FIDIC Books
Dear Sir,
We give notice of a future probable event or circumstance, which may adversely affect the work, increase the Contract price or delay the execution of the Works. We draw your attention to [*describe the circumstances or event*].
This notice is issued in accordance with Sub-Clause 8.3.
Yours faithfully

Sometimes the Contractor becomes aware of a probable future event or circumstance which may adversely affect the work, increase the Contract Price or delay

---

[7][2003] BLR 280.

Example : Unforeseeable physical conditions

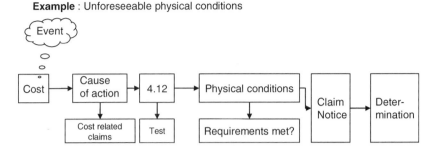

Fig. 21.2 Claims' procedure I

the execution of the Works. If so, he shall promptly give notice of such an event or circumstance. Such a notice is also known as a early warning.

If the Contractor considers himself to be entitled to a claim, the first step is for him to give notice (Sub-Clause 20.1) in accordance with Sub-Clause 1.3 (Fig. 21.2). This notice is important because:

• Everyone involved becomes aware that there is an event or circumstance where extra time or payment may be owed to the Contractor.
• Proper contemporary records must then be kept and agreed, to avoid future argument.
• Alternative measures may also be possible to reduce the effects.
• The matter may possibly be resolved at an early date.
• If the event or circumstance turns out to be of insignificant effect, then it is not necessary to follow up the notice with a formal claim.

As a rule claims related to extension of time and of additional payment under any clause of the contract or otherwise in connection with the contract must be notified within a delay of 28 days. Beware that Sub-Clause 19.2 provides a shorter period of 14 days in the event of Force Majeure circumstances. Within this delay a first notice shall be given. In any case the Contractor must provide to Employer's Engineer written notice of the claim for additional payment and time extension within 28 days after becoming aware of the occurrence of the event giving rise to claim (Sub-Clause 20.1). If the Contractor fails to comply with this notice requirement, his entitlement to the claim shall lapse.

The Claim notice must indicate basic details, in order to inform the Engineer about the scope of the claim and to enable him to give instructions, if necessary. The notice shall therefore meet the following requirements:

• It shall describe the event or circumstance in order to enable the Engineer to put the issue on record and to take measures, but also in order to enable the Engineer to investigate the matter while it is current.
• However, the notice need not state time or amount claimed or contractual basis of claim.

- It shall comply with Sub-Clause 1.3, i.e. in writing and properly delivered.
- It shall be included in the progress reports – Sub-Clause 4.21(f) – the report must list notices given.

There is no immediate response required from the Engineer (Employer) – but a simple acknowledgement is normal.

To the extent that a third party to the contract, the Engineer, has been nominated to determine claims, the parties to the contract shall notify him of any claims to which they consider themselves to be entitled to . He is then in charge of firstly approving or disapproving any claim and to determine it, if necessary. He shall do this with regard to all circumstances, which means that he will have to take into consideration all facts:

- Reported in the monthly reports
- Reported in contemporary records
- Reported in labour reports
- Stated in the claim notification
- Obtained at site visits and inspections
- Reported in early warning notifications concerning probable future events which may effect progress of the works and the contract price
- Reported in the Programme

In order to ensure that the parties and the Engineer may reach reasonable, informed, and skilful decisions, FIDIC contracts provide a sophisticated system for communications and documentation of relevant facts, events and circumstances. This system and the resulting duties as to documentation and reporting have to be recognised and respected at all times, because Judge Sanders also concluded in the Falkland case that it would be perverse if a contractor who had failed to comply with the terms of the contract should then be allowed to produce non-contemporary records to support a claim, particularly as these could not properly be investigated by the employer at a later date. The rights of the employer to inspect the records at the time the claim arose were fundamental to the FIDIC procedure. Failure to comply with the reporting duties leads to the foreclosure of claims.

By notice of a claim the claim determination procedure becomes initiated, which is described in Sub-Clause 3.5. According to Sub-Clause 3.5 and 20.1 the following shall happen:

- Contemporary records shall be kept which may be inspected by the Engineer
- A fully detailed claim must be submitted within 42 days of the event (or other agreed time)
- Provision for continuing claims and submittal of their details
- Within 42 days of receiving the claim with details the Engineer shall respond with approval, or with disapproval and detailed comments.
- The Engineer shall determine under *Sub-Clause 3.5* any time extension or additional payment to which the Contractor is entitled under the Contract.

- Each payment certificate shall include such amounts for any claim as have been reasonably substantiated.
- Any other specified requirements must also be satisfied (see Sub-Clause 19.2)

The Engineer may request any necessary further particulars, but shall nevertheless give his response on the principles of the claim within 42 days. Thus there is a time limit imposed on the Engineer to reply to a claim.

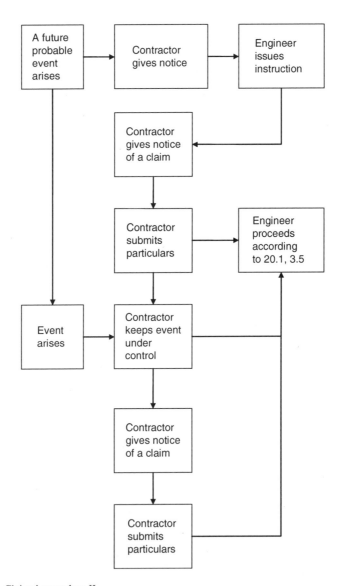

Fig. 21.3 Claims' procedure II

Once having approved or disapproved a claim the Engineer shall attempt to reach an amicable settlement. If he fails to reach an agreement he is obliged and entitled to determine the claim. Any determination issued by the Engineer will be binding on the parties until revised by DAB or arbitration. Any agreement or determination must be notified to the parties. It is suggested that any settlement which failed to become notified according to Sub-Clause 3.5 is not yet valid, even though the settlement was signed. Otherwise the danger arises that the Engineer will have no knowledge about the settlement. Moreover the notification requirement ensures that the day of validity of the settlement can be clearly identified. Each party shall give effect to each agreement or determination unless and until revised under Clause 20. Thus the date from which any agreement is binding must be clear (Fig. 21.3).

21.3 Claim Review and Preparation

Contractual claims arise where contractors consider that they are entitled to additional payments over and above those which are already included in the accepted contract amount or to extension of the already agreed time for completion. Claims should not be confused with the consequences of any Variation. Variations must be dealt with separately, although in principle Variations will also result in a determination subject to Sub-Clause 3.5 by the Engineer or Employer as the case may be.

Such kind of monetary claims are part of the Contract Price and therefore anticipated costs. However the entitlement to additional payment is usually subject to the condition that a formal claim is presented within the time limits provided by the contract. But despite this fact the parties have already agreed to additional payments at the date of the conclusion of the contract. Thus claims are nothing more than the crystallisation of an anticipated, not yet specified, part of the Contract Price.

In principle the agreed Time for Completion is open for extension claims, because nobody can anticipate what will happen during the whole course of the works. To the extent that the contract provides claims for time extension the parties have agreed in advance the possibility of extending time for completion. If an event occurs which entitles the contractor to submit a claim for time extension, his claim crystallises anticipated but not yet identified and specified additional time for completion.

In this sense claims are nothing more than a legal feature or mode by which the parties to a contract attempt to crystallise the final contract price and time for completion. However they have to be presented under the procedural rules provided by the contract, which makes it sometimes difficult to pursue the claim. The reason why claims have to be presented in a special way lies in the word crystallisation. Crystallisation means that the parties have to show the claim, to make it obvious that a claim exists. This does not yet explain why claims are often time barred. The reason for this lies in the necessity to bring evidence and the need of the employer to make the necessary financial arrangements. Thus claim management is nothing arbitrary or superfluous. It is the process within which claims must be crystallised.

Claim identification and initiation followed by claim preparation, submission and negotiation are critical issues, in particular because parties to a contract must usually comply with claim procedures and delays. In a construction contract of any complexity, the conditions are the hub or engine room of a contractual wheel or vessel comprising a myriad of documents and contractual provisions. The conditions give life to, and allow to be focused and co-ordinated, the contract documents and the obligations that those documents give rise to.[8] Claims may arise at all times until completion of the works and even later. Handling of claims may require management, technical and economic skills and experiences during the whole contract period. However academic research (Vidogah and Ndekugri 1998, pp. 363–372) has shown that:

- Claims management is still performed in an ad hoc manner.
- Contractors' management information systems are ill designed to support claims.
- The products of basic good management practice, such as diaries, timesheets, and programmes, often are inadequate in content even if available.
- Some aspects of claims are impossible to quantify with precision even with the best information available at reasonable cost.

It is thus fundamental to establish an effective and continuous claim management for the site, which must be enabled to identify, initiate, prepare, submit and negotiate claims of all kind and matter. Researching and preparing claims is a complex process based on information which must be collected, managed and if necessary shared with others. It is strongly recommended to start preparing claims registers and collating relevant information, documents, data and facts from day one of the project, which means from the day of the date of receipt of the tender invitation, because claim relevant events may even arise before the submission date which are no more relevant for the tender but which may affect cost and time for completion.

However, claim management is more than merely collating facts. All relevant information must be scrutinised, assessed, evaluated and technically checked. Relevant information may influence not only the progress and sequence of the works but also cost and profit. All decisions must be taken on a daily basis, which means that the programme and calculation have to be updated in a timely manner. This requires for all information obtained by the contract manager to be checked very quickly and reliably. At the end of this process a report on each event must be established which, if necessary will be also the document based on which a claim must be submitted to the other party. This process may involve engineers, technical experts, designers, lawyers, architects and quantity surveyors reviewing the facts as described above. This requires the formation of a management team and the

---

[8] Joinery Plus Ltd v. Laing Ltd [2003] EWHC 213 (TCC) (15 January 2003).

development of a systematic approach to the management issues in order to ensure that the team will be capable of building up a picture of the claim event supported by records, reports, expertises, measurements and calculations. The claim justification data developed from this process will substantiate the claim and assist the contractor, engineer and the employer in their efforts to understand and decide on the cause, effect and quantum of the claim.

Note the following aspects of this typical wording in FIDIC Books (see Booen 2001):

- "the Contractor shall give notice . . .": which is obligatory, but a failure to notify may be due to him not having suffered delay and not having incurred Cost.
- "the Contractor . . . shall be entitled . . .": which is not stated as being subject to anyone's opinion.
- "Subject to Sub-Clause 20.1 . . .": the second and the final paragraphs of which may affect the Contractor's entitlements.
- "An extension . . . if completion is . . . delayed . . .": so it should be calculated by reference to the delay in completion. Sub-Clause 10.1(i) defines the extent of work to be completed within the Time for Completion, which must include the matters described in sub-paragraphs (a) and (b) of Sub-Clause 8.2 but may exclude minor outstanding work and defects which will not substantially affect use for the intended purpose, as permitted in Sub-Clause 10.1(a).
- "Payment of any such Cost . . .": which is the Cost attributable to the event or circumstance, excluding Costs which are not attributable thereto.
- "Plus reasonable profit . . .": this phrase is included in Sub-Clauses which relate to failure by (or on behalf of) the Employer, and not to other risks.

Beware that claims exist either under the conditions of the contract or alternatively are based at law. There is no such thing as an extra-contractual claim. The Engineer (FIDIC), Supervisor (DC4), Project Manager (NEC3) or certifier has no power to grant "ex gratia" payments. Despite this, this type of claim is sometimes used and useful to draw the attention of the employer and/or the engineer to the fact that additional payments are required without any contractual background. Although this may be a waste of time, because the Engineer is not allowed to grant payments without any relevant claim basis, it introduces a bargaining factor for use in future negotiations concerning payment. Moreover it may at times be wise to grant an ex gratia payment in order to avoid time-consuming disputes and to support a contractor who otherwise may fail to complete the works for economical reasons. Ex gratia payments may be done without admission of liability.

It is a fundamental feature of FIDIC forms of contract that all claims as to additional payment and extension of Time for Completion are subject to determination by the Engineer (or the Employer). Under civil law this may lead to complicated discussions. In France it has been held that a clause according to which the involved architect was vested to settle disputes is null and void.[9] It is

---

[9] Cour de Cassation (commerciale), 09.03.1965, Bull.civ. IV no. 175.

therefore extremely important to understand the role of the Engineer as defined by Clause 3 FIDIC. Although a claim only crystallizes through a determination by the Engineer the claim itself already exists whether at law or by virtue of the contract. The Engineer's power is not at all conclusive and subject to further control by the DAB and arbitration.

Hence claim review and preparation involves a complex task which must be structured and managed. The claim manager or claim management team should have clear competences and follow a road map, including but not limited to:

First Step: Data collecting

- Gather and identify all contractual, legal and management requirements as to the documentation and necessary evidence of claims, such as:

  - Reporting requirements (Sub-Clause 20.1)
  - Communication requirements, e.g. notices (Sub-Clauses 1.3, 8.3)
  - Record filing requirements
  - Early warning proceedings (Sub-Clause 8.3)
  - Evidence rules
  - Programming requirements (Sub-Clause 8.3)
  - Assessment standards
  - Notification requirements and delays (Sub-Clause 20.1)
  - Cut off periods

Second step: Claim identification

- Thoroughly study the whole contract documentation (including Specifications, BoQ, Employer's Requirements) in order to identify all possible claims and its conditions, including Variation probabilities
- Carefully gather all complementary legal claims and their conditions
- Extract and record from documentation the data relevant to each claim situation
- Establish manuals for standard situations

Third step: Communication system

- Establish an early warning system as to facts which may adversely affect the work, increase the Contract Price or delay the execution of the works
- Beware that claims must usually be notified after the Contractor should have become aware of it
- Review on a daily basis actual progress compared with the programme
- Submit a revised programme if necessary having regard to all relevant circumstances, including critical path issues for probable future events

Fourth step: Claim assessment

- Establish a claim relevance check system (arguable case system), ensuring that all incoming data, information, documents, instructions, approvals, drawings, etc., will be checked as to their claim relevance (claim warning system)

- Establish internal communication systems and ensure that all members of the claim management team become involved, including decision makers
- Establish a review system for claim relevant information, data, instructions, etc., ensuring that the influence on time, cost and profit will be carefully and reliably estimated and that all necessary steps will be initiated to overcome the situation by other means than a claim. This will probably include technical and economic considerations and efforts to reduce the claim relevance of the given event or circumstance.
- Check any probable claim situation against the contractual and legal background

Fifth step: Managing claims

- Ensure that identified claims will be carefully managed and reported from the day of the date of receipt of the relevant information and the any notification delay will be surveyed from now on
- Keep contemporary records (Sub-Clause 20.1)
- Prepare cost analysis, including but not limited to a comparison of actual working hours against hours included in tender in relation to total project, identification of overtime hours, identification of plant, equipment, overhead and direct costs compared against tender estimates and determine cause of delay and related extra costs
- Review critical path and analyse changes on the critical path and the impact of the claim relevant information on the critical path, identify concurrent delay
- Determine and assess risk allocation and related responsibility and liability for delay and/or extra cost
- Prepare calculations including:

  - A comparison of delay damages and acceleration cost
  - An analysis of costs of disruption
  - Determination of costs of all changes
  - Determination of costs caused by prolongation of time for completion, including overheads, liquidated damages, etc.
  - Determination of loss of interest on capital used due to delay, disruption, additional work, late payment, etc.
  - Determination of eventual design costs

- Prepare claim documents, including but not limited to

  - Contract documents, Particular and General Conditions, Proposals, Requirements
  - Specifications
  - Drawings
  - Relevant communications
  - Photographs
  - Schedules
  - Previous Dispute Adjudication Board decisions

- Previous claim determinations and instructions
- Previous claim settlements
- Bills of quantities
- Calculations
- Cost analysis

Sixth step: Claim prosecution

- Notify each identified claim according to the requirements of the contract (Sub-Clause 20.1) with summary of the claim containing a brief description of the factual basis of the claim and (if possible) the amount sought, make sure that the claim can be identified and distinguished from parallel and previous claims; make sure that the claim has a cause of action
- Update the programme, if necessary
- Substantiate the claim according to the requirements of the contract with quantum calculation, entitlement analysis, a chronology of events and communication presented in a table format indicating:

  - When the event or circumstance giving rise to the claim became aware or should have become aware
  - When the claim work was reported
  - When the claim work was started
  - When the claim work was completed
  - Working hours
  - Which material has been used
  - Which personnel has been used

Seventh step: Claim procedure

- Wait for approval or disapproval of the claim (Sub-Clause 20.1)
- Start negotiations with endeavour to reach agreement (Sub-Clause 3.5)
- Wait for claim determination (Sub-Clause 3.5) or take appropriate steps if the Engineer remains silent, e.g. constitute a dispute
- Analyse any notified claim determination as to the impact on time, cost and profit
- Restart event assessment and claim analysis, if necessary
- Update Programme
- Keep delays for letter of dissatisfaction (Silver Book, Gold Book) or notice of intention to start Dispute Adjudication under control if necessary

Eighth step: Dispute Management

- Check availability of Dispute Adjudication Board
- Check all previous adjudication procedures and decisions
- Check all previous determinations
- Prepare eventual Dispute Adjudication
- Start Dispute Adjudication

- Check availability of the DAB
- If necessary initiate the DAB appointment
- Prepare referral

- Check any DAB decision
- Take all necessary further steps for decision review (arbitration requirements)

Beware the comments given in *McAlpine Humberberoak v. McDermott*:[10]

- Theoretical calculation, formulae, and rules of thumb do not provide proof of anything.
- Hypothetical assumptions and calculations might be satisfactory for preliminary issues of principle, but hard facts, visible and proved, are needed to substantiate claims for reimbursement.
- Whether measured in time or money, damage must be proved by hard evidence.

German courts also require a strict duty of substantiation, such as when the complaint "printer documentation" was considered insufficient because the buyer "was held to specify the defect of the documentation so precisely that misunderstandings were impossible and so that the seller could clearly discern what was meant;" the alleged ambiguity of the term "printer" prevented the defect from being clearly specified.[11] As a rule a claim must be presented in such a way that the judge will be able to check whether there is a case to be heard. This means that the claimant shall present all of the facts and circumstances (the particulars) which form the basis of the claim in a clear and logical way. Otherwise the judge will reject the claim for lack of substantiation. He is not obliged to build up the claim from the documents which the claimant has submitted to the court.

It is worthy to note that according to Sub-Clause 20.1 Payment Certificates shall (only) "include such amounts for any claim as have been reasonably substantiated as due under the relevant provision of the Contract". However the Engineer should not directly rely on this provision because of its duty to make a fair determination. Instead he should first request any necessary further particulars as provided in Sub-Clause 20.1.

21.4 Claim Notice

Claims are usually subject to claim notices. It is common practise for a first set of contractual rules to provides the contractor's obligation to give notice. A second set of provisions states the consequences resulting from failure to so. Under most internationally used standard forms of contract the giving of notice is a condition precedent of an entitlement to a claim irrespective of the extent to which the

---

[10] (1992) 58 BLR 1.
[11] BGH [1997] NJW-RR 690, 691 sub II.2.(b)(bb).

contractor is under an obligation to inform the Engineer or the Employer of all relevant news.

Sample: Claim Notice

- To [Engineer]
- *This letter is only suitable for use with FIDIC Yellow Book*
- Notice number [*insert number*]
- Dear Sir
- This notice is issued in accordance with Sub-clause [*insert Sub-Clause*] and

  - as the case may be in accordance with Sub-Clause 20.1.

- We became aware of:

  - an error or defect of a technical nature in a document which was prepared for use in executing the Works (Sub-Clause 1.8)
  - an error in the Employer's Requirements (Sub-Clauses 1.9, 5.1)
  - Unforeseeable physical conditions (Sub-Clause 4.12)

- We hereby give notice of a claim under the Contract or in connection with the Contract. We draw your attention to [*describe the circumstances giving rise to the claim with dates and other details as necessary to identify the claim*]. We consider that these circumstances entitle us to a claim for:

  - damages/cost/quantum meruit [*delete as appropriate*] against you
  - cost
  - cost plus reasonable profit
  - extension of Time for Completion

- Yours faithfully
- Contractor

According to Sub-Clause 20.1 FIDIC the Contractor shall give a notice of a claim if he considers to be entitled to any extension of the Time for Completion and/or any additional payment. He shall do so as soon as practicable, and not later than 28 days after the Contractor became aware, or should have become aware, of the event or circumstance giving rise to the additional payment of extension of Time for Completion. By doing so he shall describe the event or circumstance giving rise to the claim. Again, subject to Sub-Clause 8.3 the Contractor shall promptly give notice to the Engineer of specific probable future events or circumstances which may adversely affect the work, increase the Contract price or delay the execution of the Works.

The Contractor is thus under an obligation to give notice of specific probable future events or circumstances to the extent specified in Sub-Clause 8.3. Failure to do so will constitute a breach of contract. Whether the Contractor is also obliged to give notice of all events and circumstances which in addition he considers entitles him to any extension of the Time for Completion and/or any additional payment is questionable. It could be argued that the notification of a claim is discretionary subject to timing requirements and consequences of non-compliance. If this would be correct, the Contractor would not be in breach of contract when he fails to give notice of an event or circumstance relative to which he might put a case. However the intention seems to be to put the Contractor under the general obligation to give notice of any event and circumstance which may adversely affect the work, increase the Contract price or delay the execution of the Works. Only this understanding is in line with Sub-Clause 8.3 according to which the Contractor shall report all events and circumstances and not only those which may have a probable future effect on the works. And only this understanding will ensure that the Engineer and/or the Employer will subsequently, continuously and in particular contemporarily be informed about all events and circumstances which may adversely affect the work, increase the Contract price or delay the execution of the Works. In order to ensure an effective contract management it would not be enough to include all events and circumstances in the monthly report.

In Sub-Clause 8.3 there is no clear message as to the set out of time running. The meaning of "prompt" remains unclear. It could probably best be explained by the wording "without undue delay" or "as soon as practicable". By contrast under Sub-Clause 20.1 not the event itself but the Contractor's awareness of the event triggers time running. One means of control in so far will be any prompt notice under Sub-Clause 8.3. However the difficulties in determining the exact moment when it can properly be said that the Contractor became aware or should have become aware of an event or circumstance are considerable.

As previously stated time runs from awareness of the event or circumstance. This wording is unambiguous. However, a notice shall only be given, *if* the Contractor considers himself to be entitled to any extension of Time for Completion and/or any additional payment. Thus Sub-Clause 20.1 requires a notice of the Contractor only if he considers the underlying event as an event which entitles him to an extension of Time for Completion and/or an additional payment. Consideration is essentially a result of deliberation or of attention and examination or moreover a matured opinion. Under Sub-Clause 20.1 the Contractor has to make up his mind in connection with legal and/or contractual matters. Hence the requirement of a notice is subject to a previous thought process. It is difficult to know at which point in time the process has begun and when it was completed. But it seems to be logical that the Contractor will not be able to make up his mind *before* he became aware of the underlying event. Thus the logical timeline is that the Contractor becomes aware of an event or circumstance and he then starts to make a consideration. If this is correct, there is a discrepancy in Sub-Clause 20.1 because according to sentence 1 of paragraph 1 of Sub-Clause 20.1 the duty to give notice depends on whether the Contractor considers himself to be entitled to a claim while according to sentence 2 of paragraph 1 of Sub-Clause 20.1 the Contractor shall give notice earlier than this, namely "as soon as practicable, and not later than 28 days after he became aware, or should have become aware, of the event or circumstance", the latter being in fact the basis of its consideration.

It is common sense that a document should have the meaning which it would convey to a reasonable man having all the background knowledge which would reasonably have been available to the parties. It follows from the clear wording in Sub-Clause 20.1 that the Contractor shall give notice to the Engineer, describing the event or circumstance giving rise to the claim. The following sentence starts with the words "The notice". However it is suggested that it should be read as "This notice". Accordingly Sub-Clause 201.1 should be understood in the way that the Contractor shall give a notice of a claim, describing the event or circumstance giving rise to it, as soon as practicable and not later than 28 days after the Contractor became aware, or should have become aware, of the claim (of the event or circumstance "giving rise to the claim"). If this would not be correct, the Contractor would be under the duty to give notice of any event or circumstance without any prior reflection in order to ensure not being late while he deliberates the matter. For the avoidance of doubt, the above mentioned construction of Sub-Clause 20.1 does not mean that late considerations would be justified or excused in any case. In fact it is suggested that the Contractor will be under the duty to make up his mind in a timely manner. In doing this he shall take into consideration when he became aware, or should have become aware, of the event or circumstance giving rise to the claim. Failure to comply with this office will lead to the foreclosure of the claim. Thus we would suggest that the Contractor is safe if he gives notice of an event or circumstance giving rise to a claim as soon as practicable and not later than 28 days after becoming aware of it, to the extent that he was able to make up his mind. Time runs therefore after awareness of the event, but not earlier than the time needed to consider the entitlement to a claim (Fig. 21.4).

Moreover the question may arise whether there is a difference between a notice of a probable future event and the notice under Sub-Clause 20.1. The problem becomes apparent if the Contractor knows very early that an event or circumstance will occur, in particular when the future probable event is inescapably caused by an event which already occurred unless the chain of cause and effect is interrupted by further future events. In other words it is arguable that the Contractor should give notice of a claim even though the event did not yet appear

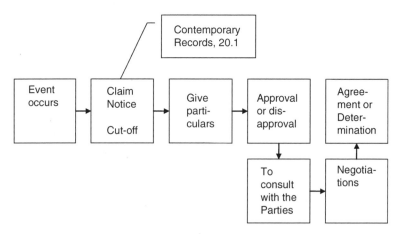

Fig. 21.4 Early warning and claim notice

if the degree of probability that the event will occur is seemingly very high. We would suggest that the wording of Sub-Clauses 20.1 and 8.3 is clear in so far. The Contractor shall give notice of a claim not later than 28 days after he became aware, or should have become aware, of the underlying event or circumstance. An event or circumstance which has not yet occurred but is likely to occur falls within the scope of Sub-Clause 8.3.

Finally the difficulty arises in determining when the Contractor *should have become aware* of an event or circumstance. The intention of the wording is reasonably clear but it is not without complications. It is intended that the Contractor shall ensure that he becomes aware of all relevant events and/or circumstances in a timely manner. Otherwise it would be arguable that there was no person on the site or that specialist contractual and legal advice was not available earlier than at the date when the Contractor actually became aware of it. The critical test is whether the Contractor has arranged effective precautions. Whether or not he has made appropriate arrangements depends certainly on the circumstances of the particular case. However a minimum standard of diligence and care should be required.

Apart from the above delineated construction issues, the question may arise of which company representative's knowledge is required to establish company knowledge. Is it only the state of mind or knowledge of the companies' directors which should be treated as company knowledge? Or is it arguable that the knowledge of the site manager, the claim manager or of other contractor's personnel on the site constitutes awareness of an event or circumstance? It is suggested that the answer to this question is clear. According to Sub-Clause 4.3 the Contractor shall appoint the Contractor's Representative and shall give him all authority necessary to act on the Contractor's behalf under the Contract. If the Contractor's Representative is to be temporarily absent from the Site during the execution of the Works, a suitable replacement person shall be appointed. To the extent that the Contractor's Representative has delegated any of his powers, functions and authority he shall give notice to the Engineer. Thus apart from the companies' directors the Contractor's Representative and his delegates are the persons who are addressed to become aware of any events or circumstances under the contract. But care should be taken. The wording of Sub-Clause 4.3 presupposes that the Contractor's Representative and/or his delegates are permanently available on the Site. If not, the Contractor will be deemed to have become aware of the event or circumstance earlier than he effectively becomes aware of it.

In a summary, FIDIC provisions can be broken down as follows:

- The Contractor is under a permanent obligation to give notice of probable future events or circumstances which may adversely affect the work, increase the Contract price or delay the execution of the Works
- The Contractor is under a permanent obligation to give notice of events or circumstances which may adversely affect the work, increase the Contract price or delay the execution of the Works
- If the Contractor considers himself to be entitled to any extension of Time for Completion and/or additional payment, he shall give notice of the event or

circumstance, describing the event or circumstance, as soon as practicable and not later than 28 days after he became aware, or should have become aware, of the event giving rise to the claim
- Time runs from the awareness of the event or circumstance to the extent that the Contractor was able to make up his mind
- Awareness means the awareness of the Contractor's Representative or his delegates

A copy of the notice should be given to the Employer (see Sub-Clause 1.3).

21.5   Documentation Requirements

It is critical to comply with the contract to the maximum extent possible. This means that all documentation requirements have to be followed by the contractor.

- General rule: *Document all deviations from the plan!*
- Keep contemporary records if required by the Contract (Sub-Clause 20.1 FIDIC)

  - Delays
  - Increased costs
  - Unforeseen conditions and events
  - Oral instructions
  - Number and location of the work-force

21.6   Presentation of Claims

Claims can be presented in a variety of ways and most contractors have their own particular forms for claim presentation. Despite this some general remarks may be helpful:

It may be wise to summarise the claim briefly at the beginning of the claim presentation in order to inform the Engineer and the Employer quickly about the relevance of the claim in order to save both of them having to read through a vast number of pages without appreciating the precise purpose of the notified claim until the end. It is therefore quite common to start with a short introduction giving an outline of the claim and to substantiate the claim later.

Any claim submission should not only be substantiated as to the factual background but also as to the legal background. It is common practice to state the relevant clauses in a logical context and to give further support on legal issues, if necessary. Otherwise the Engineer will have to investigate the contract, laws and civil codes in order to identify the claim basis. This will take time and may lead to errors. Thus a claim submission should state the subject matter of the claim in detail in order to bring the Engineer as close as possible to the Contractor's understanding of the claim.

Particulars of the claim should be accompanied by supporting data and records, such as site maps, photographs, site diaries, weather reports, instructions, programmes, drawings, correspondence, wage sheets, invoices, etc. It is useful to refer to clearly identifiable appendices.

The way in which financial analysis should be presented is not generally defined. It depends on the circumstances which structure of analysis is appropriate. Most financial analyses compare in a detailed manner the costs anticipated by the Contractor when tendering with the costs incurred when actually doing the work.

21.7 Claim Avoidance

As a rule claims are not welcome. Price and time certainty is something of high value for employers and financial institutions. It is therefore not astonishing that construction contracts comprise terms as follows:

> No alterations shall be made in the work, nor shall any charge be made by contractor for extra work, without the prior written approval of such by owner. If contractor claims that any instruction from the owner involves extra costs under the contract, or will delay the completion date of the work, contractor shall give owner immediate written notice of such and shall first obtain written approval by owner of such additional charge and new completion date prior to commencing such work.

However, such clauses may be waived. Waiver can generally be based on acts such as conduct by the owner or employer that indicated no written change order would be required or oral orders by the owner or employer (Sweet and Schneier 2004, sect. 21.04 H). Also a claimant may rely upon the principle that the law never compels a person to do something which is useless or unnecessary.[12] In the judgment of Lord Denning in Rickards v. Oppenheim[13] it was held:

> In order to constitute a waiver there must be conduct which leads the other party reasonably to believe that the strict legal rights will not be insisted upon. The whole essence of waiver is that there must be conduct which evinces an intention to affect the legal relations of the parties. If that cannot properly be inferred, there is no waiver.

The judge continued to say:

> If the defendant, as he did, led the plaintiff to believe that he would not insist on the stipulation as to time and that if they carried out the work, he would accept it, and they did it, he could not afterwards set up the stipulation as to time against them. Whether it be called waiver or forbearance on his part or an agreed variation or substituted performance does not matter. It is a kind of estoppel. By his conduct he evinced an intention to affect

---

[12] See Barrett Bros (Taxis) Ltd v. Davies Lickiss and Milestone Motor Policies at Lloyd's, Third Parties [1966] 1 WLR 1334 at 1338.

[13] [1950] 1 KB 616 at 626.

their legal relations. He made in effect a promise not to insist upon his strict legal rights. That promise was intended to be acted upon and was in fact acted upon. He cannot afterwards go back on it.

US courts go even further to find that a contractor may recover payment even without fulfilment of the written notice requirement, where an Employer makes changes which are outside of the scope of the contract and amount to a breach of the contract (see Furst and Ramsley 2006, note 11-005). In the case of Nat Harrison Associates, Inc. v. Gulf States Utilities Company[14] the US court identified four situations where a requirement for written notice may be deemed waived by the owner. Those include:

(1) When the extra work was necessary and had not been foreseen;
(2) When the changes were of such magnitude that they could not be supposed to have been made without the knowledge of the owners;
(3) When the owner was aware of the additional work and raised no objection to it; and
(4) When there was a subsequent verbal agreement authorizing the work.

However, the best rule is to comply with the contract provisions and work with a change order in hand. The court may make the contractor wish he had complied with the claim notice requirements despite the inequity of the situation. Also the aforementioned opinion of the US courts seems to be far from that in England.

21.8   Extension of Time Claims

A considerable number of events can be a source of delay and disruption to the project and may be an "excusable delay" entitling the contractor to an extension of time for completion. Typically, a construction contract includes certain clauses dealing with possible delays that affect scheduling and completion of the project. These clauses discharge the contractor or subcontractor of responsibility for certain delays – often referred to as "excusable delays" in order to mitigate such harsh consequences beyond the control of the contractor. The first thing a contractor or subcontractor should do upon experiencing a delay is to provide notice according to the contract:

- Under FIDIC Red Book 1999 edition, a contractor encountering exceptionally adverse climatic conditions will have *28 days* to provide written notice (FIDIC Red Book, sub-clauses 8.4, 20.1) after becoming aware of the possibility of a weather delay claim.

---

[14] Nat Harrison Associates, Inc v. Gulf States Utilities Company 491 F.2d 578 (5th Cir. 1974). rehearing denied, 493 F.2d 1405 (5th Cir. 1974); see also Roff v. Southern Construction Corporation, La.App., 3 Cir., 163 So.2d 112, 115–116 (1964).

- Under a FIDIC Red Book 1999 edition, a contractor encountering any operation of forces of nature which is unforeseeable or against which an experienced contractor could not reasonably have been expected to have taken adequate preventive precautions will have *28 days* to provide written notice (FIDIC Red Book, sub-clauses 17.4, 17.3, 20.1) after becoming aware of an instruction to make good damage or loss to the Works caused by weather.
- Under a FIDIC Red Book 1999 edition, a contractor encountering any natural catastrophes such as hurricane or typhoon will have 14 days to provide written notice (FIDIC Red Book, sub-clauses 19.2) after becoming aware of such circumstance and further *28 days* if he suffers delay or incurs cost by reason of such event or circumstance after becoming aware of the possibility of a weather delay claim.
- Under AIA Document A201, a contractor encountering adverse weather conditions or flooding that are not foreseeable or atypical for the period of time will have *21 days* to provide written notice (AIA Section 4.3) after recognizing the possibility of a weather delay claim.

In order to assemble such a claim, the contractor must collect the applicable scheduling or programming documents for the project and comparative weather data from the National Weather Service or similar. Daily job logs, progress reports and contemporary records are important and must include weather information and should document the personnel, material, and equipment and progress of the work and how they are impacted by the (unforeseeable) event. Accordingly, an "as planned" and as build schedules can be assembled to illustrate the progress and delays on the progress. Most importantly, pictures and videos are extremely valuable in making this claim.

Beware that the benefit to the contractor of EOT is only to relieve the contractor of liability for damages for delay (usually referred to as delay or liquidated damages) for any period prior to the extended contract completion date. The benefit of an EOT for the employer is that it establishes a new contract completion date, and prevents time for completion of the works becoming at large (SCL 2002, p. 5). By consequence EOT clauses create a win-win situation between the parties to a construction contract. From a contractor's perspective EOT has the nature of a defence against delay damages and from the employer's perspective the clause prevents time for completion of the works becoming at large.[15] This has been recently confirmed by HHJ Davies in Steria:[16]

> ... In my judgment an extension of time provision confers benefits on both parties; in particular it enables a contractor to recover reasonable extensions of time whilst still maintaining the contractually agreed structure of a specified time for completion (together, in the majority of cases, with the contractual certainty of agreed liquidated damages, as opposed to uncertain unliquidated damages). So far as the application of the contra

---

[15] See ERDC Group Ltd v. Brunel University [2006] EWHC 687 (TCC) (29 March 2006).

[16] Steria Ltd v. Sigma Wireless Communications Ltd [2007] EWHC 3454 (TCC) (15 November 2007).

proferentum rule is concerned, it seems to me that the correct question to ask is not whether
the clause was put forward originally by Steria or by Sigma; the principle which applies
here is that if there is genuine ambiguity as to whether or not notification is a condition
precedent, then the notification should not be construed as being a condition precedent,
since such a provision operates for the benefit of only one party, i.e. the employer, and
operates to deprive the other party (the contractor) of rights which he would otherwise
enjoy under the contract.

In order to reduce the number of disputes relating to delay, contractors are often
obliged to submit a properly prepared programme showing the manner and
sequence in which the contractor plans to carry out the works. According to Sub-
Clause 8.3 the programme should be updated to record actual progress and any
extensions of time granted. If this is done then the programme can be used as a tool
for managing change and determining periods of time for which compensation
may be due.

In the course of claim assessment by programming, experts and non-experts
alike frequently use the term "critical path". It is fundamental to have a precise
definition of what it and associated terms mean. What is known as the Critical Path
Method is frequently used by the construction industry both in the United States, the
United Kingdom and elsewhere in planning construction projects and in analysing
the causes of delay. The critical path can be defined as "the sequence of activities
through a project network from start to finish, the sum of whose durations determines the overall Project duration". It can only reliably be deduced from the
mathematical sum of the durations on the contractor's programme to be completed
in sequence before the completion date can be achieved. HHJ Toulmin makes the
point that this is an important cautionary finding where witnesses are convinced,
without the benefit of any such analysis, that they know where the critical path
lies.[17] Thus Critical Path Method requires detailed and sophisticated analysis and in
complex projects it is unlikely that a critical path can be identified inductively, i.e.
by assertion.

As previously mentioned the programme should show the manner and sequence
in which the contractor plans to carry out the works and the related periods of time
for each activity. It is of course possible to affect the critical path by allocating some
activities a longer time than is necessary, thus keeping them on the critical path.
This protects other activities from being on the critical path. Such time assigned to
an activity, which is longer than the shortest time that is reasonably necessary to
undertake that activity, can be referred to as "float". The term "float" is often used in
the alternative sense of the length of time before an activity becomes on or very
close to the critical path.

Thus the relationship between the critical path and the events occurring during
the completion period is an important consideration and should be addressed in all
delay cases. It is fundamental that the critical path becomes redrawn at the point in
time immediately preceding the relevant event in order to enable the parties and the

---

[17] Mirant Asia-Pacific Construction (Hong Kong) Ltd v. Ove Arup and Partners International Ltd &
Anor [2007] EWHC 918 (TCC) (20 April 2007), at no. 122.

engineer to judge with a degree of accuracy its effect on the programme. Beware that the approaches to concurrent delay in the United States, Canada, New Zealand and England are different from each other (compare, Morgan 2005, p. 54 et seq.). Depending on the contract, float may be owner-owned or contractor-owned. The SCL Protocol quotes that "unless there is an express provision to the contrary in the contract, where there is remaining float in the programme at the time of an employer risk event, an EOT should only be granted to the extent that the employer delay is predicted to reduce to below zero the total float on the activity paths affected by the employer delay".

Although the FIDIC Rainbow Edition does not provide network techniques, they merely imply the use of it.[18] Firstly only delay on time for completion usually entitles the contractor to EOT. Secondly Sub-clause 8.3 provides detailed programming by the contractor, who "shall submit a detailed time programme to the Engineer". Each programme shall include:

(a) The order in which the Contractor intends to carry out the Works, including the anticipated timing of each stage of design (if any), Contractor's Documents, procurement, manufacture of Plant, delivery to Site, construction, erection and testing
(b) Each of these stages for work by each nominated Subcontractor (as defined in Clause 5 [Nominated Subcontractors])
(c) The sequence and timing of inspections and tests specified in the Contract
(d) A supporting report which includes:

(1) A general description of the methods which the Contractor intends to adopt, and of the major stages, in the execution of the Works
(2) Details showing the Contractor's reasonable estimate of the number of each class of Contractor's Personnel and of each type of Contractor's Equipment, required on the Site for each major stage

Thus the information required is extensive and presupposes that the contractor has planned the work in detail. In particular the contractor has to show the anticipated timing of each stage of design (if any), Contractor's Documents, procurement, manufacture of Plant, delivery to Site, construction, erection and testing. Even though the FIDIC documents do not require the use of project management software the contractor shall obviously enable the engineer and the employer to identify the critical path.

In daily practice Windows analysis is the most widely accepted method of critical path analysis. The critical path analysis will identify at a given date which important aspects of the project are falling behind the programme, particularly if they are on or close to the critical path, what if any is the impact on other aspects of the programme and where additional resources need to be placed. It will also

---

[18] The FIDIC Orange Book 1995 appears to be unique in requiring expressly the use of network techniques.

demonstrate where activities are ahead of what is planned and enable a decision to be taken on whether planned activities need to be rescheduled.[19] It is finally also used as a tool for analysing, as at the given date, what has caused any delay that has occurred and what is the extent of that delay.[20]

21.9 Money Claims

The entitlement to any additional payment depends mainly on the risk allocation within the contract. Risks may result in cost and the entitlement to additional profit. However, it is an erroneous assumption that an extension of time is automatically linked to additional payment. In any case cost must be distinguished from profit. Both elements are usually defined by the contract. These definitions may have a significant impact on the performance of the contract when it comes to valuation of claims. Definitions can be as such:

> "Cost", "costs, losses and claims" and "the amount to be added to or deducted from the Contract Price" or the valuation of new prices within the Conditions of Contract, other than prices that can be valued from the Schedule of Prices or based on the Schedule of Prices shall be valued in accordance with the Schedule of Cost Components included in Schedule 11 of this Contract.[21]

Extra work of the kind contemplated by the contract will usually be paid for in the manner provided by the terms of the contract. If the contract does not provide any rates, according to English law, payment will be a reasonable sum.[22] According to German law remuneration for work is deemed to have been tacitly agreed if in the circumstances of the case it is to be expected that the work or service is to be performed only against remuneration. If the amount of remuneration is not specified and a tariff exists, the tariff rate of remuneration is deemed to have been agreed; if no tariff exists, the usual remuneration is deemed to have been agreed.

It is similar for work outside the contract. It depends on the contract whether any new rates have to be fixed by reference to rates shown in the tender or not. There is, subject to applicable law, no implied term which entitles the employer to ask for disclosure of the contractor's internal calculation. But of course the contract may expressly refer to rates included in the tender documents. However if the contractor has made an error in his pricing of the tender for a lump sum contract and there are no grounds for rectification, these rates cannot be rectified or disregarded on the

---

[19] Mirant Asia-Pacific Construction (Hong Kong) Ltd v. Ove Arup and Partners International Ltd & Anor [2007] EWHC 918 (TCC) (20 April 2007), at no. 129.

[20] Mirant Asia-Pacific Construction (Hong Kong) Ltd v. Ove Arup and Partners International Ltd & Anor [2007] EWHC 918 (TCC) (20 April 2007), at no. 130.

[21] Yorkshire Water Services Ltd v. Taylor Woodrow Construction Northern Ltd [2004] EWHC 1660 (TCC) (08 July 2004).

[22] See British Steel Corporation v. Cleveland Bridge and Engineering Co Ltd [1984] 1 All ER 504.

basis of there being an error,[23] unless the contract provides an express power to make an adjustment for pricing errors (Furst and Ramsley 2006, note 4-053).

In any case FIDIC books provide for a considerable number of cost claims, such as:

- Under FIDIC Red Book 1999 edition, a contractor prevented from access to or possession of the Site will have *28 days* to provide written notice (FIDIC Red Book, Sub-clauses 4.12, 20.1) after becoming aware of the event.
- Under FIDIC Red Book 1999 edition, a contractor encountering unforeseeable physical conditions will have *28 days* to provide written notice (FIDIC Red Book, Sub-clauses 4.12, 20.1) after becoming aware of the possibility of additional cost. However, a previous prompt written notice is required.
- Under FIDIC Red Book 1999 edition, a contractor encountering fossils will have *28 days* to provide written notice (FIDIC Red Book, Sub-clauses 4.24, 20.1) after becoming aware of the possibility of additional cost.
- Under FIDIC Red Book 1999 edition, a contractor incurring cost from complying with instructions concerning any tests will have *28 days* to provide written notice (FIDIC Red Book, Sub-clauses 7.4, 20.1) after becoming aware of the instruction.
- Under FIDIC Red Book 1999 edition, a contractor incurring cost as a result of changes in the Laws will have *28 days* to provide written notice (FIDIC Red Book, Sub-clauses 13.7, 20.1) after becoming aware of the change.
- Under FIDIC Red Book 1999 edition, a contractor incurring cost from rectifying loss or damage as a result of an Employer's Risk will have *28 days* to provide written notice (FIDIC Red Book, Sub-clauses 17.4, 20.1) after becoming aware of the cost. However, a previous prompt written notice is required.
- Under FIDIC Red Book 1999 edition, a contractor encountering a Force Majeure event will have *28 days* to provide written notice (FIDIC Red Book, Sub-clauses 19.4, 20.1) after becoming aware of the cost.

21.9.1 Cost

According to FIDIC Conditions the Contractor is entitled to additional costs including overhead (see Sub-Clause 1.1.4.3) but excluding profit for expenses encountering unforeseeable physical obstructions or conditions (Sub-Clause 4.12); encountering fossils or other specified objects of archaeological or geological interest (Sub-Clause 4.24); suspensions ordered by Engineer for reasons other than Contractor's default or because needed for proper execution of works or by reason of climatic conditions (Sub-clause 8.9), termination upon outbreak of war (Sub-Clause 19.6). In other cases the Contractor is entitled to additional costs plus reasonable profit resulting from tests required by Engineer but not provided for in

[23] Henry Boot Construction v. Alstom Combined Cycles [2000] BLR 247, CA.

the contract (7.4); uncovering work where no defect exists (Sub-Clause 11.8); termination or suspension upon Employer's default (Sub-Clauses 16.4, 19.6); Employer's failure to give Contractor possession (Sub-Clause 2.1); damage to works or Contractor's equipment or other expenses arising from specified Employer's risks (Sub-Clause 17.4); rise in costs of labour or materials (Sub-Clause 70.1) and subsequent legislation (Sub-Clause 13.7).

In most situations the Contractor will only be entitled to payment of any additional cost. Cost should be clearly distinguished from the price and rates:

- Purely cost related risks can be defined as those which can result in changes to the contractor's project cost, hence having an influence on his profit margin. Such risks include for example variation orders, cost escalation (related to wages, materials, etc.), changes in laws and regulations, tax rate increases, insurance premium increases, exchange rate fluctuations, embargos, shipping and transportation risks, etc.
- Physical risks comprise those events or occurrences which prevent or delay physical completion of the works. They include access to the site issues, site conditions, earthquakes, exceptional adverse climatic conditions, etc.
- Ability related risks are those events or occurrences that prevent or delay completion of the works other than physical obstructions, such as defective work, inadequate labour, strikes and lock-outs, war, riots, shortcomings as to materials and equipment, etc.

FIDIC contracts define the term "cost" as follows (Cl. 1.1.4.3):

"Cost" means all expenditure reasonably incurred (or to be incurred) by the Contractor, whether on or off the Site, including overhead and similar charges, but does not include profit.

According to the New Dictionary of Civil Engineering "cost" means:

Required expenditure on resources incurred in producing and selling an output, i.e. payment or expense to buy or obtain goods or services.

Changes and occurring events may cause direct and indirect financial consequences. The evaluation of such consequences is subject to a determination by the Engineer (Sub-Clause 3.5) who shall make a fair determination with regard to all relevant circumstances and in accordance with the Contract. Thus it is the Engineer who shall consider the meaning of Cost. Guidance for the support of the valuation process with regard to the consequences of events and changes is presumably the same as set down by the courts for the evaluation of damages or the determination of the price (see above).

Under Common and Civil law the guiding principle, when considering breaches of contract, is that recoverable damages shall not be too remote, though many differences appear in detail. Under Civil law the guiding principle, when considering the amount of the remuneration which the parties did not agree on, is that the remuneration shall be reasonable. Under Common law the *quantum meruit* may be recoverable, which is equal to "what it is worth". It has been established in

Thorn v. London Corp[24] that a contractor who is requested to undertake further work for which no price has been agreed will be titled to a reasonable amount, which being outside the Contract shall not be valued by reference to its terms. In so far the speech of Bowsher J in Laserbore v. Morison Biggs is worth to be cited:[25]

> I return to the approaches of the respective experts, the "reasonable rates" basis on the one hand and the "costs plus" basis on the other. I take the "reasonable rates" basis used by the plaintiffs' expert to be Saville J's "fair commercial rate for the services provided". In a competitive market, one would expect both approaches to result in much the same figure, particularly if one accepts that someone who competes by providing high quality rather than low cost should receive a higher remuneration on both tests. Tenders are usually built up on a costs plus basis and the acceptance or rejection of tenders sets what can be viewed as the market rate. But one problem for the plaintiffs is that they did not expect to have to prove their claim on a costs plus basis and they have not kept records sufficient to prove their claim in that way.
>
> I am in no doubt that the costs plus basis in the form in which it was applied by the defendants' quantum expert (though perhaps not in other forms) is wrong in principle even though in some instances it may produce the right result. One can test it by examples. If a company's directors are sufficiently canny to buy materials for stock at knockdown prices from a liquidator, must they pass on the benefit of their canniness to their customers? If a contractor provides two cranes of equal capacity and equal efficiency to do an equal amount of work, should one be charged at a lower rate than the other because one crane is only one year old but the other is three years old? If an expensive item of equipment has been depreciated to nothing in the company's accounts but by careful maintenance the company continues to use it, must the equipment be provided free of charge apart from running expenses (fuel and labour)? On the defendants' argument, the answer to those questions is, "Yes". I cannot accept that that begins to be right.

Definitions of the term "cost" are quite difficult to find. Economically Cost can be classified as direct costs (raw materials and direct labour) and indirect costs (or overheads). The definition in Sub-Clause 1.1.4.3 specifically excludes profit but includes overheads and similar charges. Usually cost means all expenditure properly incurred by the contractor, whether on or off the site, including overhead and similar charges. However it does neither specify the treatment of supplier discounts and other benefits that contractors might receive (Huse 2002, note 5-39) nor does it specify the treatment of other aforementioned benefits. Cost should therefore be understood as reasonable market rates for services provided. In addition the term Cost should be read together with Sub-Clause 17.6 according to which neither Party shall be liable for loss of profit, loss of any contract or for any other indirect and consequential loss or damage. It is suggested that it follows from Sub-Clause 17.6 that claims falling under the second limb of the principles stated in Hadley v. Baxendale[26] are excluded. Thus the term Cost will not include any consequential losses but only those items falling under the first limb of Hadley v. Baxendale. Whether the term expenditure covers all heads of claims, which in general fall under the first limb of Hadley v. Baxendale, remains open. But the wording of

---

[24] Thorn v. London Corporation (1876) L.R. 1 App. Cas. 120, HL.

[25] Laserbore Ltd v. Morrison Biggs Wall Ltd (1993) CILL 896.

[26] Hadley v. Baxendale (1854) 9 Ex. 341.

Sub-Clause 1.1.4.3 appears to include financial charges (as mentioned in the FIDIC Contracts Guide), overheads (as expressly mentioned in Sub-Clause 1.1.4.3) and presumably loss of productivity covering additional labour and machinery cost.

The question may arise whether the term "cost incurred" can be extended to include the recovery of future or anticipated cost, which has recently been denied by Justice Forbes.[27]

In principle all costs have to be shown to be incurred, moreover reasonably incurred. The FIDIC Contract's Guide states that overhead charges may include reasonable financing cost incurred by reason of payment being received after expenditure. Some of the cost causes of action are linked to particular conditions. Sub-Clause 4.12 is inextricably linked to the preceding Sub-Clauses 4.10 and 4.11, which set out the Contractor's responsibility to make its own surveys, inspections and interpretations of the submitted data. Hence, it is not the tender computation that is the starting point for any cost evaluation. Instead is the available data and the standard of care to be applied during surveys, inspections, etc.

21.9.2 Profit

The definition of "profit" or "reasonable profit" is certainly open to interpretation, because it is not a defined term. According to the New Dictionary of Civil Engineering "profit" means:

> Profit is either economic profit or accounting profit. Economic profit is the residual return after all costs have been met, not including return to land or capital. Accounting net profit means the profit [before or after tax] the residual after deducting all money costs.

Profit margin mark-ups are not necessarily those included in the original tender. It is presumed that reasonable profit should be foreseeable and capable of justification. Clear guidance as to this issue is difficult. The calculation of profit margin mark-ups is often subject to applicable law and court practice.

The FIDIC Guidance for the Preparation of Particular Conditions suggests an amendment to sub-clause 1.2 in order to elucidate the phrase "cost plus reasonable profit". The FIDIC example states that reasonable profit would be one-twentieth or 5% of the cost.

Which heads of claims are covered by the term "profit" is subject to further discussion. Whether it includes all heads of claims falling under the second limb of Hadley v. Baxendale must carefully be considered. If read in the context of Sub-Clause 17.6 it would be difficult to argue that the term "profit" also covers items which fall under the second limb of Hadley v. Baxendale.

---

[27] Yorkshire Water Services Ltd v. Taylor Woodrow Construction Northern Ltd [2004] EWHC 1660 (TCC), at no. 65.

21.9.3 Loss of Productivity Claims

It is a widely spread erroneous assumption that an extension of the Time for Completion is automatically linked to additional payment (Thomas 2001, p. 93). On the other hand it is beyond doubt that an extended Time for Completion usually results in additional cost. Under all FIDIC forms the Contractor's obligation is tied into a programme. Sub-Clause 8.1 of the Red, Yellow and Silver Forms requires the Contractor to proceed with the Works with due expedition and without delay. Sub-Clause 8.3 of the Red, Yellow and Silver forms requires the Contractor to proceed in accordance with the programme, subject to his other obligations under the Contract. If it becomes obvious that actual progress falls behind the programme, the Contractor must submit a revised Programme.

Sub-Clause 8.6 of the Red, Yellow and Silver Forms gives the Engineer (Employer under the Silver Form) the power to instruct the Contractor to submit a revised Programme with revised methods to expedite progress and complete within the Time for Completion. The power arises if actual progress is too slow to complete within the agreed Time for Completion, or if the progress has fallen or will fall behind the Programme. There is no such power if the cause is one of the matters which entitles the Contractor to an extension of Time for Completion subject to Sub-Clause 8.4. However if Sub-Clause 8.6 applies the Contractor is required to adopt the revised methods which are stated to include increases in the working hours and/or increase in resources and/or goods. The revised methods are at the Contractor's cost and risk and he is liable for the Employer's additional costs incurred in addition to any delay damages.

Sub-Clause 8.4 being the main Sub-Clause for all extension of time issues does not provide for any additional payment in favour of the Contractor. Nor is there any particular clause allowing for an entitlement to loss of productivity. However it should be noted that under FIDIC contracts there are a number of particular claim clauses which combine EOT claims and cost claims. In such cases additional cost (such as overheads and other similar cost) are already covered by the FIDIC clauses.

21.9.4 Legal Claims

FIDIC does not prevent the parties from relying on the law. Thus additional legal claims may arise depending on the facts. There are various examples of such claims:

According to common law, in the event that an Employer is aware of a project condition but fails to disclose and/or misrepresents the existence of such a condition to the Contractor, damages may be claimed. Thus, where an Employer who possesses superior knowledge, which it fails to disclose and damages result, the Employer may be liable for those damages that result from the failure to disclose.

For example, in a situation where a contractor is delayed as a result of undisclosed physical obstructions which were known to the Employer, the Employer's failure to disclose may make them liable for resulting damages. However, where the Contractor knew or should have known about the undisclosed conditions, the Contractor's claim will be dismissed.

If according to Egyptian law (art. 658 para. 3 Civil Code) the economic balance between the obligations of both, the Employer and the Contractor collapses owing to general extraordinary incidents that were not taken into account when the Contract was signed, and a as result the basis on which was founded the estimation of the contractual agreement came to falter, the judge may pass a judgment ruling that either the remuneration be increased or the contract be rescinded.

Also a Contractor may consider that the Employer has, under the governing law, to pay the quantum meruit rather than to refer to the variation regime of the contract.

It is crucial to ascertain any probable legal claims in advance. Unfortunately in current practise legal causes of actions are quite often ignored until a dispute arises. This is too late, and this for multiple reasons. The first reason lies in Sub-Clause 20.1 according to which a claim shall be notified within 28 days. The second reason is lack of documentation and evidence. The legal cause of action may require to show evidence for facts which the Contractor considered to be irrelevant or moot. The third reason is that adjudicators and arbitrators are not completely free to consider arguments which are completely new and which in fact constitute a new dispute. Difficult questions concerning the scope of the dispute that was referred for adjudication may then arise.

21.10   Gold Book

The DBO does not change the claims' procedure completely, but adjusts some of the details of the existing claim procedure concerning Contractor's claims, in particular the following:

Firstly the clear time bar for the notification of claims has been slightly defused. Hereafter the Contractor may submit details for justification of late submission to the DAB for a ruling. If the DAB considers the circumstances to be such that the late submission was acceptable, the DAB has authority to over-ride the given 28-days-limit. It is however presumed that there is an implied standard of good faith, excluding excuses which are within the control of the Contractor. Thus justification of late notification might be given if the Contractor was unambiguously unable to notify the claim within the delay stated in Sub-Clause 20.1.

Secondly in future the Contractor will be obliged to substantiate his claim within the time for substantiation, which has been fixed to 42 days. Otherwise his claim will be deemed to have lapsed. Late submission of details may be remedied. The Contractor may justify late submission and submit the details to the DAB for a ruling. Here also justification requires the presentation of circumstances which are beyond control of the Contractor.

Thirdly it seems to be clear that failure to comply with Sub-Clause 20.1 lit. b (Contemporary Records) will have a negative impact on a claim. The Contractor's claim will stand and fall by the quality of the evidence and the time within which it is produced (Glover and Hughes 2006, note 20-008).

Fourthly, if the Parties are dissatisfied with any determination of the Employer's Representative they may issue a notice of dissatisfaction within 28 days of receiving the determination. Otherwise the determination becomes final and binding.

Fifthly if the Employer's Representative remains silent more than 42 days after a substantiated claim has been submitted, either party may consider that the claim has been rejected by him and either Party may refer the matter to the DAB (Sub-Clause 20.1 lit. d subparagraph 2).

Sixthly the DBO form distinguishes between claims which may arise until issue of the Commissioning Certificate and those which may arise during the Operation Service Period. Whilst Cost can be claimed at completion stage according to Sub-Clause 9.3 subject to Sub-Clause 20.1 no such reference to Sub-Clause 20.1 is made as to compensation claims covered by Sub-Clause 10.6 lit. b. However, in most case reference to Sub-Clause 20.1 has been kept, for example in Sub-Clause 10.4 or Sub-Clause 18.4 lit. b or Sub-Clause 10.7. It is also noteworthy that extension of Time for Completion is not recoverable during the Operation Service Period and that Sub-Clause 10.6 provides for a particular compensation claim to the extent that the Contractor may recover cost and losses including loss of revenue and loss of profit, terms which are not defined in the Contract. Anyway it is critical to also establish a daily claim management during the Operation Service Period.

Thus in principle the claim procedure has been maintained, albeit in a slightly adjusted format. It is obvious that the new claim procedures require strict compliance with the given time schedule in order to avoid inconveniences, and this until the end of the whole procedure. An overabundance of tactical considerations and prolonged procedures should be avoided (Fig. 21.5).

Nevertheless, the new wording gives rise to some additional remarks. It might be argued that it is no longer necessary for the Employer's Representative to proceed

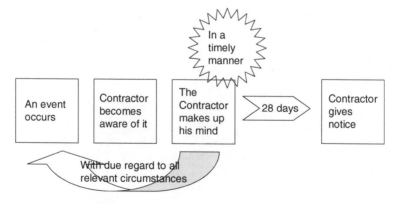

Fig. 21.5 Contractor's preliminary considerations

in accordance with Sub-Clause 3.5 if the Contractor fails to give full supporting particulars of his claim. The reason for this lies in Sub-Clause 20.1 lit. d. According to the wording of this Sub-Clause the Employer's Representative shall proceed in accordance with Sub-Clause 3.5 "within 42 days after receiving a fully detailed claim". Hence, there is no obligation to make a determination as to any claim which has not been substantiated. On first sight this might not lead to a problem, because it is clear from Sub-Clause 20.1 lit. c that in the event of failure to give full particulars the Notice shall be deemed to have lapsed. However there is an issue, if a dispute arises, as to whether a claim has been fully substantiated or not. In this event the Employer's Representative should issue a determination (rejection) in order to open the way to the DAB. If he remains silent the new Sub-Clause 20.1 lit. d subparagraph 2 applies. The Contractor may then consider that the claim has been rejected by the Employer's Representative and refer the matter to the DAB. In this case the

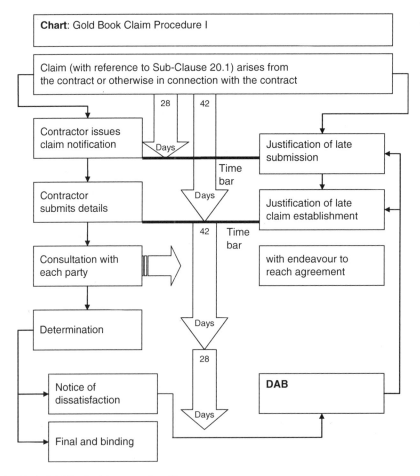

Fig. 21.6 Gold Book claim procedure II

next issue arises. According to the new Sub-Clause 20.1 lit. d paragraph 4 a Notice of dissatisfaction must be given, otherwise the determination will become final and binding. In the particular case that the Employer's Representative remains silent because he considers that the claim was not yet fully substantiated he may withhold its determination because Sub-Clause 20.1 lit. d only applies on the condition that the claim was fully detailed. However, if he was wrong and the claim was fully detailed Sub-Clause 20.1 lit. d applies. In this case the Contractor shall give within 28 days' a Notice of dissatisfaction in accordance with Sub-Clause 20.6. On the other hand Sub-Clause 20.6 presupposes a Notice of dissatisfaction. Hence, the Contractor is only allowed to refer a matter to the DAB if he has issued a Notice of dissatisfaction. It is therefore strongly recommended to issue a Notice of dissatisfaction within 28 days, if the Employers Representative does not respond in accordance with the determination procedure, even though the claim has not been sufficiently substantiated (Fig. 21.6).

Compared with the 1999 edition the claim procedure for claims of the Employer has not been touched, although the World Bank found it more balanced to insert a time bar for Employer's claims in its MDB Red Book harmonised edition. However Employer's claims are no longer dealt with in Sub-Clause 2.5 but in Sub-Clause 20.2. Moreover it should be emphasised that for the first time even Employers must comply with a cut-off period. In the event of dissatisfaction with a determination made by the Employer's Representative, the Employer must give a notice of dissatisfaction within 28 days after receiving the determination. Otherwise the determination shall be deemed to have been accepted.

References

Booen P (2001) The four FIDIC contract conditions: claims and adjustments of the contract. Presented at the Seminar "FIDIC Global Conditions of Contract", New Delhi, January 2001. http://www1.fidic.org/resources/contracts/booen_k.asp

Bunni NG (2005) FIDIC forms of contract, 3rd edn. Blackwell, Oxford

Furst S, Ramsley V (2006) Keating on construction contracts, 8th edn. Sweet & Maxwell, London

Glover J, Hughes S (2006) Understanding the new FIDIC red book. Sweet & Maxwell, London

Huse JA (2002) Understanding and negotiating turnkey and EPC contracts, 2nd edn. Sweet & Maxwell, London

Morgan DB (2005) International contract management. Gower, Hampshire

SCL (2002) SCL Delay and Disruption Protocol. Society of Construction Law

Sweet J, Schneier MM (2004) Legal aspects of architecture, engineering and the construction process, 7th edn. Thomson, Toronto

Thomas R (2001) Construction contract claims, 2nd edn. Palgrave, Hampshire

Vidogah, Ndekugri (1998) Improving the management of claims on construction contracts: consultant's perspective. Construct Manage Econ 16(3):363–372

Chapter 22
Disputes

The settlement of disputes is covered by Clause 20. FIDIC has introduced a two-step or indeed three-step procedure for the purposes of dispute settlement (Fig. 22.1). At the outset any dispute has to be referred to the Dispute Adjudication Board (DAB). Sub-Clauses 20.5 then provides for a last attempt of dispute avoidance and amicable settlement. Finally the dispute may be referred to arbitration (Sub-Clause 20.6).

22.1 Introduction

Whenever possible, it is advisable to solve any differences or disputes by amicable settlement, since disputes are time-consuming and expensive. Most international contract forms therefore provide express stipulations through which the parties to them attempt to avoid disputes. Some of them even require endeavours to be made to reach an amicable settlement before any difference or dispute can be referred either to the courts or to arbitration. As both court and arbitration proceedings are expensive and time-consuming the business community has developed so called alternative dispute resolution (ADR) proceedings, which are either used exclusively or as compulsory interim proceedings, thus baring the referral to courts or arbitration until these preliminary proceedings have come to an end.

FIDIC has at a very early stage adopted the concept of alternative dispute resolution. Since 1995 the Orange Book provides Dispute Adjudication as a regular feature of dispute resolution. The concept was maintained when FIDIC published the 1999 Rainbow Edition. A more sophisticated set of rules has been adopted in the new Design, Build & Operate form of FIDIC, also referred to as the Gold Book or DBO form. Ever since then Dispute Adjudication is recognised as a useful and appropriate feature of dispute resolution. Naturally, other dispute resolution concepts exist, some of which are also used by FIDIC. For example the FIDIC White Book still refers to mediation.

Traditionally disputes were initially determined by the Engineer within 84 days of reference, then by arbitration under ICC Rules (Sub-Clauses 67.1, 67.3 FIDIC, 4th edition 1987). Arbitration had to be noticed within 70 days of Engineer's

A.-V. Jaeger and G.-S. Hök, *FIDIC-A Guide for Practitioners*,
DOI 10.1007/978-3-642-02100-8_22, © Springer-Verlag Berlin Heidelberg 2010

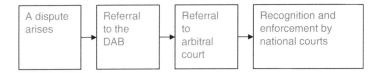

Fig. 22.1 Procedural steps

decision or after the period for such decision had expired (Sub-Clause 67.1). The 1999 series of the Books, following the Orange Book 1995, has changed this dispute resolution system. The Engineer is no longer a quasi-arbitrator and has been replaced in so far by a Dispute Adjudication Board (Sub-clauses 20.2, 20.4).

If any dispute arises the parties to the contract may refer it to the Dispute Adjudication Board. A nomination procedure for the appointment of the DAB members is ruled in Sub-clause 20.2. The DAB has full power to open up, review and revise any certificate, determination, instruction, opinion or valuation of the Engineer.

22.2 Dispute Resolution Methods

22.2.1 Introduction

Quite a sophisticated system of alternative dispute resolution has been developed over the last 25 years which covers all types of mediation, dispute reviewing and dispute adjudication.

22.2.2 Mediation

Mediation is in many ways a "new kid on the block" and has increased in popularity only in the last couple of decades. It is in truth not really a procedure by which a dispute becomes settled by the so called mediator. Mediation is aimed at leading the parties to an amicable settlement of their difference or dispute. Thus the role of a mediator is different from that of a judge or arbitrator. He tries to provide the necessary support for an amicable settlement without any procedural background and restrictions. The parties share relevant information and meet in both confidential discussions with the mediator and face to face with each other, as deemed appropriate. According to the CEDR (Centre for Effective Dispute Resolution) definition, mediation is a flexible process conducted confidentially in which a neutral person actively assists parties in working towards a negotiated agreement of a dispute or difference, with the parties in ultimate control of the decision to settle and the terms of resolution. Key features of mediation are:

- Mediation is voluntary.
- However, refusal to mediate can give rise to cost sanctions.

- Courts actively encourage parties to consider mediation.
- Mediation is confidential and "without prejudice" (nothing said in the mediation is subject to evidence legislation of the lex fori – admissible as evidence in subsequent legal proceedings).
- The mediator facilitates the process but the parties are and remain responsible for the outcome.
- Any settlement reached during mediation is binding once put into writing and signed by the parties subject to the governing law: According to German law (see Sect. 779 Civil Code) a settlement by means of which the parties' dispute or uncertainty about a legal relationship is eliminated is ineffective if the set of facts used as a basis according to the contract's contents does not correspond to reality and the dispute or uncertainty would not have occurred if the facts had been known.

Mediation is presumed to have a number of advantages over litigation and arbitration proceedings:

- *Avoids premature litigation* in case of simple misunderstandings.
- *A wide variety of settlement options* can be achieved in mediation over and above monetary settlements, including options which at court are not available (e.g. specific performance).
- *Confidential* – as any facts remain completely confidential.
- *Cost effective* – compared with litigation processes, mediation is a less expensive route to resolving disputes.
- *Excludes jurisdictional issues.*
- *Gives parties control* over the process and the outcome, which means that they are completely free to shape the mediation process.
- *Informal and flexible* – the process to suit parties' needs without any prejudice to further judicial proceedings.
- *Information sharing* – Relevant information is shared by each party and the mediator, prior to the mediation.
- *Mediation can protect and maintain business relationships* far more effectively than litigation.
- *Mediation can run alongside litigation*, or the parties may prefer to put the litigation process "on hold" while they mediate.
- *Quick* – most mediations are arranged within a few weeks (and can be arranged even more quickly) and the formal mediation session usually lasts for one or two days only.

This is the reason why for example the FIDIC White Book recommends CEDR mediation procedures for the settlement of disputes arising from a consultancy agreement. CEDR, founded as a non-profit organisation in 1990 with the support of The Confederation of British Industry (CBI) and a number of British businesses and law firms, to encourage the development and use of Alternative Dispute Resolution (ADR) and mediation in commercial disputes, is a London-based mediation and alternative dispute resolution body. CEDR Mediator Training Skills is widely thought to be the best in the world.

22.2.3   Dispute Review

Dispute Review Boards (DRBs) are also a very appropriate means for solving *disputes* in the course of the project development. Dispute review consists of a procedure wherein the dispute reviewer takes no decision but provides his opinion on the merits of the case. Usually he issues a non-binding recommendation, which the parties may use in order to reach an amicable settlement based on a clear legal position. Dispute review evolved from the former role of the engineer as decision-maker in the first instance under various standard forms of construction contracts, such as the old FIDIC Red Book 1987 (fourth Edition). For example, earlier editions of the FIDIC contracts provided that disputes were to be determined in the first instance by the Engineer under the contract. The Engineer's decision was binding upon the parties until it was reversed by arbitration. The European PRAG dc4 form still uses this feature.

Some think that dispute review is the superior way of resolving-and even avoiding-disputes. Meanwhile arbitral institutions have endorsed such procedures. For example, the American Arbitration Association (AAA) and the International Chamber of Commerce (ICC) have each issued procedural rules for dispute review boards. Also the Dispute Review Foundation (DRBF) promotes Dispute Review as a favourite means of dispute resolution. Dispute review boards can comprise a single person or a panel of three or even five members. Generally speaking, it is wise to keep the number of members to an odd number, so that it is possible to achieve a split or majority decision should the panel not reach unanimity. The members of a Review Board are (or should be) independent to the parties and are expected to be able and experienced to take the initiative in investigating and ascertaining the facts and law related to the dispute. Dispute Review Board members are also often required to possess expertise and skills in the type of project/ industry in question.

However, Dispute Review Boards lack the advantage of rendering a decision which is binding on the parties. There is always an underlying possibility that negotiations do not lead to an amicable settlement and the parties have wasted a lot of time for no discernible result.

22.2.4   Dispute Adjudication

Dispute Adjudication is the most recent form of alternative dispute resolution but likely to be the most successful and satisfactory one at the same time, because it is very effective. Unlike dispute review dispute adjudication leads to a decision of the adjudicator on the merits of the case which becomes temporarily binding until revised by either an arbitral or a state court. Due to its success in some jurisdictions such as in England and Wales, in some jurisdictions of Australia and New Zealand and in Singapore, dispute adjudication legislation has been set in force. Usually dispute adjudication starts by a notice of reference to dispute adjudication, whose purpose is to warn the adverse party of the intention to start dispute adjudication and which is a precondition for the appointment of the adjudicator, if necessary (say, if the parties did not agree to a permanent adjudicator during the whole phase of contract execution). At a second stage the referral to adjudication follows, containing a written statement by which the claimant substantiates the merits of the case and defines its demand. The adjudicator will hear the case and provide the defending party with an opportunity to answer to the complaint. Depending on the adjudication agreement of the parties he may obtain evidence, require expert advice and visit the site. Once having heard the parties the adjudicator will render a decision which he shall notify to the parties. The decision usually becomes temporarily binding until revised by subsequent arbitration or court proceedings. The adjudicator's decision is neither an arbitral award capable of enforcement under the New York Convention, nor does it have the status of a court judgment. Instead, the decision is binding only as a matter of contract between the parties. Failure to comply with a temporarily binding adjudication decision constitutes breach of contract and the appropriate method of enforcing an adjudicator's decision is by way of an action for breach of contract unless ruled otherwise by national law. Depending on the applicable law the winning party may obtain a summary judgement or similar in order to enforce the adjudication decision. This is for example the case in England and Wales.

Examples of dispute adjudication clauses can be found in FIDIC Conditions, NEC forms of contract and MF/1 forms as well. It is today quite common to agree to dispute adjudication and parts of the industry even consider lack of a dispute adjudication clause to constitute a deal breaker.

22.2.5 Arbitration

At one time arbitration was seen as the only and unique alternative to the court system. Accordingly for a long period of time arbitration was the only means to escape from court proceedings. It has since become a common method of dispute settlement and national legislation usually accepts clauses by which the parties to a contract derogate court proceedings in favour of arbitration. If the parties to a contract have agreed to arbitration the national courts usually lack jurisdiction. By consequence a national court will reject any complaint brought before it.

If any dispute or difference arises, the parties have to refer it to the agreed arbitration. Arbitration does not mean that there is a worldwide accepted international arbitral court providing a number of arbitral judges waiting for work. Referring to arbitration usually means that the parties agree to an arbitration procedure according to a named procedure such as the ICC procedure rules or the UNCITRAL procedure rules. These sets of rules provide all necessary regulations as to the nomination of the arbitrators and the proceedings itself. Most often national law provides complementary provisions as to arbitration which must be taken into consideration by the arbitrators and the parties. In the event of a conflict of laws the arbitrator will apply the national rules of the so called lex fori, which means that the law of the country will apply in which the arbitrator has to do its work.

22.2.6   Summary

Choosing the right form of dispute resolution is a critical aspect when preparing international contracts. Jurisdiction of a court or arbitral court strongly influences questions of applicable law. Procedural law including regulations as to evidence and service of documents can have big influence on the result of any dispute. Time consuming proceedings should be avoided but the advantages of quality of dispute resolution should not be underestimated. It is thus a tremendous task to find the best solution for each contract. There is a broad freedom of choice and a widespread offer of all forms of dispute resolution. It can be presumed that recommendations as to the form of dispute resolution and clauses concerning jurisdiction issues which can be found in international standard forms are well considered and usually suitable for the disputes arising during the execution of the contract. However it is worthwhile researching different forms of dispute resolution and the advantages and disadvantages of any place of jurisdiction. Common pitfalls are:

- The choice of a forum in a country which does not adhere to any multilateral or bilateral convention on recognition and enforcement of foreign court decisions or arbitral awards (e.g. New York Convention on the recognition and enforcement of foreign arbitral awards 1958).
- The choice of a forum in a country which restricts choice-of-law-clauses.
- Accepting exclusive jurisdiction of a court, if the lex fori of the court provides a single language for the pleadings, which is different from the ruling contract language. In such a case all contract documents, communications, plans, etc., must be translated in the court language, which produces considerable interpretation risk.
- Accepting jurisdiction of a court without deep knowledge of its procedural usages and rules.
- Accepting a place of jurisdiction whose legislation requires the obtaining of special visas for lawyers and witnesses.

22.3   FIDIC Dispute Adjudication

22.3.1   Introduction

All FIDIC Books recommend Dispute Adjudication as a regular means of dispute resolution. All disputes must be referred to the Dispute Adjudication Board (DAB) before arbitration is admissible. Sub-clause 20.4 FIDIC Books provides that any dispute shall be referred to the DAB. Thus a dispute must already be constituted before it becomes referred to the DAB. The DAB must verify whether a dispute has already become apparent. If not the DAB shall reject the referral. In addition the DAB must examine whether it has jurisdiction to decide the dispute. As dispute adjudication is usually a purely contractual dispute resolution method, the test is, whether there is a contract and whether the dispute has arisen from the contract or in connection with the contract. As the Procedural Rules give power to the DAB to decide upon its jurisdiction, the DAB itself has to confirm its jurisdiction or to dismiss the dispute in the event of lack of jurisdiction. There is no jurisdiction if the DAB has already decided on the dispute. However a number of exceptions have been confirmed by English courts in this matter. If for example a decision concerning the evaluation of works has been made by the DAB and defects appear later on, the DAB might have jurisdiction to decide once again.

During the whole decision-making process the DAB is bound to the construction contract and the appended Procedural Rules for Dispute Adjudication. According to this contractual framework the DAB shall comply with rules of natural justice and fairness. Thus the DAB shall hear the parties, take evidence if necessary and inform the parties about its proper investigations and methods which are intended to be applied. It is inherent to the concept of dispute adjudication that in the event of failure to comply with the rules of jurisdiction and natural justice, such a DAB decision should not be enforced. It is submitted that the settlement of a dispute ex aequo et bono (*Latin* for "according to the right and good" or "from equity and conscience") rather than on the basis of law, results neither from the nature of the dispute, nor from lacunae in international law, but solely from the decision or agreement of the parties to reach such a solution.

The DAB shall make its decision within a pre-determined time frame. FIDIC suggests that the DAB shall render a decision within 84 days. Although it cannot be excluded for the DAB to take an erroneous decision within such a short period of time, it shall be binding on the parties until reviewed by an arbitral court. However as already mentioned failure to comply with the principles of natural justice and jurisdiction would prevent the decision to be enforced by an arbitral court.

Unfortunately the administrative work of a DAB is often underestimated. The chairman of a DAB must manage the whole work of the DAB. Immediately after the appointment of the DAB members the chairman must introduce a set of internal rules, through which the internal communication and work will become structured. If and when a dispute arises it is up to him to inform the other members of the board about the complaint. But he must also arrange and prepare the site visits and meetings with the parties and the engineer. Finally the whole DAB must decide upon further procedural rules if appropriate in order to ensure a fair and transparent procedure. It might be reasonable to set out delays for written submissions of the parties, the number of admissible experts and the manner in which witnesses shall be heard. It is also recommended that a DAB gives itself a code of conduct, by which for example the contact of the board members with the parties is structured and limited. It should be ensured that all members of the board are informed about contacts with the parties and that no private relations are maintained or initiated.

22.3.2   Function and Role of the DAB

Although in Common law countries the distinction between a person who has an expertise in valuation matters, exercising the role of an independent expert on the one hand, and a quasi judicial role, on the other hand, is well recognised, this question might be an issue in Civil law countries. As to into which category a particular individual falls, in any particular case, depends on what the parties who have invited him to carry out a task for them intended his function to be. This, in turn, is to be gleaned from the agreement between them, as the result of which the DAB assumed his task. Having regard to the language of Sub-Clauses 20.2 et seq. and the Dispute Adjudication Agreement the DAB acts in a judicial capacity. The purpose of the aforementioned Sub-Clauses, properly construed, is to provide the machinery for arriving at a fair decision which shall be derived from the submitted and ascertained facts in accordance with the contract and the applicable law when a dispute arises. The essential prerequisite of a judicial role is that by the time a matter is submitted to a DAB for a decision, there should be a formulated dispute between at least two parties which its decision is required to resolve. It is not enough that parties who may be affected by the decision have opposing interests – still less that the decision is on a matter which is not agreed between them. As such it is entitled to invite the parties to make submissions. In brief it can be said that there should be a dispute or a difference between the parties which has been formulated in some way or another. This dispute or difference shall be submitted by the parties to the DAB to resolve in such a manner that it is called upon to exercise a judicial function. The parties have been provided with an opportunity to present evidence and/or submissions in support of their respective claims in the dispute; and they have agreed to accept his decision.

However, the DAB's function is not merely that of deciding disputes. In any case a permanent DAB, as recommended in the Red Book and quite often also appropriate for a Yellow Book contract, shall also attempt to avoid disputes or to settle them at an early stage. FIDIC Books therefore allow the DAB to give opinions and recommendations, if both of the parties jointly require the DAB to do so. Quite often the main services of a permanent DAB consist in such kind of dispute avoidance services.

22.3.3   Appointment

According to Sub-clause 20.2 there are different procedures available for the appointment of DAB members. The parties may agree on the members or they can leave it open until a dispute arises. In such cases the FIDIC Books refer to the FIDIC's President's list as a nominating body (see Sub-clause 20.3 and the Appendix to Tender). But the parties are also free to choose a different nominating body. However, it is worthwhile to underline that the appointment should be distinguished from the commitment of the DAB. The DAB will only become active if a Dispute Adjudication Agreement will be executed.

22.3.4 Dispute Adjudication Agreement

Once the members of the DAB have been appointed the parties to the contract shall execute a tripartite agreement with each of the members of the DAB. A DAB is only ready for work if the parties to a FIDIC Book contract have signed with each member of the DAB a tripartite Dispute Adjudication Agreement, which is included in the Books, and if the Employer and the Contractor have given notice to each member of the DAB accordingly. Failure to give notice within six months after entering in the Dispute Adjudication Agreement makes the Agreement void and invalid (Fig. 22.2).

The tripartite agreement shall comprise the Dispute Adjudication Agreement, the General Conditions of Dispute Adjudication Agreement and the Procedural Rules. All of these documents are included in the FIDIC Books.

It is critical to know, that only by means of the tripartite agreement the parties agree on the so called Procedural Rules which are intended to be binding on the DAB. However, the General Conditions of each of the Books do not directly refer to the Procedural Rules but only to the General Conditions of Dispute Adjudication Agreement contained in the Appendix to the General Conditions. Sub-Clause 4 lit. e) of the General Conditions of Dispute Adjudication Agreement then refers to the Procedural Rules, which the members of the DAB warrant to comply with.

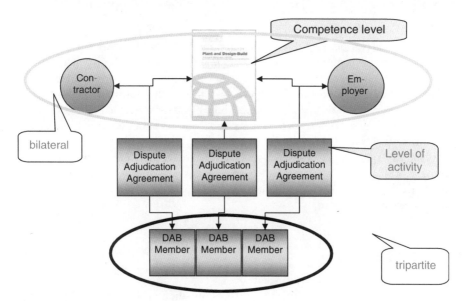

Fig. 22.2 Dispute adjudication structures

The Dispute Adjudication Agreement provides a whole and comprehensive set of rules for Dispute Adjudication and establishes a contractual relationship between the members of the DAB and the parties to the contract. Most of the issues are already pre-determined, except for the remuneration of each of the members. The remuneration is left open for negotiation.

22.3.5   Dispute Avoidance

FIDIC's overriding intention is to avoid disputes whenever possible. This attempt is illustrated by numerous provisions within the General Conditions. Thus for example the Engineer shall consult with each of the parties in an endeavour to reach an agreement (see Sub-Clause 3.5). When there is a permanent DAB in place the Procedural Rules provide for periodical site visits of the DAB and it is envisaged that issues should be discussed at early stage. It is suggested that once a dispute has arisen and the DAB is in place the DAB shall proceed in an endeavour to reach agreement, although this is not yet expressly stated in the Dispute Adjudication Agreement or in the General Conditions. If the DAB fails to reach an amicable settlement and a decision has been rendered Sub-Clause 20.5 provides for a further attempt to settle the dispute amicably.

Under the Gold Book reference can be made to Sub-Clause 20.5 according to which a joint referral to the DAB for assistance is possible.

22.3.6   Referral of a Dispute

If a dispute arises between the parties in connection with, or arising out of, the Contract or the execution of the Works either Party may refer the dispute in writing to the DAB. Such reference shall state that it is given under Sub-Clause 20.4. Although the Books do not provide much guidance for the drafting of such a referral there is a clear idea how to do this. The referring party shall contend the underlying facts in detail, give complete and detailed information about the dispute, previous determinations and DAB decisions, show evidence for all disputed facts and explain its legal arguments. Care must be taken for the referral to cover only those issues which have been indicated previously in the notice of intention to refer a dispute to Dispute Adjudication. Subsequent unilateral changes of the dispute are not permitted.

22.3.7   Jurisdiction

The first thing a DAB will do is to verify its jurisdiction. Jurisdictional issues are often complicated and once arisen will lead into intense discussions. The first issue can be the objection that no dispute exists. The second issue may lie in a wrongful appointment of DAB members. The third issue can be that there is no contract or that the dispute falls beyond the scope of the contract. The latter may appear if claims arise from an instruction which in fact required an amendment to the contract which the parties failed to agree on. Sometimes it will also be critical to determine whether a defence will fall within the jurisdiction of the DAB. One of the most important jurisdictional issues is whether any omissions of the Engineer will constitute a dispute and in particular the exact point in time when this event is considered to have arisen. It is worthy to note that the Employer will be in breach of contract if the Engineer refrains from proceeding in accordance with Sub-Clauses 20.1 and 3.5. However this knowledge will not solve the problem arising form the inactivity of the Engineer. It has been held that a dispute will be constituted if a claim has been made which has subsequently been rejected (ICC International Court of Arbitration Bulletin 74). In *Fastrack Contractors Ltd v. Morrison Construction Ltd*,[1] HHJ Thornton QC, at paragraphs 27–29 has stated:

> A "dispute" can only arise once the subject matter of the claim, issue or other matter has been brought to the attention of the opposing party and that party has had an opportunity of considering and admitting, modifying or rejecting the claim or assertion. In order to constitute a dispute, a claim must have been made which has been rejected

It is therefore suggested that a dispute will be constituted once the Contractor has informed the Employer about the fact that the Engineer remained silent for more of 42 days and that due to this fact he considers that a dispute concerning the issue as detailed in the notice will be constituted.

Jurisdictional issues shall be decided by the DAB itself (FIDIC Procedural Rules at rule 8 lit. b). It has "kompetenz-kompetenz", which is a German word, meaning the ability of an arbitral tribunal to rule on the question of whether it has jurisdiction. The principle of kompetenz-kompetenz is well established in international arbitration, and is accepted in many national laws, such as in England by section 30 of the Arbitration Act 1996.

Jurisdictional issues should be carefully examined and reasoned. English courts sometimes attempt to refuse to rule on the enforcement of DAB decisions for the reason of lack of jurisdiction.

Most adjudications relate to payment and extension of time claims. However, a FIDIC DAB is empowered to open up, review and revise any certificate, decision, determination, instruction, opinion or valuation of the Engineer (Rule 8 Procedural Rules). If a dispute arises between the Parties in connection with, or arising out of, the Contract or the execution of the Works, including any dispute as to any certificate, determination, instruction, opinion or valuation of the Engineer, either Party may refer the matter in writing to the DAB for its decision (Sub-Clause 20.4). Thus the right to refer a dispute to the DAB is not limited to claims. It is clearly

---

[1] [2000] BLR 168.

not necessary for a complaint to have been considered by the Engineer under Sub-Clause 3.5 in order to create a dispute, unless it refers to a matter about which notice must be given under the Contract (Totterdill 2006, p. 301).

22.3.8 Procedure

Sub-Clause 20.4 and the Procedural Rules lay down the procedure for the DAB. In a summary the procedural steps are as follows (Figs. 22.3 and 22.4):

- The referral to the DAB includes all relevant information concerning the dispute.
- The DAB will issue directions concerning the procedure and a time schedule.
- Both parties will make available to the DAB any further or complementary information or facilities which it may require.
- The DAB may decide to conduct a hearing to obtain evidence and/or to consider submissions on the dispute from the Parties.

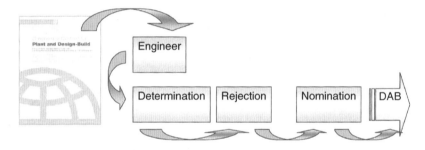

Fig. 22.3 Determination–nomination–decision

Fig. 22.4 Dispute resolution stages

- The DAB shall give its decision within 84 days or any other agreed period, from the date of the dispute reference is received by the chairman of DAB.
- If either Party is dissatisfied with the decision of the DAB or if the DAB fails to give its decision within the aforementioned period, it can issue a notice of dissatisfaction within 28 days. If the Parties fail to do so, the decision becomes final and binding.

A DAB seems to be a quasi arbitral panel. It does not have the full powers of an arbitral court and the principle of *res judicata* (meaning the preservation of its effects in further disputes) will not apply to its decision. However a DAB should follow the principles of natural justice and therefore recognise the maxim of *audi alteram partem*: "let the other side be heard". Proceedings should be conducted so they are fair to all parties. There is however broad contractual freedom to shape the procedure making it convenient to the parties. The Procedural Rules which are included in all FIDIC Books do mirror the principles mentioned above and should be strictly followed. They authorise and empower the DAB to set out its own procedural rules to the extent that they do not contradict with the Procedural Rules as incorporated by the Dispute Adjudication Agreement. Thus in practice the DAB will set out its own procedural rules and plan the procedure. At the outset the DAB will meet in order to ensure its ability to work. It is useful to have clear guidelines of working and to set out such guidelines for all of three members. The DAB members will for example agree on matters as how to proceed if one of its members speaks the local language and whether these skills will be used, how, and to what extent. In bigger cases it may be useful to share the work and to meet before the audience in order to bring together the results of the work. The DAB may also set out rules and instructions to be followed by the Parties during the proceedings. It may for example prove to be helpful to set out cut-off periods for the presentation of facts as otherwise the Parties may attempt to present new facts at a late stage which may cause significant problems in ensuring that the maxim *audi alteram partem* is adhered to. It may also be wise to give exclusive authority to the DAB Chairman to require further information and comments from the Parties. Otherwise the possibility is left open for the DAB members to issue sany manner of request without having previously discussed it with the other members of the DAB.

In summary the DAB will hear both of the parties and obtain evidence if necessary. The DAB is permitted to use inquisitorial measures in order to collect all necessary information. Having heard the parties the DAB will meet in private and prepare its decision which must be notified to the parties. The decision will be in writing, with supporting reasons.

Burden of proof issues should be solved in accordance with the applicable law. In practice adjudicators will apply the principle of balance of probabilities. This means that one party's case need only be more probable than the other. The corollary of this is the rare occurrence when the evidence is evenly balanced. In that case, victory goes to the defendant as the burden of proof is with the plaintiff, who initiates the proceedings.

22.3.9 Applicable Law

An apparently widely ignored subject matter of Dispute Adjudication is the issue of the applicable law (see Hök 2008 p. 323 et seq.). Dispute Adjudication on the international level is in principle a purely contractual feature. Although the parties to a FIDIC contract usually agree to the governing law, the issue of the determination of the applicable conflict of laws principles remains open to discussion. Actually the DAB has power to settle disputes "in connection with, or arising out of, the Contract or the execution of the Works". This means that the DAB has to ascertain the applicable law prior to making a decision, in particular if the cause of action is not contractual but based on tort or on other fields of the law. It is suggested that the DAB may then rely on the conflict of laws regime of the seat of arbitration. As Dispute Adjudication is purely contractual and the DAB is deemed not to be acting as an arbitrator it does not have its proper lex fori. By contrast a temporarily or finally binding DAB decision must be dealt as a matter of legal fact, being binding on the parties according to Sub-Clause 20.4. In other words, according to Sub-Clause 20.4 the parties to the contract have promised to each other to give effect to the DAB decision, which is a contractual obligation governed by the proper law of the contract, whether the DAB decision is based on the proper law of the contract or on tort law. Moreover, if the decision is dealt as contract shaping act by a third party, the DAB, the proper law of the contract governs the effect of the decision. In any case the DAB is under the permanent duty to ascertain the applicable law because its power to settle disputes exists only according to the law and does not allow the DAB to consider *ex aequo et bono*. If a prevailing party intends to enforce a DAB decision it is submitted that the arbitral court has to apply the proper law of the contract. However as to any procedural requirements the arbitral court will rely on its proper lex fori. Thus the lex fori of the said arbitral court will define the standards of control, such as the requirements of natural justice and the elements of jurisdiction.

22.3.10 Reaching a Decision

Reaching a decision means to decide upon the dispute in question. This means that the DAB is required to decide the law. Thus a DAB will have as a first step to examine whether the case is justified by contractual and/or legal provisions. It is beyond doubt that the parties will have to support this attempt. Whether the parties are in fact under the duty to enable the DAB to make a legally reasoned decision or not is open to discussion. As I would say that the law is obvious and usually accessible the DAB must rely on its power to ascertain the matters required for a decision (see rule 8 of the procedural Rules) and is thus under the duty to ascertain the law. This would be in line with Sub-Clause 20.4 where it is clearly stated that the DAB shall decide upon disputes in connection with, or arising out of, the Contract, which means that all legal issues must be decided as well, because as a rule a contract is based on law.[2]

In principle the DAB will have to consider whether the facts as presented to and investigated by the DAB will justify the contested claim or issue according to the applicable law and contractual provisions. If the facts remain disputed the DAB must obtain evidence to the extent necessary. It will have to take in consideration that Sub-Clause 20.1 partially excludes the presentation of witness evidence, namely in so far as contemporary records should have been kept. As civil law and common law lawyers usually adopt a different approach as to the manner in which witnesses should be heard, it is strongly recommended to clearly determine in advance whether cross examination, which is the interrogation of a witness called by one's opponent, which is preceded by direct examination (in England, Australia and Canada known as examination-in-chief) and may be followed by a redirect (re-examination in England, Australia, and Canada) is permitted. Usually the DAB will consider evidence according to the principle of the balance of probability. The applicable substantial law will however determine which of the parties bears the so called burden of proof.

Finally the DAB will render its decision, which has to be reasoned according to Sub-Clause 20.4. The reasons shall show that the DAB has followed the procedural rules which are binding on the parties and has presented its arguments in a logical way. The parties should be able to understand the guiding principles of the decision and the weighting of the respective arguments.

22.4 Issues

Those FIDIC users who have identified the advantages of and the opportunities afforded by Dispute Adjudication will usually follow strictly the guidelines for Dispute Adjudication which is inherent to all FIDIC contracts. But there is still a considerable number of FIDIC users who have not yet identified these advantages and opportunities. As a consequence in daily practice there are many attempts to circumvent Dispute Adjudication, which can be summarised as follows:

* The Employer deletes the DAB clauses, which first of all is regrettable but often also leads to considerable problems if and when this is done in a manner which is inconsistent with the remaining clauses.
* Either the Employer or the Contractor decline to nominate the members of the DAB, which will be an unapt and ineffective attempt to circumvent the DAB because of Sub-clause 20.2
* Either the Employer or the Contractor refuse to undersign the tripartite Dispute Adjudication Agreement, which is a more effective attempt at dispute resolution avoidance, because in principle the General Conditions and the Procedural Rules

[2]See Musawi v. RE International and others [2007] EWHC 2981 (Ch).

do not provide any help in this event. One could argue that Sub-clause 20.3 applies. But this Sub-clause only deals with the appointment of the DAB members and does not provide any guidance as to the situation where one of the parties refuses to sign the tripartite agreement. One could also argue that Sub-clause 20.8 applies. However this Sub-clause applies whenever there is no DAB in place, whether by reason of the expiry of the DAB's appointment or otherwise. In fact there usually is a DAB in place according to Sub-clauses 20.2 and 20.3 either by reason of a joint appointment or by nomination through FIDIC. However, if the parties fail to sign the tripartite Dispute Adjudication Agreements the DAB will not commence its work. A second critical point is that the Dispute Adjudication Agreement includes a number of procedural rules which are not binding on the parties should they fail to sign the agreement. Only the Dispute Adjudication Agreement, including the General Conditions of Dispute Adjudication Agreement, refers to the Procedural Rules (for Dispute Adjudication). The latter are not at all mentioned in the General Conditions of Contract, or more precisely are only mentioned by reference to General Conditions of Dispute Adjudication Agreement contained in Appendix to the General Conditions (see Sub-clause 20.2). It has been argued that the situation will be overcome by virtue of the FIDIC contract the parties have entered into (Owen and Totterdill 2008, p. 38 et seq.). But this seems not to be true. The mere fact that the parties entered into a FIDIC contract and agreed all of its terms does not render signing a tripartite Dispute Adjudication Agreement needless. This requirement arises clearly from Sub-clause 20.2. As Dispute Adjudication is a purely contractual dispute resolution method, there is a need to agree on the Procedural Rules, which are not included in the main contract. Failure to do so will lead to the objection that there has been a procedure without the consent of the other party. The mere fact that this party has originally agreed to accept Dispute Adjudication as such will not be a sufficient basis. It is therefore suggested that in the event of failure to sign the tripartite Dispute Adjudication Agreement the only way out is to refer a dispute to arbitration in accordance with Sub-clause 20.8 in order to request a decision that replaces the missing consent to the tripartite Dispute Adjudication Agreement of the defaulting party. However this is a solution which is based on German law, where it is possible to sue for the issue of a declaration of intention according to Sect. 894 German Civil Code, where it is said that in the event that a debtor is by judgment compelled to make a declaration of intention, the declaration will be deemed as given as soon as the judgment became final. Whether this solution is arguable under common law is open to discussion. In principle it seems that there is no similar adequate remedy under common law. If not, the only way out is to directly refer the substantial dispute to arbitration and sue for the additional cost caused by party who failed to sign the tripartite Dispute Adjudication Agreement. We would not agree with the opinion that there is no specific need for a tripartite Dispute Agreement. Although it is right that subject to Sub-clause 20.2 the referring Party is already bound to incorporate by reference the General Conditions of Dispute Adjudication Agreement contained in the Appendix to the General

Conditions there is still a need to agree to the remuneration of all of the three board members. As the failing Party will finally be bound to pay one-half of this remuneration it should be allowed to contest the amount agreed by the referring party unless it has signed itself the tripartite agreement, because estoppel and good faith arguments (see Sect. 242 German Civil Code) will not help in this regard.

It could therefore be a good idea to directly incorporate the Procedural Rules in the Contract either by reference in Sub-clause 1.5 or by reference to the Procedural Rules in Sub-Clause 20.2. The wording could be as follows:

> Disputes shall be adjudicated by a DAB in accordance with Sub-clause 20.4. The Parties shall jointly appoint a DAB by the date stated in the Appendix to Tender *and sign the tripartite Dispute Adjudication Agreements contained in the Appendix to these General Conditions.*

It seems also to be a good recommendation to insert an additional clause in Sub-clause 20.3 as follows.

> In the event of failure by one of the Parties to sign the Dispute Adjudication Agreement the appointed DAB shall nevertheless act on the basis of the Dispute Adjudication Agreement contained in the Appendix to these General Conditions. The Party who has signed the Dispute Adjudication Agreement has to ensure payment of the members of DAB subject to Sub-Clause 20.2.

Finally a Sub-clause will be useful by which the nominating body will be empowered to finally determine the remuneration of the DAB members:

> In the event of failure of one Party to sign the Dispute Adjudication Agreement the appointing entity or official named in the particular Conditions shall, upon request of either Party determine a reasonable remuneration of the DAB members.

The reasons for objecting DAB's are manifold. In some Eastern European countries the cost of DAB's are contested and not been considered to be reasonable. Others consider that a DAB procedure is useless because only an arbitral award will be recognised as a real decision which can be accepted as evidence with regard to public budget law. Moreover some Employers fear that they will be bound to a DAB decision even though it seems to be obvious that it is erroneous. Again, others consider that the strict time schedule for the DAB leads to so called ambushing, which will mean that the Contractor, having prepared his claim with care, will present it for example one day before Christmas in order to overtake and to fleece the Employer who will presumably not be able to prepare his defence on Christmas and thus be in an extremely uncomfortable situation.

22.5 Dispute Adjudication in Civil Law Countries

FIDIC Dispute Adjudication is an internationally recognised means of dispute resolution, which is practised worldwide. However for example in Germany ADR is in principle scarcely used and dispute adjudication remains largely unknown.

Most disputes arising from construction contracts are still brought before state courts, and more seldom before arbitral tribunals. The German legislator although encouraging conciliation has not yet introduced a legal framework into the German legal system allowing for and supporting modern methods of dispute resolution apart from arbitration. Only conciliation as a procedural feature of dispute resolution is partially ruled by law (Sect. 15a EGZPO, Sect. 797a, 794 Civil Procedure Code). In addition the feature of expert determination is widely used.

Parties willing to practise Dispute Adjudication thus encounter several problems. The most important ones are the following:

- Enforceability of dispute adjudication agreements
- Jurisdiction (Dismissal of complaints at court)
- Binding effects of DAB decisions on the parties

22.5.1 Enforceability of Dispute Adjudication Agreements

Naturally, German law recognises the principle of contractual freedom. Thus the parties to a contract are free to enter into a Dispute Adjudication Agreement. Whether they are allowed to do so by incorporation of trade terms or only by bespoke terms is one of the first issues. According to Sect. 307 paragraph 1 German Civil Code provisions in standard business terms are invalid if, contrary to the requirement of good faith, they place the contractual partner of the user at an unreasonable disadvantage. An unreasonable disadvantage may also result from the fact that the provision is not clear and comprehensible.

German courts have continuously held that arbitration clauses and expert determination clauses may be invalid subject to Sect. 307 German Civil Code. In particular expert determination clauses in construction contract standard forms are invalid.[3] The reasoning for this is that the courts believe that such a clause allocates an unreasonable risk to the client, that he may suffer disadvantages from an incorrect expert determination (see Palandt and Heinrichs 2009, note 144).

There is no doubt that dispute adjudication is a speedy mechanism for settling disputes in construction contracts on a provisional interim basis, requiring the decisions of adjudicators to be enforced pending the final determination of disputes by arbitration, litigation or agreement. The timetable for an adjudication are very tight. Many would say unreasonably tight, and likely to result in injustice.[4] Thus it could be suggested that under German law dispute adjudication clauses are in principle invalid and not enforceable. As Sect. 307 German Civil Code applies even to commercial contracts, Sub-Clauses 20.2 et seq. FIDIC would be invalid in

---

[3] [115] BGHZ 331; OLG Düsseldorf [2000] NJW-RR 279.
[4] Macob Civil Engineering Ltd v. Morrison Construction Ltd [1999] EWHC Technology 254 (12 February 1999).

all types of construction contracts apart from their inclusion in a bespoke contract. However, this result would not embrace the nature and shape of FIDIC dispute adjudication. According to Sub-Clauses 20.2 et seq. the DAB settles disputes on a provisional interim basis. The decisions of the DAB remain open to review by arbitration. By contrast, an expert determination subject to German law is usually final and binding unless it is manifestly inequitable according to Sect. 319 German Civil Code. This is fundamentally different from a DAB decision. It is therefore suggested, that Sub-Clauses 20.2 et seq. FIDIC are in principle valid, although they are contained in standard business terms.

22.5.2 Jurisdiction

The next issue is whether a German court will have to dismiss any complaint filed with it in a matter that is subject to a dispute adjudication clause. According to Sect. 1032 paragraph 1 German Civil Procedure Code German courts shall dismiss any complaint brought before them that is subject to an arbitration agreement. However, no such similar rule exists for dispute adjudication. Mr Chern (2008, p. 44), by referring to a decision of the Federal Court from 1998,[5] points out that the German courts have ruled that dispute board type procedures are enforceable. Actually the Federal Court has held that if a contract contains a conciliation clause a claim brought before the court prior to such conciliation attempt is inadmissible. However, the Federal Court decision applies only to conciliation clauses and not to expert determination clauses. In the event of an expert determination clause the courts have either granted a stay order or dismissed the claim as at present not due.[6]

22.5.3 Binding Effects of DAB Decisions on the Parties

According to Sub-Clause 20.4 the DAB decision shall be binding on the parties unless reviewed by arbitration. It becomes finally binding if neither party notifies a declaration of dissatisfaction within 28 days after receipt of the decision. In the event that the parties have deleted Sub-Clauses 20.6 et seq. the question arises whether the winning party may enforce the DAB decision at court. Unfortunately this will be a difficult issue to determine. German law does not contain the instrument of summary proceedings and summary judgments. Thus the courts will have to consider the nature of a DAB decision in order to get advice from the law on how to handle the DAB decision.

---

[5] BGH [1999] NJW 647.
[6] KG [2005] IBR 719; see Hök (2007, p.426).

If it has the nature of an expert determination subject to Sect. 317 et seq. Civil Code it will be treated as an amendment to the contract from which the dispute arose.[7] The claimant shall then establish a fully detailed complaint showing that he is entitled to the claim which has been decided by the DAB. According to Sect. 319 Civil Code the court has the power to verify whether the determination is manifestly inequitable. In this event the inequitable determination is replaced by judgment. It should be noted that the same applies if the third party (the DAB) cannot reach the determination or does not want to or if it delays it.

However, one of the main features of an adjudication is that there is a dispute between two or more persons who agree that they will refer their dispute to the adjudication of some selected person (the DAB) whose decision upon the matter they agree to accept. The DAB has disputes submitted to it for decision. The evidence and the contentions including any defences of the parties are put before them for its examination and consideration. Both, the contentions and the evidence put before the DAB identify the issue which is not pre-determined. The DAB therefore exercises a judicial function.

Thus, there is some doubt whether under German law a DAB decision can be considered to have the nature of an expert determination in the sense of Sections 317 et seq. of the German Civil Code. It is true that the DAB is required to act impartially and that an expert should act fairly und impartially. However, the circumstance that an expert must act fairly and impartially does not make him comparable to a DAB. Instead, for a DAB to become active a formulated dispute between at least two parties must exist. There shall be an opportunity to present evidence and/or submissions in support of the respective rights and claims in the dispute. There are submissions to the DAB either of a specific dispute or of present points of difference or of defined differences that may in the future arise and there is agreement that its decision will be binding on the parties. None of this is true about the expert who is merely carrying out its ordinary business activity. There is no dispute before him. The parties do not submit evidence as contentious to him. He merely makes his own investigations and comes to a decision. The DAB is, however, permitted to take the initiative in ascertaining the facts and the law as to the referred dispute. It may, therefore, conduct an entirely inquisitorial process, or alternatively it may, invite additional submissions and representations from the parties. In addition it may gather evidence, hear witnesses and make site visits. It may also rely on its own skills and knowledge as well as on expert and witness statements. Finally FIDIC has introduced an intervening provisional stage in the dispute resolution process. Crucially, it has made it clear that decisions of a DAB are binding and are to be complied with until the dispute is finally resolved. By contrast an expert who acts according to Sections 317 et seq. Civil Code is usually not under an obligation to consider the submissions of the parties, to ascertain the law and to hear witnesses. On the other hand his determination is usually final and binding. He is not bound to the contentions of the parties and to procedural rules.

---

[7] OLG Frankfurt [1999] NJW-RR 379.

Thus Sect. 317 et seq. Civil Code does not mirror completely the role and the powers of a DAB.

Again, according to Sub-Clause 20.4 the DAB shall not be dealt as an arbitrator or arbitral tribunal. However, if the DAB decision is neither an expert determination nor an arbitral award, the question remains as to what is the true nature of the DAB decision. It is suggested that it is something in between both of them, which is a fundamentally new concept for German law.

22.6   New Features

As in September 2008 FIDIC has published the new Design Build and Operate Form, also referred to as the Gold Book, some new features will enhance the discussion. FIDIC took advantage of this event to slightly change the procedural framework.

The success of Dispute Adjudication is undeniable. To some extent lack of it has already become a deal breaker (see Koentges 2006, p. 311). It is therefore not surprising, that FIDIC clings to Dispute Adjudication (Fig. 22.5).

However some particularities have to be stated and emphasised.

Firstly the term of "Dispute" has been defined in Sub-Clause 1.1.31. The aim was to make clear that a Dispute may exist even if the Employer's Representative remained inactive. At first sight the definition might be a bit too narrow thus limiting the access to the DAB more than necessary. In fact, it might even be argued that a Dispute presupposes a "claim" in the sense of any entitlement to extension of Time for Completion or additional payment, which has been rejected and that other kinds of disputes are therefore excluded from the scope of the wording. However the term "claim" is not defined although used as a heading or marginal word in Sub-Clause 20.1. It is submitted that it means an assertion of a right to money, property or to a remedy (Bunni 2005, FIDIC forms, p. 293), because headings and other marginal words shall not be taken into consideration as provided in Sub-Clause 1.4. Also Sub-Clause 1.1.31 should be read in conjunction with Sub-Clause 20.6. It then becomes noticeable that other kinds of disputes other than those arising from a claim in its narrow sense may be referred to the DAB as well.

Secondly during the design build period the DBO DAB will be a permanent DAB which shall be appointed by the date stated in the Contract Data, whilst during the Operation Service Period a one member DAB shall be appointed. Thus the permanent DAB will be installed only until the issue of the Commissioning Certificate or at the latest until the DAB has given its decision to a dispute and the appointment of the permanent DAB expires at the date of issue of the Commissioning Certificate unless otherwise agreed in the Contract Data. However some of the claims to which the Contractor is entitled during the Operation Service Period have to be notified in accordance with Sub-Clause 20.1, which may lead to disputes and the need for rulings by a DAB according to Sub-Clause 20.1. This is the reason why Sub-Clause 20.9 provides a special Operation Service DAB.

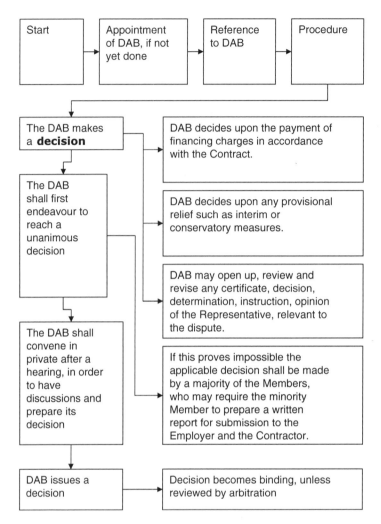

Fig. 22.5 FIDIC DBO adjudication-overview

Thirdly Sub-Clause 20.5 encourages the parties to avoid disputes. The Parties may jointly refer matters to the DAB to seek informal assistance by the DAB, a possibility which is not new but which has been set out more clearly.

Fourthly the scope of services of the DAB has been enlarged. For the future the DAB is involved in preliminary questions of claim determination in the way that the Contractor may seek for an overruling decision in the event of late claim notification or late submission of details. Finally any dispute shall be effectively treated. Thus the parties will be obliged to refer a dispute to the DAB within the time limits stated in Cl. 20.6. Hence by contrast to the 1999 edition in the future the parties are no longer allowed to collect disputed claims and to start multiple proceedings at the very end of the project. As aforementioned Cl. 20.5 encourages the parties to avoid disputes by jointly informal reference of matters to the DAB. Such informal assistance may take place at any time and may lead to non binding advice. In the event that the parties expect the DAB to give a decision, it shall be binding on both parties, who shall promptly comply with it. Failure to comply with a DAB decision may lead to direct arbitration. In so far it is new that FIDIC has filled up the gap which presumably exists in the 1999 edition as to those decisions which are not yet finally binding (Bunni 2005, p. 272).

Further an interesting new approach can be found in Sub-Clause 20.6. Employers in particular have sometimes criticised that decisions that lead to payments have to be rewarded despite the fact that they are wrong. Actually such kind of decision is subject to control by arbitration but there is always a risk that the beneficiary of such provisional payment will become insolvent. English courts have for several times granted the paying party a stay of execution where the successful claimant is in liquidation or where evidence is produced showing serious concerns that the claimant will not be able to refund sums claimed if the adjudicator's decision is later overturned in arbitration.[8] In other jurisdictions court decisions against which appeal is allowed, will only be declared as provisionally enforceable on giving of security to be determined as to the amount.[9] FIDIC has recognised this reasonable concern and allows from now on the paying party to require the payee to provide a security in respect of such payment, if either party issues a notice of dissatisfaction concerning the DAB decision.

Remark: It is recommended to add that the security should be in a form attached to the contract in order to avoid disputes about the terms of the security. It might be reasonable as well to add the following: In the event that the payee is unable to give security or is able to do so only by suffering substantial hardship or harm, the DAB may declare the decision on motion as provisionally enforceable without giving security.

Furthermore a supposed gap has been closed. As the Rainbow Edition 1999 did not provide any delay for giving a determination the question arose whether the Contractor could refer a dispute to the DAB or not, if the Engineer remained silent. According to the DBO wording the Employer's Representative is now held to issue any determination within a given time limit of 42 days. Failure to do so will lead to the following scenario. After expiry of the delay for determination the Contractor may issue a notice of dissatisfaction, which he should do within the 28 days' delay, which runs from the day of expiry of the determination delay. By consequence a dispute will be constituted which opens the way to the DAB. For precaution an express rule has been added stating that if the Employer's Representative fails to determine within the given time limits, either Party may conclude that the claim is rejected and that it may refer a dispute to the DAB (Fig. 22.6).

---

[8] Herschel Engineering Ltd v. Breen Properties Ltd [2000] BLR 272; Bouygues (UK) Ltd v. Dahl-Jensen (UK) Ltd [2000] BLR 522, CA.

[9] See Section 709 German Civil Procedure Code and the exceptions in Section 708 German Civil Procedure Code, specially concerning default judgments or judgments given in a trial by record (which is a special procedure limiting the means of evidence to documents).

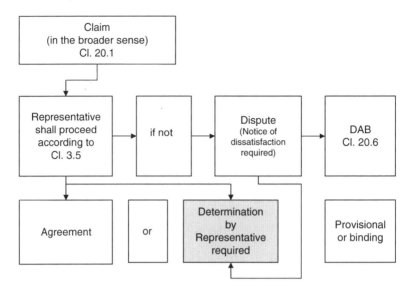

Fig. 22.6 Determination procedure

Finally it will no longer be possible to use tactics. If a dispute has been constituted it must be referred to the DAB within 28 days of issuing the Notice of dissatisfaction. If the dissatisfied Party does not refer the dispute to the DAB within the said period of time, the Notice of dissatisfaction shall be deemed to have lapsed and the determination becomes final and binding (Sub-Clause 20.6).

It can be summarised that the new procedural rules are in line with the basic idea that all claims and disputes shall be settled when staff and equipment are still on the site. The aim is still to avoid prolonged disputes. However the new rules will require more diligence and care than was previously the case. It is beyond doubt that contract administration has once again become more sophisticated.

References

Bunni NG (2005) FIDIC forms of contract, 3rd edn. Blackwell, Oxford

Bunni NG (2005) The gap in sub–clause 20.7 of the 1999 FIDIC contracts for major works. ICLR 272

Chern C (2008) Chern on dispute boards. Blackwell, Oxford

Heinrichs H (2009) in: Palandt (ed) Commentary to BGB, 68th edn. C.H. Beck, München

Hök G-S (2007) Engineer und Dispute Adjudication Board in FIDIC–Verträgen: Entwicklung, Grundlagen und rechtliche Einordnung. ZfBR 416, 426

Hök G-S (2008) Zur international privat- und verfahrensrechtlichen Behandlung des Schiedsgutachtens und DAB – Spruches. ZfBR 323

Koentges H (2006) International dispute adjudication – contractors' experiences. ICLR 306

Owen G, Totterdill B (2008) Dispute boards. Thomas Telford, London

Totterdill BW (2006) FIDIC user's guide, 2nd edn. Thomas Telford, London

Chapter 23
Samples

Sample I: Notice of Commencement Date

To [Contractor]

This letter is only suitable for use with FIDIC Yellow Book

Notice number [*insert number*]

Dear Sir

- This notice is issued in accordance with Sub-clause 8.1:

  - We give notice to the Contractor of the Commencement Date. The Commencement Date shall be the [*insert date*].
  - For precaution: If the above specified Commencement Date falls within the 7 days' notice the Commencement Date shall be the seventh day after you receive this notice.

Yours faithfully

(Engineer)

A.-V. Jaeger and G.-S. Hök, *FIDIC-A Guide for Practitioners*,
DOI 10.1007/978-3-642-02100-8_23, © Springer-Verlag Berlin Heidelberg 2010

Sample II: Notice of an Event or Circumstance
To [Engineer]

This letter is only suitable for use with FIDIC Yellow Book

Notice number [*insert number*]

Dear Sir

- This notice is issued in accordance with Sub-Clause [*insert Sub-Clause*] and as the case may be in accordance with Sub-Clause 20.1.

We became aware of:

- An error or defect of a technical nature in a document which was prepared for use in executing the Works
- An error in the Employer's Requirements
- Unforeseeable physical conditions
- A shortage, defect or default in the free issue materials
- Fossils, coins, articles of value or antiquity, and structures and other remains or items of geological or archaeological interest found on the Site
- New applicable standards coming into force in the Country after the Base
- An instruction of the Engineer
- Specific probable future events or circumstances which may adversely affect the work, increase the Contract Price or delay the execution of the Works
- The fact that we are prevented from carrying out the Tests on Completion
- The fact that we are prevented from carrying out the Tests after Completion
- Unreasonably delayed access to the Works or Plant
- Changes in the Laws or in such interpretations
- The fact that the Works have been suspended
- A risk listed in Sub-Clause 17.3 which results in loss or damage to the Works, Goods or Contractor's Documents

on [*insert date*].

- We hereby give notice of a claim under the Contract or in connection with the Contract. We draw your attention to [*describe the circumstances giving rise to the claim with dates and other details as necessary to identify the claim*]. We consider that these circumstances entitle us to a claim for:

- Damages/cost/quantum meruit [*delete as appropriate*] against you
- Cost

- Cost plus reasonable profit
- Extension of Time for Completion

Yours faithfully

(Contractor)

Copy: A copy of this notice will be sent to the Employer according to Sub-clause 1.3.

Sample III: Notice that Work Is Ready
To [Engineer]
This letter is only suitable for use with FIDIC Yellow Book

Notice number [*insert number*]

Dear Sir

- This notice is issued in accordance with Sub-clause [*insert Sub-Clause*]:

    - We give notice that work is ready and not yet covered up, put out of sight, or packaged for storage or transport.
    - We give notice of the date after which we will be ready to carry out each of the Tests of Completion [*insert date*].
    - We give notice that the Works are ready for any (other) Tests on Completion.

Yours faithfully

(Contractor)

Copy: A copy of this notice will be sent to the Employer according to Sub-clause 1.3.

Sample IV: Notice of Approval
To [Contractor]
This letter is only suitable for use with FIDIC Yellow Book

Notice number [*insert number*]

Dear Sir

* This notice is issued in accordance with Sub-clause 5.2

    * We give notice to the Contractor that the Contractor's Document [*insert specification*]:
        * Is approved without comments
        * Is approved with comments
        * Fails (to the extent stated) to comply with the Contract
    * We instruct you that further Contractor's Documents are required [*indicate documents*].

Yours faithfully

(Engineer)

Sample V: Instruction

To Contractor

This letter is only suitable for use with FIDIC Red Book
and Yellow Book

Instruction no. [insert number]

Dear Sir

We herewith formally instruct you according to Sub-Clause 7.6:

- To remove from the Site and replace any Plant or materials which is not in accordance with the Contract
- To remove and re-execute any other work which is not in accordance with the Contract
- To execute any work which is urgently required for the safety of the Works

In particular we instruct you [*choose the appropriate remedy*] to remove, to re-execute and/or to execute [*describe the Plant, material or work*].

Yours faithfully

(Engineer)

Sample VI: EOT Claim Following Variation
To Engineer, if Variation
This letter is only suitable for use with FIDIC Yellow Book
and Red Book

Claim Notice [Number] under Sub-Clause 20.1

Dear Sir

We confirm the receipt of your instruction no. [*insert number*] from [*insert date*]. We consider this to constitute a Variation.

In accordance with Sub-Clause 8.4 of the General Conditions of Contract, we herewith give notice of a claim for extension of Time for Completion.

Yours faithfully

(Contractor)

Copy: A copy of this notice will be sent to the Employer according to Sub-clause 1.3.

Sample VII: Rejection of Work
To Contractor
This letter is only suitable for use with FIDIC Red Book and Yellow Book

---

Rejection no. [insert number]

Dear Sir

We herewith formally reject according to Sub-Clause 7.5:

- The below specified Plant
- The below specified Materials
- The below specified workmanship

[*Specify the Plant, Material or workmanship*]:

- Which is found to be defective
- Which is found not to be in accordance with the Contract

According to Sub-Clause 4.1 you shall design (to the extent specified in the Contract), execute and complete the Works in accordance with the Contract and with the Engineer's instructions, and shall remedy any defects in the Works. According to Sub-Clause 7.1 the Works shall be carried out:

- In manner specified in the Contract
- In a proper workmanlike and careful manner, in accordance with recognised good practise
- With properly equipped facilities and non-hazardous Materials

We consider that [*give reasons*] ....

Yours faithfully

(Engineer)

Sample VIII: Application for Taking-Over Certificate
To [Engineer]
*This letter is only suitable for use with FIDIC Red Book
and Yellow Book*

Notice number [*insert number*]

Dear Sir,

- This notice is issued in accordance with Sub-clause 10.1:

    - We apply for a Taking Over Certificate.
    - We remind you, within 28 days after receiving our application to proceed in accordance with Sub-Clause 10.1 and issue the Taking Over Certificate.

Yours faithfully

(Engineer)

Sample IX: Letter from Engineer, if Employer's Approval Is Late
To [Employer]
This letter is only suitable for use with FIDIC Red Book
and Yellow Book

Notice number [*insert number*]

Dear Sir,

I refer to my request for approval concerning Contractor's claim no. [. . .], which I received on [. . .]. I have consulted with the Parties and negotiations were in vain. I also have submitted a draft for a determination on [. . .].

It would be appreciated if you would give me a response to my request within due time, because according to Sub-Clause 1.3, I shall not unduly delay any determination.

I am sure you will appreciate that this matter must be referred to you. However, you have promised to the Contractor that any determination shall not be unreasonably withheld or delayed.

Yours faithfully

(Engineer)

Annotation: Even if the Contract discloses any restrictions as to the powers of the Engineer there is still the obligation to not unreasonably delay any determination. The Employer will be in breach of contract if he interferes with the duties of the Engineer, even though the Contractor has accepted that Employer's approval is required for any determination under Sub-Clause 3.5.

Sample X: Determination
Engineer to Parties: Determination
This document is suitable for use with the FIDIC Yellow and Red Book

---

Claim [*insert number*] related to project [*insert project name*]

Dear Sirs,

I hereby give notice of my determination as to claim no. [*insert number*]. With regard to all relevant facts and circumstances I determine that the Contractor is entitled to [. . .] days of extension of Time for Completion.

I have given my approval/disapproval with comments on [. . .].

I have consulted with the Parties who have submitted the following statements:

[*insert details of statements*]

The Contractor has submitted

- particulars
- supported by evidence,
- including contemporary records,
- which I have monitored.

The Contractor has given notice of [. . .] on [*insert date*]:

- This was in time because he became aware of the relevant facts on [. . .].
- This was not in time because became aware of the relevant facts on [. . .].

In accordance with Sub-Clause [. . .] the Contractor is entitled to extension of Time for Completion. In accordance with Sub-Clause 8.4 the relevant event must have an impact on an activity which lies on the critical path. Both requirements are met: [*Insert reasons*]

Yours faithfully

(Engineer)

Sample XI: Notice of Dissatisfaction with a Determination of the Engineer
To [other Party with copy to the Engineer]
This letter is only suitable for use with FIDIC Red and Yellow Book

---

Notice number [*insert number*]

Dear Sir

- This notice is issued with reference to Claim notice no. [insert number]:
    - We give notice that we are dissatisfied with the Engineer's determination dated on [*insert date*].
    - We give notice that the Engineer failed to render its determination within due time after receiving the claim notice no. [*insert number*] and supporting particulars on [. . .].
    - We consider that failure to render a determination in due time constitutes a dispute under Sub-Clause 20.4. For precaution we rely on the fact that consultations and negotiations were in vain.

Yours faithfully

(**Contractor**)

Annotation: To the exception of the Silver Book a notice of dissatisfaction with a determination by the Engineer is not required. However, it may be helpful to constitute a dispute in order avoid the objection "there is no dispute". In the event that the Engineer fails to make a determination in due time it is strongly recommended to give such a notice.

Sample XII: Notice of Referral of Dispute
Contractor to the Chairman of the DAB: Referral of dispute
This letter is suitable for use with all FIDIC Books

Dispute [*insert number*] related to project [*insert project name*]

Dear Sir,

We hereby present the annexed referral of dispute no. [*insert number*] to the DAB.

Yours faithfully

(**Contractor**)

Sample XIII: Chairman of the DAB to Parties: Establishment of the Procedure
To [Parties]
This letter is suitable for use with all FIDIC Books

Dispute number [*insert number*]

Dear Sirs,

We refer to no. 5 lit. (a) of the Procedural Rules according to which the DAB has the power to establish the procedure to be applied in deciding the dispute. The DAB has taken the unanimous decision that the following procedural rules will be set in force and established:

1. The Chairman is empowered to make directions.
2. The Parties shall comply with the Chairman's directions within 3 days after receiving any such direction.
3. No experts will be heard by the DAB which are not appointed by the DAB.
4. Submissions can be made either in the ruling language or in the local language.
5. The Chairman's decision can not be overridden by the other members of the Board.
6. A retainer of 10,000 € for each Member of the Board shall be paid in advance to each Member of the Board

Yours faithfully

Annotation: The procedural rules contained in nos. 4–6 are presumably in contradiction to the powers of the DAB.

Sample XIV: Notice of Dissatisfaction with a Decision of the DAB
To [other Party]
This letter is only suitable for use with FIDIC Yellow Book

Notice number [*insert number*]

Dear Sir

This notice is issued in accordance with Sub-clause 20.4:

- We give notice that we are dissatisfied with the DAB's decision dated on [*insert date*].
- We give notice that the DAB failed to render its decision within the period of 84 days (or as otherwise approved) after receiving the reference no. [*insert number*] or payment.

Yours faithfully

(**Contractor** or **Employer**)

Annotation: This notice must be given within 28 days after the concerned Party has received the decision. If the concerned Party fails to give notice of dissatisfaction within 28 days his right to refer the dispute to arbitration is lapsed.

Sample XV: Addendum
[To be signed by both Parties]
*This document is only suitable for use with FIDIC Yellow
and Red Book*

ADDENDUM NO [. . .] TO CONTRACT NO [. . .]
This Agreement made the   day of **XXXXX**
Between   of   (hereinafter called "the Employer") of the one part,
and   of   (hereinafter called "the Contractor") of the other part

Whereas the Employer and the Contractor have agreed for the execution and
completion of the Works and the remedying of any defects therein as under
the Contract Agreement for the **construction of a cofferdam** dated on 24,25
November 2007,
   Whereas the actual progress of the Works has fallen behind the expected
progress due exceptional adverse weather conditions, unforeseen physical conditions and a Variation, **The Employer and the Contractor agree** as follows:

1. In this Amendment words and expressions shall have the same meanings as
   are respectively assigned to them in the Conditions of Contract referred to in
   the aforementioned Contract.
2. In consideration of the claims for extension of Time for Completion submitted
   by the Contractor to the Engineer until today, the Contractor hereby covenants
   with the Employer to extend Time for Completion by 35 days, in conformity
   with the provisions of the Contract. Time for Completion as referred to in
   Sub-Clause 1.1.3.3 shall be . . . **days [Time for Completion + EOT]**.
3. The Employer hereby agrees with the Contractor, in consideration of the
   aforementioned agreement that all claims relating to extension of Time for
   Completion shall be settled. A new programme shall be submitted by the
   Contractor. If and when progress of the works falls again behind the programme
   dates as updated in accordance with the Contract, Sub-Clause 8.4 shall apply.

This settlement shall not extend to claims relating to cost and profit resulting from
any delay or disruption settled according to number three of this Agreement.

   In Witness whereof the parties hereto have caused this Agreement to be executed the day and year first before written in accordance with their respective laws.
   SIGNED by: for and on behalf of the Employer in the presence of Witness:
Name: Address: Date: SIGNED by: for and on behalf of the Contractor in the
presence of Witness: Name: Address: Date:

Annotation: The extent of the addendum must be carefully checked. The addendum refers to "all claims relating to extension of Time for Completion". If during
negotiations the Contractor has given notice of new and additional EOT claims,
they would be covered by the addendum even though not having been taken in
consideration as to the result.

Chapter 24
Delay Schedule

The 1999 FIDIC Books include various contract management provisions. Among these provisions some include delays which must strictly be followed in order to avoid disadvantages:

Event or circumstance	Sub-clause	Delay	
Advanced payment (*employer*)	14.7	42 days/21 days	After receiving the letter of acceptance or after receiving the performance security
Approval or disapproval of a claim (*engineer*)	20.1	42 days	After receiving the particulars of the claim
As Built documents	5.6 (YB)		Prior to Taking Over
Change of technical standards and regulations	5.4 (YB)		After coming in force
Claim notice	20.1	28 days	After becoming aware of the event (should have become aware)
Claim with continuing effect	20.1	Monthly	No clear starting point
Commencement date	8.1	42 days	After receiving of the letter of acceptance
DAB decision (*DAB*)	20.4	84 days	After receiving a referral
DAB Site visits (*permanent DAB*)	DAB procedural rules	Intervals of 140 days	
Design review period	5.2 (YB)	21 days	After reception of the contractor's document
Determination (*engineer*)	3.5, 20.1	No delay indicated. Approval or disapproval within 42 days	After reception of particulars of the claim

A.-V. Jaeger and G.-S. Hök, *FIDIC-A Guide for Practitioners*,
DOI 10.1007/978-3-642-02100-8_24, © Springer-Verlag Berlin Heidelberg 2010

Event or circumstance	Sub-clause	Delay	
Early warning	8.3	promptly	
Final payment (*employer*)	14.7	56 days	After receiving the final payment certificate
Final statement	14.11	56 days	After receiving the performance certificate
Inspection	7.3	Without unreasonable delay	Upon notice by contractor
Interim payment (*employer*)	14.7	56 days	After receiving of the statement
Interim payment certificate (*engineer*)	14.6	28 days	After receiving if the statement
Interim statements	14.3	Monthly	
Monthly reports	4.21	Monthly	
Notice of commencement date	8.1	7 days	Prior to commencement date
Notice for inspection	7.3		Whenever work is ready and before it is covered up
Notice of errors in technical documents	1.8	Promptly	After becoming aware of it
Notice for tests on completion	9.1	21 days	Notice of the date after which the contractor will be ready to carry out the tests on completion
Notice of a force majeure event	19.2	14 days	After becoming aware of the event (should have become aware)
Notice of dissatisfaction	20.4	28 days	After receiving the DAB decision
Notice of dissatisfaction	3. 5 (SB)	14 days	After receiving of any determination by the employer
Notice of intention to attend the tests (*engineer*)	7.4	24 h	
Notice of unforeseeable physical conditions	4.12	As soon as practicable	After becoming aware
Operation and maintenance manuals	5.7 (YB)		Prior to commencement of tests on completion
Performance security	4.2	28 days	After receiving of the letter of acceptance

Event or circumstance	Sub-clause	Delay	
Programme	8.3	28 days	After reception of the notice of commencement date
Request to provide reasonable evidence for financial arrangements (*employer*)	2.4	28 days	After receiving any request from the contractor
Retention monies (first half) (*employer*)	14.9		On the date when the Taking-Over Certificate is issued
Retention monies (second half) (*employer*)	14.9		On the expiration of the defects notification period
Scrutiny of employer's requirements	5.1 (YB)	Appendix to Tender	Specified in the Appendix to Tender
Statement at completion	14.10	84 days	After receiving the Taking-Over Certificate
Substantiation of a claim	20.1	42 days	After becoming aware of the event (should have become aware)
Suspension by contractor	16.1	21 days	After receiving the notice
Termination by convenience (*employer*)	15.5	28 days	After receiving the notice or the date on which the employer returns the performance security

Additional delays may be found in the FIDIC Gold Book:

Event or circumstance	Sub-clause	Delay	
Appointment of auditing body	10.3	182 days	Prior to commencement of operation service
Commencement date	8.1	42 days	After receiving of the letter of acceptance
Determination of a claim (engineer)	20.1 lit. d	42 days	After receiving a fully detailed claim or any further particulars
Notice of dissatisfaction	20.1 lit. d	28 days	After receiving the determination
Notice of commencement date	8.1	14 days	Prior to commencement date
Referral of dispute to DAB	20.6	28 days	After issuing a notice of dissatisfaction

Index